THE
DE GAULLE
REVOLUTION

by

ALEXANDER WERTH

Le pronunciamento est un acte de décadence.
On ne peut se substituer à un peuple.
Charles de Gaulle

Programme pour demain: De Gaulle à la Place
de la République.—*Le Canard Enchaîné*.

GREENWOOD PRESS, PUBLISHERS
WESTPORT, CONNECTICUT

Library of Congress Cataloging in Publication Data

Werth, Alexander, 1901–
    The De Gaulle revolution.

    Reprint of the ed. published by R. Hale, London.
    Includes index.
    1. France—Politics and government—1958–
2. Gaulle, Charles de, Pres. France, 1890–1970.
I. Title.
DC420.W47 1976   944.082'092'4   75–31477
ISBN 0–8371–8508–4

Originally published in 1960 by Robert Hale Limited, London

Reprinted with the permission of Robert Hale & Company

Reprinted in 1976 by Greenwood Press,
a division of Williamhouse-Regency Inc.

Library of Congress Catalog Card Number 75-31477

ISBN 0-8371-8508-4

Printed in the United States of America

CONTENTS

PART III

THE FRANCE-DE GAULLE HONEYMOON

PART IV

INTO THE FIFTH REPUBLIC

PREFACE

"I t'll only be an episode," said Pierre Mendès-France the day de Gaulle became head of the French Government on June 1, 1958. But this —still unfinished—episode is particularly difficult to "place" in the long history of France. As the *Canard Enchaîné* said on the eve of the Khrushchev visit to France:

Mongénéral will have a bit of a job explaining to his visitor just what kind of régime this is. It isn't a democracy; it isn't really a republic; it isn't a monarchy either; nor is it, strictly speaking, a dictatorship. Perhaps it would be simplest if he just told him it was a *Mon Archie* - in two words.

De Gaulle has flippantly been likened to Louis XIV, and more seriously to Napoleon III and even to Pétain; but perhaps one may also say, without any disrespect, that de Gaulle has really proved to be a more successful— M. Doumergue.

In February 1934 the anti-parliamentary riots resulted in the formation of a "national government" by the aged ex-President of the Republic, who had been specially brought back to Paris to symbolize "national reconciliation", and to put an end to the rioting that had broken out on the famous night of February 6. Egged on by one of his ministers, M. André Tardieu, old man Doumergue soon afterwards began to play about with the idea of setting up a "presidential republic". But in this he failed. The working-class reaction to the "Fascist riots" of February 6 had been very strong, and was, before long, to lead to the formation of the Popular Front; also, there was still some life left in the old Third Republic, and, within a few months, Parliament forced Doumergue out of office. Uttering threats and imprecations, the old man returned to his country retreat near Toulouse, and was scarcely ever heard of again. For all that, Doumergue claimed to have "prevented civil war" in France in February 1934.

While there are certain superficial similarities between the situation in 1934 and that in 1958, the differences are great, too. First of all, the rebellion against the Republic did not, as in 1934, start in Paris; it started outside France—something that had never happened before in the whole of French history. Secondly, the Third Republic in 1934 still appeared to have full control of the Army and even of the Police, despite the highly suspect behaviour of certain police chiefs like M. Chiappe. Thirdly, not only were the working-class (and the Left in Paris generally) still ready to "defend the Republic", but provincial France also reacted very vigorously against the "Paris troublemakers" and against the "Fascist threat", and looked upon the Doumergue Government as an uneasy and purely temporary compromise, after which the Republic would, before long, "return to normal". No doubt, men like Sarraut, Chautemps and Daladier—who contrasted so unfavourably with impressive leaders of the previous decade, such as Poincaré and Briand—were not enhancing the prestige of the Third Republic; nevertheless, there was still something of a republican *mystique* in the country; and the February 6th riots had done a good deal to strengthen it. In 1958, on the other hand, for reasons which will be explained in the following narrative, what little republican *mystique* was still left in the country had worn extremely thin: for one thing, the Left was sharply divided; and, worse still, the last few leaders of the Fourth Republic—Mollet, Bourgès-Maunoury and Gaillard— were doing even less to maintain the Republic's authority than had done men like Sarraut, Chautemps and Daladier in the early 1930s. These leaders of the Fourth Republic were in the unusual position (the Third Republic had known nothing like it) of being under the constant pressure of Algiers and the Army in Algeria. Throughout its whole brief history, the Fourth Republic had, indeed, been, more or less, hampered and handicapped by colonial wars—first by the war in Indo-China, then by trouble in Tunisia and Morocco, and finally by the war in Algeria. First the "lobbies" had kept these wars and conflicts going; by 1956, the Army itself was beginning to exercise its pressure on the governments in a more direct and menacing way. J.-P. Sartre put it even more strongly: "*For 13 years,*" he wrote, "*France was ruled by its War Lords.*"

Finally, when it came to an explosion in May 1958—in many respects a worse explosion than that of 1934—the new "saviour" was of a different stature from the rather nondescript politician that M. Doumergue had been all his life. De Gaulle was not "popular" in the ordinary sense; but he was the genuinely Great Man who had perhaps been half-forgotten, but who, in an extreme emergency, could still be available. He was there to "save the situation" just as, in his own way, Doumergue had "saved" it in 1934.

But, unlike Doumergue, de Gaulle was not prepared to be used as a mere expedient to relieve the temporary headache of the Republic; also, unlike Doumergue, he was given a free hand to "rebuild the State". He produced an incongruous new Constitution but, without looking at it too closely, 80 per cent of the French people endorsed it.

Serious students of France have often wondered whether the French people have really been, throughout their history, or at least since 1792, consistently republican and democratic; were there not times when they had hankered for a Strong Man, or, at any rate, readily submitted to one? Saltykov-Schedrin, the great Russian satirist, visited France in the late

1870s, and spoke then of "this Republic without republicans, but with fat bourgeois in front, at the back and on the flanks":

No doubt, it is now argued that the Republic has one capital and unalienable advantage: and that is *suffrage universel*. I am not denying it; we in Russia have nothing like it. But, first of all, they already had this precious *suffrage universel* in the days of the Bandit[1] and every time he wanted it, it replied YES. And even today these products of the *suffrage universel* who sit in Parliament are not all that different from the products of the *suffrage restreint* of which the *chambres introuvables* in the days of Charles X and Louis-Philippe used to be so proud. Therein also lies one of the not very heartening mysteries of French history. . . .

As for the working-class, Saltykov-Schedrin added:

Latterly, there has been some talk in Paris of a new movement, the purpose of which is to put an end to the domination of the bourgeoisie. Since the amnesty, the working-class districts seem to have livened up, but nothing definite can be said about their modest aims, their temperament and their chances of success. So far, we have heard a lot of big and rather frightening words, but with no real substance or passion behind them. . . .[2]

This was written in the days of the *République des Ducs*. Later there were times—during the Dreyfus Case, for instance—when the Republic showed much greater vitality; yet one cannot but wonder whether there have not been many occasions when the alleged French devotion to the Republic and to democracy was only skin-deep, and whether the Second Empire, the *République des Ducs*, the Clemenceau régime, Vichy, and finally the present de Gaulle régime, are not, in their own way, as "typically French" as were the "good" years of the Republic. . . . What the Russian satirist wrote in the days of the *République des Ducs* has today an extraordinarily topical ring. . . .

True (except in Algeria, with its abominable *camps d'hébergement*), the de Gaulle régime is not a barbarous régime, as some of its authoritarian predecessors were. The de Gaulle of 1958—a man different in many respects from the de Gaulle of 1947—had the sense to realize that, for a smooth working of *his* republic, it was essential to preserve one thing to which, in all circumstances, the French continue to be devoted: and that is at least a semblance of personal freedom. The Frenchman likes to be able to say what he likes; and he has an illusion of freedom if he can buy the Fascist *Rivarol* and the howlingly irreverent and bean-spilling *Canard Enchaîné* and the Communist *Humanité* at his kiosk.

But personal freedom is one thing, and political freedom is another; this political freedom the French practically renounced in their referendum vote of September 1958; everything was, in effect, handed over to the

[1] Meaning Napoleon III.
[2] *Complete Works*, vol. 8, pp. 175–6 (St. Petersburg, 1906).

Great Man and to the technicians and other collaborators he chose to select; soon it became obvious that, under the Fifth Republic, parliamentary life and political democracy had been reduced to a rudimentary level. The radio and big-circulation press were becoming wholly conformist; Parliament was becoming less and less of a training-ground for future political personnel; the running of the country, starting with de Gaulle's government itself, was being increasingly entrusted to an ill-defined oligarchy of "technicians" and "bureaucrats", so much so that a high official in a Ministry or a *chef de cabinet* was often a far more powerful man than the Minister himself, especially if the latter was still only a "politician". As time went on, practically all the key posts in the de Gaulle government were handed over to "non-political" personages. This peculiar "modernization" of the French State had perhaps its advantages; but it had very little connexion with parliamentary democracy, or even with democracy *tout court*. Much could, of course, be said of the unrepresentative character of the *chambre introuvable* elected in November 1958; nevertheless, with the role of the Member of Parliament reduced to nothing, it was scarcely surprising that certain sections of the highly discontented peasantry in the early months of 1960, instead of sending angry letters to *their* deputy, as in the past, should have begun to look for "help" and "advice" that might come to them from violent Fascist demagogues, like Poujade or Dorgères d'Halluin.

Explosions of anger like the Amiens riots of February 1960, were not important in themselves, but they pointed, all the same, to the danger of scrapping the traditional safety-valve of public and especially parliamentary discussion.

It is, however, too early to attempt any final assessment of the de Gaulle régime. No doubt de Gaulle himself lent a certain international authority to France which she lacked in the days of Mollet, Bourgès or Gaillard; he could do with impunity certain things which they could not do—for example, more or less normalize France's relations with Tunisia and Morocco, treat NATO roughly, or adopt a progressive policy in Black Africa. But on a major issue like Algeria de Gaulle's sincere attempt to find a solution was constantly hampered by the same forces which had weighed so disastrously on the governments of the Fourth Republic. A large part of the story that follows is concerned with the different solutions with which de Gaulle successively played in his Algerian policy—solutions ranging from a very reluctant, but still virtual endorsement of "integration" (*tous des Français à part entière*) and the "economic bribery" of the Algerians (Constantine Program) to the search for an elusive Algerian "Third Force"—which the "cooked" Algerian election of November 1958 failed to produce—and the ambiguous "self-determination" offer of September 1959, to be followed, after the Algiers riots of

January 1960, by three new landmarks: (1) the "token" crushing of the *ultras* in both Algiers and Paris (arrest of Lagaillarde and de Sérigny, eviction from the government of that "May 13" top revolutionary, Jacques Soustelle); (2) de Gaulle's visit to the Army in Algeria where, in the course of his famous *tournée des popotes*, he virtually endorsed its "military victory first" slogan; and (3) a return, on June 14, to the seemingly dead "self-determination" offer and another invitation to the Algerian nationalists to send representatives to Paris to discuss a ccase-fire. This time the FLN leadership responded favourably; the first official contacts were made at the end of June.

Soustelle, Bidault and the other *ultras* promptly reacted to this, now openly attacking de Gaulle. The profiteers of "May 13" around de Gaulle were doing their best to sabotage the talks. The Army was silent—for the time being, but the *ultras* were now hoping that it would again force de Gaulle to submit to its will, no matter how strong his international reasons were, since the breakdown of the Summit, for wanting to free France of her Algerian millstone without delay, and no matter how favourable public opinion in metropolitan France was to de Gaulle's "new" policy.

As this book goes to press, some progress towards a settlement is in sight at last; on the final outcome of these first official contacts with the Algerian Rebellion the whole future course of France—and of the de Gaulle régime—will largely depend.

De Gaulle is no doubt a great man, who saved France from serious trouble, and perhaps disaster, in May 1958—no matter how questionable his methods were in assuming this role of "saviour". The régime he established after that was not a healthy one; one could not but wonder whether this replacement of even a bad republic by a good *Mon Archie*, without representative political *cadres* capable of fully controlling the Army and the Police, would not gravely damage France in the end. But perhaps the true greatness of de Gaulle still remains to be demonstrated; the real test —peace in Algeria—should come in the next few months.

This story deals chiefly with the dramatic circumstances in which the de Gaulle régime came into being, and with the psychological and material conditions which made this spectacular change possible. It deals far more with the complex human, rather than legalistic, aspects of this extraordinary episode of French history—with the various human reactions to de Gaulle, rather than with his virtually unread and improperly applied Constitution.

And although this story has no exact precedent in the whole history of France, it is, judging from the behaviour of its *dramatis personae*, a very French story, complete with typically French loves, hates, ambitions, resentments, fears, and those various complexes from which France has suffered ever since the disaster of 1940. Moreover, the régime has presented a curious combination of an anachronistic kind of "monarchy" with certain features of "21st-century" technocratic rule, the latter having many points of resemblance with what is happening in other countries, both East and West. But to a truly modern development of France—even with a "king" on top—the Algerian war remains the biggest and most truly anachronistic obstacle of all. And despite his doubts and hesitations, de Gaulle knows it.

Paris, July 1960.   A.W.

PART I

BEFORE MAY 13:
THE ANTI-AMERICAN REVOLT

1. WAS IT A REVOLUTION?

SOME have said that the so-called French Revolution of May 1958 was totally unnecessary; others that it was quite inevitable. These two conceptions do not necessarily exclude one another. Broadly speaking, it was unnecessary, when viewed from the French-Metropolitan point of view, and inevitable when looked at from the "Algiers" angle.

This "Algiers" point of view used to be put forward with particular vigour by de Gaulle's future Prime Minister, M. Michel Debré. But then, after all, he must be classed among the Algiers plotters. In June 1958 he asserted that, during the previous month, France "had longed for the paratroopers". Nothing is further from the truth; yet this incredible statement still does not invalidate M. Debré's other argument to the effect that if the Algiers "revolution" hadn't happened in May it would, inevitably, have occurred in June, July or August.

The current—and, I believe, perfectly legitimate—"metropolitan" view, on the other hand, is that there was nothing in May 1958 which made the French people feel that any drastic changes were urgently necessary. With the Communist Party weak and isolated, and the working class tending to become a-political, the French bourgeoisie did not for a moment feel, as it did in 1851, that its property and prerogatives were in any way threatened, and that a Man on Horseback was needed to save it from the Reds. Nor was there in France anything even remotely resembling the acute economic crisis which, with its six million unemployed, brought Hitler to power in Germany in 1933, or even that nation-wide frustration from which Italy suffered around 1920–21—a feeling which paved the way for Fascism and Mussolini. France, on the contrary, was relatively prosperous. Technically, the country was developing at a reasonable rate; its economic expansion was progressing, though unevenly; there were more cars per head of population than almost anywhere else in Europe; the birth-rate was high, and there was practically no unemployment. No doubt, there were weak spots: the housing shortage was the worst of them. But had France been asked before May 13 whether she wanted the "system" scrapped, the answer would have been No.

True, there was Algeria; but how seriously did Algeria really bother the French people, or interfere with their everyday lives?

Some, like M. Maurice Duverger,[1] for instance, have gone so far as to argue that, though a constant irritation, Algeria was, in reality, merely a side issue—a tedious problem which would have to be settled, one way or another, sooner or later. The crisis of May 1958 was brought on by a revolutionary situation *in Algeria*; but there was *no* revolutionary situation *in France* to correspond to it. And if, in the days that followed the Algiers *putsch* of May 13, there was a "Revolution" in France, too, it was created quite artificially by one thing only: *by the threat of a civil war, which practically nobody wanted.* And it was in order to avert this that the people of France accepted de Gaulle.

The Algiers plotters, whether the civilian and military *ultras*, or "Gaullists" like Delbecque and perhaps even Soustelle, aimed at the establishment of an authoritarian Right-wing dictatorship in France; and they were *using* de Gaulle for that purpose. French opinion, on the contrary, vaguely sensed that the de Gaulle of 1958 was no longer the would-be dictator of 1947. He came to symbolize not so much drastic *change* as an *escape from drastic change*: the preservation, as far as possible, of the *status quo*. Hence the ease, and the almost general relief, with which de Gaulle was almost unanimously "accepted" in May 1958—an acceptance to be confirmed by the September referendum. He was, in fact, "accepted" even by most of those who voted No as a matter of principle. It is an ironical thought that if, in 1851, Louis-Napoleon "saved" France from the Reds, de Gaulle—at least on a short-term view—saved France from Fascism in 1958.

When we say that Algiers was "revolutionary" in May 1958, and that France was not, this does not mean that "Algiers" did not have its accomplices in France itself. And by far the most serious phenomenon was the incipient revolt of the Army and the Police, which enormously aggravated the threat of the Algiers rebellion spreading to metropolitan France. The Algerian paratroopers were no danger to the Republic so long as they could not rely on the support of the Army and the Police in metropolitan France. But once these had become unreliable, the Fourth Republic was doomed.

This Fourth Republic had, especially since 1956, done its best to dig its own grave. The gravediggers of the Republic were not only the Algiers colonels or M. Soustelle, but also some of the "republican leaders" of France—Mollet, Lacoste, Max Lejeune, Bourgès-Maunoury, and many others. They had done nothing to assert the authority of the Republic; instead, they had cringed to its worst enemies. The hushing-up of the "Bazooka Affair" by M. Bourgès-Maunoury was quite a symbol of the dread in which the leaders of the Fourth Republic stood of the Army and the Algiers thugs.

If Revolution means social change in the first place, then what happened

[1] *L'Express*, October 2, 1958.

in France in May 1958 can scarcely be called a revolution at all: it was to lead to major structural, but not social changes. A counter-revolution then—something like Vichy, which marked a departure from the "republican tradition", no matter how feebly this was represented by the Fourth Republic in its decline? Yes and no; Algiers had hoped for a genuine counter-revolution; de Gaulle gave it only a limited one, but with certain unmistakable "reactionary" characteristics like the enormously reduced role of Parliament and the Vichy-like departure from the great principle of the *école laïque*, despite the traditional republican verbiage contained in the Constitution of the Fifth Republic:

La France est une République indivisible, laïque, démocratique et sociale.

In a sense, de Gaulle represented in 1958 a *liberal* element in the conflict of forces in France and Algeria. But, on a long-term basis, he inevitably also represented an anti-liberal element.

At the end of 1959 the *Canard Enchaîné* published a brilliant imaginary conversation between Ike and de Gaulle, which went like this:

Ike: Let me tell you, Charlie, you've got a goddam nerve holding *me* responsible for the failure of your so-called "Algerian policy". For every time you make one of your noble and splendid speeches that swing wide open the gates of hope, your Debré hastens to shut them with a bang. . . . And when it isn't Debré, it's your generals. "Nothing has changed," they say, "we're staying on." . . . And Bidault goes to Algiers to rouse the rabble against you. Let me just tell you this, Charlie: you expect us—I mean me, Macmillan and Khrushchev—to tremble in our shoes in your presence. You almost expect us to stand to attention in your august presence! But there's not a thing you can do to get your own generals or colonels to obey you. . . . I'm sorry, Charlie, to be so frank.

De Gaulle: I don't care, Ike, what you say. Only let me just tell you this: What reason have you for saying that my Prime Minister, my generals, even my Bidault, are disobeying me? How do you know that they aren't so many pawns I have cleverly arranged on my chessboard? How do you know this isn't part of the game to keep my régime going? A Mollet here, a Soustelle there; a Mauriac here, a Massu there; a Michelet here, a Bidault there; and after every liberal appeal I make to Ferhat Abbas, there's a trumpet blast from my generals. Remember, Ike, it was Algeria that brought me to power; it was Algeria that finished off the Fourth Republic, not to say the Republic *tout court*; it's Algeria, too, which had reduced my people to that state of blessed docility and impotence into which it had already fallen under Pétain. It's only thanks to the Algerian war that I am able to carry out the present *école libre* operation. . . . Of course, I'm all for peace, but in good time, when my régime, my faithful vassals and my army will have drawn all the advantages to be drawn from a situation they could never otherwise have hoped for, and when they'll have firmly established themselves in the conquered territory . . .

Though entertaining enough, was this "imaginary conversation" a

correct assessment of de Gaulle's powers, and did it not attribute to him
a degree of political cunning which he, in fact, lacked? What happened
only a few days later—the conflict with Pinay and the veiled threats the
Minister of Finance uttered on being sacked, and, soon afterwards,
General Massu's challenge to de Gaulle's authority—clearly showed that
de Gaulle did not have over the chessboard the full control he thought
he had. And even though, at the end of January 1960, he won a victory
over the Algiers *ultras*, it still did not mean that the Army had submitted
to his authority unconditionally.

What can be said at this stage in all fairness is that, even though he did
set up a curiously "amphibious" régime in France, full of inherent
dangers, he tried gradually—*very* gradually—to weaken the forces that
were preventing him from reaching a settlement in Algeria. He swung
right one day, and left the next, but, on balance, he seemed, by the middle
of 1960, to have weakened the *ultras*. With Soustelle driven out of the
government, and with public opinion in metropolitan France mainly
favourable to de Gaulle, the latter's position seemed stronger *vis-à-vis* the
civilian and military *ultras* than ever before. Still, the day the FLN's first
official emissaries arrived in Paris, de Gaulle had not yet won the game—
far from it. In fact, soon after, he again became distressingly ambiguous.

2. THE COLONIAL CURSE

ALTHOUGH, in the words of M. Duverger, Algeria was only a side-
issue to metropolitan France, it was, nevertheless, one which had
poisoned the whole French political atmosphere for at least two
years before the May 1958 revolution. This war had already cost 7,000
French lives (not to mention perhaps hundreds of thousands of Algerian
lives[1]) and about £2,000 million, including about a thousand million
dollars in foreign exchange. And this Algerian war was the last in the
long series of colonial wars which, practically without a break, France
had been waging ever since the end of World War II.

I need not here go over the ground already covered in other books,
which dealt in great detail with the seven-year war in Indo-China, and
with the ruthless French attempts to suppress the liberation movements in
Tunisia and Morocco.[2] In the context of the present story, by far the most
significant event was that which occurred in Morocco in the summer
and autumn of 1955: the famous "revolt of the Generals", who rebelled
against M. Grandval, the Resident-General (appointed to Rabat by the

[1] The Algerian "Government" spoke in 1959 of 1 million Algerian dead, including
civilians.
[2] See the author's *France 1940–1955* (London, 1956) and *The Strange History of Pierre
Mendès-France and the Great Conflict over French North Africa* (London, 1957).

Faure Government), because of his unnecessarily "liberal" tendencies, and openly defied the orders that were being sent them by the government of M. Faure. These generals were encouraged in their disobedience by the French settlers in Morocco, by certain right-wing emissaries who kept on travelling to Rabat, and—though in a less blatant manner—by President Coty himself. The generals were determined to keep Arafa, the puppet sultan, on the throne, and did not finally give up their attempt until the Glaoui—until then "France's best friend"—had suddenly declared himself in favour of Sidi Mohammed Ben Yussef's return. . . .

But until that time the generals in Morocco had still hoped to hold down Morocco by force, whatever else the French Government was planning. What happened in Morocco in the summer of 1955 may be regarded as a small-scale rehearsal of the Algiers rebellion of May 1958,[1] and it is significant that at least one "rebel" general in Morocco—Miquel —should have hovered threateningly in the background throughout the May 1958 crisis.

In a matter of less than three years, France had "lost" Indo-China, Tunisia and Morocco. In the meantime, on November 1, 1954, the Algerian war had started in a small way through what came to be known as the Aurès Rebellion. This was not entirely a spontaneous uprising; behind it was a secret organization, with Ben Bella as one of its leaders. It took place at a moment when the French troops in Algeria were unusually scarce, many of them having been sent to Indo-China and not yet having been repatriated.[2] Nevertheless, throughout 1955 it still remained a fairly small-scale guerrilla war, though August was marked by some savage massacres and counter-massacres. It was these massacres which deeply affected M. Jacques Soustelle who, in the previous January, had been sent by Mendès-France to Algeria as Governor-General. Soustelle was a Gaullist[3] but had, in January 1955, the reputation of a "liberal" and "Left-wing" Gaullist. His attitude to the Algerian problem was hesitant at first, and he and the European diehards of Algiers did not at first take to each other; it was not until the August massacres that Soustelle himself became a fanatical *ultra*, who was now more and more convinced that France's only hope was to be uncompromising in her struggle against both Islam and its British, American, Egyptian and Russian accomplices; Soustelle soon convinced himself, indeed, that there was an international conspiracy to oust the French from North Africa

---

[1] This "generals' rebellion" is described in the author's *Strange History of Pierre Mendès-France*, pp. 209–32.

[2] It was the "Indo-Chinese" frustration of these troops, after their return to North Africa, which was to prove, as we shall see, a major psychological factor in the May '58 rebellion.

[3] By "Gaullists" at that stage we mean former members of the RPF who had remained in the "Social Republican" party, and who, though not officially supported or sponsored by the General, continued to think of his return to power as a desirable possibility.

altogether. The solutions·for Algeria he proposed in 1955 and the early part of 1956 were "integrationist" half-measures, which could neither impress the Moslems nor unduly alarm the Europeans, who knew that Soustelle's heart was now in the right place. And whatever measures were ultimately to be applied to Algeria, Soustelle held, by the end of 1955, that "restoring order" must have top priority. After the French General Election of January 2, 1956, he was given a tremendous send-off by the European community of Algiers, who saw in him the best defender of their interests against the Algerians.

3. THE ALGERIAN TANGLE

At the time of the January 1956 Election, practically the entire Algerian *élite*—including even the most docile of Algerian politicians who had until recently sat in either Algerian or French assemblies—had expressed their solidarity with the Rebels—or at least their sympathy for them. The sympathies of the ordinary Algerian population were becoming even more outspokenly pro-Rebel.

It is true that for a short time—a very short time—hopes had been raised amongst Algerians by the formation of the new "Republican Front" Government under Guy Mollet, the Socialist leader, with Pierre Mendès-France, the Radical leader, as his Minister of State without Portfolio. Mollet was planning to send the relatively liberal General Catroux as Resident-Minister to Algiers.

But this plan was abandoned after Mollet's famous visit to Algiers on February 6, 1956. The Europeans of Algiers came out by the thousand that day to demonstrate against their "surrender" and their "betrayal" by France which they were expecting from Mollet and his Government. Needless to say, this demonstration was much less spontaneous than it looked; with the complicity of the Army and the Police, Fascists like Biaggi and the local Poujadists had for days been busy preparing it. It was on that day that Mollet, *abandoning the role of arbiter between the French and Moslems in Algeria, openly took the side of the French*. Impressed by the large numbers of "ordinary" and "humble" Europeans who had first pelted him with tomatoes and had then implored him to defend them against the Arabs, Mollet took the fatal step of "surrendering to the Street". He cancelled the Catroux appointment and sent as Resident-Minister to Algiers M. Robert Lacoste, hale and hearty and earthy Lacoste, whose very first objective was to get into Algeria as many troops as possible. He was content to fight the rebels; he cared nothing for fighting on the "second front" against the colonialists, with whom he developed the most cordial relations in the next two years.

The essence of Lacoste's policy was "pacification" and little else; in fact it was not a *policy* at all, merely an expedient. Every few weeks he would come forward with assurances that the war in Algeria was only a matter of a few months; or that France was now fighting the "last quarter-of-an-hour" of this war. He was not interested in any negotiations with the rebels; and although, inside the Socialist Party in France, there was a strong current in favour of such negotiations, Mollet's attitude to them remained highly ambiguous. When, in October 1956, the first serious attempt was made to bring a negotiated settlement nearer, this time with the help of the Tunisian and Moroccan Governments, it came to nothing because, ignoring all international rules, the Algiers diehards (and in the first place, Socialist Max Lejeune, whose action was then promptly endorsed by his chief, M. Lacoste) had the plane in which the Algerian delegates were travelling to the Tunis conference diverted from its course and captured. Ben Bella and the other Algerian delegates were sent to the Santé prison in Paris.

Soon afterwards came that Suez adventure which had an important bearing on the situation in Algeria. First of all, European-Algerian opinion, with Lacoste at its head, was convinced that, by crushing Nasser, a quick end could be put to the Algerian Resistance. Secondly, *the failure of the Suez expedition—in which the French paratroopers, notably under General Massu, had been particularly active—had a devastating psychological effect on the French Army.* They blamed both Britain and America for this new fiasco, and it made them more determined than ever to hang on to Algeria and enter into no negotiations with the Rebels. Dominating factors in the Algerian situation, particularly in the city of Algiers, were the "paratroop mentality" and the strong Fascist and racialist leanings among the European community. Another peculiarity of all these people's mentality was their attitude to France: it was the duty, the sacred duty of the Metropolis to defend "French Algeria"; at the same time they resented any interference by Paris with the "Algerian order". Every French Government, including de Gaulle's in '58–'60, was to come up against this resistance.

For what, essentially, was this order? 25,000 Europeans owned over a quarter of the arable land, and most of the best land at that. The food consumption amongst Algerians, according to an FAO report in 1948, represented, on the average, 1,450 calories and there had been little change for the better since then; only 19 per cent of Moslem children went to school and, at Algiers University, there were, in 1954, 4,548 Europeans and 557 Moslem students. Hunger had driven some 400,000 Moslems to look for work in France. Short of enormous French investments and a very different distribution of wealth (to which most Europeans were violently opposed), there was little hope of raising the standard of the Algerians. The country—in relation to its population—was poor in economic resources, unless (and this was a major French economic argument for clinging to Algeria) the Sahara were, as was prophesied far and wide, to prove a source of boundless wealth.

The mentality of the paratroopers was not necessarily identical with that of the European civilians; on the contrary, there was a strong touch of contempt in the paratroopers' attitude to the *jeunesse dorée* and some of the more blatantly smug loafers and war-profiteers amongst the community of settlers. But on one point they saw eye-to-eye: they despised French democracy, and bitterly hated the intellectuals. If, to the Europeans of Algeria, the National Assembly was a constant source of danger to their rights and privileges, to the paratroopers, the "politicians" and the "intellectuals" were, in some way, to blame for all the humiliations the French Army had suffered—whether in 1940, or at Dien Bien Phu, or in Tunisia or Morocco. . . . And now—what were the Deputies up to in Algeria?

Actually, the National Assembly wasn't "up to" anything. Throughout 1956 and 1957—as before—there was always a solid majority to support the Algerian war by every financial and military means. The National Assembly, largely dominated by the colonialist Right, indeed, invariably overthrew any government showing the slightest sign of "weakness". Mendès-France was overthrown on the Algerian issue in 1955, Bourgès-Maunoury in 1957, Gaillard in 1958. This anti-intellectual and anti-democratic attitude has often been compared with a not dissimilar attitude of the Nazis. This may be unfair; and yet the paratroopers had, over the years, acquired something of the "*élite* mentality" of Hitler's S S; they looked condescendingly, if not with positive distaste, at the ordinary conscript soldiers from France, whom they regarded as mere auxiliaries, whereas they, the paratroopers, were the hardened soldiers who, together with the Foreign Legion, had done most of the tough fighting in Indo-China, and who now again, in Algeria, were doing practically all the real fighting against the FLN. This feeling amongst paratroopers that they were bearing the brunt of this perhaps senseless war—for "Paris would again let them down", one of them told me—was one of the things I found most striking during my visit to Algeria in 1956. But in 1956 this feeling had not yet been fully rationalized in political terms.

The exceptional position of the paratroopers was a point Pierre Clostermann was to stress in his speech at the National Assembly at the now historic meeting of May 13, when he drew a clear distinction between the real fighting troops in Algeria (mostly paratroopers and the Foreign Legion) and the rest. This "superiority complex" of the paratroopers and their sense of "mission"—and, more particularly, that of some of their younger officers and their colonels—often had an unmistakably

Fascist quality. The very fact that paratroopers had been latterly employed for police and "Gestapo" work, and that it was they who had been entrusted with the task of winning "the battle of Algiers"—which they did accomplish in 1957 by stamping out Algerian terrorism in the city by every conceivable method, torture included—had given them a special position in the French Army not unlike that of the S S in Hitler's Wehrmacht. It had also made them extraordinarily popular with the European population of Algiers, who, since the early months of 1956, had suffered from sporadic acts of terrorism on the part of the Algerian nationalists. The local commander of the paratroopers, General Massu, a man who had joined de Gaulle in the Chad early in the war, who had done service in Indo-China, had conducted the paratroop operation in the Suez Canal zone, and had latterly won the "battle of Algiers" by the most ruthless methods, thus became something of an idol of the European population of Algiers.[1]

I shall not attempt here to examine in detail the extremely complex and contradictory elements of whom "European Algiers"—which engineered the French Revolution of May 1958—was composed. It is enough to say at this point that "European Algiers" was composed of, broadly, the following elements, all of them, with the exception of a few liberal intellectuals, belonging, in French terms, to the Right or Extreme Right.

On the civilian side: the big colonialist interests; the medium colonialist interests; the much larger mass of *petits blancs*, all of whom were sharing in varying degrees in the colonialist cake; thus even the smallest Government official was receiving a 30 per cent bonus (*le tiers colonial*) over and above the salary he would be getting in France; the "white" trade unions, such as Force Ouvrière, which were just as colonialist in their attitude to the Arabs as most other whites; a particularly noisy and active part of the European community consisting of

---

[1] On the face of it, in view of his defence of torture, Massu would appear to have justified the description of him as "the Himmler of Algiers"; but I have also heard him described as a "man of great personal courage, but a particularly stupid type of Blimp". Some have described him as "a highly complex and tortuous character", who agreed to torture with only the greatest reluctance and after "trying it out on himself" (though with a time-limit—which, of course, makes all the difference); he has also been referred to as "a devout Catholic", though one married to a Jewish lady (the former wife of the very Gaullist Me. Torrès)—a questionable combination in a race-conscious city like Algiers—and moreover as a man with a sneaking sympathy for the Arab underdog, and a dislike of the *gros colons* and of Algiers "teddy boys"; unlike them, he is said to have been favourable to a policy of liberal reforms in Algeria, and to have considered himself a "republican general", out of sympathy with genuine Fascists like General Faure.

When all this is taken into account, one cannot entirely reject the theory according to which Massu acted on the spur of the moment on May 13 in taking over from the "teddy boys" the Government-General building they had invaded, and in deciding to preside over the Committee of Public Safety, thus at least taking over this Committee from the civilians—and from the more outspokenly Fascist colonels (like Thomazo and Trinquier) serving under him, who had encouraged what was in effect a Fascist *putsch* by the Algiers riff-raff.

university and lycée students and the "lower middle-class" riff-raff, largely symbolized by the "teddy boys" of Bab-el-Oued and other European suburbs of Algiers; to all these people, with rare exceptions, the preservation of their colonialist privileges was one of the things that France was expected to fight for; amongst a high proportion of these people, Fascist (Poujade, Biaggi, etc.) and near-Fascist influences (Soustelle) were strong.

The "Algiers crowd" as such was "Mediterranean", easily aroused, changeable, and suffering from a sort of political infantilism, with exaggerated momentary enthusiasms and momentary fears and even panics. A perfect crowd for demagogues to work on.

On the military side, there were the conscripts from France, to most of whom their time of service in Algeria was merely a drudgery,[1] and whose role in the May events appears to have been pretty passive, though some officers and soldiers appear to have responded rather sharply to the "ultimatum" Massu sent to President Coty, and to have formed (though without any practical effect) Republican Defence Committees during the following days. But the bulk of the hardened troops and particularly the paratroopers, were disgruntled about Paris—which, they feared, might again do a "Dien Bien Phu" on them—this time a "diplomatic" one, as Lacoste had so often said, and so add to the idle sacrifice, the shame and the disgrace of the French Army. A proportion of the paratroopers, especially their colonels, were Fascist-inclined, and there was definite connivance between them and certain civilian Fascist groupings amongst the European Algerians. The Algerian territorial units were all on the side of the *ultras*, and also working in agreement with *some* paratroop colonels.

There was, in Algiers, an almost inextricable tangle of all kinds of secret societies, "networks", etc., in which both civilians and soldiers were involved.

4. PARLIAMENT AND ALGERIA

ALMOST exactly a year separated the Algiers *putsch* of May 1958 from the overthrow of the Mollet Government in May 1957. This Government, which had emerged from the Left election victory of January 1956, had failed completely to stop the Algerian war, despite all its election pledges. After Mollet had surrendered to the Algiers mob on that fateful February 6, 1956, he was given special powers by Parliament, even the Communists voting for them—for the sake of maintaining the Left majority. A few intellectuals argued that these powers were excessive, and, not trusting Mollet half an inch, they feared that they would merely empower the Government to continue the Algerian war indefinitely. Which is precisely what happened.

But in 1956 the mood in France was in favour of "keeping Algeria for

[1] This was later to change, when the officers proceeded to subject conscripts from France to a learned process of "conditioning", so that many developed something not unlike a "para" mentality and even a positive taste for brutality.

France", after all the humiliations she had suffered in Indo-China, Tunisia and Morocco. What soon afterwards came to be known as "National-Molletism" represented a mood of nationalist exasperation in France which not only allowed the Algerian war to be perpetuated, but also enabled Mollet to embark, amidst almost universal applause, on the Suez adventure. And, in all the numerous National Assembly debates on Algeria during 1956, the two men who invariably received the loudest applause were Lacoste and Soustelle.

Largely for the benefit of UN, Mollet devised in January 1957 his famous triptych: Cease-fire, elections, negotiations for a new Algerian statute; but this proved little more than a platonic gesture. So the deadlock —and the war—continued throughout the Mollet régime, which ended in May 1957. Mollet was succeeded by Bourgès-Maunoury, a Suez diehard. His chief claim to fame was the toughness with which he handled the "defeatist" press—notably papers like *L'Express* and *France-Observateur*, which were confiscated on several occasions. But this did not help him; for when he proposed a mild programme of reforms for Algeria, known as the *loi-cadre*, the Right and Extreme Right (together with the Communists) overthrew him. Some of the Centre groups were also divided.[1]

It was this unholy alliance of the French Colonialists and the Communists which was chiefly responsible for that proverbial "government instability" from which France suffered during the year preceding the Algiers *putsch*. No doubt, it was hard for the Communists to vote for men like Mollet, Bourgès-Maunoury, or Gaillard; but when, finally, in May 1958, they decided to support Pflimlin in the name of the "defence of the Republic", it was too late.

---

[1] It should be recalled that the National Assembly, which had been elected in January 1956, was composed, by the end of 1957, as follows:

EXTREME LEFT:	Communists, 142. (Thorez, Duclos.)
	Progressistes, 6. (Cot.)
LEFT:	Socialists, including small affiliated groups, 97. (Mollet, Deixonne, Pineau, Lacoste, etc.)
LEFT CENTRE:	UDSR (*Union démocratique et socialiste de la Résistance*), 20. (Pleven, Mitterrand.)
	Radicals, 42. (Mendès-France, Bourgès-Maunoury.)
CENTRE:	RGR (*Rassemblement des Gauches Républicaines*), 14. (Faure.)
	Gauche démocratique, 13. (Badie.)
	Regroupement africain, 16. (Senghor.)
	MRP (*Mouvement Républicain Populaire*), 75. (Pflimlin, Bidault, Teitgen.)
RIGHT:	*Républicains sociaux* (Gaullists), 20. (Soustelle, Chaban-Delmas, Triboulet, Dronne, etc.)
	Indépendents, 89. (Pinay, Pierre André, Isorni, etc.)
	Paysans, 11.
	Paysans d'action sociale, 8.
EXTREME RIGHT:	*Union de Fraternité Française* (Poujadists), 30.
	Others (Fascists, ex-Poujadists, etc.), 8. (Dides, Le Pen, Tixier-Vignancour, etc.)

5. TUNISIA SMOULDERING

BOURGÈS-MAUNOURY was succeeded, in November 1957, by thirty-eight-year-old Félix Gaillard, who had distinguished himself by a certain virtuosity as Minister of Finance in the previous Government; being married to the widow of a multi-millionaire newspaper king gave him that extra bit of assurance he needed to look like one of the rising young political leaders of France, and like the most dangerous rival of Mendès-France inside the (now pretty dilapidated, but perhaps still "revivable") Radical Party.

But Gaillard had bad luck. Algiers was in a state of ferment. All sorts of strange things had been going on there, among them the attempt to assassinate General Salan, the Commander-in-Chief. Also, there was more and more screaming at Algiers about Tunisia having become a "rebel sanctuary", through which supplies from all kinds of suspect sources were reaching the FLN. In France, on the other hand, "National-Molletism" had largely abated in 1957, and people were becoming increasingly bored with the Algerian war. But then something happened —just as Gaillard had taken over—to arouse not only the most violent passions in Algiers, but also to revive some of the old chauvinism in France itself.

In November 1957, to bolster up its popularity with the Arab world, and for fear of seeing any still "reliable" and "pro-Western" part of it turn to the East for help, the U.S.A. (followed by Britain) decided to send arms to Tunisia, ostensibly in order to arm the young Tunisian Army—which the French were (understandably) in no hurry to do.

This decision produced an explosion of rage in Paris. Tunis was a hotbed of FLN activity, and had been that ever since the summer of 1956. Bourguiba, though "a friend of the West", was under constant pressure from the Tunisian trade unions, from the FLN leaders themselves, and from important elements in his own Neo-Destour party who were strongly pro-Algerian, and who felt that they could hasten peace in Algeria only by supplying every possible kind of aid to the Algerian rebel forces; the most important thing was to maintain a constant flow of arms across the Tunisian-Algerian border. Bourguiba scared Washington by telling it that if he absolutely prohibited such help, he might well be faced with a pro-Algerian rebellion in Tunisia itself, and be replaced by a "Nasser stooge" like Salah Ben Yussef, who had, ever since his escape in 1955, been agitating against Bourguiba's "Westernism" from Cairo.

The French did not have the slightest doubt (and all the information from Tunis showed that their certainty was not unfounded) that a large proportion of the American and British equipment "for the Tunisian army" would, in one way or another, find its way to the Algerian rebels.

There were angry demonstrations in Paris outside the U.S. Embassy against the "murder of our boys" with American weapons. M. Gaillard protested both to London and Washington, but did not press his point very hard, in view of the rosy hopes he had of securing a loan of several hundred million dollars in the U.S.A. by the end of the year.

The loan, negotiated by M. Jean Monnet, was duly granted in January; but the deliveries of American arms to Tunisia rankled all the same, especially with the French army generals in Algeria, and with the Europeans there. Lacoste was becoming increasingly furious with that "Tunisian sanctuary" from which the arms were now flowing to the FLN, and he blamed Britain and the U.S.A. in no uncertain terms for prolonging a war which, by the end of 1957, he said, the French had as good as won. . . . In Tunisia, too, in some cases just across the Algerian border, the FLN had established army camps and training centres.

The state of public opinion in Paris in January was extremely confused, and the atmosphere unhealthy. M. Gaillard was making statements on North Africa, which might mean anything or nothing; in an interview with *U.S. News and World Report* he said there could be no question of granting Algeria independence, "at least not in the near future"—a qualification which aroused great anger in part of the right-wing press.

Altogether, he seemed between the devil and the deep sea. Half-heartedly, he produced a new programme of liberal reforms for Algeria and felt that this new version of the *loi-cadre* might be a step in the right direction—though whether it would stop the war in Algeria he was not at all certain. As a sop to the *ultras* he showed himself, like Bourgès before him, tough with the "defeatist" press. The January number of J. P. Sartre's *Temps Modernes* was seized by the police for printing a *reportage* by an Italian journalist on the Algerian rebels; similarly, a whole issue of *France-Observateur* was seized. On the other hand, members of the Gaillard Government never ceased talking of the boundless prosperity which the Sahara would bring to France. At Touggourt, on January 9, M. Max Lejeune, Minister of the Sahara, said that France would become, thanks to the Sahara, "the third-greatest world power as regards fuel resources."

Yet the war was still going on. Every day the papers published accounts of 50, or 100, or 150 rebels having been "put out of action". Some were saying that the rebels were now feeling completely exhausted, and were about to give up the struggle; others were arguing that they were merely "hibernating" and preparing for a new offensive in the spring.

The electrified barbed-wire line along the Tunisian border was being rapidly built; nevertheless the French generals in Algeria continued to draw the government's attention to the supplies that continued to reach the rebels from Tunisia.

In connection with various frontier incidents, relations between France and Tunisia were severely strained; but M. Gaillard, warned by the United States, was still anxious not to break off relations with Tunisia. The most serious of these incidents concerned Algerian rebels who, allegedly penetrating into Algerian territory from their Tunisian hide-out near Sakhiet-Sidi-Yussef on January 15, captured four French soldiers and killed several others. Sakhiet was soon to become a world-famous place.

The incident came up for discussion in an angry debate at the National Assembly on January 20, when a Gaullist, M. Dronne, declared that General de Gaulle alone had sufficient prestige and authority both to end the war in Algeria and normalize relations with Tunisia and Morocco. This was almost the first time that the "de Gaulle solution" was mentioned. M. Soustelle, while protesting against the allegation that he had advocated, either at the famous November meeting at the Salle Pleyel (where he had spoken together with M. Morice and M. Bidault), or anywhere else that Tunisia "should be reconquered", now violently attacked the government for its "feeble" attitude to Bourguiba:

"If Tunisia continues to be a belligerent, then we must, on a local scale, and by military means, undertake the necessary action, not in order to reconquer Tunisia, but to neutralize the fellaghas on Tunisian soil. . . . Six months ago we should have appealed against Tunisia to the UN."

And then came this first attack by the *ultras*—an attack to be taken up a few weeks later by M. Lacoste himself—against the French diplomatic service which was both defeatist and "under the thumb of the United States". One cannot emphasize too strongly even at this stage the frantic anti-Americanism of the French *ultras*; it was to play a decisive role in the propaganda which led up to the May explosion.

"Why," said M. Soustelle, "should the Tunisians have any respect for us if certain officials of the Quai d'Orsay are disloyal? Recently, they circulated a defeatist memorandum in favour of abandoning Algeria, and had it published in a Neo-Destour paper in Tunis."

M. Soustelle also regretted that, at the recent NATO negotiations, the French Government should not have made it plain to the USA that it could have no missile sites in France unless the USA fully supported France in Algeria.

"The whole Atlantic alliance" (M. Soustelle said) "is rotten with American anti-colonialism. The USA is willing to sacrifice its European allies in its ridiculous search for Arab friends, on the ground that this is being done in the name of anti-Communism. In reality, Communism is in full progress in the ex-colonial countries, and at the recent Cairo conference the USSR was running the whole show: there's the result of Mr. Dulles's foreign policy!"

On the following day, the foreign policy debate continued and M. Pineau, the Foreign Minister, also sharply criticized Bourguiba, saying that if there were any further incursions from Tunisian territory, France would have to react "in a legitimate state of self-defence".

In itself, this was not very explicit; but the military in Algeria knew that they were unlikely to be disavowed by the Government, still less punished, if they took the law into their own hands. . . . M. Gaillard, for his part, added that the attitude of the Tunisian Government was "inadmissible", and that its protestations of friendship were of little value if it could not control its own military trucks, the shipping in its ports, and the arms traffic. . . . Despite this verbal toughness, M. Soustelle was not satisfied with the Government, and voted against it. However, the government got through with 334 votes to 226.

At the beginning of February, the National Assembly, after a Third Reading, passed the *loi-cadre* for Algeria which did, however, little more than lay down some general principles for various types of representative assemblies in Algeria, not all of them equally democratic, since in some the European and Moslem communities were to be represented on a fifty-fifty basis. Moreover, as in the case of the *Statut d'Algérie* of 1947, which had never been applied, the actual *application* of the *loi-cadre* was left to subsequent government legislation by decree. Liberal papers like the *Monde* and Algiers liberals like M. Jacques Chevallier feared that these reforms would, as usual, fall between two stools—be unacceptable both to the *ultras* and to the Moslems, who had long lost faith in French promises.

6. THE GATHERING STORM: THE BOMBING OF SAKHIET

STRANGE things were happening in both France and Algeria during those days that preceded the French air-raid on Sakhiet on February 8. The Algerian rebels, after a long lull, had become active again, and there were numerous bloody engagements in which many French lives were lost.

On January 23, the *Monde* published an extraordinary document: an official Notice fixing the rules of "psychological action" in concentration camps in Algeria (called politely *camps d'hébergement*). This "psychological action", the purpose of which was to turn Algerian suspects and other prisoners into wholehearted supporters of "French Algeria", was, it was claimed, closely modelled on the "brain-washing" techniques that had reached such a high degree of perfection in Communist China.

Among French liberals this kind of thing produced the most lamentable impression, coming, as it did, on top of the agitation by the Comité Audin, a committee of university teachers which alleged (with more than enough evidence at its disposal) that Marcel Audin, a lecturer in mathematics at Algiers University, had been tortured to death by General Massu's paratroopers.[1]

---

[1] What was the *affaire* Audin? At 11 p.m. on June 11, 1957, paratroopers arrested at his Algiers home, without a warrant, Maurice Audin, a lecturer at the Science Faculty of Algiers University, who was also working on a doctor's thesis for the University of Paris. After he had been taken away, his wife and his three children were kept under house arrest for the next four days.

Born of an Algerian mother and a French father, Audin had lived at Algiers since 1940. Being an exceptionally brilliant mathematician, he was appointed assistant to Professor Possel in 1953, and his thesis, which everybody considered quite outstanding, was defended in his absence in Paris on December 2, 1957, i.e. long after his arrest and disappearance. As a student, Audin had joined the Algerian Communist Party; under the special powers given to the Mollet Government, the Algerian authorities could, after the dissolution of the Party, take action against him—put him under house arrest, or even send him to prison before his being charged with "subversive activity" by an examining magistrate.

On the strength of a Lacoste circular, Audin was "taken in charge" by the paratroopers, and this was officially announced in the press on June 22 which said that, "under a prefectoral decision, he had been placed at the disposal of the commanding officer of the Bouzaréah sub-sector". On the same day, Audin's wife received a note from M. Pierre Maisonneuve, head of M. Lacoste's secretariat, confirming this, and adding that Audin was "in excellent health". On June 27 another member of Lacoste's staff confirmed to a prominent Paris ournalist, M. Louis Martin-Chauffier, that Audin was still at the paratroop headquarters at El Biar. But on July 1, Colonel Trinquier (of whom we shall hear much more later as one of the leaders of the May 13 putsch) informed Mme Audin that her husband, while being transferred from one place to another, had escaped.

Now came months of lying and hedging on the part of the authorities. On July 2 Maisonneuve confirmed to Mme Audin what Trinquier had told her: Audin had "escaped". But the Government hesitated to adopt this version; questions asked about Audin's fate at the National Assembly remained unanswered; it was not until December 30 that, in a letter to the President of the Senate, Lacoste personally confirmed Audin's "escape".

The "Committee for the Safeguard of Rights and Freedoms" solemnly set up by the Mollet Government on May 10, 1957, could produce nothing conclusive; but independent inquiries made by M. Pierre Daure, Rector of the University of Caen, and Me. Maurice Garçon, the famous Paris barrister, showed that the "escape" story was an extremely fishy one.

What is more, two witnesses, who were among Audin's fellow-prisoners between June 11 and June 21, namely, Henri Alleg and an Algerian, Dr. Hadjaj, emphatically stated that they knew that Audin had been subjected to torture between June 12 and 18, and that he was in such a physical state that he had to be hidden away during the visit of inspection paid to the "sorting-out centre" of El Biar by General Zeller. a member of the Safeguard Committee.

The Audin Committee, in February 1958, specifically charged two paratroop lieutenants and two paratroop captains with having tortured Audin. And it asked the pertinent question: How, in the physical condition he was in, could he have "escaped"? Also, since these four officers were now accused of murder, why weren't they saying anything to destroy the charge?

In France the revelations and charges by the Audin Committee had aroused the strongest feelings, especially in teaching and university quarters. But it was obvious that the successive French Governments, frightened of the Army, were trying to hush up the whole thing. It is true that in December 1957 Lacoste hypocritically declared that he "was most anxious

What added still further to the general uneasiness was the publication, by the *Editions de Minuit*, of Henri Alleg's *La Question*, on February 13. In this short book, Alleg, editor of the near-Communist paper, *Alger Républicain*, gave a horrifying account of the tortures he had undergone for a whole month at the hands of General Massu's paratroopers. He was still in prison at Algiers, and his manuscript had been smuggled out. The thing that revolted people most was not so much the tortures themselves as the terrifying mentality of the young French soldiers who were doing this "work". What a hideous effect was the atmosphere of Algeria having on these young people who were now glibly boasting of being "the Gestapo"? Sixty-seven thousand copies of the book were sold in France in a few weeks, before the Gaillard Government decided to seize the remaining copies.

The publication of this book created in France a particular distaste for Algeria and its generals and professional soldiers; similarly, it caused a tremendous irritation in military quarters in Algeria against the "spineless" Metropolis, and contributed greatly to the mutual antipathy between Paris and Algiers. . . . Later, in May, at the height of the "paratroop panic", it may well have increased many people's nervousness at the thought of a "civil war", which came to be identified with Massu's methods. De Gaulle rather than torture any day! A current wisecrack was that, as part of his "psychological action" in France, Massu himself had written the Alleg book!

Everything in February seemed to pile up all at once to create violent animosity between "Paris" and "Algiers". Not only were the widest sections of liberal opinion shaken by the *Comité Audin* and by the Alleg book, but the whole French political world was overwhelmed by the French air-raid on Sakhiet on the morning of Saturday, February 8. Parliament and the press were, broadly speaking, split into two factions: the "pro-Algiers" and "pro-Army" people on the one hand, and the "anti-Algiers" people, who were also highly critical of the Army, on the other. The Government, too, was split: Lacoste representing the "Algerian" viewpoint, and Pineau, the Foreign Minister, who was aware of all the international complications to which Sakhiet might lead, sharply condemning this Tunisian "Guernica", as many were now beginning to call it. The Premier, M. Gaillard, uneasily hovered between the two, and finally sided with "Algiers".

that the whole truth be discovered", but when Mme Audin's lawyer, Me. Borker, wanted to go to Algiers "to study the dossier on the spot", the Paris Préfecture de Police, on February 3, 1958, refused him a permit to go to Algiers. In the months that followed more and more evidence piled up to show that Audin had been murdered in the torture-chamber. Worse still, the officer, who was openly accused of having, in a fit of rage, strangled Audin with his own hands, was to be given in 1959 a high military decoration.

In the small town of Sakhiet there were two Tunisian anti-aircraft batteries, and, at some short distance from Sakhiet there were alleged to be two "fellagha hideouts". The raid by twenty-five French (American-made) bombers on the town on the Saturday morning—which also happened to be market day—was scarcely of any military value, and the killing of seventy-five people, including some thirty children in the local school, was intended by the French military authorities, who had ordered the raid, to be a warning to the Tunisian Government. Apart from the dead, there were over one hundred wounded, many of them children. The report of General Salan, following almost immediately upon the raid, spoke of only military objectives having been hit, and of mostly Algerian fellaghas having been killed; but both the diplomats and the journalists who were rushed from Tunis to Sakhiet told a very different story, a familiar story of wartime "frightfulness". The stories told afterwards by the more diehard French papers about the Tunisian authorities having "secretly buried" a very large number of Algerian fellaghas killed at Sakhiet were just an invention. . . .

The bombing of Sakhiet had immediate international repercussions: Bourguiba demanded the "immediate evacuation" of all the French troops (some 20,000) still stationed in Tunisia, and even from the French naval base of Bizerta; he also decided to lodge a complaint against France before the UN Security Council. The US Government, anxious to avoid having to "choose" between France and Tunisia, started examining other procedures whereby the Franco-Tunisian conflict might be solved, among them the possibility of a "good offices" mission. In Tunisia, during the days following the Sakhiet raid, French troops were "confined to barracks" and the Tunisian authorities declared that they would not allow any French ships to dock at Bizerta. M. Masmoudi, the Tunisian Ambassador in Paris, was recalled by his Government, but several Left-wing personalities, among them M. Mendès-France, gave him a cordial send-off. More significant, before leaving, M. Masmoudi made a point of visiting General de Gaulle, after which de Gaulle had the following communiqué issued on the evening of February 10:

General de Gaulle received in audience on February 9 M. Masmoudi, the Tunisian Ambassador, who had expressed the desire to say good-bye to him before leaving for Tunis. The General listened to what the Ambassador had to say on the recent frontier incidents, as well as on his Government's views concerning a North African settlement, in so far as this concerned the Tunisian Republic. The General replied to M. Masmoudi that he wished the Tunisian Government would not allow the present difficulties to ruin the future chances of a Franco-Tunisian association. In General de Gaulle's opinion, such an association is more desirable than ever both for the West and for the world at large.

Why, one may well wonder, did M. Masmoudi specially go to see the

Defence, M. Chaban-Delmas, had boasted of having at last "wiped out a rebel hideout in Tunisia"; M. Lacoste had made a threatening speech at Constantine on the night before the raid; while the Foreign Minister was greatly distressed about the whole thing—especially from the international point of view.

In the National Assembly debate on that Tuesday, February 11, the Government was sharply attacked for the Sakhiet raid by members of the Left and the Extreme Left (Duclos, Hovnanian, Cot, Naudet).

A long speech was also made by M. Mendès-France, in which he went over much familiar ground (Indo-China, Tunisia, Morocco), and said in conclusion why he had "embraced the Tunisian Ambassador"; he had done this because he was determined that the breach between France and Tunisia should soon be healed. And, rather to the embarrassment of the Right, he added:

> And the greatest comfort, the finest justification of my attitude is to be found in the statement in which General de Gaulle, without the slightest trace of hatred and rancour, defined the spirit in which, looking at the future, we should treat the present crisis, so that this temporary quarrel does not lead to divorce. . . . We continue to believe in the French Union, which would include countries that are now independent. Our ambition is greater than yours.

The speech was, in a way, singularly "Gaullist"; it was curious how, in that whole debate, Mendès-France should have been the only one to invoke the authority of de Gaulle—that very de Gaulle against whom he was to turn after the General had been brought into power by the Algiers Insurrection. . . .

But the really essential question was raised, though very much *sub rosa*, by M. Deixonne, the official spokesman of the Socialist Party who, while claiming that M. Lacoste could not be responsible for what had happened, clearly hinted that M. Chaban-Delmas, the Minister of Defence, had been fully informed of the impending operation, and had approved it. In other words, *there was already an "Algiers government" inside the Paris Government*, with the result that the right hand did not know what the left hand was doing. Commenting on this, the *Monde* remarked that the question raised by M. Deixonne amounted to this: "*Is there an occult government which is running Paris from Algiers*, or (which amounts to the same thing) is the Army dominating the Government?" In short, opinion in Paris was becoming increasingly aware, in the light of the Sakhiet incident, of the *disobedience* of Algiers.

But to return to the Gaillard speech: he made out a fairly strong case against Bourguiba, notably over his "lack of co-operation" at the time of the January incident near Sakhiet.

After that Gaillard openly and blatantly "covered" the Sakhiet bombing. The decision, he said, had been taken by the local command; their

"hermit of Colombey"; what made him think that de Gaulle
before long, have a decisive role to play in France? The idea that de
might soon be called upon to "arbitrate" in the North African
had been gaining ground in some quarters, both on the Left and
Right. Mendès-France, in particular, who was in close contac
Masmoudi, had often spoken of de Gaulle as "perhaps the only solu

The Gaillard Government, as already said, was at sixes and seven
the Sakhiet raid. On February 11 Mr. Joseph Alsop published i
New York Herald-Tribune an interview given him the day befor
M. Christian Pineau, the Foreign Minister. In this interview the follo
statements were attributed to M. Pineau:

> The bombing of Sakhiet was a deplorable mistake;
> General Salan had perhaps been misinformed of the real nature of the opera
>   he had been asked to approve;
> There was no doubt that the whole village had been destroyed;
> The Government had authorized the Army to pursue Rebel bands into Tunis
>   territory, but this authorization did not cover an operation like Saturda
>   air raid on Sakhiet;
> General Salan had probably been simply asked to approve a minor operatio
>   such as the elimination of a machine-gun site;
> The Americans, who had had plenty of trouble in the past with the "Man
>   churian sanctuary" during the Korean war, could well appreciate the stat
>   of mind of the French Army with regard to the "Tunisian sanctuary".

Although, in view of the commotion this interview produced inside
the Government, as well as amongst the Socialist ministers, M. Pineau
(without much conviction, it is true) flatly denied having said all this to
Mr. Alsop—much to the latter's indignation—there was little doubt that
these were, in fact, his views. M. Lacoste, highly incensed by the alleged
Pineau statement and, more generally, by the attitude of the French
Foreign Office (whose secretary-general, M. Louis Joxe, had expressed
to the US Ambassador his "personal regrets" for what had happened),
also violently attacked the French journalists who had "fouled their own
nest" by telling what they had seen at Sakhiet.
Pineau argued that, to improve France's international position in this
sorry business, it was essential that she at least pay compensation to the
victims of the Sakhiet raid—a proposal which greatly annoyed M.
Lacoste. Guy Mollet, trying to reconcile the two views, characteristically
said that the raid ought to be condemned, but in a manner that would not
play "into the hands of either the defeatists or the Algerian rebels", and
which would also "take account of the mentality and the point of view
of the military in Algeria".
Gaillard himself was in an awkward spot. His "Gaullist" Minister of

2

objectives were the anti-aircraft machine-guns at Sakhiet itself and the FLN installations at a mine near the village. . . .

The Army had used its right of legitimate defence; this right had been given it by the present Government and by its predecessor; until now, this right had been used with the greatest circumspection; the raid on Sakhiet, though it succeeded in destroying an important FLN centre, had unfortunately also caused some casualties amongst the civilian population.

Now, taking up his military "sources of information", Gaillard added: "*But our information shows that most of the casualties belonged to FLN units.*" If all this happened, it was the fault of the Tunisian Government which, willingly or unwillingly, had become a belligerent.

Our armed forces' essential aim was to destroy military objectives. Only enemies of our country can believe that this retort had any other purpose. Centuries of our military tradition suffice to confirm what I am saying.

At the meeting the Socialists held soon afterwards, there was something of an uproar against such intellectual dishonesty; Gaillard, scared of the Army and of Chaban-Delmas, had "covered" them both; had adopted their version of the Sakhiet raid (complete with the fabricated story of the FLN casualties) and had even gone so far as to say that it was in the best French military tradition! Afterwards, it was whispered that, much as Gaillard hated doing it, he had no choice: *had he disavowed the Army the effect in Algeria might have been "incalculable"* . . .

Among the MRP there was also a strong feeling against "covering so immoral and reprehensible an act" as the Sakhiet bombing; and M. Robert Schuman abstained from voting for Gaillard—as a warning. A similar stand was taken by M. Edgar Faure and M. Paul Reynaud. Though full of mental reservations, a 335 to 179 majority (with 49 abstentions) nevertheless gave Gaillard its—albeit grudging—support. . . .

Gaillard was scared of Algiers—though, at the same time, he also tried to avoid a breach with the United States. His fear of Algiers expressed itself in all kinds of strange ways during the weeks that were to follow: he had managed to create in Paris a sort of McCarthyite atmosphere. Drastic action was taken against any papers which did not toe the Algiers line or were "insulting" to the Army, while foreign correspondents, such as Nora Beloff of *The Observer*, who were "giving France a bad name abroad" by dwelling on "the truth about Sakhiet" or on highly shady trials of "terrorists", or on torture and concentration camps in Algeria, were threatened with expulsion.

7. THE MOST UNPOPULAR MR. MURPHY

WE shall now try to trace the main landmarks of the negotiations that were going to be conducted during the next two months by Mr. Robert Murphy (accompanied by the shadowy Mr. Harold Beeley of the British Foreign Office) in an attempt to bring about a satisfactory Franco-Tunisian settlement, after the breach that had followed the raid on Sakhiet. As will be clearly seen, this Mission was to prove decisive in precipitating the Algiers *putsch* of May 13.

The Gaillard Government and the Tunisian Government agreed to the Anglo-American "good offices" mission partly for identical, partly for diametrically opposite reasons. The United States Government had impressed on both parties its reluctance to see the conflict debated at UN. On this point, both governments were, broadly speaking, in agreement: neither Tunisia (in view of the frontier violations) nor France (in view of Sakhiet) had a foolproof case to take before UN.

But the differences started when it came to Algeria. The French Government never ceased to emphasize that it would on no account allow the "good offices" mission to meddle in the Algerian problem, which was an "internal French affair". Bourguiba, on the other hand, was anxious to extend the "good offices" to Algeria, and there is little doubt that he had in Mr. Murphy a sympathetic audience. Although Mr. Dulles and other American leaders swore that nothing was further from the truth than insinuations to the effect that the USA was trying, in some way, to supplant France in North Africa, Bourguiba was clearly suggesting to the Americans that, with things going from bad to worse in North Africa, it would be in the interests of the Free World if the French, as an "occupying" power, cleared out of Tunisia altogether, *and the naval base of Bizerta be handed over to NATO, i.e. in effect to the United States.*

A large part of French opinion was acutely alarmed by these manœuvres; it was currently said that the whole thing "stank of oil" and that the Americans "wanted to grab the oil wealth of the Sahara". The nightmare of American oil tycoons outwitting the French with the complicity of Bourguiba, and so turning North Africa into an American sphere, was terrifying enough to prompt the Soviet Ambassador to call at the French Foreign Office to say that the Soviet Union would much rather see the French keep Bizerta than see it handed over to NATO and the USA! The Russians also took the significant step of intimating their worries to de Gaulle, Mr. Vinogradov, the Soviet Ambassador, personally calling on the General in the rue Solférino during his weekly visit to Paris.

The situation created in Tunisia by the bombing of Sakhiet was both alarming for France and deeply humiliating. In addition to "marooning" her soldiers and closing to French ships the harbour of Bizerta, the Tunisians proceeded to expel "undesirable" French citizens, many of whom had lived all their lives in Tunisia, and to close down numerous French consulates. A few days after Sakhiet, the Tunisian Government appealed to the Security Council; this was followed by a French "counter-appeal" against Tunisia. Anxious to avoid an embarrassing discussion of the Franco-Tunisian dispute at UN, the United States, as we have seen, proposed the procedure of a Good Offices mission, and Mr. Robert Murphy took on the job on February 20.

In a statement to the *Monde* President Bourguiba emphasized once again that the Algerian war was the source of all evil and that "a semi-internationalization among the members of the family was better than a complete internationalization"—which clearly implied that he would see NATO (i.e. the USA) rather than U.N. control Bizerta.

Murphy was in a difficult spot. French opinion was extremely distrustful of him. The Communists talked about him as an American imperialist agent anxious for the USA to take over from France in North Africa; almost exactly the same line was taken by the Right, with "Socialist" Lacoste at their head. Even the "liberals" in France were distrustful of Murphy: to them, he was the man who, back in 1942, had conspired in North Africa, together with Vichy's Admiral Darlan, against the Free French and de Gaulle.

For all his dashing manner, thirty-eight-year-old Félix Gaillard was now having great difficulty in impressing his authority on anybody; more and more people were beginning to wonder, after their experience of Bourgès-Maunoury, and now of Félix Gaillard, what advantage there was in having an unusually young man at the head of the Government; a venerable old hand like M. Queuille couldn't be less effective, but at least his old age and experience might carry some weight. And, needless to say, the ineffectiveness of a man like Gaillard added weight to the arguments in favour of "bringing back de Gaulle"; it was in February and March that the "de Gaulle solution" started taking shape at the back of many people's minds . . .

Murphy spent the next two months travelling between Tunis, Paris and London. Because of the suspicions aroused in France as to his real intentions, he had to watch his step. Gaillard had been very emphatic in telling him that, in the French view, Algeria was not covered by the Good Offices Mission's terms of reference. In Tunis, Murphy said, after his first meeting with Bourguiba, that the very first thing he was trying to achieve was "a psychological *détente* between Tunis and Paris". It was learned that Bourguiba had "wanted to talk Algeria" to Murphy; but that Murphy said that the first thing to do was to "prevent any further incidents". After his second meeting with Bourguiba, Murphy refused to say anything, while Bourguiba stated: "We talked about Algeria."

After a further meeting, Bourguiba said he had suggested to Murphy that "NATO take over the Algerian problem". At the same time he had declared himself opposed to the creation of a *glacis*—a No-man's Land—along the Tunisian-Algerian border.

To the irritation caused by all this in France were now added feelings of anger and anxiety; just because the Tunisians were "belligerent", the FLN had been able to resume their military operations on an unusually large scale; on February 27, it was learned that in the Constantinois, close to the Tunisian border, there had been heavy fighting, in which 200 Algerians were killed—but also 50 French paratroopers were killed, and 40 wounded. No doubt, the official figures showed that, apart from this particularly costly engagement, the French losses were usually much smaller than those of the FLN: thus, in February, 3,948 fellaghas had been "put out of action", against 297 French dead. All the same, "thanks to Tunisian aid", French losses were mounting.

Murphy continued his talks in Tunis. On March 1 he said that he was carefully excluding Algeria from his Good Offices Mission; but the French press reported that day that, according to the *New York Times*, "an American solution" to the Algerian problem was "being prepared".

Returning to Paris on March 3, Murphy said his talks with Bourguiba had been "very encouraging"; they had discussed the position of the French troops in Tunisia, and had avoided as far as possible discussing Algeria, though the question of the No-man's Land had, inevitably, given Bourguiba a chance of talking in terms of the *préalable algérien*—i.e. the need to stop the Algerian war before anything solid could be built at all. . . .

The French in Algeria were meantime working themselves into a frenzy over Murphy. On March 4 Lacoste added fuel to the flames with his speech at Philippeville, in which he made no secret of his hostility to the whole Good Offices venture, and in which he violently attacked Tunisia for supplying the rebels with arms. He sharply criticized Bourguiba's objections to the No-man's Land, saying it would only be a few kilometres wide, and would involve the evacuation of no more than five hundred families on either side of the border—so it was no use talking of the "inhumanity" of the scheme.[1] Lacoste, at the same time, advocated an increase in the number of French troops in Algeria.

A few days later, Lacoste said at a Cabinet meeting that the Good Offices Mission "had had a disastrous effect on the Moslem population of Algeria". Gaillard, for his own part, assured the Cabinet that the sole purpose of the Murphy mission was "to enable the French to resume negotiations with Tunisia". There was a clash inside the Government

---

[1] It was not till early in 1959 that it became common knowledge that the policy of "evacuating" Algerians from operational zones had resulted in $1\frac{1}{2}$ million persons being "displaced". Many of these were living in conditions of starvation or near-starvation.

between Lacoste and Pflimlin, the Finance Minister, who was unwilling to increase the total expenditure for the sake of Algeria; in the end a compromise was reached, whereby certain budget cuts elsewhere would be devoted to the costly business of strengthening and extending the defences along the Algerian-Tunisian border. . . .

Gaillard, while unwilling to risk unpleasantness with the USA by discouraging Murphy more than necessary, was now trying to appease the Right in France by starting another major police operation against the "defeatist press". M. Chênebenoit in the *Monde* of March 7 violently protested against Gaillard's "McCarthyism". The confiscation of "defeatist" papers was going too far. If that was the way Gaillard felt, it would be more honest to set up a censorship, and have done with it.

If the only people who are now allowed to speak are the *raison d'état* people, then say so! . . . If what's needed is a *Directoire* of Duchet, Morice, Bidault and Soustelle, then let's have it. *It now looks as though there were two governments in France—the official Government, and an occult government, with its headquarters at Algiers, and with Lacoste at its head.* . . .

Inside France, he argued, the Right could now do anything with impunity; all the government's thunder was reserved for the Left. Encouraged by so much tolerance, the Right were developing marked Fascist and racialist tendencies.

There was more and more talk of de Gaulle as a "solution".

Inside the Socialist Party the Left-wing opposition was beginning to gain ground. There was a strong tendency to go back to the "orthodox theses" of the Republican Front programme of the 1956 election, complete with a "liberal" solution of the Algerian problem. Many Socialists were alarmed by the growing Fascist tendencies on the Right; the attitude to de Gaulle was also hostile; as the *Populaire*, the official Socialist paper, put it, the French Socialists had a great respect for de Gaulle as leader of the Free French during the war, but the greatest dread of de Gaulle, head of the RPF (the "French People's Rally" of 1947), "one of the most colossal enterprises for the demolition of democracy that France had ever known".

No one could quite see *how* de Gaulle could be brought into office; there was, clearly, no majority to support him at the National Assembly. Nevertheless, as Maurice Duverger put it in the *Monde* of March 8, the question of de Gaulle's return was no longer a matter of *how?*, but a question of *when?* Would de Gaulle be brought back while there was still hope of solving the Algerian problem, or would he be brought back when all was already lost? He thought that, although most of the political leaders were against de Gaulle, the rank-and-file might well follow de Gaulle "in certain dramatic conditions".

On March 8 Gaillard produced a plan which failed to impress

anybody—one for a West-Mediterranean Community and for a West-Mediterranean defence pact.

It was a sort of Western variant of the Baghdad Pact, which would include France, Tunisia, Morocco, Spain, Italy and other NATO powers directly concerned; it also provided for the "joint exploitation of the Sahara" by France and the countries of the Maghreb (Tunisia and Morocco, as well as Algeria, whatever the latter's status might be). The whole thing had a half-baked look; the Defence Pact was based on an old Plan concocted in Madrid, and now heated up by Mr. Dulles. The whole idea received very little support. In England, the *Yorkshire Post*, for instance, dismissed it as "an indigestible fantasy"; in France, both the Left and the Right were, though for different reasons, highly suspicious of the scheme; questions were asked what object would be served in allowing the USA, Franco Spain, Italy and other countries to meddle in North African affairs, all the more so as the military contribution to the Defence Pact of countries like Morocco and Spain could only be negligible. Others were asking whether this Pact wasn't intended as the sugar coating for the pill of Algerian autonomy, which French opinion was refusing to swallow?

Liberal opinion in France was equally critical; it was bad enough to abandon Tunisian-Moroccan mediation in the Algerian affair in favour of American mediation; it was worse still to get half a dozen other countries, including Franco Spain, mixed up in it; all of them would want their brokerage. Gaillard, while denying that his Plan was intended to internationalize the Algerian affair, thought it would make it easier for Murphy to complete his mission and would speed up the normalization of France's relations with Tunisia and Morocco.

This half-baked scheme did not enhance the Government's authority.[1]

8. THE REVOLT OF THE FRENCH COPS

BUT worse was to come. On March 13 Paris was to witness the unprecedented spectacle of over 1,000 policemen demonstrating and rioting outside the National Assembly, uttering anti-parliamentary and even anti-Semitic cries.

The policemen's demonstration, which, to begin with, was held in the inner court of the Préfecture de Police, was at first concerned with a relatively trivial matter—the "danger bonus" (owing to the presence in Paris of numerous Algerian terrorists) of 260 francs—or about 5s.—a day which, they alleged, had been promised them by the Government, and which they were still not receiving, as well as some other financial claims. But as the meeting grew rowdier, and as the Prefect of Police,

---

[1] It is, nevertheless, curious to observe that later, under de Gaulle, some of his ministers liked to play with the idea of an "economic zone" including Spain and Italy and based on the oil and mineral wealth of the Sahara.

M. Lahillonne, refused to receive a policemen's delegation in these conditions, over 1,000 men, some in uniform, others in civilian clothes, marched to the National Assembly, which, for several hours, was "besieged" by this crowd of angry cops, many of whom threatened and insulted any Deputies they happened to sight, calling them loafers and parasites who were "getting 300,000 francs a month for doing nothing". M. Roches, a high Police official, who tried to persuade the demonstrators to disperse, was kicked and beaten up. Mobile gendarmes were meantime "defending" the Assembly against an invasion by the policemen. A delegation of these was finally admitted into the Assembly, where they were given assurances that their case would be examined by the Committee of the Interior.

But it was quite obvious that the demonstration was not an "economic" but a political one. There were strong Fascist currents in the Police, and these Fascist elements had their own men in Parliament—the ex-*commissaire* Dides, M. Le Pen, former leader of the Poujadist group, and M. Tixier-Vignancour, an old Vichyite and the most dynamic of all the Right-wing witch-hunters.

While the "siege" of the Assembly was in progress, M. Bourgès-Maunoury, the Minister of the Interior, declared that the behaviour of "certain persons in the Police" was "quite intolerable"; all the more so as the decision to give them full financial satisfaction had already been taken. However, he did not wish to discuss the matter until fuller information on what had happened had become available. There were cries of "Resign!" All hell broke loose when M. Dides rose to "answer the Government". Dides who, together with Tixier-Vignancour, ranked as the principal instigator of the demonstration and as one disposing of a Fascist police network of his own, was howled down by the greater part of the Assembly, and the meeting broke up in disorder.

This anti-parliamentary demonstration by over 1,000 Paris policemen was, clearly, a sign of the times; some very disquieting things were going on below the surface. Chênebenoit in the *Monde* blamed the Government for it:

For months now, there seems to be an unwritten rule about political demonstrations: complete indulgence towards the "super-patriots", and extreme toughness towards "defeatists". Right-wing meetings are allowed, Left-wing meetings —even the most moderate Left-wing meetings—are prohibited. No one trying to overthrow the régime is treated as a Rebel any more; only those are treated as Rebels who show up the weaknesses of the Government and the régime. (*Le Monde*, March 15.)

The Prefect of Police resigned as a result of this demonstration; disciplinary measures were taken against a number of police officials; but M. Bourgès-Maunoury, the Minister of the Interior, decided not to give up his post. The episode, though unimportant on the face of it, was nevertheless highly indicative of the Government's loss of authority, and was a warning to everybody (which is precisely what people like Dides wished it to be) that *the police could not be depended on by the Fourth Republic* in all circumstances any longer. There were many who, two months later, remembered what had happened on that 13th of March . . .

There were other straws in the wind; in a Paris by-election, caused by the death of M. Marcel Cachin, the veteran Communist leader, M. Alexis Thomas, a fanatical advocate of French "Algeria", who devoted a large part of his election propaganda to denouncing the USA, won a resounding victory over all his opponents. About the same time, the Right started a violent campaign against Murphy's "good offices"; a large and noisy meeting was held on March 18 at the Salle Pleyel, at which M. Soustelle, M. Bidault and other "Algerian" diehards spoke.

Nevertheless, Gaillard wanted the Murphy Mission to continue; what he was now asking Murphy to secure from Bourguiba was a neutral control of the Tunisian-Algerian border.

Thanks to the counsels of moderation coming from M. Pinay, the Right of the Assembly decided not to provoke a Cabinet crisis before the Easter recess; and at the end of March Gaillard felt that his government was safe for a few more weeks. . . . He little knew.

9. ALGIERS HITS OUT AT MURPHY AND GAILLARD

EASTER Sunday in 1958 fell on April 6; despite some sporadic railway strikes, there was a tremendous exodus from Paris during the first days of April, which suggested considerable indifference to M. Gaillard's difficulties, and to all the countless ups and downs of the Murphy-Beeley mission.

This impression was, however, deceptive. Wittingly or unwittingly, Gaillard had, somehow, with the help of a large part of the press, managed to *divert public animosity in France from himself to the United States, as personified by Murphy.* What struck me most during the Easter holidays I spent in the Dordogne was the vociferous anti-Americanism, even among the most un-politically-minded.

Needless to say, this feeling had been largely encouraged by the local provincial press, particularly by the *Sud-Ouest* of Bordeaux which spoke in glowing terms of the "immense vistas of French prosperity" arising from the wealth of the Sahara, and, day after day, spoke in the most venomous tones of Mr. Murphy. *La France-Nouvelle République,* reflecting the views of M. Chaban-Delmas, Mayor of Bordeaux (and Minister of Defence in the Gaillard Government!) was equally violent.

On April 3, after another visit to London and another meeting with Gaillard, Murphy and Beeley went back to Tunis, where they were now going to make another effort to make Bourguiba see reason. The French Government was now demanding that Tunisia accept control on both sides of the frontier by neutral observers, and under the auspices of UN, before any Franco-Tunisian negotiations could be resumed. Bourguiba, under FLN pressure, was reluctant to agree to this, saying that Tunisia was not, after all, at war with France—which was, it must be said, a pretty feeble argument. The question now was whether, to cover himself in the eyes of the FLN, Bourguiba was not hoping that such control would in the end be *imposed* on him by UN? There is actually little doubt that the French Government had succeeded reasonably well in putting Bourguiba in the wrong; France's diplomatic position seemed, at any rate, much better now than at the time of Sakhiet. But the fundamental problem of Algeria had not been tackled, and the USA Government (briefed, it was suspected, by Mr. Murphy himself) was unwilling to get tough with Bourguiba, even though, on the question of frontier control, he obviously had a very poor case. . . . What is more, *the French were beginning to suspect the United States of encouraging the Algerian Rebels to set up something in the nature of a provisional government*; and the Tangier conference which was to take place at the end of the month between representatives of the Tunisian Neo-Destour, the Moroccan Istiqlal, and the Algerian FLN was awaited in France with some misgivings. . . .

Bourguiba's "counter-proposals" did not help much. He obviously did not want the "good offices" to fail; but while he was opposed to UN observers being stationed along both sides of the frontier, he thought it would be a good thing if their control were extended to "the whole of the Algerian war". Bourguiba, though more reasonable than before on the other points of the agenda (French control of Bizerta, neutral control of Tunisian airfields, reopening of the French consulates, etc.) would not commit himself to frontier control. He said it was "useless"; men and arms would "get through anyway"; he also warned Murphy that if the "good offices" broke down, an Algerian Government would be set up. Yazid, the FLN representative in New York, for his part, said that if the Murphy mission failed, "friendly delegations" would see to it that a meeting of the General Assembly was called; such a meeting, he said, would be essential anyway, if UN observers were to be sent to the Algerian-Tunisian border. . . . There were some disquieting developments in Morocco, too. Apart from the Tangier conference that was being feverishly prepared, and which was promising to produce nothing good from the French point of view, Ben Barka, the Istiqlal leader, was threatening that "Morocco, too, could turn to the Arab East"—which meant ganging up with Nasser. . . . Altogether, there was a growing feeling in France that, not without American encouragement, the whole Arab world was beginning to gang up against her. . . . Bourguiba even felt that, at this juncture, he could ignore a special message sent him by Mr. Dulles.

Gaillard, a little childishly, decided to ride the high horse. He was not available in Paris when Murphy and Beeley had returned from Tunis. He "invited" them to travel all the way to his château at Barbezieux, in the Charente-Maritime, miles from anywhere, where he was spending his Easter holidays. Foreign Minister Pineau, M. Joxe, Secretary-General of the Quai d'Orsay, and the British and US Ambassadors were also summoned to the meeting.

It was this meeting which marked the beginning of the end of the Gaillard Government. Gaillard who, before the Easter recess, had assured the National Assembly that the control of both sides of the frontier was the indispensable condition which Bourguiba would have to accept, now discovered from Murphy's account that that was precisely what Bourguiba had *not* accepted. He had, however, made a large number of other concessions, and Murphy strongly advised Gaillard to accept these, and leave the frontier problem for further discussion.

In a sense, the conflict that now broke out between Gaillard and the National Assembly was a dual conflict between "technocrats" and "nationalists" and between "soft Algerians" and "hard Algerians". Gaillard, working in close contact with Jean Monnet (who had, only a few months before, secured a large loan from the USA) thought, it was widely suggested, that *he might now become the blue-eyed boy of the State Department, and get America, in one way or another, to help to normalize French relations with Tunisia and Morocco and, eventually, to help in an Algerian settlement, which would be favourable to France.* (This was to underrate the intensity of anti-American feeling that Murphy had created in France.) Both Gaillard and Pflimlin, his Finance Minister, were very worried by the financial complications that were piling up as a result of the war in Algeria, and thought that, before very long, they might have to appeal, once more, for American aid. To put an end to Murphy's "good offices" would be a dangerous thing to do in the circumstances, all the more so as the US Government was desperately anxious to "save" Bourguiba. . . .

The Tunisian proposals were such that Gaillard decided he could not accept them on his own responsibility, all the more so as the Right-wing ministers in his Government were now up in arms against Bourguiba.

A full-dress Ministerial Council was to be called on the Friday, and President Coty was specially asked to cut short his vacation at Mentone. Coty duly flew back to Paris. But Friday produced another sensation:

Gaillard received a personal message from President Eisenhower, strongly urging him to use his "common sense" and reiterating the classical American arguments in favour of Bourguiba.

The Ministerial Council was postponed until the Saturday, and it was to last from 9.30 in the morning till late in the evening. There was sharp disagreement between Gaillard and the Right-wing members of the Government who, at one stage, tried to win over President Coty to their point of view. Finally, however, it was decided to accept the "good offices" proposals as a "basis of discussion"; to "reserve the right" to submit the frontier question to the Security Council or NATO (the Right ministers had at first pressed for a French "indictment" of Tunisia at UN); and, to call Parliament on Tuesday, April 15—i.e. long before the end of the Easter recess.

The disagreement between Gaillard and the Right-wing ministers was, indeed, so fundamental that Parliament was, in fact, being called upon to "arbitrate" in the dispute, despite the nominal "unanimity" of the Government at the end of the twelve-hour Ministerial Council on that Saturday.

The supporters of "French Algeria" were furious with Gaillard. The five points of the Murphy-Beeley proposals they thought "suicidal" for France to accept. These were:

EVACUATION: All French troops stationed outside the Bizerta perimeter are to be evacuated in accordance with a time-table to be agreed upon by France and Tunisia.

BIZERTA: While not contesting Tunisia's sovereignty over Bizerta, France shall negotiate with Tunisia a new status of Bizerta before the regrouping of the French troops now in Tunisia.

AIRFIELDS: Neutral observers shall be stationed at the four airfields in South Tunisia—Sfax, Gafsa, Gabès and Remade—to see to it that these are used only for peaceful purposes.

CONSULATES: Certain French consulates in Tunisia which were closed in February may now be reopened.

EXPELLED FRENCH CITIZENS: The Tunisian Government will reconsider individually the case of all the 600 French citizens "removed" from their residences in Tunisia, and will decide whether it is safe for them to return.

These proposals, said M. Bidault, were "a threat to France's national independence". M. Debré, de Gaulle's future Minister of Justice and then Premier, spoke angrily of "Munich". M. Soustelle declared at Lyon, at a meeting of Social Republicans (Gaullists):

The so-called "good offices" have been turned into a lopsided sort of mediation, essentially hostile to France. Through intolerable pressure, we are now expected to abandon the Tunisian airfields without getting anything in return. After that we'll be expected to abandon Bizerta and Algeria itself.

What they [the USA] are trying to do is to liquidate completely our positions in North Africa. They refuse to raise the real problem: Bourguiba's belligerency by the side of the FLN.

The oil trusts want to squeeze us out of the Sahara. . . . We must say No to all this.

A particularly violent meeting was held at Toulouse. Here an organization calling itself the National Association of North African and Overseas Frenchmen, largely composed of North African repatriates, held its first "regional congress"; its president, General Vésine de la Rue, former commander of the French cavalry in Morocco, went so far as to call for a violent uprising in France itself:

Today there are one thousand of us here; but before long there shall be fifty thousand or a hundred thousand of us to howl in the streets and outside Parliament!"[1]

The hostility of the Right (and of a very large part of the Press) was such that when the Assembly met on Tuesday, April 15, M. Gaillard had few illusions that his Government could survive. From the very start he felt that it was no use to try to "reason" with the Right: they had decided on his execution in advance.[2]

Both Gaillard and Pineau, his Foreign Minister, were, rather obviously, on the defensive.

Gaillard said that it would, of course, be possible to reject the Murphy Plan, and take the whole matter before UN; but this might take a long time, and the growing impatience of the French troops marooned in Tunisia might present a real danger. He denied that the Government was not making a "free choice", and that it had surrendered to "certain foreign pressures"—a remark which produced this interjection from a member of the Right: "*Come on; you'd better read Ike's letter to us!*" Gaillard also argued that to accept the Murphy Plan as a basis of discussion with a hope of later also settling the question of the frontier control was preferable to a simple solution like the occupation of Tunisia—which would inevitably result in that internationalization of the Algerian problem which the Right dreaded most of all.

[1] General Vésine de la Rue said that there were 240,000 "repatriates", mostly living in South-West France, and most of them having come from Morocco and Tunisia.

Many, used to "colonial" privileges, were extremely discontented, and never ceased talking about their having been "betrayed" by the Republic. Numerous French commentators remarked at the time that these North African "repatriates" represented a strong Fascist nucleus in France.

[2] As will be seen, de Gaulle later came to an agreement with Tunisia largely on the lines of the "Murphy proposals"; Pineau in July even argued that the uproar against Murphy had been worked up artificially as part of the conspiracy against the Fourth Republic. (See Part III, 10.)

Pineau also did not seem very sure of himself.

He praised the proposal for the neutral control of five airfields in Southern Tunisia, though he admitted that this did not solve the question of what was to be done if the Rebels used the twenty-five other Tunisian airfields, and "Tunisian air-space generally"; but this, he argued, was part of the "Algerian problem" which was outside Murphy's terms of reference. Bourguiba's refusal to consider joint Franco-Tunisian control of the Tunisian-Algerian border he attributed merely to "the political situation inside Tunisia"; in other words, it was dangerous for Bourguiba to accept the French proposal; and the Americans had obviously not pressed him to do so.

While Pineau denied that there could be any question of "internationalizing" the North-African problem, he nevertheless spoke of an "Atlantic solution" which he intended to discuss at the next NATO meeting in May. And he concluded obscurely by saying:

Certain discussions on North Africa have become indispensable. But this Western solidarity must exercise itself in the best moral and political conditions, so that we avoid the isolation of France, which would be incompatible with the political and economic conditions of our time . . .

The whole debate that followed was marked by a noisy anti-Americanism, which, a little comically, was shared by both the Right and the Communists.

M. Jacques Duclos (Communist) said that the Government had refused at the end of 1957 the "good offices" of Tunisia and Morocco; and this had resulted in "American intervention".

The USA, he said, had now imposed on France their own "good offices", with the discreet threat of "cancelling the loans that had been granted us". So the Government was now submitting to the demands of the American imperialists, in virtue of the commitments made by M. Jean Monnet, who had negotiated the French loans in the USA. It was Monnet who "had brought the Americans and the British into North Africa". The agreement made by Murphy could quite easily have been made in direct talks between Paris and Tunis, without this American interference and without British and Americans being stationed on the Tunisian airfields. It was stupid of Gaillard, said Duclos, to bring the Americans into it; and, anyway, the real problem—that of stopping the war in Algeria—was not being tackled; on the contrary, Gaillard was planning, as he had himself admitted, to intensify this war. The propaganda for this war was in full swing; the *colons* of Western Algeria had agreed to pay a levy of 1,000 frs. per hectare to "support the parliamentary action of persons like M. Duchet and M. Soustelle". And the Gaillard Government, he concluded, was so discredited that nobody wanted to be identified with it, neither the Right nor the Socialists . . .

M. *le Pen*, the ex-Poujadist leader and a noisy Fascist, much to the delight of the Communists, declared that *of the American menace to France and the Soviet menace, the American one was by far the greater of the two.* He argued in favour of getting out of NATO.

"We get the hardest and dirtiest blows from those who call themselves our allies; we have become a sort of Anglo-American protectorate; Uncle Ike's latest friendly summons proves this conclusively."

More moderate in tone, though equally sharp, was another anti-American attack from the Right—that of M. Pierre André, who said that France ought to get out of NATO.

"We cannot be all at once valid allies on the Elbe and people who are being perfidiously stabbed in the back by our allies in Algiers and Tunis. . . . We must not yield to Bourguiba's blackmail, and our allies must obtain his absolute neutrality."

After speeches from other Right-wing members, who took a similar line, M. Soustelle launched his attack on Gaillard and on the USA:

M. Soustelle: After the failure of the "good offices", the only thing that would explain the Government's present policy is Eisenhower's letter. (*Loud cheers on extreme Right and on numerous Right and Centre benches.*)
M. Gaillard: That's penny novelette stuff!
M. Soustelle: So you say you haven't yielded to outside pressure?
M. Gaillard: I have not, and I repeat it.
M. Soustelle: The fact is that you've obeyed a summons, and this will happen again. Where, I ask you, is French policy decided—in Paris or in Washington?
M. Gaillard: I am shocked that a man of your ability should use such arguments.
M. Soustelle: Please, let's not have any of this synthetic indignation when you deal with facts that stare us in the face!

The duel went on for a long time. Gaillard accused Soustelle of wanting to occupy Tunisia; Soustelle denied this, but said once again that if no real neutrality was imposed on Tunisia, and the Murphy policy was accepted by France, it could only lead to the loss of Algeria.

It was clear that the whole Right was in sympathy with Soustelle; and despite the solemn warning made towards the end of the sitting by M. Gaillard that the overthrow of his Government would lead to an inextricable parliamentary situation, and to financial and economic difficulties, his Government was nevertheless overthrown by 321 votes to 255.

It was chiefly Soustelle, supported by other speakers of the Right, who had obtained this result. His "anti-Americanism" had been of decisive importance on this occasion.

It is significant that M. Michel Debré led a parallel onslaught on the

Government at the Senate: like Soustelle he played the anti-American string:

"There is now a clear danger that the British and Americans will dominate the Atlantic Alliance, and that Germany will dominate Europe. The Government of M. Gaillard is unworthy of representing France."

And so the Right, largely led by M. Soustelle, managed to overthrow another government of the Fourth Republic.

The Murphy Mission was so unpopular in the country that Gaillard received only very half-hearted support from both the Socialists and the MRP. All that M. Deixonne (Socialist) found to say was that the Atlantic Pact was, after all, France's "only shield against Soviet aggression", and that "one shouldn't be too hard on the United States." Which only produced "angry interruptions from the Right".

10. DE GAULLE IN THE WINGS

AFTER the fall of the Gaillard Government, there began that interregnum which was not to end until May 13, the day of the Algiers *putsch* and of the investiture of M. Pflimlin by the National Assembly in dramatic circumstances which we shall describe in a later chapter.

One of the strangest things about this long and dreary Cabinet crisis was that the name of General de Gaulle was still only seldom mentioned. To most people, he remained a possibility, but only a remote possibility. Without a great movement of public opinion in his favour, there was no chance whatsoever of de Gaulle being invested by the National Assembly. The Socialists, in particular, looked upon a de Gaulle Government as a dangerous adventure.

De Gaulle had, indeed, been out of the limelight for a very long time. His quasi-totalitarian movement, the *Rassemblement du Peuple Français* had enjoyed great support in October 1947; in the 1951 election it still counted: 120 "Gaullists" were elected to the National Assembly. In March 1952, as was to be expected (for countless "ordinary" conservatives and even Vichyites had taken advantage of the de Gaulle label between 1947 and 1951), twenty-seven of the Gaullist deputies split away from the RPF group, and went to the rescue of M. Pinay, the prospective Right-wing Premier, who was then to remain at the head of the Government throughout the greater part of 1952. In 1953, after a severe setback suffered by the Gaullists in the municipal elections (when their poll, compared with 1947, had dropped from nearly 40 per cent to a mere

10 per cent), de Gaulle withdrew, as it were, his official patronage from what was left of the "Gaullist Party" in Parliament, and went into semi-retirement, concentrating on writing his memoirs, and only occasionally coming to Paris to give a press conference as he did at the height of the controversy over EDC and the rearmament of Germany.

In November 1953 he made this strange confession, which I quote in *France 1940–1955*:

Think by how many failures my public life has been marked! First I tried to persuade the civil and military authorities to endow France with an armoured force which would have spared us an invasion. I failed. After the disaster of 1940 I urged the Government to go to North Africa and evade the enemy. In vain. . . . I failed at Dakar. After our victory I endeavoured to maintain the unity I had formed around myself. But this unity was broken. Later, in grave circumstances, I again tried [by forming the RPF], and failed once more. . . . If these failures had been mine, they would have been of no importance; but they were also the failures of France. True, from time to time, there were successes. . . . And yet, during the darkest moments of the war, I sometimes wondered: perhaps it is my mission to represent in the history of our country its last upsurge towards the lofty heights. Perhaps it is my lot to have written the last pages in the book of our greatness. . . .

De Gaulle had a sense of mission, and a sense of history—though not always an infallible one. He spoke of his failures. Some of them were due to the stupidity, cowardice and shortsightedness of others; but had not some of de Gaulle's failures been caused by his own serious mistakes?

No doubt he was right long, long ago, in 1934, to have advocated a strongly mechanized French Army—though whether this, in itself, would have prevented a German invasion is still exceedingly doubtful when one considers the human and industrial potential on the two sides. Whether he was right or wrong to have advocated the transfer of the French Government to North Africa in June 1940 is arguable. Nor is it certain that it was entirely the fault of the "system"—and not, at least to some extent, the fault of de Gaulle's excessive authoritarianism in those days—that the experiment of 1944–46 had come to so premature an end. But there is no doubt that de Gaulle made several major mistakes: his policy of "greatness" in 1944–45 was, in a sense, "anachronistic": his "Poincarist" attitude to Germany could not succeed in the face of American opposition; his attempt to hold an even balance "between East and West" could not, in practice, work, since France was financially dependent on the USA; even more open to criticism was the preference he gave to Pleven and inflation against Mendès-France and monetary reform and austerity; another great error of de Gaulle's was his decision to reconquer Indo-China, which was at the root of the disastrous eight-year-long Indo-Chinese adventure; but his greatest error (as Mauriac was to say) was his attempt to set up his totalitarian RPF in 1947. This failure of the RPF, which is described in great detail in *France 1940–1955*, was primarily due to de Gaulle's disregard of certain French ways of living and ways of thinking, his failure to realize that although the French are often offensive about parliamentary institutions, the Parties are an essential expression of the inevitable diversity and divergence of interests. Nor was the Goebbels-like theatricality that the RPF developed at one stage either in harmony with the French attitude to politics, or, for that matter, with the personality of de Gaulle himself. He was a great and respected figure, and the role of cheap demagogue which he assumed in the heyday of the RPF did not suit him. And so, after the "Communist menace"—against which the RPF was primarily directed—had receded, a large part of the RPF clientele preferred the more easy-going ways of the Fourth Republic, and looked to the comfortable, wholly unheroic M. Pinay for salvation, rather than to de Gaulle—all the more so as things had settled down in France (largely thanks to Marshall Aid), and the danger of a Communist revolution was just about as remote as that of a Soviet invasion. It was only when these *seemed* to be threatening France that nearly 40 per cent of the French voters in the 1947 municipal elections sought temporary refuge under the de Gaulle umbrella. . . .

During the years that followed—and even as late as the beginning of 1958—de Gaulle had become a sort of historic monument. A noble figure—but one who, somehow, didn't fit in anywhere. He belonged to a glorious episode of the past. Occasionally, somebody would remember de Gaulle. A man like Mendès-France—a very severe critic of the Fourth Republic—would occasionally daydream about de Gaulle coming back, and putting the house in order—but again provided he had a clear programme, and didn't try to "rule by compromise", by sticking into his Government all the Pinays and Mollets and Teitgens of the Fourth Republic[1] . . . To the younger people de Gaulle meant very little, except as a historic figure. Among the "classical" Right, among men like Pinay he was, if anything, disliked. He had "collaborated" with the Communists in 1944–46; he had put all sorts of wrong ideas into the heads of Negroes and Algerians with his speeches at Brazzaville and Constantine, during and just after the war. . . . At Algiers in 1956 I found nothing but hostility to de Gaulle on the part of the Europeans there: "We've had enough of him here—no more, thanks."

I have analysed elsewhere, at considerable length, the personality of de Gaulle. There is no doubt that the cultivation of his own personality is something to which he has given much time and attention throughout his life. His little book, *Le fil de l'épée*, written as long ago as 1932, is a real handbook for a great leader of men. Aloofness, prestige, the capacity

[1] See author's conversation with Mendès-France recorded in *The Strange History of Pierre Mendès-France*, pp. 317–18.

of keeping secrets and of saying little are among the rules which are lengthily discussed in *Le fil de l'épée*. For instance:

The passion to act by one's self is accompanied by a certain roughness. The man of character embodies the harshness inherent in his effort. His subordinates feel it, and often suffer from it. Such a chief is distant, because authority does not go without prestige, and prestige does not go without distances being kept.

Or else these rules on "prestige":

Prestige arises from an elementary gift, from a certain natural aptitude which cannot be analysed. The truth is that certain men carry with them, almost since childhood, a certain aura of authority. . . . Yet such a natural gift must, like any other natural talent, be developed. And, in the first place, prestige cannot go without mystery, for people feel no reverence for anything with which they are too familiar. . . .

Hence de Gaulle's belief in secrecy, in verbal brevity (*"imperatoria brevitas"* the Romans used to say), in the technique of keeping people guessing, in the virtues of silence, *"splendeur des forts et refuge des faibles"*. Hence also the cultivation of the pose and gesture:

". . . for is there not a connection between a man's inner strength and his outward appearance? . . . Every page of Caesar's *Commentaries* shows how carefully he measured his public gestures. And we also know how careful Napoleon was to produce the greatest effect with his public appearances . . ."

What an insight into de Gaulle's manner, both in May 1958, and afterwards when he became Premier and kept France—and Algeria—guessing, for months and months!

And again:

"Where did one ever see a great human task being performed without a man of character feeling the irresistible urge to·act? . . . Nothing would have been achieved if counsels of base caution or suggestions of cowardly modesty had prevailed. . . . Indeed, those who do great things must often ignore the conventions of a false discipline . . .

All these rules had worked with extraordinary precision at certain moments in de Gaulle's career—in 1958, but also in the past, for instance, on that 18th of June, 1940, when, knowing exactly what he was doing, he put himself at the head of the French Resistance . . . even before there *was* any Resistance.

Also, he had succeeded in building up his prestige in such a manner that, by 1944, he had become the undisputed leader of France, and the autocratic ruler of a republican government. His prestige, his personality, more than any legal prerogative, gave him that extraordinary position in 1944–45. He inspired personal respect, even personal awe; this respect and this awe were even shared by his Communist ministers, who often secretly complained that they were somehow feeling helpless in his presence. . . .

It was strange, indeed, that confession of failure that de Gaulle was to make a few years later, in 1953. And then, in 1955, he seemed finally to have retired from public life to Colombey-les-deux-Eglises. He wrote his memoirs; he received occasional visitors; what little he said they interpreted in a variety of ways. Perhaps nobody knew exactly what de Gaulle was thinking: what was he thinking of the Algerian war? Did he think that his own political role was at an end? Or was he waiting for the time when, inevitably, he would feel once again that "irresistible urge to act"—of which he had spoken back in 1932?

And who were the "Gaullists"? After the split in the RPF in 1952, and especially after their disavowal by de Gaulle in 1953, the "Social Republicans" as they had now come to call themselves in Parliament, seemed a motley crew, representing nothing very definite. If, in 1952, many "Gaullists" went over to Pinay, in the 1956 election a large part of the Gaullist rank-and-file went over to the Radicals, or the classical Right or—to Poujade. The "Gaullists", who had 120 deputies in the National Assembly in 1951, were now down to 21.

It looked for a while as if a couple of million Frenchmen, who had voted for de Gaulle, a noble figure, now preferred to him a cheap tub-thumping demagogue like Pierre Poujade. . . .

The unofficial "Gaullists" were not numerous any longer. And it was hard to say to what extent they represented de Gaulle at all. There were "Left-wing" Gaullists like Clostermann or Debû-Bridel; there were a few "Right-wing" Gaullists like General de Bénouville; there was the special case of young and dashing Chaban-Delmas, a perpetual fixture in almost every Government of the Fourth Republic, even in Mendès-France's; and there was the even more special case of Soustelle, who had become the No. 1 Cabinet-wrecker since 1957. To what extent, if at all, was he representing de Gaulle's point of view? What contacts, if any, were there between Soustelle and de Gaulle in 1956, 1957 or in the early part of 1958? Was to Soustelle the return of de Gaulle to power an end in itself, or merely a means of carrying out his (Soustelle's) own policy? That, for a very long time, was to remain the biggest mystery of all in the dramatic events of April and May 1958.

It is important to dwell on another crucial point concerning de Gaulle. For three years—from 1955 to 1958—de Gaulle had been "meditating" in his retreat at Colombey. Had he not been meditating on his past career and, above all, on his past errors and past failures? Had he carefully examined the reasons of the failure of the RPF in particular? If so, that would largely explain the different methods and different manner he adopted in 1958. The RPF was vitiated by a number of psychological errors of the first magnitude: had de Gaulle now made up his mind not to repeat these?

For one thing, had not the RPF acted *too independently of Big Business*? This was another error not to be repeated.

And another point: de Gaulle knew that the Algerian problem was becoming more and more inextricable, and seemed convinced that only a man of his exceptional, indeed unique, authority could settle it. But such passions had been aroused over Algeria that no ready-made solution could be proposed right away; only by observing the rules of the utmost secrecy, as described in *Le fil de l'épée*, could anything be achieved at all. To avoid any explosion, it was essential, for a very long time, to keep *everybody* guessing. Only a man of de Gaulle's prestige could possibly do this. And, when it came to the point, what had only been sterile *procedure* before (such as Mollet's "cease-fire, elections, negotiations" triptych) could perhaps become a live *policy* in the hands of de Gaulle. . . .

All this, of course, appeared much later. But who could say with any certainty what de Gaulle represented in April 1958? A noble figure—yes. But—to only too many—the Hero of the Liberation was also the man who had set up (fortunately unsuccessfully) the RPF, the most ambitious machine (as the Socialists said) that had yet been devised in France in peacetime for strangling democracy. . . .

11. SOUSTELLE GETS BUSY

DARK, dynamic, saturnine, nearly always wearing dark glasses, Jacques Soustelle looked both like Danton and like Jacques Doriot, the French Nazi (and ex-Communist) leader. As its Secretary-General, he had been very active in the RPF. Though reputed, until 1955, as a "Left-wing" and "socially-minded" Gaullist (not that the RPF had ever succeeded in winning over the working class) he had, as we have seen, become during his Governorship of Algeria the most notorious Algiers diehard, and later became the *tombeur*—the "chucker-out"—of any government that showed, in his opinion, the slightest sign of "defeatism". As Walter Lippmann remarked, during a visit to Paris in April 1958, no government in France could survive which showed any inclination to negotiate with the Rebels, so strong was the pressure of "Algiers". "Algiers" had, indeed, its own representatives inside the Government; in the case of the Gaillard Government, the most obvious ones were Lacoste, the Minister of Algeria, and M. Chaban-Delmas, the

Minister of Defence, who was himself working in close contact with M. Soustelle. It was to Soustelle's organization, the USRAF, that Chaban-Delmas had "lent" one of his assistants, M. Delbecque, who was to become the most prominent "Gaullist" in the early stages of the Algiers rebellion of May 13 and was to play probably the most decisive rôle of all in diverting the "activist" *putsch* into "Gaullist" channels—much to the dismay of the more extreme, but rather simple-minded, Algiers thugs.

Both Lacoste and Chaban-Delmas saw in the "good offices" mission a danger sign of the first magnitude. Soustelle was in complete agreement with them. Not content with merely digging the grave of the Gaillard Government in Paris, he was directly concerned with the "European resistance" in Algeria itself, and despite his past "social-mindedness" and the disagreements he had had, in the early days of his Governorship, with the colonialist *ultras*, any ally who, like himself, stood for "French Algeria" was now good enough for him.

M. Alain de Sérigny, the bald-headed, bespectacled editor of the *Echo d'Alger*, was a power in the land. Not only was his paper the daily gospel of the bulk of the European community of Algiers, with its constant denunciations of "defeatism" in France and its cult of "French Algeria", but M. de Sérigny occupied, as it were, the central position in the "Algeria Lobby", which—directly or indirectly through M. de Sérigny—was being supplied with very considerable funds from the *gros colons* and other colonialist interests in Algeria. M. de Sérigny had been *persona gratissima* with the Vichy régime, and had received the *francisque* at the hands of Marshal Pétain himself. Despite some lip-service he occasionally paid to "progress", de Sérigny represented the crustiest type of old-time colonialism, and any progressive reforms in Algeria since the war had been consistently sabotaged by the *Echo d'Alger*. He had been both personally and in his paper consistently hostile to de Gaulle, whom he thought to be a man with a lot of high-falutin' and muddled ideas about treating the Moslems liberally, and with a total misunderstanding of the said Moslems. *L'Echo d'Alger* stood for the complete preservation of all the old colonialist privileges, for a conservative paternalism towards "tame" Moslems, and the most savage repression of any real Algerian nationalism. It had, of course, been violently hostile to the liberal policy Mendès-France had applied to Tunisia,[1] and thought that this pampering of the Tunisians was very largely responsible for having undermined the "docile" mentality of the Algerian masses. For it was only a few months after Mendès-France's famous visit to Tunis in July 1954 that the Aurès rebellion—the starting-point of the Algerian war—had broken out.

---

[1] It is true that in August 1954, while most of the hardened French troops were still in Indo-China, *L'Echo d'Alger* seemed at first favourable to the concessions Mendès-France had made to Tunisia. It thought them inevitable in the circumstances.

Although both M. Lacoste, the Minister of Algeria, and M. Soustelle may well have had some mental reservations about M. de Sérigny, they did not hesitate to co-operate with him. Despite the discontent in the French Socialist Party over Lacoste's failure to fight on the "second front", too (i.e. not only against the Algerian rebels, but also against the colonialist *ultras*), the "Socialist" Minister of Algeria was determined to remain on the best of terms with the powerful M. de Sérigny, who had a finger in every European pie in Algiers (as well as in a good many pies in Paris, too). Moreover, the *Echo d'Alger* never stopped singing the praises of M. Lacoste, "the Clemenceau of Algiers", and savagely attacked any liberals, like M. Chevallier, the Mayor of Algiers, who attempted, on a number of occasions, to get Lacoste to talk to the FLN. Lacoste still believed in the virtues of "pacification", talked about the "last quarter of an hour" and considered that, apart from a few token "reformlets", the primary condition of any Algerian settlement was the complete military rout of the Rebellion. This view was, of course, fully supported by M. de Sérigny, who thought that such a rout was the pre-condition of any settlement which would be sure to safeguard the colonialist privileges he represented.

No doubt Sérigny had a few mental reservations about Lacoste and vice versa; Lacoste, in particular, had the incongruous idea that not only de Sérigny, but also all the Fascist and Poujadist rabble of Algiers were fundamentally "good Frenchmen", and that, far from being "run" by them, it was he who was controlling them—partly by working "through" Sérigny.

Sérigny also had considerable influence in Paris, and had his own particular allies in Parliament: virtually the whole Right, including the Poujadists (who had a large following in Algiers) and, more particularly, certain prominent public figures like M. Bidault, M. Morice, M. Duchet and, the most influential and dynamic of them all, M. Soustelle. Not to mention the more disreputable type of Fascist and witch-hunting politicians like Dides and Tixier-Vignancour.

In July 1958 M. de Sérigny published a little book, called *La Révolution du 13 mai*, which lifts at least a corner of the veil that had been hiding from public view the cloak-and-dagger stuff that went on both in Paris and Algiers, particularly after the Gaillard Government had agreed to submit to the Anglo-American "good offices" mission.

Mr. Murphy, despite all the denials he was making, was, according to M. de Sérigny, determined to "settle the Algerian problem"—in a manner wholly unsuitable to France. This was pointed out, almost as soon as the "good offices" mission had been established, by M. Soustelle in an angry article, which the *Echo d'Alger* published on February 27. Simultaneously, M. Lacoste, in a speech at Philippeville said that, although the Algerian rebellion had been virtually defeated by the end of 1957,

Tunisia was now being turned into an arsenal which would supply vast quantities of arms "from the East" to the rebel forces—not to mention the arms already delivered to Tunisia by Britain and the USA. In the second week of March, there was more and more talk of Murphy and Beeley being, in due course, replaced by Mr. Hammarskjoeld—which, in M. de Sérigny's view, would mean not merely "good offices" but a regular internationalization of the Algerian problem. He was, he said, "very worried". Although the Right wing of the Assembly were conducting a "patriotic" policy, many influences, both domestic and foreign, were working the other way.

Something had to be done. Sérigny phoned Soustelle, "who, for two years, had been the real spearhead in the battle for French Algeria".

The meeting was arranged at the Hôtel Ruhl at Nice on March 15. Four other prominent "Gaullists" were present: Roger Frey, Triboulet, Michel Debré and Edmond Michelet. (The last two were to become members of the de Gaulle Government in June and all of them in December.)

First of all, they discussed the urgent necessity of "solidly implanting in Algiers a local section of Soustelle's USRAF network", and a rapid agreement was reached on this. The USRAF had a high official, a M. Regard, stationed at Algiers, and, during the next few weeks, he was going to "exercise his lucid activity in favour of the movement". But the "essential question" to be discussed at that meeting at Nice was de Gaulle. Sérigny said that Soustelle and other "Social-Republicans" had, for a long time now, talked of de Gaulle as *the* solution; but what were the chances of bringing him back to power?

Not that M. de Sérigny, an old Vichyite and anti-Gaullist, was necessarily enchanted with the prospect of a de Gaulle régime; but, he argued, things had come to such a pass that de Gaulle might be the only solution. The Government, he said, was at sixes and sevens: everybody knew that, though both of them Socialists, Lacoste, the Minister of Algeria, and Pineau, the Foreign Minister, were conducting "diametrically opposite policies" in respect of Algeria and the "good offices".

"But," said de Sérigny to Soustelle, "can you tell me whether de Gaulle has the same views as ourselves on the Algerian problem and on the future of that province? . . . Is de Gaulle, in fact, in favour of integration? My attitude will be determined by the answer you give me.

"No doubt, I have every reason to suppose that de Gaulle approves of your attitude—your speeches at the National Assembly, your articles, etc. . . .

"But—here's the point: *you fully realize that [European] Algerian opinion is very badly prepared for a return of de Gaulle.* This is a fact which, however, within the means at my disposal, I am prepared to modify. . . . But I should like you to get in touch with General de Gaulle and get him to explain to you what he feels about the points I have mentioned, and how he envisages his legal return to power."

It is at this point that the mystery deepens. On March 28 de Sérigny received a letter from Soustelle. Sérigny does not quote the letter textually; but summarizes it as follows:

"The General" (Soustelle wrote *in effect* [*en substance*]) "looks at it from a historian's and thinker's point of view, rather than in terms of immediate action. Moreover, he thinks he has no chance of taking part in any real action, and that's why he doesn't want to talk. 'What's the good of talking,' says he, 'without acting?' He is convinced that the political parties have placed insuperable obstacles to his return to power. He has no illusions about the régime and thinks it will submit to internationalization and surrender in the end. He hopes, all the same, that France will maintain her influence in Algeria up to a point, and that better days may come, when her radiance will increase once again in North Africa.

"This doesn't mean that de Gaulle is satisfied with so dismal a prospect and that he isn't interested in the struggle conducted against secession. But he is uncertain about *integration* because he doubts whether the Moslems would accept it favourably. On the other hand, he thinks that pacification ought to be conducted with the greatest energy, but accompanied by a great social, educational, psychological and political effort. This stage should lead to integration (which he desires) but it should also correspond to the real aspirations of the Moslem population. . . . The General is struck by the sharp conflict between Left and Right and considers that whatever he may say or do, he will always be misinterpreted, annexed or rejected."

All this was remarkably vague; and for a long time it remained a mystery whether Soustelle had actually seen de Gaulle or not before writing to Sérigny. Sérigny, for his part, was only too well aware that if, after the fall of the Gaillard Government, President Coty had called on de Gaulle to form the next Government, "he wouldn't have had a hundred votes"—and, says he, most of the Right would have been against de Gaulle, too. So at first the old Vichyite, though still protesting against Murphy and Beeley, hesitated to come out in favour of de Gaulle; it was not till the 11th of May that he wrote his famous editorial in the *Echo d'Alger*: "Speak up, General, speak up quickly. Your words are worth actions . . ." This meant that, for the first time, the Vichyite and ultra-colonialist *Echo d'Alger* decided that the time had come when it could *use* de Gaulle. That was two days before the Algiers *putsch*.

No doubt, a man like Sérigny and one like Soustelle did not have quite the same approach to the Algerian problem; but their positions were, by March 1958, so close that they were natural allies . . . at least for a time. And both were *using* de Gaulle—though, again, not necessarily for the same final purpose. De Gaulle was to become during the weeks that followed a rallying point for those anxious to preserve their colonialist privileges in Algeria; for those anxious to overthrow the Republic in France; for those thinking in terms of an authoritarian or presidential régime; even for those (mostly in Algeria) who were planning a military-

Fascist dictatorship in France. And, later, for all those for whom de Gaulle was a "lesser evil".

In any case, it is significant that the conspiracy, which was to lead to, or at any rate, take advantage of, the May 13 *putsch*, should have reached a highly active stage soon after Sakhiet and the appointment of the Murphy "good offices" mission. The conspirators had another important ally in M. Robert Lacoste, who never ceased dropping the darkest hints at the disastrous results for Algeria of America's "intervention" in North Africa. . . . All the same, the case of Lacoste is not quite as straightforward as Soustelle's: he was in the Government, he was a member of the Socialist Party, and he had certain inhibitions about taking an active part in the conspiracy, of the existence of which he was, however, fully aware, and which, in fact, he had encouraged by his whole attitude.

12. THE CONSPIRACY

THIS book is not primarily concerned with the endless details of the conspiracy—the multiple conspiracy—which brought de Gaulle back to power on June 1. In a large number of more or less tendentious books this side of the story has already been described in minute detail; the most important of them, so far, is *Les 13 complots du 13 mai*, by Merry and Serge Bromberger, star reporters of the *Figaro* and of *France-Soir*.

Why *thirteen* plots? One rather suspects that this was merely part of a catchpenny title. Fundamentally, there were only *two* plots—that of the Algiers "activists" and that of the de Gaulle network, or rather, the "Gaullist" network, since de Gaulle, according to the Brombergers, seemed scarcely aware of what was going on. A point which, as far as possible, we shall try to elucidate later.

The "13 plots"—or 15 or 18, it doesn't matter—were, in fact, ramifications of the two main plots. Moreover, these two *main* plots often overlapped, the "activists" and "Gaullists" sometimes working hand-in-hand, but at other times sharply competing.

The Brombergers, who glory throughout their 450-page book over the way in which the "plotters" outwitted the Fourth Republic, start their story by enumerating the principal authors of the "13 plots".

First of all, a small group: a handful of men who were constantly thinking of de Gaulle even though, in the eyes of so many of his contemporaries, he was becoming an historic fossil. With the Fourth Republic rapidly decaying, they were convinced that the moment was near when they could bring de Gaulle back to power.

Who, then, were these men?

First of all, Olivier Guichard, de Gaulle's *chef de cabinet*, who acted as such during de Gaulle's weekly visits to Paris, but who, during the rest of the time "was working on a job which would have seemed impossible without this long preparatory 'undermining' process"; Jacques Foccart, his assistant; further, Senator Michel Debré, "who was constantly foretelling the decay of the régime, and organizing its fall"; Jacques Soustelle, "who never ceased to demonstrate the impotence of the régime, and was No. 1 champion of French Algeria". It was also he who had taken the "Gaullist" Trojan Horse to Algiers.

Who were the other plotters, some consciously working for the return of de Gaulle (whatever the exact purpose of this) and others doing their plotting—at first—without reference to de Gaulle?

According to the Brombergers, these were the principal among them: President Coty who, by May 5, had already decided that de Gaulle alone could save the situation and who, on that day, made a discreet attempt to get in personal touch with him. A very important role in the story of the overthrow of the Fourth Republic is also attributed by the Brombergers to Biaggi, who liked to describe himself as "a spermatozoon of spontaneous revolution" and who, as "the personification of extremism", had organized the Algiers riots of February 6, 1956, as a result of which Guy Mollet abandoned his role of arbiter between the two communities. After that, as the Brombergers rather gleefully remark, "*Algiers became the capital of France, and the lobbies of the National Assembly were replaced by the pavements of the rue Michelet.*"

Biaggi (of whom the Brombergers give a highly romantic description— "he used to order his breakfast in Latin, and could converse fluently in Latin with a priest on the Corsican parentage of Christopher Columbus" —though more typical of him, perhaps, were the thug commandos under his control who used to break up Left-wing meetings, not to mention his organization of the February 6, 1956 riots in Algiers)—Biaggi seems, to all appearances, to have had a foot in both camps—that of the Algiers "activists" and that of the Gaullists; when, a few days after May 13, Biaggi arrived in Algiers, he found, however, that the Gaullists were rapidly gaining control of the Committee of Public Safety, and they preferred to get him out of the way, by temporarily sending him to—the Sahara. He was a little too influential to their taste with the "Algiers rabble"—with the students, schoolboys and "teddy-boys".

It was these who, under the leadership of Pierre Lagaillarde were, on the afternoon of May 13, to start the Algiers *putsch* by invading the Government-General building. Lagaillarde was not their only leader; he was a member of the "Group of Seven"—Lagaillarde, Martel, Crespin, Dr. Lefebvre, a restaurant proprietor called Goutailler, and Orthiz (both of these members of the Poujade organization in Algeria) and a lawyer called Baille. It was these people who, persuaded that Delbecque was preparing a *putsch* for the 14th, decided to forestall him a day earlier, before Pflimlin had been invested by the National Assembly.

These Seven were sure that Delbecque had prepared his *putsch*, together with General Gilles at Constantine, Colonel Bigeard at Philippeville and General Cogny who would seize the Ministry of National Defence in Paris. (Bromberger, *op. cit.*, p. 160.)

And, after the Committee of Public Safety had been formed (at first without the Gaullists):

Delbecque ran into Lagaillarde who, with a twinkle in his eye, said: "I admit I put on your little play a little before the scheduled time!" . . . Delbecque said nothing; but it is certain that it was not till the middle of the night, or the following day (May 14)—in any case, not till the anxiously awaited arrival of Soustelle—that the Gaullist operation was to be launched. (*ibid.*, p. 190.)

It is already clear from this that Delbecque, representing both Soustelle, the top "Gaullist", and Chaban-Delmas, also a "Gaullist", but at the same time still Minister of Defence in the Gaillard Government (still nominally in charge) had established contact with certain Army leaders (Gilles and Bigeard)—though not with Trinquier and Thomazo, the paratroop colonels, who were working hand-in-glove with the "teddy-boys"; it was *this putsch* which was to be "covered", as we shall see, by General Massu, though it is fairly obvious that he had not been "in on it" from the start himself. . . .

Who, then, according to the Brombergers, were the other plotters? They mention Chaban-Delmas, who was doing his utmost "to canalize towards de Gaulle the agitation existing in the Army"; they also mention General Cogny, who was "supposed" to be preparing a military *putsch* in Paris and whose name was, at any rate, being constantly conjured with in the "war of nerves" against the moribund Fourth Republic. The role of General Cogny is among the more obscure in this whole story: Cogny, as commander of the French troops in Morocco, and an Indo-China veteran, was regarded by certain Algiers *ultras* as the strong man, and the attempt made in 1957 to assassinate the "flabby" Salan had as its principal motive his replacement at the head of the French Army in Algeria by General Cogny. The would-be assassins broadly hinted (though without any very clear proof) that Cogny had instigated the "operation" against Salan.

The Brombergers also mention various other secret societies and organizations which were mixed up with the revolution—the "Grand O", whose principal members, General Chassin, General Cherrières and a Dr. Martin, "were teleguiding their Algerian troops from Paris" and "were preparing military *putsches* in France itself". They also mention the CANAC, the *Comité d'Action national d'anciens combattants*, "the fighting force of Soustelle's USRAF", but under the command of one Sanguinetti, a close associate of Biaggi's.

Here was a clear case of "Gaullist" and "activist" plotting overlapping.

Leading roles in the conspiracy (as it turned out) were also to be played by Generals Massu and Salan, not to mention Thomazo and other paratroop colonels, who had been "in on it" from the start.

The Brombergers also attach some importance to the *anciens d'Indochine*, the Indo-China veterans who were ready at any moment to start major trouble in Paris.

But, somehow, nothing much ever happened in Paris, which was not in a mood for that kind of thing—a point which the Brombergers tend to minimize.

But if the "street movements" in Paris never amounted to much, the Brombergers, nevertheless, think that the Army leaders in Metropolitan France could have done all sorts of things if they had wanted to.

The Pflimlin Government was threatened by a military revolt in France itself, they say:

There was General Ely, Chief of the General Staff; there was the "Colonels' Club" at the Ecole Militaire; there was Colonel Gribius who was in command of all the clandestine army action in Paris; there were the tanks at Rambouillet and at St. Germain-en-Laye, and 20,000 CRS (militarized police) ready to don military uniform at any moment, and itching to carry out a *putsch* in Paris. . . , There was also General Faure, the hero of the first military conspiracy in Algiers, who was ready at any moment to bring his tanks from Germany to Strasbourg. And there was General Miquel, in charge of "Operation Resurrection".

General Miquel, one of the "rebel generals" in Morocco back in 1955, was the commander of the Toulouse military district. His plan was to occupy all strategic points in Paris with the help of the above-mentioned 20,000 CRS men, and to send paratroopers from the South of France and from Algiers to occupy Le Bourget and Orly airfields and other strategic objectives in the Paris area. According to the Brombergers, Miquel reluctantly "postponed" the execution of this plan, after de Gaulle's famous announcement that he had "embarked on the regular process of forming a Government"—a statement which, as we shall see, he claimed to have made precisely in order to prevent such a Paris *putsch*. But the Brombergers stress the scepticism and disbelief with which Miquel received this announcement, and the eagerness with which he would "start again" on the following day if de Gaulle made no visible progress.

The others, according to the Brombergers, who contributed to the success of the Revolution were Pflimlin, who gave up the struggle, rather than continue it in alliance with the Communists; and, of course,

Guy Mollet, whom the Brombergers describe as "the most French of
all the French" (a phrase, ironically enough, once used by Pétain to
describe Charles Maurras!). He played an extremely complex double or
triple or quadruple game, for the sole purpose of bringing de Gaulle to
power. "In him were concentrated all the contradictory feelings of the
French nation, and the greatest honour in his life was to have been
received by de Gaulle at Colombey."

In the subsequent narrative we shall deal less with all the ins-and-outs
of all this cloak-and-dagger stuff (much of which did not come into the
open until much later) than with what was happening on the surface—
i.e. in the Paris streets, in Parliament, among ordinary people. We shall
deal with the manner in which ordinary people were reacting to the May
events, and with the manner in which they were being conditioned by
radio and the press.

Ultimately, the exact relationship existing among all these various
conspirators is less important than the outcome of all this plotting. And
the biggest question that still remains practically unanswered is this:
HOW MUCH DID DE GAULLE HIMSELF KNOW OF WHAT WAS GOING ON?

With the exception of one journey (in the plane given him by President
Truman) to various French overseas territories, where he was enthusiastically received, de Gaulle had been in semi-retirement at Colombey-les-
deux-Eglises ever since 1953. He was disgusted with a large number of
Gaullist deputies who had ratted on him in March 1952 by voting for
Pinay. In 1953 he withdrew his patronage from the Gaullist deputies
altogether; in 1956, there were only twenty-one left. For all that, during
his Wednesday visits to Paris he used to see a lot of people—Louis Joxe,
the Secretary-General of the Quai d'Orsay, was a frequent visitor; high
officials would go to see him; so would various foreign Ambassadors,
among them the Soviet and American Ambassadors; he was, say the
Brombergers, "the best-informed man in France", a curious comment
when one considers that, in May, *he was not supposed to have any idea of
what was going on in Algiers*!

Whom then, during the critical period which started in February 1958
with the bombing of Sakhiet, did he see? According to the Brombergers,
he saw, as we know, the Tunisian Ambassador, M. Masmoudi, before
the latter's return to Tunis, following the Sakhiet raid; he also saw the
Soviet Ambassador; soon afterwards, he received Lacoste, who complained to him about the Murphy Mission; among many other visitors,
he received (on March 27) Roger Stéphane of *France-Observateur* (of
all people); he received a delegation of Soustelle's CANAC; but since
he and Soustelle were not seeing eye-to-eye on integration, he is not
supposed to have seen the latter until the beginning of May; he also
received about the same time General Lecomte, head of the Ecole de

Guerre, himself in close contact with the "Colonels' Club"; earlier, in March, de Gaulle received Delbecque, and in April, Chaban-Delmas; on May 5, he received Neuwirth, who was, a few days later, to become Delbecque's right-hand man in Algiers. In all these talks, de Gaulle was supposed to have remained wholly non-committal, speaking in riddles, but still suggesting that he would be available if France needed him. But the whole suggestion of the Bromberger story is that he took no part at all in preparing the Algiers *putsch*.

A year later, on June 3, 1959, Tréno in the *Canard Enchaîné* drew attention to the fact that the Government had declared that June would be "Information Month", and that M. Roger Frey, the Minister of Information, would visit a number of provincial centres and talk on "information". "It will be the truth, the whole truth, nothing but the truth . . ."

"Fine!" said Tréno. "Now at last we are going to learn how, a year ago, General de Gaulle came to power. Countless books and articles have been written about it; and from all these it appears that hundreds of friends of General de Gaulle, hundreds of disciples of General de Gaulle, hundreds of employees of General de Gaulle, hundreds of domestics of General de Gaulle scattered throughout the political life of the country, scattered throughout the Army, the Police, the Secret Service networks, etc., etc., were secretly preparing the General's return to power, but that the General knew nothing—just nothing at all. It was like mother's birthday when the little ones are secretly preparing for Mummy her present and her bunch of flowers, with her knowing nothing, absolutely nothing about it.
"'General!'
"'Yes, my dears?'
"'General, we've got a surprise for you. Just look what we've put on this tray for you!'
"'But how *lovely*! The keys of the Elysée! But, my dears, you *shouldn't*!'
"Perhaps M. Frey will tell us a different story; at least we hope so."

13. MR. MURPHY AND THE CABINET CRISIS

IT is an ironic thought that if the Gaillard Government had been overthrown two months before, this overthrow would have been interpreted as a disavowal of the Sakhiet raid, which it had "covered". But now, in April, Gaillard was overthrown for *not* wanting to break off relations with Tunisia, and for wishing to accept the Murphy-Beeley proposals as a basis for discussion.

Algiers had clearly played a decisive part in the overthrow of Gaillard. As Fauvet put it in the *Monde*:

Despite its clandestine nature, the action of the Europeans of Algeria and of the Army circles had a great deal to do with the fall of the Gaillard Government. Some of the speakers in Parliament are in a good position to know it, and numerous deputies and senators have plenty of evidence. Before complaining of Parliament interfering with its prerogatives, the Government of the Republic ought to try to defend itself against the civil and military pressure groups (*féodalités*), which either disinterestedly, or for financial motives, are taking over the role of the decrepit State, both in Metropolitan France and in North Africa. . . .

Cabinet crises had been a chronic ailment both under the Third and the Fourth Republic. But, with the 1956 Assembly, they had become unusually troublesome. This was the third crisis within a year, and it was clear that a mere reshuffle of ministers (which was what the formation of a new Government so often amounted to in the past) would no longer work the trick. The time seemed ripe for a "fundamental change". But such a change could mean only one of two things: either a final surrender of the Paris Government and of Parliament to the blackmail of Algiers, or a showdown. And yet, there seemed no majority for either. Those who were anxious to toe the line of the Algiers *ultras*—men like Soustelle and Bidault—had no chance of obtaining a majority in Parliament; a Government openly advocating negotiations with the FLN was unlikely to obtain a majority either—except with Communist support, and no Radical, MRP or Socialist leader was going to risk that. So the prospective Premiers were again reduced to looking for some intermediate solution, which would hold out the hope of an eventual though ill-defined settlement in Algeria without, at the same time, annoying either the Army leaders or the Algiers *ultras*.

Despite this apparent *immobilisme* on the Algerian issue, there had, nevertheless, been a certain evolution in the attitude of both the Socialists and the MRP. Inside the Socialist Party the feeling had grown that it was high time Lacoste, now apparently completely under the thumb of the *ultras*, be recalled from Algiers. He had long been a liability to the Socialist Party, both from the point of view of the rank-and-file, and from that of the Socialist International which had become violently critical of both Mollet and Lacoste.

What was shocking Socialist opinion abroad (particularly in Britain and Scandinavia) was not only Lacoste's close association with the colonialists, his determination to go on with his "pacification" policy, and his violent attacks on Britain and the United States in connection with the "good offices" mission, but also the apparent indifference with which he was reacting to the torture so widely practised in Algeria, and stories of which were now penetrating into a large part of the press in Britain, America and other allied and neutral countries. The very bad international reputation the French Socialists were gaining abroad and also the evolution inside the French Socialist Party in favour of a negotiated settlement in Algeria had gradually persuaded Guy Mollet that it was high time the Socialists put an end to Lacoste's reign in Algiers. And the only convenient way in which they could do it (i.e. without openly disavowing Lacoste) was to refuse to join in the next Government, in which case Lacoste (short of his leaving the Socialist Party) would automatically be withdrawn from Algiers.

It would be tedious to discuss in detail the attempts made by President Coty to solve the crisis. But, in view of what was to happen in May, a few landmarks should be mentioned. Since Soustelle was *le tombeur* of the Gaillard Government, i.e. the man most directly responsible for its overthrow, the obvious course was to call on him to form the next Government. This Coty decided not to do—much to the disgust of the Algiers *ultras* like M. de Sérigny. Not that they thought for a moment that Soustelle could find a majority to support him in Parliament; but had he been called upon by the President of the Republic, he could at least have made a resounding public statement over the radio. As it was, all he could do was to express the opinion, but only in a purely individual capacity (not over the radio) that the President should call upon General de Gaulle. In the circumstances, this statement had no far-reaching effect; for if the "Gaullists" and the Right could overthrow governments, they were in no position to "make" governments without the agreement of the Socialists, and at this stage (April 18–20) the Socialists declared themselves wholly opposed to a return of de Gaulle, which could only mean "a dangerous adventure".

It is worth noting that *there was as yet no widespread support for de Gaulle*. True, Edgar Faure declared himself favourable to a de Gaulle Government; but the two leading members of the "classical" Right, M. Pinay and M. Duchet (the latter very much an "Algiers Lobby" man) were still against.

Anyway, with the first round of the cantonal elections taking place on the Sunday, April 20, President Coty decided to postpone his choice of a candidate, precisely because such a prospective Premier would be in a position to use the radio for election propaganda. The Socialists were particularly anxious that Soustelle should not be given a chance to speak on the radio—chiefly because it would have given the Communists a chance to come out in the local elections as the "defenders of the Republican régime".

These communal elections, despite all the trouble there had been in Parliament, *were to reveal an astonishing stability in the mood of the country*; the only important change they marked, compared with January 1956, was the heavy losses suffered by the Poujadists. The percentages of votes cast for the various parties were as follows:

Communists and other extreme Left	23·4
Socialists and other Left	20·2
Radicals, etc.	15·2
MRP	10·6
Right	23·4
Gaullists	3·5
Poujadists	2·2
Others	0·8

In the second round a week later, there was a common "gang-up" against the Communists, *but no signs of any awareness of a "Fascist danger"*. This was a very curious phenomenon barely a fortnight before the Algiers *putsch*. There was no real desire for change in Metropolitan France. . . .

But to return to the Cabinet crisis. Before President Coty had called on anybody to form the next Government, a major bomb was to explode in Paris: Mr. Murphy, by giving a "background" press conference to American journalists in Paris on the evening of April 17, clearly suggested that France had not necessarily escaped the "internationalization" of the Algerian problem, merely because M. Gaillard's Government had been overthrown. Nothing was "on the record", but the Paris edition of the *New York Herald-Tribune* of April 18 and several papers in the USA reflected Mr. Murphy's views. Although Murphy did not advocate the formation of an "Algerian Government", he thought that it might be a good thing if, at the forthcoming conference at Tangier between the FLN, the Moroccan Istiqlal and the Tunisian Neo-Destour, a "coherent FLN group" were formed, which could enter into negotiations with the French Government. They might, Murphy suggested, negotiate on the basis of Mollet's famous "triptych" of January 1957—cease-fire, elections, negotiations for a new statute.

There was some speculation on whether Murphy had been recently in contact with representatives of the FLN, and whether he had found these more moderate than the FLN paper, *El Moujahid*, which had just rejected the proposals made by the Tunis paper *Action* for internationally-controlled elections in Algeria. The FLN paper said that the Algerian nationalists would "on no account accept elections in Algeria, not even under international control, so long as the national territory of Algeria had not been completely liberated". Mr. Murphy, whatever his latest information, cannot have thought that this was the last word of the FLN. The suggestion that he had made his statement merely out of pique—because his "good offices" had been turned down—was rejected by most French observers, who argued that Murphy had merely said what the State Department had had at the back of its mind for a long time!

The French Government—though now merely a caretaker government

—was furious. M. Pineau, the Foreign Minister, "immediately summoned" Mr. Amory Houghton, the US Ambassador, "to demand an explanation from him". As a result, some rather vague assurances were given by Washington to the French Government about there having been no "change in American policy". But these official assurances were accompanied by a large crop of comments in the US Press "expressing the gravest doubts as to France's ability to solve the Algerian problem" (*Le Monde*, April 21).

The Murphy statement naturally affected the French political parties. Those who had supported Gaillard felt he had been quite right to dread a stiffening in the American attitude as a result of the rejection of the "good offices" mission; those who had voted against Gaillard thought they were doubly right not to have yielded to American demands.

Characteristic of this Right-wing position was the commentary in *L'Aurore*, complaining of the "devilish perseverance" with which the USA was trying to hand over the whole of North Africa to a "frenzied pan-Arabism", after having already saved Nasser and "made the Free World lose the Middle East".

On the other hand, voices favourable to a more "realistic" policy started coming from some unexpected quarters; in London the *Economist* went so far as to say that, *unless the 150 French Communists were included in the Government majority, the French National Assembly could never get away from the blackmail of the Algeria lobby.*

The French Communists, for their part, were getting alarmed at the Americans becoming the "protectors of the Algerian people"; the only way of nullifying such "dangerous manœuvres" was for France to enter into negotiations with the FLN. . . .

Not until Sunday evening, April 20, did M. Coty finally decide to call on M. Bidault to form the next Government. He was one of the four leading "Algerian diehards" in Parliament, the other three being M. Morice, M. Duchet and M. Soustelle. M. Morice had refused to run; M. Duchet was a senator, and so unsuitable; while M. Soustelle was too violently disliked in Parliament.

M. Bidault, one of the three MRP members to have voted against Gaillard, had for a long time conducted a violent campaign against any policy of "surrender", and had latterly become almost a foreign body in his own party, the MRP; here his chief opponent, and a supporter of a "liberal" policy in Algeria, was M. Pflimlin. The whole Right was, of course, favourable to a Government under an Algerian diehard like M. Bidault; but the Socialists were against him, while the majority of the MRP, under the influence of M. Pflimlin, refused to support M. Bidault and to "take on any additional risks in North Africa"—M. Bidault being known to be in favour of a much stiffer policy towards Tunisia, though he continued to deny that he had ever said that he "wanted to sleep in Bourguiba's bed". The governing body of the MRP voted against the formation of a Bidault Government by 28 votes to 25 and two abstentions. It was obvious from what had happened that there was no *ultra* majority at the National Assembly. This fact was carefully noted in Algiers, *where it was decided not to think any longer in terms of Parliamentary arithmetic. . . .*

M. Bidault himself said after the MRP meeting that Algeria would remain his primary concern.

"We must save it from the FLN cut-throats, from pan-Arab ambitions and international intrigues. . . . We must prevent Tunisia from using her independence as a weapon against us. . . . I am convinced that a majority will soon exist to support my policy."

"And," he added ominously, "*such a majority exists in any case in the Nation . . . and amongst our soldiers . . .*" One of the major reasons why the MRP did not support Bidault was that he was including Soustelle in his Government; and Pflimlin said, a few days later, that Soustelle was quite capable of "risking a war against Tunisia".

The next phase of the Cabinet crisis was dull and colourless, with the dull and colourless M. Pleven as the next candidate. At first President Coty had thought of calling on M. Mitterrand, a notorious Algerian "liberal"; but, although he thought him "one of the most intelligent people in Parliament", he decided, in the end, against Mitterrand, "*owing to the threats that had come from Algiers*".

M. Pleven, despite his record as an Indo-China diehard, had, on the whole, the reputation of being reasonably liberal on the Algerian issue; but he now decided that he could only succeed in forming a Government by being all things to all men. He wanted all the national parties (i.e. all except the Communists) to agree on a "Common Charter" for Algeria; the trouble was that this "Charter" was mostly a collection of negatives: No secession; No independence; No internationalization; No foreign interference, etc. He said he would ask America for "assurances"; he even thought he would go to see Ike about it; also, he thought that the NATO powers must recognize the integrity of France's Algerian territory. "In certain conditions" he thought there *might* be talks with the FLN. He conferred with General Salan, with M. Chaban-Delmas, the Minister of Defence, with Marshal Juin. He went into the question of the financial cost of maintaining all those troops in Algeria. He looked both businesslike—and strangely unreal and unrealistic. He wanted to adopt a new procedure—that of submitting his "Algerian Charter" to the Assembly *before* forming the Government. . . . M. Le Troquer, the President of the Assembly, doubted whether this was constitutional.

14. ALGIERS ON THE MOVE—THE TANGIER CONFERENCE

WHILE M. Pleven was messing about with all these wishy-washy schemes, important things started happening at Algiers. A bomb was thrown at the US Consulate at Algiers, blowing off the arm of an Algerian charwoman—truly an innocent victim of History. A few days later it was learned that numerous "patriotic associations" of Algiers, including M. Soustelle's USRAF, had decided to hold a demonstration in Algiers on April 26. M. Lacoste, who rushed back from Paris to Algiers that morning, held a conference with Massu and other generals, and then broadcast an appeal repeating what he had said before—namely, that such a demonstration would be "useless and inopportune"—adding significantly: "The mobilization of the people in the streets must be reserved for solemn occasions or for moments of great danger. Neither applies today." He then assured his listeners that he had seen Pleven, the prospective Premier, and had informed him of the absolute determination of Algiers not to permit any foreign interference in Algeria.

Although Lacoste had officially prohibited this demonstration, it nevertheless took place. Fifteen thousand people, many of them belonging to Soustelle's USRAF, marched through the streets, carrying banners saying *"A bas le régime! L'armée au pouvoir!"*; whereupon they were congratulated by the Prefect of Algiers on the "perfect order" that had been maintained throughout the demonstration! Only about ten Moslems took part in it.

It was later learned that the real organizer of the demonstration had been M. Léon Delbecque, representing, as it were, both Soustelle and—Chaban-Delmas, still a minister in the Gaillard Government!

This demonstration of Saturday, April 26, was certainly a landmark: the fact that M. Serge Baret, the Prefect of Algiers and so the representative of the Paris Government, had *congratulated* the members of a demonstration which had been *prohibited* by the Minister of Algeria, was highly significant; better still, he had agreed to forward to the Government the resolutions passed by the demonstrators!

The position of M. Lacoste was becoming shaky at Algiers; or else he was playing a double game—nobody was, as yet, quite certain which was true. . . . Sérigny, at any rate, asserted that Lacoste had been all in favour of this demonstration, and had called it off only at the last moment at the insistence of Paris, but without great conviction.

The leading part in organizing this demonstration had, as said, been played by Soustelle's representative, M. Delbecque. It was the USRAF which had distributed the leaflets calling on the people of Algiers to demonstrate, and which had also drawn up the motions calling for the formation of a Government of Public Safety. There was, however, at that stage, no mention of de Gaulle. Did not some of these people think of Soustelle, rather than de Gaulle, as the head of this Government? M. de Sérigny, who dwells at some length on this demonstration, says that "personally he had not the slightest faith in M. Pleven", who "would negotiate with the FLN and, in the end, abandon Algeria" (*op. cit.* p. 13).

There was certainly no sympathy for Pleven at Algiers. Feeling against Parliament there had not yet risen to fever pitch. This, however, was to happen only a few days later, when suspicions were confirmed that, in order to remove Lacoste from Algiers, the Socialists were now refusing to join the Pleven Government.

What added a few further points to the temperature of Algiers was the news coming from Tangier, where the conference of the Neo-Destour, the Istiqlal and the FLN had ended in a manner highly favourable to the Algerian Rebels. This conference "for the unification of the Arab Maghreb" recorded in its resolutions the three parties' "complete identity of views on the nature, the development and the inevitable outcome of the war in Algeria". They "solemnly proclaimed the unquestionable right to independence by the Algerian people, sole condition for the settlement of the Franco-Algerian conflict".

The "political parties", the same resolution continued, "will render the Algerian people in their struggle for independence the total support (*soutien*) of their respective peoples and the support (*appui*) of their governments."

The FLN was recognized at Tangier as "the sole representative of Fighting Algeria", and it was recommended that, after consultation with the Tunisian and Moroccan Governments, an Algerian Government be constituted.

A further resolution called on foreign powers to stop helping France materially in her war against Algeria, and still another demanded that French forces cease using Tunisian and Moroccan territory as "bases of aggression against the Algerian people" and generally denounced the presence of French troops in Tunisia and Morocco as incompatible with these countries' sovereignty.

Finally, the Tangier conference recommended the possible formation of a North African Federation, and the setting up of a Consultative Assembly of the Arab Maghreb—an Assembly composed of representatives of local national assemblies in Tunisia and Morocco and of the CNRA, the National Council of the Algerian Revolution (an advisory body of the FLN, composed of fifty-four members, whose names had never been disclosed).

The members of the Tangier Conference were careful not to associate either Egypt or the United States with their aims; the emphasis was throughout on the future "federal" unity of the three North African Arab countries; and the treatment of the FLN as an equal of the Neo-Destour and the Istiqlal, together with the promise of aid and support, created the impression, in both France and Algeria, that, by and large, all the three countries of North Africa had now ganged up against France, despite the somewhat ambiguous wording of the resolutions as regards the Tunisian and Moroccan *Governments* proper. It was not clear to what extent these Governments, as distinct from the parties largely running them, were committed to "supporting" the Algerian rebels. . . . Here a loophole was left for maintaining diplomatic relations with France; nevertheless, the Tangier resolutions (which, as the *Monde* said, "will soon take the shape of political, economic and trade union institutions") had, especially in Algiers, the effect of another violent psychological shock. The current view in Algiers was, of course, that all this had been encouraged by the United States, in its determination to cultivate this "pro-Western Arab bloc"—at the expense of France.

15. SOCIALISTS AND MRP GO "ANTI-ALGIERS"

IN PARIS, oddly enough, the feeling was gaining ground that M. Pleven would inevitably form the next Government. Parliamentary arithmetic seemed to favour him. He was taking his time over it. He was negotiating with everybody, drawing up long-term plans, including plans for a one-year Plenary Powers Bill, the purpose of which would, among other things, be to avoid further inflation, to freeze prices and wages, to restrict imports and consumption by the rich, to improve France's disastrous balance of payments, etc., etc. It makes ironical reading to find that the flabby M. Pleven was thinking in terms of "forming a hard Government, composed of men whose authority would symbolize a genuine determination to impose fair sacrifices on all".

Since he was still anxious to include all the "national" parties in his Government, he continued to be inevitably vague as regards Algeria, where the Tangier Conference had created a number of new diplomatic, if not military, problems. His ten-point programme was a collection of commonplaces which were meant to be acceptable to everybody and meant very little in practice.

The next important thing to happen was the meeting of the National Council of the Socialist Party on May 2. Here the (long-expected) decision was taken not to enter M. Pleven's Government, but merely to support it. Although, at heart, Guy Mollet was anxious that the Socialists should participate in the Pleven (or any other) Government, he felt that the unity of the Party could be maintained only if it were no longer directly associated with the handling of Algeria.

Mollet had just returned from a meeting of the Socialist International in London, which had recommended a negotiated settlement in Algeria; while Mollet himself was full of mental reservations on this score, he was aware of the strong current inside the Socialist Party in favour of such a course. Also, there was Lacoste; and there was some very strong feeling in the Party in favour of getting him out of Algiers. He symbolized the fruitless policy of "pacification". Moreover, in a statement to *L'Express* of May 2, Lacoste had violently attacked M. Pineau, the Foreign Minister, and had referred to the French Foreign Office as *une bande de cons*, who had committed nothing but *conneries* in their handling of Tunisia:

"The last thing to do was to plead guilty over Sakhiet, to mumble and stutter the way our diplomats did. They just got cold feet! They got into one hell of a panic. Their one obsession now was to show that we had no intention of invading Tunisia. So they invented that ridiculous stunt—their frontier control. Everybody was so proud! By insisting on frontier control they were going to demonstrate that Bourguiba was intervening in Tunisia, but that we were guaranteeing Tunisian sovereignty! . . . And then, when Bourguiba went too far, he screamed for American help: 'Oh, sir, the Communists will come!' And, of course, the Americans fell for that one. And now they tell you you've got to choose between Bourguiba and Communism in North Africa! Communism is attractive to under-developed countries that have just acquired their independence. And Bourguiba won't stop it, any more than the King of Morocco. . . . Nor are the Americans going to triumph in North Africa. They haven't got the method. The only people who know how to handle Algeria, with real comprehension and a sense of detail, is us. And not the Americans, leaning on a thin reed like Bourguiba . . ."

For the rest, Lacoste said that if only he got 30,000 more well-trained troops, he could finish the war very quickly. He was going, with the help of his local Moslem "delegations", to hold elections for territorial assemblies on June 8 in all the pacified areas. And after that France could talk "with the Algerian people", and not with the FLN. . . . He had already pacified practically all the major cities, and the "battle of Algiers" had been "a magnificent thing"; "as for the price we had to pay, I shall explain all this in my memoirs when I am given time to write them. . . ." So much for the paratroopers and their "Gestapo". . . .

This reference to "memoirs" was probably a hint that he would soon be out of office.

The Socialist decision not to join in the Pleven Government or any Government comprising the Right, or to form any Government them-selves, marked the end of the Lacoste reign in Algeria. President Coty didn't know what to do. Should he ask Pleven to persist—even without the Socialists? Or should he ask an MRP leader to try to form the Government? Finally, he asked Pleven to make another attempt. But opinion in Paris—and even more so in Algiers—was growing impatient; again the name of de Gaulle began to appear in various newspapers—in *Combat*, in *Paris-Presse*, even in the *Monde*, where, on May 6, General Billotte published a long article in favour of a de Gaulle Government. De Gaulle was no dictator; de Gaulle was respected by everybody; de Gaulle's name meant a lot to the Algerians, etc. Two days later, another writer, M. Michel Massenet, argued in the *Monde* against the Socialist slogan: "De Gaulle means a dangerous adventure."

"An adventure? And why not if it's the noble adventure of our reconquered destiny, of our reconquered history? A de Gaulle adventure may mean a fresh start for France. But the present régime can only mean decay."

And, as already said, President Coty himself was, by this time, trying to establish secret contacts with de Gaulle.

However, on May 7 Pleven succeeded in getting a Government together; but not for long—for just a few hours. Now it wasn't the Socialists, but the Radicals, who rebelled, and decided to withdraw their three ministers—MM. Berthoin, Billières and Maurice Faure—from the new Pleven team. Why? Because Pleven had—obviously under the pressure of certain Army generals—appointed M. André Morice Minister of Defence; and Morice was a member of the "*ultra* quartet" (the other three, it will be recalled, being Bidault, Duchet and Soustelle), and had voted for the overthrow of the Gaillard Government on the "good offices" issue. The author of the "Morice Line" along the Tunisian border believed, first and foremost, in a policy of force in Algeria. To reassure the generals and the Algerian *ultras*, Pleven had, moreover, given the post of Minister of State for Sahara affairs to M. Duchet. . . . Here was another case of a parliamentary leader submitting to the blackmail of the Army and of Algiers.

There was much speculation about that time on what Guy Mollet was really doing. Had he, as some charitably suggested, seen the light, and recognized his errors (his capitulation to the Algiers *ultras* on February 6, 1956, Suez, "national-molletism", etc.) and was he going to adopt a strong liberal line in Algeria from now on? Or was he merely (and this seemed more likely) trying to remain at the head of the Party by making a few gestures—like dropping Lacoste—but putting on the brake whenever the bulk of the Party showed signs of wanting to join in the minority's clamour for a negotiated settlement? At the Socialist Congress to be called in June, it was expected that Gazier, Defferre and Savary would draw up a joint motion which would closely follow the line supported for a long time by Defferre in favour of immediate negotiations with the FLN. It was even forecast that there would be a majority at the Congress in favour of this. So Mollet had to watch his step.

And so Pleven, who had tried for over a fortnight to form a Government, gave up. After offering the job to M. Billières and M. Berthoin, President Coty finally, on May 8, asked M. Pflimlin to become head of the new Government.

Three times already had Pflimlin been offered the Premiership, but all three times he had failed, notably in May 1957, after the fall of the Guy Mollet Government. On that occasion Mollet himself had done his best to wreck Pflimlin's chances—chiefly because he considered him too "soft" on the Algerian issue.

Pflimlin, who was born in Strasbourg in 1907, was unknown before the war. He was elected town councillor of Strasbourg in 1945, and, soon afterwards, Deputy. In the years that followed, he held ministerial posts in fourteen Governments, usually as Minister of Agriculture or, more recently, as Minister of Finance. Cold, austere, distant and humourless, Pflimlin was known as a strict disciplinarian in any Government department he headed. He expected the strictest punctuality from his officials, and late-comers would often be summoned into the Minister's presence and hauled over the coals. Some said that he had an exaggerated sense of his ministerial importance; the Prefect of a *département* he once visited later told me how he had to send the only four gendarmes he had to accompany *Monsieur le Ministre* all over the place to form, whenever necessary, his "guard of honour". M. Pflimlin was a great stickler for etiquette. For all that, he had the reputation of being a man of great integrity, a fervent Catholic, and a believer in a "liberal" solution in Algeria. The last Premier of the Fourth Republic showed some unquestionable moral courage at first; after a time, both physically and mentally exhausted, he could no longer cope with the situation, and surrendered. . . .

16. "LITTLE PLUM"—THE STRANGE CASE OF M. LACOSTE— M. DE SÉRIGNY'S CLOAK-AND-DAGGER STORY

To UNDERSTAND why the name of Pflimlin was, to Algiers, like a red rag to a bull, a few facts need recalling. Just as there had been a strong evolution in favour of a negotiated Algerian settlement inside the Socialist Party, so a similar tendency had, for some time, been developing inside the MRP; and Pflimlin was the most outspoken supporter of this policy. As we have seen, Pflimlin had done everything to torpedo Bidault's attempt on April 20 to form a Government which, in Pflimlin's view, might well extend the war to Tunisia.

Then, on May 2, Pflimlin spoke before the Conseil Général of the Bas-Rhin *département* and said:

There cannot be a real solution in Algeria other than a political solution, and I consider that no opportunity should be missed for starting talks with a view to a cease-fire.

He added, it is true, that this would have to be done "from positions of strength"; all the same—

There is nothing incompatible between this will to bring the military operations to an end and the determination to intensify our war effort, if necessary; for this may be a pre-condition for reaching a peace settlement. But we must also recognize the fact that a further increase in military expenditure may well immensely aggravate our financial and economic position.

As an economist and as Minister of Finance, he was having in mind the £600 to £800 millions which, directly or indirectly, the Algerian war was costing France every year, and the demands for increased expenditure that were being made by the generals and by men like M. Lacoste. While forming his Cabinet Pflimlin continued to speak along similar lines, though sometimes he felt it necessary, as a concession to the Right, to place the emphasis on "military victory" which would, somehow, precede, or perhaps accompany, a settlement with the FLN.

His line, however, was never sufficiently precise to reassure the Algiers diehards, who also knew only too well, especially since Lacoste had been dropped by the Socialists, which way the wind was blowing. *Opinion, in short, was rapidly evolving in favour of peace talks, both inside the MRP and the Socialist Party.* Among the "Mendès-France" Radicals there had been a strong current in favour of such talks for a long time. And any peace bid was, of course, certain to receive the support of the Communists at the National Assembly.

Small wonder, then, that Algiers was getting worried.

Let us see, then, what exactly was happening during those days preceding the 13th of May both in Paris and Algiers. First of all, there was the very strange case of M. Lacoste who had, as we have seen, prohibited—and yet tacitly tolerated—the "anti-Paris" demonstration in Algiers on April 26. Since then, many things had happened. Mollet had attended the meeting of the Socialist International in London; the National Council of the Socialist Party had implicitly decided against maintaining Lacoste at Algiers; Lacoste had openly attacked Pineau and the French Foreign Office in *L'Express*; and when it was announced that Pflimlin had been called upon to form the next Government, there was an explosion of rage amongst the *ultras* in Paris and Algiers. M. de Sérigny (who, for fear of being assassinated at Algiers by the FLN, was living most of the time at the Grand Hotel in Paris) hastened to get in touch with Soustelle as soon as the news of Pflimlin had been announced. The two, who were then joined by M. Delbecque, thought there was only one way of making Lacoste play their game to its logical conclusion: and that was to persuade him to declare that he would stay in Algiers until a Government of National Union had been formed. He was (they believed) certain to do this if he thought he would be publicly backed by de Gaulle, the obvious head of such a Government. It would mean abandoning the Socialist Party, but this had, to all intents and purposes, disavowed him, anyway.

Soustelle, fully approving of this plan, said he would "do the impossible to obtain a statement from de Gaulle".

Here was a clear example of seemingly unauthorized people juggling with the name of de Gaulle, and even speaking in his name. Nothing showed that de Gaulle had authorized them to do so—except that Soustelle *did* see de Gaulle on May 5, or so, at least, we are told by the Brombergers.

Anyway, Sérigny, Soustelle and Delbecque were so determined to get Lacoste to lead the Algiers revolt against Pflimlin that on the night of May 8, Sérigny and Delbecque took the night plane to Algiers, even though the last words Soustelle uttered over the telephone to them were only: "If Lacoste takes up the required position, there is a good chance that de Gaulle will break his silence." How did Soustelle know? What had de Gaulle told him on May 5? The next morning Lacoste received de Sérigny at the Summer Palace, and Sérigny said to him:

"You have often expressed to me your surprise at de Gaulle's silence, since de Gaulle, as you yourself so often told me, was the only man with enough authority to put some sense into our people. Today I bring you a great piece of news: if you agree to make a statement on the lines of your recent Order of the Day to the Army, and if, in this statement, you say that an immediate truce must be concluded among the Parties, and that a Government of Public Safety must be formed; if, also, you say that you will stay in Algiers until this aim has been attained, then General de Gaulle would be disposed to support you in a public statement [*serait disposé à vous donner raison dans une déclaration publique*]."

What authority did Sérigny have for making this statement, except the seemingly vague hope that Soustelle had expressed the night before?

Was Lacoste wholly taken in? His first reaction was to jump out of his chair and to exclaim:

"But that's terrific, *mon vieux*! *C'est formidable!* So Big Charles would decide to speak! It's fantastic!"

Sérigny then tells how he gave Lacoste a number of code phrases whereby he could inform Soustelle by phone whether he would make the required statement, would make it in a modified form, or not make it at all. The question whether Soustelle had any proof that de Gaulle would speak after such a Lacoste statement was not mentioned. Lacoste was, in fact, being asked to buy a pig in a poke ... if one is right in assuming that Soustelle was not arranging anything with de Gaulle, but was merely preparing for him a *fait accompli* which might (but also might not) induce him to speak.[1]

However, Lacoste did not phone Soustelle. He promised Sérigny to make the required statement, but later (according to Sérigny) under the influence of a Socialist delegation that had come to see him, and also under the influence of the officials surrounding him, he changed his mind. Were the *ultras* now going to dispense with Lacoste?

Anyway, the Army leaders were already highly active. On the night of May 9, while Pflimlin was continuing his consultations, with a view to forming his Government, General Salan, in agreement with Generals Allard, Jouhaud and Massu, sent a telegram via General Ely, the Chief of Staff, to President Coty in which he said that, in view of the danger of a policy of surrender being adopted, a "reaction of despair" might readily be produced in the Army in Algeria. That same night, too, M. Lacoste received the representatives of the various ex-servicemen's and patriotic associations of Algiers (including Soustelle's USRAF), and "all of them pressed M. Lacoste to make a public stand in favour of a Government of Public Safety". Again he dodged the issue. His press chief told M. de Sérigny that M. Lacoste would make the statement, "but not today".

Having received some further evidence of Pflimlin's "capitulationist" tendencies, Sérigny phoned Lacoste late at night to tell him about it; but again Lacoste was "unconvinced", even though (as Sérigny recalls) he had for days now uttered gloomy prophecies about the "diplomatic Dien Bien Phu" which was on the way. . . .

On the morning of Saturday, May 10, Sérigny and Delbecque flew back to Paris. They were going to see Soustelle. There is no evidence that in the interval Soustelle had been in contact with de Gaulle, or that he had received any definite assurance from him that he would support Lacoste if the latter made his statement. So, with Soustelle's approval, Sérigny decided to make his "urgent appeal" to de Gaulle himself— though in the form of an editorial to be published in *Dimanche matin*, the Sunday edition of the *Echo d'Alger*.

[1] The inevitable question arises, of course, whether there wasn't, in reality, closer contact between Soustelle and de Gaulle than Sérigny is free to disclose. But *was* there?

The next people to appear on the scene were two Algerian senators, both representing big colonialist capital: Senator Rogier and Senator Schiaffino, the shipping magnate. It was Rogier who informed Sérigny that Lacoste was back in Paris, that he had decided against attending the great protest demonstration in Algiers on May 13 against the murder of three French soldiers by the FLN, but that he had recommended "that this demonstration take on 'gigantic' proportions, and that the Town Hall of Algiers be invaded in the process." An allegation, Sérigny adds, "which was later to be confirmed to me by other friends."[1]

Whether this was true or not, Lacoste decided, in any case, to play a different game from that recommended to him by Sérigny and Soustelle's various agents: he hoped that, despite Socialist support, Pflimlin would still be overthrown, and a Government of Public Safety would be formed—but under the Premiership of Guy Mollet!

That being so, Sérigny decided that his only hope was to persuade any hesitant members of the Right to vote against Pflimlin—and so to overthrow him (on the understanding, of course, that the Communists were going to vote against the Government). However, he failed to persuade M. Mutter, in particular, against joining the Pflimlin Government, and, in any case, as we now know, Pflimlin benefited, on the night of the Algiers *putsch*, from the abstention of the Communists.

This story of M. de Sérigny's certainly throws a glaring light on the strange activities that had been going on in Algiers, during the days before the May 13 *putsch*. The Army, as was shown by Salan's telegram to President Coty of May 9, was in a state of latent revolt. The *ultras* (as well as Soustelle's USRAF) were also flooding Coty with protests and

---

[1] After the publication of M. de Sérigny's book, M. Lacoste published a variety of denials which, broadly, amount to this: while he was very anxious about the "fate of Algeria", and did not in any way discourage the planned "demonstration" of May 13, he specifically denied that he had ever advocated the invasion of the *mairie* of Algiers, or any other kind of mob violence. As regards Sérigny's proposal that he publicly demand the formation of a Government of Public Safety—a demand which, according to Sérigny, would be backed by de Gaulle—Lacoste said that he had not promised Sérigny to make any statement; "I also made them [Sérigny and Delbecque] clearly understand that I did not believe that de Gaulle had agreed to their request. Moreover, I told them that I refused to act in a manner contrary to the Constitution, and would not stay on at Algiers beyond my legal tenure of office. . . . But I also repeated that I was very anxious about Algeria and longed with all my heart for a government which would make a statement declaring without any hedging that it would defend Algeria to the end." As for the Socialists who had, according to Sérigny, "influenced" him into abandoning his proposed broadcast, the only one whom he had seen that day was M. Marzorati, who fully shared Lacoste's views on Algeria. (Cf. *Le Monde*, July 4 and 23.)

Commenting on these various Lacoste denials, Eugène Mannoni, the *Monde* correspondent, said that Lacoste had not really denied, but merely *corrected* some of Sérigny's stories.

Jacques Chevallier, the Mayor of Algiers, for his own part, *believed* Sérigny's story that Lacoste wanted the demonstrators to "invade the town hall" and—even to lynch him (Chevallier). (Jacques Chevallier, *Nous, Algériens . . .*, Paris, 1958, p. 153.)

appeals. The USRAF had also published on May 9 a leaflet, widely distributed in Algiers, which read:

Those advocating surrender have decided to eliminate once and for all the true defenders of French Algeria: Soustelle, Bidault, Lacoste, Morice and Duchet. They want to give the key posts to those who intend to abandon Algeria. After Pleven, another notorious liquidator has been called in: his name is Pflimlin.

And on the 11th, as we have seen, Sérigny came out with his famous appeal to de Gaulle. This appeal ran parallel with other "bring-back-de-Gaulle" articles in the Paris press—by old PRF Gaullists like Triboulet, and by liberals like Mauriac, who thought de Gaulle alone had the authority—not to continue the war in Algeria (which was what the Sérigny appeal meant) but, on the contrary, to stop it.

Lacoste, for his own part, left Algiers, as we have seen, not wishing to be openly associated with the "gigantic demonstration" of May 13—which he himself was, on the quiet, advocating, complete (it was alleged) with the invasion—not of the Government-General, but of the Town Hall of Algiers, which, under the leadership of M. Chevallier, remained the last stronghold of Algiers "liberalism". Lacoste went off to his native Dordogne, without making any attempt to see Soustelle (though he had promised to go to see him). At Périgueux, on the 12th, he made a highly alarmist speech, in which he again talked about the impending "diplomatic Dien Bien Phu". But meantime in Algiers he had already been written off by both *ultras* and "Gaullists", no doubt under the influence of Sérigny, Delbecque and others, who now felt that Lacoste had let them down. The Poujadists even began to attack Lacoste in their leaflets as a "pricked balloon". Referring to his refusal to leave the Socialist Party and to lead the Algiers revolt against Paris, a Poujadist leaflet on the 12th said:

"We are no longer thinking in the same terms, Monsieur Lacoste. We are thinking in terms of French Algeria. You are thinking in terms of your political career. Get the hell out of here before it's too late!"

Lacoste had, indeed, already "got out". Gaillard (still acting-Premier) asked him to return to Algiers, but he refused. Several papers also reported that when he was asked in the Chamber lobbies when he was returning to Algiers, or whether he had seen M. Pflimlin, he replied with his "characteristic bluntness": "Algiers my arse. If they don't have bloodshed there today, they'll have it tomorrow . . ."

17. ANOTHER GENERALS' REVOLT?

M DE SÉRIGNY's cloak-and-dagger stuff (which he wasn't to relate in detail until July) was something of which perhaps only relatively few people in Paris were aware. There was a good deal of information in the papers about the "anguish", the "unrest", the "nervous tension" in Algiers during that week, and about protest demonstrations that were being prepared; but all this information was rather fragmentary. All the same, by the 11th or 12th some of the more observant Paris journalists were beginning to piece together the very, very queer jigsaw puzzle. By far the best effort was that made by the *Canard Enchaîné*; its issue, dated May 14, but actually written and printed before the Algiers *putsch*, produced something that came very close to a preview of M. de Sérigny's story; it warned Paris that the Army was on the point of revolting, and that Pflimlin was going to bite off more than he could chew. Here were some of the *Canard's* points, made in its usual facetious and seemingly light-hearted style:

The Republic has suddenly begun to feel terribly wobbly.
Because of Algiers, where the Street is on the move.
With the silent blessing of Comrade Lacoste.
And because, in the background, the Army is also on the move.
And very much so . . .

The other day General Salan, the C.-in-C. in Algeria, sent a report to General Ely, the Chief of Staff in France, on the state of mind existing amongst the officers in Algeria *vis-à-vis* Little Plum.[1]
The said report clearly indicated that the said officers were in a state of frenzy about the said Pflimlin, and that he (Salan) wouldn't answer for anything. Ely hastened to take the message along to Coty, who nearly fell off his chair.

Also, Salan and certain other high officers sent a circular to the various Army headquarters saying that, until further notice, they, and only they, were in command, and that no notice whatsoever need be taken of any cease-fire talk emanating from Little Plum.

In short, the Army is, as ever, in the service of the Republic. To defend it. Or, if necessary, to strangle it.

There are some who swear that if Pleven killed off his own Government, by appointing Morice Minister of Defence, it was entirely at the insistence of the military leaders.

And the *Canard* rightly added that Pflimlin had become so conscious of this Army pressure that he had, in the last day or two, been uttering

[1] In Alsatian dialect Pflimlin means "little plum".

"tricolour" phrases, such as: "When I speak of the armistice, what I have in mind is something like the armistice of 1918, which gave Alsace-Lorraine back to France"—phrases which were not the true reflection of what he really thought.

And what is more [said the *Canard*—a point later to be confirmed by de Sérigny] Pflimlin sent an emissary, a M. Payron, to Algiers, to submit his ministerial declaration to the Army leaders. They were not impressed, and said they couldn't support the Government, if there were any kick-up in Algeria. Since when Little Plum has, indeed, been telling his friends: "If we haven't got the Army with us, then *la République est foutue.*"

What in Algiers, apart from the cloak-and-dagger stuff, was to lead up to the explosion of May 13?

On May 10 it was learned that three French prisoners had been executed by the FLN, after a trial of sorts, at which they had been accused of rape and various atrocities. Coming on top of the Tangier Conference, this execution of three French war prisoners marked a further hardening of the FLN line. For a time, the FLN were glad to avail themselves of the good offices of the International Red Cross, but they had repeatedly warned the French authorities in recent weeks that executions of Algerians would be followed by reprisals against French prisoners. The French argued that they never executed any *bona fide* Algerian soldiers taken prisoner, but only "terrorists"; but this was not very convincing. Liberals in Paris tended to regard these executions as part of the "general frightfulness" for which both sides were responsible; but it was, naturally, too much to expect Algiers to take so objective a view, and the memorial ceremony, fixed in Algiers for the afternoon of May 13, promised to produce some violent incidents.

On May 12, the "Vigilance Committee", comprising seventeen different war veterans' and other patriotic associations, called on the people of Algiers to stop all work at 3 p.m. on Tuesday, May 13, and to assemble on the Plateau de Glières in the centre of the city and to demonstrate their determined opposition to the investiture of a "wholly unacceptable government of surrender".

At 6 p.m. there was, moreover, to be an official ceremony in front of the close-by war memorial in the Boulevard Laferrière in honour of the three soldiers murdered by the FLN.

Soustelle's USRAF and other associations all sent telegrams to President Coty warning him against "identifying himself with a policy of surrender", as impersonated by M. Pflimlin.

And by this time, as we have seen, even Lacoste was not spared by some of the more extreme "activist" elements.

What then was to happen in Algiers on that Tuesday, May 13? We shall see presently.

In Paris, on Tuesday morning, a curious communiqué was published by M. Lacoste (still nominally Minister of Algeria) in which he said that, contrary to certain reports, he had not seen M. Pflimlin, and had not been asked by him to do anything. But he had yesterday (Monday)

"given the civilian and military authorities of Algiers all the necessary instructions, for the maintenance of order. . . . In accordance with these instructions, all the demonstrations in Algiers and elsewhere will be merged into one, and for the sole purpose of paying tribute to the memory of the three French soldiers executed by the FLN."

That was Lacoste's last—and entirely meaningless—message to Algiers.

In the afternoon, while the Assembly was meeting, some familiar signs of nervousness could be observed in Paris—around the Etoile, around the US Embassy in the Place de la Concorde, and especially in the neighbourhood of the National Assembly. At all these points, and along the Champs-Elysées substantial police forces had been concentrated. At 6.30 p.m. a ceremony commemorating the three soldiers executed by the FLN was held at the Etoile. A crowd of about two thousand, who had gathered around the Etoile at the time of the wreath-laying, swarmed up to the Arc de Triomphe, and after observing a minute's silence and singing the *Marseillaise*, proceeded to march down the Champs Elysées. At the head of the procession were a number of well-known Fascists, such as the ex-Poujadist deputy Le Pen. They shouted "*Vive la France!*" and "*Algérie Française!*" and also "*Les députés à la Seine!*"—in the manner of the Right-wing Champs-Elysées demonstrations of the 1930s.

Although this demonstration had been carefully organized in advance, it was in reality extremely small stuff, and the public on either side of the avenue seemed mainly indifferent. It was significant that, on the day of the Algiers *putsch*, the anti-Republican forces in Paris should not have mustered a more impressive demonstration.

Nevertheless, the two thousand who had marched down the Champs-Elysées, and had attempted to approach the US Embassy, uttering a few hostile cries, now tried to cross the Concorde Bridge, with the National Assembly across the river. There were cries of *A bas la République!* and *A bas le régime!* and then the demonstrators clashed with the armed CRS guards. Tear-gas bombs were thrown, and the demonstrators, a few of whom were injured in a police charge, were driven back. A few groups then demonstrated outside the Tunisian Embassy in the rue des Pyramides, where a few windows were broken, while others, marching down the Grand Boulevard, shouted "*A Moscou!*" and "*A bas les cocos!*" outside the offices of the Communist *L'Humanité*. That was all.

In Paris, the Algiers rebellion had merely wagged a little finger.

PART II
THE TWENTY DAYS THAT SHOOK FRANCE

1. PFLIMLIN WINS THE FIRST ROUND

EXCEPT at the very end, the meeting of the National Assembly on that historic day of May 13 was an incongruously routine affair. It was during the dinner recess, between 7.30 and 9 p.m., that the tele-printers in the now deserted Assembly lobbies started ticking away like mad with the news of the Algiers rebellion. Most deputies, who had been out dining, still did not know what had happened when they returned to the Assembly for the night session at 9 p.m. What had happened before that dinner interval?

It all started with a touch of comedy. A Poujadist deputy had died during the Cabinet crisis, and M. Le Troquer,[1] the President of the Assembly, opened the proceedings with a brief funeral oration in which he said that

"nothing appeared to destine our late lamented colleague for public life. He was, indeed, running at Poitiers a highly prosperous business in leather goods. He was elected deputy on January 2, 1956. The premature end of our colleague prevented him, in Parliament, from displaying his potentialities to the full."

Then it came to the Ministerial Declaration. M. Pflimlin, with his trenchant voice, clipping his words, read out the long document on which he had worked for several days now. He advocated a reform of the Constitution—a reform to be carried out within six months—which would greatly reduce the number of Government changes in France. Amongst his remedies was the

constructive censure motion whose authors would be obliged to present an

[1] M. Le Troquer, a V.I.P. in the Socialist Party, who had associated himself with de Gaulle in 1942–43, was elected to the Presidency of the National Assembly in 1953 after the retire-ment of M. Edouard Herriot. Though he had been sharply anti-Communist on various occasions, the Communists voted for him as a "lesser evil". Throughout the May crisis he was violently opposed to de Gaulle's return to power, resented Coty's famous threat to the Assembly to resign if de Gaulle were not brought back to power, and even for a brief moment hoped to succeed Coty as President of the Republic with the support of a "Republican majority" including the Communists.

Later, under the de Gaulle Government, Le Troquer, "the staunch Republican" was—no doubt rather deliberately—shown up as a dirty old man of seventy-four, who had taken part in the famous *Ballets roses* orgies, and a criminal charge was brought against him. However, he got his own back by showing the police a film in which an elderly relative of one of the régime's high-ups was *also* seen to attend the *Ballets Roses*. In the end M. Le Troquer got away with a suspended 1-year sentence.

alternative Government programme and name the new Premier they wished to see invested. Such a reform would allow the parliamentary system to work more efficiently, for it would restore the notion of the "working majority", without which there could be no proper democratic government.

He also proposed a revision of Chapter VIII of the Constitution, with a view to giving a higher degree of self-government to overseas territories, particularly in Black Africa.

Then he dealt at some length with the fact that "France was living above her means"; advocated the "strictest discipline in our prices and wages policy"; drew a rather alarming picture of France's balance of payments, and said he would ask for extensive powers in the financial field; among other things, it would be necessary for France to make numerous changes in her economy so as to adapt it to the Common Market. It was also necessary to raise more revenue so as to be able to increase France's "military effort in Algeria".

Then came a long statement, which the Assembly had been waiting for, on Algeria. Bombarded for days with charges of "defeatism" and "capitulationism", Pflimlin had watered down the passages concerning the cease-fire, clearly suggesting that he was not proposing anything other than what Guy Mollet had already proposed in his famous triptych of January 9, 1957: cease-fire, elections, negotiations for a new statute.
"France will not abandon Algeria," he said. As for the cease-fire, he now put it this way:

The day will come when the rebellion will have lost all hope of winning and will be ready to give up the struggle. If on that day the Government find that it is in the interests of the country to enter into conversations with the Rebels, with a view to cease-fire, it will do so. "I should like to add that, in my opinion, such talks can only take place against the background of a French victory."

The attempt to appease the Right and the Algerian *ultras* and generals was quite obvious.
More conciliatory was the final part of Pflimlin's statement in favour of improving relations with Tunisia and Morocco, and he spoke of the great possibilities of a vast Franco-Maghreb Union, all of whose members would benefit from the development of the Sahara. He did not reject *a priori* the possibility of Tunisia and Morocco using their influence with the Algerian rebels to bring about the end of the war.
After a two-hour interval between 4 and 6 p.m. (by this time the Concorde Bridge was black with police forces) the discussion on the Pflimlin proposals started with the usual snarling speech by that old Fascist and Vichyite, M. Tixier-Vignancour, who remarked that, "overwhelmed by an ocean of protests", Pflimlin had been compelled, in the last three days, to tone down his statement a great deal. All the same,

hadn't he done his utmost to prevent Bidault from becoming Premier, because Bidault "really wanted to win the war"? The Army, Tixier-Vignancour said, would not allow the kind of negotiations Pflimlin was likely to engage in. In short, nothing short of a capitulation by the Rebels would do; and when Pflimlin was trying to sound like Clemenceau, he (Tixier-Vignancour) didn't believe a word of it. He would vote against.

There was a comic interlude. In a woolly speech, M. Deixonne (Socialist), forgetting the sins of his friend and master, Guy Mollet, deplored the unreasonable French nationalism which was all that the French Right seemed capable of setting against the narrow Arab nationalism, as revealed by the recent Tangier Conference.

And then came this singular tribute to Lacoste:

"At the moment when Robert Lacoste is about to leave Algeria, I, speaking in the name of the parliamentary Socialist Party, wish to express to him our gratitude, a gratitude which should be shared by the entire nation."

Mendès-France: "In that case you should have left him there." (*Loud laughter on Left. Protests on Right.*)

But Deixonne persisted. If, he said, Algeria was going to have a happy future, it would largely be thanks to the untiring efforts of Robert Lacoste.

Had the next speaker, M. Clostermann, the famous air-ace and a former Left-wing Gaullist (though now nominally a Radical) made his speech on any other occasion, it would have caused a sensation, and aroused endless discussion; on May 13, it was of little more than academic interest.

His main point was that the whole war in Algeria had been mismanaged from beginning to end. Speaking from first-hand experience as an airman who had fought in Algeria, Clostermann said that although there were over 400,000 French troops in Algeria, practically all of these were doing sentry duty and various other auxiliary jobs, and that, in reality, *all the real fighting had to be done by some 20,000 tough soldiers—the paratroopers and the Foreign Legion.* There were vast areas—such as the Dhara and Braz region 250 km. by 25—which were wholly controlled by the Rebels. Politically, Clostermann said, the situation had gravely deteriorated; the January 1956 election had raised enormous hopes amongst the Algerians; these were dashed to the ground by the policy adopted as a result of the February 6, 1956, riots.

Then came the famous dinner recess, and when the discussion was resumed at 9 p.m. the atmosphere had radically changed. But not radically enough to prevent a number of speakers from reading out their long, typed-out orations. M. Montel (Right), in the course of a whole hour's speech, talked along the usual lines:

"What is M. Pflimlin's policy, compared with M. Bidault's policy? Why did M. Mendès-France cheer M. Pflimlin when he refused to cheer M. Bidault?"

M. *Charles Hernu* (Radical): "You are a bore. A Committee of Public Safety has been set up at Algiers. Really we have other things to do than listen to you."

But M. Le Troquer, the President of the Assembly, would have none of it. He was going to respect the sanctity of parliamentary procedure:

Please do not interrupt the speaker. Let him proceed with his demonstration as he sees fit.

Hour after hour, the prepared speeches were delivered: first by Montel, then by Senghor, the African deputy, who argued in favour of turning Algeria into an "associate state", then by M. Pierre André (Right) who started a polemic against M. Clostermann:

He has painted much too black a picture of the situation in Algeria. . . . Oran and Algiers are more peaceful today than Paris. More than half the villages have been pacified; over 7,000 French Moslems are sitting on the special delegations in the municipalities; 53,000 Moslems are fighting under the French flag or are doing sentry duty in the pacified villages; more than half a million Moslem children go to elementary schools. All this is ignored by many Frenchmen, who generalize from the fact that ten Moslem officers have deserted, or that a few Algerian footballers belonging to French football teams have run away.

M. Pierre André claimed that the French losses in Algeria had been relatively small:

Killed or died of wounds or illness: 2,374 in 1956, 3,106 in 1957, 672 in the first two months of 1958. During the same period there had been about 15,000 wounded.

It is scarcely surprising that neither Pflimlin, the prospective Premier, nor most of the other Party leaders wasted their time, after the news of Massu's *putsch* in Algiers had reached Paris, on listening to all these academic speeches at the National Assembly.

It was now that the cloak-and-dagger stuff—which was to be so characteristic of the whole twenty days which preceded the advent of de Gaulle—started in a big way in Paris, too.

Pflimlin's Government was, of course, a Coalition Government, composed of some more-or-less moderate members of the Right, notably M. Mutter, the new Minister for Algeria, anti-Mendès Radicals (among them M. Edgar Faure, the Minister of Finance); and M. Maurice Faure (Interior); Left-Centre men like M. Pleven (Foreign Affairs) and several members of the MRP, most of them hostile to M. Bidault's *ultra* policy in Algeria, among them M. Robert Lecourt (Justice) and M. Bacon

(Labour). The Minister of Defence was M. de Chevigné, a former "colonialist" diehard, whom the Left largely held responsible for the Madagascar massacres in 1947.[1]

Yet it was M. de Chevigné who was among the first to react very sharply to the news of the Algiers *putsch*:

"Just give me a few hours," he said. "I don't think this nonsense can last very long. This Army rebellion in a war situation is something I am not going to tolerate."

The first reaction of the greater part of the Right-wing members was different: they argued that it would be best, in the circumstances, if Pflimlin did not persist in getting his Cabinet approved by the Assembly, but informed President Coty that he was giving up his attempt. Some were already uttering the name of General de Gaulle; others were arguing in favour of a "broad national coalition government" under the premiership of—Guy Mollet!

There was much coming and going at the Hôtel Matignon, the Premier's residence and office, which was still occupied by M. Gaillard. Attempts were made to persuade Gaillard to bring pressure to bear on Pflimlin to give up, and to give way to a "national coalition" under Mollet. Mollet himself appears, according to all reports, to have been "interested" in the proposal.

But the news of the Algiers *putsch* had aroused certain old *lutte républicaine* instincts both among various Centre and Left-Centre leaders, and amongst the rank-and-file of the Parliamentary Socialist Party.

Whereas at the Hôtel Matignon a lively discussion was in progress among Gaillard, Duchet (of the *ultra* wing of the Right) and Guy Mollet, three other leading politicians, Mitterrand, Daladier and Edgar Faure, drove to the Premier's office to tell him that, in their opinion, Pflimlin must be invested—his refusal to go on with his effort to lead the Government would be interpreted as a capitulation to the Algiers conspirators. Gaillard, oddly enough, refused to receive them. But they then saw Pflimlin, in another office, and encouraged him to carry on.

What had actually happened during the Gaillard-Duchet-Mollet meeting at the Premier's office? The cat was let out of the bag by M. Duchet who later remarked: "We very nearly managed to set up a National Union Government." "Wouldn't Mollet play ball?" "*He* wasn't the main obstacle. The real point is that Pflimlin said that he 'would take full responsibility'."

Moreover, Mollet must have realized soon after his meeting with Gaillard and Duchet that "his" plan would not receive any support from the Socialists. He had attended the beginning of their meeting soon after

[1] See *France 1940–1955*, p. 464.

nine o'clock, but had remained non-committal. Before the meeting was ended he drove to the Hôtel Matignon, the Premier's official residence. The Socialist meeting continued, and the feeling that "the Republic must stand up to the Algiers Fascists" grew stronger every moment; and the first thing to do was to give Pflimlin whole-hearted support—if he wanted it.

Pflimlin, fully conscious by this time of the little plot that was being hatched against him, was not going to surrender.

Deixonne was sent to the Hôtel Matignon to inform Gaillard—and later, Pflimlin—that the Socialists were determined to support Pflimlin. On the other hand, the great majority of the Right "Independents" were now against Pflimlin; the question was raised whether the Right-wing ministers should stay in his Government. Only one, M. Mutter, emphatically said they must stay on. But on this question no decision was taken at this stage.

It was well after ten o'clock when M. Pflimlin and the numerous other people who had gone to the Hôtel Matignon during the last three hours (while some sixty or seventy people at the Assembly had been listening to the speeches of MM. Montel, Senghor, and Pierre André) returned to the Palais-Bourbon.

No sooner had Pierre André finished his interminable speech than M. Pflimlin asked that the sitting be suspended. It was then that M. Waldeck-Rochet, for the Communists, butted in:

Waldeck-Rothet: Up till now the Communist group has not said a single word. . . . While we are discussing the Government's investiture, events of the utmost gravity are taking place in Algiers. We now learn that General Massu . . .

M. Dorgères (Extreme Right): . . . has saved France! [*Loud protests on Extreme Left. Cries of* "Fascist!")

M. Waldeck-Rochet: After having occupied the Government building in Algiers and proclaimed the formation of a Committee of Public Safety, Massu has now sent an ultimatum to the President of the Republic. This means the creation of an illegal and insurrectionist government which means the separation of Algeria and a revolt against the Republic.

Voices on extreme Right: French Algeria! French Algeria!

Voices on extreme Left: Fascists!

M. Waldeck-Rochet: Surely, the first thing to do is to dismiss and outlaw Massu. To do this, we need the immediate union of all republicans! (*Cheers on extreme Left.*)

Voice on extreme Right: Budapest!

M. Waldeck-Rochet: Immediate measures must be taken to save the Republic!

There now followed a few minutes of complete chaos. On the Right they were shouting: "*Algérie Française!*" while the Communists were chanting in chorus: "*Le fascisme ne passera pas!*"

Finally M. Pflimlin rose to speak.

M. Pflimlin: It is quite true that things of the utmost gravity have happened at Algiers; but it is, surely, not for the Communists to save freedom and the Republic. (*Cheers on Left and Centre. Protests on extreme Left.*)

Pflimlin then asked again that the sitting be suspended, so that those anxious to save the Republic "could take their responsibilities. I am prepared to take mine," he concluded.

There followed over two hours of committee-room discussions.

When the Chamber reassembled at 1.15 a.m., M. Pflimlin, looking less hesitant than before, spoke with great firmness. After asking that those still due to speak renounce their claim, he said:

It is essential that at an hour like this France should have a Government without delay. We must save Algeria. When France is in a position of unquestionable strength, we must take any opportunity to achieve a peace, which would be the fruit of our victory. . . . We must avoid anything which might extend the conflict to the whole of North Africa—which would only internationalize it. There may be some patriots who think otherwise, but they must trust me and my ministers when we say that we shall never be tempted to abandon Algeria.

But at present we are faced with a different problem. There are Frenchmen in Algiers—men whose anxiety I can well appreciate—who have allowed themselves to be drawn into some very serious acts, and I must say it with the deepest regret, there are also certain military leaders who have assumed an insurrectionist attitude towards republican legality.[1] (*Prolonged cheers on Centre, Left and extreme Left, and on a few Right benches.*)

M. Dorgères d'Halluin: You are defending the System! Together with the Communists . . .

M. Pflimlin: A tragic divorce between the French of France and the French of Algeria must be avoided. National unity must be restored. And it can only be done within the framework of the Republic. My dear colleagues, I want you to know that we are perhaps on the threshold of civil war.

There is no doubt that these are the men (*pointing to the Communists*) who would, in the end, benefit from a civil war. Nothing will bring me closer to them.

M. Raymond Lainé (Extreme Right)*:* The Communists are applauding you.

M. Pflimlin: I call upon the National Assembly to take its responsibility at this historic hour.

Despite the attacks made on them by Pflimlin, the Communists decided to abstain in the vote. It was part of the "republican defence" movement in which they were now going to take an active—even if officially unsolicited—part.

Pflimlin was invested as head of the new Government at 3.20 a.m. on May 14 by 274 votes to 129.

---

[1] M. Pflimlin soon found that his phrase about the "insurrectionist attitude of certain Army leaders" had put him in an awkward position *vis-à-vis* Salan, Massu, etc. His subsequent behaviour towards these people was wholly inconsistent with his first—and essentially correct—diagnosis of the Algiers situation.

The result was greeted with an outburst of cheering from the Socialists, the MRP, the Radicals and a small part of the Right. Most of the Right now observed a glum silence.

Most people had been impressed by Pflimlin's firm and precise manner, and by his open condemnation of the Algiers insurrection; also by his refusal to take account of the intrigues that had gone on that night—with the participation of M. Guy Mollet, the secretary-general of the Socialist Party.

The *défense républicaine* instincts had been aroused among the Socialists, and many Radicals and MRP members. This reaction was, of course, receiving full support from the Communists. Only, would it last?

The trouble, of course, was that parliamentary arithmetic was not necessarily of any decisive importance any more. Other forces were at work. Pflimlin had spoken of the "insurrectionist attitude" of certain military leaders. Already on that Tuesday night the "Social Republicans" (i.e. the ex-Gaullist group of the Assembly) issued a statement saying that France could be saved only by "the arbitration of General de Gaulle". On the Wednesday morning, four of the principal diehards, Bidault, Duchet, Morice and Soustelle, issued a proclamation demanding the formation of a Government of "union and national salvation".

They did not mention de Gaulle's name, but Bidault and Soustelle, at any rate, were known to have campaigned for de Gaulle for some time. Events were being shaped outside Parliament.

What, then, had happened at Algiers, during the time when the Assembly was listening to academic speeches, and when, at the Hôtel Matignon, Pflimlin was fighting against those trying to replace him by an unholy and suspect coalition under Guy Mollet?

2. ALGIERS: THE MAY 13 *PUTSCH*

THE story of what happened in Algiers on May 13, 1958, has been written many times, and we shall try in this chapter to confine ourselves only to the politically relevant and significant facts, which were to play, in the weeks and months that followed, so decisive a role in shaping the future destiny of France.

Three important elements were involved in the events of May 13: the Europeans of Algiers, a community with a very strange mentality of its own; the Army; and the "Gaullist network", a relative newcomer, as we have seen.

A great deal of plotting of one kind or another had been going on for a long time; there had been an Army plot, back in 1956, conducted by

General Faure; there had been, early in 1957, the *affaire* Kovacs, when a group of European "counter-terrorists" attempted to assassinate the C.-in-C., General Salan. Kovacs, an "anti-terrorist" maniac, headed an organization called ORAF (*Organisation de la Résistance de l'Algérie Française*) which went in for tortures of kidnapped Algerians and all kinds of provocations (such as throwing bombs into churches in order to convert Mgr. Duval, the Archbishop of Algiers, to a more intolerant attitude towards the Moslems). After their attempt to murder General Salan (they missed him, but killed one of his aides) Kovacs and five of his cronies were arrested, whereupon they alleged that very many important people were behind the plot: among them Soustelle, Debré, Arrighi, General Cogny (commander of the French troops in Morocco), Griotteray, and many others. "Even if Kovacs was romancing, it still seemed to embarrass a lot of people," the Brombergers wrote in connection with his subsequent trial.[1]

General Jacques Faure, whom later Poujade made one of his Parliamentary candidates at Lyon, hoped, in 1956, to bring about "a military dictatorship, which would make France clean, beautiful and powerful"; and, together with Le Pen and other Fascists and Poujadists, who had close contacts with Dides's "network" in the Paris Police, he had hoped to carry out a simultaneous *coup d'état* in Paris and Algiers. But he talked too much, and the Mollet Government locked him up—for thirty days, and then gave him a command in Germany. Not to annoy the Army too much, the Mollet Government made up for it by also arresting and locking up for thirty days one of the rare liberal generals in Algeria, General Paris de La Bollandière, who had publicly denounced the atrocities committed by the French Army.

Especially since 1956, the French Army in Algeria, as we have seen, had been dominating the Paris Government, and had become an increasingly independent political force, which was determined to dictate its will to the French Government both before and after the May "revolution." Some of the generals were "Gaullists", others were not. As early as December 1957 General Massu told an Italian paper that "de Gaulle alone could clean up this mess". In May 1958 the Algerian Army had its active accomplices in Metropolitan France: Miquel at Toulouse, Descours at Lyon, Widerspach-Thor at Dijon, Lecoq at Bordeaux, Colonel Gribius, who was preparing a *putsch* in Paris. Miquel, who alone in France had paratroopers under his command, was particularly active; as early as January 1958 he had set up secret telephone and wireless communications among the various military commands in France and between these and Algiers (Bromberger, *op. cit.*, p. 69). The General Staff in Paris also shared in the conspiracy: General Petit went to Algiers on May 10 to inform the officers that Soustelle would soon arrive (*ibid.*,

[1] Bromberger, *op. cit.*, p. 101.

p. 144), while General Challe (who was to be arrested by Pflimlin, but was later to be appointed C.-in-C. in Algeria by de Gaulle) sent thirty-six large transport planes to Algiers on May 14 and 15 to bring, if necessary, paratroops to France; finally, General Ely, the Chief of Staff, wrote to de Gaulle on May 11 asking him to intervene, and tried to bring about the fall of the Pflimlin Government by resigning at the height of the May crisis (*ibid.*, p. 247).

The Army (and particularly the paratroop colonels) had contacts with various civilian groups in Algeria; there was close contact between Colonel Thomazo and Lagaillarde and other "activist" plotters in Algiers. These, in turn, were mixed up with men like Biaggi and ex-*commissaire* Dides's police "network" in Paris. Working in the shadows, and with more important Army contacts than a mere Thomazo, were Olivier Guichard, de Gaulle's *chef de cabinet*. Defence Minister Chaban-Delmas, Soustelle, Delbecque and other "Gaullists". It was Delbecque who went to Algiers to "convert" the Army to Gaullism. In France both Soustelle and Debré were busy: Debré concentrating in particular on heads of Government departments, prefects, etc. "Gradually, as a result of Debré's efforts, a clandestine Gaullist administration crystallized, running parallel with the official administration" (*ibid.*, p. 66). Many important people in Big Business were mixed up in all this: Delbecque himself, as a director of Motte, represented the textile industry in the North of France; Marcel Dassault was the head of a great aircraft firm; Pompidou and Couve de Murville and many other of de Gaulle's close associates represented big banking interests (Rothschild, Lazard, Mirabaud, etc.).

There were, as already said, *two* main plots at Algiers—that of the "activists" and that of the "Gaullists", though in some cases the two overlapped. The actual capture of the Government-General building at Algiers on May 13 was the work of the "activists", in particular of the "Group of Seven"—Lagaillarde (head of the Students' Federation), Martel, Crespin, Orthiz, Lefebvre, Goutailler and Baille—with their army of students, schoolboys and "teddy-boys" (known as the "blue-jeans of Bab-el-Oued"). Martel later bitterly complained that "the 'activists' ' victory of May 13 had been stolen from them." While both the "activists" and "Gaullists"—the latter in close touch with the Army—were preparing something, it was the "activists" who got in the first blow. Although both groups were enjoying financial support from Algerian business quarters, the "activists", more than the "Gaullists", represented the more traditional *colon* interests; theirs was a truly primitive and infantile Fascist ideology, with its strange cult of Massu, the not-very-complicated superman. Their greatest disappointment soon afterwards was to find that Massu was a "Gaullist" rather than an "activist".

And so, following the "general strike" order issued by the Vigilance

Committee, as a result of which at 1 p.m. on that Tuesday all shops, cafés and restaurants started closing their shutters, hundreds of "teddy-boys" from Bab-el-Oued and other suburbs began to flock into the centre of European Algiers. *As a result of months of anti-American propaganda over the Murphy Mission, their first exploit, characteristically enough, was to smash up the American Information Centre*, where they broke windows and doors, littered the street with American books and magazines and tore down and smashed to pieces the sign with the American eagle. Soon afterwards the demonstrators threw stones into the windows of the insufficiently extremist *Journal d'Alger*.

This was merely a small beginning.

What followed was more serious. To commemorate the three French soldiers murdered by the FLN, enormous crowds of Europeans had gathered in the area round the war memorial—in the large square outside the Post Office, on the monumental staircase in the Boulevard Laferrière leading all the way up to the Government-General building on top of the hill, and in the adjoining streets.

The information concerning the exact sequence of events is rather contradictory: but there were three essential "moments": Lagaillarde, the bearded young leader of the "activists", in paratroop uniform, perched on the war memorial, pointing at the Government-General building on the hill behind him, and haranguing the crowds with words to the effect that "all those rats in the Government-General building should be chucked into the sea". There were shouts from the crowd of "Pflimlin Resign!", "Hang Chevallier!" (the liberal Mayor of Algiers), *"L'armée au pouvoir!"*, and, of course, the ever-recurring *"Al-gé-rie française!"*

Secondly, there was the war memorial ceremony. It was at 6.30 p.m. that General Salan, General Massu, Admiral Auboyneau and M. Serge Baret, the Prefect of Algiers, drove up to the war memorial. Numerous Army units, carrying banners, were represented at this ceremony, and again there were cries of *"L'armée au pouvoir!"*

Thirdly, there was the "activists'" attack on the Government-General building. This seems to have occurred just about the time of the war memorial ceremony. Here, following Lagaillarde's incendiary speeches, first a small and then an ever-growing number of demonstrators adopted a threatening attitude to the CRS guards protecting the building. The first attempt was then made to break down the iron gates, but the CRS guards threw tear-gas bombs at the rioters, and, for a time, these were driven back. The commander of the CRS guards promptly phoned Paris for instructions, and was told by M. Gaillard, the still acting Premier, not to open fire. Meantime jeeps with loudspeakers were racing round European Algiers shouting: "We've been provoked by the CRS, all go up to the Government-General building." At this point, paratroopers, with Colonels Trinquier and Thomazo among them, mysteriously appeared on the scene of the incipient rioting; equally mysteriously, the CRS guards withdrew to the back of the building, and, without any resistance from the paratroopers, the rioters helped themselves to a heavy Army vehicle belonging to them, and rammed down the heavy iron gates of the Government-General building. By this time enormous crowds had gathered in the "Forum" outside the GG building (this "Forum" had never served any purpose other than being a large parking space for cars). Once the gates had been broken down, hundreds of young civilians invaded the GG building, smashing up offices, throwing files and various papers out of the windows, or setting fire to them. (Not that it was an undiluted orgy of vandalism: there were some people who kept their wits about them; thus in a distant part of the GG building all the police dossiers relating to economic affairs were mysteriously removed by somebody (Bromberger, *op. cit.*, p. 194), while, in another part of the building, certain important files—particularly some relating to the "bazooka affair"—were removed from the offices of the Sûreté Générale (H. Pajaud, *La Révolution d'Alger, les 4 fils Aymon*, p. 54).

Another man who, as we shall see, did not lose his head was Delbecque. In the midst of all the chaos, he decided that no time must be lost to give a "Gaullist" twist to what was happening.

The crowds in the "Forum" were now uttering all sorts of cries, among them *"Soustelle au pouvoir!"* A colonel, a member of M. Lacoste's secretariat, appeared on the balcony, but was greeted with a chorus of boos. Numerous officials, who had not joined in the strike, were still in the building; but in view of the threatening attitude of the young people who were now ransacking the offices (and in one part of the building they even started a fire—which was, however, soon extinguished) they began to leave the building one by one.

The next thing that happened was the arrival at the GG building of General Massu. He was loudly cheered by the crowds in the "Forum", but the first thing he did was to order the paratroopers, with Colonel Trinquier at their head, to throw the "teddy-boys" out of the building, and to take it over, thus replacing the CRS guards, who had, anyway, discreetly withdrawn after the first onslaught.

At 7.35 p.m. General Salan also arrived, but as he appeared on the central balcony to speak, he was shouted down. It was during the next one and a half hours that momentous decisions were taken inside the building, now cleared of the "teddy-boys", except some of their "representatives". Already by 8.30 (though a little prematurely) cars with loudspeakers were announcing to the people of Algiers that a Committee of Public Safety had been formed at the GG. Ten minutes later, a member of the *Comité d'entente et d'action des anciens combattants* appeared on the balcony and confirmed the news.

At 9.10 p.m., with the "Forum" still thick with people, Massu finally appeared on the balcony and announced that the following telegram had just been sent to President Coty:

I inform you of the creation of a civil and military Committee of Public Safety under the presidency of myself, General Massu [*moi, Général Massu*]. This has been formed in view of the gravity of the situation and the absolute necessity to maintain order and avoid bloodshed. We demand the creation in Paris of a Government of Public Safety, alone capable of keeping Algeria as an integral part of Metropolitan France.

Massu then called on the crowd to observe calm and discipline. "The Army," he said, "is with you with all its heart. We are in agreement with your leaders and we shall together calmly await the reply from Paris. The members of the Committee of Public Safety are inside the building now, and they will not leave until a Government of Public Safety has been set up in Paris."

Several other members of the Committee then spoke, among them Colonel Thomazo who promptly proceeded to make Salan "acceptable" by making him an "honorary rebel", as it were:

"People of Algiers," he said, "it is to the Army and its Commander-in-Chief, General Salan, that you owe this victory. General Salan was subjected to very strong pressure by the French Government, which wanted him to prohibit your demonstrations today. He replied that he would not prohibit them, because the Army held the same views as yourselves. The Committee shall stay here until we receive a satisfactory reply from Paris. I ask you all now to go quietly home."

The oddest thing of all was that this *first version* of the Committee of Public Safety included no Gaullists. Apart from Massu, it included three paratroop colonels—Trinquier, Thomazo and Ducasse; and Lagaillarde, head of the "activists". All the others belonged to the Algiers riff-raff, one of them, a certain Baudier, claiming to represent merely "the crowd".

Delbecque, on learning that the "teddy-boys" were storming the GG building, called an immediate meeting of the more-or-less "Gaullist" Vigilance Committee in the rue d'Isly. It was *he* who was now going to proclaim the formation of a Committee of Public Safety; his plan had been to do this during the night, or on the following morning, after Soustelle's expected arrival in Algiers. And then the news suddenly came through to the rue d'Isly that *another* Committee of Public Safety had already been formed at the GG. Some quick thinking had to be done. Together with Vinciguerra, Lopez[1], and one or two other Gaullists, he

---

[1] Lopez, a lawyer, was the Secretary of the Social-Republicans (i.e. Gaullists) at Oran. Vinciguerra was later to become one of the most extremist Algiers members of the UNR.

rushed to the GG, and entering the room where the new Committee of Public Safety was meeting, he declared: "I am the representative of Jacques Soustelle." Soustelle's name could not be ignored in Algiers. Delbecque and several of his associates were admitted to the Committee of Public Safety; and that is how Delbecque began to give it a "Gaullist" twist.[1]

During the night, and on the following day, largely owing to Delbecque, it seems (for he appears to have put all kinds of ideas into Massu's rather obtuse head), the Committee was further enlarged, and was made to include some Moslems—who had shone by their absence throughout the events of May 13.

What all happened during that crazy night? Again, there is much conflicting evidence on the exact sequence of events. Massu, it seems, had proclaimed himself president of the Committee of Public Safety on the spur of the moment, after receiving a nod from Salan; he seemed uncertain of himself. At first he had violently upbraided Lagaillarde and the other "teddy-boys"; then he suddenly decided to take the big risk of putting himself at the head of the rebellion. His behaviour during the night and, indeed, during the next two days, was very odd, and it was Delbecque who had to use all his persuasion to convince Massu that he was doing the right thing.

Radio-Algiers that evening was still under the control of Paris-appointed officials and was broadcasting the fullest possible news on what was going on; this news was, however, being interspersed with statements from various members of the Committee of Public Safety. At 11.15 p.m., after receiving a "very secret" message from Gaillard entrusting him until further notice with the task of "taking all necessary measures for maintaining order and protecting life and property in Algeria", Salan (without mentioning Gaillard) announced on Algiers Radio that he was "temporarily taking over the destinies of French Algeria". At midnight, paratroopers occupied the building of Radio-Algiers and an "observer", representing the Committee of Public Safety, was now appointed to censor all broadcasts. Soon afterwards a statement from General Salan was broadcast saying that the Commander-in-Chief "was acting in full agreement with the Committee of Public Safety". (Again, needless to say, the authority of Gaillard was not invoked.)

During the evening there was much coming and going in the "Forum", and at one moment it was announced by one of the paratroop colonels that Soustelle (for whom the crowd had been clamouring) was about to land. But he did not.

Then about 3 a.m. the news reached the Committee of Public Safety that Pflimlin had been invested by the National Assembly.

This news caused wild consternation among the members of the

[1] Bromberger, *op. cit.* pp. 189–91.

Committee, and Massu's first reaction was that he had made a hopelessly bad mistake, for he exclaimed, *"Maintenant nous sommes foutus!"*

It was then that Delbecque and others apparently persuaded him that no retreat was possible any longer, for at 5 a.m. (there were still many people hanging around the "Forum") Massu appeared on the balcony of the GG building. He now called on the people of Algiers "to fight till final victory" and "implored General de Gaulle to break his silence". Apart from anything else, these people now realized that perhaps *de Gaulle alone could enable them to save their own skins.*

Massu now also angrily proclaimed that Soustelle had on two occasions, in the last two days, been prevented from leaving for Algeria; but that he had now "gone into hiding", and that it was hoped that "he would join us in the course of the day".

Then, again returning to the new de Gaulle theme, Massu said that if he was now appealing to de Gaulle, it was because de Gaulle alone could now save Algeria from that "diplomatic Dien Bien Phu"—to which Lacoste had referred so often.

"And pending the arrival of M. Soustelle," Massu said, "the bureau of the Committee of Public Safety is constituted as follows: General Massu; M. Delbecque, representing M. Soustelle; M. Madhani; and M. Lagaillarde."

Madhani was a Moslem (who seemed to have appeared from nowhere in the last few hours); and Massu now suddenly declared that "he was proud to say that the people of Algiers had, during this historic day, demonstrated the perfect brotherhood between the European and Moslem populations, united under the French flag".

Coming from Massu, the "Himmler of Algiers", this was new indeed; but it was, clearly, the beginning of "Operation Fraternization", another of Delbecque's fertile ideas.

It was also at Delbecque's insistence that some other Gaullists joined the Committee of Public Safety—M. Neuwirth and M. Flasch among them. No doubt he also encouraged the admission to it of Alain de Sérigny, the powerful editor of the *Echo d'Alger*, who had for years been handling *colon* propaganda funds, and had for some time, as we have seen, been plotting with Jacques Soustelle. Lagaillarde and the "teddy-boys" did not much care for the turn things were taking. Neuwirth who, in the next few days, became a sort of "minister of information" of the Committee of Public Safety, claims that, on one occasion, he would have been murdered by the "teddy-boys" if he hadn't quickly pulled out his own gun. . . .

3. COTY CALLS ARMY TO ORDER—
"IS THIS FASCISM?"

O N THE Wednesday morning, May 14, Paris was stunned by what
had happened. Newspaper kiosks were taken by storm. The sale
of *France-Soir* that day trebled, and shot up to some three million
copies. With communications with Algiers having been cut off during
the night, some of the morning papers were still uncertain of what
exactly had happened. *Paris-Journal* carried a headline saying that General
Salan had been arrested by the Committee of Public Safety. Of all the
morning papers, *Parisien Libéré* alone came out pat in favour of a de Gaulle
Government. *L'Humanité* came out with a banner headline:

ALERTE AU FASCISME!
Coup de force à Alger.

At 11 a.m. there came out the first edition of *France-Soir*, with a vast
headline:

COTY: I ORDER THE ARMY OF ALGERIA TO OBEY.

In this message, as "head of the armies" in virtue of Article 33 of the
Constitution, the President of the Republic appealed to the patriotism
and common sense of officers and soldiers of all ranks serving in Algeria

"not to add to the ordeals of our country by creating a cleavage among Frenchmen
in the face of the enemy. Any breach of discipline can only benefit those whom we
are fighting. . . . I order you to follow the path of duty under the authority of the
Government of the French Republic."

At frequent intervals this order was broadcast, followed by the playing
of the *Marseillaise*.

What struck many was that the order *did not contain even an implicit
threat of reprisals should the order be disobeyed.*

M. Pflimlin gave a short broadcast on Wednesday morning, in which
he said that the responsibility for what had happened in Algiers "would
be established". He complained about the Government's intentions in
respect of Algeria having been "systematically misrepresented". The
Government was aiming at "peace through victory".

But soon the ambiguities started. Pflimlin announced that he had
entrusted General Salan with the task of maintaining order in Algiers.

Salan issued a statement in the morning saying that he was taking over
"provisionally" the civil and military powers in Algeria. The Committee
of Public Safety would act as a *liaison* between the Army command and
the population.

He called on the population to go back to work.

Simultaneously, the Committee of Public Safety was distributing leaflets calling for further demonstrations. The appeal ended with the words:

"Show everybody, show Pflimlin that this was not a flash in the pan."

In Paris the Police were active. Soustelle, though a Deputy with parliamentary immunity, was placed "under the protection of the Police", ostensibly because he had been threatened with death by Algerian terrorists, but in reality to prevent him from going to Algiers to "provide a brain" (as the phrase went) to the Algiers insurrection.

About 150 members of four extremist Right-wing organizations were arrested during the night and in the morning of the 14th.

But already Pflimlin was beginning to experience some difficulties inside his own Government. Three out of four of his Right-wing ministers—Ribeyre, Bescary-Monsservin and Garet—resigned; the only one to stay was M. Mutter, the Minister of Algeria. As a member of the CNR he had had a fine Resistance record during the war and, though a conservative, was a genuine Republican. But there was no question yet of his going to Algiers, where he might well have been lynched, and where, for the present, he was being ambiguously represented by General Salan.

Inevitably the question arose of bringing the Socialists into the Cabinet.

On the night of the 14th, despite the Government ban on all street demonstrations, some three or four hundred young men marched down the Champs Elysées shouting "Gouvernement de Salut Public!", "De Gaulle au pouvoir!" and "Algérie Française!" A number of arrests were made. Similarly, the Communists arranged a demonstration in the Place de la République; about one thousand people assembled there, shouting "Massu au poteau!" and "Le fascisme ne passera pas!" The Police were much rougher with the Communists than with the others. . . .

The 14th being a Wednesday, de Gaulle had, as usual, come to Paris on his weekly visit. He stayed at his office in the rue Solférino, and it was said that he had seen nobody except a representative of Plon, his publishers. . . .

The situation was full of dangerous ambiguities. No one could tell whether Paris had the means of controlling Algiers; also who, in Algiers, was the real master now?

Soustelle had not yet arrived in Algiers, and de Gaulle had not yet broken his silence. Below the surface there continued a conflict between the various elements constituting the Committee of Public Safety; also, there seemed to be a further conflict inside the Army between the "moderates" and the "extremists"—i.e. those paratroop colonels who had so obviously supported the "activists" in their attack on the Government-General building on the Tuesday night.

On somebody's orders (Massu later claimed he didn't know whose they were)[1] an armoured unit, the UTB (*Unité Territoriale Blindée*) had arrived in the morning to reinforce the paratroopers guarding all the public buildings in Algiers. This armoured unit was looked upon as the "Pretorian guard" of the *ultras*.

This arrival in Algiers of the UTB was part of the general mobilization of the territorial forces of Algeria, composed mostly of Algerian Europeans who, having done their military service, did patrol or sentry duty once or twice a week. The total of these territorial forces was between 30,000 and 40,000. The most important unit, provided with heavy equipment, was the UTB, stationed in the neighbourhood of Algiers. Here was a curious "Algerian" touch concerning this unit:

"It had, in principle, been dissolved soon after the attempt had been made to assassinate General Salan in February 1957. There were rumours that it had been involved in this plot. The fact remains that it turned up at Algiers around the Government-General almost as soon as the Committee of Public Safety had been set up." (*Le Monde*, May 16, 1958.)

On the evening of the 14th, General Massu held, at his Army headquarters, a press conference which, despite endless ambiguities, greatly differed in style from his defiant attitude the night before. The dynamic and foul-mouthed *para* general with his Cyrano nose was now, according to some witnesses, "almost apologizing" for having taken the leadership of the Committee of Public Safety, and saying, indeed, that this was merely a "provisional arrangement" pending the arrival of the Minister for Algeria. He let it, however, be understood that the said Minister for Algeria would have to be "acceptable" to the people of Algiers.

An hour later, another press conference was held by the Committee of Public Safety, where it was announced that the Committee would stay in office until the formation of a Government of Public Safety under General de Gaulle. The journalists present pointed out that this was in flat contradiction with what Massu had just said. After many angry exchanges, Massu was finally produced and he now declared that his words had been deliberately misrepresented, and that he was in full agreement with the Committee of Public Safety. If anything was clear at all, it was that both Salan and Massu were now playing a double game, not quite knowing yet which way they were going to jump. Paris, hoping that Salan and Massu would somehow manage in the end to "restore legality", was backing the Army (as represented by them) against the *coup d'état* elements.

[1] According to M. and S. Bromberger (*op. cit.*, pp. 195–6) it was Lagaillarde who, distrustful of the Gaullists (and of Salan), had persuaded Colonel Thomazo to bring the UTB from Rivet, an operational area, to Algiers "to protect the Committee of Public Safety". They are not sure, however, whether the order to the UTB to rush to Algiers was given by Thomazo, or "whether Lagaillarde's appeal to his friends in the armoured unit was enough in itself to do the trick".

In view of the very tricky situation in Algiers, Pflimlin thought it wiser to let Salan and Massu keep the *ultras* quiet by playing up to them. It was a shortsighted view—but did Pflimlin have any alternative?

Men like Salan and Massu had the power and authority to liquidate the Committee of Public Safety (as, indeed, Massu threatened to do on the following day) and he could probably also have gained control of the Fascist colonels (Trinquier, Thomazo, etc.). *The Army could then have negotiated some sort of "agreement" with the Pflimlin Government. But what was to complicate matters immensely (and had, indeed, complicated them almost from the outset) was the de Gaulle factor. Between more or less open submission to the Government of the Republic and an all-out Fascist revolution which was easy enough to bring about in Algeria, but would prove an extremely risky enterprise in France, there was this third solution: the de Gaulle Arbitration, the de Gaulle Compromise. And, to the Army leaders, more than to the Algiers "activists", this was very tempting.*

Paris was bewildered by what had happened. Already the intellectuals were becoming divided. On the afternoon of May 14, the front page of the *Monde* published two articles of sharply conflicting tendencies. M. Beuve-Méry, while calling on Parliament and the Government to enforce "republican legality" everywhere and by every means, seemed to doubt whether they would be capable of doing it. And should Parliament prove its incapacity, then—there was only de Gaulle. The big question, however, was whether de Gaulle approved, or not, of the Algiers insurrection.

On the face of it, what did it matter? The legal Government of the Republic had been invested by Parliament by a large majority. But years of doubt in the Fourth Republic had clearly paralysed by this time the "republican faith" of the most influential of Paris editors. And it made little difference if, on the same page of the *Monde*, Maurice Duverger wrote:

Until yesterday the country did not believe in the Fascist menace. The recent cantonal elections showed that the country was more conscious of a Communist than of an extreme-Right menace. . . . Now France has understood. The Algiers *ultras* are rapidly succeeding in creating a Left majority in France. In ordinary circumstances, Pflimlin would never have obtained the abstention of the Communists. . . . The majority of the French of Algiers (though not necessarily of Algeria) are ready to overthrow the Republic. But the great majority of Frenchmen in France are deeply attached to it.

The Algiers generals should know that France's economic and social structure has gone well beyond the era of pronunciamentos.

He then said that there would be civil war only if the Algiers rebellion was not crushed. There was not much time to lose; *but the Pflimlin*

Government still had a chance to treat the matter with the utmost energy, and to make the Algiers rebels realize that it would not surrender to them as Mollet had done in February 1956. . . . "If the Republic yields to the insurrection, then, in a few days, civil war will replace the Republican order . . ."

In other words, no establishment of a Fascist régime was conceivable in France. France would resist . . . and there would be civil war.

The de Gaulle factor—the "third solution"—was deliberately omitted by Duverger as a possibility; he was, unlike Beuve-Méry, still unwilling even to consider it. He was still believing in the *"lutte républicaine"*, even if it meant (as it inevitably did) a *rapprochement* with the Communists.

The three trade union federations—the Communist CGT, the Socialist Force Ouvrière[1] and the Catholic CFTC—held numerous meetings and declared themselves to be in a "state of alert".

But was the working class going to react sharply against the "Fascist menace"? That remained to be seen, and already it was clear that the de Gaulle factor was confusing the issue. Altogether, this factor was disturbing the ordinary rules of the game. Pflimlin had a solid parliamentary majority at last, and *the "incapacity" of Parliament*, which Beuve-Méry feared, *had ceased to be a problem; as far as Parliament was concerned, Pflimlin had greater authority than any government had enjoyed for a long time.* The Communists who had abstained on May 13 were going, in the subsequent votes, to give Pflimlin their full support, in the name of "republican defence" and "republican legality". And even if one did not "count" the Communist votes (a dangerous precedent set up by Mendès-France on the eve of his Indo-China peace negotiations in 1954), Pflimlin still had a handsome majority to support him against the Algiers rebellion.

He spoke firmly on the radio; he spoke firmly in Parliament—but two questions remained unanswered: was he, in fact, *doing* anything about Algiers? And what was his attitude to de Gaulle?

In Algeria the Committee of Public Safety was doing things which no self-respecting Republican Government could tolerate: at Oran, for example, the Prefect, M. Lambert (i.e. the lawful representative of the Paris Government) was beaten up by rioters and was forced to hand over his powers to the local military commander. Other officials were being dismissed and displaced, without Paris being consulted.

During the short "date-fixing" meeting of the National Assembly on Wednesday morning, May 14, M. Mitterrand warned the Government that there was no time to lose; immediate measures, he said, must be taken to stop the arbitrary dismissal of prefects in Algeria by men who

[1] According to Bromberger (*op. cit.*, p. 30), André Lafont and other leaders of the Socialist trade union federation were, in fact, members of the "Gaullist network", plotting for de Gaulle's return together with Debré and certain generals.

"represent, only too benevolently, infuriated mobs who make no secret of their deadly hostility to the lawful Government of the Republic and its leader". He expressed serious doubts about General Salan.

M. Ramadier (Socialist) said, as Mitterrand had already done, that the Government derived its authority from the solid support of Parliament; he referred to the riots of February 6, 1934, when Léon Blum, though not in agreement with the Daladier Government, said he would vote for it "to defend the Republic".

A Right-wing member: And then there came the climb-down, and you sent for old man Doumergue to get you out of the mess!

The Right were, clearly, looking forward to a more or less extra-parliamentary solution.

Despite Mitterrand's appeal that Parliament be informed without delay of what the Government was doing, M. Robert Lecourt, the Minister of Justice, got the Assembly to agree that the discussion be postponed till Friday, the 16th.

On that day, May 14, Pflimlin was negotiating with both the Right and the Socialists. He wanted both Mollet and Pinay to enter his Government. If not Pinay himself, at any rate his Right-wing colleagues were laying down impossible conditions: Lacoste must be sent back to Algiers, and Bidault (who had voted against the Government and had, in fact, declared himself in agreement with the Algiers rebels) be given an important Government post. In the end, Pflimlin had to abandon his attempt to gain the support of the Right, who were as good as asking him to surrender to Algiers, and had to be content with the entry of four Socialists into his Government—Mollet as Vice-Premier, Moch as Minister of the Interior (in place of M. Maurice Faure, Radical, who was given another post), M. Gazier as Minister of Information and M. Max Lejeune as Minister of State. These appointments were made official on the 15th.

The appointment of Moch, though hated by the Communists, who had not forgotten his ruthless treatment of the strikers in 1947 and 1948, had a reassuring effect at first. As head of the police, Moch had been tough not only with the Communists but also with de Gaulle's RPF back in 1947–8, when they proceeded to hold "little Nuremberg" meetings all over France.

4. DE GAULLE SPEAKS AT LAST—
KEEPING UP THE FICTION OF SALAN AS THE
"REPRESENTATIVE OF PARIS"

APART from the entry of the Socialists into the Pflimlin Government, the 15th was marked by two much more sensational events. That morning, General Salan, addressing 15,000 people in the "Forum" of Algiers, concluded his speech by crying *"Vive la France! Vive l'Algérie Française! Vive de Gaulle!"*[1]

Why "de Gaulle"—when Salan was supposed to represent in Algiers the Government of M. Pflimlin?

Secondly, de Gaulle, in a cryptic written statement issued to the press in the afternoon, announced:

The degradation of the State inevitably leads to the alienation of the peoples associated with France, to confusion in the fighting forces, to national dislocation, and to the loss of independence. Faced with problems too hard for a régime of Parties to tackle, France has, for the last twelve years, been following a disastrous road.

In the past, the country, from its very depths, entrusted me with the task of leading it to its salvation.

Today, with the new ordeals facing it, let the country know that I am ready to assume the powers of the Republic.

The reaction to this was what was to be expected. Enthusiasm in Algiers, especially amongst the soldiers; rather less amongst the all-out Fascists, who did not care for de Gaulle's—albeit lip-service—reference to the Republic. In Paris, a highly critical attitude among all supporters of "republican legality"; it was particularly noted that there wasn't the slightest condemnation in de Gaulle's statement of the Algiers rebellion. He was clearly expecting the Army to support him wholeheartedly.

Nervousness in Paris had grown. There was a slump in French shares on the Bourse, and a sharp rise in the price of gold and foreign currency. The black-market rate of the dollar shot up from 453 to 465.

Amongst housewives, there was a run on grocery shops; it had already begun on the 14th, but now it took on alarming proportions. They started hoarding coffee, sugar, oil, macaroni, tinned milk, etc., in large quantities. In one shop I saw a woman carrying off 100 kilos of sugar in a taxi. Not until a few days later did grocers start "rationing" purchases, refusing to sell more than one kilo of sugar to any one customer. Some shops had run completely out of certain "durable" foodstuffs.

The Right-wing press, above all *Paris-Presse* and the *Parisien Libéré*,

[1] It was soon learned that Delbecque, who stood behind him while he was ending his speech, prompted him at the last moment to add the *"Vive de Gaulle!"*

started building up de Gaulle in a big way as "The saviour of France and the man who had given her back the Republic".

A curious aspect of this re-emergence of de Gaulle was, as already said, the fact that he enjoyed only a limited personal popularity, and was, to younger people—for instance, people of twenty or even twenty-five— little more than an historical name.

To others, he was a rather nebulous figure—who had played no part at all in public affairs for over three years; who, before that, had merely made occasional pronouncements of no great consequence, though full of anti-British and anti-American cracks, and whose organized following of 1947-49 had dwindled to something very insignificant.

Although, for the last two or three months, there had been a good deal of agitation in some Right-wing political quarters and in a few—not very widely-read—weeklies, notably *Carrefour*, in favour of bringing de Gaulle back, it was still important, at least for the benefit of the younger generation, to whom de Gaulle meant very little, to re-create the de Gaulle Legend.

On May 16, Eugène Mannoni, the correspondent of *Le Monde* (who was soon to be locked up by the military authorities of Algiers for several days) wrote from there:

M. Alain de Sérigny, editor of the *Echo d'Alger*, wrote in his paper this morning: "General de Gaulle's message is just what we had hoped for." M. de Sérigny is now acting as liaison man between the Committee of Public Safety and the high Army Command. . . .

De Gaulle's message has clearly consolidated the unity of the Committee of Public Safety—a unity which seemed very uncertain yesterday. . . . It amply makes up for the disappointment caused by the investiture of Pflimlin and Soustelle's failure to arrive in Algiers. . . .

Since everybody wants to read into de Gaulle's message everything he wants to read into it, some 10,000 people loudly cheered when the message was read out to them in the "Forum". . . .

General Salan's position has been greatly strengthened by the de Gaulle message. Yesterday he had already concluded his speech by crying *"Vive de Gaulle!"*—and he had been solemnly introduced to the crowd by M. *Delbecque, who had played so decisive a role on the night of May 13 in giving a "Gaullist" character to the rebellion.*

Mannoni then pointed out that there were still some conflicting tendencies inside the Committee, where the "Fascists" were now afraid that they had been outwitted. Another report, indeed, said that the Lagaillarde boys had actually threatened Massu—now apparently working hand-in-hand with Salan—with rousing the Algiers populace against the "Gaullists", to which Massu had replied with a characteristic "throat-cutting" gesture: "You had better not try, my friend." In short, the "teddy-boys" of Bab-el-Oued had outlived their initial usefulness.

Not that the situation was by any means clear yet. Salan, wrote Mannoni, was at first believed in Algiers to have been "overwhelmed" by the May 13 *coup*; then to have submitted to Pflimlin; now it was clear that—until further notice—he was backing de Gaulle. But the question still remained how Paris and Metropolitan France were going to react to de Gaulle. *So long as this was not clear, the attitude of Algiers would inevitably remain hesitant.*

There was another bone of contention at Algiers: while M. de Sérigny was blaming Pflimlin for his "blindness and obstinacy" in not sending Lacoste back to Algiers, other supporters of the Committee of Public Safety were now booing whenever the former Minister of Algeria was mentioned. . . .

Meantime, in Paris, on May 16 the National Assembly met to hear Pflimlin's statement, and to discuss and vote on the Bill establishing for three months a "state of emergency" in France. The Bill provided an extension to France of the "state of emergency" that had existed in Algeria since the Act of April 3, 1955. It gave the Government very wide powers against anyone or anything liable to endanger public order and security and national defence.

After briefly dealing with the events in Algiers, and saying that he was not quite sure yet what General Massu's real motives were in heading the "Committee of Public Safety", Pflimlin then said that, already before the Assembly vote in the morning of May 14, M. Gaillard, who was still nominal head of the Government, had ordered General Salan to "maintain order in Algeria". General Massu had since placed himself under the orders of General Salan. But in the last few days certain very serious things had happened.

"General Salan has been dismissing civil officials without the previous consent of the Government. *This raises the grave problem of the place to be held by the Army in the national community. Until now the Army has been loyally serving the nation; now certain Army leaders seem to be acting outside this framework.*"

The excitement amongst the French in Algeria, Pflimlin said, had been worked up by certain slanderous campaigns against which the Government could only make the strongest protest. Certain men, including some who had gone there from Metropolitan France, and not belonging to the Army, had created a state of insurrection in Algeria.

This kind of activity also existed in France, Pflimlin said, and the Government had therefore decided to dissolve the *Parti Patriote Révolu-*

tionnaire, the *Jeune Nation* movement, and two other minor Fascist organizations.[1]

While concentrating on these four rather eccentric Nazi or near-Nazi organizations, Pflimlin made no reference to certain other activities—like those of the various "Gaullist" networks in Metropolitan France, such as Jacques Soustelle's USRAF.

He ended with the usual flourish about preserving republican legality; but, while referring again to the breaches of this legality in Algeria by Salan and others, he gave no indication of what the Government would, or could, do about it. And finally he said that a Constitutional Reform was now inevitable, but that this could only be carried out by Parliament itself, which would undertake this work, without taking account of any threats from outside. . . .

"I call on the republican and national majority to rally to the Government, whose duty, in these hours of danger, is to defend republican legality."

Pflimlin was loudly cheered; though looking tired and harassed, he spoke with firmness and apparent conviction. But still no one could tell how he would deal with Algeria, even with all the emergency powers in the world at his disposal.

In the discussion that followed, M. Isorni, Pétain's principal defender, paradoxically enough expressed some anxiety about de Gaulle's intentions "at this moment when the Fourth Republic may be living its last hours". All de Gaulle was interested in, Isorni said, was "*moi, de Gaulle*". He had said nothing to ease the situation in Algeria, and was merely thinking of setting up a dictatorship. Isorni said he preferred the formation of a broad "national government" to the "adventure" into which de Gaulle was going to drag France.

[1] The first of these, directed by M. Biaggi, and enjoying the support of men like M. Tixier-Vignancour, had chiefly distinguished itself in France by the activities of its "commandos", who specialized in breaking up Left-wing election meetings—notably during the Paris by-election of January 1957. But it had a large following at Algiers, where Biaggi had at his service many of the Bab-el-Oued "teddy-boys" who had played so decisive a part at the initial stages of the *putsch* of May 13.

Of some importance was also the *Jeune Nation*, of Nazi-Vichy inspiration, which had been founded by three sons of one Sidos, an aide of Darnand, the head of the pro-Nazi Vichy *milice*. Sidos was executed as a traitor at the time of the Liberation. They specialized in Paris in beating up Communist newsvendors and in scribbling *Jeune Nation* and their symbol, the "Celtic cross"—a cross with a circle round it—on the walls of the capital. They were mixed up with Biaggi and certain ex-Poujadists like Le Pen. They were racialist and anti-Semitic. It was chiefly the Biaggi and Sidos gangs who demonstrated in the Champs-Elysées on the night of May 13. The "movement" was not believed to have more than 600 or 700 active members. Later, in 1959, they began to write on walls *A bas de Gaulle*, or even *De Gaulle=Mendés*, followed by the same "Celtic cross".

The *Front d'action Nationale* and the *Phalange Française* were of only minor importance. It is significant that, apart from these minor Fascist groups, there was nothing in France (as distinct from Algeria) to resemble the large political force represented in 1934–36 by the various Fascist or semi-Fascist Leagues.

There followed a lively exchange between M. Triboulet (Gaullist), who said that de Gaulle had "re-established the Republic" and that it was monstrous that anyone should object to his saying that he was "at the disposal of the nation", and M. Naegelen (Socialist) who could not help seeing in de Gaulle's statement of the previous day a grave threat to republican liberties. Nor, said M. Naegelen, had this statement done anything to condemn those "who are separating Algeria from the Republic".

Guy Mollet, now Pflimlin's Vice-Premier, already showed that he was prepared to enter into some kind of conversations with de Gaulle. Already he was accepting him as a sort of arbiter.

"Oh, how relieved we should all be," he said, "if he confirmed the words of M. Triboulet to the effect that there is nothing anti-Republican in his statement!" Mollet then said that he would like de Gaulle to answer three questions:

(1) Do you recognize the present Government as the only legal government of France?

(2) Will you disavow the promoters of the Algerian Committees of Public Safety?

(3) Would you be prepared, if you were called upon to form a government, to appear before the National Assembly with a programme, and to withdraw if you were defeated?

And he added, significantly (for some may well have wondered *why* he was asking them), that these questions were "not an appeal, but a challenge".

As M. Bidault rose to speak, M. Maurice Schumann, Teitgen and Moisan of the MRP demonstratively left the Assembly hall.

He said he would not vote for Pflimlin, whose Government, relying on Communist votes, was not representative of a national France. He suggested that the emergency measures—which gave the Government the right to search and arrest people at any time of the day and night, and tamper with the freedom of the Press and the radio—might be used for the wrong purposes. He declared himself in complete agreement with de Gaulle, and suggested that what was wanted was a government of national safety under de Gaulle.

Duclos, for the Communists, said that de Gaulle was planning to set up a military and Fascist dictatorship; to prevent this, the Communists had decided to support Pflimlin.

Mitterrand and Daladier also spoke in terms of "republican defence"; Paul Reynaud, differing in this from most of the Right-wing "independents", proclaimed that the Pflimlin Government was the legal government of France, and must be obeyed. At the same time, he thought it was essential to bring about an urgent revision of the Constitution. It was also important, he said, that the Government's emergency powers be used not only against Fascist groups, but also against "revolutionary strikes" which might come from the Communist side.

Tixier-Vignancour was as provocative as ever in hailing the Algiers revolution which "would save both France and Algeria". He alleged that one of M. Pflimlin's ministers had said that the French Government could yet crush the Algiers rebellion by cutting off all supplies and "starving it out".

M. Mutter, Minister of Algeria, firmly denied this.

Then there was an awkward moment when in reply to cries of "Fascist!" and "Vichyite!", Tixier-Vignancour recalled that 115 Socialist deputies and senators had voted for Pétain, and that when he (Tixier-Vignancour) went to Algiers and saw M. Naegelen, who was then Governor-General, they "saw completely eye-to-eye". (It is, of course, notorious that the "Socialist" Naegelen had done more than anyone else to shelve the *Statut d' Algérie* of 1947 and to allow the Algerian election returns to be faked.)

To conclude the debate, M. Pflimlin said that the emergency measures would be used cautiously, and not "unilaterally"; he would tolerate neither a repetition of "Algiers" in Metropolitan France, nor a repetition of "Prague". And he would not count the Communist votes.

"Let the people be the judge!" M. Waldeck-Rochet (Communist) exclaimed.

Despite this statement by Pflimlin, the Communists, who had abstained on May 13, now actually voted for the Government, in the name of "republican defence".

At the Senate the same day M. Pflimlin, challenged by M. Debré, thought it necessary to specify that the emergency measures were not in any way directed against General de Gaulle personally—not that it was even for a second easy to imagine that de Gaulle might be placed under house-arrest, or that the Pflimlin Government had ever considered such a step!

"His statement," Pflimlin said, "has been given two interpretations. For my own part I refuse to believe that the man who restored the Republic could think of violating republican legality; but I am sure, at the same time, that General de Gaulle would render a great service to France by throwing some light on this point."

What, then, was the position on May 16, after the Government had secured its emergency powers by an overwhelming majority?

De Gaulle's statement had strengthened and, up to a point, unified the Algiers insurgents, where his name became a sort of banner of resistance to the Paris Government. The "Gaullists", rather than the *ultras*, were now controlling Algiers.

The Left in France, and particularly the Communists, were going through the classical motions of "defending the Republic". Vigilance

Committees were being set up; the CGT and the two other principal trade union federations were uttering warnings to the "Fascist forces". Papers like L'Humanité and Libération came out with poster-like front pages with vast headlines like the following:

MIGHTY ANTI-FASCIST WAVE THROUGHOUT THE COUNTRY
With the Communist deputies voting for the Government's emergency powers, these were passed by 461 votes to 114.

VIGILANCE, ACTION, UNITY
by the working class and the people of France
TO BREAK THE CONSPIRACY OF GENERAL DE GAULLE AND HIS ACCOMPLICES

—(L'Humanité, May 17)

The Communists were agitating in favour of a Popular Front; the other trade unions and the Socialist and MRP parties continued to be very reserved on this point. Actually, the mass of the working class—including most of those who had voted Communist—were showing no great signs of a fighting spirit. The possibility of impressing either de Gaulle or Algiers with a vast Republican resistance movement forming in France was being greatly reduced by the reluctance of the Socialists and the non-Communist trade unions to enter into any agreement for an anti-Fascist "united front" with the Communists or the CGT.

Rumours of possible paratroop landings in Paris and other points of Metropolitan France had already started.

M. Moch, the Minister of the Interior, was already conscious of this threat, and, with the police and the gendarmerie at his disposal, he was said to be "taking the appropriate measures" to forestall any such coup de force.

But what about the Army in Metropolitan France, now under the orders of the Minister of Defence, M. de Chevigné?

The total of the French armed forces amounted to about 1,200,000 men; of these about 500,000 were serving overseas (mostly in North Africa); two divisions in Germany, the rest—some 460,000 men, including 120,000 sailors and airmen—in Metropolitan France.

What was their state of mind? Although at its Cabinet meeting on May 16 the Government had received "reassuring news from the provinces" about the Republican loyalty of the Army, there is no doubt that the "regulars" and, above all, the officers, were now definitely pro-de Gaulle.

Military aircraft flying over Colombey had, in the last couple of days, made a point of dipping their wings to salute the General.

Some strange things were meantime happening amongst the high command. Two Air Force generals—Maurice Challe[1] and André Martin—were both first placed under house-arrest, and then ordered to leave Paris. General Challe was said to have "retired" to Brest, as the guest of an admiral. To protest against these measures—on which he had not been consulted—General Ely, Chief of the General Staff of the Armed Forces, tendered his resignation to the Pflimlin Government. He was obviously determined to make its position untenable. Both Challe and Martin had distinguished war and Resistance records and were known for their strong Right-wing views. Among the Air Force command there had been strong criticism of the "feeble" policy the Governments had been pursuing in Algeria, and there had been some contacts between certain top-ranking Air Force officers and Algiers extremists like General Faure who represented the *ultra* wing in the armed forces in Algeria.

It was also rumoured that Moch—the ruthlessly energetic Jules Moch—was becoming very uncertain about the police, some of whom had staged an anti-Republican demonstration outside the National Assembly only a few months before, and even about the militarized CRS guards.

There were other disturbing rumours. Foreign news agencies—notably UP—had been handed by somebody the mysterious text of an Appeal by a body calling itself "The Committee of Public Safety for the Paris Region". The Appeal was in favour of a de Gaulle Government. It bore no names or addresses.

5. "FRATERNIZATION" IN ALGIERS

MEANTIME, even odder things were happening in Algiers. The Right-wing papers on the 17th were full of glowing accounts of "tremendous" pro-French demonstrations at Algiers at which "many thousands" of Moslems were now waving tricolour flags, and shouting "*Vive la France!*", "*Algérie Française!*" and "*Vive de Gaulle!*"

It looked at first like a complete fabrication. How was it possible for any Moslems to "fraternize" with all-out *colon* racialists like Alain de Sérigny, the editor of the *Echo d'Alger*, or with General Massu, whose men had terrorized the Casbah of Algiers into complete submission with their killings and tortures?

Later, in June, André Malraux, de Gaulle's provisional Minister of Information, at his famous press conference, admitted that the first Moslem demonstrations at Algiers had been "paid for"; but that the subsequent and much larger demonstrations were "spontaneous".

[1] Later appointed C.-in-C. in Algeria by de Gaulle.

Already on the night of the 13th, a number of Moslems had been brought to the Government-General and had been included in the Committee of Public Safety; but this was not taken seriously in Paris, and was dismissed as so much window-dressing. The Moslems in question had either been paid, or, more likely, been frightened into it.

But the Moslem demonstrations on May 16 seemed to be something new, and represented a new element which was sure to be exploited politically in a very big way, both by Algiers and by the Right-wing people in Paris. For here was the suggestion of a third way: neither war to the bitter end, nor negotiations with the FLN, but reconciliation with the Algerian people—and Integration.

According to official Algiers figures, 22,000 Moslems took part in those first demonstrations on the 17th.

What was behind this highly-suspect stunt?

According to the well-informed correspondent of *France-Observateur* in Algiers (who seemed, however, up to a point, to have been taken in by it), this is what happened:

The Franco-Moslem demonstration of May 16 was no more spontaneous than had been the "demonstration" of May 13. It had been organized, and mighty well organized, *and it seems that Delbecque had been the first to think it up.*

The first thing to note is that whereas all previous popular demonstrations in Algiers had been accompanied by a few lynchings of Algerians, there was nothing like that during the last few days. Two small facts are typical of the complex nature of what had been happening. In the rue Revigo *two trucks driven by paratroopers proceeded to hold up Moslems; take away their identity cards (any Moslem without an identity card is considered an FLN man), pile them into the trucks, then make them join in the procession—after which their identity cards were returned to them.* Secondly, we saw large Army trucks, full of Moslems, and driven by a single unarmed soldier—something scarcely conceivable six months or a year ago. In other words, the methods used against the Moslems are the same, but the psychological atmosphere is different. . . .

On the morning of the demonstration paratroopers went to the Casbah, where they gave orders to the *chefs d'ilots*; then they marched numerous Moslems up to the Casbah; they also mobilized the workers down at the docks; in all this they were helped by the gangs of Alilou, a former FLN man, who had entered the service of the French Police.

How then explain the change in the psychological atmosphere? This was the explanation:

(1) At Algiers there is practically no longer any FLN organization. The mass of Moslems no longer get any political directives from anywhere. Moslems in the liberal professions have been scared into silence.

(2) The Moslems knew that the power was now in the hands of the soldiers, and, paradoxical as this may sound, they have more confidence—even now—in the Army than in the Algiers *ultras*.

(3) The meeting was taking place under the banner of de Gaulle—and his name was still popular with the Moslems.

(4) Though brought by force to the demonstration, the Moslems were pleasantly surprised and even touched by the reception given them by the population. For months they had been terrified of all Europeans; now there was, among them, a real feeling of relief.

(5) The propaganda conducted for some time past by the officers of special services like the SAS (*Section Administrative Specialisée*) and the SAU (*Section Administrative Urbaine*) had been very skilfully conducted. Its main theme was something like this:

"Believe us, we don't like the *ultras* any more than you do. . . . We shall not let you down. You now have a chance of getting far more concessions than the *loi-cadre*; therefore, you had better demonstrate your loyalty to France."

Everybody in Algiers, according to the same writer, was greatly surprised by the success of the demonstration. *On the strength of it, INTEGRATION now became the official slogan of the Committee of Public Safety.*

For the Moslems of Algeria—and we must stress once again that Algiers, with its a-political mass of Moslems, is not the same as Algeria—integration is an attractive idea: it means that under integration a Moslem will be treated the same way as a Frenchman. There is also great war-weariness in Algiers, and a desire to see the war end in almost any way.

To many men in the Army, especially to the higher officers, integration is not an empty word. They consider that if Algeria is to be part of France, then it is only fair that Moslems should be treated accordingly. When these soldiers are told that "the *ultras* will never accept it", their reply is always the same: "They'll have to accept it, even if, in the process, we have to chuck a few hundred thousand Frenchmen out of Algeria."

The *ultras* think it's just a clever trick. "If," they say, "it means 150 Algerian deputies in the National Assembly, we don't mind; we shall choose them carefully. We are all in favour of integration, provided it remains on paper. . . ."

A question which, before long, was to arise was the curious reticence observed in respect of the May 13 Revolution, and especially of the "Fraternization" orgies by the largest of the *colons*—Rogier, Schiaffino and Borgeaud, for instance—who owned immense estates and industrial interests in Algeria. No doubt, de Sérigny "represented" them on the Committee of Public Safety, but his role was never quite clear. Men like Borgeaud, Schiaffino and the rest were "Gaullist" up to a point: they thought that de Gaulle could free Algeria of foreign (i.e. American) interference. But they cared neither for "fraternization", nor for "integration", with its implication of political and economic equality. In Algiers, soon afterwards, this "reticence" of the *gros colons* was explained as follows by an industrialist:

"They are reticent, because they don't like Integration. All this business about the Moslems being 'complete Frenchmen' (à part entière) was one of those stunts thought up by the Army, and taken up by Algerian Europeans 'to make a good impression in Paris'. The trouble, after that, was that Paris *suddenly seemed to take the darned thing seriously.* As industrialists and high officials in Algeria we can tell you this: 'Nobody believes a word of it. It's like grafting a cactus on to a poplar. Integration—*real*, not bogus integration—makes absolutely no sense from an economic or budget point of view in Algeria. We are not going to bust ourselves to give the same family allowances to Arabs and Whites; the Arabs haven't the same needs. . . . Equality with these people? You might as well expect us all to wear *chechias!*" (A. P. Lentin, *L'Algérie des Colonels*, Paris, 1958, pp. 29–30.)

It did not take long to show that these "fraternization" parades meant very little; though de Gaulle was to make good use of them in his propaganda, he never could be persuaded to subscribe to "integration" as such. Personally, he also had grave doubts about the sincerity of this "fraternization".

6. SOUSTELLE ESCAPES TO ALGIERS

ON THE afternoon of Saturday, May 17, the startling news reached Paris that Jacques Soustelle had arrived at Algiers. Claiming to be ill in bed with a high temperature, he had not been seen in Paris for two days. He had not appeared at the National Assembly the day the emergency powers were discussed; and, as was soon learned, he had escaped from his police "protectors", had smuggled himself into Switzerland inside the boot of a friend's car, and had flown in a privately-chartered plane from Geneva to Algiers. His escape had been engineered by several people, most of them "Right-wing" Gaullists, such as General Guillain de Bénouville, M. Roger Frey,[1] M. Geoffrey de la Tour du Pin, a diplomat and former associate of M. Bidault's, and M. René Dumont, the business head of the USRAF.

Soustelle's "triumphal" arrival at Algiers, where the mobs had been clamouring for him for days, was not, however, as smooth an affair as had been expected. Soustelle and his companions were held up at the airfield for about three quarters of an hour; and, during the next few days, the Paris papers were full of contradictory stories of what had happened. According to some, it was the *ultras* and "activists" and Lagaillarde boys who had suddenly turned against Soustelle, since they considered that the support he would give to Delbecque would finally steal their thunder, and give their "revolution" an overwhelmingly Gaullist character. In reality, something quite different seems to have happened.

[1] M. Frey was, in January 1959, to succeed M. Soustelle as Minister of Information.

Despite de Gaulle's cryptic statement of May 15 and Salan's speech on the same day which he ended by crying *"Vive de Gaulle!"*, the Commander-in-Chief in Algeria was still hesitating to burn his bridges completely with the Pflimlin Government. Salan himself was highly distrustful of certain thugs on the Committee of Public Safety who, he had good reason to believe, had been mixed up in the "bazooka plot" to assassinate him. For two days, through a variety of emissaries, extremely complex negotiations had been going on between Salan and Pflimlin.

Salan (and other generals), not quite sure about the "legality" of what they were doing, and fearing perhaps that they might have to pay dearly for it in the end, were anxious for a "friendly settlement" with the Paris Government. Salan, therefore, was urging Pflimlin discreetly to efface himself, and make room for a "Government of Public Safety", preferably under de Gaulle but not necessarily so. In return, he was promising to keep the Army in hand.

According to Bromberger (*op. cit.*, pp. 293–5), Salan, who was joined a few minutes later by Massu, arrived at Algiers airfield just in time to meet Soustelle and his party. He had a personal dislike of Soustelle whom he suspected of having, in some way, been mixed up with the "bazooka affair". But there were more immediate reasons why he did not want him at Algiers just at that moment. He informed him that he would not be allowed to appear in the "Forum"; that it was undesirable that his presence be known to the people of Algiers, and that he would be taken to a private villa outside the town for forty-eight hours.

"We are on the point of persuading Pflimlin to resign and to make room for a Government of Public Safety. If he knows that you are here, a unique chance will be lost."

Massu took the same line at first; he said that it was in the public interest that Soustelle should not appear in public, since it was now certain that Pflimlin was going to resign at 8 p.m. that night.

Soustelle and his companions heatedly argued that Pflimlin was sure to doublecross them and that, in any case, his (Soustelle's) arrival at Algiers had been noticed by several people, and that the whole of Algiers knew by now that he was there. This, of course, proved to be perfectly true; for while Salan was arguing with Soustelle, Delbecque was sending cars with loudspeakers all over Algiers, calling on the people to gather in the "Forum", where Soustelle would shortly address them.

Meantime Sérigny and others arrived at the airport. Salan, between the devil and the deep sea, finally decided to phone Pflimlin, whom he informed of Soustelle's arrival. Pflimlin apparently merely told Salan to "continue to do his duty"—whatever that meant. Nothing was said of the Government's resignation; the conversation seems to have been short and inconclusive. Sérigny and others now urged Salan to give way, and Massu also now agreed that to let Soustelle loose in Algiers might be the best way of making Paris see reason; anyway, Algiers was already in a state of frantic excitement over Soustelle's arrival, and his mysterious disappearance would take too much explaining.

When, at 4.30 p.m., Soustelle, now shaking hands ostentatiously with Salan, appeared at the GG building, he was given a rousing reception by the "Forum" crowds. From the main balcony a dummy Pflimlin was dangling from a rope.

Soustelle's speech was more moderate than might have been expected. He said he had chosen "freedom and France"; he would do all within his powers to reunite France and Algeria. He spoke of "integration" and referred to "the nine million Frenchmen of Algeria". Later, at a press conference, he said that there was a quarrel between Algiers and the French Government, and that de Gaulle alone could settle it. He declined the offer of presiding over the Committee of Public Safety, and thought an Algerian (a very tame Algerian), Dr. Sid Cara, should become its president.

Later it was announced that Salan had made Soustelle his "political counsellor".

Salan's decision meant, in fact, his final breach with Paris, and his complete and final association with the "Gaullist" insurrection, though Pflimlin was still determined, for a few days longer, to keep up the illusion that Salan was under the orders of the Paris Government. It was not till the Corsican *putsch* a week later that he realized that the last hope of controlling Salan was lost. . . .

Whom and what, at the time of this spectacular landing at Algiers on May 17, did Jacques Soustelle represent?

We have already described his previous career: "his Leftism" before the war, particularly at the time of Munich; his very fine record as a scholar and a leading authority on Mexican and South-American history, archaeology and anthropology.[1]

We also know how he joined de Gaulle in London, where this scholar and intellectual developed an unholy liking for intelligence and police work. Later he moved with de Gaulle to Algiers, where he played a very active role in de Gaulle's victorious battle against Giraud and his American backers. He described this battle brilliantly in the second volume of his wartime memoirs, *Envers et contre tout*, published in 1950. In the late 'forties he became the chief organizer of de Gaulle's RPF; he was one of the most impressive speakers at the National Assembly; he was completely

---

[1] His works include *Méxique, terre indienne* (1936); his doctorate thesis, *La Famille Otomi-Mame du Méxique central*; *Folklore chilien*; *Méxique*; and *La pensée cosmologique des anciens Méxicains*.

"Gaullist" in his opposition to EDC and German rearmament, and was notorious for his hostility to America; his attack on American "colonialism" in Guatemala is still well-remembered by all American diplomats in Paris. In January 1955, Mendès-France appointed him (in very odd circumstances described elsewhere[1]) Governor-General of Algeria. At that time he still had the reputation of a "liberal" in colonial affairs and even of a "neutralist" in international affairs (or so, at least, *Le Figaro* thought at the time of his visit to Warsaw at the end of 1954). Though wholly out of sympathy with the *colons* at first, Soustelle soon himself became an outspoken "integrationist" and, when he was recalled by the Mollet Government soon after the election of January 2, 1956, he was given a tremendous send-off by the Europeans in Algiers, who now saw in him their best defender against the new Government's "capitulationism".

He had returned from Algeria in a highly emotional state, feeling that the Europeans there were now looking upon him as their "saviour". In Parliament he became the most eloquent defender of "French Algeria" and in March 1956, two months after his return from Algiers, he started a "movement", called the USRAF (*Union pour le salut et le renouveau de l'Algérie*) which we have already mentioned. The formation of this organization was accompanied by a number of lectures, in which Soustelle strongly advocated "integration" as the best solution;[2] at that stage several French liberals (some of them had, by this time, been bitten by the nationalist bug) supported him. It was not till later that, smelling a rat, they resigned from the USRAF.

In reality it was much less a propaganda organization than a secret network. Its business manager was a Paris industrialist, M. René Dumont, a former member of Soustelle's wartime intelligence network, the DGER.

The active members of the USRAF were chiefly mobilized from amongst former members of the DGER and of the *service d'ordre*, the militarized part, as it were, of de Gaulle's former RPF. By the middle of 1957, the USRAF thus had (according to *L'Express*) some 10,000 active members, one-third of whom were armed.

One of the aims of this organization was to "bring back de Gaulle", though, according to *L'Express*, some of its members, including its "business manager", M. Dumont, also talked of a possible "reconquest of Tunisia".

Who was subsidizing this organization? Again according to *L'Express*, Soustelle —despite a certain antipathy for the "Vichyism" of the Algiers *colons*—and their dislike for *his* talk about "integration" and the *collège unique*—established close contacts with M. de Sérigny, who had a special propaganda fund amounting to no less than 2,300 million francs. Part of this money was placed at the disposal of

[1] See the author's *Strange History of Pierre Mendès-France*, pp. 165–7.
[2] This was not the "absolute" integration, which became fashionable with some Army officers for a short time in May 1958, but a more cautious form of integration under which European interests were well taken care of.

USRAF, though the greater part of these funds continued to be used for supporting the Right-wing parties in France, notably the "Independents".

Although de Sérigny's great hope was to bring about the formation of an *ultra*
government in France, comprising Soustelle, Bidault, Morice, Duchet and
perhaps Lacoste, he realized, by February or March 1958, that this was not
practicable, and Soustelle persuaded him to back de Gaulle.

It was in February 1958 that USRAF held its first "General Assembly". This
happened after Sakhiet, and after the word had gone round that France would
soon be "ousted from North Africa by the USA". The "Committee" of the
USRAF set up at that time comprised Soustelle, Bidault, Morice, Bruyneel,
Bernard Lafay and André Marie. The real moving spirit of the organization,
however, was Soustelle himself. It was he, as we have seen, who, in February
1958, worked out a plan of campaign with de Sérigny. Also, Chaban-Delmas and
Delbecque were drawn into the plot, which, in turn, helped to gain the support
of a number of Army generals. The Prefect of Algiers, M. Serge Baret, also was
won over. The first major demonstration the USRAF organized at Algiers
took place, as we have seen, on April 26.

Thus, according to *L'Express*, Soustelle—apart from being the most powerful
advocate of "French Algeria" in France—was also head of a clandestine semi-
military organization which was supported by the North Africa Lobby, as
represented by M. de Sérigny.

In a sense, Soustelle was in a false position when he arrived at Algiers.
The European populace there had been clamouring for him on the 13th;
his "imminent" arrival was being announced by the *para* colonels. On
the 13th, when he still *could* have left for Algiers, he had preferred to stay
in Paris, thinking that he would have to act as the "chucker-out" of
Pflimlin; when he saw that Pflimlin was going to be invested, thanks to
Communist abstention, he did nothing about it. By the 14th it was no
longer possible for him to leave Paris openly. Meantime, at Algiers, all
the "Gaullist" work was being done by Delbecque, and both Massu
and (on the 15th) Salan had openly proclaimed their "Gaullism".

So, in a sense, Soustelle arrived at Algiers when the "Gaullist" operation
had already succeeded there, and it was not quite clear what role he was
expected to play. After some hesitation, he seems to have decided that his
best bet was to smooth out differences between the "Gaullists" and the
"activists"; but before long, he became the great hero of the latter, so
much so that when, early in June, de Gaulle went to Algiers, the mobs
there greeted him, more often than not, as we shall see, with cries of
"*Vive Soustelle!*" rather than "*Vive de Gaulle!*" From the moment
Soustelle set foot in Algeria on May 17 he had acted as the champion of
"Integration", the word which would not pass de Gaulle's lips. . . .

But—there was also something else Soustelle was going to do after
landing in Algiers. According to Pascal Arrighi's book (*La Corse atout
décisif*), *it was Soustelle who thought up the conquest of Corsica which was to
take place a week later.*

7. DE GAULLE'S PRESS CONFERENCE: OVERTURES TO THE SOCIALISTS

SUNDAY, May 18, was a day of waiting. Algiers, the Pflimlin Government and the general public were waiting, some with hope, others with anxiety, for de Gaulle's press conference at the Hôtel du Palais d'Orsay on Monday afternoon.

Thousands of police were concentrated around the hotel and in all the adjoining streets since about noon; M. Jules Moch, the Minister of the Interior, in person, was on the spot.[1]

To mark their hostility to de Gaulle, the Communist Trade Union Federation, the CGT, had ordered its members to stop work on the Monday afternoon, this strike to coincide with the General's press conference. The Socialist and Catholic trade unions did not support this order. Nevertheless, between 3 and 7 p.m. on Monday the Paris *métro* and several suburban lines stopped running, and so did about half the Paris buses. In factories in the Paris area the strike movement was much weaker.

Thousands of journalists and others had crowded into the vast banqueting hall of the Palais d'Orsay long before three o'clock when de Gaulle was to make his first public appearance in three years.

He looked distinctly older and his voice had a tired and somewhat mellowed tone. Though appearing slightly nervous at first, in the centre of this vast assembly of people, cameras, microphones and various TV contraptions, he soon recovered his old self-assurance, his irony and his quiet arrogance.

He recalled that, three years ago, he had decided to remain silent until such time when he could again serve the country. Since then, things had gone from bad to worse, and what was happening in France and in Algeria now might well lead to a "grave national crisis". "But," he added, "this might also mark the beginning of a kind of resurrection"— his first implicit suggestion that the Algiers *putsch* was, perhaps, a blessing in disguise.

And he felt that he could now again be "useful to France". Useful for three reasons: because, under his rule in the past, many important things had been achieved, and his "moral capital" might still count—in France, in the overseas territories and abroad.

[1] Was there going to be a Paris *putsch* that day, on the lines of the Algiers *putsch*, with CANAC (*Comité d'Action des Anciens Combattants*), the "army" of Soustelle's USRAF, various war-veterans and the Biaggi boys (a total of some 20,000 men), marching down the Champs-Elysées and capturing the National Assembly and other public buildings? Such a *putsch* was planned for that day, and the Government had no faith at all in the Police. According to the Brombergers (*op. cit.*, pp. 311–15), who always tend to exaggerate the importance of the *Paris* Fascists, the *putsch* was called off at the last moment when its organizers realized that de Gaulle was very strongly opposed to it, and would not take power "in such illegal conditions".

"Secondly, I may also be useful because the exclusive régime of Parties—will never solve the enormous problems facing us, particularly that of our association with the peoples of Africa and the different communities of Algeria. . . ."

Again, he said that the present régime, for all its good intentions, would be incapable of settling anything, and, in the end (again an allusion to Murphy!) the outside world might inflict a solution on France—and this would be the worst possible of all solutions.

Finally, he (de Gaulle) could be useful because he belonged to no Party, to no organization. "I am a man who belongs to nobody, and who belongs to everybody."

"Useful—but how? Well, just as during the last great national crisis, by placing myself at the head of the French Republic, if the people wishes it."

So much for the initial statement. Then came the questions and answers.

First de Gaulle dealt with the question of how he could "assume the powers of the Republic". He took credit for all the social, economic and other reforms which (largely under Socialist and Communist pressure) had been carried out by his Government in 1944–45. He even took credit for the nationalizations that were then carried out.

After some bitter and ironical remarks on the "reappearance of the parties" who, "like so many émigrés, had forgotten nothing and learned nothing"—after which he, de Gaulle, retired from the Government—and on the "bad Constitution" which these parties then passed, de Gaulle recalled the RPF. With the help of this movement, he (de Gaulle) had tried to create a "just and strong State"; but the régime succeeded in absorbing the representatives of the RPF one by one; "after which I was left without any weapon of legal action", and "I therefore went home."

After a few more ironical comments on the "professional saviours of the Republic" who were now saying that he was a menace to public freedoms, trade union rights and the Republican institutions—all of which deserved no reply—de Gaulle went on to answer a question on Algeria.

Murphy again! After years of bloodshed, the "system" had lately resorted to the "good offices" of the outside world. And then came this bouquet for Lacoste:

The Algerian population recently heard a man, whom I may well call my friend, and who was, at that time, Minister of Algeria, saying publicly: "We are on our way to a diplomatic Dien Bien Phu."

Paris, with its constant Cabinet reshuffles and its spectacle of helplessness and impotence, was creating a lamentable impression in Algeria:

"How, in the long run, can you expect these people not to rise? Is it surprising that these people should look for salvation other than further parliamentary combinations? And that's what has inevitably happened."

Now came the real touch of Gaullist arrogance:

"So now the Algerians shout 'Vive de Gaulle', just as the French also do in moments of acute anguish, and are yet carried on the wings of hope. What we are now witnessing in Algeria is a great movement of fraternization, which provides a psychological and moral basis for an agreement and for arrangements which are vastly better than battles and ambushes."

Thus it now appeared that the "fraternization" organized in Algiers by Delbecque—and probably Massu—had clearly played into the hands of de Gaulle. He was promising peace in Algeria—a peace based neither on military victory, nor on surrender, but one based on reconciliation! It sounded good—perhaps too good.

De Gaulle then approved the attitude of the Army—which had prevented Algeria from falling into a state of chaos, and which was sharing the Algerian population's desire to see Paris "capable of assuming its responsibilities".

While understanding and appreciating the attitude of the military command, de Gaulle then said that he wished the Army to remain "coherent and united"—at a time when there was no other coherent and united force in the country.

He then warned the Government against cutting communications between France and Algeria. And he added:

"As for the Army, it is the instrument of the State; but what we need *is* a State. ... And there's no time to lose."

That was clear enough!

Then somebody mentioned the questions Guy Mollet had put to de Gaulle. He did not bother answering these questions; but what he said was much more interesting. His attitude to Mollet was semi-ironical; he said he had pleasant memories of Mollet; he respected him; he had not always been in agreement with him, or with what he had done, or had tried to do, "but then in a régime like the present one even the best people don't get much of a chance." (*Dans le régime tel qu'il est, aucune valeur ne peut réussir.*)

"I know," said de Gaulle, "I've read in the papers Guy Mollet's questions: firstly, secondly, thirdly, fourthly. My answer is: if de Gaulle is given exceptional powers, for an exceptional task, at an exceptional moment then, surely . . . he will also have to be given these powers by an exceptional procedure. For an investiture by the National Assembly, for instance."

The compliments to Lacoste and, more significant, to Mollet had, of course, been carefully calculated in advance. He actually started reminiscing about a meeting between himself and Mollet at Arras, just after the Liberation, and said what a very fine man Mollet was. Mollet later remarked that there had, in fact, never been such a meeting! But this pleasant story was also part of de Gaulle's technique.

It was clear that de Gaulle wanted to be placed at the head of the Government by legal (albeit "exceptional") methods. He could depend on the Right and probably most of the Centre to help him into office; but the Socialists held the key. Hence these seemingly ironical compliments to Guy Mollet—complete with the clear suggestion that under a different régime Guy Mollet could show his real worth far more than before!

These overtures to Mollet were the most significant passage in the whole of de Gaulle's press conference.

De Gaulle then became ironical again, if not downright satirical.

There are some who treat as rebels the Army leaders who have not been punished by the Government and who, indeed, have been delegated governmental authority in Algeria! Now, I am *not* the Government; so why should anybody expect me, in the circumstances, to treat these Army leaders as rebels? (*Loud laughter.*) In this tragedy, one ought to be serious-minded. I'm trying to be it.

He was certainly making hay of the hopelessly false position the Pflimlin Government had placed itself in with regard to the Algiers generals.

He answered a further question on Algeria: he would, if asked to do so, act as arbiter in the conflict, but before passing his verdict he would have to hear "all the sides". But conditions would have to be created in which such a verdict could be enforced. Such conditions did not exist at present.

And finally, when asked whether he would respect public freedoms, de Gaulle said, with an air of superb disdain: "It was I who re-established these public freedoms. Do you believe that, at sixty-seven, I shall start a dictator's career?"

There were some who murmured: "What about Pétain, who 'started' at eighty-four?"

To conclude, he spoke of France's high birth-rate and its great economic possibilities, including those provided by the wealth of the Sahara. These were factors which would greatly help a strong Government to create a new, great and prosperous France. No doubt the task would be no easy one, and, if called to power, he would need the help of the men and women of France.

"I've said what I had to say. Now I shall return to my village and shall remain there at the country's disposal."

The almost general reaction to the press conference was that it was hard to see how a de Gaulle Government could be avoided. De Gaulle had spoken with terrifying self-confidence.

I saw several people after the conference, amongst them the Gaullist ex-Deputy, Philippe Barrès, who simply said: "Well, now it's in the bag, don't you think?" I said I thought it was; and I also saw Pierre Courtade of *L'Humanité*, who merely shrugged his shoulders and said: "It'll be difficult to keep him out, especially if the Socialists—or most of them— eat out of his hand; and it's beginning to look like it. He's playing a devilishly clever game, and most people prefer not to look too closely. *Ils ont la trouille . . .*"

"And the working class?" I said.

"The anti-Fascist feeling is strong enough; but the Communist rank- and-file are feeling isolated; also, a lot of the working class—let's face it—have become terribly a-political. . . . De Gaulle knows that we'll fight, if necessary; he is trying to get in without having to fight; the Socialists will rush along with the step-ladder . . ."

The effect in both Paris and Algiers was what was to be expected. The de Gaulle press conference put the lid on the Fourth Republic, as far as Algiers was concerned. Practically the whole of Algiers (including all the old Vichyite elements) now became resolutely "Gaullist". His state- ment was considered as a tacit blessing to the Algiers rebellion. This reaction was shared by most of the European population and, more important, by the Army, as well as by a considerable part (though not all) of the Committee of Public Safety.

Despite a great many mental reservations on both the "Gaullist" and "activist" side, Algiers now presented a united "Gaullist" front, and the two factions even made concessions to each other: for instance, probably at the suggestion of the Gaullists (or perhaps Soustelle) General Salan expelled from Algiers two Fascist (ex-Poujade) Deputies who had just landed at Algiers—M. Le Pen and M. Demarquet. It is true that the local Fascists like Lagaillarde were not too pleased either to see these dangerous demagogues—and dangerous rivals—arrive in Algiers. Interviewed a few hours after their expulsion from Algiers at Madrid airport by Paris Radio, Le Pen made what was probably the most apoplectic-sounding broadcast since Hitler on the eve of Munich!

On the other hand two other Deputies arrived unhindered in Algiers: M. Dronne and M. Arrighi. The latter was going a few days later to play a leading role in the Corsica *putsch* (originally thought up by Soustelle). M. Dronne, both a "Gaullist" and an Algerian *ultra*, hastened to announce at Algiers that "there must now be a Government of Public Safety in France with de Gaulle at its head".

Continuing the "fraternization" policy, General Salan issued a procla- mation calling on the FLN rebels to surrender.

"Fellaghas, join us! Union has become a reality! 150,000 Moslem and Christian Frenchmen proclaimed it on May 16 in Algiers.

"Everywhere, in towns and villages, Moslem and Christian Frenchmen are proclaiming it.

"Fellaghas, join us! Surrender your arms to the Army. *We grant you our pardon.* Take up your place in the new French Algeria."

There were more and more "fraternization" demonstrations. Right-wing papers in Paris went into raptures over them—especially over the Moslem women joining in these processions and unveiling themselves—a sign of the greatest friendship. *Later, it is true, it was discovered that most of these women were professional prostitutes—after which many respectable Moslem women, who had not worn the veil for years, now put it on again to avoid confusion!*

In Paris, the de Gaulle press conference also hastened to convert many of the more cautious papers. Though still paying lip-service to "republican legality", papers like *L'Aurore, Combat* and *Le Figaro* left little doubt that they were going to back de Gaulle wholeheartedly from now on.

8. HALF-HEARTED DEFENCE OF THE REPUBLIC

WHAT was the Pflimlin Government doing meantime? Already on the Saturday, possibly as a result of Soustelle's successful escape to Algiers, it took the incongruous measure of enforcing exit visas on all French citizens intending to leave Metropolitan France. As a result, there were during the last few days vast and angry queues of people (mostly holidaymakers, many of them merely intending to visit the Brussels Exhibition) at the Préfecture de Police. On the Monday (May 20) all foreign exchange allowances (apart from 20,000 francs in French money) for tourist travel abroad were cancelled.

Also, the Government was going to ask Parliament to renew its special emergency powers for Algeria—a problem which was going to cause some complications, especially with the Communists, who objected to any Governmental powers being "delegated" to General Salan. On the parliamentary committee where the matter was discussed, the Communist members abstained.

Where de Gaulle was concerned, the Communists and Socialists now seemed to see eye-to-eye. *L'Humanité*, on its poster-like front page on May 20, reproduced with satisfaction the communiqué published after the joint meeting on the previous day by the Socialist governing committee and the Socialist parliamentary group—which said:

General de Gaulle has demanded powers which are to be given him by an exceptional procedure, the rules of which he himself intends to lay down; he has thus turned his back on the Constitution of the Republic. . . .

In various parts of the country "Defence of the Republic" committees were being set up. At Toulouse, in particular, an important committee was formed "representing twenty-five organizations", including the various trade unions, and the Socialist, Communist and Radical parties; this, however, was still unusual.

On the other hand, there were also more and more rumours of committees of public safety being more or less secretly set up in various towns and even villages.

Despite certain symptoms of a "republican defence" movement beginning to crystallize here and there, and the seeming hostility to de Gaulle on the part of both Socialists and Communists, the French Socialist leaders were very uncertain of what they were to do. M. Pinay had, for several days already—and even before de Gaulle had spoken—been urging M. Guy Mollet to see the General. But, in Mollet's view, the time was not yet ripe for such a meeting. Pinay and other members of the Right also continued to urge M. Pflimlin to resign and to make room for a more "representative" Government—though, heaven knows, there hadn't, for a long time, been a Government with such wide Parliamentary support as M. Pflimlin's. But—even the slightest indications of a possible *rapprochement* between the Socialists and the Communists were beginning to scare them. A Popular Front—God forbid! Not that there was anything like a nation-wide movement in favour of the Popular Front—yet. Especially since Budapest, the Communists had felt terribly isolated—and, indeed, ostracized. It was even remarked soon afterwards by *Esprit*, that, but for Budapest, there would have been no Algiers: *the Algiers Rebels were sufficiently confident that France was not ripe for a Popular Front*, and so incapable of putting up any real fight for the Republic.

The meeting of the National Assembly on Tuesday, May 20, was marked at first by a strange air of unreality. The discussion on the renewal of the Government's emergency powers for Algeria went on for several hours, *without de Gaulle's statement of the previous day being mentioned by anybody*. Better still, the Assembly went out of its way to vote unanimously a motion expressing to the Army "the Nation's deep gratitude for the services it has already rendered to the unity of the country and to the banner of the Republic which will, within complete legality, emerge victorious from the present ordeal." This face-saving gibberish was even more comic when one considers that M. Deixonne (Socialist), the author of this motion, had originally referred to "restored legality"—and that the adjective was then deleted, since it suggested that the "republican legality" of the Army leaders' conduct could at any time have been questioned!

Despite the unreality of this meeting, M. Pflimlin nevertheless gave the Assembly at least one piece of solid news: and that was that the war in Algeria was still going on. He welcomed the "fraternizations" in Algeria and said that if this "remarkable phenomenon" were to spread, it might well modify the whole position in Algeria; nevertheless, he thought it necessary to remind the Assembly that "rebel activity" was going on at the same rhythm as before; French losses were as great as ever, and the FLN had latterly published a violent communiqué. In the last week (i.e. since May 13) 46 French soldiers and 447 Algerian Rebels had been killed.

Also, Pflimlin referred to "certain agitators" in Algeria who were trying to create there a "revolutionary situation"—a remark which produced from that crackpot Fascist character, M. Dorgères d'Halluin, the remark that Pflimlin was talking like the Communist *L'Humanité*.

"The Committees of Public Safety," Pflimlin said, "include not only *persons attached to our republican institutions* [!] and who are trying to exercise a moderating influence there, but also a number of extremists, who are trying to turn these Committees into instruments of subversion."

Without specifying who these "republicans" were on the Committee of Public Safety, Pflimlin then paid a tribute to the Army leaders, and particularly to General Salan who had maintained order in Algeria; the "transfer of civilian posts had *most of the time* (!) been done in agreement with the Government"; but in some cases the changes had taken place "under the pressure of circumstances"; nevertheless—

Contact was never broken between the Government and the authorities in Algiers, and we shall take the necessary measures to re-establish normal relations and to bring about a return to legality. In Metropolitan France the Algerian crisis has been exploited by certain extremists . . .

M. *Legendre* (Right): Communists.

M. *Pflimlin:* I told the Assembly that the Government would fight all extremism.

There followed a hair-splitting discussion on whether the Government had been more lenient, or not, to Communist than to Fascist propaganda, a discussion which, later in the debate, took the form of a violent dialogue between another notorious Fascist character, the *ex-commissaire* Dides (head of the vast Police "network" in Paris) and M. Jules Moch, the Minister of the Interior. This dialogue soon developed into a free-for-all tussle, in the course of which Dides accused Pflimlin of being a boor, who had "sacked General Ely as though he were a flunkey", while the Communists joined in, calling Dides a Gestapo informer, etc., etc. Dides even attacked Guy Mollet for having "failed to defend French Algeria before the Socialist International".

Pflimlin said that he intended to speed up the reform of the Constitution, with a view to strengthening the executive; in the next few days proposals would be submitted to the Assembly.

As for Algeria, Pflimlin used the phrase "new and French Algeria"—

French: because it is our right and our duty to keep it French; new: because this new Algeria will have institutions under which there will be equal rights for all, and a fair share for all the communities living on Algerian soil where the administration of the country is concerned . . .

All this sounded hollow and academic; so also did M. Moch's assurances that he had had more important things to think about than confiscating Communist leaflets: he had maintained order in Paris and *had let it be known to the outside world that there was in Paris a Government which was governing.* (*Cheers on numerous benches.*)

The Assembly did not come down to earth until Mendès-France first mentioned de Gaulle's press conference:

After recalling that he had been a devoted follower of de Gaulle during the war, he said that he and others had often asked de Gaulle in recent years to use his authority for bringing about national reconciliation. But he would not answer. . . . It was not till a seditious movement among soldiers and civilians had started in Algiers that de Gaulle decided to speak—and to justify their actions, and, at the same time, to attack the political parties. No one was more conscious of the weaknesses of these parties than he (Mendès-France); but it was unfortunate that de Gaulle should have chosen this moment for attacking them and for encouraging the Algiers Rebels just at a time when they were becoming aware of the pernicious and anti-national nature of what they had done.

M. *Legendre* (Right): The whole country will now be for de Gaulle; because the whole country is against you!

M. *Mendès-France:* At this stage General de Gaulle should have tried to strengthen the Republic, instead of attacking it. . . . And those of us who have followed and loved him, beg him now to put an end to this equivocal situation—if there is still time . . .

He concluded by calling on the Government to be firm and ruthless in the face of the seditious movement in Algeria. M. Pflimlin, for all his good qualities, had never taken a sufficiently clear line, and this had played into the hands of the trouble-makers. . . . It was high time the Army leaders were called to order and made to obey the Republic. . . . When Lacoste wrote in a Bordeaux paper that morning of "losing Algeria to save the Republic, or losing the Republic to save Algeria", he was creating a false dilemma. For there was now a clear danger of losing both.

M. Triboulet, who seemed to have become de Gaulle's official spokesman in the National Assembly, said that de Gaulle was going to play the
part of arbiter, but not in the spirit of violence which Mendès-France
was now advocating.

After numerous compliments had been paid by a variety of speakers
to the Army and its leaders, the Assembly voted the renewal of the
emergency powers for Algeria by 473 votes to 93, the Communists
voting for the Government, despite the hostility shown them by M.
Pflimlin and despite their complete distrust of the Army leaders whom
both Pflimlin and de Chevigné were praising so loudly—whatever
their own mental reservations on the subject.

M. Duclos (Communist) said that the officers and generals who were now
acting in the name of de Gaulle, should, in fact, be charged with insubordination.
What was being prepared now was a military dictatorship, and several deputies—
Soustelle, Dronne, Arrighi—had already joined the rebellion. President Coty's
order to the Army to obey should, Duclos said, be hung up in every army barrack;
French Justice should stop condoning the behaviour of rebellious generals and
seditious deputies, and the radio should stop making propaganda for de Gaulle,
the would-be dictator.

But no; Pflimlin again replied that the Army leaders in Algeria were
"defending national unity and republican legality".

In short, General Salan was "representing" the Government; and the
Assembly vote now seemed to have "consolidated" the Pflimlin Government at home. But in reality the situation continued to be extremely
confused.

Many Left-wingers I talked to in Paris during those days were obsessed
by this question: could Pflimlin, with the full weight of Parliamentary
support behind him, have "got tough" with Algiers on the 14th—for
instance, by cashiering a number of generals and colonels, and by cutting
off all supplies—including the money? What would have been the
repercussions in France? An outcry that the Army was being stabbed in the
back; that the Government was playing into the hands of the FLN? Or
would a tough line by Paris have had a sobering effect on Algiers, and so
reduced to a minimum the uproar in France about the "stab in the back"?
But supposing the Army in Algiers had continued its "insurrectionist
attitude"? It could, surely, still hold out for a pretty long time against the
FLN with what arms and money were available in Algeria. And "getting
tough"—and on the night of May 13 de Chevigné thought he could do
it—was all very well, *so long as de Gaulle hadn't spoken*, and so long as
Salan hadn't cried *"Vive de Gaulle!"* in the "Forum" of Algiers on the
morning of May 15. From that moment, the "insurrectionist attitude" of
the Army leaders had assumed a different character, an air of "respectabi-

lity", as it were. They seemed to be defending now the future of France and Algeria, and the unity of the Army. The hundreds of thousands of French conscripts in Algeria somehow didn't count. They were scarcely mentioned during those days. Surely, many of them—ordinary chaps from the French countryside and from the Paris industrial belt—couldn't possibly be in sympathy with the Algiers *putsch*. I received several letters during those days from ordinary conscripts serving in Algeria; they were disconcertingly vague, and merely suggested that the officers were all on the side of the *putsch*: "*We* don't much care for it; but there's nothing much we can do." Already the story was being circulated amongst these *rappelés* that "de Gaulle would end the war in Algeria"; it had some effect; and while many assumed towards the antics of Algiers a shoulder-shrugging, wait-and-see attitude, others more or less wholeheartedly joined in what one soldier described in a letter to me as "this dangerous, but rather exciting boy-scout movement . . ."

9. M. PINAY'S CUP OF TEA

WHAT chance, in the circumstances, did the Republic have? Was there much republican *mystique* left anywhere? The Communists sounded wholehearted in their desire to "defend the Republic"; but then they were—Communists. As early as May 14 Guy Mollet said *he would rather have de Gaulle than the Popular Front*. The Socialists were divided and uncertain; they, like the MRP, paid lip-service to the "republican legality" which the Pflimlin Government was supposed to represent, and, at the same time, accepted the fiction of Salan "representing the Republic" at Algiers.

This anomalous situation obviously couldn't last. And the Right knew it full well. For if, on the one hand, Mendès-France was asking the Government to "get tough" with Algiers (but how?), and was turning his back on de Gaulle, who had done nothing to "strengthen the Republic" in its hour of need, Pinay, on the other hand, was now arguing that the Republic wasn't really in danger, and that all that was now needed was for the Republic to come to terms with de Gaulle who alone was capable of cleaning up the Algiers mess. So for days now—in fact ever since the first de Gaulle statement of May 15—Pinay had been urging both Guy Mollet and Pflimlin to establish contact with de Gaulle. Since de Gaulle's press conference Pinay had become even more active; he thought there would be no excessive difficulty in agreeing on the "exceptional procedure" the General had mentioned; and, with the full backing of important business interests, Pinay offered to go personally to Colombey-les-deux-Eglises to prepare the ground for a subsequent de Gaulle-Pflimlin-Mollet meeting. For had not de Gaulle as good as indicated that he would like to have a talk with Mollet?

It is an ironical thought that "Little Man" Pinay—who was the first, in January 1960, to defy the head of the Fifth Republic—should also have been the first to approach de Gaulle officially with a virtual request that he put an end to the Fourth.

On Thursday, May 22, M. Pinay, accompanied by his former *directeur de cabinet*, M. Yrissou, left Paris for Colombey, where he arrived around 4 p.m. As he later said, de Gaulle had received him "very courteously" and had given him tea. (For days he was to talk about that cup of tea.) He had found the General "amiable and affable". His impression had been very good: he had spent one hour and forty minutes with the General. One can well imagine that de Gaulle must have derived a certain amount of quiet amusement out of Pinay's visit; back in March, 1952, when several Gaullists deserted the RPF and came to the rescue of M. Pinay in his investiture vote, de Gaulle had remarked: "Surely, I didn't save France to hand her over in the end to this Monsieur Pinay . . ." Now it looked as though "this Monsieur Pinay" was ready to hand France back to General de Gaulle. . . .

As he drove back from Colombey, he swept aside the dozens of journalists who had, for days, been hanging round de Gaulle's country residence, and refused to say anything. But it was soon clear that Pinay had succeeded in paving the way for the early contacts between de Gaulle and Pflimlin and between de Gaulle and Guy Mollet that were soon to follow. He had discussed with de Gaulle that "exceptional procedure" by which he could be legally "invested" for the Premiership. The real purpose of his visit was to discover what de Gaulle's conditions were. *Paris-Presse*, one of the most outspokenly Gaullist papers, described the result of Pinay's visit as follows in a banner headline on May 23:

"DE GAULLE IS NOT REFUSING TO MAKE CONTACT WITH PFLIMLIN BUT . . .
he doesn't see how he can be of use without becoming head of the Government."

It was very curious that all this coming and going between Paris and Colombey—with the implication that a de Gaulle Government could not be avoided—had started several days before the Corsica *putsch*, a *putsch* which first clearly suggested that the "Algiers Revolution" was threatening to spread to France itself. In spite of all this, Pflimlin was going through the motions of "defending the Republic". For what was the position on the day of Pinay's visit to de Gaulle?

10. SOUSTELLE IN ALGIERS

As FAR as Algeria was concerned, the myth that the Generals were acting on behalf of the Government, and behaving like "good republicans" was being kept up, in accordance with Pflimlin's latest statements to Parliament and his latest broadcast, and even after Soustelle had illegally left France for Algiers and had become Salan's "counsellor".

Though cautious at first, Soustelle did not take long to speak his mind:

"The Army and the people of Algeria," he said on May 22, "have stopped the rush to capitulate. There shall be no negotiations with our enemies; there shall be no more 'good offices'—we've had enough of that. There are today ten million Frenchmen in Algeria who want to make peace in a spirit of equality and fraternity . . . Long live French Algeria! Long live de Gaulle!"

Here was integrationism with a vengeance.

Massu also made Gaullist speeches; but the man who went furthest of all was the "representative of the Pflimlin Government", General Salan, who, after thanking those who had cried *"L'Armée au pouvoir!"* declared:

"The people of Algeria and the Army are indissolubly united. We shall march up the Champs Elysées together, and the people of France will cover us with flowers . . ."

Then Massu spoke and, dismissing as nonsense rumours of dissensions among the various leaders in Algiers, he said:

"The Army is in power here. Salan is the only military and civil boss. And he will remain that until we have achieved our object—which is the formation of a Government of Public Safety in Paris. Meantime, Soustelle is our friend and our counsellor. He is helping us with all his weight, all his culture, all his competence. There can be no misunderstanding about him, and if you hear any more stories, just tell me; I'll deal with these mischief-makers!"

It seems that some of the Army people were beginning to wonder why so many Deputies were now arriving at Algiers; wasn't Soustelle playing some game of his own, independently of the Army? Or else, were there other, even more extreme elements in France, who were trying to supplant Soustelle and join up openly with the Fascist elements, as distinct from the Gaullist elements? As already said, two Fascist (ex-Poujade) Deputies, Le Pen and Demarquet, were simply ordered to fly back to Spain as soon as they had landed in Algiers; the expulsion order had come from Salan himself—possibly with Soustelle's approval and without any

protest being made by the Lagaillarde boys, who required no rivals in
Fascist demagogy.[1]

The subsequent role of Soustelle at Algiers during the days that
followed may be briefly summarized here. He acted, officially, as
"counsellor" both to Salan and to the Committee of Public Safety, quietly
worked on his Corsica "scheme", and meantime was making countless
speeches—all along the same ultra-integrationist-cum-Gaullist lines.

To coincide with the Corsica *putsch* of May 24, an enlarged Committee
of Public Safety, the *Comité de Salut Public de l'Algérie et du Sahara*, was
formed, composed of seventy-two members, of whom only a small
minority were Moslems. A very high proportion of the Europeans were
ultras, though, for the present, more or less converted to "Gaullism".

Its two presidents were General Massu and Dr. Sid Cara; its vice-presidents,
General Jouhaud, M. Delbecque and an Algerian, M. Azem Ouali; its three
secretaries were two *ultras*, M. René Denis, Dr. Lefèvre and a soldier, Captain
Renault; its six "*attachés de liaison*" included de Sérigny, Martel, a soldier and a
Moslem; the head of its Secretariat was Colonel Ducasse; its "chief liaison officer"
was Colonel Trinquier; its head of Information, M. Neuwirth; its "head of Social
Affairs", a Mlle Antona. The other members of the committee were: All the
members of the original May 13 Committee, including Colonel Thomazo,
Crespin, Lagaillarde, Ortiz, Vinciguerra, Merlot, Baudier, Martin, Parachini, and
three Moslems; six members from Oran (all Europeans); nine members from
Constantine (including three Moslems); five members from the Sahara (including
four Moslems).

At almost the same time a "supreme organ of the Algiers movement"
was created in the form of a Triumvirate, or "Co-ordination Committee
for Algeria and the Sahara"; and this was composed of Soustelle, Massu
and Sid Cara. It was explained that, although the original Algiers May 13
Committee had been incorporated in the new and wider Committee, it
continued to exist separately as well, and the Triumvirate would help to
co-ordinate the work of the two. Lieutenant Neuwirth, in a press conference, stressed that the Triumvirate had placed itself "under the high
authority of General Salan". Thus Soustelle became an official head of the
Anti-Paris Revolt.

But to return to the "pre-Corsica" situation. The situation was, indeed,
odd. Algiers had replaced the French national flag by the Gaullist flag
with the Cross of Lorraine; even so, Parliament had granted to the
Pflimlin Government "special powers" in Algeria—which was like a
bad joke.

---

[1] Similarly, on May 16, M. Biaggi had arrived in Algiers, only to be sent off provisionally—
to the Sahara, on orders from Salan.

"There is no such thing as 'power' any more," wrote Jacques Fauvet in the *Monde* on May 21, "there are only 'powers'. Political power, moral power and military power are no longer to be found in the same hands or in the same place. Power has been dispersed. De Gaulle is at Colombey, the Government is in Paris, and the Army is in Algeria."

Who could mould these "powers" into one? Some were saying: de Gaulle only; others still seemed to think that perhaps, somehow, Algiers would get tired of this situation, and, in the end, the legal power of the central Government would be able to reassert itself. That was why Pflimlin, while interested to hear from M. Pinay what de Gaulle had to say, was now going through the motions of "strengthening the Republic" by planning to rush through Parliament a vast constitutional reform.

11. PFLIMLIN'S "GAULLISM WITHOUT DE GAULLE"

THERE was, it must be said, an uncanny feeling in Paris that Pflimlin was proposing, in all seriousness, to rebuild a house which was already on fire. Anyway, it wasn't such a simple operation—no matter how urgent it was now said to be. A variety of constitutional changes were considered; the ministerial council, which met on the 22nd, brought numerous changes into the "*avant-projet*"—or Draft Bill—which had been adopted at the Cabinet meeting on the previous day. One of the features of this *avant-projet* had been the election of the head of the Government for a minimum period of two years. Most of the ministers were favourable to this scheme; but on the following day its opponents received strong support from President Coty; and, on the Friday, the President of the National Assembly, M. Le Troquer, proposed that the whole discussion be postponed until the following Tuesday, apparently in view of the very mixed reception given to the proposals by the various parliamentary groups, and in view of the numerous criticisms and amendments that were going to be offered.

A significant comment on the proposed reform came from M. Mendès-France who thought that the Government would do better to exercise its authority, instead of merely extracting from Parliament special "emergency powers" for France, and, worse still, purely theoretical "special powers" for Algeria, and now a far-reaching constitutional reform, seemingly "cut to measure for de Gaulle", and which, at the moment, no one could tell how it would be used, and by whom. The unhealthy haste with which the Pflimlin Government was talking about rushing the constitutional reform through Parliament "in five or six days" was described by Mendès-France as "sheer Kerenskyism". Others thought that here was a desperate kind of attempt to set up a "Gaullist" type of presidential régime—without de Gaulle. Nobody, somehow, could take it terribly seriously—all the more so as Pflimlin was showing growing signs of fatigue and indecision. Sweeping constitutional changes were being planned on the one hand, and preliminary contacts were being made with de Gaulle on the other. It was all very well talking about the Republic—but *who* at this juncture was the Republic? Behind Pflimlin, there were all the Guilty Men, all the real gravediggers of the Republic— Pleven of Indo-China, and Mollet, Bourgès-Maunoury, and Max Lejeune —three of the men who had always kow-towed and capitulated to the He-men of Algiers and had, in doing so, created the present inextricable situation.

12. "ALGERIA WILL SAVE FRANCE"

THE Right-wing papers were now all for de Gaulle; and they were full of endless stories about the "Miracle of Algiers", with rapturous descriptions of the Franco-Moslem "fraternizations". On May 23 at Algiers, as we have seen, an All-Algerian and Saharan Committee of Public Safety was set up, under the joint presidency of General Massu and the tame Algerian, Sid Cara. It looked good on the face of it; but the reality was less idyllic.

In reality, out of the 72 members of this new committee, there were only thirteen Moslems. As a symbol of "integration", as a forerunner of the *Collège Unique*, the single electoral college with its implied proportional representation, the new committee made no sense.

Salan, it was now learned in Paris, had tried to delay the formation of this new organism, which could only help to show up even more than the Algiers committee did the fictitious nature of the "co-ordination" between Paris and Algiers. But he gave way in the end.

The very first speeches made by the members of this new committee showed that they intended "Algeria to save France", and to impose on France the decisions taken in Algiers.

Despite the Salan "fiction", Algiers was, indeed, acting quite irrespective of the wishes of Paris. President Coty's message to the Army had not been broadcast by Algiers radio; high officials were being dismissed without reference to the Paris Government; persons who had illegally left France were being given an enthusiastic welcome by Algiers; and latterly Algiers had started a sort of radio war against France, warning her that, as in 1943, so now again, "Algiers" had the mission of "liberating" the French Metropolitan territory—not of the Germans this time, but of the "system".

Now, on May 23 and 24, there were indications of something new having happened among many soldiers and officers in Algeria. Under the influence of the highly dynamic civilian *ultras*, many of these soldiers were coming to the conclusion that they might as well go the whole hog; they had burned their boats, and their choice now lay between "court-martial or victory". The Algerian Committee formed on the 23rd thus turned out to be just as extremist as the original committee of May 13. Here also the *ultras* were in the majority: alongside Soustelle's USRAF men, here again were numerous Poujade and Biaggi followers; on this All-Algeria committee Algiers was represented by forty-nine members and the rest of Algeria by only twenty-three. And, as already said, the number of Moslems was only thirteen out of a total of seventy-two.

Does not this suggest that the "fraternization" has in reality affected only an unkempt, down-and-out bunch of suburbanites, merely anxious for some kind of protection? . . . Whatever may have been their original intentions, men like Colonel Trinquier and M. Delbecque seem to be having the greatest difficulty in securing the support of a Moslem *élite*—even though such a large *élite* exists, as we know from the experience of M. Chevallier, who, as Mayor of Algiers, enjoyed their full co-operation.[1]

But then Chevallier, though nominally still Mayor of Algiers, was being treated by the men of May 13 as a leper. For had not Chevallier for years advocated peace negotiations with the FLN, a plan which was invariably turned down by M. Lacoste—the man, as Chevallier said, who was hated by the Arabs more than anyone in the world?

That was not the spirit in which the He-men of Algiers were going to settle the Algerian problem. They were, in fact, less interested on that 23rd of May in ending the war in Algeria than in—conquering France! That day there were more demonstrations; and now the crowds started shouting a new slogan: "LES PARAS A PARIS!" According to a correspondent of *France-Soir* an officer, who thought this was going a little too far, ordered the military band to strike up to drown these cries. But, at the same time, Colonel Lacheroy, the spokesman of General Salan, declared the same day:

"We are doing all we can to inform the people of Metropolitan France objectively on the happy evolution of events in Algeria, so that they may give us their full support. It is possible *that we may have to help our friends in France if there is no rapid de Gaulle solution*."

This item appeared in the *Figaro* under the title "A Threat?"
That same evening, in connection with numerous flights of French military planes over Tunisia (against which the Tunisian Government had already sent a complaint to UN), Lacheroy denied the rumour that Salan was preparing to "saddle his horse to ride into Tunis". He was

[1] Jean Lacouture in *Le Monde*, May 25–26, 1958.

then asked whether Soustelle represented General de Gaulle at Algiers; he said de Gaulle had not commissioned anybody to represent him. Finally, he was asked whether General Lorillot, the new Chief-of-Staff appointed by M. Pflimlin to succeed General Ely, was expected at Algiers. "No," said Lacheroy disdainfully, "Lorillot hasn't come to Algiers, and is not expected to come; and we aren't expecting anybody to come from Paris."[1]

What was cooking at Algiers during that Friday the 23rd and Saturday the 24th? They were disconcerting, all those threats and mysterious code messages from Radio-Algiers; equally puzzling were those cries of LES PARAS A PARIS! in the "Forum" of Algiers, as well as the dark hints dropped by official spokesmen, not only of the Committee of Public Safety, but also of General Salan himself. . . . What did this war of nerves portend? . . .

13. THE CONQUEST OF FRANCE BEGINS: THE CORSICA *PUTSCH*

ON THE eve of the Corsica *putsch* of Saturday, May 24—which was to precipitate the great *dénouement* within a week (and already on that Friday General Massu had declared: "In a week from now de Gaulle will be in power")—the "republican forces" in France were going through the classical motions of "republican defence" and of "calls for vigilance". The Socialist *Populaire* announced on Saturday morning the FORMATION IN METROPOLITAN FRANCE OF A NATIONAL COMMITTEE OF REPUBLICAN DEFENCE. This, it was explained, comprised the MRP, the Socialist Party, the Radical Party, the UDSR and a number of smaller formations (but not the Communists); and its purpose was to give "loyal and resolute support to the legal Government of the Republic in its struggle to maintain national unity, and to defend the republican institutions, republican freedoms and public order." The Committee included Pierre Commin and Maurice Deixonne (Socialists), P. H. Teitgen and M. Moisan (MRP), Daladier and Dulin (Radicals), Mitterrand (UDSR); it advocated "the creation of departmental 'republican defence and action committees'."

On the same day, the Communist *Humanité*, while announcing the formation of a variety of local "Vigilance Committees" which included the Communists (such committees had been formed at Toulouse, at Perpignan, at Belfort, and in a number of industrial enterprises), deplored that the Republican Defence Committee should have kept out the Communists.

[1] *France-Soir*, May 24, 1958.

Let's face it [wrote René Andrieu in the *Humanité* editorial]. You cannot defend the Republic without including all republicans in this defence. . . . Any Left-wing rally in France which is essentially anti-Communist can only be sterile, and can play only into the hands of those very Fascists whom it is supposed to fight. History has shown only too often that such disunity among the democratic forces has invariably paved the way for Dictators. . . .

And the *Humanité* contrasted the attitude of the "Republican Defence Committee" with that of M. Tanguy-Prigent, an ex-minister and now the virtual leader of the Left-wing of the Socialist Party who, on the previous day, had written in the *Monde*:

While passionately attached to the Republic and to democratic socialism, and while having been for thirty-three years a devoted and disciplined member of the Socialist Party, I still wish to express my deepest conviction: and that is that, at the present moment, *the defence of the Republic requires the coherent and resolute action of the ENTIRE working class.*

There were other significant statements on that Friday and Saturday: for example, that of M. Denis Forestier, Secretary-General of the National Union of Teachers, who warned against all the wire-pulling that was going on behind the scenes, and the purpose of which was to force the Republic "to abdicate in de Gaulle's favour by ostensibly 'legal' means."

It was the Whitsun week-end. As though smelling a rat, *L'Humanité* published at the top of its front page:

WHITSUN:
REMAIN MORE VIGILANT THAN EVER

It said that it was precisely during this holiday week-end that the Fascists might try out something. . . .

It was, indeed, during this Whitsun week-end that Algiers started its "conquest of France".

It was not till the Saturday evening that news from Corsica started pouring into Paris. Corsica—a department of Metropolitan France—was now in the hands of the Algiers Rebels.

At Ajaccio, Corte and Calvi Committees of Public Safety had been set up. Two hundred and fifty paratroopers, stationed in Corsica, had "supported" the movement, which had started that afternoon at Ajaccio.

The operation had been engineered from Algiers, and M. Arrighi, the Radical deputy, had been flown on his special "mission" to Corsica on that Saturday morning.

News from Corsica that reached Paris on Saturday night and Sunday morning was still fragmentary; but here were its main points:

Demonstrators, supported by 250 paratroopers stationed in the island, had occupied the Préfecture of Ajaccio and the *sous-préfectures* of Bastia and Corte. Committees of Public Safety, calling themselves, "Gaullist" had been set up in these and other cities.

Although at Bastia the deputy-mayor had refused to evacuate his office, and the population seemed by no means enthusiastic about what had happened, while many even booed the paratroopers, there had been no violence and bloodshed.

During the previous week there had been a number of Gaullist demonstrations at Ajaccio and a police commissioner, who had tolerated these, had been transferred to the north of France by M. Jules Moch, the Minister of the Interior. As a result, feeling was running high against Paris among the Right-wing elements at Ajaccio.

But, in any case, contacts between Algiers and Corsica had been numerous, and the *coup* had obviously been carefully engineered in advance, which may well explain the dark hints dropped during the previous days at Algiers by various spokesmen of the Committee of Public Safety.

So, early on the Saturday morning, M. Arrighi, accompanied by a *para* captain, had landed at Calvi from Algiers. He promptly established contact with the 250 *paras* stationed in the neighbourhood; in the afternoon a dozen trucks carried these men to Ajaccio, where several thousand people were in process of holding a Gaullist demonstration. When the paratroopers arrived, the crowds invaded the Préfecture and occupied other public buildings, and soon after a Committee of Public Safety was set up. The Prefect was "isolated" by the rioters.

These had met with no opposition from either the police or the *gendarmerie*. By the time M. Moch dispatched a company of CRS guards by air to Ajaccio in the evening of May 24, Ajaccio airport had already been occupied by the *paras*, and these simply disarmed the CRS men as they emerged from their transport plane.

The only real opposition came from the town council of Bastia which met under the presidency of the Deputy-Mayor, and sent a message of "republican loyalty" to M. Pflimlin.

The members of the various Committees of Public Safety in Corsica comprised numerous local politicians and businessmen, as well as several soldiers. Among these members was a nephew of General de Gaulle. They were later to be joined by some prominent figures from Algiers, notably a *para* colonel of May 13 fame—"leather-nose" Thomazo.[1] Having done his "job", M. Arrighi modestly declared at first that he would not become a member of any Corsican Committee of Public Safety, since "there were more important things for him now to do, both in Algiers and in Paris". But it was he who, on the Saturday evening, had

---

[1] He had had the bridge of his nose shot off in the Italian campaign in 1944 and the gap in his face was covered by a leather bandage.

read to the crowds outside the Préfecture of Ajaccio the following message sent to the Committee of Public Safety at Algiers:

The Committee of Public Safety set up at the Préfecture of Ajaccio sends its affectionate greetings to the Committee of Public Safety of Algeria and the Sahara and, expressing its fullest confidence in General Salan and M. Soustelle, demands the formation of a French Government of Public Safety, within the framework of the Republic, under the presidency of General de Gaulle.

The Corsican *putsch* created tremendous excitement in Algiers. The attitude to Paris became even more arrogant than before. General Salan informed General Lorillot, the new French chief of staff, that his visit to Algiers, on behalf of M. Pflimlin, was "undesirable". M. J. L. Vigier, a Right-wing Deputy who had come from Paris after seeing M. Pflimlin, tried in vain to see either Salan or Soustelle—neither would receive him. A spokesman of General Salan said that Algiers had no desire to receive any official, semi-official or even unofficial visitors from Paris until further notice. . . .

Soustelle, as already said, now at last took up an official position by becoming a member of the three-men "co-ordination committee" of the All-Algeria Committee of Public Safety, the other two members being General Massu and M. Sid Cara. Thus he identified himself officially with the "Algiers Movement".

But the most important consequence in Algiers of the Corsica *putsch* was in the realm of radio.

Already on the Friday a tremendous propaganda campaign had been launched. This took the form of a ceaseless succession of "appeals" to various parts of Metropolitan France. Corsican, Breton, Alsatian and other "regional" speakers, sometimes talking in dialect, were now calling on their kinsmen to set up committees of public safety. It was almost like the BBC during the war calling on the French Resistance to do this or that. After the Ajaccio *putsch*, Radio-Algiers became hysterically rapturous: "People of Corsica," it cried, "you have started something: you have started the Liberation of Metropolitan France." And so on, hour after hour, late into the night.

It also went in for mysterious "code" messages, which meant nothing, but were part of the war of nerves. These were chiefly the work of M. Roger Frey, a close associate of Debré's and Soustelle's, who had gone to Algiers some time before. Later, in 1959, he was to succeed Soustelle as Minister of Information.

Before dealing with the reactions in Paris to the Corsica *putsch*, it should be pointed out that, on that Saturday, a large part of official opinion was concerned not only about the Algerian situation generally but also, more specifically, about *the new threat of an attack on Tunisia.*

All Friday and Saturday French military planes, based in Algeria, had been flying all over Tunisia, one bomber flying over the Cap Bon area, north-east of Tunis itself, i.e. as far inside Tunisia as was geographically possible. Coming on top of the numerous incidents during the previous days (of which those at Gafsa airfield where five Tunisian soldiers were wounded by the crews of three French military planes were the most serious) the air incursions into Tunisia were considered by many as part of the Algiers junta's war of nerves with which they were hoping to speed up the formation of a de Gaulle Government in France. The Pflimlin Government was indeed being placed in the impossible position of having to deal with a new "Franco-Tunisian" crisis, which was being deliberately created by the men of Algiers over whom the Paris Government was losing the last remnants of even nominal control.

On the Friday, President Bourguiba in his weekly broadcast declared that "we have every reason to fear the worst", and Mr. Mongi Slim, the Tunisian Ambassador in Washington, handed to Mr. Hammerskjoeld a telegram from his Government calling his attention to the new dangers threatening Tunisia. The State Department, which received two visits from Slim, recommended "calm" to the Tunisians, being obviously afraid of taking a strong stand which might "provoke" the Algiers junta, whose coup of May 13 (Washington realized only too well) could at least to a large extent be traced back to American "interference" in North Africa at the time of the Murphy Mission.

Further, there were, as already said, reports from Algiers speaking of the threatening attitude Salan was adopting towards Tunisia. While he denied that he was preparing to "ride into Tunis", he now was reported to have said that he was not going to stand any more nonsense from the Tunisians and their Algerian friends—which was interpreted in Paris as meaning that there might be another "Sakhiet" raid at any moment. Extremist organizations were meantime calling on the military to "clean up the Algerian rebel hideouts in Tunisia", while the 15,000 French troops still stationed (in a humiliating "self-interned" condition) in Tunisia were now being constantly urged by Algiers propaganda to "break out".

The Pflimlin Government had more than enough worries of every kind on its hands; but, on the eve of the Corsica *putsch*, these new complications with Tunisia were threatening to become its biggest worry of all. Maybe Salan was not ready to "saddle his horse to ride into Tunis", but there were plenty of men among both soldiers and civilians in Algeria who had daydreamed for a long time about the "reconquest of Tunisia", and who were certainly all in favour of bigger and better Sakhiets. . . .

And besides Tunisia, Paris noted, one of the latest slogans now current in Algiers was "*Get the paratroopers to Paris!*" M. Moch was already, in all seriousness, beginning to worry about such an attempt to "conquer Paris from the air". In short, it looked on that Saturday that everything was being done in Algiers to frighten the Paris Government into sur-rendering to de Gaulle. There were rumours on the Saturday that (despite the police ban) large-scale Gaullist demonstrations were being prepared for the week-end in the Champs-Elysées. Meantime Pinay and others were urging Pflimlin to "establish contact" with de Gaulle. . . .

But let it be said at once—and this is extremely significant—that, *to the vast majority of people in Paris, the thing that mattered most was—the Whitsun week-end*. Eight hundred thousand people were reckoned to have left the capital, partly by train, but mostly by car, between the Friday night and the Sunday morning. It was hot and sunny on that Whit-Sunday. The radio, of course, had taken a very grave view of the Corsica *putsch*; Pflimlin had given a stern and blood-curdling broadcast on Corsica in his best disciplinarian manner; and yet, on that Whit-Sunday Paris looked as if nothing had happened at all. It was just a major holiday, and that was all. I spent most of the afternoon at the Bois de Vincennes, which, unlike the Bois de Boulogne, is essentially "working class". Here were the usual thousands of working-class families sitting on the grass with their litres of *rouge* and their sausage and *paté* sandwiches. There were thousands of others that day at the Vincennes zoo. I particularly re-member the scene when a monkey snatched a small girl's handbag, after which the attendant had to climb over the barrier and chase the monkey up the artificial rocks; the people roared with laughter as he finally caught the monkey and took the bag away from it, and then thumbed his nose at the disconcerted animal. These people didn't look as though they were preparing to die on the barricades in a few days. At the Porte Dorée outside the Bois, the café terraces were packed by holiday crowds; nobody was reading a paper. At the *métro* entrance a young man was distributing Communist leaflets calling for working-class unity in the face of the Fascist conspiracy of Algiers and de Gaulle; most people didn't even read them, and just dropped them on the *métro* stair, littered with these yellow leaflets which, after being well trampled on, began to look like autumn leaves. . . .

14. PARIS: THE GREAT SCARE STARTS— JACQUES DUCLOS' INDISCRETIONS

WHEREAS the public seemed extraordinarily indifferent to what was happening (and hadn't most people already decided that a de Gaulle Government would soon be in office, anyway, so why worry?) the unfortunate Pflimlin Government seemed to have been electrified into action by the Corsica *putsch*.

On the day before this *putsch* Pflimlin had given a rather incongruous broadcast on the urgent, the terribly urgent need of an immediate constitutional reform—a "Gaullist reform without de Gaulle".

"In these hours of anxiety," he began, "I know that many of you doubt the value of our institutions. Great changes are necessary. But they must be carried out in the midst of order and legality."

Legality—the magic word, the last straw to which Pflimlin kept on clinging.

"It would be intolerable," he continued, "if a minority tried to impose its will on France. Frenchmen, both in France and in Algeria, must realize that all must remain united in their respect of the laws of the Republic."

He again referred to the deplorable fact that, in the last year, France had been without a government for three months.

That is why I announced in my Ministerial Declaration that a thorough reform of the State would be carried out within six months. But today it is obvious that we must act much more quickly. It is in the next few days that we must transform our institutions. . . . The Government today tabled a Bill the main features of which were agreed upon at yesterday's Council of Ministers. Our simple object is to give duration and authority to the Government of the Republic.

First, authority:

Parliament will be able to give the Government the broadest powers. But these powers must not be subject to constant discussion and haggling. . . . So the Government shall have the power of veto to oppose to any parliamentary move liable to interfere with the execution of its programme.

Second, durability:

A government cannot do much if it is likely to last only a few months. This instability lowers our credit abroad, and it is also one of the chief reasons for the Algerian crisis. Every time the Government changes, our Algerian fellow-countrymen fear a change of policy. . . . Under our Bill, a government can no longer be overthrown except on a motion designating and setting up its successor. A Cabinet crisis cannot in these conditions be provoked by a motley coalition [of Right-wingers and Communists] who can only destroy, but are incapable of jointly constructing anything.

After a passing reference to the Communists who did not belong to the "national" community, and whom therefore he didn't want in any Government, Pflimlin ended on the usual note of "republican legality" and "republican unity".

Maybe he thought that, after this effort, he'd have a relatively quiet week-end, in the course of which he would prepare for the Constitutional Reform debate on Tuesday. But it was not to be.

By the Saturday afternoon news of trouble in Corsica reached the Government; and by the evening there was no longer any doubt of what had happened. Again, on the Sunday morning, Pflimlin resorted to the microphone. His main point was that if the Algiers rebellion was "understandable", there was no excuse at all for the Corsica *putsch*.

I feel obliged on this holiday, which should be a day of peace and joy, to address to you an appeal of the utmost gravity.

After briefly describing what had happened in Corsica, where "certain civil and military elements had substituted themselves for the legal authorities," he said:

The Algerian crisis could be largely explained by popular emotion, which was respectable in so far as it expressed the will of our countrymen in Algeria to remain French. The recent Franco-Moslem fraternizations even gave rise to the hope that this Algerian crisis, though alarming in other respects, might help to build a new Algeria.
That is why the Government, despite the reprehensible attitude of certain persons, has tried to re-establish normal relations between France and Algeria. That is why the Army and the population continue to be supplied with all they need. . . .

But Corsica? No—

Corsica—that's very different. Nothing there can justify the action taken by a handful of rebels. Today it is clear that a number of misguided Frenchmen have taken the law into their own hands and are now threatening our public liberties.
The Government, the defender of the legal order, therefore orders all soldiers and civil servants to take no orders from the illegal committees who have usurped power in Corsica.

Legal action, Pflimlin said, would be taken against anyone who had taken part in the Corsica *putsch*.

There is only one way of averting the danger: you must all rally to the Government which will defend public order, civil peace and the republican unity of the nation against all their enemies, whoever they may be.

And then came the clear warning that Corsica represented a threat of strife and civil war to the whole of Metropolitan France:
Already on the Saturday night a Cabinet council had met at the Hôtel

Matignon; on the Sunday evening a ministerial council was called to meet at the Elysée. Parliament, which was not to meet till the Tuesday to discuss the Constitutional Reform Bill, was now called to meet on Monday—for the specific purpose of raising the parliamentary immunity of M. Pascal Arrighi, one of the men who had engineered the Corsica *putsch*. Other stern disciplinary measures were decided upon against other persons, civil and military, responsible for what had happened in Corsica.

But again people wondered—how could these threats be carried out? On the Sunday, there were rumours of a battleship landing "loyal" troops in Corsica; then the rumour was denied. . . . Were there any "loyal" troops left to be sent anywhere? When Moch later proposed to send the battleship *De Grasse* to Corsica, and to land troops there, Pflimlin turned down the proposal as "appallingly dangerous".

On the Sunday morning, a press censorship was set up. Also, the Government decided to jam Radio-Algiers, whose mysterious code messages to various local authorities in Metropolitan France were beginning to worry people in the Midi.

The radio war, the jamming and the press and radio censorship, if anything, increased nervousness; for, after what had happened in Corsica, there were now persistent rumours of Committees of Public Safety having been set up in Marseille, in Toulouse, and many other places. How true was all this? People started wondering. . . . But one thing is certain: except for a tiny lunatic fringe, nobody in France was "longing for the paratroopers"—regardless of what M. Debré was to say about it a few weeks later.

It was Corsica that lent fantastic speed to the *dénouement* of the drama that had opened on the 13th of May.

Radio-Marseille went out of its way to broadcast statements by Corsican Deputies and other Corsican personalities in France, disavowing the Corsican *putsch*, but that didn't change anything in Corsica, now under paratroop rule.

The Assembly met in a feverish atmosphere on the following day, May 26. M. Pflimlin repeated almost word for word what he had already said on the radio the day before, but concluded on a slightly new note:

If certain Frenchmen doubted the existence of a conspiracy against the republican institutions, the events of Ajaccio must have been an eye-opener to them.

And now came the warning and—the confession of weakness.

I feel it my duty to tell Parliament that similar things may happen in other parts of France. That is why the Government, which must take responsibility for everything, and, in doing so, must weigh all the aspects of a problem, has not yet decided, for the present, to send new forces to Corsica to restore law and order. . . .

And he strengthened still more this feeling of helplessness by saying that, at a time like this, it was insufficient for the Government to do its duty; "to avert the danger had now become the business of the whole nation".

It sounded firm—and, at the same time, ambiguous. What was Pflimlin trying to suggest? A *levée en masse* of everybody, including the working class, against the "Fascist menace"?

And then—again he said that to demonstrate "the vitality of the Republic", it was essential that Parliament pass the Constitutional Reform Bill without delay. . . .

But the immediate problem was to raise the parliamentary immunity of M. Pascal Arrighi.

M. Deixonne, for the Socialists, solemnly declared that "the hour of Resistance had struck". (*Loud cheers on Left, Extreme Left and on some Centre benches; laughter on Right.*) He then dealt with the specific case of M. Arrighi and asked whether the Corsican Deputy had not been mixed up with the criminal plot last year to assassinate General Salan—a reference to the famous "bazooka affair".

M. Mendès-France: You had better ask M. Lacoste about that!

In the subsequent discussion, the two men to dot the i's were M. Mitterrand and the Communist leader, Jacques Duclos.

Mitterrand argued against Pflimlin's determination to treat the Algiers rebellion and the Corsica *putsch* as two distinct matters; the Corsica *putsch* was, surely, merely the second act of the same operation.

The Communists who, up till now, had been satisfied with their rather passive role of supporters of the "republican legality" represented by Pflimlin and his Government, now apparently decided that the situation was too serious to mince words any longer.

So Duclos started with the (not unnatural) question—"Why only Arrighi? Why not also Soustelle, Dronne, Le Pen, Demarquet and Berthommier—who are openly supporting the Algiers rebellion?"

Let us put an end to the fiction that the French nation is benevolently disposed towards the Algerian conspiracy. The truth is that the attack made in Corsica against the Republic by a bunch of Fascists and paratroopers clearly shows the real nature of the Algiers rebellion. . . . Only the other day General Massu boasted to an English journalist about the "means of persuasion" he could use in France itself to get rid of the Pflimlin Government.

How is it conceivable that, in these conditions, the French Government should continue to send more soldiers to Algeria whom the rebellious generals could then use for plunging France into civil war?

He then remarked that large transport planes, double-decker Bréguets, had latterly been transporting large numbers of paratroopers from Algiers to Orly, Marseille and Toulouse airports. The explanation that these were merely soldiers on leave was unconvincing.

We cannot but stress the responsibility of the Massu-Soustelle-Sid Cara triumvirate and that of General Salan who, when he talks about "marching up the Champs-Elysées", means that the Algerian Army is going to be used for strangling public freedoms in France.

And then came this fundamental criticism of Pflimlin:

If the situation is so serious, it is because the Government would not look facts in the face. M. Pflimlin has gone out of his way to excuse, to legitimize, as it were, the Algiers rebellion; and he has declared himself confident in General Salan, the very Salan about whom Massu said the other day: "Salan is sole boss here, and he will remain it until we have achieved our ends—which is the formation of a Government of Public Safety in Paris." And the head of this Government, according to the Algiers rebels, is to be General de Gaulle who has "covered" the Algiers rebellion and is now suggestively silent about the criminal Ajaccio operation. . . .
The Government goes on behaving as though there were no declared enemies of the Republic inside the Army. And what about the *paras* who staged the Corsica *coup*?

Duclos now went on to say that the South of France itself was threatened by important paratroop concentrations in various points, particularly at Mont-de-Marsan, at Pau, at Tarbes, "not to mention Bordeaux, where its Mayor, M. Chaban-Delmas, is one of the main culprits of the Algiers conspiracy." . . . It was Chaban-Delmas, as Minister of Defence, who had done so much to prepare the May 13 rebellion. . . .

If the plotters, all the plotters are to be prosecuted, here is a name to remember. . . . But the Government isn't doing anything. Instead of concentrating on the real danger points, M. Pflimlin keeps on alluding to some imaginary danger coming from the extreme Left.

Duclos was now going to say what he had to say; there wasn't much time to lose:

And I want to stress with the deepest regret that by placing obstacles in the way of a real unity of the working class and of the democratic forces of the country, the Socialist leaders are, to all intents and purposes, playing into the hands of those who, trading on our divisions, intend to inflict on France a military and Fascist dictatorship. . . .

Then he warned the Government that it was in no position to rely solely on the Army and the Police to defend the Republic; these forces were full of Gaullists. . . . "What happened in Corsica in this respect must make you think." . . . There the Prefect had taken no notice of either the Algiers propaganda addressed to Corsica, or the warnings he had received from the democratic forces here. He had prohibited a Communist demonstration, and merely relying on the Police to maintain law and order, he had got nowhere.

"Yet it is only with the help of the people that you can defend the Republic effectively."

M. *Antoine Guitton* (Right): And what happens when you turn the guns on the people, as you did in Budapest?

Duclos preferred to ignore the remark. Instead, he again said that the Republic could not be effectively defended if only too many of the "republican defence committees" that had latterly been set up, continued to exclude from them the Communist rank-and-file.

Without the people standing behind the Communist Party, you cannot effectively resist the rebel onslaught against the republican institutions. . . .

Now, this morning M. Pflimlin very rightly said that it was necessary to rouse the nation. But it's no use treating [Communist] republicans on the same footing as Fascist rebels.

We are up against the following choice: either the Government will put up an unconvincing show of resistance against the conspiracy; or else it will make a genuine effort to break it; but this it can only do with the co-operation of the entire working class and the entire nation. And if the Government fails to do this, then the working class cannot remain indifferent and will not allow the Fascists to attack our provincial cities with the help of the paratroopers. . . .

M. *Fernand Bone* (Right): The people don't give a hang. . . .

M. *Duclos:* In these grave hours, inaction becomes complicity. The clandestine committee of General Chassin, which is said to be hiding in a château near Mont-de-Marsan, is calling for an armed uprising. . . . Things are too serious for discussing constitutional reforms. Such a discussion now would make Paris look like another Byzantium, splitting hairs while the enemy is at the gates. . . .

And Duclos warned the Assembly against allowing de Gaulle to use the Army as Franco had used his to enslave Spain. He spoke satirically of the so-called fraternization in Algeria, and said that the war there was continuing just as before.

What is more, with those adventurers in Algiers, there is a danger that it might spread to Tunisia and the rest of North Africa.

And again he spoke of Bordeaux; it was reported, he said, that arms were being distributed among the Fascist elements there; a certain General Lecoq was involved; reserve officers were being told that something was going to happen in a few days. Similarly, at Clermont-Ferrand feverish Gaullist propaganda was going on amongst the troops; nor was the Air Force reliable; airmen in the district had made a habit of flying in Cross-of-Lorraine formation.

I wish to pay tribute to officers and NCO's who are loyally devoted to the Republic; but what are they to think when they see other officers and NCO's openly adhering to de Gaulle—and with complete impunity?

After quoting some violent attacks against the Government that had appeared in Army papers published in Algeria—which were demanding the immediate departure of Pflimlin (just as several Right-wing speakers in the debate had done shortly before)—Duclos concluded that "both from Algiers and from Corsica, the threads lead straight to Colombey-les-deux-Eglises. The Committees of Public Safety at Toulouse and elsewhere were supposed to have been dissolved by Moch, the Minister of the Interior; but nothing had been done."

The Prefects say they have no instructions for dealing with these people who are preparing to become the Serafinis and the Maillots of other centres. . . . At Lyon a certain Thomas, a local Fascist chief, held a meeting at 3 p.m. on Saturday where it was decided that all the Left-wing members of Parliament in the Rhône department would be assassinated. . . .
There is a lack of enthusiasm about defending the Republic not only amongst the Prefects, but also amongst the police forces. Thus at Clermont-Ferrand the military headquarters received a communication from a CRS officer at Lyon to say that "on no account would the CRS intervene against the Army". The same thing happened at Lille—which just shows that the paratroop operation of Ajaccio might succeed in other places, too.[1]

As against this, Duclos tried to show that there was still plenty of republican fervour amongst numerous reserve officers and former FFI men, some of whom, for example, had offered their services to the Prefect of the Rhône. Similarly, the CGT trade unions were ready to resist.
Yet even Duclos admitted that the "contagion coming from above" was dangerous.

Only through its irresolution will the Republic perish. It will perish if this irresolution, this fear and this fatalism were to spread to the popular masses.

He ended, however, with the usual flourish by saying that Resistance would come from the people, who would not allow the Republic to be crushed. But this conventional ending sounded singularly unconvincing

---

[1] All this closely tallied with information that became available later of plans like General Miquel's "Operation Resurrection"—providing for the occupation of Paris, on May 27–28, by paratroopers brought from S.W. France and Algeria, and by 20,000 police and CRS men.

in the light of what he had said during the previous hour. For, in fact, he had made it amply clear that *the Government could no longer rely on either the Army or the Police.* A point which Jules Moch was fully to confirm a few weeks after the capitulation of the Fourth Republic.

Several Right-wing speakers in the debate—notably M. Frédéric-Dupont—were obviously gloating over the Government's discomfiture, and kept urging it to resign, and make room for de Gaulle.

M. Tixier-Vignancour even went so far as to ask why the Government was taking action against M. Pascal Arrighi, who had, after all, done no more than travel to Corsica from Algiers in a military plane which came under the authority of General Salan—who was the representative of the Pflimlin Government!

Tixier-Vignancour was hugely enjoying the joke.

M. Pflimlin, while dodging the question of Soustelle and other "rebel" Deputies, said it was essential to take action against Arrighi, "in the name of public order and republican legality".

Having said his piece, M. Pflimlin then left the Assembly.

When finally, after a quarrelsome discussion, the parliamentary immunity of M. Arrighi was raised by 396 votes to 175, a Poujadist Deputy called Pelat, addressing the Assembly, shouted:

You're a bunch of swine.
The President of the Assembly: Really, Monsieur Pelat . . .
M. Pelat: I repeat, there are plenty of bastards here.
The President: Monsieur Pelat, I call you to order.
M. Pelat: I don't give a f——!
The President: My call to order will be recorded in the minutes.

Then it nearly came to a fight, several Socialists rushing at the offender.

When a few minutes later it was proposed that the Assembly meet again on the following morning, M. Charles Hernu (Radical) suddenly said to M. Le Troquer, the President of the Assembly:

Mr. President, are you sure we can meet tomorrow morning?
The President: Why not?
M. Hernu: According to the latest news, the President of the Republic and M. Pflimlin are at present having a meeting with General de Gaulle at the château of Champs. And if this is true (and you may soon find out, Mr. President, whether it is) then, surely, it would be best if the Assembly continued to sit.
The President: I don't agree.

Then, after going over a number of routine matters and saying that the Assembly would meet again the next morning to discuss the Revision of the Constitution, M. Le Troquer declared the meeting closed at 8.40 p.m. on that 26th of May.

15. PFLIMLIN MEETS DE GAULLE

M. HERNU's facts were not quite accurate; but they had a basis of truth all the same. For that was the night on which de Gaulle came to Paris—to confer with Pflimlin.

Duclos had been quite right to stress the gravity of the situation; he knew that, within the next few hours, in view of what was going on in the Army and amongst the Police, Pflimlin would have to choose between genuine resistance—together with the Communists—and a deal with de Gaulle. . . .

The factor he perhaps minimized was that alluded to by one of his hecklers, who exclaimed: "The people don't give a hang!" This was an overstatement; but there seemed little doubt that the bulk of the working class were neither in a heroic nor a desperate mood; and that here, too, there was a tendency to avoid the de Gaulle = Fascism equation. . . .

The press the next morning (May 27) was really mysterious. The Right-wing *L'Aurore* came out with a banner headline:

> After receiving a visitor at Colombey
> DE GAULLE IS NOW IN PARIS

after which there was a large blank space with the word "censored" in the middle of it.

After that came more headlines:

> The [Right-wing] Independents ask President Coty to call a meeting of all the national leaders and General de Gaulle.

> Three Right-wing ministers of the Pflimlin Government have virtually resigned.

> Despite opposition of the CFTC and FO [the Catholic and Socialist trade unions]
> THE [Communist] CGT (alone)
> CALLS A GENERAL STRIKE FOR 2 P.M. TODAY

And so on.

The censored passage on the front page of *L'Aurore* obviously referred to the de Gaulle-Pflimlin meeting. But neither *L'Aurore* nor any other paper that morning referred to M. Hernu's sensational announcement at the Assembly's night sitting about the mysterious meeting "between de Gaulle and Coty".

The *Figaro*, significantly, criticized de Gaulle for allowing the country to "drift towards a Popular Front", whereas it would be so easy for him to say one word to condemn the Ajaccio coup—after which everybody would "respect law and order once again". And like several other papers, it gave the greatest prominence to a message from M. Robert Lacoste (whose role since he had left Algiers was highly ambiguous) to General de Gaulle in which he said that General Salan and other "non-political patriots" in Algeria "seemed to have lost control over a bunch of adventurers and certain wildly irresponsible officers".

At the time the Government was being formed I warned some of its members about it. The Corsican affair is a direct outcome of that state of things; it has been engineered by people who, already in the past, played a nefarious role in Algeria.

And he ended by appealing to de Gaulle to use his "high authority" to maintain law and order by openly condemning the Corsican adventure.

Here already was a member of the Socialist Party who was as good as admitting that not only the Government but even the Army leadership in Algeria had completely lost control, and that de Gaulle alone could now save the situation.

But during that whole morning Paris was rather bewildered. It was living in a sort of news blackout, and no paper would at first give the slightest hint of what de Gaulle had done during the six or seven hours he had spent in (or near) Paris, before returning to Colombey at 4.45 a.m.

No one was taking the Constitutional Reform, which the Assembly was to debate that morning, seriously any longer. The night before, M. Paul Coste-Floret, *rapporteur* of the Constitutional Reform Bill Resolution, when asked what was going to happen about this "Bill", which was supposed to cut the ground from under the feet of de Gaulle, merely said: "Be your age. Things have got much too serious for messing about with that sort of thing." In other words, the Fourth Republic had already missed the bus, and it was too late for it to start reforming itself. . . . This lengthy business of constitutional reform would have to be left till more quiet times, or else be left to—de Gaulle. . . . Nevertheless, the Assembly met that morning in all seriousness, intending to pass the Reform Resolution.

All that the general public knew during that Tuesday morning was that de Gaulle had received a visit, on the previous day, from M. Diebold, Prefect of the Haute-Marne, after which the General had come to Paris on his mysterious visit.

And then, in the early afternoon, came the big de Gaulle bombshell: the statement that he had "embarked on the regular process of forming a Government".

As I wrote in my notebook that Tuesday afternoon:

So he *is* forming a government! Quick work! For he hasn't gone through any of the protocol required for forming a government. *What mystery is behind all this???* Not only did he see Pflimlin last night but, apparently, Mollet, too. What's more, he has in fact responded to Lacoste's appeal; for his statement is an implicit disavowal of the Corsican *putsch*. He asks, in fact, that nothing of the same sort should be done in any other place. And, as though he were *already* head of the Government, he "places his confidence" in General Salan and in the naval and Air Force chiefs in Algeria. Thus the Army, Navy and Air Force are made to look like respectable, moderating influences in France. . . . It would, indeed, be ironical if the wild men of Algiers were now to disavow de Gaulle! The *Monde* correspondent in Algiers writes today that de Gaulle would become "totally unacceptable" to these wild people if he entered into any sort of compromise arrangement with the Fourth Republic.

Curious, indeed, how at Ajaccio the rebels were already crying "*Vive Massu!*" rather than "*Vive de Gaulle!*" . . . And although there aren't many Communists in Corsica, the Communist Party has called upon them to start a Resistance movement. Perhaps of no great practical importance, but, tactically, a clever and significant move.

It's beginning to look as though de Gaulle were going to form his Government as quietly and peacefully as he wanted to form it.

Middle class people in the street look greatly relieved after the de Gaulle message—though they continue to be puzzled as to what is really behind it. Working class people seem fatalistic: "May be just as well if he prevents major trouble—at least for the present," a bus conductor told me. "And if Mollet has to take orders from de Gaulle now, it'll serve him damn well right."

Clearly, people *don't* want trouble and, in the last few days, especially since Corsica, there've been rather too many rumours about new "Ajaccio coups" being prepared all over the place, and about paratroopers "about to land in Paris". Apparently de Gaulle's message is partly calculated to prevent this.

Big question asked is "what kind of republican government will de Gaulle set up? Moderate at first, and thuggish later?" But, apart from the Communists who *are* worried, nobody wants to look too far ahead.

I must hand it to de Gaulle: he has a style which impresses people tremendously, and makes Pflimlin and Mollet and the rest of them look pretty puny.

Even "staunch republicans", I've noticed, are showing signs of a sort of Munich reflex—a mixture of cowardly relief and shame. . . .

This afternoon's strike was no great shakes. The working class are half-hearted. They don't trust the Government's republican ardour (small wonder). Who, indeed, wants to die (or even risk his job) for Pflimlin?

16. DE GAULLE: "I HAVE EMBARKED . . ." —POLICE AND ARMY REVOLT!

THE sequence of events on that Tuesday was truly baffling. The early editions of the evening papers were still full of mystery; thus *France-Soir* headlined:

DE GAULLE: Mysterious Conversations in Paris Last Night.

The rumour of a meeting with M. Pflimlin
has not been confirmed.
The General Returned to Colombey at 4.45 a.m.

But in the early afternoon *Paris-Presse* came out with:

DE GAULLE: "I AM ON THE WAY."

And there followed the famous statement which had been released by de Gaulle's secretariat at 12.30 p.m.:

I yesterday embarked on the regular process necessary for establishing a republican government, which would be able to maintain the unity and independence of the country.

I trust this process will continue and that, by staying calm and dignified, the country will show that it wishes this process to succeed.

In these conditions any action, wherever it may come from, which would disturb public order, risks to produce the gravest consequences. While making allowances for circumstances, I cannot approve of any such action.

I expect the land, sea and air forces to maintain the strictest discipline under the command of their chiefs, General Salan, Admiral Auboyneau and General Jouhaud. I express my confidence to these chiefs and intend shortly to establish contact with them.

And *Paris-Presse* added that Pflimlin, who had gone to the Elysée to see President Coty as soon as this de Gaulle message had been released, would see him again in the afternoon—after which the resignation of M. Pflimlin would become official. The paper then suggested that Pflimlin's resignation was, in any case, clearly implied in the de Gaulle statement.

And then it added this curious piece of information:

This spectacular acceleration in the succession of events is said to be due to a telegram from General Salan, in which he is said to have warned the President of the Republic that disasters could no longer be avoided if General de Gaulle were not called for immediately. It is even said that *certain very grave steps were going to be taken tonight.*

The Gaullist *Paris-Presse* had closer contacts with the de Gaulle headquarters than almost any other paper; and it was quite clear that behind this "speculative", "it-is-said-that" tone of this story, there were a number of hard facts. Facts which, indeed, already largely confirmed what Duclos had said at the National Assembly the night before: namely that the Police and Army had got out of hand, and that all sorts of *putsches* and paratroop landings in Metropolitan France—and perhaps even in Paris itself—*had now become a matter of hours.* Later, as we shall see, Jules Moch explained that if de Gaulle issued this statement at 12.30 p.m. on that Tuesday, it was not because he had *really* come to any agreement with Pflimlin about setting up the next Government, but because he had learned *through his own sources* that a *putsch* was being prepared for the following night (May 27–28), and that he felt that he alone could stop it

with a categorical statement that he was already "taking over". Later still
it was learned that on that night General Miquel was going to launch his
"Operation Resurrection".

And *Paris-Presse* published another singular story: It had asked
Pflimlin at noon whether he had seen de Gaulle; and Pflimlin had
answered categorically: "No." All night, it said, reporters had, indeed,
been racing round the various places where de Gaulle (who had vanished
from Colombey) and Pflimlin (who could be found neither at the
National Assembly nor at the Hôtel Matignon) might possibly be in
conference. Their search had been in vain. De Gaulle wasn't "re-
discovered" until he arrived back at Colombey at 4.45 a.m.

That Tuesday was another fantastic day at the National Assembly—
with one *coup de théâtre* after another. The morning session, it is true, could
not have been duller. Although everybody agreed that nothing was less
timely or opportune than an academic discussion on the faults and virtues
of the 1946 Constitution, the Pflimlin Government was determined to get
the *principle* of a thorough overhaul of the Constitution voted. Not—and
this soon became apparent—because M. Pflimlin was passionately
interested in demonstrating the good intentions of the Fourth Republic
to mend its evil ways, but because M. Pflimlin was—looking for a
convenient excuse to resign.

There was no fight left in the man; and now he was ready to hand over
to de Gaulle. And the main feature of the whole debate, especially after
de Gaulle's famous 12.30 p.m. message had become known—was the
duel between those who were saying that it was Pflimlin's duty to stay
and those who were saying it was his duty to go. He himself was anxious
to go; we shall presently see how he went about it.

To begin with, M. Pflimlin, after the historic night he had spent in the
company of General de Gaulle (though he still wouldn't admit that he
had seen him) said that, in the vote on the constitutional reform, he would
take no account of the Communist votes, despite the "surprising
solicitude" M. Duclos and other Communist speakers had shown for the
welfare and longevity of the Government. He wanted the principle of the
constitutional reform to be voted by "a republican and national
majority".

M. Ramadier (Socialist), without entering into the question whether
it was right or not to "count" or "not count" the Communist votes,
warned the Government against giving up at this juncture. What he
meant was that, if the Communist votes were not counted, there might
well be no "national and republican" majority to support the Government. For the bulk of the Right-wing Deputies were eagerly waiting for
the opportunity of handing M. Pflimlin the *hara-kiri* knife.

After M. le Troquer, the President of the Assembly, had read out the text of the Bill on which the vote was to take place later in the day, the meeting was adjourned from 11.40 a.m. to 4.30 p.m.[1]

But when the Assembly met at 4.30, M. Lecourt, the Minister of Justice, hastened to say that an extraordinary Cabinet meeting had been called a few minutes before, and that the Premier requested that the Assembly meet at 9 p.m.

M. Duclos then insisted on speaking.

M. Duclos: The latest statement of General de Gaulle is a matter of the utmost gravity. . . . This evening's *Monde* says: "This morning M. Pflimlin stated before the National Assembly that he would not count the Communist votes. . . . Since, in the circumstances, the outcome of the vote is highly uncertain, a Cabinet crisis may start this very evening." According to the same paper, M. Guy Mollet was also supposed to have seen General de Gaulle.

Numerous Socialists: It's untrue.

M. Duclos: I am simply quoting the paper.

M. Charles Lussy (Socialist): We deny it.

M. Duclos: I take note of your denial.

Duclos, Pierre Cot and others then started asking questions. What did the de Gaulle statement mean? With whom had he started "the regular process"; how could this "process" be started without the knowledge of the National Assembly, and without the President of the Republic having called on de Gaulle to form the next Government? Duclos then said that, having encouraged the rebellion against the Republic, de Gaulle was now preaching calm. What did all this mean?

M. Duclos: It is surely with the complicity of at least a few ministers that this attempt is now being made to impose on France a military and Fascist dictatorship. He is already speaking like a dictator, who had succeeded in usurping the powers of the Government. (*Cheers on Extreme Left, loud protests on Right*). . . . I ask you, is the Republic already dead?

Voices on Right: Yes!

M. Duclos: You heard what they said: they said Yes.

Voices on Right: De Gaulle au pouvoir! De Gaulle au pouvoir!

M. Mitterrand raised a different kind of question. He feared that, in the course of the Cabinet meeting now in progress, M. Pflimlin might resign.

M. Mitterrand: We voted him into office on the night of the 13th of May. He is bound to us by a contract. He must not try to sneak out by the back door. He must not go without our consent. . . . Oh, I know, such things have happened

---

[1] This Bill merely enumerated the articles of the Constitution which the Assembly "considered it necessary to revise": 9, 12 (par. 2), 13, 45, 48, 52, 92 (par. 3), as well as the following articles already in process of revision: 17, 49, 50, 51 and 90. These articles related to the changes M. Pflimlin had already outlined a few days before.

in the past. M. Briand had a way of giving up before a hostile vote had overthrown him; and M. Pinay did the same on one occasion in 1952. But in the present circumstances such a desertion by a Premier of his parliamentary majority would be dishonourable . . .

The Left were getting nervous.

However, in the end, M. Lecourt, the Minister of Justice, assured the Assembly that Pflimlin, having faced a more arduous fortnight than any Premier of the Fourth Republic, would not resign without having first appeared before the Assembly.

There was a nasty atmosphere at the Assembly that day. The entire Right were maliciously jubilant. As even *La Croix*, almost the official organ of the French Church hierarchy, wrote that afternoon:

The atmosphere at the Palais-Bourbon is truly horrible. All that is shadiest in French politics—the people representing Money (especially Algerian money), all those who "work" through the most dubious and corrupt deputies and the fishiest of journalists—all this scum is now suddenly proclaiming its passionate devotion to Gaullism. The old gang to whom de Gaulle was a revolutionary, others who deserted from de Gaulle's RPF are now jumping like so many fleas on the bandwagon. The tall stature of de Gaulle stands high above this filth, but his boots are spattered by it all the same. . . .

The Assembly had been so pressing that Pflimlin speak as soon as possible that it was agreed that it meet not at 9 p.m. but at 7 p.m.; however, when the Assembly met again at 7, Pflimlin was not yet available. M. Lecourt said that at 9 o'clock the Government would have a statement to make. Again there was nervousness. Duclos now wanted to make quite sure that there would be a discussion after this "statement"; the President of the Assembly assured him that there would be. . . .

17. WHAT WAS MOLLET PLAYING AT?

AT LAST came that famous night session, in the course of which a few more masks were dropped, and a good many cats let out of the bag. But before proceeding to tell this extraordinary story, it is essential to refer to an important episode that evening: *the anti-de Gaulle stand taken by an overwhelming majority of the Socialists*. The *comité directeur* and the parliamentary group of the Socialist Party met first in the afternoon, soon after the de Gaulle statement had become known. Mollet was present at the early part of the meeting. He explained why the "highest authorities" in the country had found it necessary to establish contact with de Gaulle. He described the grave dangers of the situation, and commented on the relative weakness of the "republican defence reflex", as revealed hitherto. He naturally also warned the Party against any *rapprochement* with the Communists. He even added that, in his opinion, de Gaulle had no intention of abolishing public freedoms in France.

After a brief discussion, the meeting was adjourned, but it was resumed soon afterwards. Feeling against de Gaulle was running high. After two further hours of discussion the Socialist group adopted a motion saying that it was essential for the Pflimlin Government "to remain at its post as long as it enjoyed the confidence of the majority of the National Assembly" (this meant, in effect, that the Communist votes must also be "counted"); and that *on no account* would they support the candidature of General de Gaulle.

"The very form in which he has raised the question, together with the considerations surrounding it, is and will remain in all conditions a challenge to republican legality."

This motion was carried by 112 votes to 3—the only ones to oppose it being MM. Boutbien, Marezatti and Juvenal. But, as already said, M. Mollet wasn't there to vote one way or the other. . . . This motion was going to have a very curious sequel.[1]

But to return to the National Assembly. The night session was, in effect, a major battle between the joint forces of the Gaullists (Triboulet, Bidault,[2] Lipkowski), Fascists (Dides, Damasio) and Right-wingers (Pierre André) on the one hand, and a (for once) more-or-less united Left (Socialists, Communists, Progressistes, and Left-Centre men like Mitterrand) on the other.

The ones were saying that Pflimlin must go; the others that Pflimlin must stay.

It all started with the long-awaited statement from Pflimlin.

At 4 p.m. yesterday, May 26, [he began] I received a message from General de Gaulle proposing a meeting which, he said, had become necessary in view of the exceptionally grave dangers threatening the country. I accepted his offer, and the meeting took place last night.

I agreed, because I felt it my duty not to reject an opportunity of saving our country from civil war. (*Cheers on Centre benches.*)

I asked General de Gaulle to use his moral authority to call to order those who were perhaps tempted to start an insurrection against the republican order. I did not, however, obtain, by the time the meeting ended, any assurance from General

[1] The account of the first part of the meeting, with Mollet's statement, was published in some Right-wing papers, notably in *L'Aurore* (May 28) but neither in the Socialist *Populaire*, nor in the Communist *Humanité* of the same day—which was to be a great day of "democratic resistance".

[2] Bidault, though a member of the MRP, had officially declared himself "for de Gaulle" a few days before. In the vote that night he abstained, instead of voting for Pflimlin, as nearly all the other MRP members did.

de Gaulle that he would take an immediate public stand. . . . The 12 o'clock statement came to my knowledge after it had been made public. . . .

Pflimlin expressed his gratitude to de Gaulle for the statement he had published. He then said that de Gaulle had repeated to him that he would consider taking power only by legal means.

He was willing to "meet the political leaders who would like to examine with him the conditions in which a government under his leadership could be invested".

The rest of Pflimlin's speech was deliberately ambiguous. He assured the Assembly that the Government was determined "not to create a power vacuum", and that it was to the Assembly only that he would return "the powers with which it had entrusted him". But—he attached the greatest importance to the vote on the Constitutional Reform Proposal that night; and he repeated that he was appealing "only to the Republican and national majority". With a flourish he ended by saying that it was for the Assembly to "make a decisive choice of the road the country was to follow". The Socialists and the MRP cheered thinly. Then came a voice, somewhere from the Left: "Tartuffe!" There were, of course, angry protests from the Right and from the MRP, but many felt, all the same, that, on this occasion, Pflimlin's nobly vague words were merely wrapping up the clear and precise intention of passing the buck to somebody else at the first opportunity.

Very strange was the speech of old man Ramadier. He was, to begin with, met with a storm of booing from the Right. Ramadier, though a man of no great significance, nevertheless had a way of impersonating the better qualities of the Third Republic, of its old *lutte républicaine*; he had already distinguished himself as a defender of this old Republican spirit back in October 1947, after de Gaulle's great victory in the municipal elections.[1] In the name of republican legality, he had then defied de Gaulle and his RPF, saying that the Third Force could stand up both to the Communists and to the Gaullists, who had no constitutional right to replace in any way the regularly elected National Assembly. Now again he appealed to Pflimlin not to give up:

For you to give up at this hour would be the most disquieting, the most terrifying thing to do from the standpoint of the country's future. You feel the terrible weight of the burden on your shoulders; but you realize the sacred value of that burden. Believe me, if we want to demonstrate the country's will to save itself, then we must do it through the normal workings of our institutions. . . . Even under the pressure of physical violence it would still be your duty not to give up. (*Cheers on Left, Extreme Left and Centre.*) . . . We shall be with you to defend the Republic till final victory.

[1] See the author's *France 1940–1955*, pp. 376–7.

To the advocates of Pflimlin's resignation, Ramadier's noble "Third Republic" speech was just a lot of blah. They were going to make things difficult for Pflimlin—and also for some of his ministers; they were ready for a showdown.

M. Bidault wanted to know a little more about the talks with de Gaulle. The papers, he said, had also suggested that Mollet had seen the General.

M. Guy Mollet: I am glad you are not more categorical about it. I must tell you that the story of my meeting with General de Gaulle is wholly untrue.

M. Georges Bidault: All the same, it seems obvious that General de Gaulle did not come to Paris without somebody having asked him to do so. . . . We should like to have an explanation from the Government. . . . Also, it would be absurd to imagine that the phrase he used in his statement today could have been used without his having received from the Government certain requests and assurances. . . . At least one or more members of the Government must be at the back of it. . . .

The suggestion underlying Bidault's statement was, of course, that the Government had already, in fact, handed over to de Gaulle.

The man who then proceeded to dot the i's was a Gaullist deputy, M. Jean de Lipkowski. The Government, he said, had shown its utter helplessness in trying to control the situation. To prevent the Army from "doing something irreparable" it had had to appeal to General de Gaulle.

If you had to ask General de Gaulle to intercede to protect you against your own legions, it means that you can no longer get the Army to obey you.

He concluded that there was only one solution for France: de Gaulle at once.

Duclos (Communist) started by saying that Pflimlin had really been "rather too laconic" in his story about his meeting with de Gaulle. An operation had now started, he said, to create a halo of "legality" round de Gaulle. It was the same old story again: the story of Hindenburg and Hitler and his Blackshirts (*sic*), the story of Weygand, whose troops had forced Parliament to surrender to Pétain in June 1940. . . .

Now Pflimlin, said Duclos, was longing to get out. He had chosen the Constitutional reform as a good excuse for doing so; whether the Reform Proposal was voted tonight or not, whether it was voted in the normal way, or whether he didn't count the Communist votes, he was still determined to quit. But, of course, Pflimlin would find it much easier if the Reform Proposal were simply rejected by a hostile vote from both the Right and the Communists:

Then, M. Pflimlin, it would be very, very simple for you to hand in your resignation. You would have your perfect alibi. But we are *not* going to give you that alibi, and we are going to vote for you! (*Loud cheers on Extreme Left.*)

6

In doing so, we are not thinking of the Government of M. Pflimlin, but of that majority in this Assembly—a majority which we must preserve, so that it may give the country a Government other than one under General de Gaulle.

M. Raymond Triboulet, the next speaker, represented the "pure" Gaullist case. Like Lipkowski before him, he poked fun at the Government. M. Pflimlin had said he would not create a "power vacuum". "Yes—but where's the *power?*" he asked.

Mme Duvernois (Communist): It's in the people.
M. Triboulet: M. Pflimlin, what *can* you do in the present situation?
Mme Vermeersch (Communist): Call on the people!
M. Pierrard (Communist): Arrest the plotters.
M. Ramette (Communist): Put *you*, Triboulet, in jail!
M. Triboulet: Yes, you can make speeches, and interrupt, and heckle, and threaten and condemn, but how are you going to enforce your energetic intentions? The burden on your shoulders to which M. Ramadier referred a few minutes ago—this burden, M. Pflimlin, is far too heavy for you to carry!

And, with an air of triumph, M. Triboulet added:

Take Corsica, for instance. What can you do about it, Monsieur Pflimlin? Let's face it—you can do *absolutely nothing!*

And he ended by saying that he and his friends would vote against the Government, because "the road along which M. Ramadier was proposing to take the Government could only lead to a Communist dictatorship".

Pierre Cot (Progressiste) also argued that the Government ought to remain in office. The "regular process" which de Gaulle had embarked on over the head of the President of the Republic was completely irregular. Also, it was impossible for the Government of the Republic to surrender to the Army; every Frenchman had learned at school that the most elementary duty of the Army was to obey; the Army's betrayal of this elementary rule could not be condoned by any government.

When the ship is in danger, the captain must not leave it—even if he happens to dislike certain parts of its cargo.

The "cargo" meant the Communists.

M. Pierre André (Right) and other speakers again wanted to know a little more about how de Gaulle had been induced to come to Paris. Hadn't M. Maurice Schumann been sent by M. Pflimlin himself to see him? M. Hernu (a close associate of M. Mendès-France) wanted to know what exactly Guy Mollet had been up to.

At last Pflimlin spoke. And here came a little bombshell:

M. Mollet is not here at the moment, but I don't want to lose any time, so I may tell you right now that this morning M. Mollet handed me the text of a letter he had sent to General de Gaulle.

Voices on Left: Oh! Listen to this!

M. Charles Lussy (Socialist) who, poor man, was trying to "cover" Mollet, exclaimed: "In this letter he merely refused to meet de Gaulle."

M. Pflimlin: I haven't the authority to disclose to you the contents of this letter. I shall simply summarize its conclusion—which was a pressing appeal to General de Gaulle urging him to be good enough to use his moral authority to call to order those who had rebelled against the law.

At this point the Socialists, who only a few hours before had almost unanimously decided to have nothing to do with de Gaulle, looked distinctly uncomfortable.

M. Pflimlin: As for other questions asked, it is quite true that I authorized M. Maurice Schumann yesterday morning to go to see General de Gaulle. But this visit did not take place, because meantime the General had asked the Prefect of the Haute-Marne to go and see him, and handed him a letter addressed to me. By 4 p.m. M. Diebold arrived in Paris and handed me this message.

It was in this message that de Gaulle offered to meet Pflimlin that night. Pflimlin again thanked de Gaulle for having shown his determination to preserve peace in France. . . .

A few minutes later the Assembly was called upon to vote on the Constitutional Reform Resolution, and the Pflimlin Government "won" by 408 votes to 165.

Which gave it the extremely handsome majority of 243. But, since the 408 votes included only 266 "national votes" (the rest being Communists), and since without them the "constitutional majority" of 296 votes had not been attained, Pflimlin could argue that he had been "defeated"—with 408 votes in his favour! However, it was awkward, and, as Duclos had said, M. Pflimlin had not been given a really convenient alibi for getting out.

18. THE POPULAR FRONT THAT FAILED

THEN came Wednesday, May 28, the day of the great "anti-Fascist" march between the Place de la Nation and the Place de la République. On the face of it, it was a day like any other. It was cool and sunny that morning. In the rue Halévy I could watch the usual shopping crowds pouring into the Galeries Lafayette to buy their summer clothes and their holiday equipment.

That morning the Right-wing press was expressing the "fervent" hope that de Gaulle's advent would now be only a matter of a few days. The *Figaro* headlines ran:

> M. PFLIMLIN HAS VIRTUALLY RESIGNED
> after refusing to count the Communist votes on the reform of
> the Constitution.

All the same, it was rather worried:

> It is not without anguish that we noted the fragility of de Gaulle's chances of being invested—after certain spectacular new positions had been taken up. Everybody who feels that there is only one man who can now avert the terrible dangers threatening the country are wondering today whether the Socialist Party, which almost unanimously rejected this last hope of salvation, is not taking a terrible responsibility.
>
> In Parliament yesterday the Popular Front movement showed signs of making dangerous progress; it must be said that certain equivocal statements by General de Gaulle played into the hands of these people. . . .

And it ended with a warning to the Socialists to "remember Poland", "remember Czechoslovakia".

L'Aurore was equally worried, and now screamed that there was only one hope: President Coty must IMMEDIATELY call on de Gaulle. Had it been tipped off that something was going to happen at the Elysée—that President Coty, scared of a revival of the Popular Front, was planning a decisive move?

Highly interesting that morning was the Left-wing press. The whole back page of the Socialist *Le Populaire* was made to look like a poster.

VIVE LA RÉPUBLIQUE!

> The Republic is in Danger; our freedoms are threatened! Workers, republicans and democrats, you must all respond to the appeal addressed to you by the National Action and Republican Defence Committee.
>
> All of you must come at 5 p.m. today, May 28, to demonstrate your determination not to make any deal with any dictatorship, and to reaffirm your attachment to the Republican Régime and to democratic freedoms.

The appeal was signed by the Socialist Party, the MRP, the Radical Party, the UDSR, and two of the African Parties (the Rassemblement Démocratique Africain and the Parti du Regroupement Africain). The Communists had not been asked to join in this appeal, but the front page of *L'Humanité* that morning read:

To stop Fascism, to save the Republic
ALL JOIN AT 5 p.m. TODAY
in the great anti-Fascist demonstration
BETWEEN NATION AND REPUBLIQUE

But behind the scenes something was brewing; *L'Aurore* had been right to suggest that President Coty was up to something. It was indeed learned before long that Pflimlin had paid a visit to Coty early in the morning, and had presented his resignation to the President.

"But the President told me," he declared to the press, "that he would not accept it until it was possible to form another government. Meantime, to avoid a power vacuum, I have decided fully to preserve my governmental responsibilities."

There have been various accounts of the "anti-Fascist march" between the Place de la Nation and the Place de la République that afternoon. The Right-wing papers minimized the number of people who had taken part in the march; the Communist and Socialist(!) press talked of 500,000. The Préfecture de Police figure was 150,000—an obvious under-estimate. It was a large procession—no doubt about it. Perhaps 300,000 or 400,000 people. But there was, I felt, something sad, almost funereal about the whole thing. There were few shouts; the singing of the *Marseillaise* was half-hearted; the Communists avoided any revolutionary slogans or revolutionary songs like the *Internationale*; every group carried the same dreary posters: "VIVE LA REPUBLIQUE", "NON À DE GAULLE" and "LE FASCISME NE PASSERA PAS". The Communist leaders had turned out in large numbers. The leaders of the democratic parties were few and far between. Although the MRP had invited people to take part in this protest march, scarcely any MRP personalities were to be seen anywhere, with the exception of Mme Francine Lefèvre. The only prominent figures—who seemed like future leaders of the anti-de Gaulle opposition—were Mendès-France, Daladier, Mitterrand and, amongst the Socialists, apart from Pineau and Gazier, mostly anti-Mollet men like Robert Verdier, André Philip,[1] Depreux and Tanguy-Prigent.

There were thousands of workers, many in blue overalls, and some carrying "Front Populaire" banners. Particularly numerous—and this was significant—were also the teachers representing the Syndicat de l'Education Nationale. Also several hundred students of the Union Nationale des Etudiants took part in the procession. Also a few theatrical and film celebrities, amongst them Gérard Philipe.

On and on they marched, almost in silence, most of them carrying

[1] Philip had actually been expelled from the Socialist Party in the previous February for having published *Le Socialisme trahi*, a book highly critical of Mollet's Algerian policy.

Vive la République banners. *République* . . . What did it mean—with Pflimlin, head of the lawful Government of the French Republic, ready to throw up the sponge, and with Guy Mollet, leader of the Socialist Party, busy at that very moment negotiating with Coty and General de Gaulle . . .?

In the Place de la Nation that afternoon, I talked to N., a particularly active member of the Socialist Federation of the Seine.

"I agree with you," he said. "It isn't what it should be. It's difficult, infernally difficult, after all that's happened, to arouse much enthusiasm amongst our people. They don't trust anybody—least of all people like Mollet and Vincent Auriol. They don't believe very much in the 'Socialist miracle' of last night being followed up by any decisive action. The press has tried to scare them with talk about civil war, about paratroopers landing in Paris; about the Army and the police joining in a Fascist *putsch*. People are not in a fighting mood—not yet. If the paratroopers did land, there might well be a real outburst of Resistance; but that would quite inevitably mean joining up with the Communists. There *is* no other way. In the Socialist Federation of the Seine most of us realize that that would be the only way of smashing a Fascist *putsch*. Tanguy-Prigent was quite right to say so in his article in *Le Monde* the other day; but the issue has been confused, terribly confused, by their having trotted out de Gaulle. Amongst the older people there is still a bit of a de Gaulle myth; they *prefer* to believe that he is not a Fascist, that there *is* a difference between de Gaulle and Massu. They feel de Gaulle represents the easy way out. But they feel that this procession—feeble though it is—may be useful all the same. A warning—yes, a warning to de Gaulle that he must take account of 'working class opinion'; a warning, too, to Algiers that they cannot go *too* far. After this big demonstration a paratroop *putsch* is less likely than it was two days ago. Algiers must know now that Paris *would* react. At least I hope so. But it would still need a lot more provocation to make our people fight on the barricades. The tragedy is that there has been a longstanding split in the working class. The Communists still haven't quite lived down Budapest. Our Socialist rank-and-file would be ready, in certain conditions, to forget about it; but many, only too many, of these people who are carrying these *Vive la République* banners would, at heart, be relieved if de Gaulle found an easy way out. There's not much revolutionary fervour. For one thing, an awful lot of our working class, whether Socialist or Communist, have lately become singularly a-political. They are interested in sports and scooters and television and all that sort of thing. Living conditions haven't been too bad, despite the rise in the cost of living over the past year. And also—and this is, I think, important—our younger people just don't know, as we know only too well, what Fascism means. They don't remember the 'thirties; they scarcely remember the war and the Occupation. Also, they don't feel strongly about de Gaulle; what they are thinking about chiefly is their *congés payés* which start next month. God, the Algiers Fascists certainly timed their *putsch* beautifully."

"Surely," I said, "your people can't be in sympathy with the Algiers colonels?"

"No, they're not. And yet—much as they dislike men like Massu, they really haven't had any first-hand experience of these people. They don't really know what the SS was, and they don't realize the similarity between the SS and certain paratroop formations. The Army still has, to them, a certain prestige; nationalism—'national-molletism'—has had some effect even on the working class; let's face it, they *don't* like the *bicots*. The Republic—well, yes. But what does it mean? Is the Republic of Pflimlin and Mollet worth fighting for? That's the tragedy of it. The people in this big procession today are 'for the Republic'—but in an abstract sort of way. And that isn't enough. . . . The only good thing about this demonstration is that it *may* act as a warning. If 300,000 or 400,000 people get together to protest against a de Gaulle Government, at least a good number of them *might* be ready to fight if a military *coup d'état* were attempted. No doubt, they'd be crushed by the combined forces of the Army and the Police; but after that a real Resistance might start crystallizing, and then these Algiers thugs *would* be up against a civil war situation, complete with a general strike, in which Socialists and Communists would inevitably join. But it doesn't go beyond a warning, and I can assure you that if de Gaulle goes through the motions of a 'legal' investiture, nobody's going to bother unduly. The Communists will no doubt write very angry articles in *L'Humanité*—but I doubt whether they'll go any further. . . . Their attempts up till now to arouse any great movement of protest strikes have met with only a very feeble response, as you know."

"And the Socialists?"

"Our Deputies were pretty good yesterday, in their categorical refusal to have anything to do with de Gaulle *in any circumstances*; but when it comes to the point, I doubt whether all of them, or even half of them, will stick to it. The 'civil war' scare has been worked up pretty effectively, and I fear that a 'Munich complex' is developing among a lot of people, who'll accept de Gaulle with what Blum called at the time of Munich 'a mixture of cowardly relief and shame'. And perhaps not even much shame. . . . And Mollet, you can be sure, will use the 'lesser evil' argument very effectively, and even show that the Socialist Party has a Mission in acting as a moderating influence on de Gaulle. . . . Because Mollet is convinced that the French Socialist Party must be present in *any* Government. . . . He will have de Gaulle, he would even have Massu, rather than the Popular Front. What a lot of Socialist Deputies are now saying is that, with his letter to de Gaulle, it was he, more than anybody else, who started the rot, and that *he* has been bullying Pflimlin into giving up the struggle."

Great nervous tension in Paris that day? Hardly. Somehow or other most people were already taking for granted that de Gaulle would soon be called in by Coty, though nobody quite knew yet how and in what conditions. Beuve-Méry, in *Le Monde* that day, had written an article marked by a gloomy feeling of resignation:

The Fourth Republic, which did not live decently, has not even managed to die nobly. And yet, the last meetings of the Assembly did not lack a certain dignity. At the head of the Government there's a respectable man, who tries nobly to face adversity. In Parliament a majority seems resolved to support him to the bitter end to save our institutions and our freedoms against the insurrection. . . . But the country is in no adventurous spirit, and is going peacefully about its daily business. . . . The final upsurge is just another lie. . . .

Pflimlin did not have the courage to call the rebellion by its real name . . . or to show up the true causes of the Algiers revolt—the plot that had been hatched over a long period; the natural exasperation of an army left to its own devices, and expected to perform all sorts of tasks, and held responsible for all errors and all failures. . . . And then also the monumental indifference to it all by our people. . . .

It was too late to break these bad habits. Parliament last night was no longer defending legality, but merely its shadow. . . . If Parliament and the Government are unable to cope with the sedition which is spreading like mad, it would have been better to have admitted it openly. . . . There is only one real force today: and that is the Army, which all kinds of troublemakers are trying to use for their own ends. And there's only one real moral force left: de Gaulle. . . . De Gaulle is today the lesser evil.

Such was the verdict of the most influential paper in France, famous in the past for its courage and independence. The article badly shook many of France's intellectuals. . . . One of them said to me that day: "If Beuve-Méry is capitulating, he must have some good reasons for doing so . . ."

Although, during the past week, cinemas and theatres seemed to be doing much worse than usual, I found, nevertheless, that at the Grand Opera all seats for the Russian Bolshoi Ballet had been completely sold out right up to the end of their stay, except for a few side seats "*sans visibilité*". Not much good, least of all for ballet! I went to the Shostakovich concert at the Palais Chaillot that night, and here again the hall was completely packed. The reception he received was not uproariously enthusiastic; not, however, because he was Soviet, but because his preludes and fugues were a bore, and because he played them badly anyway, and because his new Eleventh Symphony just didn't ring a bell, somehow. . . .

I met a well-known Socialist journalist at the concert; he took pretty much the same line as the man I had talked to at the Nation that afternoon.

"Pretty impressive demonstration, but——. Some funny things are going on at the Elysée tonight . . ."

19. ENTER PRESIDENT COTY—
MORE ABOUT MOLLET

IMPORTANT things had, indeed, been going on that day behind the scenes. At 10 that morning, de Gaulle, still at Colombey, was said to have received General Catroux, notorious as a North African "liberal". No one knew what the exact purpose of this visit was. Later it transpired that the reporters at Colombey had made a mistake: the visitor wasn't General Catroux at all, but *a secret emissary from General Salan*. About the same time, at 11 a.m., President Coty had a meeting at the Elysée with M. Monnerville, the Negro President of the Senate, while, in the afternoon, just about the time the great anti-Fascist demonstration in the east end of Paris was about to start, three men went into conference with the President of the Republic: M. Pinay, M. Teitgen and—M. Guy Mollet.

About the same time, at 4 p.m., de Gaulle received a short visit from Marshal Juin, after which he took his car to drive to Paris.

At 10 o'clock that night, ex-President Vincent Auriol was summoned to the Elysée, followed soon afterwards by M. Le Troquer, President of the National Assembly, and M. Monnerville, President of the Senate. Finally, at 11.45 p.m., a communiqué was published by the Elysée saying that President Coty had asked Le Troquer and Monnerville to establish contact with General de Gaulle "with a view to examining with him the conditions in which he could constitute the Government of the Republic".

What had happened during that meeting between Coty, Teitgen, Pinay and Mollet?

On the following morning the *Parisien Libéré*, scared of the Popular Front and apparently impressed by the Nation-République demonstration of the day before (even though it put the number of people who took part in it at—50,000!), described the Elysée conference as follows:

The three parliamentary leaders told the President that he would have to choose between a Government of Public Safety and the Popular Front. "For my own part," M. Coty said, "I absolutely reject this second alternative, which would plunge the country into civil war. I shall resign, rather than accept it. I shall now tell you that it is my firm intention to call on General de Gaulle. If any of you gentlemen object, I shall address a message to the Nation to inform it of the situation that has been created . . ." Naturally [the paper continued] the three political leaders could not commit themselves without consulting their respective parties."

As far as the Right were concerned, there was, of course, no difficulty; the MRP were still divided, but the paper reported that opinion in that Party was rapidly evolving in the right direction; as for the Socialists:

It is by no means impossible that they will go back on the decision they had taken the day before in a moment of complete bewilderment. In the course of a first meeting they held on the [Wednesday] afternoon, M. Max Lejeune warned them against the possible repercussions their motion of hostility *vis-à-vis* General de Gaulle might have—a motion they had passed in the absence of M. Guy Mollet.

He asked them to meet again at 9 p.m., this time in the presence of Guy Mollet.

This meeting took place, but after a speech by Guy Mollet, which we understand to have been very favourable to de Gaulle, it was decided that the meeting be adjourned till this [Thursday] morning.

The *Parisien Libéré* naturally concluded on a note of hope—the innate patriotism of the Socialists would soon triumph over their sectarian prejudices.

It was obvious that, at that Socialist meeting on the Wednesday night, Mollet had been given a pretty rough passage. Some Socialists had, in the words of *France-Soir*, come to the meeting "galvanized" by the Nation-République demonstration. Tanguy-Prigent was particularly "violent". He and others attacked Mollet for the letter he had written without anybody's knowledge to de Gaulle. Mollet admitted that he had written to de Gaulle, and read out a few extracts from his letter, though without showing them its full text.

From good sources we learn [said *France-Soir*] that in his letter M. Mollet warned de Gaulle against certain steps which might smash French unity, and lead inevitably, within eight days, or eight weeks, or eight months to a Popular Front. This, in turn, would result in the creation of a People's Democracy in France.

At the meeting, Mollet argued that there were only three possibilities—a normal parliamentary government, a government under de Gaulle, and a government of colonels. Personally he would prefer a normal parliamentary government, but if this proved impossible then he much preferred a de Gaulle government to a government of colonels.

And Mollet added that Coty had made up his mind to call in de Gaulle, since he (Coty) did not believe that after Pflimlin's resignation, a "normal" parliamentary government (except on Popular Front lines—which he wouldn't consider *on any account*) was possible any longer. . . .

So the Socialist meeting broke up.

Meanwhile, "somewhere near Versailles", the Presidents of the National Assembly and the Senate had a short meeting with General de Gaulle.

On Thursday, the 11 a.m. edition of *France-Soir* announced in a banner headline:

DE GAULLE SUDDENLY RETURNS TO COLOMBEY
AFTER SEEING LE TROQUER AND MONNERVILLE

It suggested a breakdown. It was also reported that de Gaulle was "deeply offended by the attitude taken up by the Socialist Party . . ."

On that Thursday, May 29, event followed upon event with breakneck speed. President Coty, frightened of the "obstructive" attitude shown by the Socialists, decided that there wasn't another moment to lose. In the morning he already announced that he was sending a "message" to Parliament, an almost unprecedented step. The last time it had happened was in 1924, when President Millerand announced to Parliament his resignation in this manner.

In view of the Coty announcement, the Socialist meeting that morning was adjourned, pending the President's message.

At 3 p.m. the Assembly met in a feverish atmosphere; the Chamber, as well as all the galleries, was packed as seldom before.

As M. Le Troquer, the President of the Assembly, announced that he was going to read a message he had received from the President of the Republic, the whole Assembly rose to its feet. Le Troquer was obviously hostile to Coty; he read out his message quickly, in a deliberately flat, inexpressive voice.

Here were the essential passages:

For four and a half years the State has not ceased disintegrating; and now we are on the brink of civil war. . . . After a cruel fratricidal struggle, what would remain of our France? National unity cannot be achieved in a state of anarchy, but only if the Law is respected. . . .

Now that both the country and the Republic are in danger, I have decided to turn to the most illustrious of Frenchmen, to the man who in the most sombre years of our history, led us to the reconquest of freedom and who, having created around himself national unanimity, refused to establish a dictatorship and established the Republic instead. . . .

At this point the Communists and several Socialists sat down, and there were cries of "This is Fascism!"

M. Le Troquer continued to read the message:

I am asking General de Gaulle to be good enough to confer with the Head of the State and to examine with him the necessary steps that can immediately be taken, within the framework of republican legality, to set up a Government of National Safety, and to bring about, within a short time, a fundamental reform of our institutions.

And then came Coty's warning—or Coty's "blackmail", as some were to call it:

> Should I fail in this task, then, in the absence of that moral authority which the Head of the State now requires more than ever, I shall have no alternative to handing over my functions immediately to the President of the National Assembly, in accordance with Article 41 of the Constitution.

Having got that one off his chest, Coty concluded on a note of confidence:

> May my last word be one of confidence in this admirable people of France who, after so many years of hardship and suffering in the course of their history, are faced with a chance of a magnificent revival.
> Representatives of the Nation! The destiny of our people is in your hands. With calm and dignity you will, when the time comes, make the necessary resolutions so that France and the Republic may live.

There were cheers in the Centre, on the Right and the Extreme Right. From the Left came a cry: "Long live the *real* Republic!" A voice on the Right shouted: "*Vive la France!*" The Communists and numerous Socialists then shouted in chorus: "*Vive la République! Le fascisme ne passera pas!*"

Then they rose and sang the *Marseillaise*.

The Right also rose and sang the *Marseillaise*, the Left shouting them down: "Sit down, Fascists! Down with Fascism! *Le fascisme ne passera pas!*"

It went on like this for a few minutes. Then M. Pflimlin, followed by members of the Government and by most of the Centre and Right-wing Deputies, left the hall.

It was only too obvious what had happened: the President of the Republic, frightened of both the Popular Front tendencies that were beginning to take shape, however vaguely, and of the possibility of military *putsches* in various French cities, perhaps including Paris, had decided to throw in his whole weight in favour of the de Gaulle "solution". One of the rumours most widely current that day was that M. Le Troquer, the Socialist President of the Assembly, was secretly hoping that the Assembly would rebel against Coty's "blackmail", as a result of which he (Le Troquer) would almost automatically become President of the Republic. The very gloomy account he gave that morning to the Socialist group of the Assembly of his meeting with de Gaulle on the previous night appeared to confirm this impression.

But in reality the game was up. Almost as soon as Le Troquer had read out Coty's message to Parliament—a message on which no vote was taken, and which the Assembly was merely expected to "note" (after which, in Le Troquer's phrase, the original of the message was placed in the Assembly's archives)—de Gaulle left Colombey for Paris. His constant coming and going between Colombey and Paris (a distance of over two hundred miles) showed that he was well determined to take over. . . .

Simultaneously, threatening statements and appeals to Metropolitan France to set up Committees of Public Safety continued to be issued that day by the Algiers Committee of Public Safety and by General Massu; these appeared in the French press in versions heavily cut by the censorship.

Meantime M. Mollet was up in arms against M. Le Troquer, with whom he had a stormy meeting soon after the reading of Coty's message to the Assembly. Mollet claimed to have seen M. Monnerville, the President of the Senate, whose version of what de Gaulle had said to him and Le Troquer was much less alarming: he had not spoken (as Le Troquer had done) of a "plebiscite" to be held after one year of practically absolute power. Also, according to Monnerville, the de Gaulle Constitution would be deliberated by the two Assemblies and only if these failed to agree, would it be submitted to a referendum.[1]

As we now know, the Le Troquer version came nearer than the Monnerville version to what de Gaulle actually was going to do.

That afternoon there were numerous meetings at the Palais-Bourbon among the various groups—the Socialists, the Communists, the Radicals, the MRP. At the MRP meeting, M. Pflimlin simply declared that he had acquired the full conviction that there was no alternative to a de Gaulle Government without the country being plunged into civil war.

The Communists naturally stuck to their line that there was a regular Parliamentary majority in favour of the Republic and that it must not yield to Coty's blackmail.

The Radicals were divided; many talked about "defending the Republic"; it was suggested at one point that M. Mendès-France be asked to see de Gaulle to obtain from him certain "assurances"; but he said he did not see that this could, at the present juncture, serve any useful purpose.

At the Socialist meeting, now attended by Mollet, the *malaise* was greatest of all. Mollet now stressed the very reassuring nature of de Gaulle's reply to Vincent Auriol's letter of May 26—the text of both of which had by now been made public.

Auriol had written to de Gaulle:

. . . I know how anxious you are to maintain the national unity of France. I also know that you are determined to re-establish, in a spirit of equality and human dignity, that indispensable France-Moslem friendship, without which there can be no free Algeria.

[1] If de Gaulle made this promise to Monnerville, he certainly had no intention of keeping it.

But your reply to those who, in Algeria, have rebelled against national sovereignty has aggravated the *malaise*. . . . Now the events of Ajaccio and the establishment of Committees of Public Safety all over France throw a glaring light on the real aims of some of those who have . . . diverted certain military leaders from the path of duty, have ignored the authority of the President of the Republic and have driven on rebellious and violent crowds to push forward your candidature. . . . This is a rebellion against the laws and institutions of France.

I cannot believe that you want to make the Republic capitulate and to receive illegal power from the hands of a rebellious faction. . . .

I am sure that you will do your utmost to remind of their duty those generals and officers who disobeyed their supreme chief, the President of the Republic.

And Auriol concluded that if only de Gaulle dissociated himself from the "sedition", the whole French nation would regain confidence in him and a rapid agreement would be made possible between him and the responsible leaders of the Republic with a view to granting him full powers for a limited time.

De Gaulle, in a letter that sounded deliberately conciliatory, replied that the events in Algeria had been "provoked by the chronic helplessness of the authorities"—a helplessness he had done his best in the past to remedy. His name had been invoked at Algiers, without his ever having been involved in the developments there in any way.

"Things being what they are, I proposed to form, by legal means, a Government which I believe could restore unity and discipline, particularly on the part of the Army, and promote the adoption of a new Constitution."

But, said de Gaulle, he now came up against determined opposition from the representatives of the people. And in Algeria and in the Army, whatever he now did or said, the movement had acquired such proportions that the failure of his proposal might break down all barriers and submerge the Army Command itself. And since he (de Gaulle) was determined not to accept office from anyone other than the people, or, at any rate, their representatives, it was to be feared that France was drifting into anarchy and civil war. Those who, through an "incomprehensible sectarianism", were now preventing him (de Gaulle) from saving the Republic once more, were assuming a grave responsibility. "As for myself, I shall live in a state of sorrow till the end of my days."

The Socialists seemed to be shaken by this exchange of letters. By 62 votes to 29 they agreed, in effect, that Vincent Auriol had asked de Gaulle the right questions; and that the same questions should be put to him again. Was the ice broken, and were the Socialists now anxious to enter into negotiations with the General "with whom, as the man pushed forward by the Algiers and Corsica rebellions, they would have nothing to do ever, and in any circumstances"—as they had said, only two days before?

Max Lejeune, a crony of Lacoste's and one of the Algerian diehards, was strongly agitating, together with Mollet, in favour of these "contacts" with de Gaulle.

That evening, while de Gaulle was conferring with President Coty, large crowds gathered in the Champs-Elysées, and in the Faubourg St. Honoré, to demonstrate in de Gaulle's favour. Thousands of cars, ignoring the no-hooting rule of the Paris traffic, were now hooting all over the place their . . .-- signal, meaning *Al-gé-rie fran-çaise*, or the --. . . signal meaning *de Gaulle au pouvoir*.

Decidedly, the people in cars were all for de Gaulle—as distinct from the "pedestrians" who, the day before, had walked all the way from the Nation to the République. . . .

In the Place de la Concorde, a few hundred young men tried to break through the CRS barrage on the Concorde Bridge. They were shouting *Vive de Gaulle!* and *Massu au pouvoir!* and *Les paras avec nous!* and even *Les socialos à la flotte!* (Chuck the Socialists into the river!) and *Mort aux Juifs!* (Death to the Jews!).

That night it was learned that de Gaulle had accepted Coty's offer that he form the Government. He left it to Coty himself to start the initial conversations with the "groups". He told Coty: "You had better also ask the Communist leaders to come and see you—after all, they are Frenchmen . . ."

At Algiers that night thousands of Europeans and Moslems were cheering the nomination of de Gaulle. General Massu assured the crowds that when Soustelle had promised Algeria Integration he "knew exactly what was at the back of de Gaulle's mind". The fundamental *équivoque* in the whole Algerian situation was being deliberately kept up. . . .

20. THE END OF THE FOURTH REPUBLIC— "DE GAULLE IS NO FASCIST"

BEFORE leaving the Elysée that night, de Gaulle issued a statement in which he said that he "had had the honour of meeting President Coty" to whom he had outlined the conditions on which he could form a government: after its investiture by Parliament, the Government would require plenary powers for a limited period; the right to make changes in the Constitution, such changes to be submitted to a referendum; they would deal in particular with the "separation and equilibrium of powers", and with the relations between the French Republic and "the peoples with whom she is associated"; he also suggested that such powers should be granted to the Government by a large majority; and concluded by referring to the grave dangers which made it urgent to form such a government.

On the following day, Friday, May 30, the schoolteachers of France held a protest strike; according to districts, between 50 per cent and 100 per cent took part in it. Most schools were closed for the day.

It was another of those platonic protest gestures of no practical significance.

All that day President Coty conferred with the various political leaders, in preparation for their "round-table" conference with General de Gaulle at the Hôtel Lapérouse on the following day. The Communists haughtily announced that Thorez and Duclos had refused Coty's invitation to confer with him, since they did not wish to "cover with an appearance of legality this capitulation to the Algiers and Ajaccio rebellions".

But amongst the Socialists that day the wind was rapidly changing. It was a far cry from the resolution of May 27—only three days before—when they refused to have anything to do with de Gaulle. True, that morning some of the Socialists were still in a fighting mood, and resented Mollet's sudden announcement that he and Deixonne, the leader of the Socialist parliamentary group, had been invited to see de Gaulle at Colombey that very day—whereupon they left the meeting without any further argument.

The Socialists did not meet again till late in the evening, after Mollet's and Deixonne's return to Paris. This time Mollet was positively lyrical. He declared that his meeting with de Gaulle "had been one of the greatest moments in his life", while Deixonne, in a rapturous state, went on repeating that de Gaulle was "a very great gentleman". Mollet added that de Gaulle was so fairminded that "even the Communists would vote for him, if they had any sense".

That night there were some sharp clashes between Right-wing and Communist demonstrators in the Champs Elysées, the Communists smashing up several of the cars hooting their usual *Algérie française* and *De Gaulle au pouvoir* signals. About ten Communists and two policemen were badly injured. The police appeared to be entirely on the side of the "Gaullists"—the people "in cars", as against the people "on foot".

For the past week the Paris Bourse was in a highly optimistic mood; it was assumed that de Gaulle was taking over, and financial papers openly declared: THE BOURSE WANTS DE GAULLE. Since Thursday, the day of the Coty Message to Parliament, the rise in French shares was particularly spectacular.

On the Saturday, May 31, there was no longer the slightest doubt that the de Gaulle investiture on the following day was now in the bag. That morning the Socialist group, already shaken by Mollet the night before, listened to Vincent Auriol.

The former President of the Republic, whose correspondence with de Gaulle had already done so much to mollify the wobblers, was now quite categorical in saying that de Gaulle had absolutely no intention of becoming a dictator. "He intends to maintain the Republic and demo- cracy," he said.

One Deputy, M. Leenhardt of Marseilles, asked, all the same, how Auriol could reconcile such confidence with all the harsh things he had said about de Gaulle when the latter was head of the totalitarian RPF movement in the past. The ex-President replied: "Yes, I took a very stern view of the de Gaulle of those days. In fact, he reminded me the other day of having said that I was not going to act the Hindenburg for him. But the man has changed a lot." A wisecrack current amongst the Socialists that evening was that if Auriol was contemplating a "marriage of convenience", Mollet was now thinking of a real love-match. . . .

But a large number of Socialists were still undecided, and a few remained uncompromisingly hostile to a pro-de Gaulle vote. After a long discussion, and seeing that the Party was in danger of splitting, Mollet agreed that, in the investiture debate on the following day, everybody would be free to vote whichever way he liked. The *Comité directeur*, the deputies and senators then voted—77 were now for the investiture, and 74 against; but the majority of the deputies (50 against 40) were against. Even some of Mollet's closest associates, like M. Commin and various representatives of the Nord and Pas de Calais, were against. It showed the seriousness of the inherent conflict inside the Socialist Party. . . .

At one point M. Mollet even threatened to resign his post of secretary- general.

Mollet's chief worry was that this hostility of most of the Socialist deputies would make de Gaulle throw up the sponge. The story goes that he drove to the Hôtel Lapérouse and "begged" him to go on with his consultations and his Cabinet-making, to which de Gaulle replied: "All right, I will. But you'll have to come with me." The greater part of the MRP allowed themselves to be persuaded without much difficulty.

Much stormier was the meeting of the Radicals that day. Here Mendès- France argued that he had never ceased repeating—as recently as three weeks before—that France's one great hope was the "arbitration" by de Gaulle. But de Gaulle had, in fact, given his blessing to the Algiers rebellion, and to vote for him now was like yielding to the "civil war" blackmail that both de Gaulle and Algiers were exercising against the Republic.

The opposite line was taken by Clostermann who argued that it would be wrong for the Radicals, with their sound republican tradition, to allow de Gaulle to surround himself by Socialists who were, he suggested, a bunch of hopeless opportunists.

All day that Saturday there was a constant coming and going at the Hôtel Lapérouse, near the Etoile, where de Gaulle had taken up his provisional headquarters. He argued with the various politicians (some of them, like M. Mitterrand, very hostile) in an easygoing, often even jocular vein; many of them left, feeling both puzzled and charmed by the man.

In particular, he had given Ramadier and Mitterrand the assurance that, just as in 1944, he was opposed to the exercise of any autonomous power, conflicting with that of the central Government, by the Liberation Committees set up by the Resistance, so now he would take a similar stand with regard to the Committees of Public Safety:

"As the holder of the powers of the Republic, I must, *ipso facto*, make everybody obey me. I shall never be the man of any faction." (*Le Monde*, June 1.)

As regards Algeria, he declared that it should be a Federation, holding a place in a Confederation incorporating both the Metropolis and the overseas territories (*ibid.*).

This was, clearly, in flat contradiction with the "integrationism" of Algiers.

De Gaulle also said that he would rapidly revoke the recent Emergency Law, with its censorship and other restrictions.

That evening, he was already forming his Government.

During the course of that Saturday, I received an unexpected visit from a lady, the wife of a high-up Government official, whom I had met only very casually in the past. I suspect it was part of a little propaganda drive amongst foreign correspondents.

"It's important," she said, "that people abroad should realize that de Gaulle is the best possible solution in present circumstances. It's no use identifying him with thugs like Massu or Soustelle. I know what I am talking about: de Gaulle feels the greatest distrust for Soustelle, and resents his posing in Algiers as his nominee. They have scarcely been on speaking terms lately. De Gaulle is the only man who can keep these wild men of Algiers in order—and he's going to do it. I can tell you off the record: Mollet and Pflimlin, whom de Gaulle is taking into his Government, have made it a condition of joining him that he keeps Soustelle out of it."

"But surely," I said, "Soustelle's organization, the USRAF, calls itself Gaullist."

"That's a lot of window-dressing. They are using de Gaulle's name in vain. It's difficult for him to disavow them openly just now; but he will when the time comes. . . . For one thing, Big Business in France is practically entirely for de Gaulle. They are against Fascism. They want a strong State, a managerial, modern type of State, and they don't want to antagonize the Communists. D'Astier de La Vigerie, who is on reasonably good personal terms with de Gaulle, has received some very important assurances on this point. French industrialists—the Bloch-Dassaults, banking firms like the Rothschilds and the Lazards—take a very different view of the de Gaulle régime from that taken by the North Africa lobby—and by all those other people who have been supporting Soustelle and his USRAF. There is a fundamental difference between de Gaulle's and Soustelle's attitude to Algeria. De Gaulle is a federalist, who is quite capable when the time comes of starting negotiations with all groups in Algeria, including the FLN. The integrationists, on the other hand, think they can turn the Arabs into a small minority inside a big bloc of '53 million Frenchmen'. De Gaulle is not impressed by the fraternization carnival they have, for this purpose, organized in Algiers. And he is supported by those industrial interests in France which are all in favour of winding up the Algerian war as soon as possible—and through negotiation.''

There was an uncanny feeling in Paris that Saturday night—the last night, as it were, of the Fourth Republic. De Gaulle had agreed to appear personally before the National Assembly the next day. . . . In the Grands Boulevards thousands of leaflets were being scattered from cars and lorries saying:

ALL GATHER OUTSIDE THE NATIONAL ASSEMBLY TOMORROW (SUNDAY)
TO HOWL DOWN AND . . . . . .
ANY DEPUTY (OTHER THAN THE COMMUNISTS) WHO WILL HAVE VOTED
AGAINST GENERAL DE GAULLE!

This call to violence was signed by somebody calling themselves "A group of former Resistance men". It was faintly reminiscent of that day of July 1940 at Vichy when the Doriot boys were threatening with physical violence anyone who would not vote for Pétain.

Lots of other parallels were drawn during those days between the Pétain "situation" of July 1940 and the de Gaulle "situation" now. It was related in all seriousness that on the Friday a hesitant deputy had made inquiries at the National Assembly as to how long after the vote for Pétain in July, 1940, deputies continued to draw their salaries.

Also, many deputies were remembering the heroic "Eighty" who had voted against Pétain on that 10th of July, 1940—a vote which was later to constitute a sort of new title of nobility—with a good many political advantages attached to it.

De Gaulle remained throughout those days something of a mystery still. The intellectuals were confused. Some like Bourdet and J. P. Sartre were gloomily prophesying: "After Gaullism there will be Fascism."

Much fewer were the references to the monumental failure of de Gaulle as leader of the RPF, that quasi-totalitarian movement which had tried, in 1947-48, to crush the Fourth Republic of Ramadier and Schuman.

Mauriac, who had so severely condemned the RPF experiment in the past, was now all for de Gaulle, differing in this from the *Express* editorials.

A "benefit-of-the-doubt" line was taken by other intellectuals, notably by the *Monde*. On May 31, while de Gaulle was conversing with the parliamentary groups at the Hôtel Lapérouse, Beuve-Méry wrote that it was for de Gaulle to decide whether he wanted to be "with the people" or not.

As a soldier, he knows how to give orders. But the exercise of political power is something different. As head of the Government in 1944-46, he failed. . . . As a demagogue he was swallowed up by the contradictions and the mediocrity of the RPF. And . . . around him today there is nobody—not a single team, not a single man, whose competence and prestige could equal their fidelity.

De Gaulle is alone, terribly alone. May he realize how badly he needs the support of the people!

And then this idle warning, but preceded by this prophetic glimpse into the future:

If he were to base his power on a Pretorian guard, and become the albeit unconscious slave of occult organizations and of financial interests, and if he were to create a "system" worse than the old one by covering those who today are blackmailing France with the threat of civil war, and call themselves Gaullists simply in order to enslave de Gaulle, then we shall not be with him. . . .

21. FROM "OPERATION SUPERIOR PERSON" TO "OPERATION SEDUCTION"

JUNE I was a dazzling summer day. But there was nervous tension in Paris. Thousands of police had roped off the whole area around the National Assembly where de Gaulle was to speak in the afternoon. The Concorde and Chambre des Députés *métro* stations were closed. For a long time, de Gaulle had been reluctant to "lower" himself to personally asking the despised Assembly for its vote of confidence. He thought at first of simply sending the Assembly a message, on which it could then deliberate. The Socialists and MRP leaders thought the Assembly would take such an unprecedented procedure very badly, and that it might cost de Gaulle a great number of votes. On the principle that *Paris vaut bien une messe*, de Gaulle agreed to read out a seven-minute statement, but to let the subsequent debate take place in his absence.

The National Assembly was packed when de Gaulle, looking a little nervous and uneasy, took his seat on the Government bench. He had not been in this building, which he had never liked, since that day in January 1946 when he threw up the sponge. M. Le Troquer read out the names of de Gaulle's ministers.

Then, in complete silence, de Gaulle walked up the steps of the tribune and proceeded, in a nervous voice, to read out his brief message. Again he spoke of the "degradation" of the State, the fact that the Army had been "scandalized" by the lack of authority of previous Governments, and of the danger of "dislocation and perhaps even of civil war".

It is in these conditions that I have agreed once again to lead the country, the State and the Republic along the road of salvation. Having been called upon by the Head of the State, I am now asking the National Assembly to invest me for this heavy task.

He then said that he was asking the Assembly to grant him plenary powers for a period of six months "to restore order in the State and restore hope in Algeria". But such "temporary" solutions were obviously insufficient, and it would be important for the Government to get down to the root of the trouble: an end must be put to the "confusion of power" and to the "helplessness of the Government".

Subject to your approval, the Government I shall form will promptly submit to you a Bill reforming Article 90 of the Constitution,[1] so that the National Assembly may authorize the Government to elaborate the necessary changes in the Constitution, such changes to be submitted to the people's referendum. . . . The Government will lay down the three principles which must be the very basis of the Republican régime: universal suffrage must be the source of all authority; executive power and legislative power must be effectively separate, so that Government and Parliament clearly assume its attributions, each under its own responsibility; the Government shall be responsible to Parliament.

The same constitutional reform, de Gaulle continued, would provide the "solemn occasion" for "organizing the relations between the French Republic and the peoples with whom she is associated". There was no

---

[1] It was a case of abrogating Article 90 of the 1946 Constitution providing for a complex and very lengthy procedure whereby the Cons'tution could be revised. (For text of this Article, see Philip Williams, *Politics in Post-War France*. London, 1954, pp. 434–5).

time to lose; the necessary Bills to be submitted to Parliament must be quickly voted, after which Parliament would rise until the date marking the opening of the ordinary (autumn) session.

Invested by the confidence of the representatives of the people, the Government could then proceed with its urgent tasks which would preserve "the integrity, the unity and the independence of France".

The cheers were slow in coming. Perhaps the Right and the Extreme Right did not want to "compromise" de Gaulle by marking him too obviously as "their" man; perhaps they were also a little disappointed by the vagueness—especially about the future of Algeria—as well as the apparent moderation of de Gaulle's message. Then they cheered half-heartedly, followed by the Centre—the MRP and most of the Radicals. On the Socialist benches only four were cheering: Lejeune, Lapie, Ramadier and Eugène Thomas.

After throwing a quick glance round the Assembly, de Gaulle then left, and the strange "investiture debate" began in his absence.

This started on a strange note.

M. Isorni, the man who had defended Pétain at his trial, said that, having remained faithful to the memory of Pétain, he could not, in all conscience, vote for de Gaulle. Nevertheless, he wished de Gaulle good luck, and hoped that he would bring about the integration of Algeria, and not be merely content with making her an "associate" country. And alluding to the ill-treatment the Vichyites had suffered in the past at the hands of de Gaulle, Isorni concluded: "May God protect him against himself!"

This Isorni speech was curious in many ways: it seemed to be motivated by a sort of emotional approach to de Gaulle, by unpleasant historic memories, and not by political and sociological considerations; for, ever since the RPF movement had started in 1947–48, the bulk of the ex-Vichyites in France had become reconciled to de Gaulle and many had even adopted him as "their" man. Men like M. Pinay, a former Vichyite, were members of de Gaulle's Government. Formally, nevertheless, de Gaulle would not agree to be reconciled with Vichy; he was to show this, only a few days later, when he rejected the appeal addressed to him by a Vichyite association that the remains of Pétain be at last allowed to be buried at Verdun. De Gaulle would not yield on this point: Pétain, he felt, must not be remembered primarily as the Victor of Verdun, but as the head of the Vichy régime, against which he, de Gaulle, had fought.

It was an odd debate—if one may call it that. De Gaulle had hastened to leave the National Assembly; now there sat on the Government bench three lots of men: "technicians" who had not been "compromised" by the "System"—a Prefect, M. Pelletier, who was now Minister of the Interior; a diplomat, M. Couve de Murville, who was now Foreign Minister (poor Bidault, who had fallen over himself to "join" de Gaulle immediately after May 13, and who could already see himself as Foreign Minister, had been left out); M. Guillaumat, Minister of the Armies, and a high official; secondly, parliamentarians, but sworn enemies of the "System" like M. Michel Debré, one of the leaders of the RPF in the past, who was now Minister of Justice; and thirdly, typical representatives of the "System": the four Ministers of State: Guy Mollet, the Socialist; Pierre Pflimlin, the MRP leader; M. Houphouet-Boigny, a leader of the African party of the RDA; M. Louis Jacquinot, a Right-winger; finally, men like M. Pinay (Right), who was Minister of Finance; M. Berthoin, Radical Senator, who was Minister of Education; M. Bacon (MRP), Minister of Labour; and Socialist Max Lejeune, who was to become Minister of the Sahara, and who had been closely associated with M. Lacoste at Algiers and the "activists" in the French Army[1] in their complete opposition to a negotiated settlement. Finally, there was among the Ministers M. André Malraux, who was, for a short time, to become Minister of Information; an intellectual ornament of the RPF, this one-time great writer was again planning to contribute his florid romantic oratory to the new Gaullist "revolution". As Minister of Information he was to prove a distinct failure, and, though preserving a nominal post at the Présidence du Conseil, he was soon to be replaced by Jacques Soustelle—a man who really meant business and had not, like Malraux, disgraced himself only quite recently by protesting against torture in Algeria.

Soustelle was not on the Government bench on that 1st of June; he was still at Algiers; de Gaulle had promised Mollet and Pflimlin not to include in the Government anybody directly associated with the Algiers rebellion, and least of all Soustelle—this promise was soon to be broken.

Another curious, though not a Cabinet, appointment which was to cause a good deal of comment in the next few days was that of M. Olivier Pompidou, as *Directeur de Cabinet* of General de Gaulle. Formerly a high official of the Conseil d'Etat, he had, in 1954, entered the Rothschild Bank, of which he was now director-general, besides being on the board of directors of several important companies (*Société anonyme de gérance et d'armement, Chemins de fer du Nord, Pennaroya, Francarep, Société Rateau,* etc.[2])—thus representing both nationalized industries and Big Business in the immediate entourage of General de Gaulle.

The "for" and the "against" speeches were almost evenly divided. M. Clostermann, representing "Left-wing Gaullism", exclaimed that he had "waited for twelve years for this moment". M. Georges Bonnet, of Munich fame, also supported de Gaulle, though in a speech which was very much on the "liberal" side: de Gaulle must make peace in Algeria,

[1] It was he who had taken the responsibility of preventing the Tunis conference of October 1956 between the Tunisian and Moroccan Governments and the FLN leaders, by having the latter's plane intercepted. Cf. the author's *Strange History of Pierre Mendès-France*, pp. 393–5.

[2] *Le Monde*, June 3, 1958.

and also defend France's public liberties; Parliament, he also said, had been maligned, and the whole Algiers rebellion, he said, had been a "tragic misunderstanding": Parliament had never intended to "abandon" Algeria.

Significant was the speech of M. P. H. Teitgen, the MRP leader, who enumerated the promises which, he claimed, de Gaulle had made:

The European treaties would be maintained; he would never accept the idea of having been brought into power by the Committees of Public Safety; he wished to have only those powers which had been regularly given him by Parliament; everybody in Algeria and Corsica would "be put back in his place in a spirit of order and discipline", both to be placed in the service of the Republic; trade union freedom would be respected; and de Gaulle's plenary powers would not apply to "personal rights and fundamental freedoms".

M. *Roger Roucaute* (Communist): He didn't say anything about that here!

M. *P. H. Teitgen:* These plenary powers will be limited to six months. During the parliamentary recess the committees will sit permanently in order to control Government activity. (*Laughter on Communist benches.*) The Constitutional Reform will respect and consolidate the fundamental principles of democracy: Government and Parliament will represent the will of the people; and the Government will be responsible to an Assembly elected by universal suffrage. We do not doubt the word of General de Gaulle, and shall therefore vote for him. . . .

M. Guy Mollet, refraining from raising any awkward questions about the role he himself had played in bringing de Gaulle into power, merely said that there was no time to lose: de Gaulle would go, in the next few days, to Algeria to re-establish order; it was essential that he be given the necessary authority for doing so.

More significant were the "anti" speeches. M. de Menthon, one of the three MRP members to vote against, said that he did not think that a Government brought into power by the Algiers Committees could restore national unity and the authority of the State. He recalled how de Gaulle had encouraged the Algiers insurrection and had so rendered things impossible for the legal Government under M. Pflimlin.

M. Pierre Cot said that Parliament was being driven by fear into accepting this Government; to grant constituent powers to one man was a shameful and desperately dangerous surrender. . . .

Anyway, we have no illusions about General de Gaulle himself. He will soon be dominated by the more turbulent of the people around him. Recently he said that he was "alone". He is no longer alone. There are around him some honest people who are making a great mistake in good faith; but there are around him some others who are sworn enemies of freedom and of the Republic. . . . But he will not have the working class with him. . . .

M. *Triboulet* (Gaullist): You are very badly informed. (*Laughter on Extreme Left.*)

M. *Pierre Cot:* The future will show you that you are wrong. We have more faith in the people than in Parliament.

M. Tanguy-Prigent, one of the Socialist leaders of the anti-Mollet faction, speaking with real emotion, said that while he deeply respected General de Gaulle for the role he had played in the past, he could not, in all conscience, submit to a man who had been put forward by a rebellious army to rule France.

The General is in no way an accomplice of these people; but it would be better if he had condemned the insurrection and had realized, after the Nation-République demonstration, that he did not have the whole of the people of France behind him. . . .

A Poujadist deputy: Yes, but what about the Champs-Elysées?

M. Tanguy-Prigent: I went there. I saw these people on a binge, and their pretty ladies. I suppose you prefer them? (*Loud cheers on Extreme Left, Left and Centre.*)

He said he did not believe the great social and economic problems of France could be settled by a Man of Providence; worse still, there was a danger that a vote for de Gaulle would pave the way for totalitarianism and persecution.

The two Left-wing leaders to whom the Assembly listened with the greatest attention were M. Mitterrand and M. Mendès-France.

Mitterrand began by saying that if, in 1944, Country and Honour were de Gaulle's companions, his two companions now were Rebellion and Sedition. The assurances de Gaulle had now given to members of Parliament during his preliminary talks with them had been extremely thin.

He then spoke of the Fascist adventurers who had organized the Algiers conspiracy, which had ramifications in Paris, and which had, in fact, now imposed General de Gaulle on Parliament as its candidate. No doubt, said M. Mitterrand, there were some who were now telling him that he would "join de Gaulle before long". Yes—he would join him if de Gaulle were to found a new form of democracy, if he liberated the peoples of Africa, if he maintained the "presence of France" everywhere overseas; if he restored national unity in France itself. But not now.

On the following day, the *Monde* was to speak a little ironically about both Mitterrand and Mendès-France who, it said, were taking out a double insurance: if de Gaulle succeeded, they would be with him; if he failed, they could take credit for being in the position of the "Eighty", who voted against Pétain in the famous vote of July 10, 1940, which marked the end of the Third Republic.

Mendès-France's speech was marked by his usual high analytical qualities. The Fourth Republic, he said, had fallen victim of its own faults. It had, in particular, failed to reconvert the old colonial empire to more modern forms; it had failed to replace domination by association. Colonial wars had, on the other hand, deprived France of her chance of modernizing her economy and raising her standard of living.

Yet if the Fourth Republic had discredited itself in the eyes of so many Frenchmen, it was not the fault of democracy, but of those anaemic Governments that had allowed themselves to be at the mercy of pressure groups—those very pressure groups which were again represented in the new Government of General de Gaulle. . . .

Whatever my personal feelings towards General de Gaulle, I cannot vote for him under the threat of violence and insurrection. . . . This vote is not a free, but an imposed decision.

And, alluding to the threats (like those contained in the leaflets distributed in Paris on the previous night) Mendès-France added:

I am not referring to individual threats, but to the more general civil war blackmail to which we have been subjected. . . . Capturing the name of General de Gaulle, the enemies of the Republic have gravely altered the whole significance of his "arbitration". This Government is being imposed on us by those very people who have sabotaged every attempt at a human, reasonable settlement in North Africa.

And yet, like Mitterrand, he also concluded by hoping that de Gaulle would not allow himself to be dominated by those who had brought him to power; and that he would safeguard the fundamental freedoms of the French Republic. He hoped de Gaulle would oppose any attempt to set up a totalitarian, "single-party" régime in his name. The preservation of the Republic's fundamental freedoms was the only safeguard against a Fascist dictatorship, which would only lead to civil war, and might finally lead to a Communist dictatorship. . . .

De Gaulle's investiture was approved (still in his absence) by 329 votes to 224. The Communists and *Progressistes*, of course, voted against; the Socialists were divided, 42 voting for, and 49 against;[1] so were the Radicals who also were almost equally divided (24 for, 18 against); the MRP (except three) voted for de Gaulle, so did practically the whole Right, except M. Isorni. The 30 Poujadists, ignoring the instructions of Poujade himself, voted for de Gaulle.

When the results were announced, there were cries of *Vive la République!* and *A bas le fascisme!* on the Extreme Left.

The President then announced that the Assembly would meet on the following day to discuss three Bills: the renewal of special powers for Algeria; the Plenary Powers Bill; and the Bill modifying Article 90 of the Constitution.

[1] The Socialists voting for de Gaulle included MM. Deixonne, Lacoste, Lejeune, Moch, Mollet, Neigelen and Ramadier; those voting against included Defferre, Depreux, Gazier, Gouin, Lussy, Pineau, Tanguy-Prigent, Savary and Verdier. "For" Radicals included Clostermann, Maurice Faure, Gaillard; "against" Radicals included Bourgès-Maunoury, Daladier, Baylet and Mendès-France.

On the following day, the Assembly had the surprise of seeing appear before it a new and almost unsuspected kind of de Gaulle—not the stiff, haughty and "Louis XIV" kind of de Gaulle of the day before, but one who was now determined to carry out what a Communist deputy, M. Kriegel-Valrimont, was later to describe as "Operation Seduction".

"No one had expected," wrote the *Monde* correspondent, "that he would exercise such skill, and show such gifts of diplomacy and psychological understanding—with which even his best friends had never credited him. Sitting like a good boy on the Government bench (with M. Guy Mollet beside him and looking like his secretary) de Gaulle patiently listened to the *rapporteur*. Only after that did he say in the mildest tone that either his Plenary Powers Bill would be accepted, or he would go."

Throughout his several speeches de Gaulle used—seemingly with complete sincerity—phrases like "the pleasure and the honour of being in your midst"; and it was, as the *Monde* again put it, as though de Gaulle had "made one step towards the System, while the System had made two or three steps towards him".

And, during an interval in the discussion, people could watch a sight worthy of "Molière, La Bruyère, Saint-Simon and Marcel Proust rolled into one"—countless deputies trying to get sufficiently close to the front Government bench to be able to shake the great man's hand. In particular, Georges Bonnet was seen manœuvring his way to the place where de Gaulle sat and managing to extract from him a handshake; one observer said it was "a very short and dry one", another that "it looked as though de Gaulle had touched a slug, so quick was he in withdrawing his hand".

De Gaulle's good grace and good humour were all the more surprising as the discussions on the six months' plenary powers and on the Constitutional Law laying down the "principles" of the new Constitution could not have been more confusing and irritating; amendment after amendment was being proposed, only to be swept aside, sometimes almost at once, sometimes after some obscure and hair-splitting discussions.

For all that, the discussion ended almost in an atmosphere of mutual friendship and confidence between de Gaulle and the Assembly. De Gaulle assured the deputies that his great aim was "to let the Republic continue".

It does not embarrass me at all to tell you that what will be done with regard to the new Constitution will not be done by me alone, but by the Government as a whole, in consultation with the Advisory Committee. It will be the crowning achievement of the Republic, a sequel to what already exists. (*Loud cheers on Right, Centre and Left benches.*) Will there be a principal Assembly elected by universal suffrage? But obviously there will be! What better proof is there than the pleasure and honour I feel of being in your midst tonight? (*Laughter and cheers.*) There will be no presidential régime, and the functions of the Prime Minister will not be the same as those of the President of the Republic.

It was then that M. Kriegel-Valrimont exclaimed: "After 'Operation Sedition' we are now witnessing 'Operation Seduction!' " while Mendès-France remarked that such supreme politeness was, in reality, the height of insolence.

Apart from the routine renewal of special powers in Algeria, what did the two Laws amount to?

The Constitutional Law laid down that, in drawing up the new Constitution, the Government would adhere to the following principles:

1. Universal suffrage alone is the source of power. Legislative and executive power can only be derived from universal suffrage or from its elected representatives [instances élues].
2. Executive and legislative power must be effectively separated. . . .
3. The Government must be responsible to Parliament.
4. Judicial authority must remain independent and assure the respect of the essential freedoms as defined by the Preamble of the Constitution of 1946 and the Declaration of the Rights of Man.
5. The Constitution must enable the Government to organize the relations between the Republic and the associated peoples.

The rest of the Bill concerned the appointment, partly by the parliamentary committees, of the Advisory Council with whom the Draft Constitution was to be discussed. This draft Constitution, after consultation with the Conseil d'Etat, was to be finally agreed to by a Ministerial Council, and submitted to the people's referendum. After adoption by the people it would be promulgated by the President of the Republic within a week.

This was adopted by 350 votes to 161.

The Plenary Powers Law provided that the Government could enact by decree any measures required for the "restoration" of the nation. These decrees could not, however, apply to human and civil and trade union rights, to criminal legislation now in force, or to electoral legislation. Except in cases of special urgency, these measures would be taken by the council of ministers after consultation with the Conseil d'Etat. At the end of the above six months, the decrees were to be submitted to the ratification of the National Assembly.

Simple though it all sounded, there were in reality plenty of loopholes in all this. To take the most striking example: the decrees could not concern "electoral legislation"; in other words, the Government could not decide by decree what system would be applied during the next election; on the face of it, this meant that the National Assembly would decide on the new election system, and not the Government. But what if the Assembly were not to meet before the referendum? Could not the Government, on the strength of the new Constitution, decide on the new election system, since, by that time, the old Assembly would, to all intents and purposes, have ceased to exist? Questions about this were raised during the final meeting of the 1956 Assembly, but no answer was given by de Gaulle; though M. Pflimlin did say that "the Government had no intention of deciding on the electoral system by decree or by ordinance".

At the back of many minds there was some doubt whether assurances given by Pflimlin or Mollet were really binding, as far as de Gaulle was concerned.

But, as the *Monde* put it, the Assembly was, by the end of that last meeting it was ever to hold, so charmed by de Gaulle that it committed *hara-kiri* with a smile on its lips.

De Gaulle had not, as some later said, "destroyed" the French Left. There *was* no real Left. Instead, there was a vacuum, or rather, as Mauriac was to say,

"mere phantoms of parties divided against themselves and united only in their determination to keep aloof from the Communist masses. They may have been right; but what kind of Left can there be if it is separated from the proletariat? Words and high principles. It's a lot, and it's nothing."

And not only that: the Police and the Army were on the other side. And Mollet made sure that the Left should on no account be reunited, for fear that, in the end, it might win, despite the initial advantage of the armed forces.

Thus ended the first phase of the "Gaullist Revolution".

The most significant first reaction was the acute disappointment amongst the wild men of Algiers.

De Gaulle's initial statement of June 1 had, on the whole, been well received; both soldiers and civilians of the "May 13 Movement" interpreted it as a formal condemnation of the "System", and as the first step towards liquidating it altogether.

But there was great disappointment when it was learned that important posts in the Government were going to be held by representatives of the defunct "System": Pinay, Pflimlin, Mollet, etc., while no post had been given to Soustelle or any of the other French leaders who had openly supported the Algiers rebellion.

However, many members of the Committee of Public Safety were trying to console themselves with the thought that it was necessary for de Gaulle to do a little "finessing":

"Since, they say, he was determined to observe the 'legal' forms of his investiture, he could not help including in his Government some of the leaders of the Fourth Republic, and to get their respective parties to support him. For the time being he has had to keep Soustelle out; but that won't be for long." (*Le Monde*, June 3.)

Radio-Algiers was all sound and fury: "This is the first stage; this is only our first victory. We are determined to achieve our aim, which is to make France a Great Power again. . . . We shall continue the battle relentlessly. . ."

22. THE CONFESSIONS OF M. JULES MOCH: "PARATROOPS TONIGHT?"

THE Fourth Republic had committed suicide by persuasion. Perhaps it will never be known whether on May 14—when many of the Army leaders at Algiers felt that their *coup de force* had misfired—the Government of the Republic could still have imposed its will on Algiers by drastic and spectacular action. But de Gaulle's first cryptic statement of May 15 had a heartening effect on the Algiers rebels and rendered the task of the Pflimlin Government infinitely more difficult.

In the days that followed the view was rapidly gaining ground that, short of a Popular Front movement—even if such a thing were psychologically possible—there were only these alternatives: the acceptance of de Gaulle as the "arbiter", and a "paratroop dictatorship". The French Left were, in the main, still unprepared for a Popular Front; and even those (like Claude Bourdet, for instance) who advocated it, took the heroic line that it was better to die fighting than to submit to a de Gaulle régime, which would, before long, develop into a Fascist tyranny.

But the heroic mood wasn't there—not even amongst the Communists who stood to lose more than anybody else from a de Gaulle régime.

The feeling of helplessness, both among the Government parties, and even on the extreme Left, was sharply increased by the Corsica *putsch*, and by the news blackout that followed it, when all "alarmist" stories about Committees of Public Safety being set up in Metropolitan France, and about rebellion and disobedience in the Army and the Police, were suppressed by the press censorship.

On May 26, 27, 28, there were persistent rumours in Paris of a "paratroop landing" likely to happen any moment; there was even something of a panic amongst those most likely to be exposed to the wrath of Massu's paratroopers; prominent Left-wing persons, haunted perhaps by memories of Alleg's book, are known to have avoided sleeping in their own homes. There was also a little parallel panic amongst some "nice" people, who imagined that the "Communist militia" were preparing a St. Bartholomew's Night. Algiers Radio had started the story that Jules Moch, the Minister of the Interior, had begun to arm such a "workers' militia".

These rumours—and they were not idle rumours—about the Army in France and the Police having got out of hand contributed more than anything else to the final surrender to de Gaulle—first by Guy Mollet, who started the capitulation process, partly, it is true, out of fear that a Popular Front might, before long, become a reality, if only it were given enough time; then by Vincent Auriol and others, and finally by the National Assembly itself.

The most important evidence about Corsica having been merely intended as a "dress rehearsal" for a similar and much more vast operation in France itself was produced by M. Jules Moch, M. Pflimlin's Minister of the Interior, at the "National Information Conference" held by the Socialist Party on July 6, 1958.

The most crucial day, he said, was May 27. It was during the previous night that Pflimlin had his secret meeting with de Gaulle. Ten hours later, at 12.25 p.m. de Gaulle issued his famous communiqué—"I have embarked on the regular process of forming a Government . . ." This statement was made by de Gaulle, Moch said, because he had become aware of "very grave incidents" which were expected to take place during the night of that very same day, May 27.

The whole period between the 13th of May and the investiture of de Gaulle on June 1 fell, Moch said, into two distinct periods. Up to the 23rd, the situation was dominated by the Algerian rebellion. After the Corsican *coup* of the 24th, France itself was in danger of being engulfed in civil war.

Moch recalled that it was only very reluctantly that he accepted the post of Minister of the Interior; nevertheless, in view of the gravity of the situation, he saw no alternative to accepting Pflimlin's offer.

He was armed with exceptional emergency powers—more important ones than those at the disposal of any other Minister of the Interior; and he thought, at that time, that he had a sufficient armed force at his command to maintain law and order. He was anxious to avoid two things: a "Franco *coup*" (i.e. a military *putsch*) and a "Prague *coup*", which might have become possible if a "workers' militia" had been allowed to take shape.

But the trouble, Moch said, was that, when it came to the point, neither the Army nor the Police could be relied upon.

A certain number of generals, who were Regional Commanders—in at least four out of the nine Metropolitan regions, and radiating over nearly one-half of the territory—had made no secret of being in complete sympathy with Algiers.

"I shall read you a note I received at that time from one of our comrades (I shall just omit the names):

'General X, Commander of the X region, called a meeting of all his officers on the night of May 24–25 and informed them that he was in complete agreement with Algiers. Measures of both a general and an individual nature had been decided upon (such as the arrest of Prefects, of politicians, etc.) and would be carried out at a given moment. He argued that the Army must on no account allow itself to be divided. . . . Therefore, the Army in Metropolitan France must do as the Army in Algeria had done—i.e. seize power.'

"This view was shared by the three other regional commanders I have mentioned," Moch said.

The Prefects were all at sixes and sevens; they did not know whether to arrest the suspect generals, and whether, if they did, the generals' deputies would not do the "job" in any case; the arrest of these generals might, in fact, only have precipitated the tragedy.

Instead, we had to resort to minor subterfuges, such as getting the Minister of Defence to summon the suspect generals to Paris just at a time when we thought they might start their action.

As for the paratroopers, Moch said that there were about 13,000 of them in France, chiefly concentrated at Pau, Mont-de-Marsan, Bayonne and Perpignan;[1] both officers and men were in a highly excited state, and were itching to copy the example of Algiers and Ajaccio.

Similarly, in the Air Force, the great majority of both officers and men were of the same frame of mind. And even the *gendarmerie* were far from safe.

After quoting several more instances of this unreliability of the Army, Moch concluded that during those days the Government was in constant fear of a repetition of the Ajaccio *coup* at several points of France. The ordinary conscripts were of little consequence in all this, because most of them were serving either in Germany or in Algeria.

More serious still, the Police were not much more reliable either.

"I am ashamed to say," said Moch, "that the Police was thoroughly diseased. Some of you will no doubt remember the scandalous demonstration held by the Parisian Police outside Parliament some months ago, when they shouted the most abominable slogans" [like "throw the deputies into the Seine!" and "Death to the Jews!"].

"Ex-police-commissioner Dides, himself a deputy since 1956,"[2] said Moch, "was controlling a not very numerous, but very active police network; and, from the outset, I had the impression that the Prefect of Police, though not personally guilty, had lost his grip over the Paris

---

[1] These were under the command of General Miquel, with headquarters at Toulouse. Miquel, a North-African *ultra* was, as already mentioned, planning for the night of May 27–28 his "Operation Resurrection". It was "postponed" as a result of de Gaulle's famous statement of May 27: "I have embarked . . ."

[2] On the role of Dides in the smear campaign and witch-hunt against "defeatism", see the author's *Strange History of Pierre Mendès-France*, pp. 98–9 and 271–2. According to Bromberger, *op. cit.*, the great majority of the 20,000 ordinary policemen of Paris belonged to the "Dides organization".

Police. Whenever there were Gaullist demonstrations, the police were on the side of the demonstrators."

"In short, I could not count on the great majority of the Paris Police.

"The so-called Mobile Gendarmerie were no better. Many of its men had fought at Dien Bien Phu; they had been in Algeria; they had that Army complex—a complex created by our defeat in 1940 and then reinforced by Dien Bien Phu, by Suez and all the rest of it. . . .

"This Gendarmerie completely ratted on the Government in Corsica.

"The State Police of the Sûreté Nationale were better; but their numbers, thinly spread over a large number of cities, could not be very effective. As for the militarized police, the CRS, who, in 1947–48, had been the backbone of the Republican Order [in keeping down both the Gaullists and the Communists[1]], these also were partly demoralized. They had stayed for too long in the unhealthy atmosphere of Paris, where they had joined in some regrettable demonstrations; and the attitude of those I had sent to Corsica proved far from heroic: they just placed themselves at the service of the military mutiny."

Thus, according to Moch, both Army and Police were thoroughly unreliable.

But not only that—the civilian authorities, too, had become more than doubtful.

"The Prefectoral Corps—and I say it with regret, and weighing my words—was no longer what I had known it to be eight years ago. . . . The rapid succession of ministers had created a sort of cliqueyness amongst the Prefects and their assistants, and the Prefectoral Corps no longer presented the same cohesion as in the past."

In Corsica there were six Sub-Prefects or Secretary-Generals, and only one of them had remained faithful to the Government when it came to the point. The rest simply ignored his (Moch's) categorical instructions and the Secretary-General of the Ajaccio Préfecture placed himself in the service of Colonel Thomazo, who had given himself the title of "Civil and Military Chief of Corsica". The Sub-Prefect of Calvi had concealed from the Prefect of Corsica (at Ajaccio) the arrival at Calvi that morning of M. Arrighi, the chief organizer of the *putsch*. This *putsch* was, indeed, going to be carried out with the complicity of practically all the main prefectoral officers in Corsica. Moch quoted numerous examples in addition to those already mentioned; the only men to have defied the Rebels were the sub-prefect of Sartène, the Mayor of Sartène and the Deputy-Mayor of Bastia. But the Sub-Prefect of Bastia had submitted just as the others had done. . . . Similarly, the Prefect of Corsica himself, though not exactly "collaborating" with the paratroopers, simply allowed himself to be replaced by Colonel Thomazo.

[1] See the author's *France 1940–1955*, pp. 362–8 and 415–8.

These events in Corsica had tremendous repercussions in Paris, though the general public was still scarcely aware of all their implications.

Tuesday, May 27, Moch repeated, was an absolutely crucial day.

"Pflimlin, as I already said, had seen de Gaulle up till 2 a.m. on the previous night, after which de Gaulle returned to Colombey at 5.15 a.m. I am not betraying any secret in telling you that Mollet and I were supposed to attend this secret meeting; but I had made it a condition that de Gaulle disavow the Corsican *putsch* first. This de Gaulle refused to do on the following grounds: 'I can disavow only once . . . and if this has no effect, I cannot disavow a second time.' This he said to Pflimlin, who went to the meeting alone. . . .

Pflimlin reported his conversation to Mollet and Moch; he had discussed with de Gaulle the "disavowal" of Corsica and had received from him the above reply; then he had discussed with him the possibility of a broader meeting—also a secret one—with the various Party leaders; but that was all. So when, at 12.25 p.m., the famous de Gaulle communiqué was issued—"I have embarked on the regular process . . ."—Moch's first thought was that Pflimlin must be really furious—

It made him out to be a liar. He had never said anything to us about any sort of transfer of power to de Gaulle having been discussed that night—all of which made little sense, anyway, since de Gaulle had not even seen the President of the Republic.

But—

It is correct that on the morning of May 27, and, to be precise, about two hours before the publication of the de Gaulle communiqué, I had received confirmation that a very serious movement was to take place that very night. . . . This information I received not from the Police services, but from foreign diplomatic services which had collected this information and which thought it their duty to pass it on to the French Government. . . . The Government concluded that this operation was to happen *that very evening*. In my diary I noted down: "Landing to night?" and "Paratroop insurrection?"

"And now I must tell you," said Moch, "that I received the news of the de Gaulle communiqué with a feeling of immense relief. For after this communiqué I was sure that nothing would happen that night. . . . I have not talked to de Gaulle since then, except for a conversation concerning the disarmament problem; but I am convinced that he was in possession of the same information as I was, and, roughly, about the same time."

And Moch concluded by saying that, in his opinion, only de Gaulle could now restore order and discipline in the Army; also, it was only he who was likely to instil into the officials of the Prefectoral Corps and of the Police the conviction that their primary duty was the defence of the Republic . . .[1]

[1] *Bulletin intérieur du Parti Socialiste SFIO, juillet* 1958, pp. 10–13.

PART III

THE FRANCE–DE GAULLE HONEYMOON

1. DE GAULLE IN ALGERIA—"I HAVE UNDERSTOOD YOU"

Not everybody in France heaved a sigh of relief the day de Gaulle was granted practically unlimited powers by Parliament; but few can have genuinely mourned the passing of the Fourth Republic. What is more, as time went on, there was a growing feeling that de Gaulle had greatly mellowed since he was last at the head of the Government, back in 1946; that, despite his very-superior-person manner, he was not going to do anything reckless; that he was keeping a finger on the country's pulse, and was perfectly conscious of its reluctance to see a sharply authoritarian or, worse still, a dictatorial, Government set up. Among the first things he did was to revoke several of the emergency measures taken by the Pflimlin Government, among them the press censorship. Throughout the summer, there was a happy feeling that, under de Gaulle, France had, in some ways, become a freer and more self-confident country than it had been during the last years and, especially, months of the Fourth Republic. And there were times when it seemed that, far from identifying himself with the men of the 13th of May, he was slowly, but surely, going to put them in their places, and reassert the authority of the central Government of Paris. It was also obvious that the *ultras* in Algeria were more or less openly hostile to de Gaulle, who, almost immediately, came to symbolize in their eyes an unhealthy kind of compromise between their "national revolution" and the now seemingly defunct "System". Much less certain, however, was the question of the de Gaulle–Army relationship.

It was, of course, natural that, having been put in power by Algiers, de Gaulle should hasten, as head of the new Government, to go on a pilgrimage to this "source of power"—and, as the *Monde* put it, "purify it, if possible".

This first de Gaulle visit to Algiers marked the beginning of an incredibly long, complicated and tortuous process, the ultimate aim of which was, in de Gaulle's view, peace in Algeria. But was it, as so often seemed, a straightforward conflict between a "liberal" de Gaulle on the one hand and an "anti-liberal" Algiers and an almost equally "anti-liberal" Army on the other?

What, then, was the position in Algeria, three weeks after the 13th of May? The truth is that, since that day, the official authorities had very largely been replaced by the Army—and by a variety of unauthorized persons who had formed wholly irregular committees of "public safety". Of these, the most important one was the "Committee for Algeria and the Sahara", an enlarged version of the original May 13 Committee. In the smaller localities, the CPS's were merely organisms controlled by the Army; but the big Algeria and Sahara Committee, composed of both soldiers and civilians, seemed determined not to fade out, whatever de Gaulle thought of it. Apart from "Gaullists" like Delbecque, there were on this committee, as we have seen, a large number of wild men—people like Martel, Lagaillarde and Dr. Lefèvre, who had a great influence over the "Algiers street", as well as certain paratroop colonels, who were looking upon the "de Gaulle solution" as merely a first step towards a Fascist revolution in France. Massu, while unwilling to defy de Gaulle openly, was nevertheless making statements which suggested that de Gaulle could not depend entirely on his sense of discipline. "*General de Gaulle,*" he told the *Daily Telegraph* on June 2, "*must decide in favour of integration.*" Although competent observers were extremely dubious about the Franco-Moslem "fraternization" which the Army had staged, the fact remained that the Army had adopted "integration" as its slogan, and that this had also been accepted (no doubt with many mental reservations) by numerous Europeans most hostile to it in the past.

As for the colonels like Godard, Trinquier and Lacheroy, their work, which has often been described as having been inspired by the reading of Mao Tse-Tung, consisted primarily, as far as Algeria was concerned, in an *encadrement des masses* by a system of "parallel hierarchies"—both on a territorial level and (since May 13) on a "party" level, each "population unit" (block of houses, village, district, province) being "framed" (*encadré*) by members of what was, in effect, a military-fascist group of activists. This work of *encadrement* had been started about a year before, and produced the most spectacular results in the city of Algiers where the activists and their Moslem agents had scared the Moslem population into complete submission. Many of these colonels had at the back of their minds the possibility of extending this system to France itself, in the name of "anti-Communism".[1] While some of these ideas had been borrowed from Mao Tse-Tung, others were not unlike those practised under the Nazi régime, with its network of "block guardians" (*Blockwarte*) at the base of the Nazi pyramid.

No less important was the fact that in a large number of Army units,

[1] In May 1959, Marshal Juin, General Massu and General Challe (by this time C.-in-C. in Algeria) started talking quite openly about the *encadrement* of France and of "stamping out sedition" there, as a preliminary to the "inevitable showdown between East and West". These fantasies received no support from de Gaulle himself.

and particularly amongst the paratroopers, both the war in Algeria and the May 13 *putsch* had created a feeling of independence, a superiority complex and, indeed, something of an "ideology".

As Jean Lacouture significantly remarked:

Since May 13 the Army has become a sort of "Party", with a "political conscience" of its own.[1]

We shall examine later this phenomenon of the Army as a "Party"— something that had never happened in France before.

It was curious how, on the eve of General de Gaulle's arrival in Algiers, orders should have been given to replace the paratroopers who had been guarding the GG, the Ministry of Algeria, since May 13 by more reliable Naval Infantry units.

No doubt de Gaulle's arrival at Algiers on that 4th of June was celebrated as a great day of victory by the people of Algiers. The crowds greeted him with Mediterranean exuberance; the streets were a sea of tricolour flags, and the streamers and confetti were expended with all the generosity of Fifth Avenue. But they cried not only "*Vive de Gaulle!*" but also "*Vive Soustelle!*", and, more frequently still: "*Algérie française!*" These crowds did not know that de Gaulle had firmly committed himself in Paris to not taking Soustelle into his Government. Nor were they aware at first that de Gaulle was being accompanied by two members of his Cabinet. When this became known, there was much grumbling about "the System" being still alive. Also, an unfavourable impression was created by the pointed manner in which de Gaulle received the diplomatic corps and the "legally-constituted bodies" of the city of Algiers, among them the representatives of the Town Hall, the Church and the University, before seeing the Committee of Public Safety, whose members were presented to him by General Massu.

Massu said to de Gaulle that the Army had adopted Integration as its ideal and he asked de Gaulle to eliminate the remnants of the "System," and people who had been "finally discredited in the eyes of the country", and to look upon the Committees of Public Safety as the most reliable supporters in that peaceful revolution which he (de Gaulle) was now carrying out, and as the real "civil backbone" of this revolution.

Although, on leaving the Summer Palace, the members of the CPS declared themselves delighted with de Gaulle, he actually is now known to have replied extremely frigidly to Massu's "appeal". Indeed, soon afterwards a communiqué was issued on de Gaulle's behalf saying that, to avoid any misunderstandings, he himself would speak to the people of Algiers that evening.

[1] *Le Monde*, June 5, 1958.

Long before de Gaulle was due to speak from the famous "Forum" balcony, 200,000 people (nearly all Europeans) had crowded into the "Forum", and were harangued for a couple of hours by various members of the CPS, such as M. Denis, who exclaimed:

We've got to finish with the whole damned system, and we've got to finish off all those swine. . . .

Later, a rather more moderate speech was made by Salan, and another by Soustelle, who exalted the heroism and unanimous enthusiasm of the ten million people of Algeria. "They all want to remain French, and it is thanks to their determination that General de Gaulle is with us today, a day of happiness and glory!"

Finally, at 7 p.m. de Gaulle appeared on the famous balcony. A few seconds before, the two ministers accompanying him—M. Jacquinot and M. Max Lejeune—were stopped on the stair by members of the CPS and pushed into an office and locked up. The representatives of the "System" were not to be allowed on to the "Forum" balcony. De Gaulle, who did not hear about this until later, was extremely angry. There was also another *contretemps*: the French State Radio had sent its own professional broadcasters from Paris to cover the de Gaulle visit; but they were not allowed into Algiers broadcasting station, and the events of the day were reported by the amateurs who had taken over the station on May 13 on behalf of the Committee of Public Safety. The radio-commentaries were extremely amateurish ("*mais c'est inoui, cet enthousiasme, c'est incroyable, c'est formidable*", etc.) but, more important, the whole emphasis was not on the enthusiastic reception given to de Gaulle, but on the "*inoui*" and the "*formidable*" ovations that the presence of Soustelle were producing everywhere.

"*Je vous ai compris* (I have understood you)", de Gaulle began. The phrase was enough to cause the Algiers crowds to burst into several minutes' frantic cheering.

I have understood you [he repeated]. I know what happened here. I know what you wanted to do. The road you have thrown open in Algeria is the road of renewal and of fraternity.

The "renewal", he said, must in the first place apply to the institutions of France; and the "fraternity" was symbolized by "the magnificent spectacle" of the different communities "joining hands". (Not that there were many Moslems present, holding anybody's hands.)

Well, I take note of all this and I declare, in the name of France, that from today, France considers that in the whole of Algeria there is only one category of inhabitants—only complete Frenchmen (*à part entière*), all having the same rights and the same duties.

Which means that the roads must be opened to those who had them closed to them before. Those who had not the means of living must be given these means now. Those whom human dignity was denied must be treated with dignity now. Those who doubted whether they had a homeland must no longer doubt that they have one.

After paying a warm tribute to the ardour, discipline and "the magnificent work of understanding and pacification" of the Army, de Gaulle said that the Army would be the guardian (*le garant*) of the movement that had developed in Algeria.

The Army knew how to dam the current and to capture its energy. I express my confidence to the Army. I count on it both now and in future.

In three months all the "complete" Frenchmen, including the ten million Frenchmen of Algeria, would vote together, as a single electoral body (*au collège unique*) to decide their own destiny.

And then came the key phrase: "With these elected representatives, we shall see what to do about the rest." (. . . *nous verrons comment faire le reste*). It meant that after the election the French Government would confer with the lawful representatives of Algeria to see what status was to be given to the country.

But what about the FLN? De Gaulle appealed to them, too. He wanted them also to vote. Out of despair, they had taken up arms against France; it was a courageous battle—"for there is no lack of courage in this land of Algeria"—though a cruel and fratricidal one.

"I, de Gaulle, open to them the gates of reconciliation! Never have I felt more than I do tonight how beautiful, how great, how generous France is! *Vive la République! Vive la France!*"

Well, that was that. There was no mention of "French Algeria". Nor had de Gaulle mentioned "integration". The "rest" would be decided upon after the Algerian people had—on a basis of electoral equality—duly elected their representatives; and "the rest" meant—everything. The future of Algeria would not be settled either unilaterally by Paris, or by the screaming in the Algiers "Forum".

The speech was nevertheless full of obscurities. Would the FLN give up the struggle? Had de Gaulle subscribed to "integration" (without mentioning it) as it was understood by M. Soustelle, or had he left the door open for the adoption of some kind of Federation, when the time came to "decide about the rest" with the "elected representatives" of the Algerian people? And, above all, how would the "complete" Moslem Frenchmen be elected? No doubt, the Army would "control" the Algiers Movement; but what was really going to be its attitude to this Movement?

And what was going to be its attitude to de Gaulle? Nor had the Algiers populace received any satisfaction as regards Soustelle; two days later de Gaulle announced that he himself would be "Minister of Algeria"; he said nothing about the future of Soustelle, whom Algiers wanted appointed to that post. . . .

An FLN spokesman at Cairo rejected de Gaulle's speech as even a "basis of discussion". Ferhat Abbas at Geneva, though less trenchant, argued that de Gaulle had, in fact, spoken of "integration", even though without using the word. The Algerians wanted to be Algerians, not bogus Frenchmen.

At Constantine, where de Gaulle, accompanied by Salan and Soustelle, spoke to crowds containing a much higher proportion of Moslems than at Algiers, he used practically the same words as on the previous day. Again his speech was interrupted by cries of "*Algérie française!*", "*Intégration complète!*" and "Soustelle!" So much so that, on one occasion, Soustelle himself felt obliged to wave at his supporters to shut up.

De Gaulle was finding all this increasingly irritating, and decided to take a firm line with the Committees of Public Safety at the next convenient opportunity. This soon presented itself. At Oran, where he went after a brief visit to Bône, a spokesman of the local CPS, a M. Carlin, addressing de Gaulle, read out to him the following "petition" on behalf of the committee:

Complete powers should be delegated in Algeria to General Salan;
All French laws should apply in Algeria;
The Government should rest its authoirty in Algeria on the Committees of Public Safety;
An end should be put to the régime of Parties and to foreign interference;
The members of the Committees of Public Safety should take part in a grandiose patriotic demonstration in the Champs-Elysées in Paris on June 18.

Looking more and more impatient as M. Carlin was pouring forth his demands, de Gaulle finally exploded:

None of you people seems to realize that authority[1] must remain unquestioned in Algeria. In any case, it has all my confidence.
You gentlemen will *not* continue to make a revolution. Your job is to win over people's minds to national unity, to the reform of France, and to support for General de Gaulle, without trying to force his hand, and within the framework which I shall set down.

---

[1] He did not specify whether he meant the authority of the State or of the Army, though later he spoke of the "authority of the Army".

And continuing rather less harshly, de Gaulle said:

There is one matter of capital importance: the contacts to be established between the two communities. Things must be done in such a way that the ten million French Algerians should not have the slightest doubt that they *are* French. You have to take a lofty view of things, since you ought to be models of intellectual honesty, loyalty and national discipline. . . . The Army must control everybody, and, in particular, it must control you. Do not force its hand; don't even look as though you were trying to do so.

And, in reply to the demand that the "Parties" be dissolved, de Gaulle bluntly said:

And don't you waste your energies on any such vendettas. France cannot be made without all Frenchmen taking part in the work.

This curbing of the Committees of Public Safety was not intended for Algeria only. It was M. Delbecque, Soustelle's right-hand man in person, who, on the very day before de Gaulle's Oran statement, had prepared a broadcast for Radio-Algiers against the "princes of the system" who were "hoping to strangle the Algiers Revolution". These were the blood-curdling threats Delbecque was going to address to France:

In France, the Committees of Public Safety will come out of hiding, and will rally round the National Committee. . . . They will, up to the time of the referendum, conduct propaganda. . . . They must checkmate all the manœuvres and tricks of the moribund "System" against national unity. . . . Having met the principal representatives of these committees, I can assure you that these men are determined to see it through. . . . Metropolitan France has not yet fully understood the meaning of the Algerian people's revolution. . . . Yet I felt that in Paris a new generation of patriots had risen, and that this generation was determined to put a final end to the "System". . . . This new France, solidly linked with the Army, which, for fifteen years, has been carrying the banner of Youth, will regroup itself behind the Committees of Public Safety.

In this script there was no mention of the name of General de Gaulle. General Salan prohibited the use of this broadcast on Radio-Algiers and finally it was transmitted only by some private radio stations. But it got into the press all the same.

What, then, were these "clandestine committees of Public Safety" to which Delbecque had been referring? How much of all this was bluff?

A few days before his Algiers broadcast, M. Delbecque had told two journalists that "in a few days, a National Committee of Public Safety will be set up, that is, as soon as we have completed our inquiry concerning the 320 Committees of Public Safety which have already informed us of their existence". But did they really exist? As the *Monde* of June 6 put it:

> Up till now a few of them have officially announced their existence—those of Tarbes, Toulouse, Lyon and the Rhône Department. There are other numerous bodies which send out, chiefly to the press, all sorts of leaflets signed by unknown names; it is hard to say whether any of this is serious or even authentic. In particular there is something calling itself the "CPS of Paris", and whose communiqués are signed "on behalf of its Central Committee" by somebody calling himself "Captain Way"—an obvious pseudonym; no address is given. . . . These communiqués should, however, be examined in the light of the statements made by M. Delbecque, and also of Colonel Thomazo's press conference at Bastia on June 2 in the course of which he said: "We know that the Committees of Public Safety will become more and more important in France in helping General de Gaulle to revive the country's greatness."[1]

As we have seen, there was practically no agitation in France during the May crisis on the part of any Fascist "activists"; there was no evidence that these were numerous, except possibly in places like Toulouse, where there were several thousand "North African repatriates" with a truly pathological hatred for the Republic, or Lyon, where M. Soustelle had been particularly active.

And although there was not much evidence of Committees of Public Safety being very active anywhere in France, or having any sort of serious following, the question nevertheless was to arise among political observers only a few weeks later: was there not *a deal* underlying the appointment of Soustelle to the post of Minister of Information? Delbecque had announced in his Algiers broadcast that the very first task of the Committees of Public Safety in France would be to conduct propaganda for the Referendum; did the "deal" not consist in shutting up the Committees of Public Safety in return for handing over French radio and television (on certain conditions) to M. Soustelle? One condition being that this radio and TV propaganda was to be essentially "Gaullist" and not just propaganda for the "Algiers Revolution" and against the "System". . . .

In June, at any rate, these Committees of Public Safety in France, whatever their real strength, were taken fairly seriously by what was left of "republican opinion". In the absence of Parliament, de Gaulle had now assumed the airs of a King of France, governing with the aid of a "Crown Council"—his Cabinet largely made up of former members of the defunct "System". Was there not a danger, it was asked, that the "activists" of the Committees of Public Safety might not establish some sort of rival authority, possibly with the complicity of certain Army elements, which

---

[1] A few days later "Captain Way" made his identity known; he was a small Paris businessman, apparently of no importance whatsoever.

would then try to set up a "single party"—a party whose "barons" would try to save the "King" from his "republican" Crown Council? On a short-term basis, these fears proved unjustified. There were, nevertheless, to be two significant developments in the coming months: (1) the appointment of Soustelle to the post of Minister of Information, and (2) Soustelle's attempt to revive the RPF, followed by his attempt to get de Gaulle to adopt an election system which would have greatly favoured this new RPF . . .

After Oran, and before returning to France, de Gaulle made another speech at Mostaganem in which he used, for the first time, the phrase *"Algérie française"*—a phrase he had, until then, carefully avoided. This added to the confusion, both in Algeria and France, that had already been caused by some of de Gaulle's utterances. In Paris, some commentators dismissed it merely as a slip of the tongue.

And again, at Mostaganem, de Gaulle spoke of there being "only one kind of citizen in Algeria":

I give you my word of honour, and I proclaim it in the name of France, that there are only complete Frenchmen here, fellow-Frenchmen, fellow-citizens who will henceforth walk through life hand in hand. . . .

And, in three months, de Gaulle reiterated, the ten million Frenchmen of Algeria would take part on an equal footing in expressing the national will (a reference to the Referendum and the subsequent elections).

It sounded good; but would these words put an end to years and years of enmity between the two communities, to the widespread anti-Arab racialism of the Europeans, including the *petits blancs*; also, what did equality mean so long as one community had a *per capita* income ten times larger than the other?

And all this was still a far cry to that (albeit highly ambiguous) "self-determination" offer de Gaulle was to make to Algeria in September 1959. One can just imagine how "self-determination" would have been received in Algiers in June 1958!

On the last day of his visit to Algeria de Gaulle sent a letter to General Salan appointing him Delegate-General of the Government in Algeria, and confirming him in his functions as Commander-in-Chief in Algeria.

"You shall communicate directly with me, to whom you are subordinated, and who will, inside the Government, take responsibility for Algerian affairs"—

which meant, in effect, that he, de Gaulle, was Minister of Algeria, with Salan as his deputy.

In this letter de Gaulle also instructed Salan to maintain and, when necessary, to "re-establish the workings of regular authority". Salan was also empowered to remove from Algeria any officials whom he considered unsuitable "in present circumstances". As for the Committees of Public Safety, de Gaulle gave Salan the following instructions:

These committees, which spontaneously came into being in the course of recent events, cannot, obviously, and in any circumstances, impinge upon the functions of the regular authorities. They can, however, under your control, usefully employ themselves at unifying public opinion and particularly at creating contacts between the various Algerian communities.

What, then, was the net result of de Gaulle's first visit to Algiers? Had he achieved all that he had set out to do? Had he fully restored the authority of the French State in Algeria, that very strange country whose European community always expected and demanded help and support from France, while, at the same time, resenting "Metropolitan interference"?

It was, unfortunately, obvious that de Gaulle had not succeeded, by his mere personal presence, in putting an end to the "Algiers revolution". He had, however, stressed the absolute necessity of "restoring legality" and—and this is where complications were likely to arise sooner or later—*he had entrusted the Army with this task*. If he assumed that the Army was unconditionally "for de Gaulle", was he being naïve—or did he have no other choice? Or was he hoping that, if not at once, at least gradually, he would win over the Army?

De Gaulle must, in fact, have realized that not everything was quite "straight" as far as the Army was concerned. He must have been unpleasantly surprised when, after telling Salan that he was proposing to dissolve the Committees of Public Safety, the Commander-in-Chief strongly urged him not to do so. In the circumstances, de Gaulle did not press the point, and confined himself to laying down, in his letter to Salan, the general principles concerning the future, purely "auxiliary", role of the CPS's.

On the face of it, the Army, as represented by Salan and Massu, *seemed* to be willing henceforth to take orders from de Gaulle. On the CPS's the reaction was much more mixed: it was not even possible any longer to distinguish very clearly between "Gaullists" and "activists" (or *ultras*). M. Neuwirth, a Gaullist, and official spokesman of the Algiers committee, declared himself in full agreement with de Gaulle and said that "the aims of the movement had been attained". He even specified that the main task of the CPS's was now to prepare the Referendum—a Referendum which would finally liquidate "the System", and would give France a new Constitution "which would be compatible with the Atomic Age" *(sic)*. But another "Gaullist" and a close associate of Soustelle's, M. Delbecque, as we have seen, persisted in thinking that this was only "a beginning". However, having been reprimanded for his broadcast by both Salan and Massu, he agreed that this had been "rather on the blunt side", and he also assured the generals that if he was going for a few days to Paris, "it was only on family business".

And certain other anomalies continued, even after the CPS's had had their new (and limited) role clearly defined by de Gaulle. M. Chevallier, the liberal Mayor of Algiers, who had been driven out of office by the May 13 *putsch*, was not reinstated;[1] while Radio-Algiers continued to be run by agents of the Committee of Public Safety. . . . The great question now was whether Salan, who had not been able to do much so long as he represented only M. Pflimlin, and whose authority Algiers was reluctant to recognize, would now be able, as de Gaulle's official delegate, to dictate his will to the European community and to the *whole* of the Army, including the Fascist colonels? Or would his position continue to remain slightly ambiguous? Or, finally, was not he going to continue to play a little double game of his own?[2]

But what about the ordinary European population, and what about the Moslems?

The prevalent impression amongst the Europeans was that de Gaulle had accepted "integration", since he had constantly spoken of the "ten million Frenchmen of Algeria", thus, in their view, subscribing to their precious theory that instead of the Europeans being a minority in an Algeria of ten million people, the Moslems would become a minority in a France of fifty-three millions. De Gaulle's "*Vive l'Algérie française*" at Mostaganem tended to convince them that he had been converted to their way of thinking—though there continued, needless to say, a prejudice against de Gaulle's use of the phrase "single college".[3]

---

[1] Chevallier had sent his official resignation, as Mayor of Algiers, to General Salan just before de Gaulle's visit. Normally, after what de Gaulle had said, Chevallier should have been reinstated and his resignation refused; but the "activists" had shown him such hostility that neither he himself nor Salan thought it wise for him to stay on as head of the Algiers municipality.

[2] That is precisely what he *was* going to do until finally de Gaulle withdrew him from Algeria and "kicked him upstairs".

[3] The *collège unique*, meaning equal electoral rights for both European and Moslem voters, in place of the "two electoral colleges" one of which, in terms of representation in the Algerian Assembly weighed several times more than the other, was a heresy against which the *ultras*, like de Sérigny of the *Echo d'Alger*, had fought tooth-and-nail right up to May 13. If these people were now paying lip-service to the *collège unique* as an inevitable corollary of "fraternization", and of that "equality" of which de Gaulle never stopped talking, it was no doubt because they still believed that the Army would act as the necessary "corrective" in handling the voters in such a way that the great disasters prophesied by opponents of the *collège unique* would be prevented. Which is precisely what was to happen both in the Referendum of September 28 and, more blatantly still, in the general election of November 30.

As for the Moslems, all that could be safely said at that time was this: neither had they been indifferent to de Gaulle's visit; nor, on the other hand, had there been any genuine "miracle" of fraternization.

The only miracle (wrote Alain Jacob in the *Monde* on June 8) is that no acts of violence should have been committed against the Moslems by our European "revolutionaries" on May 13 or on the following days. But there is no reason for supposing that most of the Moslems look with any favour upon "integration", as understood by our Army officers. . . . All that can be safely assumed is that the Moslems still believe in the possibility of General de Gaulle proposing something out of the ordinary. . . . But there is not much time to lose. The FLN in Cairo have rejected de Gaulle's proposals; does it follow that the Algerian nationalists, to whose courage de Gaulle paid several tributes, will refuse to talk?

And Jacob concluded that if only there were fair elections in which the Algerian nationalists could freely compete, there might be a settlement between the French and the genuine representatives of the Algerian people whom the election would bring into the open. As we shall see, that is precisely what de Gaulle wanted to happen; but his instructions were to be sabotaged both by the European "activists" and, worse still, by the Army itself.

De Gaulle's return to Paris from Algeria on Saturday, June 7, did not mark the end of his difficulties with the Committees of Public Safety. A few days later, the Committee for Algeria and the Sahara passed unanimously a motion in which, broadly speaking, it adopted those very demands which de Gaulle had sharply rejected during his visit to Oran, as well as some others.

The motion asked that no municipal elections be held in Algeria before the Referendum; that the *loi-cadre* be declared null and void; that "any administrative organisms emphasizing the particularism of Algeria" (and so, incompatible with "integration")—such as the Ministry of Algeria and the Ministry of the Sahara—be abolished, and, finally, that the political parties be dissolved, since these were "instruments of vested interests and factors of disunity".

The odd—or not so odd—thing is that this motion was approved by General Salan—even though it criticized those very municipal elections which he himself had favoured. No doubt, with Algeria in a state of war, there were some strong arguments against holding municipal elections;[1]

---

[1] There was, clearly, no proper basis for holding these municipal elections. In the city of Algiers, only some 20,000 out of the 200,000 prospective Moslem voters held voters' cards, while in the countryside, where the French were, more or less, in control, the military authorities were very far from having completed the population census; in other areas, controlled by the FLN, these had, in many cases, confiscated or temporarily "retained" identity cards and similar papers. Nor had most of the Moslem women been registered as voters anywhere.

but the rest of the CPS's document betrayed an "ideology" which was quite rightly described as "Vichyite"—all the more so as the passage in the motion condemning the political parties was accompanied by a glorification of virtues based on "the profession, the family, the commune and the province".

And the worst of it was that many soldiers had taken part in drawing up and voting this motion.

De Gaulle reacted sharply. In a message to Salan he described the motion of June 10 as "unfortunate and irresponsible" (*fâcheux et intempestif*); he pointed out to Salan that he had no business to approve or disapprove of such a motion; and ordered him to tell the "people concerned" that the task he (de Gaulle) had undertaken required a calm and reasonable attitude and "the loyal support of all who wish to help me to save the unity, the integrity and the independence of the country".

In Paris, de Gaulle's sharp reply to the Algiers Committee was generally welcomed; many commentators argued that even if the "wild men" amongst the civilian members probably continued to be troublesome, the officers and generals would, at any rate, submit to de Gaulle. And, without the support of the military, the civilians couldn't do much. . . .

What perhaps made all this Algiers campaigning against the political parties a little awkward for de Gaulle was that they were borrowing some of their ideas not only from Vichy, but also from the programme of de Gaulle's own RPF of 1947–53. De Gaulle had, however, made it plain that he had no intention of returning to the RPF policy or RPF tactics—which had proved unacceptable to Metropolitan France.

As regards the presence on the Algiers Committee of both civilians and soldiers, it is worth noting that already on June 12, two days after the famous motion of the Algiers Committee, the question arose whether de Gaulle was to order the military to get out of the Committees of Public Safety. He thought of doing so, but then—decided against . . . for the present. It is probable that since he was determined at any price to maintain the "unity of the Army", he was just not absolutely sure whether the more extremist elements amongst the military—particularly the paratroop colonels like Trinquier (the man who did more than any other to lend military support to the *putsch* of May 13)—would obey, and he preferred not to take a chance.[1]

About the civilian members of the CPS there was some renewed speculation after their motion of June 10: it was thought that the numerically stronger Algiers "activists" and *ultras*, loudly voicing their disappointment over certain aspects of the de Gaulle visit to Algeria, were now overruling the "Gaullists"—not that these, as we have seen from the

---

[1] Among the seventy-two members of the CPS for Algeria and the Sahara, fifteen were soldiers: General Massu (President), General Jouhaud (Vice-President), General Mirambeau (Sahara); eight colonels (amongst them Trinquier and Thomazo), and four captains.

behaviour of some of them, like M. Delbecque, were necessarily more "moderate".

Complicated though the whole Algiers set-up was, one thing was fairly clear after de Gaulle's return to Paris; and that was that he had not entirely succeeded in "stopping the Algiers revolution"; that there were mighty few people in Algiers whom he could trust, but that he was hoping gradually to impose his authority on the Army. Not that the behaviour of this— judging from the way Salan had acted on June 10—could be regarded as completely reliable either.

2. PARIS IN JUNE—MALRAUX'S PRESS CONFERENCE: "NO MORE TORTURE"

OPINION in France, and particularly in Paris, was much more favourable to de Gaulle than were the Europeans of Algiers, despite all the show of popular enthusiasm that had accompanied his visit there. Paris, on the contrary, was taking de Gaulle very calmly. He seemed to embody a reasonable solution to the dangerous crisis of May; Big Business was reassured; the bulk of the press was wholly favourable to the General; the bourgeoisie, without being frantically enthusiastic about him, saw in him a guardian of the *status quo* to which he was promising to add some method and order. People on the Left, who had darkly prophesied that de Gaulle was merely "a first step to Fascism", were, if anything, reassured by his seemingly liberal manner, both at the National Assembly and during his Algerian tour; his *Roi de France* airs, so different from the airs of a vulgar plebeian dictator, had a certain pleasing historical quality; at heart, a high proportion of the French have a soft spot for royalty, while the little anti-parliamentary side in every Frenchman's heart derived some amusement and enjoyment from the numerous stories that were current about de Gaulle's way of discussing business with his Cabinet ministers, the survivors of the "System". He was a good listener: he liked to be informed, but, having been informed, he then took a decision, and nobody dared to object. Thanks to his natural role of arbiter, the time spent on discussions was much shorter at Cabinet meetings than it used to be. He was never offensive to his colleagues; often a light gesture of impatience was enough to put a man in his place; and, coming from de Gaulle, any little sign of approval or praise was doubly appreciated. While he liked to listen, and did not mind allowing himself to be influenced, he seldom entered into long discussions himself, before announcing his decision. With a slightly weary and very-superior-person air he would sometimes outline a whole policy by merely dropping a few hints. When, at one Cabinet meeting, a minister expressed grave apprehensions lest genuinely free elections in Algeria might result in some real Algerian nationalists (who would demand Independence) being returned, de Gaulle merely said: "That wouldn't worry me at all; on the contrary, it would suit me." Then, in case he hadn't been fully understood, de Gaulle gave an historical illustration to the point he had made:

> Rebellions can be stopped. It has happened before. Remember the *Chouans*. Bonaparte called together the *Chouan* chiefs and said to them: "No more killing. No more prisoners. No more arrests. Let's talk." It may be the same thing in Algeria. . . . I am not Bonaparte, but I believe that one ought to talk to everybody, and exclude nobody.

De Gaulle, especially during those early months, felt particularly invulnerable—at least in France; and, if he felt strongly about anything, he was determined not to yield, except on some minor points of detail—and even then only to show that he was not being dictatorial. This was particularly true in the case of the Constitution. Neither criticisms made at Cabinet meetings, nor amendments proposed by the Constitutional Advisory Committee, had very much effect on the final text of the Constitution which de Gaulle was determined from the start to push through with as little change as possible. Algeria, however, was a harder nut to crack.

Throughout the summer, Algeria and the Constitution were, indeed, de Gaulle's two principal worries. He showed comparatively little interest in financial and economic affairs (for which he had never much cared) or—at that stage—even in foreign affairs, except that he hastened to improve relations with both Tunisia and Morocco. Finance, economics, labour problems were, to de Gaulle, only auxiliary factors in his Greater Design, and he largely left these matters to the specialists and technicians— to M. Pinay, the Minister of Finance, to M. Pompidou, his *directeur de cabinet*, to the experts of the ministries concerned. One of the first things to be done after de Gaulle's return from Algeria, it is true, was to launch M. Pinay's 3½ per cent internal loan, which, being guaranteed in terms of gold against depreciation, was attractive both to big and small investors. Its proceeds were calculated to bridge the deficit for a few months. De Gaulle graciously lent himself to appealing to subscribers over the radio and TV, though he drew the line at doing any vulgar salesmanship in boosting its great financial advantages, and concentrated instead on how he, de Gaulle, had saved France from civil war, and on how it was only right that the French people should make the loan a "triumphal success".

> "This loan will mark the first stage of our revival; it will be the first proof of the Nation's confidence in itself and, may I add, of your confidence in me, who needs this confidence so much."

And, after referring to the basic soundness of France's economy, to the happy future of its young generation, to the great wealth of the Sahara, and to the overwhelming importance of the future new Constitution, de Gaulle concluded:

"The road ahead is hard but beautiful! The aim is difficult, but how great! Onward, now that we have made a start!"

Though not greatly interested in labour conditions, he showed a benevolent attitude to the trade unions; he thought, at one time, of including leaders of the non-Communist unions in his Cabinet, and he was almost offended when the leaders of the Communist CGT declined his invitation to confer with him.

Inside his Cabinet de Gaulle's apparent preference for a "liberal" policy in Algeria was shared by everybody—until the day when Jacques Soustelle was appointed Minister of Information. Striking, indeed, was the difference in both approach and temperament between Soustelle and André Malraux who, during the first few weeks of the de Gaulle régime, had been Acting Minister of Information. On the "colonialist" Right, Malraux was looked upon askance from the start, and severely criticized, especially after his famous press conference of June 24.

Malraux, the one-time great novelist, the soldier, the man of action, who seemed to love action for action's sake, and revolution for revolution's sake, who had fought both for lost causes and for winning causes, as an airman in Republican Spain, as a leader of the Alsace-Lorraine Brigade in Germany in 1944–45; who had plotted against the Germans in the French Resistance, and had faced death in a Gestapo prison at Toulouse in 1943, had, however, never been a great success as a politician. With his "poetic" appearance, his carefully-studied gestures, Malraux, as a politician, was less a romantic than a theatrical figure.

As Minister of Information in the de Gaulle Government after the Liberation, he tried to impersonate the virtues and the *mystique* of the Resistance, even long after all this *mystique* had died. As propaganda chief of de Gaulle's RPF, he had been the finest intellectual ornament of the movement; but he had a way of talking high-falutin' and pretentious nonsense about the RPF being in the great tradition of Valmy and the French Revolution, which no doubt charmed literary-minded ladies in his audience, but did not make the slightest impression on prospective voters interested in the price of steak.

At one time, at the end of 1954, he had played with the idea of starting a new "Nouvelle Gauche" movement, with de Gaulle and Mendès-France as its leading lights; he thought they could absorb the bulk of the five-million Communist vote. This absurd idea was soon dropped.

De Gaulle had a personal regard and even affection for Malraux, though one may doubt whether he took him very seriously. It is highly probable, all the same, that the main points Malraux made at his famous press conference on June 24 were made with de Gaulle's approval. Whether or not it was intended to reassure "republican opinion" in France, it is doubtful whether it reassured anybody—for there was something wildly unrealistic about the whole presentation of the Malraux case. On the other hand, there was quite enough in the press conference to get a part of the Right-wing press into a fury, and to make it recommend, as politely as possible, the removal of Malraux from the Ministry of Information.

After answering a number of specific questions, such as "Do you intend to suppress the political parties?"—to which Malraux replied that there had never been any question of doing so[1]—he then made the following points:

The de Gaulle Government represented the *continuity of the Republic;* this did not mean, however, that it would remain inactive until the time when the Fifth Republic was set up. It was not a caretaker government, and it knew that *France, the paralytic, wanted to walk again.*

"When I speak of France," said Malraux, "I include in it those who marched on May 28 from the Nation to the République. That is, those who demonstrated their attachment to the French Republic, not to the Russian Republic."

He couldn't quite resist delivering this side-kick at the Communists, though since June 1 de Gaulle himself had carefully avoided resurrecting the "separatist" slogan.[2]

And then:

Today there are men who want the Republic without General de Gaulle; there are others who want General de Gaulle without the Republic; but the majority of Frenchmen want *both* the Republic and de Gaulle.

And then came this "mystical" Malraux way of speaking of "the

[1] The constant assertions that de Gaulle had *never* advocated the abolition of the political parties was one of the major quibbles of the de Gaulle régime of 1958. Both the explicit and even more so, the implicit aim of de Gaulle's RPF—with its constant denunciation of the Parties as the source of all evil, and its refusal to recognize the fact that the disappearance of all parties (except a single party) meant, in effect, dictatorship—was, in fact, the suppression of the parties, and their replacement by a single "rally".

At his press conference on November 12, 1947, de Gaulle said quite explicitly: "The RPF (the French People's Rally) will continue to extend and develop *until it embraces the entire nation,* except, of course, the Communists who have not made it their business to form part of the nation, a few odd 'general staffs' [of the Parties] without troops, and a few cranky individuals." If this was not a "single party" programme, one should like to know what is! (*cf. L'Année Politique,* 1947, p. 129; also J. Debû-Bridel's *Les Partis contre de Gaulle* (1948) rubbing in this point, page after page.)

[2] At the height of the Cold War, the RPF used to treat the French Communists as "separatists".

people" as a kind of historical abstraction: he said that de Gaulle represented neither the motorists of the Champs-Elysées, nor the pedestrians of the Nation-République demonstration; on June 18 the whole people of Paris were present in the Champs-Elysées to hail de Gaulle: the people of the Republic and the people of the Nation. Not really a very good pun if this was meant to be both an allusion to the East-end march, and another way of saying that both the Right (*Nation*) and the Left (*République*) were there.

I shall digress for a moment. The truth is that on June 18, when, on the anniversary of his famous London broadcast, de Gaulle drove up the Champs-Elysées, standing in an open car, there were scarcely any "East end" elements in the crowd at all; while the "West end", too, had not turned out in force, and the cheering which de Gaulle received that day from the not very numerous—mostly well-dressed—people along the avenue was, if anything, surprisingly half-hearted. It was as though people were waiting to see what he would do before they went into frantic raptures.[1] For one thing, nobody was quite certain that he was really solving the Algerian problem.

Malraux also announced that he would soon speak himself to "the people of Paris" from "one of the squares which form part of our history since the Revolution"; and he would proclaim to the people of Paris: "We are not your enemies." All this sounded rather theatrical and unrealistic—as, indeed, M. Malraux's two not very happy experiments in that line—on July 14 in front of the Hôtel de Ville, and on September 4 in the Place de la République—were to show.

After that Malraux embarked on a long harangue about the miracle of "fraternization" in Algeria.

He admitted that "in all probability" the first groups of Moslems who had gone in for "fraternization" after May 13 had been bribed; but then—making a highly dubious historical assertion—Malraux said that, after all, the Battle of Valmy was won because the Duke of Brunswick had been bribed by Danton; yet, *after* that, the armies of the French Revolution won many genuine victories, like those of Fleurus and Jemmapes; in the same way, the great "fraternization" movement had later also become perfectly genuine—and 1½ million Moslems [Malraux asserted] had flocked from all over Algeria to welcome de Gaulle. The Moslems, he said, had been fascinated by the promises made by de Gaulle in the speeches he had delivered during his Algerian visit.

And then Malraux announced the strange plan for turning one of the departments of Algeria into a "test case":

[1] Jacques Gascuel's Right-wing newsletter, *Perspectives* was probably not far wrong when it wrote on July 5: "Where do we stand a month after de Gaulle has formed the Government? It would be untrue to say that the country is following him with wild enthusiasm. The great majority of people are happy to have escaped the danger of civil war; and now they are watching the development of the de Gaulle 'experiment' with sympathy—but no more. And not perhaps without a touch of anxiety."

It would be done in co-operation with Tunisia and Morocco, and would be "chiefly financed" out of the resources of the Sahara—a point which was to be severely criticized on the ground that the Sahara was only at an early stage of capital investment, and that there weren't any "resources from the Sahara" to speak of which could be used to develop Algeria!

Nor was it very clear what exactly Tunisia and Morocco were to do about the development of this "sample department" on the lines, as M. Malraux put it, of what the US Government had done in the Tennessee Valley.[1]

Rather more interesting was the suggestion that after the establishment of a new relationship between France and Algeria (and Malraux emphatically avoided the use of the word "integration") "federal bonds" would be established between France, Tunisia and Morocco; was this not a hint that de Gaulle himself preferred federalism to integration in the case of Algeria, too?

Then, returning to his old style of the RPF's propaganda chief, and quoting almost word for word speeches he had made years ago, Malraux talked of France's need "to find once again a mission in the world": France had been greatest of all, not in the reign of Louis XIV, but at the time of the Crusades and of the French Revolution, when she "radiated" throughout the world. It was almost embarrassing. So was also this conclusion on the "miracle" of France and Algeria:

We call on France to tell the world, first in a soft voice, and then, soon perhaps, loudly: "Look what France and Algeria are doing together!" and then to tell the fellaghas, and after that Egypt: "Now see if you can do any better!"

And, to stress the miraculous nature of the fraternization, Malraux produced this gem for an anthology of political cretinisms: "Yes, the Algerian Moslems are crying '*Algérie française!*' " Has anyone ever heard of the Pakistanis shouting "*Pakistan anglais!*"?

For the end, Malraux reserved this choice bit: *he admitted that torture had been practised by the French in Algeria.* Had he, indeed, not himself protested, along with other leading writers, against the confiscation by the police, on orders from the Gaillard Government, of Alleg's book, *La Question?*

"To my knowledge (or to your knowledge, for that matter)," he said, "no act of torture has been committed in Algeria since General de Gaulle's visit there."

But lest there were still some doubts, Malraux now invited, in the name of the Government, France's three literary Nobel Prize winners, MM. Mauriac, Martin du Gard and Camus, to constitute a commission and go to Algeria, with the personal accreditation from General de Gaulle.

[1] This "test case" was never to be put to any test at all.

This was a piece of incredible *naïveté*—or a piece of bluff. How could these three writers find out anything? Anyway, Martin du Gard was, by now, a dying man; Mauriac was an old man, certainly not used to a job of this kind; and, in any case, he expressed great scepticism about the effectiveness of any such a prefabricated inquiry; and, in the circumstances, Camus (who was on a cruise in Greece at the time) also showed no interest in pursuing the matter.

Still, as a gesture, it was not unimportant; *the de Gaulle Government had formally condemned torture*—which is rather more than the last Governments of the Fourth Republic had done, who, when challenged, never went beyond "deploring certain excesses". Many felt, however, that the gesture would have been more effective if it had been accompanied, for instance, by the transfer to France and the release of a tortured prisoner like Henri Alleg. This would have been a more effective lesson to the Massu boys than the threat of a visit from three Nobel Prize winners.

M. Soustelle, who had been in Paris for some time now, and who had had several meetings with de Gaulle and had also, at de Gaulle's request, "informed" the other members of the Government on the situation in Algeria, also gave a press conference at the Hôtel Lutetia that week. He was still in a rather ambiguous position, and spoke in a "purely personal" capacity. Striking, though, was the great moderation with which he now spoke.

He said he was in favour of "integration" only in so far as it was the opposite of "disintegration"; but suggested that "the people of Algeria" were for integration and not federalism; at the same time, it was wrong to get into a panic about the cost of giving "equal rights and equal duties" to the Algerian population and improving their economic condition; about half the resources for carrying out such a policy would come from Algeria itself, and only a small proportion from the French State budget. Of the Committees of Public Safety M. Soustelle merely said that they were "an emanation" of the Algerian population, thus suggesting that they did not exist in France; and he fully agreed with de Gaulle about the limited role they were to play in future.

The impression among journalists at the press conference was that Soustelle was reassuming the role of de Gaulle's close associate, and that, in spite of the promises de Gaulle had made to Mollet and Pflimlin, Soustelle would soon begin to play an important part—though no one quite knew what it would be. Some thought he might be appointed Ambassador to Washington, all the more so as he made a point in declaring that there had been much misunderstanding about his alleged "anti-Americanism"; if France, he said, was going to "save Algeria", it would be for the good of the whole Free World.

There was much talk in Paris, during those days, about the "rivalry" between Malraux and Soustelle; and, despite the great moderation Soustelle had displayed at his conference, it was obvious that Algiers greatly preferred him to Malraux and his "indiscretions". The executive committee of the "University Movement for the Maintenance of French Sovereignty in Algeria" issued a motion sharply condemning M. Malraux

for obviously "not having realized yet that Algeria was just as much part of France as was Brittany, Burgundy or Provence"; for having treated "fraternization" frivolously, without realizing the "profound political thought underlying it"; for having spoken of torture, as though it had been a common practice in Algeria; as for Mauriac, "who lacked all moral authority", "neither the population of Algeria nor the Army could possibly tolerate an official visit from him."

The *ultras*, under the command of M. Lagaillarde, were, indeed, becoming troublesome in more ways than one; a few days before de Gaulle's second visit to Algiers, schoolboys and students, instigated by M. Lagaillarde, were tearing down de Gaulle's portraits put up by the Army.

Not that the Army was being all that "Gaullist"; six generals, suspected of "republican sentiments", were removed from their posts, and sent back to France; on the other hand, Colonel Trinquier, the right-hand man of the Committee of Public Safety, was still at Algiers, and had not been transferred to France, despite instructions sent from Paris to that effect.

Another curious episode showing that different people around de Gaulle were pulling in different directions was that concerning the interview given to Jean Daniel of *L'Express* by Krim Belkacem, the principal military chief of the FLN. Belkacem had made peace proposals to the French Government through Daniel. He was asking de Gaulle to "make a few gestures": to recognize the FLN as a regular army, and to treat FLN prisoners accordingly; to release Ben Bella and the other rebel leaders who had been in prison in France since October 1956; and to enter into peace negotiations with the FLN. Before being published, this statement was communicated by the paper to de Gaulle; after that, with M. Malraux's approval, it was published. Thereupon, on instructions from the military authorities, the paper was seized. M. Malraux was very annoyed at not having been "consulted".

These rivalries were to continue throughout the summer and, after the appointment of M. Soustelle as Minister of Information, M. Malraux's role became, for a time, little more than decorative. He was allowed to speak to a few thousand "loyal Algerians" at the heavily-guarded "open-air meeting" outside the Hôtel de Ville on July 14, and again, this time together with de Gaulle, at the famous pre-Referendum meeting in the Place de la République on September 4; both meetings were outstanding failures. After that Malraux was chiefly used as a sort of "cultural ambassador" who was sent all over the world to create good will and to "represent" France at various official functions. The eminent author was, in M. Soustelle's view, excellent for foreign consumption. Later, he devoted most of his energies to reorganizing the French theatres.

3. DE GAULLE TRIES TO WIN OVER THE ARMY

DE GAULLE was fully aware of having failed, during his first visit to Algeria, to "stop the revolution"; so three weeks after his return (which were chiefly marked by an agreement on the gradual withdrawal of French troops from Tunisia, and the "normalization" of France's relations with both Tunisia and Morocco) he decided that he would have to pay another visit to Algeria at the beginning of July.

The extremists in Algiers were continuing to be troublesome. The *Monde* of June 30 spoke about the reactions to de Gaulle "amongst the men of May 13" ranging from "reserve to open hostility". These people were looking askance at the *rapprochement* with Tunisia and Morocco; worse still, they were impatient with de Gaulle for having given no encouragement to the pursuit of the "May 13 Revolution", and for not having "abolished the System" in France. Nor had de Gaulle abolished the *loi-cadre* or any of the signs of "Algerian particularism", such as the Ministries of Algeria and the Sahara. Also, Algiers was now upset by the rumour that de Gaulle was thinking of appointing to a Government post M. Farès, former President of the Algerian Assembly, a "moderate nationalist" who might act as a link between the French Government and the FLN. Though, in 1955, Farès was still an "integrationist", he joined, at the end of that year, in the "rebellion of the 61" Algerian deputies and other representatives,[1] and had subsequently advocated negotiations with the FLN.

It was obvious from this that, even if de Gaulle was anxious to establish any contacts with the FLN, he was meeting with objections and obstruction from the Army, not to mention the Algiers "activists". One of the oddest things about the whole situation was a certain unreality that surrounded all these hair-splitting discussions on "integration", on "equal rights and duties", and "fraternization"; and this unreality arose from the real state of mind of the Moslem population which was, somehow, left out of account in all this planning. Occasionally only would some surprising news reach Paris from Algeria which seemed to suggest that there was an Algerian reality which had little connection with Algiers politics.

[1] See *The Strange History of Pierre Mendès-France*, p. 290.

Nothing surprised people in Paris more, for instance, than the news that on June 30, hundreds of Moslem women staged a *genuinely* spontaneous demonstration outside the Préfecture of Algiers: they were begging that their husbands, sons and brothers be released from internment camps, or that they be at least allowed to communicate with their families, who had not heard from them for many months. They also carried banners demanding that the death penalty be abolished.

This demonstration assumed a rather violent form, and some of the women-demonstrators smashed the headlights and windscreens of several stationary cars; several dozens were rounded up "so that their identity could be checked".

Those who set an example of mighty street demonstrations will perhaps be surprised to see the Moslem community imitating them. The reactions of the police will no doubt have shown that equal rights have not yet been extended to the right to demonstrate in the streets.[1]

Or else there were the reports of those from the Algerian countryside, or even from towns other than Algiers, which drew a very different picture of Algerian reality.

An anonymous correspondent in the *Monde* on the same day warned French opinion against generalizing merely from the example of Algiers:

Looking at Algeria from Algiers, and looking at it from say, the Constantinois, are two very different things. . . . Algiers just has no idea what people do and what people think in the *bled* or in medium-sized towns like Djidjelli, Sétif, Guelma, etc. In these places, the Europeans have no great illusions: the Moslems, to them, are very elusive, and they continue to hanker for independence. The Army can impress the Moslems, or rather, it can impose its will on them; people over thirty have still a respect for the French Army; but even if the non-Europeans seem to "yield", the effects of the "psychological shock" of May have already very largely worn off. Young Algerians (twenty to thirty) continue, on the whole, to be completely "nationalist"; and to them "fraternization" and "integration" mean nothing at all. . . .

The Europeans, in these areas, look upon "integration" of the two populations, equal rights, the Single Electoral College, and all the rest of it as a plain disaster—unless, of course, with the help of the Army and the civil administration, the elections are faked once again. In fact, it is very difficult to imagine how such elections can *not* be faked. . . . And it's no use talking about "Moslem opinion" merely on the strength of what Moslems *with jobs* (such as the hand-picked members of the *délégations spéciales*) will tell you. . . . I don't want to be pessimistic, but the situation is not as brilliant in our part of the world as the Committee of Public Safety is trying to make out. Far from it . . . (*Le Monde*, July 1.)

And if there was much misunderstanding of Algeria in France, so there was also a great misunderstanding of France in Algeria. Amongst the

[1] Jean Lacouture in *Le Monde*, July 1, 1958.

"activists" in Algeria and even among Army officers, there was a completely distorted view of conditions in France; many of them imagined, on the strength of reading the Algiers press, that France was "rotten with Communism", and that if it hadn't been for the "May Revolution", the Reds would be playing the same role in France as the FLN were in Algeria!

Batna, Sidi-bel-Abbès, Fort-National, Tizi Ouzou; it was in these places, far from the madding crowds of the "Forum" of Algiers, that de Gaulle spent most of his time during his second visit to Algeria, between July 1 and 4. Sidi-bel-Abbès is the headquarters of the Foreign Legion; Batna and Fort-National are deep inside Algeria, close to the "front". It was in the Batna area that the Insurrection started, far back in November 1954.

On this second visit, de Gaulle made a point of "visiting" the Army—especially the units stationed in the "danger zones".

Only a day before his arrival at Fort-National in Great Kabylia, there had been a bloody engagement barely three miles away. De Gaulle, who was well, but not enthusiastically, received by mixed crowds of Moslems and Europeans, made much the same kind of speeches as before. Thus, at Tizi-Ouzou he paid tribute to "the courage and intelligence of Kabylia", adding:

This land of Algeria deserves a great and prosperous destiny. She can have it, but on condition that the men living here, and the men living in France are fraternally associated.

Also, there, as elsewhere, he stressed the importance of the Referendum, in which all Algerians, men, as well as women, would take part. Their approval of the Constitution would seal the bonds between France and Algeria.

At Sidi-bel-Abbès, he visited the museum of the Foreign Legion, and paid a tribute to their gallantry, and to the sacrifices they had made in Indo-China, where they had lost 10,000 men and 309 officers. Throughout, he said, they had acted as soldiers, keeping aloof from politics.

In the *bled* he spoke, in a familiar manner, to numerous officers and soldiers; and observers concluded that, except for a few hotheads in the Army, he had won over the bulk of the French forces in Algeria—"even most of the paratroopers".

At Algiers, after his tour of the "front", de Gaulle pointedly ignored the "politicians" and again talked only to the soldiers. He saw about a hundred officers, but refused to receive a delegation of the Algiers-Sahara Committee of Public Safety, comprising M. Delbecque, M. Neuwirth, M. Denis and others. He said he "hadn't time to see them". Massu was received by the head of the Government in his capacity of Prefect of Algiers, and not as President of the Committee of Public Safety. When Massu nevertheless presented de Gaulle with another, rather peremptory "motion" from this Committee, de Gaulle took it very badly. Nor did he have time to see a delegation from the Socialist and Catholic trade unions; these were told to discuss their problems with the unfortunate Guy Mollet, who had been ordered by de Gaulle to accompany him on this journey, and who had been booed by the Europeans on several occasions. Nor, for that matter, had the Europeans shown much enthusiasm for de Gaulle himself; they seemed to resent the fact that he had spent his time talking to the Army, and had practically ignored the civilians, and that most of his speeches seemed to be addressed to the Moslems.

What is more, de Gaulle was not taking the organized type of "fraternization" seriously any longer. As the *Canard Enchaîné* put it:

> Throughout the journey, Great Charles seemed in a nasty mood. He had the impression that these people were trying to take him for a ride with all their fraternization and integration-of-souls stuff, and all that. . . . Departing from his Bossuet style, he used some plain barrack-room expressions in commenting on the CPS type of "fraternization".
>
> . . . Altogether, after this second journey to Algeria, the General's *entourage* seems reasonably happy: the Army seems to have "rallied" to de Gaulle, and will carry out his orders. Wilder men like Colonels Trinquier and Ducasse and General de Reuilly have been transferred *extra muros*. But there still seem some doubts about the "Gaullist loyalty" of at least three military personages: Goussault, head of the Psychological Action; Lacheroy, head of Salan's Information Service, and —Salan himself, who is being very closely watched from the Hôtel Matignon, even though "the utmost confidence" is being shown him in official communiqués.

A very curious point, when one considers the future course of the de Gaulle–Salan relationship—sharp orders to Salan on October 9, Salan's disobedience, Salan's removal from Algiers in December, complete with de Gaulle's protestations of undying friendship, gratitude and devotion. . . .

According to the *Canard*, de Gaulle was also getting rather tired of all the stories about the miraculous effects of Goussault's "psychological action", modelled, it was said, on techniques perfected by Mao Tse-Tung, and known in Algiers as the "Massu-Tse-Tung" method.

> Goussault has sent round circulars to modernize the "material of application" of the said "psychological action": little tricolour flags to be waved during fraternization rallies; records of martial music; pots of paint for adequate inscriptions; microphones and loudspeakers to magnify the enthusiasm.

And what de Gaulle also didn't much care for was this:

Since de Gaulle became head of the Government and announced that the Moslems were "complete" citizens (à part entière), the Psychological Action people now invariably refer to Moslems as "part entière". Recently Colonel Godard, head of the Algiers police phoned an SAS officer in a place between Algiers and Constantine: "To organize a fraternization rally, I need three truckfuls of 'part entière' and fifty women." The SAS officer said he couldn't supply so many women; that part of the country was much too traditionalist. "I suggest ten women and—to make up for the others—four truckfuls of part entière." "I need fifty women." "No, sorry." "Yes, I tell you." In the end the SAS officer had to refer the matter to Paris. . . .[1]

De Gaulle made no public speech at Algiers, but only recorded one which was to be broadcast after he had left; this speech did not greatly please the *ultras*.

In it he seemed to ignore the political aspects of the Algerian problem, and concentrated instead on its economic aspects, saying, in the process, that the laws concerning the protection of rural labour should be strictly observed: a warning to those *colons* who were not even paying their Algerian labourers the miserable minimum wage. And he referred, though still only in general terms, to the industrialization of Algeria, to the development of housing and education, and said, in conclusion, that three decrees were about to be published instituting the *collège unique* in all Algerian localities with a view to the coming referendum and election, and giving the vote to Algerian women for the first time.

This reform was particularly disliked by the *ultras*; but it was also looked upon with some disapproval by the more traditional Moslem elements.

In the military field, de Gaulle discussed with the high command a change of strategy in Algeria; Salan was reported to have informed the head of the Government that only by replacing the static doctrine of *quadrillage* and by sending 80,000 more highly-trained French troops to Algeria, could the areas of continued resistance be "finally" mopped up. Chief among these were the Aurès and Nemenchas regions, parts of Kabylia, the Collo peninsula, Hodna, Ouarsensis and the Tlemcen mountains.

During the following days much criticism was to be heard in Algiers of de Gaulle's failure, once again, to speak of "integration"; the Government's decision to give Algeria the same postage stamps as France (the first example of "integration") merely seemed to add insult to injury.

---

[1] *Le Canard Enchaîné*, July 9. As usual, I am not apologizing for quoting so "frivolous" a paper; the *Canard* was, in July 1958, a particularly refreshing oasis in a desert of newspaper conformism, and as well-informed as ever. During the next two years of the de Gaulle régime it became the best-informed and most uninhibited of all Paris papers.

4. THE ARMY AS A "POLITICAL PARTY"— "REVOLUTIONARY WAR" THEORIES

How had the French Army become *an independent political force?* No doubt, it had attempted, in the past, for example at the time of the Dreyfus Case, to play a political role of its own; but, in the end, it was forced to submit to the authority of the State. But the war in Indo-China had started in the Army a process which was finally to crystallize in Algeria into something of paramount importance. The Army became a *Party*, complete with a propaganda machine,[1] as well as with a precise political programme: integration of Algeria, de Gaulle's return to power, vote of a new authoritarian Constitution (to begin with). Secondly, the Army was in possession of an elaborate *state apparatus*, comprising the SAS (*Section administrative spéciale*) officers, combining social and welfare work and administrative duties in the Algerian country-side, and those very generals and colonels who, after May 13, either substituted themselves for the civilian authorities, such as Prefects, or closely controlled them. The Army had also, since 1957, taken over police duties on a large scale.

None of this had come suddenly, of course. Slowly, almost imperceptibly, the Army had, already under the Mollet-Lacoste régime, started taking over the authority of the civilians in Algeria; after May 13, this political power of the Army came out into the open.

Of course, of the half-million soldiers in Algeria, not all were in agreement with this departure from the old tradition, under which the Army was in the service of the Republic. But the greater part of the Army had been duly indoctrinated, while the rest followed as a matter of ordinary military discipline. In Metropolitan France, the Algerian Army had its accomplices, so much so, as we have seen, that, at the height of the May crisis, the Government of the Republic found itself, in fact, deserted by the armed forces.

At the time of de Gaulle's second visit to Algeria—and what he "visited" on that occasion was chiefly the Army—much was made of the fact that the Army had "submitted" to de Gaulle, as distinct from certain civilian *ultras* in Algiers. Was not this a deceptive impression? As J. M. Domenach was to write:

The truth is that the officers are submitting less to a government than to a man with exceptional prestige, who is, moreover, "one of them". But is not all

[1] This comprised a bureau of "psychological action", a press printing hundreds of thousands of copies (thus *Le Bled*, the Army paper in Algeria, had, by May 1958, the highest circulation of any French weekly circulating in Algeria), a radio and cinema service of its own, highly-specialized officers, such as the "psychological officers" in Algeria, officers for Algerian affairs, etc.).

this rather precarious? For what would happen if de Gaulle were suddenly to disappear? What other man would be able to be "invested" by the Army, the way prospective Emperors were during the decline of the Roman Empire? . . . It would not take much to persuade the Army, encouraged by the precedent of May 13, to impose its own policy on France, by using once again the threat of military intervention.[1]

What was the process whereby the *cadres* of the French Army, as well as certain specialized troops, notably the paratroopers, had become "politicized"? There appears to be general agreement that the decisive factor in this process was the war in Indo-China. This war had started as one of de Gaulle's "prestige operations"; later, the French Army in Indo-China had become a pawn in an intricate inter-party game in France, with a shady background of speculation and profiteering, in which the Gaullist RPF was no less involved than the Socialists and the MRP.[2] Then this army became a tool of French foreign policy, a pump for extracting dollars from the USA in the "Free World's struggle against Communism". Finally, without the Army having had much to say in any of these political, financial and diplomatic operations, the war had to be wound up in humiliating conditions after the disaster of Dien Bien Phu.

In the course of that cruel and bloody war, the proverbially "silent" officers and soldiers had done a good deal of thinking; and the conclusions most of them arrived at were not (as one might have expected) that this kind of colonial war was senseless, but that

(a) there was nothing wrong with the war in itself; (b) that the French Governments had behaved ineptly and incoherently, and in a manner insulting to the Army in Indo-China; (c) that this army understood what this kind of war was about, whereas Paris had understood nothing; and that, in any similar war elsewhere, the *policy* of the war should be determined by the Army, and not by Paris.

The war in Indo-China ended in the summer of 1954. For the next six months, France was extremely short of troops in North Africa—which was one reason, by the way, why Mendès-France hastened to grant Internal Autonomy to Tunisia—a step which, at first, was fully approved as something inevitable even by a diehard Algiers paper like *L'Echo d'Alger*. When the Algerian rebellion started in November 1954, it was, as Jacques Chevallier argued,[3] because the Algerian nationalists decided that now was the time to strike: the French had not yet had time to bring the bulk of their hardened troops back from Indo-China. It cannot be too strongly emphasized *that the bulk of the officer cadres and most of the hardened troops who, in subsequent months, were to begin to pour into Algeria*

[1] *Esprit*, November 1958, p. 634.
[2] See chapters on Indo-China war, the Bao Dai experiment and the *Affaire des généraux* in the author's *France 1940–1955* (London, 1956).
[3] Jacques Chevallier, *Nous Algériens*, pp. 126-7 (Paris 1958).

were men who had fought for years in Indo-China. These men were embittered against the Republic; also, many of the officers had evolved certain half-baked theories of their own about the true nature of what they considered to be "revolutionary wars"; and it was these theories which they began to apply in Algeria, where they were determined to avoid the mistakes and failures of the Indo-China campaign. Later, *the Suez fiasco was to add to their bitterness against the Paris Government.*

The officers who had fought in Indo-China had, indeed, acquired the idea that "modern" wars were essentially different from the trench warfare of 1914–18, and even from the *blitzkrieg* of 1940; that present-day wars—especially in colonial territories—were "revolutionary" wars, and required an entirely different approach. Ever since returning from Indo-China, and particularly in 1957–58, it was fashionable among French officers in Algeria to talk about Mao Tse-Tung, and about the primary importance in modern warfare of "psychological action". This psycho-logical action was primarily to be applied to the "natives", and to colonial peoples in revolt; but gradually the idea also gained ground that a parallel psychological action could be exercised on the French in Algeria, and, ultimately, on France itself. But the idea of embarking on such "psychological action" in France did not perhaps occur to anybody until after May 13. What was this "psychological action"?

It was defined as follows by the notorious Colonel Trinquier (formerly of Indo-China) in a statement to Associated Press in September 1958:

What we have to do is to organize the population from top to bottom. I don't care if you call me a Fascist; but we must have a docile population, every gesture of which shall be subject to our control.

It was, indeed, on the basis of these conditioning and "brain-washing" theories that the "psychological services" of the French Army in Algeria decided that the FLN's slogan of *independence* must be countered by another, and equally simple slogan: and that was *integration*. No doubt, the methods used by the different elements in the Army varied greatly from place to place. The "psychological action" ranged from the paternalist and often genuinely friendly activity of the SAS officers in remote spots of the Algerian *bled* (with their concentration on medical and educational work, and their often authentic belief in a land reform to be carried out at the expense of the *colons*), to the activity of certain other formations, whose "psychological action" consisted in terrorizing the population, complete with the Gestapo methods rendered notorious throughout the world by a book like Henri Alleg's *La Question*.

Underlying the whole conception of a "revolutionary" war which the French Army was supposed to be conducting in Algeria there was, of course, a gigantic quibble. Mao Tse-Tung in China, Ho Chi-minh in

Vietnam, it was argued, had, with their propaganda and their "revolutionary war" tactics, rapidly converted the amorphous peasant masses of China and Vietnam to a *"revolutionary outlook"*. Thus, it had not been difficult to convert (!) the Vietnam peasantry to the policy of Independence.

The French Army, which used to be *la grande muette*, had become *la grande bavarde*, especially since May 1958; and the "psychological colonels" in particular delighted in writing books, articles and essays, and giving interviews about their "psychological warfare". Thus, in June, Colonel Goussault wrote an article in *Atlantique Nord* in which he took as his starting-point the simple assertion that the FLN had been trained by Moscow, and had a Marxist-Leninist conception of "revolutionary wars". The French Army could not resort to such totalitarian methods, and had to distinguish between various groups of the Algerian population—which it was essential to "organize and instruct".

The four main groups were (1) the *douars* (villages), (2) the young people, (3) women, and (4) war veterans. The most important was the organization of the villages; "men of the right sort of character" who would soon become fervent partisans of French Algeria, were, Goussault said, being given a rudimentary administrative training, and also enough military training to organize the self-defence of the village against the FLN, as well as to build up an essential little "information network". These "village chiefs," he said, had for some time been trained in "formation centres"; after returning to their villages, they could be depended on to act in the best interests of "French Algeria". The young Moslem generation was beginning to receive similar training in a *"Centre de formation de la jeunesse d'Algérie"*, set up in the spring of 1958. The "village chiefs" and the young people thus "formed" and "conditioned" would, in Colonel Goussault's view, act as indispensable links between the Army and the population. The colonel admitted that for the two remaining groups—the women and the war veterans—nothing much had yet been done.

Colonel Trinquier, in a lecture given on June 7 to the students of Algiers University, spoke more particularly of his experience in "taming" the Casbah of Algiers (which had, for a long time, been infested by FLN terrorists).

He described the elaborate technique by which the Moslems were bribed or terrorized into spying on each other; when the lists of inhabitants in every house were drawn up, "the women were particularly helpful" in supplying the information. And it was thanks to this network of spies and informers, Trinquier concluded, that it had not only been possible for the Army to keep complete control over the Arab population of Algiers, but also to organize the great fraternization demonstrations in May—the political consequences of which had proved so important.

Trinquier, Thomazo, and some other colonels had made themselves famous in France through the part they had played in the events of May 1958.

Goussault, whom we have just quoted, and Lacheroy, were the chief "ideologists" of the "revolutionary war" which, they claimed, the French Army was conducting in Algeria. Lacheroy, polished, well-groomed, was a familiar figure at Algiers. He was head of the Army's information, press and propaganda services, and the real head of the *"collège des colonels"*; his immediate assistant was Goussault,[1] head of the Fifth Bureau, the military department specially concerned with "psychological affairs".

Lacheroy is a dominant personality; he speaks in a polished, deliberately unctuous manner, but, when necessary, his tone becomes harsh; when that happens the "thugs" serving under him—men like Thomazo and Trinquier—and even Colonel Godard, head of all the Police services of Algeria, eat out of his hand. (*L'Express*, June 26, 1958.)

Lacheroy's great regret was that de Gaulle had not been installed at the head of the Government by the direct intervention of the paratroopers. *L'Express* quoted him as saying:

We could have done it in three days. There would have been a few hundred dead; the party leaders would have fled in a panic; the trade union leaders would have been muzzled; it would have been the end. Instead, de Gaulle has brought back what we would have swept away. He has frustrated and disappointed us. But we shall never retreat. Our revolution—which is our revenge for Indo-China, Tunisia and Morocco—will safeguard the future of France and her overseas possessions for a hundred years. . . . (*ibid.*)

He deplored the fact that, during his first visit to Algiers, de Gaulle had brought with him two of his ministers, Jacquinot and Lejeune, "for whom we had already dug graves in an Algiers garden"; and that he should be planning to bring Mollet to Algiers on his second visit.

Lacheroy, whose official title, in June 1958, was "Chief of the Psychological Action and Information Service of National Defence and the Armed Forces", had written a book, called *La guerre révolutionnaire*. Much of this book was amateurish and even childish in its starry-eyed discovery of the "revolutionary war tactics" of Bolshevism. "A revolutionary war," he said, "is one you conduct among the mass of the people, and in which you have to capture the masses."

So he proceeded to present Vietminh's methods, as he had observed them in Indo-China, as worthy of imitation by the French in Algeria:

[1] Lacheroy's immediate assistant, Colonel Goussault, who had been taken prisoner by Vietminh at Cao Bang in 1950, had some first-hand experience of Chinese and Vietnamese "brainwashing" methods.

"Among the arsenal of words, Vietminh chose one which corresponded more or less (!) to its own war aims, and which also greatly appealed to the masses—and that was the word *Doclap*, which, in Vietnamese, means 'independence'. After that, everything became *Doclap*." And he added: "Fear is a pretty good way of keeping a war going; but enthusiasm is even better."

On the brainwashing of prisoners, Lacheroy was not very explicit; he thought the first phase—that of "flattening a man out"—was easy enough; the second phase, that of "indoctrinating him", was often more difficult; *sometimes you succeeded, but sometimes the chap died in the process.*

The colonel's historical erudition was perhaps a little weak: thus, he suggested that, before 1945, there was really "nothing" in Indo-China to create a revolutionary situation; things just began to pop, as it were, because of a few people "who had specialized in that kind of thing". And, after that, came the magic "Operation *Doclap*". From which he concluded:

(1) The Army must take an active, indeed, a dominant, part in politics; and that is what happened in Algeria since May 13: generals had replaced the prefects; and the wives of generals had taken over the direction of the social work.
(2) The Army should have "parallel" civilian organizations in the "total" and "revolutionary" wars that were now going on; as far as the Europeans in Algeria were concerned, this "parallelism" had worked very well, except for a few unfortunate misunderstandings, for instance, when a bunch of civilians, in their revolutionary ardour, nearly bumped off General Salan; but when it came to the Moslem population, the system did not work too well.
(3) The Moslem population should be converted, with the help of a "key slogan". Vietminh had succeeded remarkably well with its "*Doclap*" (independence) slogan; why then, Lacheroy argued, shouldn't the French Army succeed equally well with the Arabs by firing their imagination with the word "Integration"?

As J. F. Rolland remarked, with a touch of irony, perhaps they would have done better to try another word, which would correspond "more or less" to the real aspirations of the Moslem Algerians; if, instead of *indimadj* (integration) they had talked of *istiqlal* (independence) *"they might have been surprised by the extraordinary success of their revolutionary war tactics!"*[1]

All things considered, the "psychological action" services of the Army had proved infinitely more effective in conditioning the Army itself than in converting the Moslems. Men like Lacheroy had done a great deal to prepare the Army psychologically for the political role it was to assume in May 1958. The uproar in France and, especially, in the outside world over Sakhiet had helped to "revolutionize" the relatively unpolitical

[1] *France-Observateur*, July 31, 1958.

Air Force, which saw in these attacks an insult to itself; the "anti-torture" campaign in France and abroad, which became particularly strident in February–April 1958, was treated by the "psychological services" as a highly organized smear campaign against the French Army as a whole, while the investiture of Pflimlin was, as we have seen, interpreted as the prelude to another stab in the back for the French Army.

When we say that the "psychological warfare" among the Moslem masses was much less successful, we are not trying to minimize the considerable amount of good will that, in many distant corners of Algeria, the SAS officers often succeeded in creating despite difficult conditions. But these were still exceptions, rather than the general rule.

The fact that de Gaulle later removed from Algeria over 1,000 officers who, in his opinion, had been too closely associated with "May 13" (among them Salan and Lacheroy) did not in itself mean that the Army had abandoned its political ambitions or its new political philosophy.

There is, however, another aspect which cannot be ignored. Apart from the Army's political ambitions, it also had a strong vested interest in the Algerian war continuing. All officers and NCO's were receiving much higher pay in Algeria than they would in France. Thus cases are known of captains (with a large family in France) receiving (with full keep) as much as 320,000 to 350,000 francs *a month* (roughly £3,000 a year). This was, in French—or, indeed, any—terms, a quite fantastic salary; moreover, the chance of being killed in Algeria was very small.

5. DE GAULLE'S "SPLIT PERSONALITY"?— THE SOUSTELLE APPOINTMENT

A T THE beginning of July, a month after de Gaulle had formed his Government, Paris seemed quite happy about the way things were going. He had "normalized" relations with Tunisia and Morocco; he had shown that he was out of sympathy with the lunatic fringe of Algiers. The comforting M. Pinay at the Ministry of Finance had been reasonably successful with his gold-guaranteed loan, which produced enough cash to help the Treasury through the next few months—till after the Referendum. As the somewhat tepid reception given to de Gaulle on "de Gaulle Day" on June 18 had shown, there was no frantic enthusiasm in the country for the man, but rather, a feeling of confidence and of genuine gratitude for his having prevented serious trouble in May.

But what the man really stood for nobody quite knew. Intellectuals tried, as far as possible, to analyse de Gaulle, and even to psychoanalyse him. One conclusion reached was not that he was playing a "double game" between Paris and Algiers, but that he was something of a split personality; also that there was really no "Gaullism" as such, but a clash of two "pseudo-Gaullisms". The crowds of the Algiers "Forum", with their cries of "Soustelle!" were really Fascists at heart, i.e. pseudo-Gaullists. The parliamentary parties, who had "accepted" de Gaulle, were also pseudo-Gaullists, though of a very different kind. And, during this first period, it seemed, de Gaulle was neither repudiating, nor identifying himself with, either of these pseudo-Gaullisms.

"For as long as possible," wrote Edgar Morin, "de Gaulle will perpetuate this double personality; only in doing so can he act as arbiter between two radically different sociological conceptions. Both of these forces are, however, continuously pressing him to make a choice. . . .

"In France there is an economic and sociological dynamism which is trying to transform political and social relations after the American and British model. . . . This aims at economic expansion . . . at a weakening of the class conflict . . . at close collaboration between the executive and the power *élite* (high finance, big industry, State and private technicians, top bureaucrats, trade union leaders). . . . In short, a middle-class civilization directed by a power *élite*, and one in which a reformist working class would be fully integrated in the nation. . . .

"As against this, there is the dynamism of Algiers, which wants a completely new system of government, based essentially on the Single Party, already symbolized by the Committees of Public Safety. . . . This system is supported by the bulk of the Army, which, after fifteen years of colonial wars, is angry with the Republic, and is prepared to help in the building of a military-Fascist régime which it would then impose on Metropolitan France. . . ." [1]

The curious thing, as the same writer observed, was that France and Algeria seemed to have developed in two watertight compartments: Algerian economy had not been affected by France's neo-capitalist tendencies; it had remained an essentially colonialist and racialist economy. Similarly, post-war France had (as distinct from the France of 1934–35) *failed to produce a Fascist or near-Fascist mass movement of any kind.* And so the contradiction continued *between the neo-Fascism of Algiers and the neo-Capitalism of France—*

"But while France was treating Algeria as a side-issue, not showing any real determination to embark on an all-out war of reconquest, French Algeria was preparing to conquer France with the ultimate object of fully reconquering Moslem Algeria. . . . Between these two forces, de Gaulle should be able to act as a super-arbiter; but the trouble is that he does not fully control the machinery of the State, since the real power of the State—the Army and the Police—is under the influence of one of the two conflicting forces." (*ibid.*)

The odd thing was that the "French de Gaulle" (as distinct from the

[1] *France-Observateur*, June 19, 1958.

"Algiers de Gaulle") now seemed to be trying to do what Mendès-France had already attempted. Like Mendès, who had tried to reform the Fourth Republic and invigorate its economic structure, de Gaulle now also surrounded himself by a brains-trust of technicians and economists; was offering Government posts to trade union leaders; was even willing— which was going further than Mendès—to talk to the Communists and the CGT. All this was suggesting a desire for social peace, and a respect for individual and collective freedoms. Compared with Mendès-France's abortive attempt to reform the Fourth Republic, de Gaulle had the great advantage of being able to do the same thing without being sabotaged by Parliament. The great question was whether this authoritarian power, potentially beneficial to France, would not, in reality, be subjected to dangerous pressures from Algiers.

Whether he liked it or not, de Gaulle had to reckon with Algiers. It was that, rather than a definite preference for neo-Fascism, which made de Gaulle take, on July 8, the spectacular step of appointing Soustelle Minister of Information.

During his last visit to Algeria, the clamour for Soustelle had been louder than ever and, on one occasion, he finally gave the assurance that "before long" Soustelle would be given a highly important appointment.

But the appointment of Soustelle was rather a lot to swallow.

Men like Mollet, Pflimlin and Vincent Auriol, who had done so much to persuade France to accept the "de Gaulle compromise" at the end of May, had the greatest distrust of Soustelle, and had extracted from de Gaulle, before giving him their full support, at least one firm promise: and that was that Soustelle would not be included in the Government. To numerous persons Auriol declared that this guarantee had finally persuaded him that de Gaulle was "a good risk".

When, in the middle of June, Soustelle returned to Paris, de Gaulle raised the question of giving him a Government post; Mollet, Pflimlin and several other ministers, outraged by de Gaulle's *volte face*, threatened to resign. De Gaulle decided he had better wait. So he waited till the end of the Information Conference held by the Socialist Party at the beginning of July; like the general public, the Socialists were in an optimistic mood, and it was best, at that stage, not to shake them out of their euphoria.

But now that this is over [Bourdet, one of de Gaulle's sharpest critics, wrote on July 10], he thinks he can take another step forward without too much risk. And what risk *is* there? The Socialist Party is sufficiently well chloroformed not to cause any major trouble. Also, the policy of the "lesser evil" is sure to continue to work according to its own logic. Mollet, Pflimlin and their friends are sure to argue that they would lose all influence with the general if they abandoned their seats to Soustelle and his friends. . . . I am prepared to bet that the next cheering thought that will occur to them will be: "Soustelle will be much more dangerous outside the Government than inside; the republican ministers (including, de Gaulle, of course) will be in a good position to keep an eye on him . . ."[1]

His conclusion was that the appointment of Soustelle showed that de Gaulle, with the bulk of the "essentially anti-republican" Algerian Army on his side, but anxious to give it "an additional guarantee", could afford to ignore the Left; that this was a concession which would be greatly appreciated by both the Army and the *ultras*; that, until the Referendum, neither Soustelle nor anybody else would do anything outrageous to shake out of its torpor the "great a-political mass of Frenchmen", on whom the success of the Referendum ultimately depended; but that it was useful to start right now building up the machinery of the future authoritarian and "psychological" régime; and no man could do this more effectively than Soustelle, with radio and TV at his disposal. (The fact that de Gaulle had finally to get rid of Soustelle could, of course, not be anticipated in 1958.)

The immediate problem for Soustelle was to "condition" French opinion to a "massive" pro-de Gaulle vote in the Referendum; but this task, as was soon to become apparent, was going to be preceded by a drastic reorganization of the radio and TV services, with the implantation of "Soustelle men" in the French propaganda services, many of them drawn from the old propaganda machine of the RPF. No doubt, Soustelle was not given the job unconditionally; the propaganda was to be "Gaullist"; it was not to glorify unduly the "13th of May"—which, in terms of the Referendum in France, would have been a bad psychological error, anyway. It is also probable, as has already been suggested in an earlier chapter, that Soustelle was asked to use his influence in silencing, as far as possible, the various "committees of public safety", which (according to Delbecque) were very numerous, especially in provincial France, and divert their activities into "legal" channels.

The reactions to the Soustelle appointment were, of course, what was to be expected. At Algiers, and particularly on the Committee of Public Safety, it was greeted with wild enthusiasm as "a final approval by de Gaulle of May 13"; in reply to a rapturous telegram from the Committee, Soustelle cabled: "Your confidence will be of great help to me in the heavy task awaiting me"; at the other extreme, the Communist press was, of course, all sound and fury; the Socialist *Populaire*, under the unexciting headline, "The Premier Makes New Government Appointments", tried to argue rather sheepishly that "the appointment of M. Soustelle today is not nearly as significant or important as it would have been a month ago". And it added—"We can say without any irony that since yesterday Paris and Algiers are united in the same Government team"—which, it then suggested, was "inevitable" and perhaps all to the good.

Perhaps the most curious reaction came from the *Figaro*, the organ of the conservative bourgeoisie; it recalled that Soustelle's "militant action" had played a decisive role at Algiers in May; his appointment to "a post which, by its very nature, is an arbitration post, has profoundly surprised us". Alongside this editorial was a curious article recalling that Hitler, too, used to thunder against the "system" of the Weimar Republic; and that the Nazis invaded Vienna crying "down with the system"; this word, said the *Figaro*, should be eliminated from the official vocabulary. Its attitude was, in a curious way, comparable to that of the Deutsch-Nationale to the Nazis! Hugenberg versus Goebbels, as it were. . . . It is, indeed, odd how in the next few months the *Figaro* came to represent a sort of Left wing of the French Right-wing press; its most spectacular performance, as we shall see, was the highly critical attitude adopted in its columns by M. André Siegfried to de Gaulle's Draft Constitution. It might also be recalled that the *Figaro*, with its partly "Vichyite", partly "Third Republic" outlook, had, in 1949, assumed a hostile position in relation to de Gaulle and the RPF—notably by publishing that year the posthumous anti-de Gaulle *Memoirs* of General Giraud. During that period it played an important part in detaching "good conservatives" from the wilder men of the RPF; Soustelle was one of the wildest among them. The *Figaro's* old hostility to the RPF suddenly re-emerged with the appointment of Soustelle to the Ministry of Information.

6. A BASTILLE DAY THAT BECAME AN ALGIERS DAY

AT THE height of the May rebellion in Algiers, General Salan had declared: "The day is near when we shall all march up the Champs-Elysées and the people will cover us with flowers." And that—apart from the flowers—is precisely what happened on July 14, the traditional *fête nationale* of the Republic. Salan was there; Massu was there; other rebel generals were there. Although, only ten days before, de Gaulle had not parted on the best of terms with the civilian extremists on the Algiers Committee of Public Safety, he went out of his way to show the greatest lenience and benevolence to the military leaders of the May Rebellion. On the eve of July 14 General Salan received a high decoration; Massu (already appointed shortly before Prefect of Algiers) was promoted to the rank of *général de corps d'armée*; General Jacques Faure, who had headed an abortive anti-republican conspiracy back in

1956 (after which he had been put under arrest for a month and then transferred to Germany, and who later ran as a Fascist candidate under the patronage of Poujade in a Lyon by-election), was now sent back to Algeria with great honours and put in command of the highly important military region of Tizi-Ouzou. There were many other military and administrative promotions among persons who had played a major role in the May 13 rebellion. On the other hand, men faithful to the Republic, like M. Louis Périllier, Prefect of the Haute-Garonne (Toulouse), who had "tolerated" Left-wing demonstrations against the Algiers rebels in May, were relieved of their posts.

All Left-wing demonstrations and processions to mark Bastille Day were prohibited both in Paris and in provincial France. In Paris the day was made to look like the apotheosis of the May 13 rebellion. On that morning 18,000 troops marched up the Champs-Elysées, among them 4,000 men—mostly paratroopers—who had been specially brought from Algeria to Paris. Also, 4,000 Moslem ex-servicemen and 2,000 young Moslems had been brought from Algeria to take part in the parade.

The "protocol" aspect of the parade was rather odd. General de Gaulle was unwilling to figure in it as "No. 4" personage, i.e. after the President of the Republic and the Presidents of the National Assembly and the Senate; and the subterfuge was thus devised whereby he would quickly review the troops by driving in an open car up to the Etoile and back with President Coty, whereupon he would step into another car, which would take him to the airfield; from there he would fly to Toulon to preside over a great Naval Review.

This part of the programme lasted scarcely a quarter of an hour, and the regular (or rather, most irregular) July 14 Review took place after he had already left Paris. In the parade the paratroopers aroused, of course, the greatest attention, and there were numerous cries from the middle-class crowds along the pavements of "Algérie française!" and "Vivent les paras!" Rather more uncertain were the reactions to the Moslem ex-servicemen, most of them wearing native clothes, and heavily decorated with medals, and many of them elderly and even very old men. As for the 2,000 hand-picked "young Moslems", a few mistakes must have been made, for as they filed past the official tribune, a few of them suddenly unfurled white-and-green flags of the FLN and shouted "A bas l'Algérie française!"; the effect was so startling that nothing happened at first; only half a minute or so later were the offenders pounced upon by the Police and quickly whisked off; nobody quite knows what happened to them afterwards. One of them was a mere boy of fifteen, who trembled with both fear and excitement as the Police took him away.

The parade on the morning of the 14th and the festivities during the rest of the day were supposed to symbolize "fraternization"; but this was scarcely a success. During several days before July 14, there had been

numerous terrorist acts in Paris against soldiers, policemen and particularly against "collaborating" Moslems; and both the military and civilian
Moslems who had been brought to Paris were everywhere under heavy
army and police protection—notably in the Place de l'Hôtel de Ville
where the Moslems—none looking in the least cheerful—were brought
in the afternoon to hold a parade, and to listen to speeches by M. Vigier,
President of the Paris Town Council, M. Michelet, Minister of War
Veterans, M. Azem Ouali, President of the Mayors of Kabylia, who
delivered his speech in three languages—French, Arabic and Kabylian—
M. André Malraux and others. After that they attended a reception at
the Town Hall. M. Ouali declared in all three languages that Integration
was the only possible solution for Algeria—

From now on we are a people of 53 million inhabitants, with the same duties
and the same rights. Long live France and Algeria united for ever! Long live the
Army and the Republic! Long live de Gaulle!

And M. Malraux made another of his lofty speeches, in which he
coupled the names of Jaurès and General Leclerc; assured his listeners
that, since de Gaulle had taken over, Fascism had not advanced, but
retreated in France; and exalted all the wonders that France would do
"for Algeria". But his speech ended on a note of warning, followed by a
note of conciliation:

Let those who have been demonstrating to defend a republic other than the
French Republic do their demonstrating in Budapest! But to those who thought
they were defending the French Republic against us . . . to those our France calls
out: "I call you all to come unto me—those who have defended me, and those
who think they are fighting against me!" And in the case of these, I shall appeal to
their noblest fear: and that is that France will revive without them. . . . They want
a Republic without de Gaulle, just as others want de Gaulle without the Republic.
But both France and Paris want the Republic with General de Gaulle. . . . That is
the Republic that France wants, because for ten years, France lost her habit of
hoping; she will allow no one to frustrate her hopes now. May the System of
Misfortune disappear for ever. And long life to the Republic to which de Gaulle
has restored, for the good of France, the fraternal face of hope, and, for the good
of the world—and within a mere six weeks—the face of pride. . . .

This kind of speech may sound odd in translation; it sounded just as
odd in the original. Soustelle was determined to allow Malraux to have
as little to do with the radio as possible. "*Ces discours ronflants,*" he would
say, "*cela ne fait pas sérieux . . .*"
In view of the Algerian war, there had been no dancing in the streets
and no fireworks on July 14 during the two previous years; this year, to
celebrate, as it were, the "Algerians' visit" to Paris, these austerity rules
were abandoned; and the greatest open-air *bal* of all was held in the

Esplanade des Invalides, where the 2nd Armoured Division had organized a vast *kermesse*, the proceeds of which were to go to the Division's "welfare fund". Here paratroopers in their red berets and soldiers of the Foreign Legion were particularly numerous. Many of these had that army-of-occupation look on their faces. . . . Almost everywhere people merely wanted to dance and see the fireworks on the Seine. However, in the rue de l'Ecole-de-Médecine, there was a *"Grand bal républicain"*, organized by various "republican committees" of the theatre and the radio, and guarded by groups of young men wearing the Phrygian bonnet and a *sans-culottes* rig-out. They were selling (illicit) reprints of Alleg's *La Question*. This was one of the few minor protests against the *14-juillet* having been turned into a *fête* which was, in fact, clearly intended to celebrate the Victory of Algiers. . . .

Here and there, especially in the working class quarters (which, however, also had their open-air *bals*) one could hear an occasional bitter comment; but it was a mostly a-political day of dancing and merriment for all that; and most people decided not to get ruffled that day by the huge headlines that overshadowed the *14-juillet* news, that King Feisal and Noury Said had been murdered in Baghdad that morning, and that a new régime had been set up in Irak. . . .

7. THE IRAK–LEBANON WAR SCARE

DURING the next few weeks the attention of the world was no longer centred on France, but on the Middle East. France's role in this crisis was only a very minor one; and de Gaulle was, clearly, not satisfied with his allies' attitude. The United States had not consulted France before landing troops in the Lebanon; nor had Britain consulted her before sending troops to Jordan. The French cruiser *De Grasse* was sent to Beirut; but no French forces were landed, and, soon afterwards, the ship was recalled. It was even reported that the American authorities had made it clear that the French were "not wanted" in the Lebanon, even though President Chamoun had addressed an SOS to France just as much as to the others. . . . De Gaulle was all the more annoyed about this as, earlier in the month, both Mr. Dulles (who had come on a flying visit to Paris specially to meet him) and Mr. Macmillan had assured him that France would be consulted about any steps to be taken in the Middle East. Later in the month, de Gaulle's annoyance was reflected in his unwillingness to conform with either the British or the American response to Khrushchev's proposal for a Summit Conference. Whereas the US Government wanted to leave it to the Security Council to organize such a Summit Conference, and the British Government was arguing in favour of a meeting of the Security Council, with the Big Four heads-of-government present, de Gaulle declared himself entirely opposed to any such public meeting, and favoured a much more secret and discreet four-power meeting, more in keeping with Khrushchev's original proposal: "all meet Monday at Geneva"—except that, in reality, de Gaulle was willing to agree to such a meeting, but only provided it had been "carefully prepared in advance". In the end, largely as a result of Chinese objections, there was no summit meeting of any kind; but a significant by-product of the July crisis and of the lack of co-ordination shown by the USA, Britain and France was de Gaulle's dispatch of Couve de Murville to Bonn and Rome: since France had been cold-shouldered by Britain and the USA during the Irak–Lebanon–Jordan crisis, perhaps she would carry more weight in future if backed by "Little Europe".

The Middle East crisis [the *Monde* commented on July 29] has provided General de Gaulle with the opportunity to formulate his conception of Europe. In his view, this must no longer be a mere assembly of institutions and a bunch of economic agencies; it must organize itself with a view to creating a common front which, going beyond mere politics, would represent the conception of a common civilization. It is not a case of creating a Third Force between the two blocs. It's a case of Europe, as part of the West, asserting itself more than it has been able to do up till now. The present international situation has provided France with a good opportunity to act in this direction . . .

We shall hear more about this "build-up of Europe"—especially in connection with the subsequent de Gaulle–Adenauer meetings, and the Anglo-French clash over the Common Market. But it is significant that de Gaulle's (formerly half-hearted and uncertain) "Europeanism" should have received a fresh impetus from the "inconsiderate" attitude shown to France at the time of the Middle-East crisis of July 1958. De Gaulle had never quite forgotten how in 1945 the British had turned the French out of Syria, while he (de Gaulle) was head of the French Government; and both the Anglo-American arms deliveries to Tunisia in the winter of 1957 and the Anglo-American "good offices" mission of February–April 1958 continued to rankle. . . .

On July 23 the *New York Times*, commenting on the bad humour in Paris, said that the French Government had made it plain to the US Government that it was in no hurry to agree to the establishment of missile sites on French territory. . . .

Striking, in the same context, was, throughout the Irak–Lebanon crisis and the negotiations for a "summit" meeting, the relatively favourable attitude shown to de Gaulle by the Soviet press. This was not to change until after de Gaulle's first meeting with Adenauer; it was only after that, and on the eve of the French Referendum of September 28, that Khrushchev made a sledge-hammer attack on de Gaulle and the French

"Fascists". This would scarcely have happened but for that de Gaulle–Adenauer meeting ten days before. . . .

Also, to avoid any repetition of the "Lebanon episode", de Gaulle sent in September a secret memorandum to London and Washington demanding that France be included in a "Three-Power Directorate" which would take political and strategic decisions on a world scale. The British and American response to this was unenthusiastic.

8. GRUMBLES FROM THE ALGIERS LUNATIC FRINGE

ALTHOUGH de Gaulle's second visit to Algeria had created the (not perhaps altogether correct) impression that he had, by and large, won over the Army, it was obvious that, among the civilian "activists" on the Committees of Public Safety, a good deal of pro-Fascist agitation was continuing. On July 22, fourteen members of the Committee of May 13 published a "manifesto" advocating the creation in France of a "corporatist state". Drawn up by Dr. Lefèvre, an Algiers Fascist, and signed by MM. Orthiz, Montigny and other extremists (many of them belonging to the Poujadist organizations in Algiers), this "manifesto" was a singular mixture of old Vichyite ideas ("*famille, travail, nation*", a variant of Pétain's "*travail, famille, patrie*") and certain soap-box slogans used in the 1956 election by Pierre Poujade.

It advocated the complete suppression of the "political parties" which, it said, were showing a tendency to revive again (with the implication that de Gaulle was being outwitted by the "System"), and declared that "between a return to the System and the Fascist temptation, we must choose the corporatist State"—after which the broad outline of a purely Fascist constitution for France and a "wholly integrated" Algeria was given.

General Salan and General Massu, as well as the majority of the Committee of Public Safety, dissociated themselves from the "manifesto"; nevertheless, this "lunatic fringe" document could not be dismissed as entirely insignificant; it was, as it were, "a caricatural expression of certain strong and highly organized, though more discreetly-expressed tendencies existing within various 'civic action' movements in Algeria and a number of professional and youth organizations".[1] It was perhaps partly to emphasize his total disagreement with these views that General de Gaulle had a long meeting, a day after the publication of the "manifesto", with M. Jacques Chevallier, the liberal Mayor of Algiers, who resigned

[1] Jean Lacouture in *Le Monde*, July 24.

after the May rebellion. M. Chevallier, who had throughout been Lacoste's enemy no. 1 in Algiers, was a firm believer in the fundamental friendship the Algerian people felt for the French—a friendship which, in his view, Lacoste had done his best to destroy. Certain of Chevallier's paternalist or, rather, "fraternalist" ideas were obviously to be reflected in de Gaulle's famous Constantine Programme of the following October —a programme which was to arouse such resentment among the Algiers *ultras*.

Meantime, throughout July, sporadic fighting was continuing in Algeria, with heavy losses on both sides. A severe blow was dealt to certain French "fraternization" enthusiasts by the inglorious end of the "Bellounis experiment". "General" Mohammed Bellounis had, for about a year, been the head of the "National Army of the Algerian People", which was supposed to have fought against the FLN on the side of the French. The "Bellounis Army" had been an invention of M. Lacoste's; but, before long, the French High Command became increasingly doubtful about the value of the experiment. Heavily armed by the French, Bellounis's 3,000 or 4,000 men, after playing something of a double game, and massacring, in the process, several thousand Algerians, finally crossed over to the Rebel side, with Bellounis himself following, rather than leading them. And then it was learned that on July 14 Bellounis himself was killed by a French patrol in that very area in the South-Algérois where his "army" was supposed to fight the Rebels and protect the "oil line" between Touggourt and Biskra. . . .

9. THE BAZOOKA TRIAL: ACT I

ON July 25, after a short but stormy session, the Paris Military Tribunal, presided over by M. Olmi, adjourned *sine die* the trial of René Kovacs and five other men belonging to an "anti-terrorist" organization in Algiers who had attempted, on January 16, 1957, to assassinate General Salan, the French Commander-in-Chief in Algeria, by firing a bazooka shell into his office. Salan, as already said, happened to have gone out, but one of his aides, Major Rodier, was killed and another officer wounded.

This bold exploit was going to be attributed to the "ubiquity" of the Algerian terrorists; but, only a few days later, the Algiers police discovered the real culprits. Everything was done at the time to hush up the affair, and the trial of Kovacs and his companions kept on being postponed. Finally, however, on July 24, the case came before the Paris Military Tribunal. Kovacs was brought in on a stretcher; and, from the start, the two principal counsel for the defence, both of them notorious Fascists,

Me. Tixier-Vignancour and Me. Biaggi, pleaded that Kovacs was not in a fit condition to give evidence, despite the opinion of the medical experts that the skin disease from which he was suffering was not serious. It was for this reason that the defence had made no arrangements for the fifty-seven witnesses for the defence to appear in Court. Tixier-Vignancour, defying the opinion of the medical experts, gave gruesome clinical details about Kovacs's "blood-stained stools", "putrid breath" and so on, and finally dangled before the Court a bulging envelope containing peelings of Kovacs's skin which the sick man had scraped off his body as a result of the "intolerable itch" from which he was suffering. When none of this quite convinced the Court, Tixier-Vignancour and Biaggi resorted to another argument: they were not going to discuss anything in the presence of the "treason press"—the representatives of *Le Monde*, *L'Express* and *Libération*—and demanded that the case be heard *in camera*. Surprisingly—or perhaps not so surprisingly—the Court agreed to this. And, an hour and a half later, the Court was so impressed by what had transpired during the secret session that it agreed to the "provisional release" (*liberté provisoire*) of all the six accused. "Despite the gravity of the case," the Court stated, "the arguments produced during the *in camera* session have enabled the Court to show benevolence to the six men."

What was behind all this? The indictment, read out at the beginning of the session, i.e. before the Court was cleared, recalled the main facts:

On January 16 a bazooka shell was fired from a house facing the headquarters of the 10th Military Region at Algiers; it was fired straight into the office of General Salan. He was absent at the time, but the shell killed Major Rodier and wounded Lieut.-Colonel Basset.

The principal culprit was René Kovacs (34), former lieutenant of the DGER, the secret police service, and a former swimming champion, now officially established as a physician in Algiers. Actually, he did not practise, and the sources of his apparently substantial income were unknown. The other five were typical *petits blancs* of Algiers. Together they belonged to a counter-terrorist organization called the ORAF (*Organisation de Résistance pour l'Algérie française*).

If they decided to assassinate General Salan, it was because they had convinced themselves that Salan was "a slave of the System" and was thus betraying the ideals of French Algeria. They also wanted to create a "psychological shock" and kill two birds with one stone: get rid of Salan, and impress upon public opinion the extraordinary temerity of the Algerian terrorists, and so cause the war against them to be intensified.

The indictment said that it "wasn't necessary to dwell on the question where the bazooka and the shells had come from", but went on to say that the six conspirators had tried out the bazooka on lonely beaches, and had attained a degree of precision which explained how they had succeeded in firing the shell through a window from a considerable distance.

On the face of it, the whole enterprise was the work of a handful of fanatical cranks. But was there not something to which the indictment had not referred? Was there not somebody behind this attempt to eliminate Salan?

It was not until Tixier-Vignancour's "medical" arguments in favour of postponing the hearing were rejected by the Court that he lifted, in insidiously threatening tones, a corner of the veil by saying:

I intend to cite 57 witnesses. And if this case is to be discussed in detail, we've got to get to the bottom of it, so that nothing is left unsaid. The witnesses for the defence will give evidence on the context of the bare facts and on *the extremely close links between these facts and the major plan that gave birth to them.*

He then asked that the hearing be adjourned till November 9. By that time, the political situation in France would be clarified, and would be less liable than now to influence the verdict; it would also give the defence enough time to bring all the witnesses together. . . .

And then came another touch which obviously made the Court nervous:

I asked General Salan whether he thought it would be right that Kovacs should die in prison. And, *with his perfect knowledge of the whole case,* General Salan replied that it would not be right. Surely, it is only too obvious that *the men in the dock represent the Army. But neither the heart nor the head of the plot is here.*

And he added that it was probably just as well, because there were times when it was best not to discuss certain events in public, and, above all, in the presence of the enemy (meaning the Left-wing press). In short, it was no use washing one's dirty linen in public.

Tixier-Vignancour left very little doubt about the meaning of his words. If there was to be any spilling of beans, nobody would be spared— neither politicians nor Army leaders. . . . What were the secrets which Tixier-Vignancour threatened to reveal if the trial were brought to its bitter end? He had clearly suggested that the men implicated were not mere Fourth Republic politicians, but persons ranking high in the Army and under the de Gaulle régime, and that some very important people had hoped to benefit from the death of Salan.

A few days after the "first" Kovacs trial, *L'Express* published a pro-visional inquiry into the whole affair. M. Philippe Grumbach, the author of the article, made the following points:

What, he asked, were those terrible secrets which had enabled Kovacs's lawyers to speak so arrogantly at the trial and to obtain, after the Court had been cleared, so "benevolent" an attitude from the judges *vis-à-vis* a band of assassins?

Who were "the head and the heart" of the plot?
And then:

The bazooka affair is so serious that it must not be hushed up.
The truth is that names have been mentioned; men have been—perhaps unjustly
—compromised. Rumours have been circulating in administrative, military and
political quarters. . . . For instance, a very high-ranking officer and a colonel have
both been accused of having embezzled important funds for their own ends. A
former premier, a former minister are alleged to be constantly blackmailed, since
their mail was intercepted. . . . And *the link among all these stories is the bazooka
affair*.

Unfortunately, said Grumbach, the matter was not so simple. For one
thing, certain very important and pertinent documents had disappeared
in Algiers at the height of the May rebellion; so even if General de Gaulle
himself wanted to be fully informed, it was not certain that the documents
could now be provided.

The fact remained [said Grumbach] that, in March 1958, Tixier-Vignancour
had forwarded to the examining magistrate a long memorandum containing some
"specially grave revelations" made by his client, René Kovacs. Kovacs alleged,
for example, that a "very high-ranking officer" and certain prominent political
leaders had been negotiating for a long time, with a view to organizing an insurrection, to be headed by the officer in question.
   According to Kovacs, the said officer said to the politicians that it was important
to get Salan out of the way; he even suggested that he have dinner with him, and
bring him after dinner to the garden of the Hôtel St. Georges at Algiers; "only
you'll have to aim well".
   This plotting went right back to December 1956, i.e. a month before the actual
attempt to assassinate Salan.
   It was at that time that General Faure, deputy to General Manceaux-Demiaux,
commanding general of the Algiers region, and himself commanding the local
territorial units and in close touch with the civilian *ultras* of Algiers, called, on
December 24, on M. Paul Teitgen, Secretary-General of the Préfecture of Algiers.
He declared to him that the republican régime was leading France and Algeria
to a catastrophe. The territorial armoured unit of Maison-Carrée [which was to
play so important a part on May 14] was ready to act, and all the officers had been
informed of what they were to do.
   According to Faure, Salan could be won over, while Lacoste could be put out of
harm's way. Republican generals like Paris de Bollardière and Huet could be
"neutralized". Certain of Lacoste's officials could be arrested. Once the *coup*
succeeded, Salan would join; the commander of the Air Force in Algeria, General
Frandon, had already been won over, Faure claimed.
   Faure's purpose in visiting Teitgen was to secure the full support of the Police.
   Teitgen informed Lacoste of what had happened. Faure came to see Teitgen
again on December 30, and here talked to him for one hour and thirty-five
minutes, explaining exactly how the *putsch* would take place.
   A secret tape recording was made of his statement. Teitgen thereupon left for

Paris, complete with the tape recording, and informed Guy Mollet (then Premier) of what was going on. Thereupon Faure was summoned to Paris, and arrested soon afterwards.

Already at the end of 1956 the Guy Mollet Government knew that a plot was being hatched in Algiers.

Yet Faure's friends in Paris soon persuaded the Government that a complete revelation of the "Faure story" might only encourage sedition in the Army.

It so happened that about the same time General Paris de Bollardière had openly condemned certain terrorist methods (including torture) used by the French Army. So he also was summoned to Paris, and to cancel each other out, as it were, *both* the rebellious general and the republican general were put under arrest for a month.

For the first time, the "Army blackmail" had worked perfectly.

As for the famous tape-recording, it had mysteriously been tampered with, and the more "dangerous" passages had been blurred out.

The "Faure Plan" having failed, the "Kovacs gang" decided to act. The "high-ranking officer" referred to in the Tixier-Vignancour memorandum was consulted, but would not commit himself. Since Salan also assumed a non-committal attitude, it was decided to liquidate him, in the hope that the extremists' friends in Paris would secure the appointment, in Salan's place, of a "more energetic" chief. . . .

Then, on January 16, 1957, came the attempt to kill Salan. It failed, and soon afterwards, the Police trapped Kovacs and his accomplices.

Then a new kind of blackmail started. A Paris evening paper published a statement by one of their lawyers saying that Kovacs had merely acted on behalf of a "Committee of Six" sitting in Paris and comprising leading civilian and military personages. The paper also said that, according to Kovacs, numerous generals and colonels, bankers and businessmen, senators, deputies and Cabinet ministers were mixed up with the affair.

Lacoste meantime was trying to minimize the affair, attributing it to a "handful of fanatics", while, at the National Assembly, M. Soustelle accused the Government of "fabricating non-existent conspiracies".

Fearing a sharp reaction from the Army, the Governments of the Fourth Republic preferred to dismiss Faure's statements as "a few indiscretions" and the bazooka affair as the work of a handful of fanatics.

The serious attempt by M. Mitterrand, M. Mollet's Minister of Justice, to get at the full facts was sabotaged by the Ministry of Defence.

Yet already in February 1957 another plot had been discovered by the Police, with a certain Sauveur Lauratou at its head; a close link was established between this terrorist organization and the Kovacs gang; during the inquiry into this case, it was established that the Kovacs gang had torture chambers of its own at the Villa des Sources, near Algiers, and that certain other persons were involved in these activities, notably members of another extremist organization, the CRF, the *Comité de la Résistance Française*. Two of these, Crespin and Martel, were now members of the Algiers and Sahara Committee of Public Safety. . . .

Grumbach's conclusion may be summed up as follows:

The names of the all-powerful Committee of Six, which pulled the wires in Paris, as well as the names of many others who had been preparing for years the May 13 revolution—and who were, more or less, implicated in the bazooka affair—are known to many persons in high authority; but it is for the Courts to make them appear publicly and answer whatever charges may be brought against them. The truth, however, is that while many, though not all, the military revealed their game on May 13, the civilians remained in the shadow. Hence Tixier's threat to spill the beans.

And why, Grumbach asked, should a Vichyite like Tixier-Vignancour feel strong enough to blackmail the de Gaulle Government? Why should he be able, speaking in the name of a gang who killed a French officer, to talk about its being "a family affair" among "French patriots"?

Is it not because he thinks that, just as the last three Governments of the Fourth Republic preferred to hush up the affair, so the de Gaulle Government will do the same, to avoid too much unpleasantness of one kind or another?

He ended, however, on an optimistic note. "This time," he said, "Tixier-Vignancour may have gone too far." He recalled that since the Kovacs case was adjourned *sine die*, M. Guillaumat, de Gaulle's Minister of the Army, had, as head of the military Office of Prosecutions (*Parquet militaire*), ordered that the case be reopened in August.

Alas! as we shall see, a sufficiently large number of powerful persons thought it in their interest that the case should *not* be reopened. By the time things threatened to get really hot, it was discovered that the "dying" Kovacs had escaped to Spain, complete with his skin disease, his "bloody stools" and—all those very, very awkward secrets. . . .

10. THE SOCIALIST "INFORMATION CONFERENCE" OF JULY 6

DE GAULLE, as we have seen, had waited for the end of the Socialist "Information Conference" of July 6 before announcing the appointment of Soustelle to the post of Minister of Information. This Socialist meeting is of considerable interest. We have already dealt with the explanations given by Jules Moch at this conference as to why, in view of the latent revolt in the Army and the Police in May, there was no choice for the Socialists other than to bring de Gaulle quickly into power.

Least interesting, perhaps, at this conference was the long speech by Guy Mollet. who argued throughout that he had done "the right thing", besides going over much of the already familiar ground and skating, in the process, over some long stretches of very thin ice.

Ex-Foreign Minister Pineau, along with several others, explained once again why he had voted against de Gaulle's investiture. He spoke with some bitterness of the perfect ease with which de Gaulle had now made a settlement with Tunisia, giving her even *more* than Murphy's and Beeley's "good offices" mission had recommended (in particular, no international control of the Tunisian airfields had now been provided for), and yet doing it with complete impunity, and with scarcely a murmur from anybody—not even from the wild men of Algiers. Was not this, he said, just another illustration of the chronic conspiracy that had gone on against the Fourth Republic?

THE LACOSTE VERSION

The most interesting speeches made at the Conference were those dealing specifically with Algeria. Robert Lacoste complained of the attacks that had been made on him in the Socialist Party and of the great discourtesy with which so many were now treating him. He was, throughout, on the defensive, trying to argue that he had done a wonderful job in Algeria, but had received no thanks for it. Most striking of all, throughout his speech, was perhaps the fact that he was entirely concerned with his relations with the Army and the Europeans, and that he showed no interest at all in the Moslems—rather confirming the opinion of Jacques Chevallier, the Mayor of Algiers, that Lacoste was, among the Moslems, the best-hated of all Frenchmen.

Lacoste recalled that as long ago as September 1956 he had warned the Government that the Army could not be absolutely relied upon. If, he wrote at the time, there were any attempt to abandon Algeria, the Army would, "at least morally", join in the revolt. A year later, he informed the Government of a dangerous ferment among the younger officers, though the high command fortunately still appeared to be reliable; General Massu, in particular, had been very helpful in preventing a demonstration against the first *loi-cadre* project. On the other hand, he already then thought the Algiers Police wholly unreliable.

He then recalled how, at the beginning of May 1958, he had warned the Socialist Party against any talk of negotiations with the FLN; all this talk was discouraging and annoying the Army, and it was no use expecting soldiers to fight in such conditions. . . . Yes, he *had* used the phrase "a diplomatic Dien Bien Phu"; he had not coined that phrase himself; it had been invented by Cairo radio, and represented the great hope of the FLN. Before that, in February and March, *he had warned the Government of the disastrous impression the Anglo-American good offices mission* was creating among the Europeans in Algeria; in April, after the fall of the Gaillard Government, he declared that European opinion in Algiers was convinced that, in any case, the stage had been set for the gradual abandonment of Algeria. He thought there would be some violent protest demonstrations, and the extreme nervousness of the Europeans was fully shared by the younger officers in the Army.

What added to the Europeans' exasperation, said Lacoste, were the long-drawn-out Cabinet crisis of April–May, the failure of Bidault (who was trusted by the Europeans) to form a Government, the Socialist Party's decision not to join any new Government (which was interpreted as a change in the Socialists' Algerian policy) and, finally, all the sniggering in the *Monde* and other papers about the "dropping" of Lacoste. . . .

The great protest demonstration of April 26, Lacoste said, had been chiefly organized by M. Delbecque, who was the *chef de cabinet* of M. Chaban-Delmas, the Minister of Defence.

In that capacity he enjoyed a sort of immunity against which M. Lacoste could do nothing. He could, for instance, land at any military airfield without anybody being informed. Among the other organizers of the April 26 demonstration there was also Colonel Trinquier; he (Lacoste) had, despite much opposition from Salan, got rid of him in the past, by having him transferred to France; but in March 1958 he was surprised to learn that Chaban-Delmas, as Minister of Defence, had sent him back to Algeria, where he was to replace Colonel Bigeard on the Tunisian border.[1] It did not take long before Trinquier's unit came to Algiers, ostensibly on leave. Trinquier and Delbecque and other extremists in Algiers had deliberately ignored Lacoste's prohibition of the April 26 demonstration.

Throughout this part of his narrative Lacoste clearly indicated *that Chaban-Delmas, Minister of Defence, Mayor of Bordeaux, and one of the "Gaullists" who was always ready to play the Trojan horse in any Government of the Fourth Republic,*[2] (and who was later to become President of the Fifth Republic's National Assembly) was one of the men in Paris who had been particularly active in preparing the Algiers revolution. . . .

While denying that he had tried to stir up any agitation in Algeria in his own favour and against his departure, Lacoste nevertheless said that, at Oran, on May 8, 35,000 people "implored" him to stay on. But neither these appeals, nor the overtures made to him by Delbecque and de Sérigny, Lacoste said, could shake his loyalty to the Socialist Party. Greatly differing in this from the account given by de Sérigny, Lacoste claimed that he dismissed as "totally absurd" Delbecque's

---

[1] Bigeard, though a legendary hero among the French paratroopers, had, it seems, ostentatiously *not* taken part in the Algiers *putsch*, and had remained aloof of the whole 13th of May movement. Soon after the formation of the de Gaulle Government, he was relieved of his command in Algeria and transferred to France. Delbecque nevertheless claimed that he was a member of that "Gaullist" group which would have struck out on May 14 if it hadn't been forestalled by the "activists" the night before.

[2] He had even been a member of the Mendès-France Government in 1954.

and de Sérigny's suggestion that de Gaulle was expecting him (Lacoste) to rebel against Paris before making any far-reaching statement himself.

Then, with a great display of bitterness, he described how he left Algiers, without any honours being rendered him, "as though I had not served this country for twenty-seven months with all my heart and soul . . ."

Those who trusted me there, now thought me a traitor; and those facing me here now think me a Machiavelli. . . .

And then Lacoste recalled how, on the night of May 13–14, after the revolt had broken out in Algiers, General Ely said—in the presence of several ministers—that, in his opinion, there was only one man who could still fully restore the discipline of the Army, and that was Lacoste—provided he left for Algiers immediately. But it came to nothing.

He also claimed that, on the evening of May 13, while talking to Massu on the phone, he warned him against the unconstitutional step he had just taken in accepting the presidency of the Committee of Public Safety. " 'Massu, watch your step,' I said to him."

But who, then, according to Lacoste, had started the May 13 *putsch*?

I had known for a long time that there were explosive elements in Algiers; and now nobody was going to stop the explosion. The Army had no intention of stopping it. But the actual explosion was organized by people who had certainly subversive political ideas. The attack on the Government-General was carried out by a bunch of people I would call *neo-ultras*—a bunch of young, wild and very active people who, in the last analysis, were a tool in the hands of the "colonels". I do not believe that either Salan or Massu knew anything about it.

Indeed, at 9 o'clock that evening, Salan called Delbecque a thug [*voyou*], while Massu said to Colonel Thomazo: "You knew there was going to be this *bordel*; why did you do nothing to stop it?" Here were certain elements who, following the classical rules of secret and subversive action, had for weeks been manipulating irresponsible masses. . . . Together with this action went a variety of plots in Metropolitan France itself . . ., while in the Army there were many who were firmly opposed to any Government that might be tempted to negotiate with the FLN.

And Lacoste recalled that in his own *département*, the Dordogne, the local Army commanders had told the Prefect that he need not depend on them to maintain law and order; they were going to take orders only from their chiefs "in the Army hierarchy"—from which Lacoste concluded that there was a military plot in Metropolitan France, too.

The fact remained, said Lacoste, that although the Algiers revolt had been organized by a whole series of (often unconnected) plots, the movement was unquestionably a *popular movement*. And after saying that he was going to explain the details of all this in a book, Lacoste concluded both in sorrow and in anger:

> I rejected the chance of an easy popularity. I was the so-called "proconsul" who had refused to lead the revolt of ten million Algerians against the Republic. I left Algiers discreetly, almost like a guilty man, only to see before me now a number of faces from which all traces of friendship have vanished. Great is my sorrow, but I shall do my duty to the end. . . .

WHAT DID THE MOSLEMS REALLY THINK?

Not once had Lacoste mentioned the Moslems. It was typical of the man, whose main, if not sole, concern throughout his "proconsulate" in Algeria had been to "pacify" the country and keep the Europeans happy. This large gap in his story was to be filled at the Socialist Conference by a man whose name was not given, and who was discreetly described as "a comrade from Constantine"; this Socialist had obviously mixed, infinitely more than Lacoste had done, with the Moslem population; and he had some valuable information to give both on the state of mind of the Moslems before, during and since the May 13 revolution, and on that of the ordinary French conscripts, of whom so little was ever heard. Unlike many other *petit-blanc* Socialists in Algeria, this "old Socialist *militant*", as he described himself, had at least tried to understand the Moslem point of view.

He did not mince his words.

The Moslem masses, he said, turned against France after "our comrade" Mollet's visit to Algiers on February 6, 1956, when Mollet did nothing to oppose the *ultras* who had organized that famous demonstration against him.

The distrust of the Moslems deepened still further after the appointment of Lacoste to Algiers.

Lacoste had, throughout, ignored the old Socialist *militants* of Algeria, who would have helped him to avoid many errors; he had not realized, for example, that it was essential to purge the administration of all the resolute enemies of the Moslems, and of all those officials who were hostile to Socialism and to the popular masses. . . . No doubt, the Mollet Government was right to have sent 400,000 troops to Algeria, but that, in itself, was not enough. Any reforms that were decided upon were inadequate, and were, in any case, sabotaged by the officials. The experiment of the "*délégations spéciales*" had been a failure and had given rise to sordid negotiations between the administration and the Moslem candidates to municipal posts.

The Moslems, he then said, could have no faith in France; although a Socialist was Minister-Resident, all the old colonialists and reactionaries continued to run the country. In the circumstances, the *loi-cadre* made no impression on the Moslems; nor were they impressed by what was going on in Paris, with Parliament dominated by the Right-wing reactionaries.

For a long time, in Algeria, there had been much talk of a Fascist plot. It was said that a meeting had taken place in August 1957 at Palma, Majorca, by a large number of persons, from both France and Algeria, among them de Sérigny, Delbecque, Lagaillarde, big French employers, and some soldiers. Their aims were said to be—(1) to abolish the Republic; (2) to set up a Fascist or authoritarian régime, with possibly the Count of Paris at its head; (3) to settle the Algerian problem by exterminating a few hundred thousand Algerians; (4) to invade Tunisia and wipe out all the Algerian rebels there. . . . Also, we learned from good sources that three milliard francs' worth of food was to be bought from Spain to feed the European population of Algiers in the event of a probable breach between France and Algeria.

After dwelling on the great nervousness caused in Algeria by the "good offices" mission and by Lacoste's "diplomatic Dien Bien Phu" prophecy, the "Comrade from Constantine" said that the invasion, by a bunch of young thugs, of the Government-General building on May 13 *was entirely the work of the paratroop colonels.* It was, indeed, such a colonel who had ordered the CRS guards to withdraw, after these had easily repelled the first attack; and it was a paratroopers' truck which, used as a battering-ram, broke down the gates of the building and let in the crowd of young people, who then proceeded to ransack the offices of the Government-General. . . . But the real tragedy was that none of this would have been possible, had not the ringleaders somehow put it into people's heads that all this was being done to "save Algeria".

And even later, when many began to see clearly what was behind it all, the mass of the people did not react. Some actively joined in the movement, others— including Socialists, I regret to say—joined Committees of Public Safety, either spontaneously or out of fear. . . .

And whatever the exact role played by the top-ranking officers, there was no doubt that the younger officers, especially the paratroopers, were all in sympathy with the *putsch*.

No doubt there were also some officers who were frankly revolted by what was happening; but, as regards the ordinary conscripts, they were mostly out in the *bled*; they were chiefly interested in "leave and grub".

The CPS was formed at Algiers on May 13; similar committees were formed at Constantine and elsewhere on the following day. The Constantine committee consisted mostly of old Pétainists, former members of the Pétain Legion, big *colons* and other colonialists, most of whom were, in fact, strongly prejudiced against de Gaulle at first. . . . There followed several days of complete confusion; but the arrival of Soustelle was of decisive importance in making the "de Gaulle" slogan acceptable to most. The "comrade from Constantine" then confessed that, even to the not very numerous sincere democrats and Socialists in Algeria, de Gaulle came to symbolize a lesser evil. . . .

It was the extremists on the Committees of Public Safety who now felt disturbed; the Socialists of Constantine, on the contrary, welcomed de Gaulle, as well as Mollet's decision to enter the de Gaulle Government.

What, during this period, had been the attitude of the Moslems? A large number of paratroopers arrived at Constantine on April 27. and proceeded to terrorize the Moslem population, rounding them up in the streets, making numerous arrests, and subjecting them to the worst humiliations. But then, suddenly, Algiers proclaimed the "Integration" slogan.

To the "comrade from Constantine" the slogan, though it reduced tension for a time, made no sense. *If there were honest elections in Algeria, there would be ninety or a hundred FLN or separatist Algerians sitting in the National Assembly in Paris; while the cost of economic integration would be quite prohibitive.* And the Moslems to whom he had talked of "integration" just didn't believe in it. They thought it would be just another swindle, especially with the place run by the thugs of the Committees of Public Safety. The famous "fraternization" rallies had been a swindle, too, he said: *"We who were there know what methods were used to organize these grandiose mass demonstrations."*

The "comrade's" conclusion was, however, on the vague side. He was in favour of undertaking a "vast military operation" to wipe out the last remnants of the FLN; on the whole, de Gaulle still enjoyed some prestige with the Moslems, and perhaps he could gain their confidence if he resolutely embarked on a campaign against the old colonialist privileges— which was more than any governor-general in the past had ever tried to do. It was important to strengthen freedom and democracy in Algeria.

All of which was scarcely very conclusive. . . .

"you've got no socialist theory"

Many other speakers took part in the Conference, many of them Socialists who had voted against de Gaulle, among them Pineau, Gazier, Verdier, and Depreux. Perhaps the most vital criticism of the "optimistic" or "pessimistic" attitude the various speakers had adopted towards de Gaulle came from Jean Rous who tried to get down to fundamentals, and deplored the lack of any theoretical and analytical basis to the discussion:

Before the war, we used to engage in doctrinal and analytical debates, whether we had been brought up on the ideas of Blum or Marx, Jaurès or Trotsky. Now, faced with Gaullism, we talk about it in terms of mere anecdotes; or we are just guided by sentiment. We overlook the fact that here is a phenomenon very similar to that "Bonapartism", which Marx analysed so brilliantly in his *Civil War in France.* If only we would read our classical texts, we would soon realize that Gaullism, like Bonapartism, is a highly ambiguous system, comprising certain positive aspects, but containing also some highly negative and dangerous features;

and the dangers are of a nature which finally lead to military or personal dictatorship.

What Rous meant was that, charmed or dazzled by certain remarks or attitudes of de Gaulle, *a man like Mollet was incapable of seeing the de Gaulle phenomenon in any sort of historical perspective*; maybe a "good" man in himself, de Gaulle still represented certain social and historical forces which were fundamentally hostile to all that Socialism was meant to stand for.

Mollet did not answer Rous on this occasion; but he was going to answer him indirectly in September when, at the Socialist Congress, he drew the distinction between his own "realistic socialism" of today and his "theoretical socialism" in the past. . . .

Some other highly valid points were made. Not only "integration", but the concept of Algerians becoming "complete Frenchmen"—*Français à part entière*—were criticized as impractical and demagogic. Thus M. Rimbert (of the Seine Federation) said:

[The Algerians] can never become "complete" Frenchmen. Not because de Gaulle or any other member of his Government is against it, but because it means in practice that France would have to reduce her own standard of living by 30 per cent; and those who scream loudest about '*Algérie française*' would be the first to reject this sacrifice. . . .

Since the Socialist meeting of July 6 was only an "information conference", and not a Congress, no resolutions or motions on the future policy of the Socialist Party were discussed; this work was left for the Socialist Congress that was to meet early in September. But a few days later the Socialist *comité directeur* (meeting in the absence of M. Mollet) expressed the wish that the Committees of Public Safety in Algeria and elsewhere be dissolved. Needless to say, the Government took no notice of this any more than it did of various other Socialist requests.

11. CONFUSION ON THE LEFT

(a) THE LEFT "RALLY"

ALTOGETHER, the Socialists and, indeed, all the Left-wing parties and organizations seemed to be deeply demoralized by what had happened. It is true that, on July 7, some important members of the non-Communist Left laid the foundations for a new political group or, rather, "rally", when forty-one persons went to a meeting called by M. Daniel Mayer, president of the *Ligue des Droits de l'Homme* (who, being in total disagreement with the Socialist leadership, had resigned from the National Assembly earlier in the year). This new "rally" took the name of *Union des Forces Démocratiques*, and its "provisional bureau" was composed of a number of university men, such as the *doyen* Chatelet, M. Jean Hippolyte, director of the *Ecole Normale Supérieure*, MM. Mendès-France, Mitterrand, and some members of the Left wing of the Socialist Party, notably Edouard Depreux, Alain Savary and Robert Verdier, as well as André Philip, who had been expelled from the Party in February, on account of his book, *Le socialisme trahi*. On whether this new organization was to have long-term objectives (such as the creation of a new "Labour Party"—which appeared to be M. Mendès-France's idea) or whether its immediate purpose was to put up a major fight against the adoption of the new de Gaulle Constitution (which was then in process of being drafted) was not finally decided. Mendès-France, in particular, took the view that it would be largely a waste of time to fight against the Constitution, which was certain to be adopted by a large majority of the electorate, but that the new Left-wing organization had better try to gain some seats in the subsequent election—an argument which met with the obvious objection that, once the Constitution had been adopted, the forces hostile to de Gaulle would not stand much of a chance in the election. . . . The question of any possible co-operation with the Communists, either during the Referendum campaign or in the subsequent general election, was scarcely touched upon: most members of the new *Union des Forces Démocratiques* still thought in terms of "rallying" the forces of the non-Communist Left.

(*b*) THE COMMUNISTS: "IT'LL BE TERRIBLY DIFFICULT . . ."

For their own part, the Communists also held an "information conference" at Montreuil a few days later. The atmosphere was rather morose, and M. Maurice Thorez and other speakers made no secret of the "terrible difficulties" the Party would face in trying to explain the dangers of the new Constitution to the working class. The general euphoria, following the "bloodless revolution" of May, and the general respect for de Gaulle, were shared by a large part of the habitual Communist voters.

To show up the "de Gaulle myth", Thorez went out of his way to recall how de Gaulle had resigned in 1946, since "he could not resign himself to governing with a sovereign Assembly, or to working with ministers who would be anything other than his office boys". He was already then becoming the spokesman of the old Vichyites, who, soon afterwards, were going to form the backbone of the RPF.

Without dwelling on the fact that it was the "Third Force" which had, in reality, prevented de Gaulle's RPF from seizing power in 1947–8,

Thorez attacked the MRP and the Socialists who, throughout the history of the Fourth Republic, had "weakened democracy" by ostracizing the greatest working class party, the CP. It was also they, he said, who paved the way for de Gaulle's return to power.

Turning to the problem of Algeria, Thorez ridiculed the "sinister farce" of "fraternization" at a time when General Salan was clamouring for 100,000 more troops to be added to the half-million troops already there. He denied that de Gaulle had any intention of making peace in Algeria.

The aim of the Referendum, said Thorez, was to establish a presidential régime in France, in which the President would be all-powerful. The voting in the Referendum would be done without any proper knowledge of the new Constitution, without any discussion, without the possibility of any counter-proposals being made; the whole thing would be "a mockery".

Thorez regretted that the non-Communist Left (the *Union des forces démocratiques* in particular) had not shown greater eagerness to work hand-in-hand with the Communists. And his final words were like a prophecy of a lost battle:

> The superhuman effort we must make is necessary not only in order to strengthen our Party. We must do wonders in a very short time to enlighten and organize the masses. A great and very hard ideological and political battle has begun. Between now and October 5[1] we must prove ourselves capable of explaining to the inhabitants of even the most remote hamlet of our country the stakes in this battle, and the true significance of the Referendum-plebiscite; we must know how to answer the flood of lies pouring out of the Government radio and the Government-inspired press.

And he called on every Party member to work, with all his heart, for the closest united action between Communists and Socialists, and all the other democratic forces in the country; only such unity could finally rout the rebel forces. . . .

12. SOUSTELLE AGAIN ON THE MOVE— THE RADIO PURGE

IF THE confusion was great amongst both the non-Communist Left and the Communists themselves, the "Gaullists" had, obviously, a much clearer plan of action. On July 17 it was announced that M. Jacques Soustelle, the Minister of Information, was about to found a new move-

---

[1] The date of the Referendum was at first fixed for October 5, to be changed later to September 28.

ment called the URF (*Union pour le renouveau français*); its personnel
would, in the main, be that of the old USRAF, which Soustelle had
founded in March 1956 and which, as we have seen, had played a decisive
role in the May events. This new organization, it was stated, would
"give its full support to any action aiming at the renewal of the institutions of the Republic", and would conduct a vigorous campaign in favour
of the new Constitution.

This organization was, in fact, the nucleus of that UNR Party which
was to be formed after the Referendum, and was to become the great
victorious "Gaullist" party in the November election.

Parallel with this setting up of a powerful propaganda machine for the
Referendum, Soustelle (who seldom spoke in public and preferred to act
in the shadowy background) also fully reorganized the radio and television
services now under his complete control. Even the meek and mild Socialist
Populaire was getting alarmed by the extent of M. Soustelle's powers.
"The unlimited nature of the powers entrusted to him resemble those
which were shared in Algiers by Colonel Lacheroy and M. Neuwirth," it
wrote on July 20. And there seemed, indeed, little doubt that the "spirit
of May 13" was pervading all M. Soustelle's activities. His secretariat
at the Ministry of Information was composed of "May 13" men, among
them the said M. Neuwirth, who was to "organize" for the radio and the
press the information about Algeria; here also were most of the old leaders
of the USRAF, who were now going to act under the banner of the
above-mentioned URF.

After his appointment as Minister of Information, M. Soustelle did not
take long to purge radio and TV, replacing numerous "good republicans"
(many of them now branded as "crypto-Communists") by his own men,
notably M. Terrenoire, formerly his right-hand man in the old RPF.
M. Soustelle's guiding idea was that radio and television (both State-
owned) were a "national service". While, for the time being, heterodox
speakers were not to be eliminated entirely, the time to be given them was
to be exceedingly short; if they did not watch their step, they were to be
cut out altogether. Thus a statement by M. Daniel Mayer, president of the
Ligue des Droits de l'Homme, was banned, because it spoke of "sedition" in
Algiers. Similarly, one staff member was rapped over the knuckles by
M. Soustelle himself for having passed a news item which had referred
to the rise in the price of steak, without specifying that this rise was
"sporadic and accidental".[1] Not only did M. Soustelle's team control the
actual radio broadcasts and TV shows, but they set up a special service to
watch the opposition press, and another to control cinema newsreels,
and still another to establish close contact with all the press and information services of other Government departments, with a view to controlling
them. As we shall see, radio and TV under Soustelle's guidance and control

[1] *France-Observateur*, July 31, 1958.

were to play an absolutely decisive role in securing a nearly 80 per cent vote "for de Gaulle" in the Referendum in September, and in obtaining an overwhelming victory for the UNR in the General Election in November.

As regards the radio propaganda for the Referendum, extremely little was said about the Draft Constitution itself; it was thanks to the radio, more than to anything else, that the Referendum on the Constitution became in effect a plebiscite for de Gaulle. . . .

Among M. Soustelle's many tasks was that of "co-ordinating the press, documentation and information services" of all the Government departments; and in all these, it was now alleged, he had his own men, who were keeping an eye on the various ministers and their assistants; he was particularly anxious to prevent any activity by "Left-wing Gaullists"[1] who were likely to do all the wrong things.

Radio and TV continued, throughout August, to be purged. When challenged on this score by a group of deputies (forming part of the Press Committee of the National Assembly) M. Soustelle resorted to the classical argument that he had to get rid of "Communist and pro-Communist elements". This was little more than an excuse. French radio had already undergone several "purges" since 1946. On the RTF (French radio and TV) there were, according to *L'Express*, 250 professional journalists; only eleven of these belonged to the Communist trade union federation (CGT), and had long ago been given "unpolitical" jobs, and been carefully removed from anything even remotely connected with news on any of the three programmes. For over ten years French radio had kept clear of anything like Communist-tainted information.

So in reality it was not a case of replacing Communists by "objective reporters"; it was a case of replacing *anybody* by persons with an RPF background, or by others whom M. Soustelle had some particular reason to trust. Thus, Me. Henry Torrès, an old RPF man, was appointed president of the *conseil supérieur* of the RTF in place of the late Professor Paul Rivet; most important of all, M. Terrenoire, a leading RPF figure, became supreme boss of all the news services in place of M. Gayman. Gayman gave an interview to *Le Monde* in which he referred to himself as No. 1 scapegoat, adding that if he was a Communist before the war, "*M. Soustelle and M. Malraux were not far off it either.*"

With an eye to the Referendum campaign a special post of Secretary-General for Information was created for M. Paul Bodin, "technical

[1] *France-Observateur* of August 28 alleged that M. Michelet, Minister of War Veterans, had arranged a commemorative ceremony on the anniversary of General von Choltitz's capitulation to the French Army and Resistance in August 1944; a number of Communists who had played a leading part in the liberation of Paris were to be invited. Such "broad-mindedness" was too much for M. Soustelle, and his "representatives" inside M. Michelet's ministry cancelled the invitations to the Communists! Michelet was very angry about this interference in his Ministry by the "Soustelle network".

adviser" on M. Soustelle's staff; the foreign news service was entrusted to M. Maurice Ferro, who had quarrelled with the *Monde* some years before and had since been active on Right-wing papers like *Paris-Presse*, *L'Aurore* and the short-lived *Temps de Paris* (which had tried to "sink" the *Monde*). And so all the way down the scale. But sacking people was not enough; and, in order to intensify radio propaganda during the coming Referendum campaign, new jobs were created, and M. Soustelle's department received for the purpose an additional Government grant of 225 million francs. Radio-Algiers (now called France V) was handed over by Soustelle to "May 13" men.

Secret rules were now laid down in the daily briefings: for example, Colombey-les-deux-Eglises was not to be mentioned, because it "irritated" the General; certain speeches (for instance, M. Duchet's "integrationist" speech at Algiers) were to be quoted throughout the day; M. Mendès-France's journey to China was not to be mentioned; no opposition speeches or newspapers were to be quoted, except the clumsier utterances in the Communist press; altogether, the impression was to be given that the entire opposition was Communist; new Left-wing organizations like the *Union des Forces Démocratiques* were to be ignored altogether; even statements by the *Centre de la Réforme Républicaine*, a "Left-wing Gaullist" organization, were to be ignored. All favourable comments on de Gaulle at home or abroad had to be played up.

All this suggested that the Ministry of Information was rapidly becoming the Ministry of Propaganda.

Closely connected with the work of the Ministry of Information was also that of the CDF, the *Centre de Diffusion Française*, an organism set up in 1957 and dependent on the "*documentation et diffusion*" service of the Premier's office. Its initial purpose was to "spread French culture abroad". Now, in connection with the Referendum, its budget had been increased to 3½ milliard francs; one of its immediate aims was "to buy time on peripheral wireless stations like Radio-Luxembourg and Radio-Europe No. 1 which must, at the same time, undertake not to open their studios to propaganda by any of the opposition parties".[1]

The same organization was also planning to embark on a major "psychological action" to influence the press during the Referendum campaign, and even some "psychological specialists" of the Army in Algeria were specially brought to Paris for the purpose.[2]

[1] *L'Exprees*, August 28.
[2] *ibid.*

13. "OPERATION CHLOROFORM"

WHEN we speak of the general euphoria that marked those first months of the de Gaulle régime—a euphoria which did so much to produce the treble victory of the Referendum, the General Election and the election of de Gaulle himself to the Presidency of the Republic—we can scarcely deny that there was, in all this, an element of confidence trickery. Commentators have gone so far as to speak of "Operation Chloroform". One of the biggest shots of dope was, of course, administered to public opinion by M. Pinay, whose successful loan of June–July 1958 made it possible to postpone those fairly drastic financial measures which the public were going to get *after* they had said three times Yes to de Gaulle.

In a broadcast, only a few days before the publication of the Draft Constitution, M. Pinay drew an optimistic picture of France's economic and financial position. He recalled that the loan had produced 324 milliard francs, of which 293 milliards were "fresh" money; that the Bank of France had bought 150 tons of gold, the equivalent of 170 million dollars. While the subscriptions to this loan were open, there had been no decline in the subscription to Treasury Bonds or in savings banks deposits. For the rest,

> M. Pinay indicated that he intended to steer a careful course between the extremes of deflation and inflation, rigid planned economy and "blind and inhuman liberalism"; and said he would aim at happily balancing wages and prices, revenue and expenditure, and imports and exports. While admitting that there had been a certain rise in the cost of living in recent months, the stabilization of prices, he said, was now "well on the way". The foreign exchange situation had also greatly improved, thanks to the repatriation of capital, the sales of gold and the generally more favourable foreign attitude to the franc. Without suggesting that all difficulties were over, M. Pinay nevertheless indicated that the general outlook was favourable.

One thing, in any case, was certain: whereas the Gaillard and Pflimlin Governments were both dreading the rapidly-approaching day when France would have to face a major foreign-exchange crisis—for her foreign exchange reserves were rapidly running out—the "return of confidence" in June–July and the successful Pinay Loan had now postponed the day of reckoning. The absence of any explicit reference to this "day of reckoning"—which did finally come in December—helped enormously in maintaining in France that holiday mood which marked the first few months of the de Gaulle régime.

14. THE PRELIMINARY DRAFT CONSTITUTION

I T WAS on June 12, i.e. barely ten days after forming his Government and almost immediately after completing his first journey to Algeria, that de Gaulle presided over the first meeting of that "Interministerial Council" which was to draw up the text of the Preliminary Draft Constitution. This Council was composed of the four Ministers of State and M. Debré, the Minister of Justice.

Contrary to expectations, de Gaulle—despite his years of meditation on the "flaws of the system" and on "the absence of the State"—had not himself produced any Draft. He merely laid down before his five ministers some of the general principles which he wished to see incorporated in the new Constitution. His *exposé* was followed by numerous discussions. A number of his original suggestions were discarded altogether; others were modified. The Prime Minister's powers, on the face of it, were to be greater than what de Gaulle had at first proposed. Also, some new ideas were adopted, such as the creation of a Constitutional Council of nine members.

The final text of the preliminary Draft Constitution, which was published on July 29, and submitted to the deliberations of the Advisory Constitutional Committee (the CCC) meeting at the Palais Royal, was, in the main, drawn up by M. Debré, in agreement with de Gaulle and his four Ministers of State, among them M. Mollet and M. Pflimlin.

We shall deal later with the final text of the Constitution, as it emerged from the August deliberations of the CCC and the Conseil d'Etat, and was to be finally approved by the electorate on September 28. Except for some mostly minor details, it does not greatly differ from the preliminary Draft of July 29. The significant comments on this preliminary Draft did not, indeed, concern themselves with details but, rather, with the general principles of the document.

The biggest flaw which most careful commentators noted was that the Constitution was, somehow, *quite inseparable from the person of General de Gaulle*; that the particular form it had taken had been dictated by circumstances, and by the existence of the unique "de Gaulle phenomenon".

"Circumstances and the existence of one man," wrote A. Chênebenoit in the *Monde* of July 30, "will have created an *ad hoc* régime. Paradoxically, the man for whom the Constitution has been specially made to measure may well prove the best safeguard against the dangers inherent in the Constitution. But it is not at all certain that such a Constitution will prove suitable in the near future, still less in a distant future; for if there were no de Gaulle, the Constitution would never have assumed this particular form."

And while assuming that, in the last resort, the "Monarch" would always submit to "the will of the people", Chênebenoit seemed to dread the danger of a *de facto* authority (meaning, no doubt, the Army) forcing the President to submit to its will, an eventuality against which the Draft Constitution did not seem to provide sufficient guarantees.

What were the other reactions? The bulk of the Right-wing press, without going into any details, merely asked its readers in effect to assume that the Constitution was good, and its acceptance essential to the salvation of France. And that, whether one liked the Constitution or not, the choice now lay between "de Gaulle and civil war" or "de Gaulle and the 'colonels' ". True, in the *Figaro* (where the publication of this article was to cause a major internal row), the aged M. André Siegfried published a very severe criticism of the preliminary Draft Constitution, stressing in particular the following points:

The legislative role of Parliament was reduced to a bare minimum; apart from a limited number of subjects, all matters were settled by the Government. "This," Siegfried said, "goes far beyond the decree-laws and *lois-cadres* of the past; it's a case of conferring on the Government quasi-permanent plenary powers. Here we are no longer in the republican tradition, and this becomes even more serious when we find that [under Article 14 of the preliminary Draft] the President of the Republic can, on his own initiative, and merely after consultation with the Prime Minister, and without his signature, 'take all the measures required in given circumstances'. Such discretionary and completely uncontrolled powers are contrary to a century-old tradition."

And he expressed the pious hope that the CCC would have enough authority to amend, with de Gaulle's consent, these, and a number of other provisions. He also thought there was much ambiguity about the respective roles of President and Premier; was there not a danger, he asked, that the Premier might be merely the President's rubber stamp?

The Left-wing intellectuals were, of course, highly critical, too. Claude Bourdet described it as—

"clandestinely monarchist and anti-democratic in virtue of the circumstances of its birth. . . . With its arbitrarily-appointed Consultative Committee, with its referendum on a confused and complicated text, which no Assembly of any kind has been given a chance to discuss, this Constitution is in the old monarchist and Bonapartist tradition under which the Prince is always best served by himself. . . . There is no more democracy about it than about the Constitutions of 1799, 1814 or 1852, the last-named with the same old plebiscite 'stunt' attached to it . . ." (*France-Observateur*, August 22.)

Concentrating on the powers of the President, the Communist *Humanité* also attacked as "undemocratic" the election of the President by an overwhelmingly reactionary "college of *notables*" (Article 4); it

9

demonstrated that, under Article 6, "all the executive power would be concentrated in the hands of the President". The Communist paper also objected to the "virtually unlimited powers of the President" to dissolve the Assembly. He merely had to take the "opinion" (*avis*) of the Prime Minister, his own creature, as well as those of the Presidents of the two Assemblies; but need take no notice of them.

Like André Siegfried, it made the most, of course, of the "truly hair-raising Article 14".[1]

"Need we recall," it said, "that it was such a 'threat to public order' that Louis-Napoleon used as his pretext for carrying out his *coup d'état* of December 2?"

It is curious how this, as well as all other critical comments, dwelt chiefly on the President's powers to clip the wings of Parliament; when later, in November, the general election (thanks largely to the peculiarities of the new election system) produced an overwhelmingly Right-wing *chambre introuvable*, some of the same commentators openly or secretly consoled themselves with the thought that, under the Constitution, the President would *fortunately* be able to limit the damage such an Assembly might be well tempted to cause!

The CCC (*Conseil Constitutionnel Consultatif*) which was given till August 17 to examine the Preliminary Draft Constitution (after which it was going to be given a further examination by the Conseil d'Etat), was treated throughout with a good deal of irony. It was composed mostly of jurists and of members of the National Assembly and the Senate; its chairman was the perennial M. Paul Reynaud, now eighty years old, and it met at the Palais Royal, in a large room adorned by a large oil-painting of Napoleon III! General de Gaulle made it plain to the CCC that he was willing to discuss some minor amendments, but would not agree to any fundamental changes in the text of the proposed Constitution. Occasionally the press would report a major concession the CCC had succeeded in extracting from de Gaulle; thus, it was reported that he had agreed to make the entry into force of the provisions under the famous Article 14 (President's Emergency Powers) dependent on a favourable vote by the Constitutional Council, but this proved to be untrue. The most he would agree to was that the emergency powers could come into force only after the "constitutional organs had ceased to function normally".

The most important difference between the Provisional Draft Constitution and the Draft Constitution of September 4 actually concerned

---

[1] This article was to be partly toned down in the final text; the President's discretionary powers could apply only if the machinery of government had "broken down"; but whether it had "broken down" or not, was, ultimately, for the President himself to decide. All the same, a common interpretation of this final text was that, in fact, this Article could come into force only in the event of war or civil war.

overseas territories which, in the second version, were allowed, under the famous Article 86, to opt for independence; this was a major change which de Gaulle had apparently made entirely on his own initiative; it was under this Article that Guinea was able to proclaim her independence after rejecting the Constitution.

The Left-wing press treated the CCC with irony (*L'Express*, in particular, commented on the superb ease with which the worthies of the Fourth Republic were adapting themselves to the new régime); while the Government press took a certain malicious joy in relating how de Gaulle "twisted the whole lot of them round his little finger". Despite all their good resolutions about this or that particularly "dangerous" Article, they very quickly submitted to de Gaulle. He had only to speak to them like a half-strict, half-jocular uncle, and they ate out of his hand. "They were charmed into submission. . . . They were dazzled. . . . They were fascinated by the man . . ." It was in these terms that the papers described the effect de Gaulle had on them all—Reynaud, Pleven, Maurice Schumann, Edgar Faure and the rest of them—in the course of his final meeting with the CCC.

For example, the wish expressed by the CCC that there be a Referendum on the actual election system to be applied in November was simply brushed aside by de Gaulle—who had, indeed, already made up his mind that the Government, and only the Government, would decide on this— regardless of what Mollet and Pflimlin had promised the old National Assembly, ostensibly on *his* behalf.

15. ALGERIAN TERRORISM IN FRANCE

WE NOW come to a factor which undoubtedly greatly contributed to the "safety first" urge which, on September 28, was to determine de Gaulle's overwhelming success in the Referendum. And that was, in the midst of the general euphoria of the summer of 1958, the outbreak of widespread Algerian terrorism in Metropolitan France. This started in a big way during the last week in August. As distinct from the sporadic terrorism against an occasional soldier or policeman in the past, or the bloody feuds and "settlement of scores" among various Algerian factions in France,[1] the terrorism this time

---

[1] The main rivalry was between the FLN and the "Messalists"; the followers of Messali Hadj, the GOM of Algerian nationalism, who had been interned in France for several years past, were still numerous in Metropolitan France, though the movement had apparently very little influence left in Algeria. Much of the FLN gunning in France was directed at Algerian café proprietors and others who, for political or other reasons, were unwilling to contribute to the FLN's war chest, which was being regularly replenished with more than just "voluntary" contributions from a very high proportion of Algerians working in France.

assumed major proportions, was obviously directed "from above", and appeared to be carefully co-ordinated. It now looked as though the FLN had decided to extend their terrorist tactics to France on an increasingly large scale. Thus the night of August 24–25 was marked by fires, explosions and acts of sabotage in fifteen different points in France. At Toulouse, at Marseille, at Narbonne and several other places, millions of litres of petrol were destroyed in spectacular fires started by Algerian saboteurs. That night, as well as during the weeks that followed, French soldiers and policemen were being arbitrarily assassinated by Algerian gunmen all over the country. On that night of the 24th alone four policemen were murdered by Algerian gunmen in Paris. Some days later, a young soldier was shot dead in a corridor of the Montparnasse *métro* station. Such shootings were to become a daily occurrence, and were going to cause growing nervousness among the French population. The danger of railway sabotage at the height of the holiday season seemed particularly terrifying.

What was behind all this?

For over two years, the French Police had been rounding up and arresting numerous FLN ringleaders in France; yet the fifteen major acts of terrorism on the night of August 24–25 suggested to the French Police that they had failed to "decapitate" the FLN's terrorist organization in France. It was also known that one of the central organizations of the FLN for France was operating from Germany, and was so outside the reach of the French authorities.

In 1955 there were estimated to be 250,000 Algerians in France; but since then their numbers had increased to 400,000 or even 450,000.

The Algerians in France, still only few before the war, had, driven on by poverty and hunger, come there in increasing numbers since the Liberation. Most of them were working in mining and industry, usually doing the more "difficult" and "unpleasant" jobs. Many were fully, others partially unemployed, and constituted a sort of fluid labour reserve, with all the characteristics of a sub-proletariat. Most of the Algerians lived in appalling housing conditions, some living in regular *bidonvilles*, others sharing sordid hotel rooms for which they often had to pay incredibly high prices. The wretched condition of so many of the Algerians, even though many of them were earning regular industrial wages, was due to several factors: they were sending a high proportion of their pay to their families in Algeria; many were mercilessly exploited by hotel proprietors; and latterly the FLN had been levying contributions on them.

They were no better off morally than materially. The hostility towards North Africans was almost general, and not least among the French working class. Even to many a Communist *militant*, with all his anti-colonialism, an Algerian was still a "Wog"—a *raton* or a *bicot*, living in filthy conditions, and known for his filthy habits—whether real or imaginary. Except for "the very lowest type of prostitute", the women in French working class areas were particularly prejudiced against the "North Africans". They were rowdy, they were supposed to carry guns and knives, and they made it unsafe to go about the streets at night. It must be said that, even long before the Algerian war had begun, part of the press—and notably a paper like L'Aurore—had done much to create the legend of the terrible "criminality" among the North Africans in the Paris area; any case of assault or robbery which had not been clarified at once was almost automatically attributed by these papers to "North Africans". In reality, the police records up to 1955 showed that if the incidence of petty crime, like thieving, was high amongst the Algerians in France, the number of murders and other major crimes committed by them was remarkably low.

Since the Algerian war had begun, the Algerians in France (who, for a variety of reasons had now been joined by 150,000 or 200,000 of their fellow-countrymen, some of whom were simply trying to escape from the general insecurity in Algeria) became more suspect than ever.

But what chiefly marked the first three years of the Algerian war in France itself was the numerous gunning incidents amongst the Algerians themselves, a result of the hostility between the FLN and the MNA (the "Messalists"), who represented the more moderate wing of the Algerian nationalist movement, and one which had been disavowed (together with their veteran leader, Messali Hadj) by the FLN leadership.

In the last few years, the FLN had, according to the French Police, succeeded in setting up a major terrorist organization in France. Forty thousand men were said to be armed, some of them with tommy-guns. The reasons why the FLN had found no difficulty in recruiting all these men were, according to L'Express, as follows:

Both the physical and moral conditions which these people found in Paris, Lille, Metz or Marseille are often worse than what they were back in Algeria. Unemployment, the necessity to take the hardest jobs, the cramming of these people into sordid hotel rooms and bidonvilles, the constant police raids and round-ups, the difficulty of postal communications with their families in Algeria and the growing racialism of the European population were making it easy for the FLN to recruit thousands of desperadoes amongst the Algerians in France. (L'Express, August 28.)

It seems that, on the question of "extending the war to Metropolitan France" the FLN leadership in Cairo and Tunis was sharply divided for a long time. The statement attributed in 1956 to Ferhat Abbas that "we shall, if necessary, carry the war to French territory" was denied by the Algerian leader; but others, like Abade Ramdane (who died in Tunis in 1958) considered that terrorist action in France was essential as part of the Algerian war effort. As against this, it was argued that such terrorism could only unite a strongly divided French opinion against the FLN, and would also meet with no sympathy in the USA and elsewhere. So, throughout 1956 and the early part of 1957 the slogan "leaflets rather than hand-grenades" continued to represent the essence of FLN tactics in France. But even after the leadership of the "French Front" was changed in the spring of 1957, the emphasis was still on propaganda and internal organization, rather than on bomb-throwing. The liquidation of the rival Messalist organizations was decided upon; but if any Europeans were occasionally murdered, this was the work of individual fanatics, rather than the result of any instructions from above.

There seemed very little doubt, however, that the series of terrorist acts at the end of August 1958 reflected a change of policy amongst the FLN leadership. The purpose of this change was apparently both psychological and military. The feeling of insecurity in France was calculated to encourage "let's-end-the-war" currents in France itself, and to compel the authorities to keep in France large numbers of those very armed forces for which the French command in Algeria had been clamouring. Even if the French resorted to the extreme (and logical) preventive measure of interning or repatriating *all* the Algerians in France, this would suit the FLN perfectly well: repatriation would mean an ever-growing ferment among the Moslem masses in Algeria, while the internment of several hundred thousand people in French concentration camps would have the most unfavourable repercussions in the Free World.

On August 26 in Cairo Ferhat Abbas confirmed that a new policy had been adopted by the FLN in France. The FLN could no longer rely on a trong and effective French Left-wing opposition to the war in Algeria; de Gaulle's "liberalism" in respect of Algeria was proving ineffective; and orders had now been given to the FLN organization in France not to attack civilians, but "to weaken the military and economic potential of France".

How strong was this FLN organization in France? The Police reckoned that, out of some 400,000 Algerians in France, about 50,000 were members of the FLN; of these some 20,000 could be considered as "activists"; and, out of these, some 5,000 represented "the hard core".

It was reckoned that there were about 10,000 FLN "cells" in France, which was divided into five or six *willayas* or regions, with an elusive itinerant chief for each of these *willayas*. According to other information there stood at the head of each region not one man, but a small committee of three or four men.

The general organization of the movement appears to be a mixture of Communist techniques, principles derived from Mao Tse-Tung's "revolutionary war", certain tricks learned from the French Resistance, and others adopted from various police services. Its purpose is to create a State within the State, and this aim has been at least partly achieved. The organization is sufficiently strong to be able to tax practically all the Algerian workers in France, and so to collect a yearly total of four to five milliard francs. . . . Part of this money is used for buying cafés and hotels serving as meeting-places for the organization; for buying cars and scooters to give mobility to the various "networks"; for buying arms in Belgium, Germany and Italy, and for maintaining political contacts through Switzerland.[1]

The French Government and Police reacted sharply to the attempt to "extend the Algerian war to France". Thousands of Algerians were rounded up in Paris, Lyon, Belfort, Marseille and other cities. Several vast "sorting-out centres" were created in Paris alone, the largest of them at the Vélodrome d'Hiver, where several thousand suspects were to be held *incommunicado* for weeks. The press was not admitted to the Vél' d'Hiv' or any of the other "sorting-out centres", and, after a while, *Libération* and a few other papers cautiously hinted at "some pretty terrible things" going on there, and at "dead bodies" being discreetly removed at night. However, even the Communist press said very little; public feeling had been roused against the Algerian terrorists and, indeed, against Algerians generally; the vague fear that they would "start throwing bombs into cinemas and cafés" and "start wrecking trains" was very widespread.

Despite these precautionary measures, Algerian terrorism was to continue throughout most of September. Its most spectacular performance was the attempt made on September 15 to assassinate M. Jacques Soustelle, whose car was attacked in broad daylight by two gunmen in the crowded avenue Friedland, near the Etoile. Another spectacular piece of terrorism was the alleged attempt to blow up the Eiffel Tower; here, it was reported, a time bomb was discovered behind a seat in the ladies' lavatory on the Tower's top platform. . . .

This Algerian terrorism was badly timed from the FLN point of view; it greatly contributed to swelling the Yes vote in the Referendum, and played into the hands of the French diehards. If the FLN leadership realized their mistake, they did so too late.

16. THE BAZOOKA TRIAL: ACT II

BEFORE its grand finale in October, the Kovacs affair came up for a second time in August. M. Guillaumat, the Minister of the Armies had insisted that the "bazooka affair" come before the Paris military tribunal without delay. But when the Court met on August 18, Kovacs

[1] *Le Monde*, August 29.

wasn't there; a few days before, in a Troyes nursing home, he had under-gone an operation for appendicitis; a medical expert, whom the prosecu-tion had sent to Troyes to examine the patient, declared that, although the appendix operation was "useful", it had not been urgent. Nevertheless, it was "justified". He was unable to say how long it would take for Kovacs to be well enough to appear in Court. Since Kovacs was the "soul of the plot", the prosecution proposed not to deal with the other accused until Kovacs became available again, and to adjourn the case; but it demanded that Kovacs be, meantime, placed under arrest. The defence violently protested; in view of the state of his health, it was "more essential than ever" for him to be free. The Court agreed with this, and decided that "in view of the accused's state of health, on the strength of which he was granted 'provisional freedom' on July 24—a state of health which has since become worse—the Court 'considers that there is no case for delivering against Kovacs a warrant for his arrest'." We shall see later how this comedy ended.

Meantime the public remained extremely sceptical about Kovacs's "delicate state of health", and the question asked in some papers was who exactly was going to "control his convalescence"? It also seemed very odd that the Court's decision seemed to imply the incapacity of prison hospitals to look after Kovacs without endangering his life! The *Monde* talked about "the shrieking anomalies of this trial". There continued to be hints about the defence "blackmailing" certain important persons—particularly in the Army—who had known all along of the planned attempt to assassinate General Salan.

17. DE GAULLE IN BLACK AFRICA

To de Gaulle, Algeria was an infernal problem which, he soon realized, could be solved only gradually, and with infinite patience. In the case of Black Africa, the obstacles in the way of "moving with the times" were less serious. De Gaulle was fully conscious of the Awakening of Africa, and took the reasonably progressive view of "enlightened capitalism" that the independence of the Black-African countries (with the possible exception of South Africa) was only a matter of years, and that, in the long run, Europe's best chance in Africa was "to leave in order to stay".

On a more short-term basis, however, de Gaulle's journey to Africa was marked by two major anomalies.

The first concerned the Constitution itself. In deciding that the peoples of France, Algeria and Black Africa and all other territories under the

French flag were to vote on the same Constitution in the same Referendum, de Gaulle had created a highly confused situation. For in voting for or against the Constitution, the peoples of France, Algeria and Black Africa were in fact voting on altogether separate and different issues. France was asked to accept or reject a semi-presidential constitution; the Algerians (as it turned out) were told that they were voting for or against "integration"; the peoples of Black Africa, for greater autonomy or even independence. Significant, as we shall see, was the decision of the Madagascar Communists to vote *for* the Constitution since they considered it a step in the direction of national independence! In doing so, they were also contributing to the vote in favour of a semi-presidential régime *in France*!

There was a second very strange aspect to the journey. It almost looked as though, in leaving Paris for Africa, de Gaulle had not yet entirely made up his mind what he was going to offer the overseas territories. And it was not till the second stage of his journey—at Brazzaville—that he explicitly produced a new policy which was promptly described by both critics and admirers as a "bombshell". This bombshell consisted in letting every overseas territory have its independence right away, if it rejected the Constitution. He had referred to "secession" before, but it was not entirely clear what he meant.

Before he had left Paris, de Gaulle did not seem to have seriously considered so "extreme" a solution. He thought more in terms of consolidating the principle of "internal autonomy" already contained in M. Gaston Defferre's *loi-cadre* of 1957. He had, if anything, been irritated by the PRA's Congress at Cotonou, with its clamour for "immediate independence"; and before the Constitutional Advisory Committee he had declared earlier in August:

> The overseas territories are not States. We must therefore have a federation. It might even be called a confederation in view of certain special agreements that may have to be made, taking account of the special position of certain territories, Madagascar, for instance. But these are just words; and I prefer to stick to "Federation".

And while rejecting the principle of independence, he admitted that of "secession"—with the clear implication that any territory that had "seceded" would thereby forfeit any French financial aid. Whereupon some African leaders spoke of "blackmail".

After much quibbling over the respective significance of "federation" and "confederation" on the CCC, de Gaulle proposed a new word: Community, a term that had been used by the part of the RDA (*Rassemblement Démocratique Africain*) favourable to federalism.

9*

De Gaulle's journey, as we shall see, was marked by a rapid evolution towards an increasingly generous solution: if, in Madagascar, he did not go any further than promising the Great Island that it could again become "a State", he went much further with his "Brazzaville bombshell".

De Gaulle's first stop, at 4 a.m. on August 21, was at Fort-Lamy, in that very Chad Territory which, under its Negro governor, Félix Eboué, had been the first to join the Free French in 1940. After being welcomed by M. Toura Gaba, the Acting Premier of the Chad Territory, who said that, as in the past, the country was determined to give France its "fullest help and co-operation", de Gaulle made the first public speech in which he used the word "Community".

A new dawn will rise in a few days; it will herald a day of work, efforts and hope—a day which shall be known by the name of "Community". The peoples of Metropolitan France and those of the overseas territories shall join their efforts. . . . There will be a terrible lot to do in this hard and difficult world, but we shall march together along the same road, and live with the same hopes in our hearts.

He referred to the Chad Territory as "a land of brave and loyal men". Then he flew off to Madagascar.

Since the massacres of 1947, when after the killing of some two hundred French people, the punitive expedition of General Garbay resulted in the death of what was commonly estimated at about 80,000 people, the Great Island had now more or less settled down to normal.

The head of the Madagascar Government, M. Philibert Tsiranana, took the view that Madagascar was "not yet quite ripe for independence"; his chief objection to independence was the island's precarious economic position, with a highly adverse trade balance; for several years there had been a slump in its mining, while its agriculture had not yet been sufficiently developed for export purposes.

There were, in August 1958, thirteen political parties in Madagascar, some of only very small influence, but ranging from supporters of "independence at any price" to those favourable to maintaining the closest possible bonds with France.

The nationalist *élite* [wrote *Le Monde* on August 22] has been strongly influenced by the Missions, and there is sharp competition between Catholics and Protestants. While the Catholics are fairly moderate, the Protestants are much more intransigent. They mostly belong to the Hovas, an aristocracy which dominated the island during the second half of the nineteenth century, and who dominate the inland parts of the island. There are sharp rivalries between them and the coastal populations. . . . The two leading nationalists are Catholics, M. Rokotonerina, the mayor of the capital, Tananarive, and M. Rabemananjara, a former deputy still under arrest in France.

It was he who, together with two other parliamentarians, Rovoahangy and Raseta, had been arrested in 1947 in connection with the Madagascar rebellion and sentenced in highly suspect conditions in the famous Tananarive Trial. Since then—early in 1958—he had been excluded from the amnesty, and the Madagascar nationalists felt strongly about this. These more "extreme" nationalists wanted, among other things, independence for Madagascar, combined with loose "confederal bonds" with France; and a complete amnesty for all political prisoners.

Despite these differences, there was in Madagascar, as in most African territories, a strong prejudice in favour of de Gaulle. Arriving at Tananarive on the morning of August 21, he was warmly received by the populace, and, speaking before the Representative Assembly, he declared: "We shall offer Madagascar all the imaginable possibilities. The texts to be proposed to the peoples shall exclude no solution, not even secession." M. Tsinarana, the nationalist leader, argued in favour of voting Yes in the Referendum, but implied that Madagascar should become independent five years later. He thought the new Constitution was a step in the right direction, but asked de Gaulle that the Annexation Law of 1896 be explicitly repudiated by France.

De Gaulle gave no such clear assurance; but, on the following day, he was more explicit than before on Madagascar now being able to become a State once again. Pointing at the palace of the last queen of Madagascar, Queen Ranavalo, de Gaulle exclaimed:

Tomorrow you will become a State, just as much as you were when this palace was inhabited.

What, if you say Yes in the referendum, will be the future relations between France and Madagascar? They will be those of a Community. Under this new system Madagascar, the other overseas territories and Metropolitan France, will enter freely and spontaneously into a Federation, that is, inside the same political, economic and, if necessary, security organization. . . . But if Madagascar does not wish this, she can choose her own way by separating herself from France and the other territories.

But by saying Yes in the referendum, you will vote for a great future. . . .

You will once again become a State. . . .

He then enumerated the various Government departments for which Madagascar would be solely responsible. It was, in short, an offer of home rule (or "internal autonomy"), the details of which would, however, not be worked out until after the Referendum.

On the whole, the reaction to de Gaulle was warm and even enthusiastic; particularly when he referred to Madagascar "again becoming a State". Nor was his talk with a delegation of the opposition parties without effect. They received, however, no satisfaction on the two points they felt so strongly about: M. Cornut-Gentille, the Minister for Overseas

Territories, who was accompanying de Gaulle, merely said that the revocation of the Annexation Law was "implied"; whereas, as regards Raseta and the two other leaders still under arrest in France, it was indicated that nothing could be done—at least not until after the Referendum.[1]

Most of the Madagascar parties appeared, nevertheless, more or less favourable to the Yes vote, even, as already said, the small local Communist party. More reserved were the Independence Congress, the Union of the Madagascar People, and other nationalist formations. There was also something of a cleavage between the Protestants and Catholics (each with a following of about one million people each—i.e. about half the total population); the Catholics being, on the whole, more favourable to the Constitution than the Protestants.

It was at Brazzaville, in the heart of Black Africa, that de Gaulle had made his famous speech of January 30, 1944, in which he had promised the Africans associated with France both prosperity and home rule. The 1944 promises had largely remained a dead letter; but it was Brazzaville again which de Gaulle now chose for making his most sensationally explicit "African" programme speech.

Here, in French Equatorial Africa, there was a genuine "Gaullist" tradition, dating back to 1940; among certain native tribes a real "cult" of de Gaulle had developed, so much so that not only a special brand of rice, but also countless children were named after him—*Ngol* being the local version of his name.[2]

No doubt, conditions had changed since 1944. At that time, in his famous Brazzaville speech, which was, as it were, the theoretical cornerstone of the African "emancipation" policy of the Fourth Republic, he had still assumed a "paternalist" attitude:

"The French nation alone can proceed, when the time comes, to those structural reforms in the French empire; and this it will do, conscious of its own sovereignty."

But the Fourth Republic had never, in fact, done much to give any legal form to these promises, even though the creation of new "statutes" for the African territories was implied in the Constitution of 1946. M. Gaston Defferre's *loi-cadre* had come too late to be of much effect.

The situation now called for a more "modern" approach; and de Gaulle was fully aware of it. It was no longer possible for France to "grant" these territories the new forms of government they needed; in de Gaulle's opinion, it was essential to find a voluntary basis for the new Community.

[1] When, some months later, Raseta was allowed by de Gaulle to return to Madagascar, the military at Jibuti—ignoring de Gaulle's orders—sent him back to France.
[2] *Le Monde*, August 24-25.

Speaking at Brazzaville, de Gaulle was more precise than he had been at Tananarive. After recalling the role Brazzaville and French Equatorial Africa had played in the history of Free France, de Gaulle produced this bombshell:

"Some say: 'We have a right to be independent.' To these I reply: Yes, you have; and anyone wanting his independence can have it. The Metropolis will not stop you. Any territory can take its independence by saying No on September 28. That will mean that it does not wish to take part in the Community, but desires to secede from it. It will mean that it wishes to follow its own road, at its own risk and peril."

What followed was perhaps even more important. The vote of September 28, said de Gaulle, was not binding for all time:

"If within a certain time, a territory feels that it is capable of carrying all the burdens and taking all the responsibilities of independence, then let its elected Assembly, and if necessary, its people, through a referendum, say so. I guarantee in advance that should this happen in any territory, France will not stop it."

He added, however, that, since the Community implied great economic and other burdens for France, France also would be free to "break her Community bonds with this or that territory".

He concluded by referring to the great dangers threatening Africa, particularly those coming from Asia, where there were "great human masses" driven on by hunger; but, as usual, such a movement was "covered by ideology"—and behind this ideology there was a "new imperialism".

There were, among the Africans, two outstanding leaders whose names were familiar in France: one was de Gaulle's Minister of State, Houphouet-Boigny, the Ivory Coast "federalist"; the other was Sekou Touré, the Guinean champion of independence. De Gaulle's Brazzaville speech was, paradoxically enough, favourably received by both currents of the RDA (the *Rassemblement Démocratique Africain*) to which both these leaders belonged. De Gaulle had, in a way, succeeded in pleasing both factions: for while using the magic word "independence", he stressed at the same time that independence also implied responsibility—for which, in the federalists' view, Black Africa was not quite prepared yet.[1]

If all went well for de Gaulle at Brazzaville and Abidjan, Houphouet-Boigny's stronghold, de Gaulle came up against the first difficulties at Conakry, the capital of French Guinea. It is true that the reception he was given by the people was, outwardly, as friendly as in other places, and even more picturesque. A member of the Government had organized

[1] With the constitutional changes in 1960 allowing "independent" countries like Mali and Madagascar to remain in the community, Houphouet-Boigny abandoned his hostility to independence.

a vast "Negro Ballet" which danced all along the way from the airfield to Conakry, as de Gaulle, with Sekou Touré by his side, drove into the city. But the cheering and the cries of "Sili" (meaning the Elephant, symbol of the RDA party) were intended for the immensely popular Guinean leader rather than for de Gaulle.

At the great public meeting at Conakry that day, de Gaulle had to sit through a harangue from the dynamic young Guinea leader, which was different from any of the other speeches of welcome he had heard throughout that African trip. His speech was an impassioned diatribe against colonialism: he declared that he and his people "preferred poverty with freedom to wealth without dignity".

"Was this African, implacably determined to claim his rights," a startled French reporter wrote, "and demanding the creation of great African states, with Dakar and Brazzaville as their capitals; was this African the lieutenant of M. Houphouet-Boigny who, only a few hours earlier, had assured General de Gaulle at Abidjan that African independence was not the best means of attaining a higher standard of living for the African masses? . . . Yet this black man clad in white, hammering his words, was like the personification of primeval Africa rebelling against all past and present humiliations. . . . And sitting beside him, and looking pale and tired, was General de Gaulle, who seemed less affected by the fiery words of the orator than by the gusts of frantic cheering rising from the back of the hall. . . ." (Le Monde, August 27.)

And when de Gaulle rose to reply, "he was no longer the same man we had seen at Brazzaville and Abidjan. He seemed weary and upset."

He reiterated that Guinea, like all the other territories of Black Africa, was free to say No on September 28; but he used the usual arguments to show that it was in her interests to say Yes.

"He spoke," wrote Jean Lacouture, "like a man carrying on his shoulders the heavy burdens of a long destiny; he spoke as the representative of that old Europe, which was proud of its past, but was now anxiously wondering whether its role in the world was at an end. . . . Instead of engaging in cheap polemics with Sekou Touré, he merely spoke of his faith in the co-operation between the two continents; and he spoke with serene melancholy. . . ." (ibid.)

In a statement later issued to the press, Sekou Touré specified that "if Guinea was to approve of the Constitution, it was essential that it should explicitly state, not only in its preamble, but also in its text, that the overseas peoples had a right to independence without any restrictions". He suggested that there were a "lack of frankness" on the French side, and various mental reservations.

For all that, most French observers still believed at the time that Guinea would, in the end, vote for the Constitution, since she stood to suffer economically if she did not. When, in the end, she proved to be the only

French overseas territory to turn down the Constitution, there was an uproar in France against the "machinations of Britain and of the British Intelligence Service".

At Dakar, the capital of Senegal, de Gaulle confronted a different kind of opposition. Here, in the enormous Place Protet in the centre of Dakar, he was literally howled down by some five thousand African workers, waving their red flags with a black star, and many of them shouting "Down with de Gaulle". Most of these Africans were members of the PRA (the *Parti du Regroupement Africain*,) the *Parti Africain de l'Indépendance*, and other nationalist groupings; and of the UGTAN (*Union Générale des Travailleurs de l'Afrique Noire*) trade union federation; here also were some young intellectuals and students, and a few Communists. Most of these people, according to French observers, had come from the *bidonvilles* around Dakar, and belonged to an embittered African subproletariat. De Gaulle made only a brief statement, in which he sarcastically remarked that "the gentlemen carrying all those banners and slogans are perfectly free to vote No".

The meetings de Gaulle later had at Dakar with "responsible African leaders" proved more satisfactory; and they all "deplored the discourtesy" with which he had been treated earlier in the day.

For all that, the visit to Senegal—so important to France's economy and so important in the past for the contribution it had made to France's military strength—had not been a great success, despite the "brilliance" of the vast reception given to 1,500 people at the High Commissioner's Palace, at which de Gaulle was able to converse informally with the various African leaders.

M. Guillabert, vice-president of the territorial Assembly of Senegal and a leading member of the PRA, apologized to de Gaulle for the "regrettable incidents" earlier in the day which, he said, were incompatible with African and Senegalese hospitality, and had been caused by "alien subversive elements".

From Dakar de Gaulle flew to Algiers.

What did the African trip add up to? It was clear that the head of the French Government had been warmly received in Madagascar, enthusiastically received in Brazzaville and Abidjan; but much less so at Conakry and Dakar. There was no doubt about the vote in Madagascar and in French Equatorial Africa; much more doubtful was going to be the vote of Guinea; but M. Houphouet-Boigny, the most wholeheartedly "federalist" leader, had secured the support of most of the sections of the RDA in both West and Equatorial Africa. Apart from some popular feeling against France (attributed by some observers to "anti-European racialism", and by others to Moslem-Algerian influence), which clearly existed among the sub-proletariat of a city like Dakar, political opposition came not only (as already said) from the RDA section of Guinea, but also from the PRA (*Parti du Regroupement Africain*) in both Equatorial Africa and its Senegal stronghold. Most of these opposition groups, while admitting the principle of "confederation" (as distinct from "federation") were very insistent that the African territories' right to independence at any time be explicitly stated in the Constitution. De Gaulle's verbal assurances on this point they found insufficient. Whereas a prominent Senegal leader like M. Senghor was as emphatic on this question as Sekou Touré, there was, nevertheless, another factor playing in favour of the Yes vote in Senegal; and that was the fear of isolating the country from the rest of West Africa which (with the exception of Guinea) was certain to approve of the Constitution.

At the end of his African tour, de Gaulle was given a particularly cool reception in Algiers. There were few flags in the streets; most Europeans were away on holiday; and, at the airfield only two members of the Committee of Public Safety (and both of them "Gaullists")—General Massu and M. Neuwirth—were there to meet the head of the Government. None of the members of the "Committee of 14" turned up. De Gaulle made no public appearance throughout his three days at Algiers, but stayed practically all the time at the Summer Palace, where he received a succession of "representative" visitors belonging to the various sections of the population. For fear of FLN reprisals, no names of these visitors were published. But de Gaulle was anxious to collect some first-hand impressions on the various moods existing in Algeria. It was not until after he had left for Paris that his recorded address to Algeria, opening, as it were, the Referendum campaign there, was broadcast. Its wording was remarkably vague. True, it treated "from Dunkirk to Tamanrasset" as a single geographical and "human" entity; and drew a distinction between "France and Algeria" on the one hand and the rest of French Africa on the other; but it vaguely referred to a future "statute" of Algeria, and made no mention of "integration". All that the speech did, in effect, was to urge all the inhabitants of Algeria to vote Yes in the Referendum, both for their own good, and for the good of France. Also there recurred the phrase about all Algerians being "complete Frenchmen"—*à part entière*—and another about Algeria developing "in a French framework"—whatever that meant.

The *ultras* had again plenty to grumble about—which they did. Their "intellectual guide", Dr. Lefèvre, attacked the Constitution on more general grounds, declaring that it said nothing about integration, or about the abolition of the political parties; moreover, it maintained the "criminal" principle of *laïcité*. According to Lefèvre, his own doctrine was inspired by Salazar, Maurras and the Papal Encyclicals; and de Gaulle, he said, was the man who had proved to be the main obstacle in the way of a "logical development" of the May 13 Revolution. He also said that, while he was going to support the Yes vote in the Referendum, he would afterwards run "corporatist" and anti-Gaullist candidates in the Election. He described de Gaulle's Black-Africa policy as "the very worst we have yet had."

"Lunatic-fringe" stuff? Yes and no. For, as the *Monde* observed:

All local observers agree that these ideas are making headway, both among students, where the weekly, *Energie nationale*, has been building up José Antonio Primo de Rivera as a model, and among the ordinary European masses, where this kind of propaganda goes down well. . . . (*Le Monde*, August 31.)

Whatever else could be said of de Gaulle's African trip, people were impressed by the extraordinary physical endurance he had shown during that long journey at the very height of the African summer. Also, as time was to show, this was de Gaulle's first decisive step towards that "Commonwealth" which began to take shape in 1960.

18. THE DE GAULLE CONSTITUTION[1]

NO SOONER had de Gaulle returned to Paris after his exhausting African tour than he presided over a number of Government meetings at which the final touches were put to the official text of the Draft Constitution of the Fifth Republic. Divided into a Preamble, fifteen Chapters and ninety-two Articles, this text of the Constitution did not, except for its African provisions, greatly differ from the original draft published at the end of July.

To take its most salient points:

"The French people," said the *Preamble*, "solemnly proclaim their attachment to the Rights of Man and the principles of National Sovereignty as defined by the Declaration of 1789, confirmed and completed by the Preamble to the Constitution of 1946."

In accordance with these principles, and the principle of the free determination of peoples, the Republic offers to those overseas territories which express the will to adhere to it new institutions based on the common idea of liberty, equality and fraternity and conceived with a view to their democratic evolution.

[1] In this chapter—which is no more than a brief summary of the main points of the Constitution—I usually quote, with the authors' kind permission, the translation by Peter Campbell and Brian Chapman, as published in their book, *The Constitution of the Fifth Republic* (Oxford, Blackwell, 1958). For full details of the Constitution see *De Gaulle's Republic* by Philip Williams and Martin Harrison and *The French Fifth Republic* by Dorothy Pickles.

Then came Chapter I:

Art. 1 said that the Republic and the overseas territories which had freely adopted the Constitution—i.e. by voting YES in the Referendum—would together form a Community.

Most of this first chapter sounded equally reassuring to all liberal and democratic ears:

Art. 2 declared that France was an "indivisible, secular [*laïque*] democratic and social Republic". It guaranteed "equality before the law to all citizens, regardless of origin, race or religion" and "respected all beliefs".

The national flag was the blue-white-red tricolour, and the national anthem the *Marseillaise*. The Republic's motto, was, as before, "Liberty, Equality, Fraternity".

In short, all the trappings of the Republic would be the same, as distinct from Vichy, when the old three-word motto was changed to "*Travail, Famille, Patrie*".
France's underlying principle was "government of the people, by the people, for the people".

Art. 3 said that national sovereignty belonged to the people, who would exercise it through their representatives, or by way of referendum. . . . Suffrage may be direct or indirect, as laid down in the Constitution. It is always universal, equal and secret.

There had been a good deal of discussion and haggling over the next article, *Art. 4*, both on the CCC and at the *Conseil d'Etat*, which insisted that the recognition of political parties be explicitly stated in the Constitution, and not left to the whims of any subsequent legislation.
This Article now read:

Political parties and groups may play their part in the expression of the suffrage. They develop and act freely. They must respect the principles of national sovereignty and democracy.

There is no doubt that for the drafting of this *Art. 4* some of the more anti-Communist members of the CCC were largely responsible. The Article meant to convey the idea that "freedom cannot be used against freedom". It was argued that the spirit in which this Article was drawn up was the same as that which had inspired the final Article of the Universal Declaration of Human Rights adopted by the General Assembly of UN in 1948.
The Algiers *ultras*, for their part, who considered the political parties as the root of all evil, and remembered some of de Gaulle's own utterances

on the subject in the past, were particularly dissatisfied with this Article. On the other hand, Left-wing commentators did not care much for the last sentence, which suggested the possibility of giving a "constitutional" basis to any future discrimination or persecution, notably against the Communists.[1]

Chapter II (*Arts. 5 to 19*) concerning the President of the Republic was a particularly long one.

It stated that the President "ensured that the Constitution was observed", and "intervened in order to ensure the proper working of the public authorities and the continuity of the State".

"He is the guardian of national independence, territorial integrity, and respect for Community agreements and for treaties."

Art. 6 concerned the election of the President for seven years "by an electoral college composed of the members of Parliament, the members of the general councils of the Departments and of the Assemblies of the overseas territories, and representatives elected by municipal councils".

There followed a long list of these "electors".

This was something new, except that it remotely savoured of the election of senators under the Third Republic, with the preferential treatment given to the rural, as distinct from the urban, areas.

Thus, the mayors of small rural communes of less than 1,000 inhabitants were among the "grand electors" of the President of the Republic; in comparison, large cities were heavily under-represented on the "electoral college", numbering about 100,000 members.

There followed some of the most vital provisions of the Constitution:

Art. 8. The President . . . appoints the Prime Minister. He removes him from office if he tenders his Government's resignation. On the proposal of the Prime Minister he appoints and dismisses the other members of the Government.

This final draft of the Constitution made it clear (the first draft had left some doubt on the subject) that the President could *not* get rid of the Prime Minister—except (indirectly) by dissolving the Assembly.

Art. 9 said that the President presided over the Council of Ministers, and *Art.* 10 that the President promulgated laws within a fortnight of their transmission to the Government, after their final adoption.

But here was something new:

[1] Oddly enough, it was a small Fascist organization, the *Parti Révolutionnaire*, representing the *Jeune Nation* movement, against whom this Article was first applied in practice in February 1959.

"Before this period has elapsed he may ask Parliament for a further debate on the law or any of its articles. This request cannot be refused."

Art. 11 concerned the referendum machinery, and read as follows:

At the proposal of the Government during the session or at the joint proposal of the two Houses . . . the President may put to a referendum any Government bill which concerns the organization of public powers, approves a Community agreement, or authorizes the ratification of a treaty which, though not contrary to the Constitution, would affect the working of the institutions.

The future alone would show to what extent the President could "engineer" a referendum if he wanted one. With a docile government, there should be no difficulty.

Then came *Art. 12*—the "dissolution" Article:

This provided that the President could dissolve the National Assembly "after consulting the Prime Minister and the presidents of the Houses", i.e. in reality on the strength of his own decision. A new general election was to be held not less than twenty and not more than forty days after the dissolution. There could be no new dissolution within less than a year after the preceding one.

Art. 13 dealt with the special new powers of the President, in addition to his right of dissolution. He signed ordinances and decrees and deliberated at the Council of Ministers. He made appointments to all the civil and military posts of the State.

Such appointments had to be countersigned by the Prime Minister; everything indicated, however, that, unless conditions radically changed, the Premier would be a very obedient de Gaulle man.

The article specified that he appointed councillors of the Conseil d'Etat, the Grand Chancellor of the Legion of Honour, ambassadors, prefects, representatives of the Government in overseas territories, generals, rectors of universities and directors of civil service departments.

Art. 14 said that the President accredited Ambassadors and other diplomatic representatives; and *Art. 15* that he was "head of the armed forces" and presided over the high councils and committees of national defence.

And now came the highly controversial "dictatorial" *Art. 16* (the *Art. 14* of the preliminary Draft, which had aroused so much excitement). This, in its final form, now read:

If there is a serious and immediate threat to the institutions of the Republic, the Nation's independence, its territorial integrity, or the fulfilment of its international undertakings, and the constitutional machinery of the Government breaks down, the President of the Republic takes the measures that the situation demands, after officially consulting the Prime Minister, the presidents of the Houses and the Constitutional Council.

He informs the Nation by a message.

These measures must be designed to ensure that the constitutional machinery of government shall be fully restored as soon as possible. The Constitutional Council is consulted about them. Parliament meets as of right. The National Assembly may not be dissolved while the emergency powers are in force.

The CCC proposed that an emergency situation could not be proclaimed by the President without the Constitutional Council's approval; this the Government rejected. The Council was to be "consulted", but no more. It was also the CCC which—this time more successfully—asked that Parliament remain in session in such an emergency, except in the event of *force majeure*, but this last phrase was not specifically included in the Constitution.

Art. 17 gave the President the right of reprieve.

Art. 18 said: The President . . . communicates with the two Houses of Parliament by messages which he reads, and which cannot be debated. Outside the session, Parliament is recalled specially for this purpose.

Art. 19 said that all acts of the President, except those governed by Art. 8 (par. 1), 11, 12, 16, 18, 54, 56 and 61, must be countersigned by the Prime Minister and, when appropriate, by the responsible ministers.

(These articles concern the appointment of the Prime Minister and the acceptance of his resignation; the dissolution of the National Assembly; referendum; emergency powers, messages to Parliament, references of treaties to the Constitutional Council; presidential appointments to the Constitutional Council; reference of laws to the said Council.)

Chapter III on "The Government" consisted of only four Articles:

Art. 20.—"The Government formulates and executes national policy. It has at its disposal the administrative services and the armed forces. It is responsible to Parliament as prescribed under *Art. 49* and *50*."

Art. 21.—The Prime Minister directs the work of the Government. He is responsible for national defence, and ensures that the laws are carried out. Subject to *Art. 13* . . . he appoints to civil and military posts.

(The rest of the article dealt with cases when he could delegate his powers to others, or when the President delegated his powers to him.)

Art. 22 dealt with the countersigning of the Prime Minister's acts by other ministers.

The most "revolutionary" Article in this Chapter was *Art. 23*.
This said:

"No one may be a member of the government and at the same time serve as a member of Parliament or as a professional representative on a national body, hold public employment, or exercise any professional activity."

The text of the preliminary Draft had spoken merely of the incompatibility of the two functions of minister and member of Parliament; this incompatibility had now been extended to other functions as well; de Gaulle strongly felt that a minister must become as independent as possible of his party and his constituents, and that he should feel no divided loyalty in the event of a conflict between Government and Parliament. Under the new text, moreover, he was also to abandon practically all other jobs.

Under the "organic law" provided for under Art. 25, a minister was going to be replaced, in his deputy's seat, by his "shadow", who had stood for "conditional" election at the same time as himself.

The "incompatibility" article had another aspect: Parliament was no longer necessarily to be a "school of ministers", as it had been under the Third and Fourth Republic, and was intended to open a wide passage to the Government bench to technicians, professional diplomats, etc. It was one of de Gaulle's ways of fighting the proverbial *"république des camarades"* with its *"valse des portefeuilles"*. In reality, it was essentially anti-parliamentarian.

Chapter IV (*Arts. 24 to 33*) was called "Parliament".
This was composed of the National Assembly and the Senate.

"The deputies are elected by direct suffrage. The Senate is elected by indirect suffrage. It represents the territorial bodies of the Republic. French citizens overseas are represented in the Senate."

Art. 25 stated that an "organic law" would lay down the details concerning the number of deputies to be elected, their remuneration, replacement, etc.

Art. 26 dealt with parliamentary immunity, under which no member of Parliament—whose immunity had not been raised—could be arrested except *in flagrante delicto*.

Art. 27 (a departure from former practice) virtually abolished parliamentary vote by proxy and provided that (with rare exceptions) anyone voting in Parliament must be personally present.

Art. 28 said that Parliament would hold two ordinary sessions a year, a total of about $5\frac{1}{2}$ months—which was much less than under the Fourth Republic.

Art. 29 provided that extraordinary sessions of Parliament could be called by the Prime Minister or by the majority of the members of the National Assembly for the purpose of discussing an agenda settled in advance. An extraordinary session called at the request of the majority of the National Assembly must not last more than twelve days; a new extraordinary session could be called only by the Prime Minister within a month of the decree of closure of the previous extraordinary session.[1]

Art. 30 to 33 dealt with secondary matters.

Chapter V (*Art. 34 to 51*) concerned "The Relations between Parliament and the Government", and contained some of the most controversial clauses.

[1] The first major row between Parliament and de Gaulle occurred early in 1960 over this Art. 29. A majority of the Assembly had demanded an extraordinary session to deal with the agricultural crisis. Interpreting the Article in what was thought to be a highly arbitrary manner, and without consulting the Constitutional Council, de Gaulle simply "rejected" the Assembly's demand, though it was not at all clear that, constitutionally, he was entitled to do so.

Art. 34 proclaimed that "laws are voted by Parliament", and then gave a long list of items which were subject to this procedure: civil rights, taxation, crime, currency, electoral system for Parliament and local assemblies, nationalization, denationalization, defence, local government, education, labour, trade union rights, etc. (Taxation and the electoral system had been specifically included at the suggestion of the CCC, but even this list limited Parliament's legislative powers and increased those of the Government.)

Art. 38 was equally important.

"To carry out its programme," it said, "the Government may ask Parliament's permission to issue within a fixed period ordinances regulating matters normally within the scope of the laws. Ordinances are promulgated by the Council of Ministers after consultation with the Conseil d'Etat. They come into force on publication, but become void if the bill ratifying them is not submitted to Parliament before the date fixed by the enabling Act."

Art. 39 merely said:

The Prime Minister and members of Parliament have the right to initiate laws. . . . Government bills . . . are tabled in either House. Finance bills are submitted in the first instance to the National Assembly.

But here came the snag: Under *Art. 40*—

Bills and amendments proposed by members of Parliament cannot be tabled if they entail a decrease in revenue or an increase in expenditure. (This, obviously, enormously limited any parliamentary initiative.)

Some of the following Articles were particularly important in showing the extent to which the Government had the whip-hand over Parliament:

Art. 45 said: "Every bill must pass through both Houses so that, if possible, an agreed text may be reached. If the Houses disagree and the bill is not passed after two readings in each House, or after a single reading in the case of bills declared urgent by the Government, the Prime Minister can call a joint committee of the two Houses . . . to draft agreed provisions for the clauses in dispute.

"The Government may then submit the joint committee's text to both Houses. No amendment may be tabled without the government's permission.

"If the joint committee cannot agree on a text . . . the Government may, after a further reading in both Houses, ask the National Assembly to decide the matter . . ."

Art. 47 said that an organic law would prescribe the procedure by which Parliament would vote *on finance bills*.

"If the National Assembly has not concluded its first reading within forty days of the bill being tabled, the Government submits the bill to the Senate, which must vote on it within a fortnight. The procedure is that described in *Art. 45*.

"If Parliament has not finished with the bill within seventy days, *the provisions of the bill may be put into force by ordinance*."

This was, obviously, one of the most authoritarian Articles of all.

The next paragraph said that if a draft budget had not been tabled soon enough to be promulgated before the start of the financial year, the Government would ask Parliament . . . to levy taxes and allocate by decree funds to services already approved. But—"the limits laid down in this article are valid only when Parliament is in session."

Art. 48 made it clear that the Government virtually dictated its agenda to Parliament:

"Government bills and private members' bills agreed to by the Government are placed on the order paper of each House *in an order of precedence laid down by the Government.*"

This was something entirely new.

So also was the next paragraph saying that "at one sitting a week priority is given to private members' questions and the Government's replies".

In practice, as was later to be seen, the Government opposed any discussion of its answers, which were given in a take-it-or-leave-it spirit. The CCC's attempt to give Parliament greater freedom in fixing its agenda, at least once a week, met with no favourable response from de Gaulle and Debré.

The next two Articles concerned Parliament's powers to overthrow the Government. *Art. 49* read:

"The Prime Minister . . . may seek the support of the National Assembly for the Government's initial programme or, subsequently, for a declaration of its general policy.

"The National Assembly registers its lack of confidence in the Government by voting a motion of censure. Such a motion may be tabled only if it is signed by at least one-tenth of the members of the National Assembly. No vote can be taken within forty-eight hours of the motion being tabled. A motion of censure is carried only if it receives the votes of an absolute majority of the members of the National Assembly. Only the votes in favour of the motion are counted. If a motion of censure is not carried, its sponsors cannot table a second motion of censure in the course of the same session, except in the circumstances envisaged in the following paragraph.

"The Prime Minister . . . may make the Assembly's vote on a text a matter of confidence. The text is then regarded as adopted unless a motion of censure, tabled within twenty-four hours, is carried under the conditions prescribed in the previous paragraph.

"The Prime Minister may ask the Senate to approve a declaration of general policy."

THE DE GAULLE CONSTITUTION

The text of the Draft Constitution did not make it clear whether the Government must resign if defeated by the Senate.

Finally, *Art. 50* said:

> If the National Assembly carries a motion of censure or withholds approval of the Government's programme or general policy, the Prime Minister must tender his Government's resignation to the President of the Republic.

The preliminary Draft had limited this obligation to resign merely to the specific motion of censure; even so, it was clear that it would not be easy for Parliament to overthrow a government.

The brief Chapter VI (*Art. 52 to 55*) on "Treaties and International Agreements" concerned the President's supreme role in negotiating and ratifying treaties, and the cases in which such treaties could be ratified only in virtue of a special law. The text clearly suggested that the Constitution *gave the President very considerable powers in the field of secret diplomacy.*

Chapter VII (*Art. 56 to 63*) concerned the Constitutional Council, an altogether new feature.

> It "is composed of nine members, appointed for nine years and not re-eligible. Three members are appointed by the President of the Republic, three by the president of the National Assembly, and three by the president of the Senate. In addition, former Presidents of the Republic [i.e., in 1958, MM. Auriol and Coty] are *ex-officio* life members of the Council. The president is appointed by the President of the Republic and has a casting vote."

Art. 57 dealt with "incompatibilities"; a member of the Constitutional Council could not be a minister or a member of Parliament. Other incompatibilities would be settled by an organic law.

> *Art. 58, 59, 60 and 61* enumerated some of the CC's functions.
> *Art. 62* said: "If a provision is declared unconstitutional, it cannot be promulgated or come into force. There is no appeal against decisions of the Constitutional Council. They are binding on all public authorities and on all administrative and judicial authorities."

Chapter VIII, concerning the Judicial Authority (*Art. 64–66*), stated that the President of the Republic had to safeguard the independence of the Judiciary.

> He presided over the *Conseil supérieur de la magistrature*, which made recommendations for the appointment of judges of the *Cour de Cassation* and of the First President of the *Cour d'Appel*. It was also consulted on the appointment of other judges, and on reprieves, etc. It was also the disciplinary council for judges.
> *Art. 66* specified that "No one may be arbitrarily detained. The judicial authority,

guardian of personal freedom, ensures that this principle is observed in accordance with the law"—a phrase which seemed to have certain limitative implications.

Chapter IX (*Art. 67–68*) concerned the High Court of Justice composed of members of the two Houses, and intended to deal with certain crimes and offences committed by members of the Government while in office "and by their accomplices" and defined as "plotting against the safety of the State". The President of the Republic could be tried only on a charge of high treason (a charge which, legally, however, had never been clearly defined).

Chapter X (*Art. 69–71*) concerned the Economic and Social Council, an advisory body; and Chapter XI (*Art. 72–76*), the "Territorial Collectivities" (communes, departments and overseas territories).

Chapter XII (*Art. 77 to 86*) was particularly important in the light of de Gaulle's African journey; it dealt with "The Community".

Art. 77: Within the Community the States are autonomous; they administer themselves . . . democratically and freely. All citizens are equal in law, whatever their origin, race or religion. They have the same duties.

Art. 78: The Community's jurisdiction includes foreign policy, defence, currency, common economic and financial policy and policy concerning raw materials.

It also includes, subject to special agreements, the supervision of justice, higher education, the organization of external and common transport and of telecommunications.

By special agreement the Community's competence in respect of any member can be widened or narrowed.

Art. 80 said: The Community has as its President and representative the President of the Republic. Its organs are an Executive Council, a Senate and an Arbitration Court.

Art. 81: The member-states of the Community take part in the election of the President of the Republic in accordance with Art. 6 . . .

Art. 82: The Executive Council of the Community is presided over by the President of the Republic. It is composed of the Prime Minister of the Republic, the heads of government of each of the member states . . . and ministers charged, on behalf of the Community, with matters of common interest. . . . The organization of the Executive Council is settled by an organic law.

Art. 83 dealt with the Community Senate, which would sit twice a year, one month at a time. Its legislative powers were very limited and its functions appeared to be mainly advisory. Its composition and rules of procedure were to be settled by an organic law.

Art. 84 dealt with the Arbitration Court of the Community, and *Art. 85* with the procedure whereby common institutions "may be revised by identical laws voted by the Parliament of the Republic and the Senate of the Community".

Then came the important *Art. 86*, clearly inspired by de Gaulle's Brazzaville speech only a few days before; this Article read:

A change in the status of a member-state . . . may be requested either by the

Republic or by a resolution of the legislative assembly of the State concerned, confirmed by a local referendum organized and supervised by the institutions of the Community. The actual change is effected by an agreement approved by the Parliament of the Republic and the legislative assembly concerned.

A member-state may become independent by the same means. It then ceases to belong to the Community. (However, under the 1960 revision of the relevant articles, "independence" and "membership" even no longer incompatible.)

Art. 87 added that "the special agreements applying the present chapter must be approved by the Parliament of the Republic and the legislative assembly concerned".

It was under this Article that Guinea proclaimed her independence after voting No in the Referendum.

The one-article (*Art. 88*) Chapter XIII concerned Treaties of Association; this provided that either France or the Community "may conclude agreements with States wishing to associate with it to develop their civilization". This vaguely-worded article referred primarily to any possible future "associations" in Africa.

After proclaiming her independence, Guinea invoked this Article, claiming the right still to be "associated" with the Community.

Chapter XIV (*Art. 89*) dealt with the procedures for revising the Constitution: it could be initiated either by the President of the Republic on the advice of the Prime Minister, or by members of Parliament.

"A bill proposing revision must be voted in the same terms by both Houses. The revision comes into force when it has been approved by a referendum. No referendum is required when a government reform bill is submitted by the President to a joint meeting of the two Houses of Parliament, sitting in Congress.

The bill is approved if voted by a three-fifths majority.

No attempt at revision may be initiated or continued when the territorial integrity of the State is in danger.

The republican form of government may not be the object of a proposed revision.

Finally, Chapter XV (*Art. 90–92*) dealt with the transition period between the promulgation of the new Constitution and the establishment, within four months, of the new institutions of the Republic (six months in the case of the Community). An exception was made in the case of the Senate; until the middle of 1959 the members of the old Council of the Republic would act as "senators", pending the election of the Senate under the new system. "Organic laws to settle the final form of the Senate must be completed before July 31, 1959."

The last Article of the Constitution (*Art. 92*) gave the Government unlimited powers during the four-months' transition period:

"Legislative measures necessary for setting up the institutions and, until they are set up, for ensuring the proper functioning of public authorities, will be issued by the Council of Ministers, after consultation with the Conseil d'Etat, as ordinances having force of law."

During the period in question "the Government is authorized to fix, by ordinances having the force of law . . . the electoral system for the Houses set up by the Constitution. . . . The Government may [also] take all those measures which it considers necessary to ensure the life of the nation, the protection of citizens and the defence of public liberties".

The CCC had wanted the electoral system to be submitted to a referendum, but the Government rejected this proposal, despite the fact that the plenary powers law of June 2 had expressly excluded the electoral system from the scope of powers given to the Government (*cf.* Campbell and Chapman, p. 58).

         ★   ★   ★

This unwieldy document, as we shall see, was to be approved on September 28 by nearly 80 per cent of the French voters—the vast majority of whom had never even looked at it. The Referendum was, as everybody agreed, more in the nature of a plebiscite; people voted "for" or "against" de Gaulle.

In the chapters dealing with the Referendum campaign we shall see what were the principal objections raised by the critics of the Constitution. Here it is perhaps sufficient to make the following points:

The Draft Constitution represented, on the face of it, a compromise between the purely "presidential" principle of de Gaulle's "Bayeux Constitution" of 1946 and certain liberal principles of the French republican tradition; but, as a net result of this compromise, the powers of the President were still enormously increased, and those of Parliament seriously curtailed—though to what extent exactly future practice alone would show. One of the peculiarities of the 1958 Constitution was precisely the fact that, at the time the electorate was voting on it, *it was practically impossible to say how it would work in practice under de Gaulle, and even more so after de Gaulle*. In particular, it was far from clear what the exact relationship would be between the President, the Prime Minister and Parliament, though, obviously, the President's powers would be far greater than they had ever been. As Paul Bastid, an eminent jurist with a long experience of both the Third and Fourth Republic, wrote:

Exceptionally strong means are placed at the President's disposal. His authority is above constitutional machinery . . . and supersedes the separation of powers. In addition to classical prerogatives . . . he possesses extensive attributes which assure him an active role. He appoints the Prime Minister . . . who is merely his foremost collaborator. On the proposal of the Prime Minister, he appoints and dismisses the other members of the Government. In principle, he makes appointments to civil and military offices. [As in the past] he presides over the Council of Ministers, *but it is obvious that his authority will be greater, since the Government emanates from him and him alone, and there is no need for him to be bound*

by factors deriving from the parliamentary situation. In international affairs, he recovers
the power to negotiate treaties, which the 1946 Constitution had taken away from
the Head of the State.[1]

In short, Paul Bastid said:

Under the new Constitution, the Head of the State is much more powerful than
the Head of the State in any of the previous Republics, *including those of Louis-
Napoleon Bonaparte and MacMahon.* The high office of President, as at present
established, was devised for one man. It represents *an entirely new element in the
French constitutional system*, a fact which can only be explained by circumstances
and the prestige of General de Gaulle. (*ibid.*, p. 151.)

Apart from that, the Draft Constitution was, in his view, both *"complicated and full of obscurities"*. Parliament's chances of overthrowing the
Government had, obviously, been enormously reduced (threat of dissolution, the complicated machinery of the censure motion, etc.), and
it was not even clear by what majority the Government could be overthrown. And although the Constitution was reintroducing an apparently
more effective bicameral system in France than under the Fourth Republic,
the exact role of the Senate had not been made clear by the September
text.

Bastid also commented on "the severe and systematic precautions
that had been taken against Parliament"—

They can be explained by the wish to prevent a return to former methods . . .
[But] the separation of the Executive and the Legislative appears a one-way
separation since, although *the Legislative is prevented from encroaching on the Executive,
the contrary is far from true.* Moreover, the procedure of interpellation seems to have
been discarded, since Art. 48 provides that only one meeting per week shall be
reserved for questions.

And it is, after all, interpellations which, in the last ninety years, had been
the life-blood of French parliamentary activity!

No doubt, from the Government's point of view, interpellations were a
waste of time and a nuisance; but without them, as future practice was to
show, the virtual abolition of interpellations meant the almost complete
silencing of parliamentary criticism and control, and the suppression of
many awkward facts which would have given rise to long—and sometimes fruity—discussion under the Third and Fourth Republic.

Looking a little ahead, how much parliamentary discussion was there
going to be of those various scandals, in which the Fifth Republic was to
prove quite as rich (if not more so) as the Fourth and the Third Republic?

What Bastid, as an old parliamentary hand, perhaps overrated at the

[1] Paul Bastid in *Inter-Parliamentary Bulletin*, 1958, p. 150 (Geneva).

time was the extraordinary indifference to Parliament in the country—an indifference that was noticeable both during the Referendum campaign and the election campaign, both of which assumed the nature of a plebiscite. The antipathy to Parliament was, if anything, increased by the *chambre introuvable* which emerged from the system used in the November election; Parliament was, even much less than usual, a faithful reflection of the electorate's wishes. Nor did the increased salaries of the deputies (over 4 million francs a year) increase their popularity; it was as if de Gaulle had killed two birds with one stone: he was adding to the deputy's disrepute, and was, at the same time, making him particularly docile *vis-à-vis* a President wielding the weapon of dissolution.

Paradoxically, too, it was the extreme Right, with its anti-Parliamentary tradition, which was largely controlling this first Assembly of the Fifth Republic; the Left, on the other hand, felt that it had been grossly swindled in the Election. Not that part of the Left wasn't itself largely to blame. It was Mendès-France, after all, who had started all the agitation in favour of a return to the "anti-Communist" *scrutin d'arrondissement* which, in November 1958, resulted in the election of the most reactionary Chamber since 1871.

Two other fundamental objections to the Constitution were, of course, these: (1) It left the question of Algeria completely open; in the circumstances, this was reasonable; but then why make Algeria take part in the Referendum? And (2) What if de Gaulle were suddenly to die? Who other than he could "wear" this Constitution with impunity? And, indeed, could *he* wear it indefinitely without its wearing him down?

19. SEPTEMBER 4: PLACE DE LA RÉPUBLIQUE —BLOODSHED

BLOODSHED—not much of it, but still bloodshed—was to mark the official opening of the Referendum campaign by General de Gaulle in the Place de la République on the afternoon of September 4. The whole thing, as de Gaulle was amongst the first to realize, had been badly arranged. Why September 4? Why Place de la République? September 4 happened to be the anniversary of the turbulent and chaotic birth of the Third Republic; it was hard to say whether this was a good reference or not; 1870 was remote, and the date itself did not stick in many minds as a landmark of any particular significance. No doubt, September 4 was a "republican" date, but not one that was cherished or revered. But the fact that de Gaulle was to speak in the Place de la République, on the fringe of working-class Paris, had already been foreshadowed by M. André Malraux in his famous press conference back in

June. De Gaulle was, in Malraux' conception, to address "the people of Paris". Since de Gaulle was "above party", it was right and proper that, after having appeared in various ceremonies in the West-end, he should also appear in the same capacity in the East-end, and speak to *le peuple*, to the heirs of the French Revolution and of the Commune of 1871. This whole paternalist conception was both childish and amateurish. Unless the organizers of the thing had meant it as a deliberate little provocation.

For several days workmen had been busy erecting a large platform in the middle of the Place de la République, the whole of it surmounted by a gigantic gilded V, which stood for both Victory and the V-th Republic.

As the *Canard Enchaîné* delightfully put it:

PROGRAMME POUR DEMAIN . . .	DE GAULLE A LA PLACE DE LA REPUBLIQUE

As an "address to the people of Paris", the whole ceremony was a failure from the very start. Early in the afternoon, all the numerous streets leading into the Place de la République were roped off by thousands of police. Only some 6,000 or 7,000 persons holding invitation cards, which were checked half a dozen times by the successive police cordons, were allowed into the Place de la République at all. *Le peuple* was kept at least two hundred yards away from the square; and nobody had even taken the trouble to put up loudspeakers, so that the "goats" could hear the General speak.

In the square itself the "sheep", well-surrounded by a variety of troops and police, and with a military band playing martial music from time to time, largely consisted, ironically enough, of representatives of the defunct "system", including such lights as M. Joseph Laniel, M. Georges Bidault, M. René Mayer and other deputies, senators and ex-Ministers. The men of the new "System" were there, too, in large numbers, headed by M. Soustelle and M. Triboulet, as well as the "amphibians" like Guy Mollet and Pflimlin. The ceremony started with a little piece of paternalist demagogy, when about a hundred working men were awarded the Legion of Honour.

This ceremony was accompanied by a speech from M. Berthoin, the Minister of Education, another amphibian, who exalted the virtues of the Republic, managed to bring in Gambetta, and Jules Ferry, and Jean Jaurès, Galliéni, Lyautey and Clemenceau, and paid a special tribute to "the workers of the mine, the workshop, the factory and the field" to whom France owed so much, and on whose best representatives the Government was happy to confer the highest distinctions with which the Republic could honour her sons. And he concluded by pointing to the

corpulent 1889 statue of the Republic in front of the huge V-erection
and reminded his audience that "she was a mother to us all".

By this time, shouts of "*Non! Non à de Gaulle!*" and "*Le fascisme ne
passera pas!*" could be indistinctly heard from the distance—from beyond
the five or six police barriers in the rue Turbigo and the rue du Temple;
and a few toy balloons, with NON written on them, began to float placidly
across the Place de la République. The scandalized guests tried not to
notice them.

The next star-turn was M. Malraux. Speaking this time with the
deliberate trace of a "proletarian" *faubourg* accent, M. Malraux produced
another rehash of the old RPF-French Revolution themes.

Turning a blind eye to the police cordons, he started by proclaiming
that the People of Paris were here; they had come to meet de Gaulle in
the Place de la République:

> Le peuple de Paris est là.
> Pour la France, merci, témoins!

Then came variations on the same old theme: Jemappes, the Convention, de Gaulle, Rivoli, Austerlitz, de Gaulle, "*soldats de l'An II qui firent
danser l'Europe au nom de la liberté . . .*" "And in 1941 de Gaulle said:
'*Liberté, égalité, fraternité*' . . ."

"No!" cried Malraux, "the memory of the Republic was not a memory of
easy living, still less was it one of ministerial combinations. It was not even the
romantic memory of 1848, or of the upsurge of the Commune; it was, and still is,
the memory of the Convention, it is our nostalgia for that forward rush by a
whole people towards its historic destiny. Fraternity—yes, but fraternity in labour
and hope. . . . Danton and Saint-Just proclaimed that the Republic meant the
control of the Government by the men elected by the people; they did not say
that the Republic must mean paralysis . . ."

Now, he said, an immense hope had risen—a hope of greater social
justice; there would now be unemployment insurance. And what had
once been the colonial empire would now become the Community:

"The country knows that the Fifth Republic carries with her luck and hope,
while the Fourth had become a synonym of failures and surrenders."

And he ended with a great dramatic flourish. As General de Gaulle's
black limousine drove up, Malraux, copying the slogans of the Free
French Radio of London, exclaimed:

"Many of you used to hear, night after night: 'LONDON CALLING. LES
FRANÇAIS PARLENT AUX FRANÇAIS. HONNEUR ET PATRIE. YOU WILL NOW
HEAR GENERAL DE GAULLE.' And now it is 'PARIS CALLING. HONNEUR ET

PATRIE. HERE, AT THE RALLYING POINT OF THE REPUBLIC, AT THE RALLYING POINT OF HISTORY YOU WILL HEAR GENERAL DE GAULLE'."

In the distance, down the rue du Temple, the rue de Bretagne, the rue Turbigo, the police were now charging the NO demonstrators, and even some "uninvited" YES people. Toy balloons with NO written on them were dotting the sky as de Gaulle, amid cheers from the invited, raised his long arms in a V-sign and rose to speak.

He, too, spoke of the Republic, but with quiet dignity, and without any of Malraux' theatrical effects and historical gibberish. He recalled 1792 and 1848. He recalled 1870 when the Republic, that permanent French institution, "offered once again to come to France's rescue after the disaster of Sedan". And he paid a tribute to that Third Republic, which had helped France to win the First World War. But then came 1940, and it was clear then that the Republic had not adapted France to the international context of the times. On June 18 the struggle began for the birth of a new Republic; but this Republic also failed; and it was in order to save the Republic that he (de Gaulle) and his Government saved France from disaster, and had, in strict legality, undertaken the task of drawing up a new Constitution.

France had an immense task ahead of her:

We are living at a time when gigantic forces are in process of transforming the world. Unless we are prepared to become a backward and despised country, we must evolve rapidly in the scientific, social and economic fields. . . . It will be our duty, too, to restore peace in Algeria, to develop her economically, and settle the question of her place and her statute. . . . The resources of the Sahara open up to us magnificent, but complex opportunities, and the relations between France and the overseas territories will require a profound adaptation. . . . The French nation will either flourish or wither in accordance with whether the State will have enough strength, constancy and prestige to lead it along the right path . . .

And, after (very vaguely) outlining the main features of the Constitution, de Gaulle declared:

With all my heart, and in the name of France, I ask you to answer YES on September 28. If you say NO, we shall return on that very day to the evil ways of the past. If you say YES, you will make the Republic strong and effective, provided those in charge of it have the necessary will. . . . A YES vote will also show that our country wants to be united and great. The outside world will draw from this vote the necessary conclusion. It may already have drawn this conclusion. A great hope is rising. I believe it has already risen.

Vive la République!
Vive la France!

Before leaving the tribune, de Gaulle called on the audience to sing the

10

Marseillaise; then, after shaking a few hands, he rather hurriedly drove away. Those who listened to the speech on the radio or saw it on TV were given the ear-splitting cheers coming from the guests; they were given no idea at all of the hostile shouts that were coming from the side-streets; radio and TV were given recorded and filmed (and in both cases, carefully cleaned-up) versions of the ceremony half an hour after it had actually taken place.

De Gaulle himself had, however, been fully aware of what was going on, and expressed extreme dissatisfaction with those—Malraux in the first place—who had thought up this Place de la République stunt; he said he wasn't going to face this kind of thing again. Before long he decided that he would not visit any French city during the Referendum campaign in which any serious hostile demonstrations were likely to occur.

*   *   *

It would be excessive to compare the NO demonstrations on that afternoon and evening of September 4 to the great working-class demonstrations of the 1930s. But, at a rough estimate, some 80,000 or 100,000 people had gathered in the rue Turbigo, the rue du Temple and the other streets leading up to the République. Many, indeed most, were working class. They carried banners and posters saying NON A DE GAULLE, or simply NON; they raised whole snowstorms of little white leaflets with the word NON printed on them in black heavy type; they sent up coloured balloons with NON written on them; they shouted "*Non!*" and "*A bas le fascisme!*" But they were not all working class. Very numerous were schoolteachers, for instance, male and female. Numerous intellectual groups—including Left-wing Socialists, men like Claude Bourdet and others—were also there. All these people made a lot of noise, and littered the streets with leaflets, but there was nothing provocative in their behaviour. But no sooner did they come anywhere near the police cordons two hundred yards from the Place de la République than the police charged with the utmost savagery, knocking people down and kicking them, and cracking them over the heads with their batons. Shopkeepers hastened to put down their shutters, and café proprietors to take in the chairs and tables. In the rue Turbigo, near the Temple *métro* station, I witnessed three such charges; several people nearest the police were knocked down, some lying unconscious on the pavement, with blood streaming from their heads, while the others, to escape the police batons, were running into side-streets and yards, and up staircases, and being pursued by the *flics*. More brutal still than the ordinary police were the militarized CRS guards, who distinguished themselves particularly later in the evening when the demonstrations had spread to the Grands Boulevards.

During the following days papers like the *Monde* published numerous letters from eye-witnesses of various cases of police brutality, even against old women who just happened to be "in their way". The Swedish Government lodged a protest with the French Foreign Ministry against the completely arbitrary beating-up of five Swedes who had gone to look at the République counter-demonstrations and to take photographs. Later the *Monde* related that when the Swedes protested to the police against having been beaten up, they received this singular reply: "Terribly sorry, but we thought you were Dutchmen", while a *Daily Telegraph* correspondent related how he explained to a policeman who was about to hit him with a truncheon that he was English, whereupon the cop said: "*Tant mieux!*" and walloped him over the head.

The Communist *Humanité* also revealed that, in one clash, the police had used not only tear-gas, but also firearms, wounding two demonstrators, among them a Renault worker. Subsequent inquiries showed that this was true, though at first strict instructions were given to the hospital to give the press no information on the wounded men.

From the Government point of view, the République ceremony had not been a success, though both the radio and the greater part of the press did their utmost to present it as such. But the NO demonstration could hardly be called a major success either; numerically it did not amount to very much, but the brutality displayed by the police attracted more attention to the existence of a seemingly vigorous opposition to de Gaulle than it would otherwise have received. The NO demonstrators can scarcely be said to have represented a major mass movement: probably two-thirds took part in the demonstration at the invitation of the local Communist organizations, who had provided the posters, leaflets and balloons; another third was composed of non-Communist Left-wingers (teachers, intellectual groups, etc.). Some also (including many tourists and other foreigners) had involuntarily joined the NO demonstration out of curiosity.

Now that de Gaulle had said his piece, there were only twenty-three days left in which the people of France were to decide whether they were to say YES or NO. Perhaps the most characteristic feature of those twenty-three days was the verbosity of the press, the radio and the political leaders, and the reticence, cageyness and often complete silence of the general population. In many parts of the country—especially the "traditionally republican" parts—one was constantly conscious of an almost general uneasiness, uncertainty and embarrassment whenever the Referendum was mentioned. It was as if most people instinctively felt that there was something wrong about the whole thing; but that, at the same time, there really wasn't any constructive alternative to the YES vote. A very high proportion of people in such parts of the country were wholeheartedly neither "for" nor "against", though the arguments "for" outweighed the arguments "against" in the end, as we shall see.

But the days that followed the République ceremony were marked, above all, by the stands—the *prises de position*—taken by the various political leaders and groupings. The intellectual groups were divided; and so were most of the traditional republican parties.

20. THE BATTLE BETWEEN "YES" AND "NO"

(a) MENDÈS-FRANCE'S "ALTERNATIVE" TO DE GAULLE

ON THE Right, apart from the strange case of Pierre Poujade, some of his followers, and a few outspoken Vichyites like M. Isorni, everybody was decidedly for the YES vote; so was the great bulk of the MRP; the Communists (as distinct, as we shall see, from many rank-and-file Communist voters) were emphatically for the NO vote; the two political scenes of a conflict between the YES-men and the NO-men were the Radical Party and the Socialist Party.

One of the first to come out with a clear NO statement was Pierre Mendès-France, who called a press conference almost immediately after the République ceremony. First of all, he put as follows his four main questions:

(1) Were those voting in the Referendum voting on a sufficiently clear issue?
(2) What was the value of the Draft Constitution? Was it respecting the fundamental principles of democracy? Was it not potentially as impotent as the Constitution of the Fourth Republic?
(3) Would a YES vote mean that the Government action of the last four months would be continued; and would that be a good thing? Had this action brought peace in Algeria any nearer, and had it reduced or increased the Fascist danger? Would a YES vote strengthen the French Union, or hasten its dislocation?
(4) Was there an alternative to the de Gaulle Constitution? Could its critics produce something better?

Like others before him, Mendès-France dwelt on the inherent contradictions of the YES vote; an African native and a citizen of Metropolitan France, in voting YES, would be voting for different things.

After describing the altogether abnormal conditions in which Algerians were going to vote, Mendès-France said:

The votes thus obtained will be included in the final YES and NO votes; and such voting will finally discredit in the eyes of all Moslems the democratic voting procedure.

As for the voting conditions in France itself—

Never perhaps since the Second Empire has official pressure been developed to such a point. Never since then has any government mobilized the Prefects the way this one has done, so that they bring down their whole weight on the voters. Similarly, the Army leaders are strongly influencing the soldiers' vote. The radio is becoming more and more tendentious, not to mention all kinds of other tricks, big and small, mean and scandalous, that are being used.

Most serious of all is the fact that those opposed to the Constitution should not be allowed to propose an alternative.

At the same time, the opponents of the Constitution are being perfidiously accused of "having nothing to propose". . . . This situation makes it easy to create all kinds of bogeys: some are made to think that the only alternative to the Constitution will be a Popular Front led by the Communists; others are made to think that the only alternative is a conquest of France by the paratroopers and civil war. Or, finally, a return to the Fourth Republic, with its sorry heroes. . . .

In dealing with his No. 2 question, Mendès-France criticized the Constitution on various grounds; even if, at sixty-seven, de Gaulle did not want to be a dictator, what guarantee was there that his successor would have no such ambitions? He also seemed particularly concerned about the Assembly being hamstrung by the President, by the Government, by the Constitutional Committee, and, even more so, by the bureaucracy:

Everything that determines economic and social progress will, in fact, be outside parliamentary control: full employment, social security, economic organization, investments, education, research, science, etc. In all these vital fields Parliament will merely be able to "express wishes". The vital decisions, notably the fixing of expenditure, will be solely in the hands of the Government, that is, of the bureaucracy and technocracy.

Any attempt by Parliament to extend its prerogatives would come up against the veto of the Constitutional Council, solely appointed "from above"; and even in fields in which Parliament may exercise a certain power, it will still be vulnerable to Government pressure:

Should Parliament dislike a Budget submitted to it by the Government, and does not pass it in its original form within seventy-five days, then the Government can pass the budget by decree. If the Government tables a Bill of which the Assembly disapproves, then one of two things can happen: either the Government "engages its responsibility" and simply enforces the Bill if there has been no vote of censure by an absolute majority within three days; or else there is such a vote of censure, and then the President can dissolve the Assembly!

Mendès-France also attacked the Government for not allowing the people to decide on the new election system; and he made his usual plea in favour of the two-round *scrutin-d'arrondissement*.

The next point Mendès-France made was that what was going to be held would be less a referendum than a plebiscite. Countless people had confidence in General de Gaulle; but was this confidence entirely justified? Many had thought that de Gaulle could bring a solution of the Algerian problem nearer; but in reality Algiers was constantly defying de Gaulle, even though paying lip-service to him. Worse still—

The men of Algiers and their *protégés* are being honoured and rewarded for the services they rendered the rebellion, while officials and military leaders who are suspected of republican sympathies are being purged.... And the radio has become so tendentious that one is not far wrong in asserting that in this field Paris is modelling itself on Algiers. The gulf between the French and Moslem communities is wider than ever, despite all the artificial fraternization scenes and the prefabri- cated *kermesses* over which the conformist press made such a song and dance.

He then dwelt on the contradictions between *de Gaulle's generous policy for Black Africa and the colonialist policy he continued to tolerate in Algeria.* The time would come when it would not be possible to deny the Algerians what had been granted to the people of Black Africa.

He put the cost of the Algerian war at 800 milliard francs a year, and attributed to the Algerian war the inflation in France and the rise in the cost of living. Food prices in France had risen in one year by 23 per cent. The Treasury was raising money by hook and by crook, and the rich had benefited from the latest Pinay loan. This money was, in fact, being swallowed up by Algeria. And when there was talk about a great new housing programme, one could only ask: with what money? Similarly, there was no money for education. Out of the extra 80 milliards the Minister of Education had asked for, de Gaulle had granted him only 5 milliards, whereas the Algerian war was given nearly all the extra 120 milliards Algiers had demanded.

To conclude, Mendès-France said that there could be no return to the Fourth Republic, but that there *was* an alternative to the de Gaulle Constitution: if the de Gaulle Constitution was rejected, a Constituent Assembly should be elected (under the *scrutin d'arrondissement*, of course!) in November; and this should be called upon to vote, within a month, a simple and clear Republican Constitution, complete with the British dissolution procedure. And the next thing to do would be to negotiate a peace settlement with the qualified representatives of the Algerian people, with the Tunisian and Moroccan Governments lending a hand in these negotiations.

For nothing useful and valid in any field will be done in France so long as no peaceful solution in Algeria will have been loyally sought and found. What an extraordinary paradox that this most tragic No. 1 problem, which cost the Fourth Republic its life, should be passed over in silence in the Constitution of the Fifth Republic!

And he called for "a Pact among the NOES" all agreed on the above aims.

In a way, it was important that somebody should stand up and say clearly that there *was* an alternative to the de Gaulle Constitution. But the terrible weakness of Mendès-France's grand gesture—for it was, in fact, little more than that—was that, with his almost maniacal insistence on the *scrutin d'arrondissement*—which implied the virtual exclusion of the Communists from any Parliament—he was excluding from any "Pact of NOES" the only Party that was wholeheartedly NO.

There was something fundamentally false in the Mendès-France position. *L'Express* of September 11 was trying, in a half-hearted sort of way, to remedy the weakness of the Mendès-France position by using the following arguments:

Malraux had exclaimed at the République: "*Ceux qui là-bas crient Non contre la France!*" This meant that those who cried "No" were, *ipso facto*, Communist and un-French. Soustelle and his radio and the conformist press were now identifying all NO votes with Communism and FLN terrorism, the "ally of Communism". They were trying to create a conditioned reflex among prospective NO voters in favour of voting YES:

"We mustn't fall into that trap, by always doing the opposite of what the Communists do. Communists or not, all those who cried NO were the 'first resisters against Fascism'."

It sounded almost like a plea for the Popular Front! Yet at the same time *L'Express* was all in favour of the *scrutin d'arrondissement*, which could only help the Right-wing parties into power, short of a Popular Front election alliance; and this *L'Express* was careful never to advocate.

Such was the intellectual muddle and confusion on the non-Communist Left.

(b) THE SOCIALIST CONGRESS: MOLLET WINS

The Fiftieth Congress of the Socialist Party met at Issy-les-Moulineaux, near Paris, on September 11. Guy Mollet, looking tanned and in good form, and wearing starched collar and tie and a smart navy-blue lounge suit (he was now very much de Gaulle's Minister of State, and the General did not like sartorial sloppiness) seemed remarkably self-confident throughout the Congress. If, only a month or two before, there was some doubt whether he would continue to "lead" the Socialist Party, it was certain now that he had fully regained control of the "machine". The last doubts had been swept away by the decision of Gaston Defferre, head of the powerful Marseille (Bouches-du-Rhône) federation to support the YES vote.

In the past, Mollet liked to impersonate the "ordinary working-chap"[1]

---

[1] According to one of the more apocryphal stories of the end of May 1958, Mollet declared that if the paratroopers invaded France, he would die fighting "at the head of the Pas-de-Calais miners".

at Congresses, by appearing in his shirt-sleeves and braces, and no tie; not now. What is more, Mollet and the other organizers of the Congress somehow decided that it would be, if not indecent, at any rate irrelevant in the present circumstances, to bring down from the attic the dusty old photographs of Guesde, Jaurès, Blum and any of the other "great ancestors". They might have put ironical thoughts into some of the delegates' minds; it was not a good idea. So the effigies of Guesde, Jaurès and Blum were not admitted to the Congress, and the only decoration at the back of the platform was the (wholly meaningless) three-arrow emblem which the SFIO shared with the German Social-Democrats and a few other more-or-less decrepit Socialist parties of Western Europe.

Guy Mollet, who, in 1946, had led the revolt inside the Socialist Party against the "reformism" and "anti-Marxism" of Blum and Daniel Meyer and who managed, soon after, to gain control of the Party machine, made a particularly significant remark in his opening speech to the Congress:

> In 1946, I was a little too much of a theorist. Since then, I have learned a lot about people and the role they play in human affairs. . . . I now know that it is more important to count on men of action than on those who mistake revolutionary verbiage for revolution. . . .

But, in reality, had Guy Mollet ever been a "theorist"? In my two previous books on post-war France, Guy Mollet holds a very prominent place; but at no point does he figure as a "theorist" or as a man of ideas. In the light of Guy Mollet's leading role in the establishment of the de Gaulle régime in May–June 1958 (a role in which he persisted in taking the greatest pride) it is worth looking once again at the motives that prompted the activity of the French Socialist leader ever since the war.

This teacher of English at the *lycée* of Arras just before the war was still virtually unknown in the Socialist Party in 1945. He had been a war prisoner in Germany and, after his release, had played a minor role in the Resistance. But, at the time of the Liberation, he proceeded to cultivate his contacts in the Pas-de-Calais *département*, made himself popular with the miners—with whom he used to adopt rather "proletarian" airs—and was elected Mayor of Arras. Soon he also became secretary of the Socialist Federation of the Pas-de-Calais, one of the largest and most "working class" of all the Socialist federations.

First, in 1945, he distinguished himself by demanding (without success) the withdrawal of the Socialists from the coalition government under General de Gaulle. After de Gaulle's retirement in January 1946, Mollet, cold, hard and humourless, and now representing the "Left-wing" tendencies inside the Socialist Party, led the revolt, as already said, against the "reformism" of Blum and the then Secretary-General of the Party,

Daniel Mayer. In the vote on the "moral report" at the Congress of August 1946, Mollet won a resounding victory against Mayer, and became Secretary-General of the Party—whereupon nothing more was heard of the said "moral report", which emphasized too clearly the dissensions inside the Party. For Mollet's *idée fixe*, then as later, was to preserve the unity of the Party at all costs, and not allow internal dissensions to come into the open. And though heading the "Left" at that time, he knew that, in reality, in view of the imminent conflict with the Communists, the centre of gravity in the Party was rapidly shifting to the Right. Ironically enough, it was Mollet, the leader of the "Left" who, at the National Council of the Socialist Party in the winter of 1946–47, was among the first to oppose a formal resolution in favour of entering into immediate peace negotiations with Ho Chi Minh. Which meant that he was already then anticipating close collaboration between the Socialists and the Indo-China war party, the MRP. On this, as on other issues, Mollet soon became a determined opponent of the Communists. Though at first he seemed opposed to Ramadier's "expulsion" of the Communists from the last "tripartite" government in May 1947, and even demanded that the Socialists part company with the MRP, he became, only a few months later, a strong supporter of the Third Force, and a staunch ally of Jules Moch, the Minister of the Interior, the "Cavaignac" who fought on two fronts: against de Gaulle's RPF and, with even greater determination, against the political strikes that the Communist Party had then organized.

Mollet, far from being a "theorist" of any kind, was, first and foremost, an opportunist, who never stopped keeping a finger on the pulse of French public opinion. He cashed in on the growing anti-Communism of 1947–48; and he rightly saw that Marshall Aid was helping the Third Force, rather than de Gaulle, to gain the upper hand. Caught between the Communists and the RPF, Mollet decided that the Socialist Party had better ally itself with the Centre parties (the MRP and the Radicals) regardless of whether the social or colonial policy of these had anything whatsoever to do with "Socialism". Personally Mollet was never popular; in Parliament he was clumsy, awkward and ill-at-ease; but he had a way of dominating Socialist Congresses which was truly impressive. Constantly backed by the powerful Pas-de-Calais and Nord Federations, he met with little opposition; or, when he did, he used soothing and reassuring words, as he did, for example, at Lille, in June 1956, to quieten the revolt against Lacoste's policy in Algeria.

Several months before, on that fateful 6th of February, 1956 when he surrendered to the Algiers mob, abandoned the role of supreme arbiter between the two Algerian communities, and so opened the era of the growing subservience of Paris to Algiers, Mollet had thrown overboard all the lofty principles he had professed during the election campaign of December 1955, when he had fumed against "this senseless war". Mendès-France had stuck to these principles, and soon came to grief. Mollet, on the contrary, conformed readily to the nationalist and anti-Arab feeling that was then rapidly growing in France. For eighteen months he remained at the head of the Government, allowing himself, more and more, to be influenced and bossed by the Algiers *ultras*. Any of the feeble attempts he made to end the war in Algeria were sabotaged by Lacoste, Max Lejeune and the Army; and he took this sabotage without a murmur. His attitude to the Europeans of Algiers, who had pelted him with tomatoes on that famous 6th of February, and had even threatened to murder him, was very strange: in his view, the people who were hating him so much, who seemed ready to tear him limb from limb, were not "Fascists", as he had imagined, but "ordinary" Frenchmen—*petits blancs*—just the kind of people who, in France, would naturally vote Socialist. And even if many of them were "reactionaries", Mollet still felt that they were "essentially French"; and there is (as many people who know him well have told me) "a sentimental streak about Mollet"; he wants to be loved, and not least by his class enemies: hence this strange desire for a "communion of the classes" which he shares with de Gaulle.

The familiar phrase, "National-Molletism", is not an idle wisecrack. Mollet did his best to conform to that nationalist wave that was sweeping France in 1956–57—even if, in the process, it meant the enslavement of Paris by Algiers, and was to lead, sooner or later, to the disintegration of the Fourth Republic. Already in 1956–57, Mollet, like Lacoste, was essentially an authoritarian, rather than a defender of the traditional forms of French democracy. And, oddly enough, there was nothing during those eighteen months when Mollet was head of the French Government, of which he was prouder than his Suez exploit. He got it into his head that he, Guy Mollet, was going to overthrow Nasser's dictatorship. Out of an innate kind of chauvinism? No. Mollet simply felt that he had public opinion behind him; that it was the popular thing for him to do; above all, it was popular with the French Right; and the French Right had become, to Mollet, the natural ally of what French "Socialism" had now become—even though he liked to call it "the most stupid Right in the world".

Mollet was also obsessed by Communist competition. As we have seen, it did not take him long to decide, at the height of the May crisis, that de Gaulle was his man. Public opinion was, by and large, pro-de Gaulle. But while to many de Gaulle was merely a "lesser evil" (the paratroopers would have been worse), to Mollet de Gaulle meant something inherently and *positively* good. And, by a strange kink, Mollet felt, above all, that the inevitable return of de Gaulle to power would not weaken, but strengthen the Socialist Party; in loyal co-operation with the General, it would play an honourable part in the "renovation" of France; and the death of the Fourth Republic would not adversely affect the destinies of the French

Socialist Party, still ironically labelled SFIO! Let the Republic die, so long as the Party went on living!

The Congress of Issy-les-Moulineaux was marked by this desire of the Party to go on living—under the Fifth Republic, under the de Gaulle régime, no matter how authoritarian it might be. For after all—and this was something that always mattered immensely to Mollet—was not the bulk of French public opinion pro-de Gaulle? The Party, in his view, would exercise a salutary moderating influence on the régime; if it found itself in opposition, it would become His Majesty's Opposition, in the British sense. In his fairly frequent conversations with top-ranking British diplomats during this period, Mollet never failed to stress his "profound admiration" for the British political system; the Fifth Republic would, he thought, have many points in common with it. One can only wonder whether he *honestly* believed that.

A fortnight before the Congress met, Guy Mollet had already sent a *Lettre aux militants* in which he strongly defended the Constitution and urged the Socialist Party to vote YES. He also used many of the arguments he had already used at the Socialist Information Conference in July to defend his policy in May:

I considered that between the imminent danger of a reactionary dictatorship and the possible danger of an improvised popular mass movement degenerating into a civil war which could only benefit the Communists, there was a middle way: and that was the maintenance and, at the same time, the *renovation* of the Republic. . . . And even if, as some said, this was a backward step, then let me remind you that there are tactical retreats which can save the bulk of our forces, just as there can be offensives which can destroy these forces for an indefinite period. . . .

He then proceeded to justify the action of the de Gaulle Government since June, saying that, as a member of the Government, he took full responsibility for "certain nominations and promotions" (Soustelle's, Massu's, etc.), just as, in the past, he had taken responsibility for the Suez operation:

I had not consulted the Party in advance (for this would have made the whole thing impossible); but I knew that I was acting in your name.

And, sure enough, he had not been disavowed!
Having skated over this stretch of very thin ice, Mollet then wrote:

And the big questions before us are these: Is the Republic threatened? I say No. Is the republican order being slowly but surely re-established? I say Yes. Are the fundamental freedoms safeguarded? Again, I say Yes. Have our Socialist comrades, now members of the Government, been faithful to their ideal and their mission?

Without arrogance, but also without false modesty, I say Yes. And, last but not
least, have the chances of Socialist democracy in France remained intact? Without
hesitation, I answer Yes; they may even be greater than they were before, if we
know how to choose.

There followed a highly tortuous defence of the Constitution, and of
the YES vote. The main argument in favour of voting YES was, indeed,
simply this:

Supposing the NO vote wins. What are you going to do next? Are you ready to
take over the succession? With whom? With the "Communists"?[1]

As for the Constitution itself, Mollet argued that it was not dangerous
to freedom; even the famous Article 14, giving the President exceptional
emergency powers, was not dangerous in itself, for, in its revised form, it
could apply only to situations similar to those of 1940 when "the public
authorities had ceased to function normally"—which was an objective
fact, and not something that could subjectively be determined by the
President. As for the "strengthening of the authority and stability of the
Executive", the "better organization of parliamentary work", etc., these
were "all to the good". Also, the explicit introduction of the *habeas corpus*
principle into the French Constitution could only be welcomed, as were
to be the new principles applicable to Black Africa, which were in full
agreement with what the Socialist Party had always stood for. . . . On
Algeria, Mollet said nothing.

This *Lettre aux militants* had been received by its addressees with somewhat mixed feelings, as could be observed from the very first meeting
of the Issy Congress. It was clear almost at once that a split in the Party
was inevitable. Men like M. Mazier, deputy for the Côtes-du-Nord, and
M. Jean Rous (Seine), raised awkward questions like Soustelle's appointment, as well as the whole record of the Socialist Party in the colonial
field. Rous said that, ever since 1946, the Socialist Party had failed to take
an anti-colonialist stand; worse still, he accused the Party of being run on
"secretly Stalinist lines", meaning that Mollet and his bureaucratic
apparatus were dominating the Party completely. Despite the violence
of these criticisms, it was clear that Mollet was confident that the bulk
of the Party would follow him, even if a few individuals dropped out.

Nevertheless, throughout the four days' discussions, the whole atmosphere at the Congress was nervous and uneasy. It was scarcely surprising.
The Socialists (like nearly everybody else in France) were groping in the
dark during those days. The assurances given by Mollet that the Constitution was a republican Constitution, and that de Gaulle could be trusted;
the certainty expressed by Defferre that de Gaulle had every intention of

[1] The quotation marks were meant to imply that the French Communists did not represent
any political philosophy, but were merely the agents of a foreign power!

pursuing a liberal policy in Algeria and that he alone was capable of making peace there seemed to many like so much wishful thinking. In his public pronouncements de Gaulle had spoken in riddles. He was, in fact, asking France for a blank cheque. And even many of those who trusted de Gaulle were troubled by three sets of considerations:

Supposing de Gaulle died in the near future—who would rule France under the new Constitution? Was de Gaulle, even if his intentions were pure and his republicanism above suspicion (despite the unhappy RPF experiment), going to dictate his will to the Army, to the *ultras*, to men like Soustelle, whose totalitarian tendencies seemed all too evident? And—as a matter of principle—was it not wrong to continue to submit to the "blackmail of Algiers"—for was there not the same old implied threat in the invitation to vote YES: either you do, or there'll be chaos and civil war; you've got to choose between de Gaulle and Massu.

It soon became apparent that, at the Socialist Congress, there was a small number of men uncompromisingly opposed to de Gaulle and Mollet—Depreux, Savary, Verdier and a few others—but that the rest considered it expedient to vote YES in the Referendum, or else to vote NO as a matter of principle, but without leaving the Party. (These included men like Gazier, Pineau and Tanguy-Prigent.)

The speech that was awaited with the greatest interest was that of *M. Gaston Defferre*, Mayor of Marseilles and leader of the powerful Bouches-du-Rhône Federation, which was going to be decisive in swinging the great majority of the Congress in favour of the YES vote— and the maintenance of Mollet at the head of the Party. It was known that de Gaulle had specially asked Defferre to go and see him; that he had spoken to him for nearly two hours, and had completely persuaded him that he (de Gaulle) had every intention of making peace in Algeria. De Gaulle, realizing the great weight that Defferre's vote would carry at the Socialist Congress, had gone out of his way to exercise on him his powers of seduction. Defferre, who was also anxious not to lose the *mairie* of Marseilles, gladly allowed himself to be "seduced" by the General. He left the Hôtel Matignon completely starry-eyed, and as nearly convinced as was possible that de Gaulle was determined to get tough with the Algiers *ultras* and to find a liberal solution to the Algerian problem; anyway, had not his tour of Black Africa shown which way he was disposed?

The YES vote, he said, was the best way of securing peace in Algeria. De Gaulle had never spoken of "integration"—"that swindle with which we must in no way associate ourselves". De Gaulle had, on September 4, spoken of a new Algerian *statute*, which was quite a different matter.

And then came this glowing defence of de Gaulle:

"How can a man who re-established normal relations with Tunisia, who allowed arms to be delivered to Bourguiba, who has withdrawn the French troops from Morocco, how can you expect such a man to pursue in Algeria the diametrically opposite policy? . . . The Army, which has had a completely free hand all this time, has achieved nothing; and de Gaulle alone has a very good chance of restoring order in Algeria. . . . We must allow de Gaulle to get rid of the pressure the men of May 13 are still trying to exercise on him. He must be enabled to act without them, and even against them. We must abandon [Mollet's] triptych— 'cease-fire—elections—negotiations'—which has proved useless, and has merely led to the May 13 explosion. We must, instead, negotiate with those against whom we are fighting. France has never yet proposed negotiations; she must do it now."

And Defferre clearly hinted that de Gaulle had promised him to make such an offer to the FLN. . . .

After many other speeches "for" and "against" the Constitution, Mollet wound up with a two-and-a-half-hour speech, the main features of which were:

(1) His desire to preserve, as far as possible, the unity of the Party (he even appealed personally to a man like Tanguy-Prigent not to leave).

(2) His virulent anti-Communism, which had very largely determined his action in May when he had helped to bring de Gaulle back to power—even though he now swore that he had done his utmost to support Pflimlin "so long as was humanly possible".

(3) His "ever-growing confidence in the loyalty of General de Gaulle", and his fear that "de Gaulle might not be given a chance to fulfil all the tasks he had set himself". He also thought that "thanks to his great authority" de Gaulle could settle the Algerian problem; and it was no use, Mollet said, complicating his task by laying down any rigid conditions.

(4) His anger and embarrassment at the NO resolutions passed by the Teachers' Syndicate and the bulk of the (non-Communist) trade union leadership.

The Congress nevertheless ended in a clear victory for the YES vote in the Referendum. This was approved by 2,687 votes to 1,176.

It also passed a number of motions, the most important of which was on Algeria' demanding that the civil authorities be re-established in their functions; that the Committees of Public Safety be dissolved; that elections in Algeria be conducted honestly and sincerely. It asserted that the use of slogans like "integration" could not, in itself, solve anything; anyway, the word meant something quite different to a Socialist from what it meant to those who were the *most fanatical European supporters of "integration"*.

For the rest, the motion took up Defferre's arguments in favour of entering into negotiations "with the qualified representatives of the population, excluding nobody". (This was, in fact, a little vaguer than Defferre's argument in favour of negotiating with the FLN; the motion had been watered down at the insistence of M. Max Lejeune, who, in talking to me at the Congress, still declared himself proud—and a great big smirk came over his face—of having "caught Ben Bella and his chums" back in October 1956.)

Another motion passed unanimously expressed great satisfaction with the liberal spirit shown by de Gaulle in Black Africa; it implied that de Gaulle had merely adopted an attitude "which had always been that of the Socialist Party".

Most of those who had voted against the YES vote in the Referendum (even men like Pineau and Tanguy-Prigent) made it clear that they were not going to leave the Party. But a small group broke away, to form the Autonomous Socialist Party (*SFIO Autonome*).

Its leader was M. Edouard Depreux, and its members included a former premier, M. Gouin; deputies like MM. Mazier and Arbeltier; Prof. C. A. Julien, leading authority on North Africa; ex-Minister André Philip (who had been expelled from the Party earlier in the year); two prominent women-members of the Resistance, Mmes Andrée Viénot and Pierre Brossolette; M. Oreste Rosenfeld, formerly a close associate of Léon Blum's; Jean Rous, another authority on North Africa; M. Daniel Mayer, former minister, who, earlier in the year, had resigned from Parliament to become president of the *Ligue des Droits de l'Homme*, etc.

In a press conference, M. Depreux condemned Guy Mollet, "the first to have gone to Canossa-les-deux-Eglises"; he blasted the policy of Lacoste, "which embodies everything that I, as a Socialist, had sworn to fight"; and declared that the new party would conduct a vigorous NO campaign in the country, together with men like Mendès-France and teachers and trade unionists who also had decided to vote NO; it would not ally itself with "*the most stupid Right in the world*" (Mollet's phrase), but one "*which had, all the same, been intelligent enough to impose its policy on M. Guy Mollet's party*".

It was a gesture by a handful of men—mostly intellectuals; it did not greatly upset Guy Mollet; on the contrary, it rather pleased him to get rid of his more virulent critics inside the Party. Even if, inside the Party, a substantial number of people were still favourable to the NO vote in the Referendum, the outward unity of the Party—Mollet's chief concern— had been preserved. The only thing that worried him about the split was that the Socialist International might "recognize" the Autonomous SFIO as the *real* French Socialist Party, and expel Mollet's party.

Fluctuat nec mergitur had, as *France-Observateur* maliciously remarked, been the everlasting motto of both Mollet and his Government-minded Party. Mollet was going to lead his troops straight from the Fourth into the Fifth Republic; foreshadowing the adoption of the *scrutin d'arrondissement* in the next General Election, he was, many thought, already fancying himself de Gaulle's first Prime Minister!

A comic (or perhaps not so comic) little sideshow was provided at the Socialist Congress by M. Lacoste, whose role was described as follows in an ironical little paragraph in *Le Monde*:

THE SILENT ONE

Modest and self-effacing, there he was, a delegate like any other delegate. Seated among the members of his Federation, he cheered the leaders as they spoke; like a disciplined boy, he sang the *Internationale* along with the others; at the buffet during intervals he commented on the ups and downs of the Congress like anybody else. But he did not ask to speak. Even when his name was mentioned—and it was often mentioned—he remained silent and unperturbed.

Yet this delegate had governed Algeria and run the war there for thirty months. His Federation—the Dordogne Federation—gave sixty votes to the YES vote in the Referendum, and ten to the NO vote. And on the Algerian issue M. Lacoste cast sixty-two of his comrades' votes into the scales in favour of the motion condemning integration and demanding a cease-fire and negotiations. . . . [1]

De Gaulle himself was extremely satisfied with the outcome of the Socialist Congress; not so the *ultras* in Algeria. The motion on Algeria —approved, moreover, by the Socialist Federation of Algiers—produced a storm of protests. The local Gaullists (*Fédération algérienne des républicains sociaux*) adopted unanimously a motion

"violently protesting against the wording of the Socialist motion calculated to win over by intolerable concessions a minority ready to abandon French Algeria . . ."

[1] It was at the time of the Socialist Congress that the text of the letters exchanged in May between Guy Mollet and de Gaulle was finally published. In his letter of May 25 Mollet began by saying that he had never met de Gaulle and doubted whether he ever would; though, like other Resisters, he had "seen and loved him from afar". He said he had twice met de Gaulle's representative, M. Guichard, and had expressed to him his great anxiety lest the General's return to power played into the hands of the Bolsheviks. Not he (de Gaulle) was threatening freedom, but his supporters were; the Bolsheviks would benefit from the disillusionment that would follow the setting-up of a dictatorship in France; they would benefit from it "perhaps in ten weeks, or ten months or ten years—they don't mind waiting". But the letter ended with an implicit—but perfectly clear—appeal to de Gaulle to "defend Republican freedoms" and to speak up and disavow "the madmen preparing a military pronunciamento". "France is the only country in Europe in danger of a *putsch*; its authors are claiming to act in your name; and you are saying nothing."

De Gaulle answered this long and tortuous letter with a short and friendly note in which he merely said:

Mon cher président [It was afterwards noted that, in addressing Pflimlin, he used the more formal "*Monsieur le président*"]

"Your letter clearly suggests to me that we are not far from being in complete agreement on fundamentals. I regret all the more that you did not follow up your intention of seeing me. It seems to me that it is in the interests of the country's unity and, before long, of its independence, that a direct contact (no matter how discreet) be urgently established between the Government and myself, lest the situation deteriorates still further."

And of all the possible ways of concluding a letter, de Gaulle chose about the most cordial of all:

Soyez assuré en tout cas, mon cher président, de mes sentiments bien cordialement dévoués.

Charles de Gaulle.

Algiers radio, now under Soustelle's control, savagely attacked the "remnants of the System which General de Gaulle had not yet been able to exclude from his Government", while M. Georges Bidault, speaking at Tizi-Ouzou, exclaimed: "The soul of France is not represented by Congress motions, but by your courage."[1]) The motion was also severely criticized by M. de Sérigny in the *Echo d'Alger* and, in Paris, by M. Soustelle's USRAF which said that the Socialists' hostility to "integration" and their way of ignoring the "immense fraternization movement in Algeria" were calculated to distort the real meaning of the YES vote in the Referendum.

(c) MOST RADICALS ALSO FOR DE GAULLE

Despite his personal regard for Mendès-France, de Gaulle also had every reason to be satisfied with the defeat of Mendès-France and of the *mendésistes* at the Radical Congress that was held about the same time at Lyon. No doubt the opposition to the YES vote in the Referendum was, on the face of it, stronger among the Radicals than among the Socialists; 716 votes were cast in favour of the YES vote, and 544 in favour of the NO vote. The federations of South-West France, whose old-time republicanism was largely represented by the *Dépêche du Midi* of Toulouse, by its editor, M. Baylet, and even by the by no means very liberal M. Bourgès-Maunoury, were the real backbone of the NO vote among the Radicals. The Congress was marked by all sorts of strange contradictions; the "traditional" Radicals were obviously reacting sharply against all that Mendès-France had stood for, and yet they seemed to take some pride in the fact that Mendès-France's reformist zeal had already foreshadowed some of de Gaulle's reforms; at the same time, most of them implicitly condemned Mendès-France's over-liberal policy in respect of Tunisia and his hostility to the Suez adventure; by a large majority, the Congress elected to the presidency of the Party, not Mendès-France, but the more "comfortable" Félix Gaillard who, somehow, for all his youthful dash, seemed to symbolize to the "old beards" of the Radical Party a "return to normal", after all the extravagant experiments Mendès had tried to perform on the Party.

No doubt, the Constitution was severely criticized both by those favouring the YES vote and the NO vote, and the final "Declaration of the Party", though drawn up by the YES majority, had some nasty things to say about the men of Algiers and M. Soustelle, and the "one-way propaganda of the radio, TV and information services, which is quite inadmissible in a democratic régime". The Algerian problem, it also said, had

---

[1] M. Georges Bidault, who had agitated earlier and more actively than most in favour of de Gaulle's return to power, was sick at heart of having been cold-shouldered by the General throughout the May crisis and ever since his investiture by the Assembly; now he threw in his lot more than ever with the Algiers *ultras*.

not been settled; the events of May 13 had made it even more acute; and the Government did not seem to have any clear idea of how to deal with it. In his final address to the Congress, the new President, M. Gaillard— who remembered only too well all the trouble he had had with the generals at the time of Sakhiet and of Murphy's "good offices" mission— expressed some grave doubts about the loyalty of the Army, and he called on the Government to take some "drastic decisions".

And one of his last sentences was intended no doubt to mark the end of the Mendès-France experiments:

"Our Party has been in danger of dying of a spirit of intolerance."

On the Constitution itself, the Congress expressed approval, though with all sorts of reservations; M. Maurice Faure called it "Orleanist"; and M. Gaillard himself feared that it might lead to a "permanent conflict between the executive and legislative powers"; M. Mendès-France repeated the arguments he had already used against the Constitution in his press conference ten days before; nevertheless, the majority of the Congress, though worried, approved the YES vote. In the final motion on the Constitution, the majority of the Radical Party made the most of having been "the first to criticize all the weaknesses of the 1946 Constitution", and advocated the adoption of the *scrutin d'arrondissement*, which, it regretted, the Government had not yet done.

Much was made of the fact that the "real test" would come not on September 28, at the time of the Referendum, but in November, when France would elect the new Assembly.

The impression made by the Socialist Congress and the Radical Congress was that these two essential French Parties were anxious to adapt themselves to the new conditions of the Fifth Republic, and were hoping to exercise a moderating influence on de Gaulle; for was not the country, whatever Algiers thought, fundamentally republican at heart?

What really emerged from the Lyon Congress of the Radical Party were the hankering for the Party's return to its old, "normal" place in the Republic (for de Gaulle or no de Gaulle, "the Republic must continue"), and the fact that *mendésisme*, despite its brief success, first in 1954 and then during the election campaign at the end of 1955, did not represent a political force any longer, but only an intellectual attitude. If a large minority of the Radical Party favoured the NO vote in the Referendum, it was not out of devotion to Mendès-France, but in virtue of a much older, much more whiskered Republican Tradition, represented by the South-West Federations and the *Dépêche du Midi*.

(d) FRENCH TEACHERS SAY "NO"

There was one awkward event which was scarcely mentioned at the
Radical Congress, but which had produced an explosion of fury from
Guy Mollet at the Socialist Congress—and that was the fact that, in the
name of the 190,000 *instituteurs*—the primary school teachers of France—
the *Syndicat National des Instituteurs* had on September 8 unanimously
rejected the de Gaulle Constitution and had recommended the NO vote.
A high proportion of French teachers were Socialists, and had, for
generations, been looked upon as the backbone of France's republican
traditions.

Libération, overjoyed by the vote of September 8, wrote:

This decision is of the greatest importance to every republican in our country.
In our smallest villages, as well as in the overcrowded working-class areas of our
cities, the teacher is more than a mere instructor of children. The rectitude of his
life, the sincerity of his convictions, his competence and his devotion to popular
education have built up that personal prestige which have also made of him the
natural counsellor of parents. That is also why so many teachers have formed such
valuable *cadres* among Left-wing parties. Their rejection of a monarchist-inspired
Constitution is of decisive importance to all those determined to defend the
Republic. . . . It has often been said that it was the teachers of France who had
"made the Republic"; because they had *made* it, it is natural that they should have
so spontaneously risen to defend it in its hour of peril. . . .

The rejection of the Constitution by the Teachers' Federation was not
violent in its wording. It recalled that this body, the SNI (*Syndicat National
des Instituteurs*), was a "free trade union organization, independent of all
political parties and of any government", but that it stood for "the
fundamental principles of freedom, human dignity, the free play of
democratic institutions and the people's sovereignty".

Having been entrusted by its Congress of Brest to examine the Constitution and
the Referendum, its National Council had come to the following conclusions:
The preamble of the Constitution did not set down sufficiently clearly those
principles of a social Republic which were essential to a normal evolution of
France in the modern world; the Constitution did not explicitly provide for the
extension of education to all categories of the population, and this was left to the
sole discretion of the Government; the Constitution . . . placed both Parliament
and the Government under the tutelage of the President, who was also in a position
to set up a régime of personal rule. And although the Constitution contained some
"excellent principles" concerning personal freedom and the future relations
between France and Black Africa, the National Council nevertheless declared itself
opposed to the Constitution. . . . There was also no doubt that the Referendum
campaign was being conducted in an undemocratic manner, the radio and the bulk
of the press carrying out a wholly one-sided propaganda. While suggesting
that the recommendation to vote NO did not place any obligation on the members
of the SNI, the motion nevertheless said in conclusion that the rejection of the

Constitution would enable Parliament to elaborate a new Constitution on a more democratic basis, i.e. by the regularly-elected representatives of the people.

Above all, what worried the teachers was the (more than legitimate) suspicion that the de Gaulle régime would, by hook and by crook, favour and encourage religious education and the écoles libres *at the expense of the non-religious,* laïque *State schools.* If, despite the *laïcité* principle figuring in the Constitution of both the Fourth and the Fifth Republic, the former had still managed, in 1951, to pass the *loi Barangé* providing financial aid to religious schools, *the Fifth Republic was likely to go very much further in that direction.*

Not only the primary teachers' federation—the *Syndicat national des instituteurs*—but also the similar organization of secondary school teachers —the *Syndicat national de l'Enseignement Secondaire*—as well as the *Syndicat national de l'Enseignement Technique*, passed *almost unanimously* similar resolutions. The majority of university teachers and scientists (though no exact figures are available in their case) also appear to have been against the Constitution. *In any case, practically the whole of the French teaching profession had declared itself opposed to the Constitution.*

No such political stand had been taken by the French teachers since the Second Empire.

The most significant thing was the way in which radio and the pro-Government press deliberately did their utmost to hush up this awkward fact. On the day following the vote of the three teachers' *syndicats*, the three largest-circulation Paris newspapers handled the news as follows:

The Parisien Libéré made a great song and dance on page 1 about the decision of the "dissident" Radicals of M. André Morice (3,000 members throughout France) to vote YES. On the *Conseil National des Instituteurs:* two lines at the bottom of the page) and not one word about their communiqué!

In *L'Aurore*, on an inside page, merely a passing reference, in the midst of a YES article, to the "teachers' regrettable decision not to join in this movement of national unanimity".

In the *Figaro* NOT A WORD anywhere. The paper gave ample details about the NO vote of Poujade; about the YES and NO votes of various socialist committees; about YES and NO tendencies in distant Gabon; but nothing about the teachers!

This curious case illustrated better than anything else the determination of Government propaganda to suggest that only Communists and their friends (besides a few crackpots like Poujade) were going to be against de Gaulle. The unanimous NO attitude of the entire French teaching profession was such a misfit that it was best not to try to fit it in, and to say nothing.[1]

---

[1] It was not until several days later—when the fact had become widely known, despite this conspiracy of silence—that M. Thierry-Maulnier, formerly of the Royalist *Action Française*, violently attacked the teachers in the *Figaro*.

(e) THE STRANGE CASE OF PIERRE POUJADE

Pierre Poujade, poor Poujade, who had collected 2½ million votes in France in January 1956 and who now merely had to console himself with the thought that he had embodied the "spirit of May 13" two and a half years before this glorious 13th of May, who had, moreover, been deserted by his deputies in the National Assembly (these had, without further ado, simply voted for his "successor"), had been placed in a hopeless position. No doubt he still had his teddy-boy supporters in Algiers; but he had become totally redundant in France. His weekly paper, *Fraternité Française*, snarled at de Gaulle in an inarticulate sort of way—all about having become "the prisoner of the System"—"soon he'll have Mendès-France hanging round his neck, too"—and, after his African journey, about surrendering France's heritage to the cannibals.

MAKOKO . . . OU DUPONT? was how the banner headline of Poujade's paper summed up the situation, with the suggestion that, with de Gaulle's blessing, Makoko would soon (literally) gobble up Dupont. The only other prominent NO figure on the Right was Me. Isorni, the leading Pétainist in the old Assembly; what finally, he said—and more even than his loyalty to the memory of Pétain—persuaded him to vote NO was Article 86 of the Constitution enabling African territories to "secede" from France.

(f) THE COMMUNISTS ARE VERY WORRIED

And the Communists? The leaders were, clearly, worried—worried, largely, because the French working-class, the Communist rank-and-file, had also, to some extent, been infected by the general euphoria of the summer of 1958.

On Sunday, September 7, the *Humanité* held its annual open-air *fête* though not, as usual, at the Bois de Vincennes (this had been refused), but in a large park near Montreuil, Jacques Duclos' constituency. Here were all kinds of exhibits, pavilions (one of *Pravda*), sideshows, concerts, doughnut and sausage stalls, and a *grand tombola*, with a Simca and a 4-h.p. Renault as the first and second prizes.

"A gay and peaceful crowd," *L'Humanité* wrote the next day, "but conscious of the gravity of the dangers threatening our country. These 350,000 did not go to Montreuil as though it were merely a *kermesse*; their presence there was also a political act . . ."

It was, and it wasn't; for the *grande kermesse* continued for hours—long after the very brief political part of the programme had been disposed of. This took the form of a short speech by Maurice Thorez, who seemed to be in rather better physical form than he had been for some time.

He started with a eulogy of *L'Humanité*, "the great paper of Jaurès and Marcel Cachin". . . . "How, without *L'Humanité*, could we answer the vast campaign of lies and slander conducted by the men now in power?"

He denied the much-vaunted "legality" of de Gaulle's rule; he had been brought to power by violence, blackmail, fear, and the shameful abdication of Parliament. Debré himself had admitted that this was a "dictatorship". It was a régime of police terror, as could be seen from the way the police had behaved in the Place de la République only three days before.

Thorez significantly dwelt as much as possible on the "present eyewash" —de Gaulle was not the "national arbiter" he claimed that he was; he was the man of the Algiers rebels. Of course, it was an old trick of de Gaulle's always to make *promises*: to get a massive YES vote in Black Africa, he had even promised these people independence; but if *they* could be independent, why couldn't Algeria be?

Some had hoped that de Gaulle would pursue a policy of national independence; but he was a man of the Atlantic Pact; worse still, France was the only one of the great powers to refuse even to consider abandoning nuclear tests; and Debré had announced the other day that the famous Article 14 related to conditions that would be created in the event of an atomic war: "In that case," said Thorez, "the President of the Republic would be able to carry national sovereignty away with him, and leave the people to a frightful catastrophe."

After saying that a NO victory would mean the election of a new Constituent Assembly, and after making a few cracks at Mollet, Pflimlin and Reynaud, Thorez concluded:

"They cannot intimidate our people. What can Massu's paratroopers do against them? Last Thursday some of these thugs felt on their own skin how Republicans can hit back. (*Loud cheers.*) But all Republicans must remain united; and, despite the Mollets and Lacostes, who are helping the dictatorship, more and more Socialists are realizing where their leaders are going. . . . To quote the immortal words of the *Internationale*:

> *Il n'est pas de sauveur suprême,*
> *Ni Dieu, ni César, ni tribun . . ."*

A milliard men, Thorez said, were now building a happy life in the world under the banner of Socialism; Asia, Africa, South America were marching with the times; why should France put the clock back?

"France will say NO to servitude, NO to Fascism, NO to war. *Vive la République! Vive la France!"*

The people cheered, then sang the *Internationale*; then went back to the *grande kermesse*.

I talked to S. of *L'Humanité*. "A good speech," he said, "a good show; but the 1936 spirit is lacking. A lot will vote YES, out of laziness, and because they read *France-Soir* every day and listen to the radio. It's terribly difficult to persuade even a lot of our younger workers that de Gaulle is a Fascist. That African trip of his has made a hell of a big impression." "Yes," I said, "Thorez, I thought, found it a pretty tricky point to deal with." "You're damned right," S. grinned. "To make an awful lot of people vote NO *will* require, as our Central Committee repeated the other day, a 'superhuman effort'. . . . He'll get his 65 per cent.; more perhaps . . . And the old blackmail is still working. People don't want to have to fight Massu's paratroopers, if they can possibly help it. . . . Maurice's boast that *we* had beaten up a few thugs in the Place de la République was the feeblest part of his speech; the armed force is all on *their* side. . . . General strike, and all that? Sure; but it didn't work all that well last May. People are afraid of losing their jobs, and many are also the slaves of HP on their TV sets and all that sort of thing. De Gaulle will have to scare and annoy people a lot more than he has done before any serious resistance movement develops . . ."

It was a hot day, and at an open-air buffet, decorated with hammers-and-sickles, we drank iced coca-cola. "S.," I said, "your ideology is going to hell." "No, it isn't really," he said, "in spite of Coca-Cola. But we are terribly isolated; in spite of all the *main tendue* stuff we are doing, all these anti-Mollet Socialists, and Mendès-France and Daniel Mayer and Claude Bourdet boys are still scared to death of 'compromising' themselves with us. And, reassured by the fact that de Gaulle hasn't started persecuting Communists and hasn't closed down the *Humanité*, a lot of our chaps are sharing in the general euphoria. . . . Of course, there are going to be economic difficulties, but they aren't acute yet . . ."

(g) THE INTELLECTUALS ARE DIVIDED

No doubt, *L'Humanité* was screaming about dictatorship; so was *Libération*; the school teachers were against the Constitution; and so was what the *ultras* liked to call the "treason press"—in the first place *L'Express* and *France-Observateur*, though, in the former, François Mauriac was taking a pro-de Gaulle line, which wholly differed from the paper's editorial policy.

To take three significant "Left-wing intellectual" attitudes: those of Bourdet, Sartre, and Mauriac:

Bourdet (*France-Observateur*, September 25) argued as follows:

The Constitution was sure to lead to grave political conflicts; to a strangling of democracy and, before long, to the establishment of a dictatorship. De Gaulle, to appease the military, would have to become increasingly hard with the working class; a change in France's Algerian policy was extremely improbable; on the contrary, the war was likely to be intensified, and strengthen the Fascist forces.

The YES vote was based on two things: the blind faith in a man, and the fear of civil war. A NO victory would make civil war not more probable, but less probable; a YES victory would not produce immediate civil war, but the danger of having civil war *later* would be enormously increased. He admitted, however, that nothing could be foretold with absolute certainty; but, as a leading member of the Resistance, he felt that the question of human dignity should tilt the balance: just as it had been a matter of human dignity to say NO to Munich and NO to Vichy (for then, too, France was being blackmailed, though in a much more serious way, with war and a complete German occupation), so it was now a matter of dignity to say NO to de Gaulle, regardless of the (much less serious) threat of a paratroop landing.

It was clear, however, that Bourdet was speaking for a minority; and that he was conscious of it; for both Munich and Vichy had shown that French opinion had preferred to play safe. . . .

Jean-Paul Sartre in *L'Express* of September 25, in an article entitled "The Frogs want a King", used the following arguments:

People weren't going to say YES to the Constitution; they didn't give a damn about it. They were going to vote for a man. He represented the mirage of national unity. It was understandable that frustrated old women should identify de Gaulle with God; but why should active, modern, technically-trained young people want de Gaulle? Wasn't it because they vaguely felt that he represented a *policy*? But this also was a mirage.

The trouble with the Fourth Republic, apart from the "abnormal" Mendès-France interlude, was that neither Parliament nor the Governments were powerful; all the arguing about the executive or the legislative being too powerful or too weak was beside the point. The Governments (who had Parliament in tow) had, for a long time now, obeyed the Army. And although governments changed, they were, in fact, the same gang, i.e. the same government.

Gaullist propaganda which never stopped saying that the unfortunate ministers of the Fourth Republic were being terrorized by Parliament was just talking through its hat. Parliament had not forced Mollet to surrender to the Algiers mob, or Gaillard to "cover" the bombing of Sakhiet.

Back in 1946, the real executive, the authoritarian and uncontrollable executive, was Thierry d'Argenlieu, the master of Indo-China; today this executive had a hundred names: Massu, Trinquier, Lacheroy and other "colonels". *For thirteen years France had in reality been ruled by its War Lords . . .*

After the Liberation, Russia, America and de Gaulle between them had smashed the Resistance and the Left. . . . And after the humiliations of 1940 and 1945, France began to look for Greatness. And she could only find it in the "Empire". So, to sound like a Great Power, France started talking about being the defender of the Free World, Christianity and Graeco-Roman civilization . . . in Vietnam.

The Army, still suffering from the memory of 1940, tried to rehabilitate itself in Indo-China; when that failed, it clung to Algeria. And it would cling to Algeria, because, without it, the French Army would mean nothing. *The Army's sense of defeat was the life-blood of all Fascist movements . . .*

All this business about the "ungovernable System" was a lot of eyewash. The executive was in Algiers. *Perhaps* de Gaulle could do something about it. That seemed one argument for voting YES, though nobody knew what he could do. The majority of the YES voters had no enthusiasm for de Gaulle; a YES vote for de Gaulle was, to them, merely a NO vote for Massu. But de Gaulle with his New Look "system" would be just as much the prisoner of Algiers and of the Army as the old System had been. So what was the good of perpetuating this situation by voting YES for de Gaulle?

Finally, Mauriac. Just as, only two years before, he had developed a kind of "mystical" approach to Mendès-France, the Only Man who Could Save France,[1] so now he had become thoroughly mystical about de Gaulle:

In this tragedy, which is not only our tragedy, but that of the whole world, de Gaulle appears to me as the only Frenchman capable of speaking and acting in the name of us all. I daresay, on May 13, we could have chosen another road. Like one man, the people could have risen to support their Parliament and to defy the pronunciamiento. But the Left were agreed on one point only: which was *not* to join forces . . .
So what was left to us was the chance of calling in the man who would act as Arbiter among the divided French. . . . We must take him such as he has been given to us, just as destiny has shaped him. I could use another word . . . but I am also speaking to non-Christians. . . . The phrase "man of providence" has, in other contexts, been made to sound ridiculous. The fact remains that History at certain times has always produced, for better or for worse, a person through whom to achieve its ends. . . .

He compared him to St. Augustine, and then challenged the NO men to say if there was another man who could assume de Gaulle's role, "since the nation itself had proved incapable of reacting by itself".

And can any of you, his opponents, contemplate without a shudder the possibility of his suddenly no longer being there?

(*h*) THE PRESS AND THE REFERENDUM

Throughout the Referendum campaign, radio and TV were, of course, 100 per cent for the YES vote, except for those rare few minutes which were given to a number of Opposition parties. Thus, throughout the campaign, five minutes on radio and five minutes on TV was all that was allowed the Communist Party, despite its five million votes in 1956.

Apart from a few weeklies (chief among them *L'Express*, *France-Observateur* and the *Canard Enchaîné*), the two Communist dailies, *Libération* and *L'Humanité*, and, finally, *Le Monde* (which, though a YES

---

[1] See the author's *The Strange History of Pierre Mendès-France*, pp. 152-6, 246-8, etc.

paper, still allowed a good deal of space in its *Tribune Libre* to NO writers), practically the entire Paris press was more or less violently YES; in the first place the big-circulation morning papers, *L'Aurore*, *Parisien Libéré* and *Le Figaro*, and the two popular evening papers, *France-Soir* and *Paris-Presse*. Of the Paris daily press 3,600,000 copies preached YES, only 350,000 copies (i.e. less than 10 per cent) advocated NO.

The provincial press presented, broadly, a similar picture. In the chapter on the provincial press during the Referendum campaign published by Jacques Kayser and Joseph Dutter in the *Cahiers de la Fondation Nationale des Sciences Politiques* one finds the following interesting details:

Out of 101 provincial dailies (i.e. practically all in Metropolitan France) over 70 per cent were definitely for the YES vote; 7 per cent were "undecided"; some 13 per cent "non-committal", and only 9 per cent definitely NO.

Most of the YES papers made full use of Government-sponsored propaganda from organizations like the anti-abstentionist *Front d'action Civique contre l'Abstention* and the *Associations départementales du soutien de l'action du Général de Gaulle*. The YES papers fell into three groups: those (Y1) which used "passionate" phrases in their editorials like "life and death", "the future of the country is at stake", "greatest historic moment", "YES to the future", "NO to *immobilisme* and violence".

The second group of YES papers (Y2) conducted a more moderate YES campaign, and were quite explicit on the subject in their editorials. (19 per cent of total circulation.)

The third group of YES papers, instead of shouting slogans, tended more to argue, to weigh up all the pros and cons, but finally concluding that the YES vote was either the best thing, or "a lesser evil". These papers represented 40 per cent of the circulation.

The NO papers were all the Communist papers and three non-Communist papers, of which by far the most important was the *Dépêche du Midi* of Toulouse.

In its final appeal on September 26 the *Dépêche* wrote:

"We are happy not to have left a monopoly of opposition to the Communists. ... As good republicans, with a deep faith in democracy, we sincerely believe that it is our duty to say NO to the authoritarian republic. In making this crucial choice, we are conscious of all the responsibilities we are assuming . . ."

The "uncommitted" papers (13·6 per cent of circulation) avoided editorials, but much of their news was, nevertheless, presented in a manner favourable to de Gaulle. The "undecided" papers, with often contradictory editorials (7 per cent of total circulation) reflected chiefly the indecision of the Radical and Socialist elements, for which they were catering. The same study summed up its analysis of the provincial press as follows:

(Y1, Y2, Y3 = YES papers; N = NO papers; UND = Undecided;
NC1 = Non-committal, with YES bias; NC2 = Strictly non-committal)

	Y1	Y2	Y3	Total	N	UND	NC1	NC2	Total
Proportion of papers (%)	15	18	31	64	10	9	12	5	17
Proportion of circulation (%)	11	19·4	40	70·4	9	7	10	3·6	13·6

Which shows that, in the provinces, over 70 per cent of the papers were
emphatically YES, with a further 15 per cent at least implicitly YES, and
only some 10 per cent definitely NO.

(i) DIRECT GOVERNMENT INTERFERENCE IN THE REFERENDUM

In all other forms of propaganda the NO was severely handicapped by
direct Government intervention. *Graffiti*, scribbles and painted inscriptions on walls, bridges, railway carriages, etc., which had been such a
characteristic feature of all previous French elections and especially
referendums, were discouraged, if not downright prohibited as far as
NO propaganda was concerned. In numerous *départements* the Prefects
issued instructions to the police and highroad services to "erase or remove
all seditious inscriptions, such as 'NO to de Gaulle'."[1]

On September 19 most (if not all) Prefects sent a circular to all the
Mayors of their *département* saying:

"The Ministry of Information has informed me that it has distributed two
official posters in connection with the Referendum:
(1) A National Poster representing flags . . . and printed in three sizes. These
must be displayed in each *commune* . . .
(2) A poster representing a Phrygian Bonnet, with the O in the centre representing the cockade and forming part of the word OUI. . . . This is of
extra-large size and is intended for display along highroads.
Further, various groups have published a number of posters approved by the
Ministry of Information which they themselves will put up in any available
poster space.
Shortly I shall also send you posters representing Rude's *Marseillaise* [the
famous statue below the Arc de Triomphe] urging people to vote YES in the
Referendum. I call upon you to give these posters the greatest prominence in
your *commune*."[2]

In short, Soustelle was using his authority as Minister of Information
not only to subsidize YES propaganda out of Government funds, and for
using official channels for its most effective distribution and display, but
was also using official administrative machinery for helping "private"
organizations to spread their YES propaganda. The Ministry of Information
also kept a close watch on newsreels shown in cinemas; these also invariably added to the propaganda in favour of the YES vote.

[1] Quoted by *Le Monde*, September 24.
[2] Quoted by *France-Observateur*, September 25, 1958.

21. DE GAULLE, ADENAUER AND
AN ANGRY MR. K.

THE last fortnight of the Referendum campaign was marked by several events, the most spectacular of which were the first de Gaulle–Adenauer meeting; the attempt by Algerian terrorists to assassinate Jacques Soustelle; and the formation of an "Algerian Government", which had already been foreshadowed by the Tangier Conference at the end of April.

To the general public the brief visit of Adenauer to Colombey, at de Gaulle's country home, came as a surprise—though, in reality, this meeting had been the object of long preliminary discussions between Paris and Bonn. The German Government was at first reluctant, it seems, to overlook considerations of "seniority"; why should the 83-year-old Chancellor travel all the way to Colombey to visit de Gaulle, a "younger" European leader and younger man? Nor were the Germans very sure what de Gaulle stood for. The "May Revolution" in France had been received with very mixed feeling in Germany, as elsewhere in the West; Western Germany, in particular, remembered that de Gaulle had not only opposed EDC so dear to Adenauer's heart, but had also opposed the Paris Treaties of 1954 providing for the rearmament of Germany and her inclusion in NATO. In the past, he had pursued a variety of policies, ranging from his between-East-and-West or "Third Force" policy of 1945, to his rather fanciful "back-to-Charlemagne's Empire" of 1951, an empire in which France obviously intended to play the leading role. Also, the State Department had given Adenauer not too favourable an account of Dulles's meeting with de Gaulle in June; the Americans were particularly dissatisfied with de Gaulle's desire to see France included in a Three-Power "super-directorate", and her determination to go ahead with her atomic tests whenever she was ready for them, even if, by that time, an agreement to stop all such tests had been reached between the USA, Britain and the USSR. The Germans also knew that Russia was continuing to give de Gaulle the benefit of the doubt, and that the Soviet press was extremely chary of criticizing him, whatever else it said about the "Algiers Fascists". So it took weeks of diplomatic preparations to persuade the Germans that de Gaulle's heart was in the right place. What seems finally to have "converted" de Gaulle to close co-operation with Germany was the total disregard shown to France by Britain and the United States in their handling both of the Quemoy affair and of the Iraq–Lebanon–Jordan crisis of July. Also, in the course of the summer, Fanfani, with the Vatican's blessing, had done the honest broker between de Gaulle and Adenauer, and had persuaded the latter that de Gaulle was a good and loyal "European".

It was very much an old-time country-house party. After lunch de Gaulle and Adenauer talked for several hours; then they were joined for dinner by Couve de Murville, Brentano and various French and German officials. Mme de Gaulle was the hostess. The final communiqué said that the two leaders had "discussed a large number of subjects lengthily, freely and cordially"—

We are deeply conscious of the importance and significance of our meeting. We believe that the old enmity between our two countries must for ever be regarded as a thing of the past. . . . We are convinced that the close co-operation between the Federal Republic of Germany and the French Republic is the foundation for all constructive work in Europe. It contributes to the strength of the Atlantic alliance and is indispensable to the world. We believe that this co-operation must be organized and that it should, at the same time, include the other nations of Western Europe with which our countries are closely connected. We wish it to work to the advantage of all peoples as regards great world problems, and desire it to extend to the largest possible number of European nations.

On the face of it this could mean a great deal—or very little. It was not clear, for instance, what, if anything, had been decided about the Common Market to which de Gaulle was still believed to be unfavourable. All the same, the whole thing seemed to savour of Little Europe, though with a difference. Suspicions were aroused in Britain. In Germany, the press expressed, on the contrary, its "pleasant surprise"; too many Germans still remembered that de Gaulle had, in the past, advocated the ruthless dismemberment of Germany.[1] Whether he was favourable or not to "Little Europe" with its various bits of supra-national machinery, he seemed rather irritated with Britain; and the semi-official Italian press thought the meeting "highly promising".

The French Right-wing press (and, on this occasion, even the *Monde*) grew lyrical over this meeting of "Europe's two most powerful personalities"; it was stressed that no "practical details" had been discussed (such as German economic co-operation in North Africa, or Franco-German nuclear co-operation), but that questions like the Far East and the Middle East and disarmament and the possibility of a summit conference had no doubt been touched upon; though, in the main, the discussion on Franco-German co-operation had been conducted "in terms of general political, historical and philosophical ideas" and with reference to "the real historical and geographical framework of the two countries."[2]

Without meaning anything precise, this kind of Quai-inspired verbiage was, nevertheless, extremely suggestive. The anti-British and anti-American undertones, however faint, were unmistakable. . . .

[1] *Cf.* the author's *France 1940–1955*, parts 2 and 3.
[2] *Le Monde*, September 16, 1958.

Although nothing was announced about the return visit de Gaulle would pay the German Chancellor, there was little doubt that the discussion, so fruitfully started at Colombey, would be resumed before long. Probably very soon after the Referendum. Which is indeed what happened; and at Bad Kreuznach de Gaulle was to go much more thoroughly with Adenauer into a number of subjects which had only been briefly discussed during the first meeting at Colombey. In the words of *Esprit* it was the Kreuznach, rather than the Colombey visit, which marked de Gaulle's "real conversion" to Little Europe.

The most spectacular immediate consequence of the first de Gaulle–Adenauer meeting was an outburst of rage in Moscow. The Soviet press which had, ever since the May events, been extremely cautious in its treatment of de Gaulle, had become openly pro-NO ever since the Referendum campaign had started, though it still pulled its punches where the General himself was concerned. It was not till after the Colombey meeting that *Pravda* brought its heavy artillery into action—in the form of an interview with Khrushchev himself.

"Twenty years after Munich," Khrushchev said, "new efforts are being made to bring about a Franco-German *rapprochement* the purpose of which is to start a new campaign against the nations of Eastern Europe."

Apart from that, Khrushchev now expressed his disappointment with de Gaulle: a few months earlier it was still possible to entertain the hope that the de Gaulle Government "would be willing and anxious to put the Fascist rebels in their place; to end an unjust and wicked war against the Algerian people, and maintain the republican régime in France". But since the "heroes" of May 13 had been promoted on July 14, and paratroopers had been brought to Paris that day, little room was left for illusions. The situation was ominously like the German situation in 1933. Just as the Ruhr magnates had used Hindenburg to put Hitler in power, so French Big Business would now use de Gaulle for setting up a Fascist dictatorship. Already "the military clique" was holding countless key positions in France. Khrushchev sharply attacked the Constitution, and implicitly expressed the hope that the French people would reject it.

The Communist press in France published the interview in full; though whether, at heart, the Communists were happy about it may be doubted. To have Khrushchev take sides in the Referendum did not help the NO vote; and Soustelle was the first to express to Mr. K. his "heartfelt gratitude" for the support he had given to the YES vote.

22. ALGERIANS AGAIN

(a) THE ATTEMPT TO ASSASSINATE SOUSTELLE

IT WAS while Dr. Adenauer, who had stayed the night at La Boisserie, de Gaulle's country house, was about to start on his homeward journey that an event occurred which shook not only France but also Germany.[1]

At 9.30 that morning, in the Avenue Friedland, just off the Etoile, a "commando" of Algerian gunmen tried to assassinate M. Jacques Soustelle.

As Soustelle himself described the incident an hour later, with sticking-plaster covering the cuts he had received from flying glass—

While I was talking to my bodyguard and the chauffeur, I suddenly saw an arm with a revolver emerging through the open window. The barrel of the gun was seven inches from my head. I threw myself on the floor. It was then that the gun went off. When I looked up, I saw that the gunman was running away. My bodyguard and chauffeur were chasing him towards the *métro* station.

Just as I stepped out of the car, I saw another man standing on the pavement producing a tommy-gun from under his raincoat. I threw myself on the ground, and so escaped his bullets. This second gunman then ran towards the rue Tilsitt. He was covering his retreat by firing his gun indiscriminately. When this firing was over, a passer-by asked me if I was wounded, and accompanied me to the door of the Ministry . . .

His face had, indeed, been cut by flying glass, and there were two bullet-holes in his jacket.

Like the second gunman, so the first, too, fired at his pursuers, and killed one unfortunate passer-by and wounded three others. Finally he was caught inside the *métro* by Soustelle's bodyguard and chauffeur, was severely manhandled by the crowd, and taken to hospital in a serious condition. He was a 25-year-old Algerian named Mouloud Ouraghi. The second gunman, after an attempt to escape, was wounded in the stomach by a policeman, and also taken to hospital. He, too, was a 25-year-old Algerian, named Cherouk Abdelafid. Soon afterwards the police caught a third Algerian whom they declared to be an accomplice of the other two. Several other arrests were made in the same neighbourhood during the morning.

At his press conference—held only an hour later—M. Soustelle, looking grim but self-possessed, made a point of stressing that his would-be assassins belonged to "a small fanatical minority" and should not be identified with the Moslem population working in France.

[1] The news from Paris overshadowed in the German press the reports on the de Gaulle-Adenauer meeting, rather with the implication that no serious Franco-German planning was possible as long as "this kind of thing" went on.

(b) "COMMUNIST COLLUSION"

It was the Ministry of the Interior which went out of its way to make political capital out of the attempt to assassinate Soustelle, the most spectacular act of terrorism yet committed by the FLN in France.

"At a time," it said in a communiqué published in the afternoon, "when this terrorist activity is being intensively and effectively repressed, one cannot but denounce the help that these terrorist organizations of the FLN receive from the Communists, from *L'Humanité* and *Libération*. These do not hesitate to weaken the grip of the forces of law and order by conducting a campaign against the police, even though the killers attack the working population itself, which is unanimously opposed to such activities."

Although this was not a very convincing demonstration of Communist "complicity" in the attempt to assassinate Soustelle, the purpose of the communiqué was, nevertheless, to suggest in this rather vague way that there was a connection between Algerian terrorists and the Communists and their papers. . . . The very tortuousness of the sentence, when read over the radio dozens of times, helped to put this idea across:

> Communists = FLN.
> Communists = Terrorism.
> Communists = Murder.
> Communists = Treason.
> Communists = NO vote.
> Communists = Trouble awaits them.

On September 17 it was semi-officially announced that:

The competent services are studying the measures which may be taken after the Referendum in virtue of Art. 92 of the Draft Constitution authorizing the Government to take by ordinance "any measures necessary to the life of the nation, the protection of citizens and the safeguard of freedoms". (*Le Monde*, September 18.)

On the face of it, all this was aimed at suspect Algerians living in France, particularly those "without any definite sources of income". But one never could tell what mightn't be done under Article 92. Radio-Algiers promptly started attacking the "treason press".

As regards the Algerians themselves, one proposal which, it was reported, the Government was now considering was "the extension of the present 24-hour legal limit for the interrogation of suspects".

It must, of course, be said that, by and large, the general public were wholly in favour of getting tough with the Algerians; this applied not least to the working class in Paris, who in certain "Algerian-infested" parts of the Paris area had more direct contacts with the "North-Africans" than the bourgeoisie had; and who, on the whole, did not care for the *sidis* at all.

On the other hand, the attempt to assassinate Soustelle produced the kind of political reactions that might have been expected. Soustelle himself was the first to say: "Just shows that one can't negotiate with these people", a statement repeated over and over again on the radio, rather to the annoyance of Socialists like Defferre, who were supporting the YES vote precisely because they were hoping that de Gaulle would negotiate a peace settlement with the FLN. The FLN leaders, for their part, weren't making things any easier. According to a United Press report from Cairo, Ferhat Abbas told its correspondent on the day of the Etoile shooting:

These attempts to assassinate the Soustelles and Lacostes will continue. The latest attempt is not going to be the last one. The campaign we are conducting in France is achieving its object: already France has been compelled to bring troops back from Germany to protect oil refineries and other strategic objectives.

During the days that followed the attempt on Soustelle's life, there were numerous other terrorist acts in France, while the police were busy rounding up thousands of Algerians all over the place; in the Paris area alone several hundred persons were detained, and several thousands interrogated.

(c) THE "FREE ALGERIAN GOVERNMENT"

It was in this unhealthy atmosphere that the news broke on September 18 that a "Free Algerian Government" was about to be formed. The decision was announced by "a spokesman of the FLN" in Cairo. It was on the day on which M. Couve de Murville, the French Foreign Minister, declared at the United Nations that it was "not competent" to discuss Algeria, and that if there were a debate, France would boycott it, even though the bureau of the General Assembly had recommended the inclusion of Algeria in the agenda. It was "an internal French affair", and under Article 2, paragraph 6, of the Charter, UN had no right to interfere. This was the line that had already been taken by M. Antoine Pinay, the then Foreign Minister, in 1955; later, his successor, M. Christian Pineau, while unwilling to discuss Algeria with UN, had nevertheless agreed to "inform" the General Assembly on what France was doing or planning to do in Algeria. It was, indeed, largely for the benefit of UN that the Guy Mollet Government had, in January 1957, produced its famous "triptych"—cease-fire, elections, negotiations. Now it was a complete return to the old "hands-off" attitude.

There were numerous reasons why the FLN decided to set up a Free Algerian Government just at that time. The decision was intended to strengthen the Algerians' desire to boycott the Referendum; it was also meant to create international complications for France; it was certain that all the Arab countries, and in the first place Nasser's UAR, Tunisia and Morocco would recognize the Algerian Government; India, Indonesia, China and some, if not all, the members of the Soviet bloc would probably do so, too. And perhaps even some Western powers. In Tunis where, according to the *Monde* correspondent, the formation of the Free Algerian Government had been received "with enthusiasm", it was reckoned that no fewer than thirty governments would recognize it, among them two or three non-Communist European states, three Latin-American republics, all the Arab and Communist states, besides several "uncommitted" African and Asian countries. The FLN and their Tunisian friends were being distinctly over-optimistic.

The Algerian "government", the formation of which was announced simultaneously in Cairo, Tunis and Rabat, was composed of nineteen members, of whom the Vice-Premier, Ahmed Ben Bella, and the four Ministers of State, Hocine Ait Ahmed, Boudiaf, Khider and Bitat Rabah, were in jail in France.

The "prime minister" was *Ferhat Abbas* (59), a moderate Algerian nationalist who had played a prominent role in Algerian affairs for the last twenty years, first as a supporter of "assimilation", then as leader of the UDMA (*Union Démocratique du Manifeste Algérien*), in which capacity he was member of various French and Algerian assemblies between 1945 and 1955.

After the Algerian rebellion had broken out in November 1954, Ferhat Abbas hoped that the war could be nipped in the bud if the French quickly produced a plan of far-reaching reforms; and it was not till April 1956 (i.e. after Lacoste's appointment to Algiers) that, giving up all hope of an early peaceful solution, he openly identified himself with the FLN. But even in 1958 he continued to be regarded by many French observers as a "moderate", who was anxious to negotiate a settlement with the French.

Ben Bella (42), who had a distinguished war record in the French Army, had belonged since 1948 to a secret organization which ultimately prepared the insurrection of Novmeber 1954, when the French forces in Algeria were at their lowest ebb. Though regarded as being much tougher than Ferhat Abbas, Ben Bella was nevertheless willing to consider a peaceful settlement with the help of the Tunisian and Moroccan Governments when, in October 1956, he and four others had their plane—in which they were travelling to the Tunis Conference—intercepted by the Algiers authorities.[1]

Krim Belcacem (36), who had also served in the French Army with distinction, but later became one of the chief organizers of the rebellion, was Minister of the Armed Forces in the Algerian Government.

[1] See the author's *The Strange History of Pierre Mendès-France*, pp. 152-6, 246-8, etc.

Dr. *Lamine Debaghine* (41), the Foreign Minister, was considered as one of the most extreme members of the Government, opposed to any negotiations.

Dr. *Ahmed Francis* (48), the Minister of Finance, was, on the contrary, a "moderate", and a close associate of Ferhat Abbas. But like most of the "ministers" he had been a member of the CRUA, the *Comité révolutionnaire d'unité et d'action*, which had directed the rebellion at its early stages.[1]

Mohammed Yazid (34), the Minister of Information, was, like most members of the Algerian Government, a man of French culture and education; he had actually graduated at the Paris Law Faculty; both his father and grandfather had been officers in the French Army. As a member of the "Messalist" MTLD he was arrested in 1948 and sentenced to two years' imprisonment for having written an article in favour of Algerian independence. After the outbreak of the insurrection, he went to Cairo, and went from there on numerous propaganda trips abroad. By 1958 he had become a familiar figure in New York, being the "permenent delegate of the FLN at UN". He was regarded in France as one of the more moderate members of the "government".

Mahmoud Cherif (44), the Minister of Armaments and Supplies, had fought in the French Army in Indo-China. After the Algerian insurrection had begun, he became commander of the rebel forces in the vital Aurès-Nementchas region, where the rebellion had started.

The "government" also included Ministers of the Interior, of Social Affairs, of Cultural Affairs, etc.

Immediately all the Arab countries recognized the Algerian Government—the UAR, Iraq, Libya, Yemen, Saudi Arabia, Tunisia and Morocco. The only exception was the Lebanon. A few days later it was also recognized by China. Both the Tunisian and especially the Moroccan Government went out of their way to say that this would not "in any way" affect their relations with France. The French Foreign Office, while warning everybody that France would consider any recognition of the Algerian Government as "an unfriendly act", did not at this stage go much beyond that. It was apparent after a few days that the Algerian leaders' hope of being recognized by thirty countries was wide of the mark.

The Soviet Union, though very annoyed with France ever since the de Gaulle–Adenauer meeting of September 14–15 (which seemed to Moscow to foreshadow, among other things, the outlawing of the French Communist Party) seemed, nevertheless, hesitant about recognizing the Algerian "government".

On the American side, the State Department announced on September 22 that there was no question of the USA recognizing the "Provisional Government of Algeria"; nevertheless, Mr. Raymond Hare, the US Ambassador in Cairo, had a long talk with two of its "ministers", M'Hamed Yazid and Ahmed Francis. They did not come to ask for recognition by the USA, but merely "to inform the US Government of the circumstances in which the Algerian Government had been formed".

[1] *Cf. France 1940–1955*, p. 732.

One of the first acts of the "Provisional Government of the Algerian Republic" (for that was its official title) was to protest to UN against the Referendum being held in Algeria. It was, it said, "an act of international political mystification", and the Algerian Government would "oppose it by every means at its disposal". If the Referendum were held, "it might lead to very grave consequences, for which France would have to bear the sole responsibility".

The Algerian leaders further informed Mr. Hammerskjoeld that France was employing 800,000 soldiers and policemen in her Referendum campaign in Algeria, and that the Algerian people would be forced to vote at the point of a bayonet.

These protests were, as we shall presently see, perfectly justified; but there wasn't much that Mr. Hammerskjoeld could do about it. . . .

23. SMALL-TOWN REFERENDUM DIARY

IT SO happened that I spent the last twelve days of the Referendum campaign in South-west France, with my headquarters at what I shall call Vignac-sur-Vézère, a small market town of 2,500 inhabitants. On the eve of polling day, September 28, I returned to Paris.

Vignac, in the heart of the Périgord country in the Dordogne department, on the southern fringes of the Massif Central, is in a traditionally "Left" department, though its "Leftism" is mostly of a "moderate", and sometimes plainly suspect character. Among its deputies returned in 1956 there were two famous names: Lacoste, the diehard Minister for Algeria, and, secondly, a notorious pre-war figure, who after years of non-eligibility, had now made a comeback with 40,000 votes—Ribbentrop's old friend, the long-nosed M. Georges Bonnet. Both were local *notables*, which counts more than anything else in this still rather "Third Republic" part of the country. There was also one Communist deputy, and over 30 per cent of the poll had gone to the Communists, though the constituency was predominantly rural. Though no Poujadist was elected in 1956, Poujade influences were strong among the shopkeepers and for at least two years my friend the ironmonger, M. Rousset, had a VIVE POUJADE sign displayed in his shop-window in the midst of the nails and screws and pots and pans. M. Tourné, the garrulous carpenter, who also owned a more or less authentic prehistoric cave some miles away, where he took tourists in summer, and had latterly also bought one of the largest cafés in the town, was a member of the Communist Party, and No. 1 Communist in the town; but in 1956 he developed a great liking for Poujade, and, I suspect, even voted for him, because Poujade had the "right ideas" about Algeria: the only way, Tourné said, in which to end "all the nonsense" there was to kill off a million or so Algerians, and the Communists just lacked such a "constructive policy". Tourné claimed to have been very active in the local Communist *maquis* during the war, but also to have saved the life of Maurice Chevalier who, as an alleged "collaborator", had been hiding in the neighbourhood.

"I knew there'd be hell to pay if we bumped off Maurice Chevalier, so I told the chaps to lay off. . . . That was on the day when we rounded up the headquarters of the Pétain *milice*, and shot three of the fellows in the market square . . ."

People in the town were a bit doubtful about the great role Tourné had played in the Resistance, especially some of the genuine Resisters in the town, Roumany the grocer and Perroux the stonemason.

Many of the other shopkeepers were, however, *attentistes* during the war, with a soft spot for Pétain, and with little sympathy for either of the *maquis* active in the neighbourhood, the non-Communist one, and the Communist one.

The head of the local branch of the Pétain *Légion* was M. Géraud, one of the local squires, an elderly gentleman with a grey handle-bar moustache, wearing riding-breeches, a silk shirt and a bow tie. He was credited (or debited) with having negotiated the non-destruction of Vignac with the Germans as these were, in June 1944, rushing through the Dordogne to Normandy, and destroying in the process several villages suspected of Resistance activity. Quite near Vignac they thus burned down Rouffignac, and, further north, near Limoges, they massacred the whole population of Oradour-sur-Glane. . . . In May 1958 M. Géraud began to form, together with another local worthy, a Committee of Public Safety, and tried to win over the support of the five men of the local *gendarmerie*; but these told him to go and chase himself. . . .

The town council, with its seventeen members, was predominantly Radical-Socialist, though it concerned itself entirely with local affairs, and politics scarcely entered into it.

M. *le curé*, who had been both pro-Pétain and anti-German during the war, was proud of the fact that practically all the women went to his ugly big church, built around 1875, even though some of the men were still so anti-clerical that, even at a funeral, they would stay outside the church rather than go in. But even these, he told me, were, almost without exception, married in church and when they were dead, their womenfolk saw to it that they were given a religious funeral!

There were a lot of shopkeepers and artisans of various kinds in the town, and one or two little local industries had latterly sprung up, notably a fruit and vegetable canning factory on the banks of the Vézère; for weeks at the end of summer, it kept a large part of the population, especially all the old women, busy shelling peas and threading beans. Later in the autumn the same people hammered away for days, shelling walnuts. There were also several little enterprises in the town making truffled *pâtés* and other *spécialités du Périgord*. The peasants in the neighbourhood went in for mixed crops, the most important among them being tobacco. The wine, of poor quality, was only locally consumed.

It was here that I spent most of those twelve days before the Referendum.

Vignac, September 15. Took the train at Austerlitz this morning, arriving here about 7 p.m. "What the hell are they up to in Paris?" were the first words I heard at Vignac. They were uttered by M. Lalou, who runs the ramshackle old bus from the station to Vignac, about two miles away. "Why, what's wrong?" "Haven't you heard? The Algerians have tried to bump off Soustelle." "WHAT???" And he told me what he had heard on the radio, adding: "They say the Communists are mixed up in it somehow. I don't quite see how, but that's what they say . . ."

In the town they were all talking about it tonight. M. Tourné said he had very little use for Soustelle—"even though he's got the right ideas on Algeria"—but he thought it was high time they started getting tough with the *bicots*. Thank God, we haven't any here, but it must be hell in Paris. They should round up the whole damned lot and send them back to where they have come from." M. Dufour, the baker, thought, however, differently. "*Le torchon brûle*," he said, "the whole thing stinks. . . . Are you sure it isn't a put-up job? A police provocation?" I must confess that the thought had crossed my mind, too, especially when I heard the stories about *L'Humanité* and *Libération* being implicated in the attempt to assassinate Soustelle. *Reichstag Fire???* But no; it couldn't be possible. . . . It was much too close a shave for Soustelle. . . . All the same, wasn't somebody—especially the radio and the Ministry of the Interior—making good use of the whole thing in the Referendum campaign? . . .

September 16. Campaign? Well, there really isn't any campaign. At least, not here at Vignac. So far, no YES posters, no NO posters, no scribbles one way or the other. Bought large collection of papers at the Vignac paper shop this morning, both Paris and local (Bordeaux and Limoges). Tremendous headlines, especially in the Right-wing papers about the attempt to murder Soustelle.

A notice in the paper shop: "FULL TEXT OF THE DRAFT CONSTITUTION: 20 frs."

"How many have you sold?" I asked Mme Leroy.

"Three copies," she said. "People are not interested. I have tried to read it. Don't understand it. People don't have to read it; they'll vote for de Gaulle anyway."

"It's very odd," said M. Fauré, the café proprietor, who is also a Radical-Socialist member on the town council, "but nobody knows what they are voting for. Nobody, literally nobody, had read the Constitution."

"Have you?"

"*Pensez-vous!* I haven't time."

"But you are going to vote YES?"

"I don't know. I'll have to think about it," he said, getting cagey and non-committal. Then he added: "There's something to be said for de Gaulle, you know. After all, he did save us from civil war. If it hadn't been for him, there would have been hell to pay. Look at old man Géraud trying to set up in May a *comité de salut public*. Yes, even here, at Vignac. And in Toulouse and Lyon they really meant business, it was touch and go, what with all those Fascist 'repatriates' from North Africa with Toulouse as their headquarters, and with the local commander, General Miquel, threatening to march his troops on Paris. . . . My brother, who lives in Toulouse, was telling me about it when he came here a week ago."

"At Toulouse," I said, "they publish the *Dépêche*, which is one of the few all-out NO papers."

"Yes, I know," said Fauré. "We don't get it here; the train connections are bad; wouldn't get here till the afternoon; so what we get is the Bordeaux papers, and they are 100 per cent YES. . . . Anyway, my brother says the *Dépêche* doesn't cut much ice, and a lot of people have stopped reading it, because of its NO line . . ."[1]

More Algerian acts of terrorism reported in the press today. Three soldiers wounded at Joinville, one killed; other shootings at Metz and Lyon. Bombs thrown at Marseille: some dead and wounded. Angry comments heard at Vignac. No comments on Sekou Touré's announcement that Guinea would vote NO. Except from Fauré: "Didn't de Gaulle go a bit far, all the same, telling the Black African colonies they could vote for independence? . . . If they do, won't it just mean that England or America will take them over? . . ." And then: "Do you really think de Gaulle will end the war in Algeria? The radio has been saying, especially after the Soustelle business: 'You can't negotiate with *these* people.' I see the Socialist Congress has followed Defferre; and Defferre believes de Gaulle will make peace in Algeria; wonder what he thinks now, after what Soustelle has said?" . . .

September 17. Long talk with *Monsieur le curé*. "All that has happened was quite inevitable," he said. "Parliamentary government in this country was completely discredited. Just talk to some of the people here; you'll

---

[1] This was scarcely true: the circulation of the *Dépêche*, without going up, had remained stable throughout August-September. Later, it lost 4 per cent of its circulation.

see how furious they are with the deputies. Things just didn't hang together; these Government changes were quite exasperating."

"What do you think of de Gaulle and the Constitution?" I ventured.

"Things have been better since de Gaulle took over, I assure you. The Constitution—not that I have studied it closely—seems all right. It will mean stabler government. And I think de Gaulle is a man to be trusted."

"Yes, I know," I said, "he's a good Catholic. But then—Article 2 of the Constitution says that France will be a *laïque* republic; are you quite satisfied with that, *Monsieur le curé*?"

The old man smiled. "*Laïque, laïque*—it's just a word. After all, the Fourth Republic, too, was *laïque*; that didn't stop it from passing the *loi Barangé* in '51. *Cher monsieur*, believe me, this country is not feeling strongly about *laïcité* one way or the other. A great many people in this town are not very *croyant* or very *pratiquant*, but when in trouble, they still come to see the *curé*; most of the people whose fathers never came near a church, now get married in church and send their children to first Communion.

"They can talk about *laïcité* as much as they like (though they hardly ever do); but they won't start fighting on the barricades if the new Parliament passes another *loi Barangé*, a bigger and better one, as we hope.

"When I was a young man, *on bouffait du curé* in this part of the country, people swore by *le petit père* Combes. After World War I all this was largely forgotten; true, the Radicals and Socialists still used to make a lot of noise about it—about Poincaré having been married in church, and all that sort of thing. But since the last war, even our wilder anti-clericals have been terribly meek and mild. Besides, haven't you seen in to-day's paper what the French Cardinals are saying about the Constitution? They say that the word '*laïque*' in the Constitution need not prevent Catholics from voting freely on September 28." He again smiled knowingly.

"Does that mean the Cardinals are calling on the faithful to vote YES?"

"Good heavens, no," said *M. le curé*, "it merely means that it isn't at all necessary for a good Catholic to vote NO."

"Doesn't it amount to the same thing?" I said. He gave me a funny look. "No, no, it simply means that people should be guided by their own conscience, and that the word *laïque* doesn't mean as much as some imagine it might mean. A little guidance, a little guidance, that's all . . ."

Sure enough, the Cardinals did take a stand on this yesterday. It seems that some Catholics had, on the strength of this word *laïque*, been advocating abstention, or even a NO vote. In the Basque country, in particular, where Spanish influences are strong, this movement seems to have taken on quite sizeable proportions.

So today the Cardinals of France—Liénard, Gerlier, Feltin, Roques and Grente—issued the following statement:

In view of the uneasiness existing among certain Catholics in connection with the coming Referendum, the Cardinals of France, while bearing in mind the indications already given with great authority by a number of bishops to their dioceses, wish to make the following joint statement:

(1) They disapprove of the inopportune propaganda calling on Catholics to abstain, or to reject the Draft Constitution by *solely* invoking the demands of their faith;

(2) They consider that neither the absence of any reference to God (however painful to a Catholic) . . . nor the use of the word "*laïque*", which may lend itself to a variety of interpretations—though the Draft Constitution emphasized the respect of all beliefs—can prevent Catholics from expressing their will freely in respect of the Constitution. . . .

In a third paragraph the Cardinals warned the faithful against abstention, all the more so as the outcome of the Referendum affected the most vital interests of France; finally, they called on the faithful to pray and meditate before voting. The last phrase was particularly telling:

"They pray for the day when it will be possible, with the agreement of all citizens, to let the name of God figure in the text governing the institutions of France."

It seemed pretty obvious even to those ill-acquainted with the subtleties of Cardinals' pronouncements that a YES vote was more likely than a NO vote to bring that blessed day nearer.

In the next few days several bishops openly told the faithful to vote YES.

Monday, September 22. I spent a good part of this week-end listening to de Gaulle on the radio and trying to follow his Referendum campaign—which, after the fiasco of the Place de la République on September 4, he decided to limit to four of the least "dangerous" large cities: Rennes, Bordeaux, Strasbourg and Lille. In Lille alone was he liable to meet with some very severe opposition.

At Vignac on Saturday I was offered a free lift to Bordeaux—less than a hundred miles from here.

Bordeaux was black with police; the Soustelle business really seems to have scared the pants off them; and de Gaulle's plan to have a more-or-less policeless "meeting with the people" had to be abandoned. For a few seconds, in the Cours de l'Intendance, I could see de Gaulle, dressed in mufti, drive down in an open car. Later, from a very respectful distance, I could see him speak for a few minutes from the balcony of the Hôtel de Ville, with Chaban-Delmas by his side. There was a lot of cheering,

and a little booing, and cries of NO, and one young man threw into the
air a handful of NO leaflets; the police were soon on top of him, and he
was taken away with a bloody face. . . .

What did this two-day "campaign" really add up to? Radio and TV
made, of course, the most of it. But these were the things that characterized the lightning trip: (1) Again, as in Paris, the "sheep" were carefully
separated from the "goats"; tremendous security measures were taken
everywhere, so much so that the reasonably *bien-pensant* city of Rennes
found it all a little disconcerting: all this display of immense police forces
all over the place, the search of hotels, the rounding-up of "suspects", etc.
(2) Priority given by de Gaulle to the various local worthies who had been
invited by the hundred to the receptions organized in the town halls;
at these gatherings de Gaulle was "making contact" with the various local
"personalities", and asking all the right questions: thus, at Bordeaux, he
asked how the grape harvest was getting on; at Lille "whether and to what
extent they were feeling the recession", and "how much new housing
did they think they wanted"; the short speeches delivered to the more or
less "selected" crowds—10,000 at Bordeaux, for instance—were delivered
as a sort of supplement to the main proceedings. (3) The cities de Gaulle
visited were not decorated with flags, except in those places where he was
to speak, and the flags were national flags, without the Cross of Lorraine;
notwithstanding, at Strasbourg, de Gaulle laid a Cross-of-Lorraine-cum-
V-sign wreath on the war memorial. Altogether, it seems that, of the
four cities he visited, he was given the warmest reception of all at Strasbourg. (4) With the exception of Bordeaux, the Church was very prominent in all these ceremonies and receptions. At Lille, de Gaulle's native
city, he spent some time at the big town hall reception talking to Cardinal
Liénart; at Strasbourg on the Sunday morning with all the church bells
ringing he and the ministers accompanying him (among them M.
Pflimlin) drove for High Mass to the Cathedral. Here, after the Kyrie,
sung by the Cathedral choir, Mgr. Weber, the Bishop of Strasbourg,
addressed a warm tribute to General de Gaulle, and ended the service
with "a prayer for the Republic" . . . It was all vaguely reminiscent of
Pétain's visits to provincial cities.

What then was the purpose of this tour, apart from its obvious propaganda value to the press, radio and especially TV—which, as usual,
managed to "delete" a few discordant notes like the handful of NO
demonstrators at Rennes, Lille and Bordeaux "who were quickly
eliminated by the police"? It is certain that radio and TV managed to
give the impression that there was overwhelming mass enthusiasm in the
country for de Gaulle.

But what did de Gaulle actually say? The truth is that, during those four
visits to Rennes, Bordeaux, Strasbourg and Lille, he continued to talk
in riddles, to be all things to all men, but stressed on every occasion

the extreme importance of not only a YES vote, but of a *massive* YES
vote.

At Rennes he spoke of the special bonds of friendship that seemed to
unite him, especially during the war, to Brittany.

"Even this brief contact is sufficient to show me how united and patriotic the
people of Rennes are, how well they understand a question, how well they understand a situation . . ."

At the Town Hall meeting de Gaulle spoke of Algeria.

The Moslems are Moslems. But we must give them reasons for feeling that,
by and large, they are French. . . . It's a long and arduous task. There can be neither
complete independence nor integration in the sense given by many to the word. . . .

Then, in making a public speech, he referred to the grave dangers of
the international situation. He did not think a catastrophe was in sight,
but it was essential for France to be strong and united. Again he spoke of
his bonds with Rennes and with Brittany ("I feel I am among real
friends here!" *Cries of "Yes"!*) And then again:

This country has been governed by antiquated institutions, by inadequate
institutions; what has happened is merely the expression of everybody's very calm
and positive will. . . . I believe France will say YES in the Referendum, but there
is something more I want to ask of you: and that is that there should be an
immense number of YES votes, that there should be a *massive* majority. Only such
a massive and crushing majority can demonstrate the unity of France to the
outside world; then its internal solidity and its international dignity will be assured
for many years to come. It will also be a tribute to the man now speaking to you.
It is a tribute I need.

At Bordeaux, at Strasbourg, at Lille, he made similar appeals for "a
massive vote". And France's unity and France's greatness were the ever-
recurring themes. Thus at Lille:

We have all the means to be prosperous, happy and great. We have these means
within us, within our activity, within our minds and within our hearts. To
achieve our aim—and we must achieve it in a world that is hard and dangerous—
we must, first of all, reshape the institutions of the Republic in a manner which
would place the necessary means at the disposal of its responsible leaders. . . . This
is the sole object of the reform proposed to the country. . . . When you will have
voted YES how immense a new hope will rise in our hearts, in this dear, hard-
working department of the Nord, in this proud and noble city of Lille! You will
realize it, I promise you, on Monday week . . .

And at Strasbourg:

Now we all see that a straight road lies ahead of us. No doubt, it will not be easy. A great country like ours has always obstacles to overcome. Such is the price of greatness. A great future, I say. Listen to me, young men and young girls! Listen to the old man that I am, an old man who has seen so much in his life. You have a magnificent country. You are the children of a country full of greatness and with a rich future. Once and for all our economic activity has passed beyond the routine stage . . .

This "old man" theme was not overplayed, but it no doubt had its purpose, too. It linked up with the assurance he gave France in May that "one did not become a dictator at the age of sixty-seven"; it struck the right paternalist note that goes down well with many Frenchmen; it also fitted into the tradition under which old men always come to France's rescue in moments of danger: Clemenceau in 1917, Poincaré in 1926, Doumergue in 1934, finally, Pétain in 1940. The Pétain analogy was not necessarily distasteful to everybody. It was also meant to remind de Gaulle's audience that it was the relatively young men who had made a mess of the Fourth Republic. Psychologically, the "old man" theme was not irrelevant either: de Gaulle was not the popular dashing young demagogue; rather than popular in the ordinary sense, he was the respected father symbol. That is why at Bordeaux de Gaulle took it very badly when a young woman threw her arms round him and kissed him; he gave her such a stern look that, full of confusion, the damsel retreated; muttering: "*Pardon, mon général* . . ."

Vignac, September 24. Four more days to go till the Referendum, and it still isn't quite clear how big a majority de Gaulle will get. 65 per cent, as the Prefects now say; or 60 per cent, as they were saying a month ago; or *much* more, as some papers have been saying: 75 or even 80 per cent? It's hard to say, because people are extremely cagey on how they are going to vote.

Long and unusually interesting talk today with M. Legrand, the *professeur*, the secondary school teacher living at Vignac.

"I am puzzled," I said to him. "I have followed half-a-dozen general election campaigns in France and one or two referendum campaigns. People never hesitated to tell you then how they would vote; usually, they announced it for everyone to hear. But this time it's different. I have tried to 'pump' twenty or thirty people; only two clearly said which way they were going to vote: one of them a railwayman, and a Communist *militant*; the other M. Fauré, our Radical town councillor, who yesterday told me definitely he was going to vote YES. But all the others would say: 'I don't know yet; I'll have to think about it . . .' And that sort of thing. One would think they were scared of something . . ."

"You are damned right," said M. Legrand. "They *are* scared. *Ils ont la frousse.* Perhaps the most significant thing in this town is what happened last week. There were two political meetings: one for the YES vote, held by one of our *indépendant* town councillors, another for the NO vote, held by a Communist who had come here from Périgueux. Well, there were *four* people at the YES meeting, and *two* at the Communist meeting! Both were a complete washout. You will have noticed that, apart from a few posters—nearly all of them YES posters, for the printing and distribution of which not only the Government but Big Business have spent hundreds of millions—there are practically no YES or NO *graffiti* to be seen anywhere. The Prefects, it is true, have been ordered (at the taxpayers' expense, if you please!) to rub out all the NO scribbles; but in this part of the country, at any rate, there's no need for them to do anything; the NO scribbles are just as scarce as the YES scribbles. Also, people here have long memories. And they know that this is an unusual situation, something not quite 'normal'. They remember Vichy. They remember that many Vichyites had a rough time during the Liberation, and they think that if it's known that they have voted YES, they might have trouble if and when the Fifth Republic comes to an end! And those who intend to vote NO think they might get it in the neck right away, if it's known how they've voted."

"Are they absolutely sure," I said, "of the secrecy of the vote this time?"

"There again," said Legrand, "it's hard to tell. I think a good number may have some doubts on the subject. After all, they've been hearing about the extremely dubious YES vote that's going to be extracted from Algeria; and although there's always been a lot of hanky-panky about elections in Algeria, they are not so sure there won't be some hanky-panky here, too, this time. This little shadow of doubt may increase the YES vote. People are impressed by the fact that all the strength seems to be on the side of the YES people; just listen to the radio! And Soustelle, with his stories about the Communists being accomplices of the FLN, has tended to scare a few timid souls."

"But what would you say was their attitude to de Gaulle?"

"I think," said Legrand, "that there's a good deal of respect for the man. Hero-worship, no. But a great respect—undoubtedly. And a feeling of gratitude. The idea has certainly very successfully been put across that de Gaulle saved us from civil war in May. The French Algerians are heartily disliked, I can tell you, and the generals—the Massus and Salans and Miquels—are distrusted. It is felt that if anyone can keep them in order, de Gaulle can. Will he? I'm damned if *I* know; but people are prepared to take a chance on it. Also, let's face it, parliamentary government, with its Mollets and Bourgèses and Gaillards, is pretty discredited in the eyes of the people; they want a change; they want a 'strong' government, and a stable government: it's happened so often in French history before. They are ready to take a chance with de Gaulle, whom they trust . . . up to a point. There's a feeling that there isn't really much

of an alternative; for another idea that's been successfully put across is
that they've got to choose between de Gaulle and the paratroopers who
would bring civil war to France. Will de Gaulle and Soustelle and the
rest of them get tough after they've won in the Referendum? Some are
rather afraid of it. But many, as I already said, are a little scared to vote
NO—somehow or other it might be known. . . . I must say the Algerian
terrorists haven't made things any easier for the NO people; I am sure the
feeling has grown that if Algerians start shooting at Cabinet ministers
in broad daylight in the centre of Paris, a strong hand at the helm is
necessary. For there's a good deal of hatred for the Algerians in France. . . .
On the other hand, there are many who have been impressed by Defferre's
argument that de Gaulle is more likely than anybody else to end the war
in Algeria. People are sick of it, and they are clutching at this straw;
they are not sure whether he will end the war there; but the fact that he
wasn't too polite to the *Comité de Salut Public* thugs in Algiers has made
rather a good impression here. . . ."

"But, surely, this is a traditionally 'republican' part of the country, and
the Constitution . . ."

"Oh, the Constitution," said Legrand, "I don't think more than two or
three people at Vignac have read it, and even those who have aren't sure
what it all means. Yes—this part of the country is 'republican', as you say.
There was a good deal of Resistance here during the war; but, after all,
for an awfully long time people were quite happy about Pétain. And then
—after the big scare in May (and it *was* quite a scare, I can tell you), what
with rumours of paratroopers landing in Paris and Bordeaux, and Massu
setting up a Gestapo, life has, after all, gone back to normal. Economically, things are going on quite nicely, and if we are going to have new
taxes, de Gaulle will be damned sure not to introduce any till after the
general election; and people don't look very far ahead where that's
concerned."

"What about all the Poujade boys who were so numerous here two
years ago?"

"That's nothing. Although Poujade is urging people to vote NO, he
cuts no ice. Why should he? The Poujade boys were screaming for a
strong government: well, they've got one. That's the main thing to them.
In so far as Poujade has any influence left at all, it's among the 'activists' in
Algiers, who are now beginning to scream against de Gaulle; but here,
in the Dordogne, they don't matter a hang any longer. The local Poujadists
simply feel that de Gaulle and Soustelle—that is, people much smarter and
much more powerful than Poujade—have succeeded where Poujade
failed."

"In short, you think there's going to be a huge YES vote?"

"Huge?—I don't know; but a pretty big one, though how big is
extremely hard to say. People are slightly scared (the Soustelle shooting

has certainly added to the feeling of uneasiness); they are cagey and non-committal; they are keeping their thoughts to themselves. They won't even tell you very clearly what they really think of de Gaulle. At the Café des Sports the other night, they watched de Gaulle on TV doing his stuff; they looked on in almost complete silence. It was really quite uncanny. Yet I know for certain that several people there were 'pro', and a few were 'anti'; but neither made any comment . . ."

"Is the Church playing a big part in the YES propaganda?"

"Well," said Legrand, "the *curé* here is a nice old chap, as you know. A funny chap in some ways. He liked Pétain, and is a bit distrustful of de Gaulle. He's also very much against *les députés*. But, as far as I know, he hasn't been saying much, though no doubt if pressed for advice, he'd tell people to vote YES. But he hasn't said much openly. Maybe he, too, is a little scared . . ."

"And you?"

"Ah, well, people know that practically all the *instituteurs* and *professeurs* of France are against the Constitution. At least *en principe*. At the same time, many of them think the NO vote inexpedient. I am going to vote NO, but I am not ramming my views down anybody's throat; what's the good? By now everybody's pretty well made up his mind which way he is going to vote. And it isn't much use telling people that the damned Constitution is thoroughly unsound and dangerous; and what will happen if de Gaulle dies? etc., etc. In some ways they look very far ahead (hence the general secrecy), in other ways they don't. They are, in fact, voting for the *status quo*. Things have been reasonably all right in the last few months, and long may it continue. . . . De Gaulle's 'Operation Chloroform', as you called it the other day, has been a complete success. An awful lot of our good republicans—Radicals and Socialists—just don't believe there's going to be a Fascist régime in France; they don't think de Gaulle will set one up; anyway, what they say is: 'Let's give him a chance. If he betrays the Republic, then the whole of Republican France,' etc., etc. They then trot out the old *lutte républicaine* claptrap of the Third Republic. It doesn't mean much. But it's a good mental alibi. . . . And also, let's face it, they *don't* like the Communists, and that's why there was no Popular Front in May, either in Paris or anywhere else—except, up to a point, at Toulouse, where they were *really* conscious of a Fascist danger."

"So it isn't a referendum really; it's just a plebiscite?"

"Why, of course," Legrand said.

"Didn't you see in the papers today," I said, "that Jean-Paul Sartre now says that 'To vote for de Gaulle is to invite the colonels to take over'?"

"No, I haven't read the article. But if you read it to the shopkeepers at Vignac, they'd just dismiss it as intellectual acrobatics. My feeling is that most of them are convinced that it's *plain good common sense* to vote for de Gaulle, though, as we know, very few will tell you so openly."

"And what do people think of all this *grandeur française* that de Gaulle loves talking about?"

"*Grandeur, grandeur*," said Legrand, "that's just de Gaulle all over. I doubt whether it makes all that much impression. People realize only too well that there are really only two great world powers, Russia and America. De Gaulle's *grandeur* landed us in the Indo-China war; but we *have* been kicked around by the Americans, and American interference in Tunisia annoyed people quite a lot last spring, as you may remember. Personally I am not at all impressed when we are now told that *we* are going to explode an atom bomb in the Sahara next month; nor do I much care for all this hobnobbing with Adenauer. A smack in the eye for the British and the Americans? I don't know. Nobody can really make much sense of de Gaulle's foreign policy so far; but that isn't an issue, anyway, in the Referendum . . ."

Paris, Saturday, September 27. I got back to Paris last night. In the train from Limoges people were talking chiefly about Algerian terrorism. Was there a subconscious fear that the Algerians might now start derailing trains? The papers were full of stories of how "The Eiffel Tower Was Nearly Blown Up". At a Cabinet meeting on Wednesday (banner headlines about it in *Paris-Presse*) an "Anti-Terrorist Plan" was adopted; but this would not be revealed until after the Referendum when, under Article 92 of the Constitution, the Government would be empowered to "adopt all measures it considered necessary for the protection of citizens". Is this part of the pre-Referendum war of nerves, especially when taken in conjunction with Soustelle's latest utterance (also prominently featured on page 1 of *Paris-Presse*)—saying:

ALGERIAN TERRORISM IS DIRECTED CHIEFLY BY THE COMMUNIST PARTY

In the course of his speech at the Cercle républicain, Soustelle ridiculed those who were saying that the Government was interfering with the freedom of speech.

The other day M. Claude Bourdet was able, thanks to the orders I myself had signed, to scream on French television about how it was impossible for him to express his thoughts freely. (*Loud laughter.*)

The Communists, Soustelle also said, were at the back of the whole NO campaign, and he concluded on this menacing note:

"If we don't want the Fifth Republic to share the fate of the Fourth, then we must, immediately after the Referendum, act in such a way that the Communist Party will not be able to rot the new institutions, as it succeeded in poisoning the old ones."[1]

[1] *Paris-Presse*, September 25, 1958.

As for the very "funny" story about Bourdet and his five-minute TV talk as the spokesman of one of the smaller opposition parties, Soustelle was obviously just quibbling. The opposition parties, whether small or large (such as the CP with its 5½ million votes in 1956) were given five minutes each on radio and five minutes each on TV throughout the whole Referendum campaign. All the rest of the time both radio and TV were effectively attuned to YES propaganda in a dozen different forms.

Curious how Soustelle is doing most of the talking now; Malraux has been dispatched to Guadeloupe and Martinique to spread French culture and "radiation". Soustelle is said to have persuaded the General that he had better get Malraux out of the way at the height of the Referendum campaign; he might start saying all the wrong things again about the Battle of Valmy, and the phoneyness of fraternization, and about tortures in Algeria. . . .

Not that there's really much of a "campaign" in Paris, any more than there is at Vignac-sur-Vézère. The political leaders are making pronouncements for or against the Constitution; but the general public is scarcely taking any part at all in these discussions.

Yesterday (Friday) the voting started in Algeria. No doubt about it. The Army is "running" the Referendum there. The main thing for the Army is to display sufficient armed strength to make the Moslems go to the polls regardless of the FLN's threats of reprisals. Something of the *stimmung* among the Moslems in Algeria is rendered by Philippe Herreman's dispatch from Tizi-Ouzou published in Wednesday's *Monde* under the heading:

CONSIDERATIONS OF SECURITY RATHER THAN POLITICAL CHOICE WILL DETERMINE THE MOSLEMS' VOTE:

During the last three years it has always been difficult to sound Moslem opinion in Algeria. At present it's simply impossible. This latent fear, this distrust, which were slightly reduced during the events in May, are now as strong as ever. The *détente* has proved superficial and short-lived. Once more the Moslems are grimly silent. This Referendum which they would in normal times regard as a sign of confidence, as a step towards equality, as a sign of greater human dignity, is today just another nightmare to them.

In this great battle for the Moslem vote, in which the Army, with its vast propaganda machine, will fight against the FLN, with their threat of terror and bloody reprisals, it's the ordinary Moslem who is again going to bear the brunt of it all. It's no use asking these people how they are going to vote. Do they know? And even if they have a political opinion, will they dare to express it, or be allowed to express it? (*Le Monde*, September 24.)

Meantime, the Communists and other supporters of the NO vote are making people's flesh creep. *L'Express* reproduced a confidential circular this week sent to the members of the 10th Paratroop Division:

We are in the midst of a revolutionary war. When public opinion has grasped this fundamental fact, its representative will give it force of law. The necessary logical conclusions will then be drawn: the enemies of France will be unmasked and punished by a JUSTICE READAPTED TO THE NEW CIRCUM-STANCES. The Communist Party will be outlawed, and all the traitors WILL BE LEGALLY SHOT.

Yesterday it was announced that on September 30 Algiers would celebrate a GRANDE FÊTE DE L'INTEGRATION. De Gaulle seems to have been very angry about this, and the said *fête* has been called off.

Ugly shooting affair at the Simca motor works at Nanterre. Five men wounded by bullets, all of them Communists who had come to distribute NO tracts among the workers. Many conflicting versions of what really happened; but one thing is certain: the fight was between two lots of workers at Simca: the Communists and the "Americanized" and "house-trained" workers, working hand-in-glove with the management. There is little doubt that there are, among the latter, "commandos"—already known for some time past as *"les nervis de chez Simca"*. It was they who last spring savagely beat up Léon Hovnanian—Mendès-France's friend—at an election meeting, half-tearing off one of his ears and nearly blinding him. The Communist papers are making the most of it; but, apart from one man killed by Communists at Toulouse, it seems, so far, about the only really serious fight—not mixed up with Algerians—directly resulting from the Referendum campaign. At the Salle Pleyel last night, where Soustelle, Michelet, Delbecque and other "Gaullists" held a "final" pre-Referendum meeting, the hall was almost half-empty.

Another little Government trick: The UGS (*Union de Gauche Socialiste*), which is one of the major non-Communist parties of the Left, claiming 10,000 *militants*, and fairly strong in Paris, Lyon, Grenoble and one or two other places, held its first Congress at Lyon last week-end. (The *militants* include 25 per cent workers, 20 per cent teachers, 18 per cent employees, besides technicians, students and members of the liberal professions, and Bourdet and Martinet are among its leading lights.) Not perhaps a world-shaking event, but still a fairly significant new development in France. The official AFP news agency wrote exactly five lines about it. So papers with no correspondent at Lyon knew (and told) practically nothing about this Congress. It's part of the technique which consists in suggesting that *only* the Communists are against the Constitution.

Very long article by Beuve-Méry in yesterday's *Monde* saying that the staff of the paper is strongly divided on the Referendum issue, but, after weighing all the various arguments for and against, concluding in favour of a YES vote.

The "intellectual" papers are working hard on historical analogies. All over its front page *L'Express* reproduces in facsimile the text of Napoleon III's last plebiscite appeal in 1870. I doubt whether it can have much effect. . . .

Great indignation in the *Monde* against Colonel Lacheroy's statement why Radio-Algiers was not allowed to carry any NO propaganda at all. "Why should it?" he said. "There are five peripheral stations doing nothing but NO propaganda." By this he meant, in the first place, Radio-Cairo and other stations in the Arab world. "Is Nasser," says the *Monde*, "to be accepted in Algeria as the only valid NO spokesman?"

Last night on radio and TV de Gaulle wound up the Referendum campaign. Same old themes: the Referendum went beyond the mere adoption of a text. The destiny of France was at stake. . . . France's policy would now be inspired by a new spirit; a new Republic would lead France along the road of her destiny. The fact that millions of Algerian men and women were voting for the first time on a footing of complete equality would show that they had confidence in France and in de Gaulle. Also, the Referendum would demonstrate the unity of France:

"A free community of peoples will be established between France and the overseas territories; this great human mass grouped round France will be a glowing example to the rest of the world, where so many tyrannies are still in power."

And he ended with the usual appeal for a "massive" vote.

"In a world obsessed by terrible threats, how great will be the dignity of France! That is why the size of the YES majority will be of immense importance! Oh, how could anyone want to abstain!"

Last night, too, Soustelle received 140 foreign journalists and told them that, "without guaranteeing anything", he expected a 65 per cent YES vote. He denied that the Opposition hadn't been free during the Referendum campaign: one only had to look at the newspaper kiosks. As for the radio, well, said Soustelle, that was another matter.

The radio is a matter for the State. Even so, all the principal parties, including the Communist Party, were allowed to speak on the radio during the campaign.

Yes—for five minutes. And the press: about 90 per cent was for the YES vote.

Sunday, September 28. The great day has come. Posters, posters—nearly all tricolour YES posters—everywhere. A sunny day. All quiet. But queues from early morning in the numerous polling stations all over Paris. Everybody doing his *devoir civique* quietly, without fuss. Went to the Goutte d'Or district behind the Gare du Nord, known as the "Casbah of Paris". The Algerians in Paris are not voting; didn't see a single one at any of the polling stations. Nobody's forcing them to vote here; it's a different story in Algeria. . . .

A last warning by *Humanité-Dimanche*:

NO
to Dictatorship, Poverty, War and Fascism!
Vive la République!
Vive la France!

By this plebiscite, de Gaulle hopes to legalize the power he has obtained from the Algiers rebels. . . . He is continuing the war in Algeria, where the massacres of Algerians and the losses among the French soldiers have increased since June 1. This war has spread to France. . . . Men like Massu and Soustelle have been given key positions. They hope that the YES vote will enable them to extend the Fascist terror to France. . . .

And so on . . .

Soon after nine o'clock tonight the radio started giving out the first results: soon it became clear that de Gaulle had won an overwhelming victory. 70, 80, 90 per cent of YES votes. . . . Enormous crowds cheering in the Champs-Elysées as the Referendum results were being announced. . . . Colombey-les-deux-Eglises: one NO vote. Immediate wisecrack: "Must have been de Gaulle himself!"

24. WHY 80 PER CENT VOTED FOR DE GAULLE

I T WAS a far greater victory for de Gaulle than most had expected; only a few days before polling day Soustelle and the Prefects were still speaking of 65 per cent YES votes. What had, obviously, made forecasts so difficult was precisely that "cageyness" which so many observers had noted.

The most striking phenomenon was that a substantial part of the working class, including a very large number of habitual Communist voters, had now voted YES. This fact was not only played up, more than anything else, in the banner headlines in the Right-wing press announcing de Gaulle's victory, but it was also (as we shall see) closely examined and openly discussed by the Communist leaders themselves.

The figures for Metropolitan France were highly illuminating:

Registered voters	26,606,948
Votes cast	22,291,306
YES	17,666,828 (79·25%)
NO	4,624,475 (20·75%)

PARIS:[1]

Registered voters	1,717,703
Votes cast	1,452,939
YES	1,114,984 (77·6%)
NO	320,890 (22·4%)

In 1956, out of 1,445,000 Paris voters, 390,000 (27 per cent) were Communist; 132,000 Socialist; 216,000 Radical (mostly Mendès-France); 150,000 other Centre and Left-Centre groups; 75,000 MRP; 224,000 Right "independents"; 120,000 Poujadist, 88,000 other Right groups, including "Gaullists".

In the "rich" districts (8th, 7th, 16th) the YES vote was over 85 per cent (the 8th—Champs-Elysées—holding the record with 89 per cent); next came the partly less opulent 17th, 9th, 1st districts, and the "intellectual" 6th district with 80 to 85 per cent; then the mainly petit-bourgeois but also largely working-class districts—18th, 10th, 2nd, 4th, 5th, 15th, 14th and 12th with 75 to 80 per cent (the 5th is the "Latin Quarter", while the 18th (Montmartre), the 10th (Gare du Nord) and the 15th (Citroen works) have a considerable Algerian population; the Algerians did not themselves vote, but their irritating presence contributed to the YES vote);[2] next came the "East-End" proper—the 3rd, 11th and 19th districts with 70 to 75 per cent—and finally the 20th (Menilmontant) and the 13th (Place d'Italie) with 69 per cent. But the fact that even the "reddest" of the Paris districts should have voted 69 per cent was revealing in itself.

In the 13th district, for instance, there were 25,000 NO votes; in 1956 there had been 32,000 Communist votes, out of a total of 85,000.

If the total YES vote in Paris was 77·6 per cent, it was 68·1 per cent in the *banlieue*, which includes the "Red Belt" of Paris, but also some highly prosperous residential areas like Neuilly, for instance. At Neuilly there was, of course, a nearly 90 per cent YES vote. The only district where the NOES had a majority was Bagnolet (56·4 per cent of NOES); in other Communist strongholds the number of NOES was generally

---

[1] This has become very different from the rebellious, *frondeur* Paris of the Second Empire when, as distinct from provincial France, only a minority voted *for* Napoleon III.

[2] My charlady, living on the north side of Montmartre, said that her dread of Algerians at night was one of the chief reasons why she was going to vote YES.

lower than the number of Communist votes in 1956, though it would, of course, be excessive to speak of a complete rout.

Ivry (the stronghold of Maurice Thorez) had 48 per cent NO votes. Nanterre returned 40 per cent of NOES; Aubervilliers, 43 per cent; Gennevilliers, 47 per cent; St. Denis, 47 per cent; St. Ouen, Clichy and other industrial suburbs, between 40 and 45 per cent. At Montreuil, Jacques Duclos' stronghold, 17,000 out of 43,000 voted NO, as against 21,000 who had voted Communist in 1956.

Since it is obvious that a substantial number of people other than habitual Communist voters voted NO (teachers, intellectuals, some rank-and-file Radicals and Socialists, etc.) the number of ex-Communist voters who voted YES was even higher than is suggested by the comparison between the NO vote in 1958 and the Communist vote in 1956.

The map of France showing the YES and NO votes is highly instructive, too.

It was over 90 per cent in five *départements* (Meuse and Bas-Rhin (Strasbourg), in the East, and Manche, Orne and Mayenne in the traditionally conservative West). These were closely followed (85 to 90 per cent) by the bulk of the other Eastern departments: Moselle, Haut-Rhin, Vosges, Haute-Saône, Doubs, Haute-Marne, and most of the Western departments: Ille-et-Villaine, Morbihan, Loire-Atlantique, Maine-et-Loire, Deux-Sèvres, Vendée, with a few over-85 per cent "islands" elsewhere—Gironde, Basses-Pyrénées, Haute-Loire, Loire and Corsica.

The "staunch Republican South"—with its large Radical, Socialist and (since 1945) Communist vote—was, clearly, less wholehearted than "clerical" Normandy and (partly) Brittany and even more clerical Alsace. With a few exceptions, the YES vote ranged here from 80 to 64 per cent—the minimum being recorded in the Corrèze. With 36 per cent the Corrèze thus showed the highest NO vote in the whole of France (36·7 per cent Communist vote in 1956), closely followed by the Gard, the Haute-Vienne (Limoges), the Creuse and Allier departments. The industrial North (Nord, Pas-de-Calais, Aisne, Somme, etc.), where Socialist influences were strong, adopted an intermediate position with a between 70 and 80 per cent YES vote. 75 per cent, too, in the Haute-Garonne (Toulouse), despite the NO propaganda of the *Dépêche*. Over 76 per cent in the Dordogne. Between 70 and 75 per cent in the Mediterranean South, except for a higher YES vote on the "Riviera" (Var and Alpes-Maritimes) and a still higher one in Corsica, where "Algiers" influences were strong.

By and large, it may be said that the "republican" tradition south of the Loire stood up better to de Gaulle than the "class" reflex, notably in the North of France. (Here Mollet had done much YES propaganda.) And if the Communists were reckoned to have lost about 1 million of their voters, or rather 1½ millions (if account was taken of the non-Communists voting NO), the fact remained that the number of non-Communist NO votes was small, amounting to somewhere between half a million and a million, out of the total of 4·6 million NO votes.

The proportion of Radicals and Socialists voting NO was certainly much lower than the proportion of NO votes cast at their respective Congresses earlier in September. M. Verdier,[1] one of the leading NO Socialists, tried to console himself with the thought that the NO vote was relatively high (even independently of the Communists) in districts where the non-Communist NO leaders had been active (Gard, Haute-Garonne, Gers, Vaucluse, etc.) but this was something of a quibble. In the Vaucluse (72 per cent. YES vote) Daladier had cut very little ice; so had M. Baylet's *Dépêche* at Toulouse; but the most striking fiasco of the non-Communist NO vote was to be seen in Mendès-France's stronghold in the Eure (79·4 per cent YES votes). Since both the local Radicals and Socialists had recommended the NO vote, it is probable that many Communists voted YES.

Only in fourteen departments was the 1958 NO vote higher than the Communist vote in 1956.

The Communist vote slumped most heavily in the North-East—notably in the industrial Meurthe-et-Moselle (CP in 1956, 27 per cent; NOES in 1958, 15·3 per cent),[2] Haute-Marne (25·6 per cent and 13·6 per cent respectively); Belfort (35·2 per cent and 14·7 per cent), Bas-Rhin (11·7 per cent and 6·6 per cent), Moselle (19·3 per cent and 11 per cent). These showed a much bigger drop in the Communist vote than most other places did, including Paris, where there were 390,000 CP votes in 1956 and 320,000 NO votes in 1958. In the *banlieue* the respective figures were 495,000 and 410,000.

In Algeria, the Referendum also proved, on the face of it, a great victory for de Gaulle; here, despite a slightly higher number (20 per cent as against 15 per cent) of abstentions than in France (there weren't enough Army trucks to transport everybody), 97 per cent of those who did vote voted YES. But this Algerian Referendum is a very different story from that in France; and we shall deal with it separately later. The other overseas territories also voted YES, with the exception of Guinea where, out of a population of 2¼ million and out of 1·4 million registered voters, 346,000 voted NO and only 10,000 voted YES. Guinea was thus refusing to enter the French Community. Of the other overseas territories, Madagascar alone showed a fairly high NO minority in the referendum returns.

What the immediate reactions were to the Referendum results may be easily imagined. The radio and the Right-wing press were jubilant. In giant letters *L'Aurore* screamed: *OUI ECRASANT.*

---

[1] *France-Observateur*, October 2.

[2] The figures for the Meurthe-et-Moselle are particularly curious: in 1956 there were, out of 284,000 votes, 77,000 Communist and 43,000 Socialist votes; and although, in 1958, the majority of the Socialist Federation was advocating the NO vote, the total NO vote was still only 45,000, as against a 253,000 YES vote. It suggests that half the Communists and most of the Socialists voted YES. It seems that the old Lorraine nationalism—complete with the *Croix de Lorraine*—dominated all other loyalties and considerations.

AN OVERWHELMING YES:
—both in Metropolitan FRANCE (79·25 per cent)
and, despite FLN threats, in ALGERIA (97 per cent).

The Communist Party has been abandoned by its voters
a large part of whom voted for DE GAULLE.
BLACK AFRICA Rallies to the Community, but
GUINEA will ask for its INDEPENDENCE on Thursday.

And M. Robert Bony in his editorial, after rejoicing over the Communists' defeat ("now they've been reduced to their right proportions: a suspect and alien group"), declared:

"Both the Metropolis and Algeria have clearly and dazzlingly shown that they don't want Communism, and that they don't want adventure and disorder. The green light has been given to a healthier, more vigorous, more beautiful republic, fully conscious of its deep roots in the soil of France."

In its enthusiasm, *Le Parisien Libéré* went one better and said that *over* 80 per cent in France had voted for de Gaulle.

The *Figaro*, a little less exuberant, spoke of a Great Hope that had risen over France.

There was much rejoicing over the defeat of the Communists; M. Pelletier, the Minister of the Interior, said he was happy that September 28 had not been marked by a single incident or act of disturbance, but promptly added that the "vertical drop" of the Communist Party was the most important feature of the Referendum result. He added that the Constitution would come into force on October 5, and that the Government would have four months in which to set up new institutions under Article 92 and pass the new electoral law.

M. Guy Mollet hastened to express his joy over the results of the Referendum:

"I am extremely happy about these excellent results. . . . The entire country has expressed its determination to take part in the renewal of the Republic. . . . Right up to the last moment the Bolsheviks had hoped to carry with them many genuine republicans. The failure of the NO vote . . . means that the disintoxication of the workers, who had been taken in by the Stalinites, is now in full swing . . ."

Lacoste also joined in the chorus of self-congratulation, saying that the vote pointed to

"strong disapproval in the country of an artificial, anarchical and incomprehensible political life which, for only too long, had plunged it into a state of chronic helplessness and dissatisfaction."

All these utterances made out that the vote was, essentially, a positive vote, whereas, in reality, it had very largely been a negative vote—less *for* the Fifth Republic than *against* all kinds of more or less real dangers of violent change, paratroop landings and civil war.

Fear of violent change—yes; but also a desire for peaceful change, for an escape from the parliamentary disorder of the Fourth Republic, even though this Republic, under constant pressure from Algiers and the Army, was perhaps more sinned against than sinning. This desire for peaceful change was emphasized by Beuve-Méry in his cautious *Le Monde* editorial on the day after the Referendum; although he, too, had advocated the YES vote, he was careful now not to join in the official song and dance.

De Gaulle, he said, had received a blank cheque from France, largely because the French people had grown tired of the ineffectual ways of the Fourth Republic. The legitimacy of the de Gaulle régime had thus been strikingly endorsed, "and, for the time being, its powers have no limit other than the wisdom of one man".

Its powers are unlimited—and yet precarious. . . . The question asked in the Referendum was grossly oversimplified, and de Gaulle knows from his experience of 1945–46 that elections do not always produce results that are as brilliant as the Referendum which has just preceded them. . . . The RPF experiment must have taught him that, in the long run, the disinterested devotion of a handful of people is not enough. . . . De Gaulle also knows that *if, in moments of crisis, our people are happy to hand over all responsibility to a man wanting to take it on, they still remain passionately attached to the unwritten laws of freedom and human dignity.*

And Beuve-Méry ended on a note of warning: if the Algerian war went on indefinitely, and if, as a result, this liberty and this human dignity were more and more disregarded, and the economic and financial burdens grew heavier and heavier, without that economic expansion continuing which (it was only fair to say) had begun under the Fourth Republic, then there would be a violent and inevitable swing of the pendulum the other way.

How then did the NO people react?

A characteristic reaction was that of M. Jean Baylet, the editor of the *Dépêche* of Toulouse, the only important non-Communist paper to have conducted a NO campaign. As soon as the results of the Referendum became known, he declared that he was resigning his position as Mayor of Valence d'Agen, and also resigning from the *Conseil Général* of the Lot-et-Garonne department, since he had been disavowed by his fellow-citizens. In the town of which he was Mayor, two-thirds had voted YES.

Other NO men, like Mendès-France's henchman, Charles Hernu,

stressed that many people had voted YES, because they believed de Gaulle would make peace in Algeria; would he?

L'Humanité and *Libération* must have hesitated about their headlines on September 29; finally, they produced this:

L'Humanité:

THE MONARCHIST CONSTITUTION HAS BEEN ADOPTED
Millions of Frenchmen have Voted NO.

Libération:

The Constitution has been Adopted.
AN EQUIVOCAL "YES" COALITION
Gives de Gaulle a heterogeneous majority

Rather pathetically, *L'Humanité* "led" with a list of thirty-four (mostly very small) localities where the NO vote was greater than the YES vote.

It was not till a week later that the Communist Party decided to say publicly why so many habitual Communist voters had voted for de Gaulle—a fact slurred over in Fajon's editorial on September 29.

It was at the meeting of the Central Committee of the Communist Party, held at Ivry, that Marcel Servin got down to brass tacks.

"The result of the plebiscite," he said, "must be regarded as a victory of the most reactionary forces in the country. It is a very serious setback for the working class, for the democratic forces of the nation, and for the Communist Party itself."

After saying that certain non-Communist leaders (Mendès-France in the Eure, Badiou and Bourgès-Maunoury in the Haute-Garonne, Baylet in the Tarn-et-Garonne, and Daladier and Lussy in the Vaucluse) had done their best to increase the NO vote (though without very much success), Servin then came to his main point:

The YES movement has eaten into the Communist Party. In 1956 we had 5,600,000 votes. On September 28, there were only 4,600,000 NOES. It is not sufficient to say that one million Communist voters now voted YES. For if most of the NOES came from Communists, it would be both untrue and dangerous to say that the NOES that came from Socialists, democrats, Radicals and, to a lesser extent, Catholics, were negligible. That being so, it is obvious that *not just a million Communists, but more than a million voted YES*. It is a serious situation, and we've got to face it squarely. Such a thing has happened for the first time since the Liberation. One voter in five has ignored our appeal. And it isn't merely a case of voters newly-acquired in January 1956, but also of people who had voted Communist for years.

"... Many workers, particularly many of the poorest and most unhappy among them, voted for de Gaulle, because they had illusions about him."

Servin said that there were also some deeper causes why many workers had voted for de Gaulle. The election promises of January 2, 1956, had been grossly broken as a result of Guy Mollet's shameful capitulation to the colonialists. As a result, many workers, including many Communists, who had voted Left in 1956, now voted for de Gaulle out of disillusionment. They wanted things to "change". After all, there were many Communist voters who were just "ordinary chaps", and they had been carried away by this movement. No doubt they had made a grave error, for the social forces backing de Gaulle were the worst enemies of social progress and of peace in Algeria.

It would be wrong, Servin said, to look upon the 17 million YES voters as a mass of reactionaries. There were among them millions of Communists, Socialists and Radicals who would be greatly surprised if they were told they wanted Fascism and the perpetuation of the Algerian war. And it was wrong of so many Communists in factories who had loyally devoted themselves to the NO campaign to snarl at those who had voted YES, and to say that "it would serve them damn well right to get what was coming to them". There must instead be "patient and fraternal discussions".

In the final resolution passed, the Central Committee called for unity among all the democratic forces of France; expressed the conviction that time was on the side of the Communists, and that there was no ground for pessimism. But it also contained some veiled criticism of the CP in the past.

A curious passage in Servin's report concerned Algerian terrorism in France. One of the reasons why so many workers had voted YES was "the FLN's conception of the kind of struggle it had to conduct on French soil"; this was not perhaps very explicit, though clear enough. Moreover, the phrase was, significantly, more fully explained by *L'Humanité*, which quoted a Prague paper, *Tvorba*. This had said:

The violent activities of the FLN in France have not served the cause of Free Algeria. French opinion condemned this activity, and reactionary propaganda certainly made the greatest use of it to create a psychosis of fear. . . . There is good reason for saying that the bomb on the Eiffel Tower was a put-up job arranged by the police; but earlier actions by the FLN had made this possible. In present circumstances it will be easy to organize something on the lines of the Reichstag fire, complete with the subsequent prohibition of the Communist Party.

Indeed, a very similar line was taken, a few days later, by Maurice Thorez himself.

The Communist Central Committee thus confirmed what very many people felt in August and September: namely, that the FLN gunmen were helping de Gaulle. . . . It also suggested, with its *Tvorba* quotation, that the FLN gunmen had better stop this very dangerous nonsense at once. . . .

25. THE PHONEY "REFERENDUM" IN ALGERIA

IT SEEMS that de Gaulle was genuinely anxious that the Referendum should be conducted in Algeria as fairly as possible; at any rate that it should be conducted in such a way that the results would give at least an approximate indication of what the Moslem population really felt. Thus, the number of NOES might help to show how large a support the FLN was still enjoying among the people. A fortnight before the Referendum a member of the Control Commission declared, apparently in all seriousness: "I don't think there will be any question of a 90 or 95 per cent YES vote. Everything will be done in a regular manner, and the opposition will be treated with perfect respect."

The results belied this forecast. Out of 4,402,000 registered voters (a fairly high proportion of adult Moslems had, owing to war conditions and for other reasons not been "registered") 3,477,000 took part in the vote, with this remarkable result:

YES	3,357,000
NO	119,000,

or nearly 97 per cent YES votes.

How did this happen?

The FLN and Cairo and other Arab radio stations had called on the Algerian people to boycott the Referendum; the French Army, on the other hand, was determined that as many Moslems as possible—including the women—should vote. Army trucks were extensively used to "help" them to carry out their "civic duty". As said before, the Algerians in Metropolitan France did actually boycott the referendum; it is said that they had been "terrorized" into doing so by the FLN, with no counter-pressure coming from the Army. Whether they were scared of FLN gunmen or not, the fact remains that all Algerians in France refrained from voting. In Algeria, on the other hand, nearly 70 per cent of the registered voters went (or were taken) to the polling stations.

As distinct from France, where the YES and NO ballot papers were of the same colour, in Algeria the YES paper was white, and the NO paper purple. Seemingly in all innocence *France-Soir* described the following scene in a polling station in the Constantinois:

A completely ignorant Moslem woman entered, and was given the following explanation by an official:

"Here is an envelope, take one. You will put your ballot paper inside. Now, here are two piles of ballot papers. The white one is for de Gaulle; the purple one is for the fellaghas. Put whichever you want in the envelope and close it."[1]

[1] Quoted by *France-Observateur*, October 2.

In short, to vote "purple" was to vote for the outlaws. (Also, Arabs are said to regard purple as an "unlucky" colour.)

Apart from the radio and the Government press, which revelled in the "enthusiasm" with which the Moslems voted, and so defied the threats of the FLN, all reasonably honest observers agreed that the Moslem masses, war-weary and, even more so, frightened and intimidated, were everywhere playing for safety. The spectacular results were, as a rule, not obtained by the crude trickery and fakery that had characterized previous elections in Algeria, but by the Army's "psychological action".

The best analysis of what had happened was made in retrospect by Philippe Herreman, the *Monde* correspondent, who had followed the campaign throughout.

The Referendum in Algeria, he wrote, was not "faked" in the ordinary sense; but the voting was not free either.

The results were not fabricated, as they were so often in the past: that is, there was no "stuffing" of ballot-boxes with the right kind of papers, as there was in 1951. The boxes were "stuffed" by the voters themselves—to the tune of 96 per cent!

Not that there weren't some cases of "classical" faking, too. I know that at one polling station in Algiers, the European assessors reduced the number of purple papers in one box. . . . A few more such cases are being inquired into by the Control Commission. . . .

But such cases were exceptional. All the same, some Europeans are still attached to such methods, and still won't understand that a genuine 75 per cent would be far better than a suspect 97 per cent!

. . . But it is more difficult to estimate what the real proportion of YES votes would have been without the Army's "psychological action" . . . But it is certain that the Moslem did not feel completely free in his vote. He had been subjected to weeks of intensive unilateral propaganda by an army in a country at war. After four years of insecurity, such propaganda was imperative by its very nature. That was how the inhabitants of the Casbah reacted when armed soldiers came along to tell them that they were really "quite" free to go, or not to go, to the polling stations. . . .

There was no middle way between the Army's orders and the FLN's instructions. All Algerian trade unionists, moderate nationalists and intellectuals are in camps or in exile, or else with the *maquis*, and the only NO propaganda was done by foreign radios.

Thus the Moslem voter was subjected to a process of "conditioning", which went on for weeks. On polling day there was a tremendous display of soldiers and paratroopers everywhere, and the wretched Moslem scarcely knew whether all these people were there to protect him or to frighten him. It was not till he got inside the polling station that he felt "free" at last. But, says Herreman—

Having got that far, he could not but wonder whether all this freedom wasn't a put-up job, a deadly trap with a stage-setting of Freedom in which he no longer believed. . . . So to take two ballot papers into the polling booth—even if he intended to vote YES—seemed an almost reckless piece of audacity. Very frequently, the Moslem voter was simply handed his envelope with the white paper. This breach of the rules was particularly frequent in the case of illiterate Moslem women. Assessors later argued that it would have taken too long to explain everything to every voter; and one couldn't really be expected to shove a *purple* paper at them!

There was another thing. "Has voted" was inscribed in the identity card of any man or woman who had done so; anyone who had abstained thus became automatically "suspect". It was only in the concentration camps—the *camps d'hébergement*—that the Algerian prisoners decided *collectively* to boycott the Referendum; they could do this more safely than a man in a small village.

And in conclusion Herreman raised this awkward question: if 97 per cent of Algerians were "for de Gaulle" and for "integration"—or even only 80 per cent, if one took account of the abstentions, how was it possible for the FLN to continue to operate and to be supplied in such a country? The Europeans, he noted, seemed particularly pleased with the rather mythical 97 per cent as a demonstration that the Moslems were "for integration"; the Army was particularly pleased to have got as many as 80 per cent to vote. "And even if you think," members of the Army said to Herreman, "that they voted out of fear, *you should at least recognize that they are more afraid of us than they are of the FLN. Which is a victory for France.*"

Only, many Army men looked further ahead: they felt that this negative success, achieved thanks to the Moslems' fear or war-weariness, could be turned into a positive success in time. De Gaulle's Constantine programme might well prove a fruitful ground for a more trusting relationship between the Army and the Moslem population; and in the Army, Herreman reported, there were also strong currents in favour of eliminating from Algeria certain *colons* and officials, whose presence would never allow the Moslems to develop any confidence in a new order. . . .

How much of this was wishful thinking? And how many were really thinking along these lines?

Anyway, the *Monde* of October 8, with the "indiscreet" Herreman article, was duly seized by the military authorities in Algiers, despite all de Gaulle's admonishments about respecting the freedom of the press.

PART IV
INTO THE FIFTH REPUBLIC

1. THE CONSTANTINE PROGRAMME

THE short period between the Referendum and the General Election at the end of November was a particularly exciting one.

It began with another de Gaulle journey to Algeria, in the course of which he outlined the "New Deal" he had worked out for Algeria, and which came to be known as the Constantine Plan. Only a few days later, feeling obviously dissatisfied (whatever he officially said to the contrary) with the manner in which the Referendum had been conducted in Algeria, with its "Hitler-Stalin" 97 per cent YES vote, he gave emphatic new instructions to General Salan and the Army, the categorical sharpness of which flabbergasted the *ultras* and "activists" in Algeria, and produced an outburst of cheering from the "liberals" in France—even from NO people like Mendès-France, Servan-Schreiber, etc., and even an emphatic nod of approval—from the Communists! With bated breath, YES people like Gaston Defferre were now waiting for de Gaulle's next move, which was, they thought, going to initiate peace negotiations with the FLN. This move was not long in coming; it was nobly worded; but what, in effect, it implied (especially in the eyes of Algiers) was that nothing short of capitulation by the Algerian rebels would do.

It was in October, too, that France was to witness the farcical, revolting, but also highly revealing grand finale of the Bazooka Affair, with General Salan, General Cogny and other big shots giving evidence in Court— after René Kovacs, the chief accused, had already mysteriously absconded to Spain, to the great indignation of some, and much to the relief of others. . . .

It was also in October that the Government passed, under the plenary powers it had received under Article 92 of the new Constitution, the new electoral law, and that the Parties started organizing themselves for the great November contest. The most important new development was, of course, the spectacular rise of a new Party, the "Gaullist" Party of the UNR, the *Union de la Nouvelle République*.

*   *   *

During his fourth journey to Algeria, de Gaulle decided not to make his great programme speech in the crazy and artificial atmosphere of the

Algiers "Forum" but in the more "realistic" setting of Constantine, less isolated than European Algiers from the Moslem masses.

On the way there, it is true, he stopped for a short time at Oran and Algiers, where he was cheered by the crowds after the great Referendum victory; but the chief function he attended at Algiers was a "captains' dinner". He wanted to have a heart-to-heart talk with some "ordinary" young officers, who were engaged in the actual fighting in Algeria. He sent instructions to the military authorities that seventeen such "typical" officers be invited to his dinner. According to the well-informed correspondent of *L'Express*, Jean Daniel, the selection of de Gaulle's guests gave rise to "an incredible amount of intrigue and wire-pulling and, in the end, the more revolutionary and intelligent among the captains were excluded from the invitation list".[1] In what way were they "revolutionary"? These, according to Daniel, were a new brand of "liberals":

> Some of these captains had taken up a peculiar attitude to the May 13 revolution. Their great ambition was to put about a hundred of the more notorious *ultras* (among them M. de Sérigny) on a plane and send them off to France, and then to set up a Committee of Public Safety which would include liberals like M. Jacques Chevallier and Archbishop Duval, and a number of Algerian nationalists. These captains got disgusted with the whole thing when de Sérigny and the other *ultras* succeeded, in agreement with the "Gaullists"—notably Delbecque and Neuwirth —in eliminating the liberals from the Committee of Public Safety. (*ibid.*)

There is little evidence that any such "liberal" captains really attended the dinner. The line that the captains present seemed to take was that it would be wrong to negotiate with the FLN; that the Army, by having set up its "protection groups", its network of SAS "welfare officers", and the numerous "special delegations" of tame Algerians, had assumed a sacred moral obligation to protect these people against the vengeance of the FLN. The French Army, it was also argued, had "abandoned" the Catholics in Vietnam, and it must not do the same to France's friends in Algeria. De Gaulle is reported to have remarked with dry solemnity: "What makes you think that de Gaulle would ever abandon his friends?"

In short, it seems that the "typical" officers at de Gaulle's dinner party (they had, after all, been selected by the local military authorities) seemed strongly opposed to any negotiations with the FLN. It is hard to say to what extent de Gaulle was impressed, but his unfortunate "white flag" phrase in his press conference a fortnight later may well have been a concession to those captains who put above all else "the honour of the French Army".

And then, on the following day, October 3, de Gaulle made his famous

[1] *L'Express* October 9.

Constantine speech on the future of Algeria. Some 40,000 people, two-thirds of whom were estimated to be Moslems, had come to hear de Gaulle speak; they were, however, kept a good hundred yards away from the specially-erected official platform from which the General spoke. According to all reports, the Moslems remained silent throughout, while the cheers of the Europeans were rather lukewarm. The Arab translation of the speech was thinly cheered—and only by Europeans. On the other hand, the local Committee of Public Safety were in a state of fury and phoned Massu to ask him to okay a hostile demonstration against de Gaulle there and then; however, they could not reach him, and confined themselves, therefore, to sending a delegation to de Gaulle to protest against the absence of the word "integration" in his speech. De Gaulle refused to see them.

Taking the results of the Algerian referendum at its face value, de Gaulle began by congratulating himself on the fact that 3½ million "Algerian men and women" had "on a basis of complete equality" expressed their confidence in France and in himself. They had done it freely, without any coercion, and despite the threats of the Algerian fanatics. It showed that France and Algeria had thus entered into a mutual commitment.

And then came the "Constantine Programme":

It was essential that this country, so full of courage and vitality, but so difficult and long-suffering, should undergo profound transformations. The conditions of life of every Algerian man and woman must improve every day from now on.... "The whole of Algeria must have its share of what modern civilization can and must bring by way of human dignity and well-being."

And here were the measures proposed:

During the next five years at least one-tenth of all young people *in Metropolitan France* entering the State organisms, the administration, the judiciary, education and the public services, must be members of the Arab, Kabyle or Mozabite communities—and this without prejudice to an increased number of Algerians serving in similar capacities in Algeria itself.

In the same five years wages and salaries in Algeria will be put on a level "comparable to that in Metropolitan France".

In these five years, 250,000 hectares of new lands will be distributed among Moslem farmers.

In these five years, too, which will mark the first stage of the programme for the agricultural and industrial development of Algeria, the oil and gas of the Sahara will be brought to Algeria; great engineering and chemical plants will be set up; dwellings will be built for one million persons, with a corresponding development of health equipment, roads, ports, etc., and the creation of 400,000 new jobs.

In these five years, two-thirds of Algerian children will be sent to school, and

12

by the end of eight years, *all* Algerian children will go to school [as against some 20 per cent now].

During this period, the human contact—to which the Army has contributed so much—will be intensified between the two communities, not only in Algeria, but in Metropolitan France as well.

What then about the future status of Algeria? Although the above social and economic measures implied a very high degree of "integration", de Gaulle refrained from using this word, and instead went so far as to use the phrase "Algerian personality", so abhorred by the *ultras*:

"As regards the political status of Algeria, I consider it quite useless to commit myself to any particular words; a proper definition of this status will be given by the very programme we are undertaking. . . .

"In two months from now Algeria will elect its representatives in the same conditions as France. It is essential that at least two-thirds of these should be Moslems.

"As for the future, *it is natural that Algeria should be built on the dual basis of its personality and of its close solidarity with Metropolitan France.*

"It is absolutely essential that this fruitful transformation should take place. It is essential . . . for the good of the Algerian population as well as for the honour of the human race. It is essential to the peace of the world. It is in nobody's interest that a people should remain stagnant; only those can be interested in it who want to benefit from the wretched condition and the revolt of others. . . .

"And who, except France, can carry out this immense transformation? . . . She wants to do it, and she has the means of doing it. And the Algerians' vote in the Referendum shows that this work should be done together with France."

And then came this appeal to the FLN:

"Turning to those who are prolonging the fratricidal struggle . . . and who, from certain foreign capitals, go on hurling their invective against France, I want to say this: Why kill people when you must make them live? Why destroy, when your duty is to build? Why this hatred, instead of co-operation?

"Stop these absurd battles! The moment you stop them, you will see hope blossoming all over the land of Algeria; the prisons will empty themselves; and there will be a great future for everybody, particularly for yourselves!"

Then came a final thrust at those States which were fomenting the rebellion:

"There is something that France alone can accomplish. Can *you* accomplish it? No, you can't. Well then—let France do her work."

In the present state of the world, de Gaulle said, fomenting the Algerian rebellion could only lead to a new world war. That was not France's way; France had chosen the road of fraternity. And he ended—rather to the dismay of the *ultras*—by exclaiming: *"Vive la République! Vive l'Algérie et la France!"*

So Algeria and France were two distinct countries? Those with a hair-splitting disposition noted the curious fact that, in the official text, the singular *vive!* was used instead of the (grammatically much more correct but politically dangerous) plural *vivent!*

Apart from the *ultras* whom the Constantine speech infuriated on political grounds, everybody in France, one might say, made the same obvious comment: "Sounds fine, but *what is it going to cost?*" There were some grim comments on the terrible housing shortage in Paris, and de Gaulle's promise to build houses for one million Algerians. Shouldn't charity begin at home?

Moreover, was it certain that this handsome offer—which Ferhat Abbas would have joyfully accepted five years earlier—hadn't come too late?

The Moslems present at Constantine had not cheered; they had remained sceptical about the whole thing.

Numerous commentators in France proceeded to analyse the economic implications of the Constantine Programme.

The Left-wing intellectuals of *France-Observateur* and *L'Express* tended to criticize the plan as being essentially "paternalist" and "neo-colonialist", full of demagogic tricks, and loopholes, and promises which, in reality, could not be kept, short of either securing an enormous amount of foreign aid, or of restricting French consumption, by means of a rigid quasi-Fascist economy, for the benefit of Algeria. But the most vital criticism was that, in a demagogic and essentially "integrationist" way, de Gaulle was identifying a highly-developed country like France with an essentially under-developed country like Algeria, and somehow overlooking the fact that, even at its best, the Constantine Plan could not solve the chronic problem of Algerian unemployment, but, at most, stabilize it.

But other, seemingly more favourable commentators (such as Pierre Drouin in the *Monde* of October 5), while praising the "imaginative sweep" of the Constantine Programme, recalled that—

In Algeria, essentially an under-developed country, the average *per capita* income was five times smaller than in France and, if one took into account the Europeans in Algeria, it was nearly ten times smaller. The real curse of Algeria was unemployment; there was a total of one million unemployed (or grossly under-employed), which meant, in fact, nearly one-half of the adult male population. No doubt, de Gaulle was promising to create 400,000 new jobs, but the natural population increase was such that it would very nearly absorb all these new jobs, and there would still be very nearly a million unemployed. De Gaulle's housing programme for Algeria would mean that, on the average, three or four times more houses would have to be built every year than hitherto; the schooling programme also would be very costly, and where would the teachers come from? As it was, there was a severe shortage of teachers in France. The natural resources of Algeria were very poor, and oil was not enough, in itself, to lay the foundations for an industrial country. Meantime, in France, there was a yearly net population increase of 300,000—which meant over two million by 1970; here also new jobs and new schools would be needed. The Common Market, about to come into force, would create further complications for the French economy.

Pierre Drouin's conclusion (which contrasted strangely with de Gaulle's "France, France alone can do it" . . .) was that, without foreign aid, the Constantine Programme could not be carried out:

"Maybe this titanic enterprise," he wrote, "will create both in France and throughout the world a great movement of solidarity, and perhaps the World Bank . . . will soon be able to give us valuable help.
But if there is no foreign aid, then there are only three possibilities:
(1) In practice, France will not fulfil her promises—and the political consequences of this would be serious;
(2) She will not be able to control the inflation which would "integrate" France and Algeria in a particularly unpleasant way;
(3) The Government will have to restrict severely private consumption in France itself, in order to carry out the Constantine Programme . . ."

Other commentators thought the Programme was "perfectly feasible" —but on condition that the war in Algeria soon stopped. But there was just nothing to show that this condition was going to be fulfilled, though, for a short time, de Gaulle's next moves were going to give some ground for optimism. . . .

On his return journey from Algeria, de Gaulle stopped at Ajaccio, Bastia, Marseille and Lyon, where he made the usual kind of speeches, emphasizing, in each case, the quite exceptional importance of the place he was visiting at that moment. Thus, at Ajaccio, he said:

"Our country is on the threshold of a new epoch. That is what was so brilliantly demonstrated by the country, and particularly by Corsica on September 28. The French people demonstrated their unity that day and the fact that France was now on its way towards a new greatness . . . Corsica is a land where many men were born who nobly served their country, a land of brave men, where the most glorious of all Frenchmen was born." (Cries of "*Vive Napoléon!*") . . . "Our future will be great and beautiful. And I say with all my heart: Long live Corsica! Long live the Republic! Long live France!"

In more business-like Bastia he had this kind of conversation with the various mayors of northern Corsica (as reported by AFP):

The General: What do you need?
The Mayors: Water, schools, roads, houses, the means of fighting fires . . .
The General: Do you believe in the economic development of Corsica?
The Mayors: Yes.
The General: Are you interested in tourism?
The Mayors: Very much.

Unfortunately the dialogue was cut short just at the most interesting point, i.e. when it came to discussing financial resources.

In Marseille, in Lyon, the tone was lofty again.

As *Esprit* remarked, in concocting a "composite" de Gaulle speech—

> *Vive l'Algérie!*
> *Vive la Bretagne!*
> *Vive la Corse!*
>   *Marseille est éternelle!*
> *A Lyon on sait ce qu'est un homme*
> *On sait ce qu'est un travailleur*
> *On sait ce qu'est un effort—*

"Why, this might have come straight out of a poem by Aragon!"

2. THE BAZOOKA TRIAL: THE THIRD (AND LAST) ACT

BEFORE proceeding with the story of the rather spectacular moves with which, in the course of October and November, de Gaulle followed up his Constantine Programme, we must deal here with the third and last act of that fantastic Bazooka Affair which pointed so clearly to the mud and blood from which so many of the roots of the new Régime of Purity had sprung.

No doubt every régime has its scandals; the Fourth Republic had dozens of them, among them the *affaire des généraux*, with its tangle of Indo-Chinese intrigues and rackets. But here, at least, an attempt was made by two parliamentary committees of inquiry to examine all the ins and outs of the *affaire*; the Bazooka Affair, on the contrary, suggested that, threatened with "revelations", all the great leaders of the Fifth Republic preferred to let the whole business fizzle out as inconclusively as possible.

Although, during the third hearing of the Bazooka Affair, many "spectacular" witnesses appeared in Court—among them General Salan and General Cogny—nothing very new was learned. M. Olmi, the presiding judge, avoided asking any awkward questions, and, in the absence of Kovacs, the principal accused, little sense could, on the face of it, be made of anything. . . . The small fry were sent to jail, and that was all.

When the Bazooka trial was reopened on Monday, October 6, the first thing that was learned was, indeed, that Kovacs, who had been too "ill" to appear in Court in July and August, had now simply escaped to Spain! M. Olmi informed the Court that he had received a *pneumatique* from Kovacs saying that, since M. Tixier-Vignancour, his defence counsel, no longer wished, for reasons of his own, to defend him, and since, in any case, the political atmosphere between the Referendum and the coming elections seemed "inopportune" for such a trial, he much regretted not to be able to be present.

Tixier-Vignancour, for his part, had also written to M. Olmi saying that, since he had been accused by Colonel Cornu, the *commissaire du gouvernement* (acting for the prosecution) of trying to blackmail the Court, he had decided not to take part in the trial any more. There was much more in Tixier-Vignancour's display of righteous indignation than met the eye . . .

In the absence of Kovacs, the five accused—who had actually taken part in installing the bazooka and firing it on January 16, 1957, into General Salan's office, killing Major Rodier in the process, and wounding another officer—were only very small fry. Chief among them was one Philippe Castille, a French reserve officer; the rest were typical "white-trash" French-Algerians—Tronci, a watchmaker; a man called Fechoz, very nearly mentally defective; a small employee, called Geffori, and a member of the Bab-el-Oued fire-brigade, called Dellamonica.

Perhaps the only good point the defence made, in the course of their trial, was that throughout the winter of 1956–57 Algiers was the scene of continuous terrorist and anti-terrorist activity, and that it had not been difficult for Kovacs, "a man with a hypnotic and magnetic personality", to persuade them that they were doing the right thing. The arguments used at first by Castille and some of the other accused that they had merely tried to create a "psychological shock", and had no intention of killing anybody, proved remarkably unconvincing. There was no doubt what-soever that they *had* intended to kill Salan. But it was equally clear that they were not just a handful of eccentrics, who had acted off their own bat. Yet those who had, for months, moved in the background, had put ideas into their heads, had spoken of "bombs that would be detonated in Algiers but blow up in Paris", who had intrigued in favour of General Cogny's appointment to Algiers—all these strange characters, Knecht, Sauvage, Griotteray (an immediate associate of General Cogny, the French C.-in-C. in Morocco), or M. Pascal Arrighi, the Corsican deputy, who *had* had mysterious contacts with Kovacs, were not charged with anything. In the end, Castille got ten years' hard labour, and the others shorter terms.

In the course of the six-days' hearing of the case, General Cogny, in full regalia, and accompanied by his ADC, appeared as a "witness";

so did General Salan, M. Pascal Arrighi, and a few others; also a rather suggestive document by M. Lacoste was read out. Cogny denied having had the slightest inkling of the "Bazooka Affair" at the time; but he knew Major Griotteray—whom he had sent on various official missions to Algiers—as well as his two friends, Sauvage and Knecht, whom Kovacs had represented as having been "important wheels" in the plot. But Cogny denied ever having met Kovacs—

"This alleged meeting I was supposed to have had with him in my hotel room is too absurd for words. The French Commander-in-Chief in Morocco, going on an official visit to Algiers in the company of several officers, and with his time-table carefully filled in advance, doesn't sneak away to talk at length to some obscure individual. I emphatically reject this ridiculous story on which so many odious and grotesque stories have been built up.

"No doubt it is true that I received a telegram signed 'Professor Kovacs', which referred to my duodenal ulcer. I took no notice of it; in the course of my career, I have received all sorts of lunatic missives, ranging from anonymous love-letters to threats to murder me. . . . Kovacs had sent me this supposedly 'code' telegram simply to impress his associates. . . ."

Altogether, Cogny made Kovacs out to be a complete liar.

He kept on repeating that he had never met Kovacs:

"The most I can say about my visit to Algiers on December 15–16, 1956, is that I may have spent a few minutes in the hall of the hotel talking to two of his alleged 'friends', Knecht and Arrighi."

It seems that the prosecution took General Cogny's word for it. But it wanted to know a little more about Griotteray's visits to Lacoste, Griotteray having been at that time on Cogny's staff.

"Maybe they did have some political discussions," Cogny said.

At this point the prosecution produced the text of M. Lacoste's statement to the magistrate inquiring into the Bazooka Affair in December 1957. Lacoste particularly remembered a visit paid him by Griotteray some time in 1956:

"On that occasion he spoke with great venom of the Republican régime, saying that some kind of 'subversive action' might be necessary to save Algeria. . . . This kind of talk was, of course, quite current at Algiers at the time, and, re-membering the General Faure case, I warned him: 'If you think you can stab me in the back, you're making a great mistake.' . . . Some time later, however, I saw Griotteray again, and this time he told me General Cogny wanted to see me; soon afterwards, I saw Cogny, and he made it clear that he would like to succeed General Lorillot as C.-in-C. in Algeria.[1] But I thought Lorillot just the right kind of man."

[1] Lorillot was actually going to be replaced on November 13, 1956, as C.-in-C. in Algeria, not by Cogny, but by Salan.

On the following day, the Court received an indignant denial from General Cogny saying that he had never asked Lacoste for the post but that, on the contrary, Lacoste had sent an officer to him, at Rabat, on a confidential mission, to sound him on the possibility of his succeeding Lorillot.

Another "witness" to be heard was Pascal Arrighi, hero of the Corsica *putsch*, and alleged by Kovacs to have been "right in the centre of the bazooka plot":

"On December 15, 1956, I was having coffee with my old war comrade Knecht; Kovacs, who was also there, invited me to his villa. I don't see why I shouldn't have accepted the invitation. . . . Anyway, we only talked about the great anxiety caused among Europeans in Algeria by all the terrorism that was going on, and by the approaching UN debate. I certainly remember that Kovacs spoke very violently about Parliament in Paris. Our parting was rather frigid, and I have never seen him since. . . . All the 'revelations' he has produced about me are grotesque and monstrous, the fantasies of a chap who ought to be psycho-analysed."

General Salan, oddly enough, had very little to say, except that, in the firing of the bazooka, "premeditation was unquestionable". It was not true, as the defence had suggested, that he had "forgiven" Kovacs, since Kovacs and his companions were merely "misguided patriots"; he could not forgive their action; for they had killed a very fine French soldier, Major Rodier, whose widow was present at the trial. . . .

All this was remarkably vague; on the face of it, nobody was to blame for the Bazooka Affair, except a bunch of six Algiers fanatics, the chief of whom—who was going to spill the beans—had been allowed to escape to Spain. The others got their ten or five years' hard labour. . . .

All this was very odd, and it was curious how the Court missed dozens of opportunities to ask some pointed questions. For there *were* some obvious questions to ask: for instance, about the coincidence whereby so many people were all in Algiers on December 15, 1956: Kovacs, Castille and their fellow-terrorists of the ORAF; Pascal Arrighi; Knecht, close friend and associate of Griotteray, the latter a member of General Cogny's staff; finally, General Cogny himself. Arrighi admitted to have seen both Knecht and Kovacs; Arrighi also saw Cogny the same day. Kovacs claimed to have seen Cogny and to have discussed with him the elimination of Salan; Cogny denied this; but there were persons like Arrighi, who had seen *both* Kovacs and Cogny. All this, in itself, proved nothing; but suggested a great deal.

The ORAF were not just a bunch of eccentrics. ORAF was a "serious" terrorist organization, which had already distinguished itself by its bomb outrage in the Casbah of Algiers in August 1956 and much else. In the spring of 1957, at UN, M. Pineau, the Foreign Minister, still treated the ORAF bomb in the Casbah as the FLN's No. 1 outrage.

It was also in December 1956 that General Faure was preparing his abortive *putsch* with the help of the Algerian territorial units, composed of French-Algerians. As we saw before, his plot was shown up, and he was locked up for a month, and then transferred to Germany. Oddly enough, he was fully reinstated by de Gaulle, and appointed to the key post of Commander of the French forces in Kabylia. Why this promotion? Did Faure know too much—and was not his planned *putsch* part of the same operation as the Bazooka Affair?

What was the role of Griotteray? Again, the Court (as even the rather complacent *Figaro* noted) showed an "astounding lack of curiosity". Griotteray had talked to Lacoste of the necessity of undertaking some "subversive action" in Algeria; at the same time, Lacoste alleged that Cogny had expressed to him the wish to be appointed C.-in-C.[1]

A month after the strange Algiers "rally" (Cogny, Arrighi, Kovacs, etc.) the bazooka shell was fired into Salan's office. The Mollet Government and Lacoste both got scared and when the Algiers Sûreté finally caught Kovacs, he was "put through the mill", and proceeded to make hair-raising allegations. He claimed to be merely the executor of a vast design; the centre of the plot was in Paris, and its moving spirits were a "Committee of Six", including Soustelle, Arrighi and Debré.[2] The liaison between Paris and Algiers was carried out by Griotteray (Cogny's right-hand man), Knecht and Sauvage (Griotteray's former secretary).

The Mollet Government got busy. Knecht and Sauvage were arrested, while Griotteray escaped to Spain.

Was light going to be thrown on the matter at last? A judicial inquiry was started by M. Mitterrand, the Minister of Justice; but the whole matter was taken over, before long, by the Military Tribunal of Algiers. . . . It was then that long and secret negotiations were begun with Major Griotteray. It was not till Chaban-Delmas became Minister of Defence in the Gaillard Government at the end of 1957 that the negotiations were brought to a conclusion: Griotteray was asked to come to Paris, and here his case was dismissed, as well as those of Knecht and Sauvage.[3]

Soon afterwards, there was the May *putsch*, in the course of which certain highly relevant documents disappeared from the GG in Algiers. M. Guillaumat, de Gaulle's Minister of Defence, holding that the

---

[1] There seems some contradictory evidence here: did Cogny ask for this appointment while Lorillot was still C.-in-C., or after Salan had already been appointed to Lorillot's former post? Lacoste's statement above suggests that Cogny had wanted the post both *while* Lorillot was in charge (i.e. before November 13) and *after* the Faure *affaire*, i.e. in December, after Salan's appointment as C.-in-C.

[2] Later, in October 1959, Mitterrand was to make some serious allegations against Debré.

[3] Claude Bourdet in *France-Observateur*, October 16, 1958.

murder of an officer could not be hushed up, insisted that the trial of Kovacs and his men be held in Paris.

At this point Tixier-Vignancour embarked on an extraordinary piece of blackmail. In July he claimed that his client was much too ill to attend the trial; but if he were still forced to come, the defence would produce fifty-seven witnesses who would "clearly demonstrate the links existing between the planners and the executors of the operation". Tixier also demanded that Kovacs be provisionally released. This, strangely enough, was agreed to. In August, Kovacs could not attend the trial, because of a very timely appendix operation. In October he vanished. . . .
Tixier-Vignancour's attitude is perfectly understandable: he held some very high trumps. But the crime committed by Kovacs was so serious that there was little chance of getting him acquitted. So he (Tixier) could either publicly compromise many very powerful persons, or he could remain silent, provided Kovacs was allowed to escape. This second course suited Tixier-Vignancour all the better as it gave him a convenient entry into the New System, in which he would represent the sacred union of Vichyism and Gaullism . . . (*ibid.*)

And so the third act of the Bazooka Affair ended, with countless suspicions having been aroused, and not a single question having been clearly answered. Despite the laudable efforts of M. Guillaumat to have some light thrown on the matter, he received no support from his fellow-Ministers—or from de Gaulle himself. Why? Perhaps because there was a closer connection between the Bazooka Affair and the birth of the Fifth Republic than met the eye. . . .

It was finally decided that Kovacs would be tried *in absentia*. A few days later he was, indeed, sentenced to death. Which meant, of course, precisely nothing.

3. DE GAULLE GETS TOUGH WITH SALAN

WE NOW come to that short period in the history of the Fifth Republic when hopes ran high that de Gaulle would pave the way for a genuine peace settlement in Algeria. Barely ten days after the Constantine Programme, and after de Gaulle's letter to Salan[1]

---

[1] Just after delivering the Constantine speech, de Gaulle had sent a particularly cordial letter to General Salan in which he said: "I wish to express to you, in the name of the country and the Government, my entire satisfaction with the contribution made to the great success of the Referendum by the Army units under your orders. In guaranteeing security and in maintaining human and material contact [with the population] the high command, the officers and the soldiers rendered the country a magnificent service. Their efforts and sacrifices have been splendidly rewarded. It is now essential rapidly to achieve complete pacification. I have complete confidence in your pursuing that great task." (*Le Monde*, October 5-6.)

congratulating him and the Army on the splendid result of the Referendum in Algeria, readers of the French press rubbed their eyes as they read that de Gaulle had sent peremptory instructions to General Salan that all officers leave the Committees of Public Safety, and that the coming elections in Algeria be held without any faking—the implication being that the Referendum had not been conducted according to normal democratic rules. Most striking was the very sharp tone he adopted in his new letter and instructions to Salan:

Paris, October 9, 1958.

My dear General,

The Government has decided that, like Metropolitan France, Algeria shall elect its representatives to the National Assembly on November 23 next.

This election shall be carried out in Algeria on a one-ballot majority *scrutin de liste* basis.

It is in the higher interests of the country that these elections be held in conditions of freedom and complete sincerity, and that electoral lists representing all tendencies—and I mean *all* tendencies—be able to compete freely and on a basis of complete equality for securing the votes.

I must therefore ask you to conform to the directives enclosed herewith. . .

Charles de Gaulle.

These instructions were as follows:

Part I said that the elections in Algeria must be "loyally" held.

All opinions may be expressed, and all candidates may stand and conduct their election campaign, regardless of their programme; this programme being free to advocate any statute or future destiny for Algeria [i.e. even independence].

"It will be for the responsible authorities to see to it that the candidates of all parties will be free to exercise this right. No restrictions on this freedom determined by the necessity of maintaining law and order can be allowed, unless approved by the control commission. The only persons to be excluded from the electoral contest are those taking part in terrorist activity and thus subject to a criminal charge."

French and local papers must be allowed to circulate freely, unless they contain articles of a kind that would justify legal prosecution.

In Part II of the instructions to Salan de Gaulle declared:

"I attach the greatest importance to the fact that there should be a genuine competition, i.e. complete with rival electoral lists; the worst pitfall would be to run lists solely favoured by the authorities. What we should aim at is that a political Algerian *élite* should freely emerge from the Election; it is only thus that the political vacuum can be filled which has opened the way to the leaders of the Algerian rebellion."

All this was explosive enough; what, from the *ultra* and "activist" point of view in Algeria was even worse was Part III of de Gaulle's instructions. This said that officials and soldiers now stationed in Algeria, or who had been stationed there until less than a year ago, could not stand as candidates in the elections; but what's more:

"The time has come when soldiers must cease to take part in any organization of a political type, regardless of the special reasons that may have prompted them since last May to join such organizations. . . . There is no further justification for their belonging to them now. I order that they withdraw from these without delay."

In other words: Get out of the Committees of Public Safety.

Finally, in Part IV of the instructions, de Gaulle merely said that Salan was to inform him of the steps that were being taken to carry out these orders.

What was behind all this? Clearly, de Gaulle was sick and tired of the Committees of Public Safety deriving their questionable authority from the presence of numerous officers on them; and the whole principle of Army officers playing a political role quite independently of the wishes of the Paris Government was wrong. To withdraw the military members from these Committees was, on the face of it, to weaken these Committees themselves.

As regards the "loyal" elections which de Gaulle was now demanding in Algeria, he was hoping in this way to produce some "representative" spokesmen—not only extreme FLN men, but also some FLN sympathizers who might, nevertheless, be willing to enter into reasonable negotiations with France. De Gaulle was not automatically excluding the "Algerian Government" from any such talks; he was merely hoping that this "government", supplemented by some regularly elected Algerian representatives (some taking the FLN line, but others possibly not) could participate in negotiations which would primarily be conducted with the new "Algerian deputies".

Since the failure of the Algerian terrorist campaign of August–September, and since de Gaulle's great Referendum victory, Ferhat Abbas was now making more and more frequent statements to show that the "Algerian Government" was willing to enter into negotiations with the French. Thus two days before the publication of de Gaulle's instructions to Salan, Ferhat Abbas published a statement in the official FLN paper saying that his Government "was willing to put an end to the trial of strength that had been going on in Algeria for four years", and let its delegates "meet French delegates with a view to determining the political and military conditions of a cease-fire".

No doubt, the Algerian leaders had, for three years past, made such "peaceful" proposals; but they had always laid down the condition that France must, before any talks could be entered into, recognize the "independence" of Algeria.

But this time Ferhat Abbas, while suggesting that independence was his Government's ultimate objective, no longer explicitly demanded its prior acceptance by France. Obviously, he would not agree to a cease-fire without at least receiving some assurances from the French; but his relative moderation could be attributed to a number of factors: the failure of the "Algerian Government" to be recognized by a large number of powers; the overwhelming victory of de Gaulle in the Referendum; the vague hope that de Gaulle was possibly anxious to come to an agreement (shortly before Ferhat Abbas had, indeed, said: "I'd deal with de Gaulle much rather than with Mollet"); the failure and lamentable effect of the "terrorist campaign" in France; finally, perhaps, counsels of moderation from Tunisia and Morocco—and possibly also from the United States.

Clearly, there was something in the air. Unofficial contacts had gone on for some time.

The rumours of secret negotiations between the French Government and the FLN had already created acute worry among the European "activists" in Algiers. Coming on top of these, de Gaulle's instructions to Salan caused an explosion of uncontrolled rage. The Committee of Public Safety for Algeria and the Sahara met at 10 a.m. on October 14, only to be immediately informed by General Massu that he and the eleven other soldiers on the Committee were resigning from it immediately "in accordance with the orders received from the head of the Government."[1]

The civilian members of the CPS all rose to their feet and protested violently—some of them yelling that de Gaulle had betrayed "the spirit of May 13 that had brought him into power", others that he was "the prisoner of the System", others still using terms of angry abuse to describe de Gaulle's "unspeakable action"; but the soldiers (whatever their private feelings) would not listen to them; except that, according to an AFP report, Massu said before leaving: "Orders are orders, and stop making a fuss; but there are still plenty of useful things you can do without us." It may already be said that if the "May 13" generals, colonels and captains displayed great discipline in carrying out de Gaulle's orders about their leaving the Committees of Public Safety, they had every intention of interpreting in their own way his instruction concerning "sincere and loyal elections in Algeria" ... By and large, they agreed with the Algerian *ultras* that if de Gaulle's instructions were literally carried out, the Algerian deputies elected would not represent a homogeneous "integrationist" body. Other officers, however, not so closely associated with "May 13" felt that de Gaulle was perhaps right, and that it might be a good thing if the elections in Algeria produced at least a few "new men".

[1] These were General Massu, President of the CPS, Generals Jouhaud and Mirambeau, eight colonels, including Trinquier, Thomazo and Ducasse, and four captains.

But the civilians on the Committee of Public Safety would not take it lying down; they published a communiqué in which they expressed their "painful surprise" over de Gaulle's instructions, and they called on the people of Algiers to hold a general "protest strike" on the afternoon of Thursday, October 16, and to come, that same afternoon, to the "Forum" to demonstrate their anger and disappointment.

But both the "strike" and the "Forum" demonstration were to prove a failure. If, on May 13, the Algiers Europeans felt that they had the Army on their side, they had the gravest doubts on the subject on October 16. Salan and Massu (the latter acting as Prefect of Algiers) both declared their opposition to the strike and the "Forum" rally; and, inside what was left of the Committee of Public Safety, some serious clashes occurred. M. de Sérigny and M. Abdesselam resigned. The "strike and demonstration" order to the people of Algiers was, in the end, supported only by a minority of the Committee: ten members, including Martel, Ortiz, Crespin, and other representatives of the "lunatic fringe"; a larger number were against, amongst them even some of the worst "lunatics" like Lagaillarde and Dr. Lefèvre, who thought the order "inexpedient" in the given circumstances.

As was to be expected, both the strike and the "Forum" demonstration proved a complete failure; there was no "strike" to speak of, and the "demonstration" in the "Forum" amounted to no more than this: a few hundred people assembled there; engaged in heated argument; and finally came to blows. The bulk of the population, now feeling that "the Army knew best", did not budge. Not that there wasn't, in the cafés of the rue Michelet, a good deal of recrimination that day against General de Gaulle.

But if the Algiers *ultras* were in a state of helpless rage against de Gaulle, his Instructions to Salan created in France a more optimistic mood than had existed for a long time. At last, it seemed, peace in Algeria was in sight. At last, too, it seemed, de Gaulle had put the Army in its place by ordering its members to withdraw from the Committees of Public Safety.

Incredible as this may sound, the Communist *Humanité* went so far as to write on October 17: "The decision taken by General de Gaulle has quite rightly been given the most favourable reception by an immense majority of the French people." "Left-wing Gaullists", or Socialists like Defferre, who had supported the YES vote in the Referendum in the hope that de Gaulle would bring about a peaceful settlement in Algeria, were exuberantly happy at the thought that they had been right. Many NO people, too, now almost went so far as to beat their chests and to say that they had misjudged de Gaulle. Mendès-France thought the instructions to Salan "represented an entirely new factor" which might well prove of the greatest importance. . . . "If these instructions are loyally carried out, they may open a way to peace in Algeria."

A big *if*, no doubt; but, pending further developments, liberal opinion in France was immensely reassured by what de Gaulle had done. . . .

4. DE GAULLE'S PEACE OFFER TO THE FLN

THE next great landmark in de Gaulle's "peace offensive" was his famous press conference of October 23, in the course of which he dealt with the possibility of ending military operations in Algeria. His proposal fell into two distinct parts; and it was made, as we shall see, after unofficial contacts had been established for some time with the FLN leaders.

First, on the local level—

"It is up to their chiefs to establish contact with our military commanders in Algeria. When soldiers want arms to be silent, they resort to the wise old custom of using the white parliamentarians' flag. I guarantee that in such cases the [enemy] soldiers will be received and treated honourably."

Secondly, on the "government" level—

"If [Algerian] delegates are appointed to agree with the [French] authorities on the termination of hostilities, all they need do is to apply to the French Embassy in Tunis or Rabat, which will provide their transportation to Metropolitan France. I guarantee their absolute security and their freedom to leave France."

What was behind all this? When, on October 23, General de Gaulle made this famous statement which was to be given world-shaking importance in the world press and produced hopeful or enthusiastic comments nearly everywhere, he already knew that the FLN leaders had made up their minds to come to Paris. This knowledge was reflected in the second point of his proposal. There had been indirect contacts for some time between de Gaulle and the FLN leadership. This is how it was done: A close associate of General de Gaulle's had written to M. Farès, former President of the Algerian Assembly, a moderate Algerian nationalist living in France, to say that General de Gaulle would be glad if M. Ferhat Abbas came to see him in Paris. In his reply to M. Farès, Ferhat Abbas argued that such a meeting should be preceded by "a meeting of French and Algerian ministers on neutral territory"—and he proposed Rome as such a meeting place. De Gaulle's associate, who had started this correspondence, rejected this proposal of the FLN leader, since this would amount to a *de facto* recognition of the Algerian Government; he pointed

out, at the same time (and this was a weighty argument), that, in asking
them to come to Paris, de Gaulle wished to deal *personally* with the FLN
leaders. It would, however, be too much to expect him, de Gaulle, to go
off to a neutral country to meet them.

This prospect of dealing personally with de Gaulle did not fail to make
a big impression on the FLN leaders, especially after the very tough line
the head of the French Government had taken with Salan and the
Algerian Committees of Public Safety. It was agreed that three of their
leaders would travel to Paris: Ferhat Abbas, the "Premier", Krim
Belkacem, the "War Minister", and Lamine Debaghine, the "Foreign
Minister". This welcome news was transmitted by Farès to de Gaulle,
and it was even rumoured that reservations had been made for the
Algerian delegation at the Hôtel Crillon.

The trouble was that Farès, who was an Algerian patriot, but also one
anxious to bring about a peace settlement with France, had apparently
given too optimistic a view of de Gaulle's disposition to the FLN, even
going so far as to suggest that de Gaulle believed in a gradual evolution
of Algeria towards quasi-independence, though remaining a member of
the "Community". On the other hand, he convinced de Gaulle that the
FLN had resigned themselves to some kind of compromise solution, and
that, in any case, they were willing to see Algeria remain in the "Community". Farès did not make it clear that de Gaulle was, apparently,
unwilling to discuss anything beyond a cease-fire.

If Farès was stretching a few points, it was because he had deeply convinced himself that a Ferhat Abbas–de Gaulle meeting must take place at
all costs—after which progress would become rapid.

What ruined everything in the end was de Gaulle's phrase about the
"white flag". No doubt, the use of the phrase "white parliamentarians'
flag" did not suggest unconditional capitulation. But the phrase, inspired
by the Army leaders in Algeria, implied, nevertheless, a series of cease-fire
arrangements which would, inevitably, only mean in practice the
abandonment of armed resistance by the FLN.

This did not fit in with the plans of the FLN leadership. Their communiqué of October 25 was to suggest clearly that they were not opposed
to a *military truce*, but that they were against any cease-fires on a local
level and implying the disarming of the FLN units concerned. What the
FLN leadership feared was that the "white flag" technique proposed
by de Gaulle would, in fact, deprive them of their biggest trump in any
negotiations with Paris—namely, the threat of resuming military operations in Algeria. For the FLN to subscribe to the "white flag" was to
demoralize and disorganize the Algerian resistance fighters.

There were some observers who at first thought that the most important part of de Gaulle's statement was his offer to Ferhat Abbas and the
other FLN leaders to come to Paris, and that the phrase about the "white

flag" was merely added on the spur of the moment. In reality, there is every reason to suppose that de Gaulle did not "improvise" at his press conference, and that the "white flag" phrase had been carefully prepared in advance.

It is probable that, despite this phrase, de Gaulle still hoped that the FLN would send a delegation to Paris. He hoped, among other things, that the FLN would authorize certain "moderate" Algerian nationalists like Farès and Imalayen to run in the coming election; they could act as useful auxiliaries in all subsequent negotiations between the French and the Algerian nationalists; in de Gaulle's view, they would be infinitely more "representative" and more useful than the usual *beni-ou-ouis* the French Army and administration had already put forward; only a fortnight was left till the closing of the candidates' lists in Algeria, and not a single "serious" candidate had yet come forward.

No doubt Ferhat Abbas and perhaps Lamine Debaghine were at first opposed to a sharp rejection of de Gaulle's offer; but the "white flag" phrase played into the hands of the diehards—particularly the soldiers—in the "Algerian Government". In their communiqué made public on Cairo radio on the evening of October 25, they now said that de Gaulle's offer amounted to no more than a demand for "unconditional surrender"; they declared that the present French Government, like all its predecessors, was determined to keep Algeria under the colonialist heel; the Referendum in Algeria had been a "colonialist mystification", and the coming election would result in the election of French stooges who would subscribe to the "integration" of Algeria. The Algerian Government would continue to fight for the freedom and independence of Algeria, but was prepared to negotiate "a general settlement"—and not just a cease-fire—with France on neutral territory. M. M'Hammed Yazid, the Algerian "Minister of Information" in New York, declared that the cease-fire was not merely a military, but also a political problem, and it was now clear that when de Gaulle was saying "Come to Paris", he meant "Come here to surrender".

"We want to negotiate, but before negotiating, we want to know what we are to negotiate about. . . . So long as this fundamental divergence subsists between us and the French, there remains only one outlet, and that is UN. We shall defend our case at UN; we hope the French will come here, too, to defend theirs."

According to messages from Tunis, it was, in the last analysis, the military commanders of the FLN forces in Algeria itself who, after being consulted on the subject, finally caused the "Algerian Government" to reject de Gaulle's offer. . . .

Such was the disappointing end of an episode which, for a brief fortnight, had aroused many hopes throughout the world. But for the unfortunate "white flag" phrase, Ferhat Abbas and other FLN leaders would undoubtedly have come to Paris, and history might perhaps have taken a different turn. Or would it have changed nothing, in view of the French Military Command's extreme reluctance to see the war end?

At any rate, the Army, as well as the Algiers *ultras*, were relieved, rather than disappointed, by the FLN's rejection of de Gaulle's offer. The notorious Dr. Lefèvre declared that he was delighted with what had happened. "Now we know exactly what we have to do: strengthen our war effort and bring the Rebels to their knees."

What had been perhaps of decisive importance in the FLN's rejection of the offer was the "interpretation" given it by Algiers. De Sérigny's *Echo d'Alger* had said from the start: "The 'white flag' phrase means capitulation, and nothing but capitulation."

5. THE UNR AND THE CLASH BETWEEN SOUSTELLE AND DE GAULLE

UNR means "*Union pour la Nouvelle République*". That was the new "mass organization" which M. Soustelle and others had, for some time, been planning to set up immediately after the Referendum. Soustelle's idea was to capitalize the YES vote, to create, as it were, a centre of political attraction for as many people as possible in the coming election who had said YES to de Gaulle. The new organization was to be essentially *the* Gaullist Party, though de Gaulle was to state clearly at his press conference at the end of October that his name was not to be used in any party label, "not even in its adjectival form". But, as we shall see, the UNR (as well as other parties) got round this nominal veto in a variety of ways. In the end, it was the UNR which benefited greatly from being the "most" Gaullist of all the Gaullist parties, including the Mollet Socialists who, in their posters, claimed that they also were Gaullists of sorts, since they intended to co-operate loyally with the General, and had been right to do so since June.

However, most of the press, including *France-Soir*, greatly helped the UNR by specifically referring to *them* as "Gaullists".

Was the UNR to be a revival, in a slightly modified form, of de Gaulle's RPF of 1947, i.e. a potential Single Party? Although he later angrily denied this, notably in a letter to *Time* Magazine, that seems to have been Soustelle's original idea. But this, before long, came up against opposition from—de Gaulle himself.

As early as September 29, i.e. the very day after the Referendum, various "Gaullist" organizations got together with a view to forming the UNR. They were talking in terms of a "rally" (*rassemblement*). It was proposed that the UNR should include all the various "Gaullist personalities" in the country, and all the various Gaullist organizations: notably the "Social Republicans" led by M. Chaban-Delmas and M. Roger Frey; M. Soustelle's notorious USRAF; a near-Fascist organization like the *Convention Républicaine* set up by M. Léon Delbecque, etc. Although the future leaders of the UNR were not at all keen on including any "Left-wing Gaullists" in the new organization, they could not keep out men like Michelet, who was one of de Gaulle's ministers. But most of the "Left-wing Gaullists" were against joining the UNR anyway.

The primary aim of this new organization, which hastened to claim that it was "neither Right nor Left", was to nominate candidates in most of the constituencies; such candidates would be chosen, it was stated, "among the *notables* faithful to General de Gaulle". It was clear that top priority was to be given to persons who had been active in the old RPF or, before that, in Soustelle's "network" and similar organizations.

The first news of these plans caused a great deal of alarm among the liberal and Left-wing press. Thus, the *Monde* of October 1 wrote:

The great risk of this undertaking—which obviously aims at canalizing the electorate's confidence in General de Gaulle towards candidates claiming to be the only "real Gaullists"—would be to repeat the RPF adventure with all its contradictions and failures. It will be important to know to what extent General de Gaulle will, even if only tacitly, allow his name and prestige to be mixed up in the election struggle.

The new organization was, indeed, doing quick work. Already on October 3 it elected its Central Committee, composed as follows:

Chaban-Delmas, Albin Chalandon, Michel Debré, Léon Delbecque, Mme Marie-Madeleine Fourcade, Roger Frey, André Jarrot, Ali Mallem, Albert Marcenet, Edmond Michelet, P. Picard, J. Soustelle, J. Veyssière.

Although M. Soustelle had at first planned to become the leader of the new Party, it was de Gaulle himself who insisted that it be led "collectively". Officially he had nothing to do with the new Party, but when its co-ordination committee met for the first time, immediately after the Referendum, de Gaulle dispatched two "observers" of his own to the meeting. They had already done some lobbying beforehand, for when a few people present "spontaneously" proposed that Soustelle be appointed president of the new movement, there was a chorus of protests, after which Chaban-Delmas, Michelet and Debré argued in favour of "collegial leadership". Then one of de Gaulle's "observers" spoke and said on behalf of the Premier that although the latter did not consider himself in any way associated with the new Party, he took account of the fact that three of his ministers were among its leaders, and he considered the appointment of a president inopportune. And it was Frey, and not Soustelle, who was thereupon appointed secretary-general, and Chalandon treasurer.

All this fitted in with de Gaulle's little offensive against the *ultras*, an offensive which was to find expression soon afterwards in his famous "instructions" to Salan and in the preference he gave to the election system advocated by Guy Mollet over that proposed by Soustelle.

Now, who were these leaders of the UNR, of whom only four—Soustelle, Debré, Michelet and Chaban-Delmas—were well-known to the general public?

All or nearly all these people had, in some measure, been associated with the old RPF.

Thus *Veyssière* and *Marcenet*, though not workers themselves, but one, a postal official, and the other, an industrial employee, had belonged, ten years before, to the *Action ouvrière* (the "working-class action") of the RPF. Marcenet had, since then, acquired the rather doubtful distinction of having, as chief of personnel at the Simca works, organized the "anti-Communist" commando groups which, under the leadership of a certain Pigozzi, had more than once in the last few years "discouraged" any seditious or unruly movements among the workers.

Frey, belonging to a wealthy textile family of Mulhouse, had for years been secretary-general of the Gaullist "Centre des Républicains Sociaux". On May 13 he mysteriously vanished from Paris, and soon afterwards reappeared at Algiers, where he was particularly active, as we have seen, in conducting a war of nerves against the Pflimlin Government over Radio-Algiers. Outwardly, this 45-year-old conspirator was a man of charming manners and great affability.

Delbecque, of whom we have spoken on many occasions before in connection with the role he played in Algiers in April, May and June as Chaban-Delmas's representative, and who was hellbent in June on setting up, throughout France, a network of Committees of Public Safety, represented, as head of an organization called the *Convention Républicaine*, the more extreme "activist" elements inside the UNR. He belonged to the Big Business class in the North of France.

Pierre Picard was one of Soustelle's men, and had played a leading part in setting up in August the URF, the *Union pour le Renouveau Français*, a slightly revised version of Soustelle's old USRAF, itself a predecessor of the UNR.

Ali Malem, a lawyer from Batna, and the only Moslem member of the UNR's original Central Committee, had been a Messalist in the past but had latterly been won over by the Committees of Public Safety as a Moslem theorist of "integration".

Jarrot was an old Gaullist of many years' standing, an active member of the RPF and Mayor of Lux in the Saône-et-Loire department.

Mme Fourcade, who had belonged to the Gaullist intelligence network called "Alliance", had worked in close touch with Delbecque during the May crisis, and had, in particular, organized the dispatch of thousands of petitions to President Coty in favour of bringing de Gaulle back to power.

Rather a different type was *M. Albin Chalandon*, representing not only a certain section of Big Business but also of High Finance. He was managing director of the Banque Commerciale de Paris, controlled by Marcel Dassault, the aircraft manufacturer, who also owned the *Jours de France* weekly; Chalandon was also general manager of *Francarep*, the Franco-African company for oil prospection and research, controlled by the Rothschild Bank; as well as a director of the *Bon Marché* department store, where one of his fellow-directors was André Dewavrin, the famous "Colonel Passy", head of de Gaulle's intelligence service in London during the war. Chalandon was the No. 1 economic and financial brain of the UNR, whose inflationist "New Deal" (if not "near-Schachtian") policy was, before long, to lead to a clash between him and the much more orthodox M. Pinay and his principal adviser, M. Rueff. . . .

Chaban-Delmas, handsome, well-groomed, a good rugby and tennis player, and a great ladies' man, was a young *Inspecteur des Finances* at the beginning of the war. He joined the Resistance and soon became one of de Gaulle's military delegates in France. He took part in the Paris Insurrection of August 1944, acting, at that time, as a brake on the more reckless Communist leaders of the uprising.[1] In the years that followed, Chaban-Delmas became Mayor of Bordeaux and built up for himself a big local reputation; he was sufficiently "liberal" not to be disliked unduly by the working class, and sufficiently "conservative" to be liked by the traditionally stuffy bourgeoisie of Bordeaux. He had a way of being all things to all men and, though a Gaullist, gladly joined in any government, including even that of M. Mendès-France in 1954. Though he had, through Delbecque, played an extremely important part in preparing the Algiers *putsch* in May, while being at the same time a member of the Gaillard Government, he was careful, when it came to the point, not to join the "rebels" at Algiers, but to stay quietly at Bordeaux, lest anything went wrong at the Algiers end. And if all went well there, he could still claim a share of the credit for what had happened. Similarly, in the UNR Chaban-Delmas was careful to adopt a "middle" position between the "Algerian" extremism of Soustelle and Delbecque and the Catholic liberalism of Edmond Michelet, a man in the best demo-Christian tradition.

Michelet, at 58, was the oldest member of the UNR Central Committee. The son of a grocer at Pau, Michelet joined the French Army as a boy in World War I. Later, he settled at Brive, set up a wholesale business, got married, and was active in the local Catholic social movements. During World War II he entered the Resistance, was deported to Dachau, returned to France as a fervent Gaullist, and soon became War Minister in the de Gaulle Government in 1944–45. When de Gaulle later formed the RPF, Michelet, abandoning the MRP, joined the new movement wholeheartedly. As distinct from Soustelle, he represented the most liberal, "Marc Sangnier" tendencies in the RPF. Later, as a Senator, he opposed German rearmament. In May '58 he argued with his various Left-wing friends, who had taken part in the Republican demonstration of May 28, in favour of de Gaulle, who continued to personify for him all the Christian virtues of Péguy and Bernanos. In the new de Gaulle Government there was, as we have seen, something of a permanent, if more or less silent, conflict between him and Soustelle.

Perhaps the darkest horse among all the leaders of the UNR at that time was *Michel Debré.* Not that he was unknown; but the man seemed full of contradictions,

[1] See the author's *France 1940–1955*, p. 215.

and it was hard to see how a man of such violence in the recent past could become, in effect, the right-hand man of de Gaulle, the arbiter, the man of compromise and conciliation.

Born in Paris in 1912, he belonged to that *grande bourgeoisie* (partly Jewish in origin) which tended to produce doctors, lawyers, writers, university men and members of the administrative *élite*, rather than businessmen. At the age of 22, and already a Doctor of Law, he became a junior official on the Conseil d'Etat. In 1938 he became a member of the secretariat of M. Paul Reynaud, then Minister of Finance; it was here that he first became acquainted with Colonel de Gaulle. (Reynaud was one of the few politicians of the Third Republic to have taken any serious notice of de Gaulle's theories on the reorganization of the French Army.) In 1939 he married the daughter of a prominent architect, M. Lemaresquier, a Member of the Institute, and had four children.

Debré was taken prisoner by the Germans in 1940 but soon returned to France. After spending a year at Rabat as a member of the Vichy administration there, he returned to France and played an active part in the Resistance. Later, he was given an important post by the French Liberation Committee at Algiers: as head of the "Appointments Committee" he played a leading role in selecting suitable Prefects, *Commissaires de la République* and other administrators who would take over at the time of the Liberation and would, as far as possible, represent the non-Communist elements in the Resistance. In the process, he himself was appointed *Commissaire de la République* of the Angers region.

As a "rebuilder" of the State he impressed de Gaulle; it is said that already then de Gaulle saw in him something of a kindred spirit; he had a great "sense of the State", was—except in Parliament—a man of few words, fundamentally shy and reserved, and with a marked dislike for brilliant and extrovert people.

In April 1945 he became a member of de Gaulle's secretariat and was responsible for drawing up several administrative reforms, notably the statutes of the *Ecole Nationale d'Administration*. After his election failure in 1946, he was appointed to the Commissariat for German and Austrian Affairs.

He was one of the first to join de Gaulle's RPF in 1947, and was elected senator a year later.

It was, in a way, a tragedy for Debré to have become a senator and not a deputy. The Senate (or rather, "Council of the Republic") was of little importance under the Constitution of the Fourth Republic; its debates were very seldom reported in the press, and the general public knew very little about Debré. Inside the Senate he became, however, quite a "character". He took a joy in heckling and interrupting Government spokesmen; even before entering the Senate, he had publicly advocated (thirteen years before the Algiers *putsch*) a "Government of Public Safety"; at the Senate he never missed an opportunity of thundering against "defeatism", the "betrayal of France's interests", the "enslavement of France by America", etc. He violently attacked the Coal-Steel Pool and all other schemes directed against France's sovereignty; taking his cue from de Gaulle, he was a savage critic of EDC; he fumed against American bases, against American arms deliveries to Tunisia, against Euratom which was, to him, "a plot against France", against the cartellization of the Ruhr industries; no opportunity was to be missed to denounce the "defeatism" and "capitulationism" of the System. He wrote violent diatribes against the System in *Carrefour*; at the end of 1957 he started a weekly of his own, significantly entitled *Le Courrier de la Colère* ("The Courier of Wrath")— which was, however, a complete failure and barely sold 500 copies.

He had been outraged by the Murphy Mission and on the eve of the fall of the Gaillard Government in April 1958 (Debré was, by this time, up to his neck in "Algiers" plotting) he produced at the Senate one of his most violent philippics:

> How can I not but shout from the rooftops to all Frenchmen: "You are being lied to! These people are taking advantage of your simple-mindedness! You must do what your ancestors did in 1789, in 1830, in 1848. You must rebel!" Members of the Government! It is not true that there is no choice other than the military reconquest of Algeria and plain abdication! Only, tell me how, without the political authority of a Clemenceau, you can re-establish peace in Algeria? How can you restore the economic and financial position of a country which is today the debtor of the whole world! How, without the political authority of a Clemenceau, can you reform the régime? We need a Government of Public Safety; France must regain her authority in the world. . . .

Yet, despite all this violence,[1] there was something woolly and colourless in much of Debré's thinking and writing; thus his "devastating" pamphlets against the Fourth Republic, such as *Ces princes qui nous gouvernent*, published in 1957, are curiously flat and undistinguished, as compared with the brilliant, if not very scrupulous, rapier-work of a man like Soustelle.

Debré's social background is a curious mixture and has given rise to some "psycho-analytical" explanations. His grandfather was a rabbi.

> His devotion to de Gaulle is part of his extreme nationalism. It forms part of the complex caused by his Jewish origin. . . . It is not an unusual phenomenon. Like Arthur Meyer in the past, Debré is a sort of "Swann" of French politics. His father, Professor Debré, is one of the most distinguished members of the Medical Academy, linked, by his second marriage, to the La Panouse family, itself related to the steel magnates, the De Wendels. One of his uncles is chairman of the *Compagnie Générale d'Electricité*. Thus Michel Debré is a son of that Jewish *grande bourgeoisie* which has so often reacted against anti-Semitism by becoming as "super-French" as the anti-Semites. And Gaullism is, to Debré, a kind of super-patriotism.[2]

Much was said then, as later, about Debré's "dog-like devotion" to de Gaulle. The phrase cannot be taken literally; although de Gaulle had more affinities with Debré than with Soustelle, and trusted him more, Debré was at times known to pursue a policy different from de Gaulle's. Thus, at the Senate in 1955, he ignored de Gaulle's sharp opposition to the ratification of the Paris Agreements providing for the rearmament of Germany, and finally swung the bulk of the RPF group at the Senate in favour of this ratification, much to de Gaulle's annoyance; similarly, as late as 1958, he conducted a violent campaign against Bourguiba in *Carrefour* despite de Gaulle's opposition to a worsening in Franco-Tunisian relations. Later still, during his visits to Algiers, he was very much more "integrationist" than de Gaulle. . . .

---

[1] He was even accused by various people of having been involved in the Bazooka case.
[2] *France-Observateur*, December 4, 1958.

Thus the central committee of the UNR were, from the start, a rather motley crew, but, in so far as they largely represented the Resistance and the RPF, they reflected the Right-wing, rather than the Left-wing, tendencies in both.

We may open a parenthesis here. It may be said that the French Resistance consisted of three distinct elements:

the Free French Forces (FFL), the various Gaullist intelligence networks, and, finally, the Home Resistance. The FFL were a very mixed bunch, but their *cadres*— their officers and NCO's—were mostly professional soldiers, nationalist, rather than anti-Fascist in temperament. This was even truer of the Intelligence networks; many of these people were definitely Right-wing, if not plainly Fascist. On the other hand, with a few exceptions like Guillain de Bénouville, formerly of the *Action Française*, the Home Resistance was overwhelmingly Left-wing, particu-larly in the south, where the struggle was conducted not only against the Germans, but also against Vichy.

There was also a marked difference in de Gaulle's own attitude to the FFL and the "networks" on the one hand, and to the Home Resistance on the other. Whereas the first two (and, in the first place, the BCRA of Colonel Passy, which, towards the end of the war, had incorporated the bulk of all the "networks"), went in for a sort of "personality cult" of de Gaulle, the Home Resistance was a great deal more reticent. Relations between de Gaulle and the Home Resistance— and not only the Communist Home Resistance—were often strained, and de Gaulle's personal preference for the "networks" and the FFL was well reflected in his choice of "Companions of the Liberation"; despite the incomparably more numerous members of the Home Resistance, the 1,000-odd persons on whom the title of "Companion of the Liberation" was conferred (largely on the strength of de Gaulle's own choice) consist of 783 members of the small Free French Forces, of 107 members of the Intelligence networks and—of only 157 members of the Home Resistance.[1]

The backbone of the RPF was composed not of former members of the Home Resistance, but of former members of the Intelligence networks and of the Free French Forces. The same phenomenon was to be observed in the case of the UNR; when it came to the test on November 30, it was found that out of the fourteen Companions of the Liberation returned as UNR deputies, eleven had belonged to the Free French Forces or to the BCRA and only three to the Home Resistance; and of these, two were nationalists of the extreme Right, Guillain de Bénouville and Drouot l'Hermine, i.e. men who were not typical of the Home Resistance as a whole.

We shall later consider in greater detail the rank-and-file of the UNR deputies who were returned in the November election; it is enough to say here that most of them were typical of various Right-wing "Gaullist" cliques who had been revived, chiefly from the remnants of the old RPF, throughout France.

[1] Claude Bourdet in *France-Observateur*, December 4, 1958.

Not that de Gaulle wanted to revive the RPF as such. This became apparent soon after the Referendum; but at first the announcement that the UNR had been formed caused the greatest anxiety among French liberals. On October 4 Maurice Duverger sounded the alarm in an article in the *Monde* called "The Wolf in the Role of Shepherd".

He thought the formation of the UNR the most ominous development since the 13th of May. It was, of course, natural, he said, for the RPF to revive, and its central committee included some people sincerely devoted to democracy. . . . If fresh blood was poured into the French Right, maybe it would be a good thing; but, unfortunately, the UNR was not merely a new version of the RPF, but "also a means of camouflaging the action of Soustelle and his friends . . . and to pass on to the next stage of the political action started on May 13".

"No doubt M. Soustelle knows that an openly Fascist movement cannot succeed in France. . . . And that's why the wolf pretends to be the shepherd." . . . "There will be plenty of respectable republicans in the UNR, but the levers of political action will continue to be concentrated in the hands of M. Soustelle and of the 'network' he set up both before and since May 13." In short, Soustelle had an organization behind him, while the liberals had none.

Maybe the Left-wing anti-Fascist who had become an Algiers *ultra*, Duverger argued, would start evolving in the opposite direction; but this wasn't certain by any means. After all, with only 3 per cent of the country's votes behind his party, he had succeeded, by taking advantage of the Algiers *putsch*, in overthrowing the Fourth Republic; and he could not but remember the sweetness of such a victory.

"So long as Soustelle continues to enjoy sufficient power and prestige under the Fifth Republic, he will be content. But if things go wrong for him he will have at his disposal an instrument of dictatorship infinitely more powerful than what he possessed on May 13. . . . No doubt, the whole apparatus may undergo a process of *enbourgeoisement*, especially if the Algerian problem is settled. But if the Algerian war continues, the Fascist danger, roaming round the new régime, may become much more real. . . . It is all the more serious as the Fascist threat in France is not an open one, but an insidious one . . ."

It is very curious, as we look back to October 1958, how Soustelle was No. 1 Bogey Man to all liberals in France. De Gaulle was fully conscious of it, and during the few weeks following the Referendum France was to witness something of a struggle between de Gaulle and the French *ultras*, as represented by Soustelle.

As it turned out, de Gaulle miscalculated the results of the *scrutin d'arrondissement* election system to which, after several days' heated discussion among his ministers, he finally gave his blessing. The *chambre introuvable*,[1] the top-heavy Assembly with its overwhelming Right majority, was not what he had wanted.

---

[1] The phrase was originally applied to the Parliament elected in 1815 under the Restoration; it was much more reactionary than Louis XVIII himself, who was considered a "liberal" in comparison.

To him, the election, coming on top of the plebiscite of September 28, was to mark a further step in consolidating a "strong state" under his personal rule, with as little interference from Parliament as possible. In his own view, he (de Gaulle) represented 80 per cent of the French nation, whereas the Parties and the politicians—whether Soustelle, Duchet, Bidault or Mollet—represented merely what he wanted them to represent; and that was why it was essential to prevent Soustelle from bringing about a vast rally of all the Right-wing forces under the "de Gaulle" banner. De Gaulle had hoped that, in adopting the *scrutin d'arrondissement*, he would succeed in dividing the political forces in France fairly evenly—apart from the Communists, who would be simply as good as eliminated from Parliament. But between the two "extremes" —Soustelle and Mollet—he (de Gaulle) would be in an excellent position to arbitrate.

He therefore did his best to nip in the bud the Soustelle plan for creating a "Gaullist" mass movement based on an alliance of the UNR with the *ultra* elements represented by Duchet, Bidault and Morice (as well as the Algerian *ultras*), and essentially pro-Fascist in character. De Gaulle, indeed, feared that if Soustelle controlled a vast Right-wing party, he would soon start, with the help of the Army and the *ultras*, to dictate his will to de Gaulle himself.

What then was the sequence of events?

After the formation of the UNR (which the "Left-wing Gaullists" belonging to a new organization called *Centre pour la Réforme Républicaine* had refused to join), Soustelle established contact with three extreme Right-wing leaders—M. Georges Bidault, now busy forming a shadow party (distinct from the MRP) of "Christian-Democrats",[1] M. André Morice, head of a small *ultra* Radical Party (also separate from the "classical", "Valoisien" party, now under Gaillard); and M. Roger Duchet, head of the Right-wing Independents.[2] At this point de Gaulle let it be known that this vast Right-wing coalition would in no way enjoy his (de Gaulle's) patronage.

This was, in fact, a new episode in the curious de Gaulle–Soustelle

[1] Actually Bidault still remained a member of the MRP, and the latter's position in the coming election was so shaky that the question of expelling Bidault did not arise. On the contrary, the MRP hoped, in a number of constituencies, to benefit from the support of Bidault's followers in the second ballot. In some constituencies, candidates ran under the dual label of MRP and "Christian Democrat". The oddest feature of the "Christian Democrats" was the adoption of their label in the election by an extreme Fascist and Algerian diehard like M. Tixier-Vignancour, Kovacs's lawyer in the Bazooka Affair.

[2] Duchet, though president of the Conservatives or "classical" Right ("Independents"), represented its extreme Right wing, particularly in respect of Algeria. In the election he was, at least in principle, almost as opposed to the Socialists as to the Communists. Compared with Duchet, Pinay, the Minister of Finance, was considered a liberal, and the die-hard "Independents" and *ultras* could never quite forgive him his "sell-out" of Morocco in November 1955, when at La Celle-St. Cloud he "implored" the deposed Sultan to return to Rabat and promised Morocco independence.

conflict that had gone on for several months. Soustelle had obviously been working hard with the aim of becoming Prime Minister.

In his own view, he had done more than anybody to bring de Gaulle into power; but, despite some major concessions (like appointing him Minister of Information) de Gaulle was not treating him as No. 1 man of the new régime. De Gaulle and Soustelle also had different conceptions of what "Gaullism" should be. To de Gaulle it meant that, under it, he would act as a permanent arbiter among the conflicting forces in France; to Soustelle it meant the domination of France by a powerful Right-wing "rally". A top-heavy Parliament, with Soustelle as Prime Minister, would greatly reduce de Gaulle's power of arbitration.

That is why, after long and heated discussions in the Government over the new electoral system, de Gaulle finally supported Mollet against Soustelle. The Government was equally divided; Soustelle, Pinay, Debré and the other Right-wingers supported the departmental *scrutin de liste*; Mollet, supported by Pflimlin and the other MRP ministers (who, in the absence of proportional representation—this, since it would favour the Communists, was out of the question—looked upon it as a lesser evil), defended the *scrutin d'arrondissement*.

The two-ballot *scrutin de liste*, applying to large, multi-member constituencies, which Soustelle defended meant that the voters would have to choose parties, rather than men. In the first ballot, the list obtaining an absolute majority would get all the seats of the constituency. If no list achieved this, then the list at the top of the poll in the second ballot would get all the seats. In M. Soustelle's view, several lists could merge between the two ballots into a single coalition list. Thus, all the Right-wing parties could gang together, and, if necessary, also include in the coalition an MRP, a Right-wing Radical and even a Socialist. But in most constituencies this situation would be extremely awkward, especially for the Socialist: he would have to join forces with the Communist, or lose his seat, or else become a reluctant and severely handicapped ally of the Right, and, as it were, its prisoner.

Mollet fought this proposal tooth-and-nail. He hoped that, with single-member, two-ballot constituencies, the Socialists would be in a much more favourable position for gaining the support (or step-down) of the Radicals, MRP or even Communists to defeat the Right in the second round; or the support of the Right to defeat the Communists. The only disadvantage from Mollet's point of view was that under this system the Party headquarters would have little influence with the local candidate.

De Gaulle greatly preferred the Mollet system. He thought it would produce a more evenly balanced Assembly. The *scrutin de liste*, on the other hand, would compel all the Right-wing parties to form solid alliances and might well produce an "Algerian", *ultra* majority in Parliament. De Gaulle therefore much preferred to see the Socialists well-represented in the new Parliament and, if possible, belonging to a coalition government over which he could continue to rule supreme.

The ministers had been equally divided on this issue: eleven were for the *scrutin de liste* and eleven for the *scrutin d'arrondissement*; when on October 7 de Gaulle gave his casting vote to the latter, Soustelle was extremely dissatisfied and Pinay even threatened to resign. But Soustelle would not easily admit defeat. Even under the *scrutin d'arrondissement*, he thought, an overwhelming alliance of the Right-wing forces might work. De Gaulle had been playing about with the idea that the UNR would be a large centre party, which he would use to tilt the balance, one way or the other, in his "arbitration" work; under the Fifth Republic the UNR would hold a place similar to that of the Radicals under the Third. This conception was supported by Michelet and Chaban-Delmas, the latter anxious, for reasons of his own, not to annoy de Gaulle.

It came to something of a showdown at the meeting of the UNR's central committee on October 16. Soustelle had in his pocket an alliance manifesto to be signed by himself, Duchet, Bidault and Morice, all these four leaders being united on the Algerian issue. Oddly enough, Soustelle found himself in a minority, even Delbecque, belonging to the *ultra* wing of the UNR but closely linked with Chaban-Delmas, now opposing him. Soustelle then threatened to resign. This caused a moment of consternation, for it would mean a split in the "Gaullist" ranks. So de Gaulle had to save the situation. He had a long and stormy session with Soustelle on the following day, and it was finally agreed that the UNR would not fight any of de Gaulle's ministers (Socialists, MRP or Radicals) in the election campaign and that while it could ally itself with Duchet, Bidault and Morice candidates, it could also enter into alliances "with others".

De Gaulle seemed to think that he had won a great victory over Soustelle.

According to members of his secretariat the 465 Metropolitan seats of the new National Assembly would be composed as follows:

35 Communists; 45 various Left-wing groups; 120 Socialists; 45 MRP; 100 UNR; 120 "Independents" (i.e. "classical" Right).[1]

Here was wishful thinking with a vengeance. De Gaulle apparently really hoped that the Government after the election would be merely a continuation of his present Government, complete with its Mollets and Pflimlins. Soustelle and his "network" knew better. . . .

But already in October, partly as a result of all this unpleasantness between de Gaulle and Soustelle, tipsters were almost unanimous in saying

[1] *L'Express*, October 30, 1958.

that the man who would head the new French Government after the election would not be Soustelle, but the much less troublesome Debré. Among the Mollet Socialists a few still had the illusion that Mollet might perhaps be chosen; Mollet himself, taking a less rosy view of the Socialists' chances, was speaking of himself as the future leader of "His Majesty's Opposition". Especially in speaking to English friends, he liked to draw false analogies between the British parliamentary system and the system that would emerge in France under the Constitution of the Fifth Republic.

Since the Referendum and the coming into force of the new Constitution, the Government had been busy drawing up numerous ordinances and also the organic laws which were to complete the Constitution proper. Among the ordinances, one of the most important was that concerning Algerian terrorist activities; the ordinance of October 8, with its extension of the system of administrative arrest and internment and the increased "facilities" for questioning suspects marked a further French departure from the *habeas corpus* principle.

Also, in the course of October, nineteen "organic laws" were passed; one of these provided for the new election system, complete with the redrawing of the map of French constituencies; the number of these was reduced from 537 to 465 in Metropolitan France, each new constituency containing 93,000 inhabitants as nearly as possible. Communist strongholds were, as far as possible, sliced up, so as to make the new constituencies less uniformly working-class.

The other organic laws supplementing the Constitution concerned the election of the President of the Republic, the composition and duration of the National Assembly and the Senate; the "functioning of the parliamentary assemblies"; the election of senators; the salaries of members of Parliament; the vote by proxy in Parliament; the composition and functions of the Constitutional Council; the Economic and Social Council; the High Court of Justice; the Executive Council of the Community; the Senate of the Community and the French Republic's representation in this Senate; the Community's Court of Arbitration, etc.

It was decided that the general election would take place in France on November 23 and 30, and in Algeria (where there was to be only a single ballot) on November 30; that the President of the Republic be elected on December 21 and (failing an absolute majority in the first round) 28; that there be municipal elections in France on March 8 and 15, 1959, and elections to the Senate on April 26.

It must be said that public attention in France, throughout the greater part of October, was centred less on the coming election than on the death of the Pope Pius XII, the Galeazzi Lisi scandal and the election of the new Pope.

Altogether, the election campaign in France was extraordinarily slow in making a start, and the public seemed, at least at first, wholly indifferent to the whole thing. On the face of it, it seemed little more than a repeat performance of the September Referendum.

6. AN ELECTION WITHOUT IDEAS

To a very large extent it *was*, indeed, a repeat performance of the Referendum. Strictly speaking, there was no real political battle, i.e. no battle of ideas. With the exception of the Communists, a few Radicals—Mendès-France, Daladier, Baylet—and a few smaller Left-wing groups,[1] everybody was trying to cash in on de Gaulle's 80 per cent in the Referendum, and claiming credit for having advocated the YES vote.

Together with these protestations of undying loyalty and absolute faith in de Gaulle went this other theme of the election propaganda: France was going to be "renewed". Even most of the old hands of the Fourth Republic (and even of the Third, like the 80-year-old Paul Reynaud) joined in this clamour for renewal, novelty and rejuvenation. All this screaming for "new men" was not without effect; with a nearly three-years' delay, the electorate did, in fact, respond to Poujade's battle-cry of January 1956: "*Sortez les sortants!*"—"Get the old gang out!" In the end, an extraordinarily high number of deputies, many of whom had been in Parliament for years and years, were eliminated. It is true that, at the same time, a few old hands got back to Parliament, such as M. Jean-Paul Palewski and some other former RPF deputies, now riding on the crest of the UNR wave.

The UNR, the "classical" Right, the MRP, the Radicals (or most of them), the Mollet Socialists, as well as a great variety of fancy candidates, identified themselves, in varying degrees, with de Gaulle; to have the Cross of Lorraine printed on your poster, or at least the name of General de Gaulle, was, to the vast majority of candidates, the *sine qua non* of success.

That brilliant cartoonist, Maurice Henry, was not far wrong when he drew a picture of numerous candidates showing off their election posters:

---

[1] Chief among these were the UFD, *Union des Forces Démocratiques* (Daniel Mayer, Mendès-France, Mitterrand) and the UGS, *Union de la gauche socialiste* (Bourdet, anti-Mollet Socialists like Verdier, Depreux, etc.). All shared in the general *débacle* of the Left. "Autonomous Socialists" like Verdier and Depreux and men like Hernu and Hovnanian, who had been successful *mendésiste* candidates in 1956, now failed miserably.

The only numerous (though unimportant) opposition group on the Right were the Poujadists, who ran many candidates most of whom, not having got 5 per cent of the votes, were, however, to forfeit their 100,000-franc deposits. Poujade himself stood at Saumur, where he scraped together 7,000 votes out of a total of 40,000 votes. *Sic transit.*

WITH DE GAULLE FOR DEMOCRACY AND THE REPUBLIC!
WITH DE GAULLE FOR THE SUPPORT OF THE WORKING CLASS!
WITH DE GAULLE FOR INTEGRATION!
WITH DE GAULLE FOR A FRANCO-ALGERIAN ASSOCIATION!
WITH DE GAULLE FOR AN INDEPENDENT ALGERIA!
WITH DE GAULLE FOR THE DEFENCE OF CAPITALISM!
WITH DE GAULLE AGAINST THE "SYSTEM"!
WITH DE GAULLE FOR SOCIALISM!
WITH DE GAULLE FOR AN AUTHORITARIAN STATE!
WITH DE GAULLE FOR FREEDOM OF OPINION![1]

One could go on indefinitely with this list. Except for the opposition ("No") candidates, they all went in for that sort of thing. Even if the Socialists did not officially call themselves "Gaullists", they nevertheless exalted in their posters the "statesmanship" and "wisdom" of Guy Mollet in having supported de Gaulle in May, in having limited the damage, in having saved France from civil war. They spoke of the great role the Socialist Party would, together with de Gaulle, play in the Fifth Republic.

Some candidates who had advocated the NO vote—such as M. Isorni, the No. 1 Pétainist, who stood in the Auteuil district of Paris, were now almost apologizing for that NO. Isorni, indeed, made it clear that he was really heart-and-soul behind de Gaulle, though he regretted Article 86 of the Constitution which, in allowing parts of the French Union to break away, was "terribly dangerous". But, apart from that, he also was a "Gaullist", though cherishing, as before, the "sacred memory of Philippe Pétain". The suggestion was that, after all, de Gaulle had fortunately a great deal in common with the head of the Vichy State.

In so far as the election was fought at all, it was fought round the name of de Gaulle. The UNR were, of course, conjuring with this name more convincingly than the others.

In many cases the village-pump arguments, an inevitable accompaniment of the *scrutin d'arrondissement*, held an important place in the candidates' "professions of faith". The name of de Gaulle was linked with the promise of a reduction in the iniquitous water-rates of Cloche-merle, or with the promise that "I shall fight for a preferential gas rate in your commune. *Vivent les Hautes-Pyrénées! Vive de Gaulle! Vive la République!"*

Many observers of the 1958 election were struck by another curious phenomenon: its very widespread *apolitisme*. If, in 1951, the election centred round the maintenance of the Third Force in power, and the State-School problem was also something of an issue; if, in 1956, the Algerian war was undoubtedly No. 1 issue, there seemed no clear issue at all this time. Apart from the mumbo-jumbo about de Gaulle, practically

[1] *France-Observateur*, November 6, 1958.

all candidates went in for generalities, chest-beating and high-falutin' protestations of honesty, integrity, sense of public service, "civic virtue which has been so sorely lacking in the past", etc.

Thus it was quite usual to find a candidate (of almost any party) saying something like this: "My programme is simple. It can be summed up in a few words. Together with General de Gaulle, I want to defend your interests, freedom, justice, social progress and peace." In most "professions of faith" the candidates felt obliged to say something about Algeria, though sometimes—even in the case of a few Socialist candidates—even Algeria was omitted. But when it was mentioned, the candidate's "programme" on this issue was usually confined to platitudes and generalities, such as "An Algerian Pact must be concluded among all the Frenchmen between Dunkirk and Tamanrasset" (a UNR leaflet); "A French Peace based on Justice: trust de Gaulle" (also UNR); etc. The Mollet Socialists hinted that de Gaulle was, in fact, pursuing Mollet's policy in Algeria; that de Gaulle had his heart in the right place and that, with Socialist support, he would bring about a fair Algerian settlement. "We agree with the Constantine Programme . . ." and so on.

The irresponsible *apolitisme* which marked this election often went to absurd extremes; some candidates, exploiting the prejudice against the Fourth Republic, claimed to have nothing to do with politics at all:

"I have never gone in for politics and I undertake never to do it." . . .

"I am a new man, with experience, but with no political past. But I offer you my youth and my devotion . . ."

"I am a new man with no political associations. A new régime must have new men. I am one . . ."

"I have never gone in for politics and never shall. I am neither on the Right, nor on the Left. Like de Gaulle, the Liberator, I am in front . . ."[1]

There were 2,997 candidates for the 465 seats in Metropolitan France, but until a week before the first round on November 23 the election campaign was extremely slow. In Paris it was very rare to find an election meeting attended by more than 100 people; in most cases, candidates addressed empty classrooms with a dozen people present, or even fewer. Also, the multiplicity of the various candidates—particularly the various brands of Right-wing, UNR and "Left-wing Gaullist" candidates—caused a great deal of confusion at first, as well as the fact that the UNR candidates ranged from seemingly good liberals with an infinite faith in the wisdom and goodness of de Gaulle to Fascist thugs like M. Biaggi, whose inclusion among the UNR candidates M. Michelet had strongly opposed; but he was overruled by Soustelle and his friends.

A peculiar feature of the election was the relatively small place held in the election propaganda by anti-Communism, which was very potent

---

[1] Election leaflets quoted by *Esprit*, January 1959, p. 131.

in 1956 and, even more so, in 1951; the reason for this was simple; the Communists had been defeated in the Referendum and, moreover, under the *scrutin d'arrondissement*, which applied to the Paris region, as to the rest of France,[1] their chances of being returned in large numbers had been reduced to nothing.

The election was an inevitably dreary one; only in a small number of constituencies, where there was a (most unusual) clash of ideas, or a clash of colourful personalities, did the election arouse some local excitement and even nation-wide interest. The most outstanding among these were Lyon,[2] where Soustelle was planning to win an overwhelming victory in the first round by having, unlike so many other UNR candidates, secured the full support and non-competition of the "classical" Right; Bordeaux, where Chaban-Delmas was opposed (much to his delight, for this enabled him to appeal to the Left vote) by an extravagant Fascist character, General Chassin, who had, in May, played with the idea of starting an "anti-republican maquis" in the Landes country, and who was now accusing Chaban-Delmas of having been "a baron of the System" and of having behaved like a coward in May; further, there was Louviers, where Mendès-France was fighting an increasingly difficult battle against an MRP man, M. Montagne, who was claiming to represent "all the YES votes of the Referendum"; then there was Montreuil in the "Red Belt" of Paris, where, for the first time in thirty years, Jacques Duclos, the Communist leader, was in danger of losing his seat; finally, there was Arras, where Guy Mollet fraternized with the Church and went through some very strange political contortions (such as showing off an auto-graphed photograph of de Gaulle—"To my dear and loyal friend, Guy Mollet . . ."). These contortions were to become even more extravagant between the first and second round.

Apart from these little oases, France was, as *L'Express* said, "a political

[1] The PR principle which applied in the two previous Fourth Republic elections more fully to the Paris region than to the rest of France accounted for the unusually large number of Communist deputies it returned to Parliament.

[2] At an early stage of the election, Soustelle had hoped to benefit from the "scandal" arising from police revelations that a number of priests at Lyon had been harbouring and helping "Algerian terrorists". The *abbé* Carteron and others had, indeed, been doing valuable social work for years (with the full approval of Cardinal Gerlier, Archbishop of Lyon) among the Algerian sub-proletariat in the city. A number of these Algerians were arrested in 1958 and were tortured by the police, after which action was taken against the priests. When Cardinal Gerlier made a statement severely condemning "certain police officials" for the methods they used, the matter became rather awkward for M. Soustelle, and in the latter stages of the election campaign the "scandal", instead of being exploited for electoral purposes, was played down, since the stand taken by the Archbishop was liable to prejudice Catholics against M. Soustelle.

The fact remains that Lyon, a traditional stronghold of French Radicalism, where Herriot had reigned supreme for forty years, now became one of the most reactionary cities in France.

The 10 members of the Rhône department were now: 6 "Independents" and 4 UNR's. In 1956 the department was represented by: 3 Communists or *progressistes*, 1 Socialist, 2 Radicals, 1 MRP, 3 "Independents", 1 Gaullist.

Soustelle's "network", complete with "commandos", was particularly active at Lyon.

desert". Most people had no very clear idea for whom to vote—and yet, they went and voted on that Sunday, November 23, just as they had gone to vote in the Referendum less than two months before—usually with the same idea at the back of their minds: "de Gaulle and Safety First".

And yet, had France gone "Gaullist", as the UNR understood it? Was she hellbent on "French Algeria"? Had she gone anti-republican? Was it a rational political vote, or an instinctive (rather than emotional) kind of vote? In looking at the result of the first ballot, we come up against a variety of contradictory factors which makes it extremely difficult to draw any clear conclusion on the state of mind in France. But the bulk of French opinion was certainly not in favour of the *ultra* idea of "French Algeria".

The most striking fact, in that first ballot, was that the UNR had *not* swept the country. Their total poll amounted to 3·6 million votes, or 17·6 per cent of the total. This was over half a million fewer votes than the RPF had got in 1951, and very much less than it had got in the municipal elections of 1947 when nearly 40 per cent of the French electorate had rallied to it.

The following table is highly indicative:

THE PARTIES FROM 1951 TO 1958

Parties	1958 (first round) Reg. voters: 27·2 m. Votes cast: 20·5 m. Abstentions: 22·9%		1956 26·8 m. 21·5 m. 16·3%		1951 24·5 m. 19·1 m. 19·8%	
	1000's of votes	%	1000's of votes	%	1000's of votes	%
Communists and *Progressistes*	3,882	18·9	5,544	25·7	5,057	25·4
Socialists	3,167	15·5	3,181	14·8	2,745	14·3
Other Left	347	1·4	449	2·0	39	0·2
Radicals, etc.[1]	2,347	11·5	2,877	13·3	1,888	9·8
UNR or Gaullists[2]	3,604	17·9	949	4·4	4,125	21·5
MRP[3]	2,379	11·6	2,374	11·0	2,370	13·5
"Classical" Right[4]	4,093	19·9	3,086	14·3	2,656	13·5
Extreme Right[5]	670	3·3	2,817	13·1	87	0·5

[1] The Radicals proper (in so far as there was such a thing) got only 933,000 votes in 1958, the rest of the 2·3 million votes going to the RGR and other, mostly "Right Centre", groups.
[2] UNR in 1958; "Social Republicans" in 1956; RPF in 1951.
[3] Including, in 1958, M. Bidault's "Christian Democrats".
[4] Including both the "Independents" and other "Moderate" groups.
[5] Including the Poujadists in 1958 and 1956.

This table calls for several observations.

The number of abstentions was much higher than usual—a sign of a good deal of political confusion and apathy.

The UNR, as already said, did not sweep the country. It could even be argued that they had not done very much more than win over (in addition to the Gaullist vote—nearly one million in 1956) practically the whole of the Poujadist vote. Poujade's 2½ million votes in 1956 had been mostly the votes of middle-class malcontents with an anti-parliamentary and nationalist-"Algerian" bias; it was natural that these votes should go to the UNR, also claiming (more effectively than the Poujadists) to be a party of "change" and of "French Algeria". If, therefore, the UNR won over 2 million votes from Poujade in the first round, its great attraction as the "specifically" Gaullist Party produced no more than another 1½ million votes. Where from? There seems no doubt that, just as many ex-Communists voted YES in the Referendum, so at least some voted for the UNR now. It should, however, be said that the UNR did not run at all in about 100 constituencies; if it had done so, its total poll would have been much larger than it was.

A more striking victory, in a way, was that of the "classical" Right. This had obtained more than 4 million votes—a million more than in 1956—a point which M. Pinay was not going to forget. The "traditional" republican parties —the various (mostly Right-wing) Radicals, the MRP and the (mostly Mollet) Socialists—had, curiously enough, held their own, except that the Radicals of 1958 were no longer what the Radicals were in 1956, when at least a part of them were distinctly *mendésistes*, and so represented something new and dynamic.

However, in the second round they lost a very high proportion of these votes.

This victory of the "Independents" and other Right-wingers justifies, more than does the relative success of the UNR, the view that France— and Paris in particular—had shown a very marked Right-wing swing.[1]

As *L'Express* wrote a few days after this first election round:

The French did not vote for de Gaulle. They voted for the Right. Or rather they voted for the Gaullists in so far as they were on the Right, and not for the Right in so far as they were Gaullists. This was not a vote for de Gaulle of the Liberation and the nationalizations, it was not a vote for the Federalist de Gaulle of Brazzaville; it was a vote for the de Gaulle of May 15, the de Gaulle of Soustelle

[1] A detailed examination of the Paris vote showed that, whenever the electorate had the choice between a "Right-wing" Gaullist and a "liberal" Gaullist, it gave its preference to the former (thus, in the 14th electoral district in the 13th—largely working-class—*arrondissement* a Fascist like Biaggi got nearly 9,000 votes as against the 3,000 votes that went to his "Left-wing Gaullist" competitor). All the prominent "Left-wing Gaullists" were hopelessly defeated—Clostermann, Lipkowski, Debu-Bridel, etc.

The "Gaullist" label thus did not seem to have any absolute virtue: when a Left-wing Gaullist opposed a Right-wing and non-Gaullist reactionary, he almost invariably lost (Example: in the 17th district of Paris, ex-Police Prefect Baylot—a snarling diehard reactionary—wiped the floor with a liberal Gaullist with a fine Resistance record, Colonel Barbelot). Worse still, when a Right-wing Gaullist fought a Right-wing non-Gaullist, it was the latter who usually won. Thus, in the 3rd district—Latin Quarter, of all places— ex-Poujadist Le Pen got far more votes than his Right-wing Gaullist competitor.

and Massu. Not a vote for the man sentenced to death by Vichy, but a vote for Vichy.

This, perhaps, overstated the case; and, in the second round, the Gaullist label ultimately helped the UNR to secure more votes (and far more seats) than the "classical" Right; but the point made by *L'Express* is an interesting one all the same.

It was certainly striking (and a strange reflection on French political intelligence) that an "Algiers" *ultra* like Le Pen should find himself at the top of the poll in the Latin Quarter, and another like Biaggi in the 13th *arrondissement*, a Paris working-class district. A certain political fossilization of the French Communist Party, combined with the growing *apolitisme* and anti-Arab sentiments of the French working class, had much to do with it.

The drop in the Communist vote was general, though not uniform, in France.

In the Seine Department (including Paris) it had dropped from 30·1 per cent to 25·2 per cent; in the Seine-et-Oise, from 34·1 per cent to 25.9 per cent; in the Bouches-du-Rhône (Marseille) from 35 to 27 per cent; in the Rhône (Lyon) from 24·4 to 16·7 per cent; in the Nord from 27 to 21 per cent; in the Pas-de-Calais, from 31 to 24 per cent. In the industrial East and in the predominantly rural areas the losses were heavier still, with the exception of a few strongholds like Limoges and the Corrèze Department. By and large, the Communist decline followed fairly closely the pattern of the Referendum.

The fact remained that there were still nearly 4 million Communist votes in France; but there had been over 5½ million in 1956.

The first ballot produced only a very small number of final results: only thirty-nine deputies were elected in this first round. The most spectacular defeat was that of M. Mendès-France at Louviers; he attributed it partly to the smear campaign to which he had now been subjected for years, and partly to the "magic" of the YES vote, which his opponent had done his best to capitalize. Especially in the rural areas of the constituency, voters would have thought it highly inconsistent to vote for a NO man two months after voting YES in the Referendum. No amount of arguing about the danger of an *ultra* majority, which would perpetuate the war in Algeria, could make much difference.

Mendès-France's defeat was, indeed, spectacular: M. Rémy Montagne (*Union des OUI*) got nearly 20,000 votes, and Mendès-France just over 10,000; the Communist, 4,000; and the Socialist, 2,000.

Only a fortnight before, *L'Express* had written that no one in the constituency believed that a man of Mendès's standing and long association with Louviers (he had been its mayor since 1935) could be defeated. This defeat was highly symptomatic of the mood in France. Mendès's long-standing advocacy of the *scrutin d'arrondissement* had not done *him* much good. On the contrary, as the second ballot was to show, it was going to make things terribly easy for the UNR. Seldom had a man of Mendès-France's judgment made so bad a miscalculation. . . . Originally, he had hoped to keep the Communists out of Parliament; now Parliament was going to be invaded instead by a horde of reactionaries and Fascists.

Between the two rounds of the election more than half of the three thousand candidates withdrew from the contest. 1,332 candidates were now contesting the 426 seats that had remained *en ballottage*.

It was apparent after the first round that a very large number of *notables* of the Fourth Republic were in danger of being defeated, not to mention the Communist leaders, only a handful of whom had a good chance of being returned.

Everywhere the UNR were helping de Gaulle's ministers; at Arras, where they had no candidate, they gave their "patronage" to M. Guy Mollet, openly calling on voters, "in the name of General de Gaulle", to support him.

The voting in the first round was as follows:

Guy Mollet (Socialist)	17,524
G. Coquet (Communist)	11,143
R. Poudonson (MRP)	10,116
A. Lecup (Right)	5,500
P. Lebas (Poujadist)	1,780

These last two withdrew after the first round. It was now a three-cornered fight among Mollet, the Communist and the MRP man. As said before, Mollet made the most of his "Gaullism", flaunting an autographed photo of the General; he also tried to win over some Catholic votes by proclaiming on one occasion (at the risk of annoying the anti-clerical Socialists of the area) that he saw no reason why a *curé* shouldn't be head of a Socialist Section.[1] The local UNR organization and the UNR headquarters gave him their full support after the first ballot; in the end, to keep Mollet out, some three thousand Communists actually voted for the MRP man, rather than for their own candidate! The final result was as follows:

Guy Mollet (Socialist)	20,561
P. Poudonson (MRP)	17,993
C. Coquet (Communist)	8,285

[1] An embarrassed local Socialist paper "paraphrased" this as follows: "There is no reason why a *curé* should not *belong* to a Socialist section."

The Communist election tactics consisted in maintaining the CP candidates in the second round against the Mollet Socialist, but to step down in favour of non-Mollet Socialists; the only exception they made was in the 3rd district of the Nord, where they supported a Mollet Socialist in order to keep M. Delbecque out. But it was in vain. Delbecque was elected by 23,000 votes against 13,000 Socialist votes.

The UNR's election alliance with the "classical" Right, though unofficial after de Gaulle's rather stormy session with Soustelle on October 17, had fully worked in a very large number of constituencies. It had benefited both these groups at the expense of everybody else. The second ballot was much more spectacular than the first.

The Communist vote had remained almost stationary, dropping from 3·8 million votes to 3·7 millions, but (in view of the greater number of abstentions) showing an increase in the percentage in the total poll from 18·9 to 20·7 per cent. The Socialist poll dropped from 3·2 million votes to 2·5 millions; the Radicals were wiped out almost completely, their poll dropping from 933,000 to 362,000, and the MRP's poll from 2·4 million to 1·2 million. The great victors of the day were the UNR, whose poll shot up from 3·6 million votes to nearly 4·8 millions, and the Right, who increased theirs slightly from 4·1 million to 4·25 million votes.

It was clear that a very large number of people who had first voted for the various centre parties and also for the Socialists had voted in the second ballot for the "Gaullist" UNR. These had enormously intensified their propaganda between the two rounds, harping on the fact that, more than anyone else, they represented de Gaulle. The popular press and, above all, *France-Soir* (with its 1½ million circulation), kept referring in its banner headlines to the UNR as "Gaullists". The same tricks were resorted to as during the Referendum. Although the radio and TV allowed five minutes (throughout the *whole* campaign!) to all the larger parties and groupings, all the rest of their propaganda was "Gaullist" throughout, with the clear suggestion that the UNR were *the* real Gaullists.

Only 131 of the old deputies were re-elected, out of a total (for Metropolitan France) of 537. Nearly all the Communists were eliminated; so were almost countless prominent parliamentary figures of the Fourth Republic—and not only NO men like Mendès-France, Mitterrand, Gazier, Pineau, Bourgès-Maunoury, Daladier, but also prominent YES men like Lacoste, Ramadier, Edgar Faure, Defferre (the pro-Gaullist Socialist Mayor of Marseille), and even Right-wing extremists like André Morice and Tixier-Vignancour. The defeat of these was, oddly enough, part of the widespread prejudice against *anyone* who had been a deputy before!

Paris was shared out between the "classical" Right and the UNR. In all constituencies there was a well-organized gang-up against the Communists . . . and everybody else. Apart from one Right-wing "Radical", the rest of the thirty constituencies of Paris were shared by eleven men of the "classical" Right and nineteen UNR men, the former holding (or taking over) the more prosperous districts, the latter helping themselves to the working-class districts. All the eight Communists, three Socialists, four Radicals and three MRP's of Paris were out. If the Communists increased their poll in Paris from 20 to 24 per cent between the two rounds, the Radical, MRP and Radical voters had rushed in large numbers to the support of the UNR man. In most working-class districts it was a straight fight between the UNR man and the Communist.

In the *banlieue* (Seine Department other than Paris) the Communists kept five out of ten seats, Thorez, Grenier and Waldeck Rochet being among the winners, but Duclos and Fajon among the losers.[1] The CP still got nearly 36 per cent of the votes; but the most striking feature of the *banlieue* elections was the sharp rise in the UNR vote from 22 to 42 per cent between the two ballots. In short, the *banlieue* now returned 5 Communists, 2 Socialists, 2 Right-wingers, and 15 UNR men.

In the Seine-et-Oise, the UNR grabbed 11 out of the 18 seats.

It was much the same nearly everywhere. In five departments the UNR got all the seats; in about thirty, half or more than half.

But far more spectacular than the number of votes given to the UNR were the number of seats they were getting under the *scrutin d'arrondissement* system, as the table on the next page ("Metropolitan France Election Figures") shows.

Thus, taking the second ballot, it required some 25,000 votes to get a UNR deputy elected; some 50,000 to get a Socialist elected; and 370,000 to get a Communist elected. If one takes the first ballot with its more "sincere" and "spontaneous" vote, the difference is even more striking:

[1] At Ivry, Thorez barely scraped through with a 1,000 majority. At Montreuil, Duclos was defeated as follows:

1st round:		2nd round:	
Duclos (Communist)	21,049	Profichet (UNR)	29,662
Profichet (UNR)	18,218	Duclos (Communist)	21,252
Frenay ("Left" Gaullist)	10,416		
Others	2,538		

19,000 votes for one UNR seat; 78,000 for one Socialist seat; 388,000 for one Communist seat.[1]

For all that, the swing in public opinion was unmistakable. True, the UNR had not produced any sort of political doctrine on its posters, but the general impression of the November 30 vote was that, by and large, the people intended it to be another vote of confidence for de Gaulle—even though, this time, they voted for people most of whom were either unknown or forgotten, but who had the advantage of calling themselves Gaullists.

The real cuckolds of the election were the Socialists. Mollet had

[1] Under PR the results would, of course, have been very different. The following table was drawn up by the *Monde* (December 6) after the election:

Parties	Result of 1958 election	Under PR there would have been:
Communists.	10	88
Socialists	40	72
Other Left	2	8
Radicals	13	23
Left Centre	22	31
MRP and Christian-Democrats . .	57	42
UNR	189	82
"Classical Right"	132	94
Extreme Right	1	15

In a Chamber elected under PR the MRP would have held the balance. Even so, not even by the widest stretch could it be argued that there was any sort of Left majority in France.

METROPOLITAN FRANCE ELECTION FIGURES

Parties	Seats[1]		1958		1956
	1958	1956	2nd Round	1st Round	Single Round
			(in 000's)	(in 000's)	(in 000's)
Communists and Progressistes . .	10	145	3,741 (20·7%)	3,882 (18·9%)	5,533 (25·7%)
Other Left . .	2	—	—	347 (1·4%)	449 (2·0%)
Socialists . .	40	88	2,484 (13·8%)	3,167 (15·5%)	3,181 (14·8%)
Radicals . .	13	55[2]	362 (2·0%)	933 (4·8%)	2,876[2] (13·3%)
Left Centre . .	22	18	1,036 (5·7%)	1,365 (6·7%)	
MRP and Christian-Democrats . .	44+13	71	1,365 (7·5%)	2,379 (11·6%)	2,374 (11·0%)
UNR . .	189	16[3]	4,769 (26·4%)	3,604 (17·6%)	949[3] (4·4%)
"Classical" Right .	120+13[4]	95	4,250 (23·6%)	4,093 (19·9%)	3,086 (14·3%)
Extreme Right .	1	52[5]	—	670 (3·3%)	2,817 (13·1%)[5]

[1] 544 in 1956 for Metropolitan France; 465 in 1958.
[2] Including various "dissident" Radicals coming under "Left Centre" in 1958.
[3] "Social Republicans" in 1956.
[4] The first figure refers to officially-sponsored "Independents", the second to other members of the "Classical" Right.
[5] Mostly Poujadists.

imagined that by stressing their "Gaullism", the Socialists would share in the general triumph of the "national" parties. Like the Radicals, "those suicidal maniacs", as the *Monde*[1] called them, the Socialists had pressed for the *scrutin d'arrondissement* without wanting to realize that it could benefit them only if they had a hard-and-fast election arrangement, either with the Communists, as in 1936, or with the Right, UNR, etc., and provided they headed in a very large number of constituencies the poll of all the "national" parties. . . . But it so happened that, in most cases, the poll was headed by the Right or the UNR, and either the Socialist candidate dropped out spontaneously, or was more or less dropped by the voters in the second round. When the choice lay between voting UNR or Communist, the majority of voters voted UNR; if, in the second round, there was a three-cornered fight, the Socialist usually found himself only poorly supported by voters anxious to "vote usefully", i.e. to keep out one of the two extremes. And since the Mollet Socialists insisted on their "Gaullism", some voters reflected: If so, why not go the whole hog and vote for *the* Gaullists?[2]

Who were all these new men, these 189 deputies of the UNR? Rather a mixed crew, and yet very unlike the mob of mostly grocers and butchers and other small shopkeepers Poujade had sent to Parliament in January 1956. There was method in the way they had been selected.

Broadly speaking, nearly all had, in the past, been associated with the RPF. Some of them were soldiers and politicians, more or less directly associated with the Algiers *putsch*.

In Paris, for example, the eighteen UNR deputies included M. Moatti, a former RPF deputy and former president of the Paris municipal council; M. Malleville, who was a member of M. Michelet's secretariat; Colonel Bourgoin,

---

[1] *Le Monde*, December 2, 1958.

[2] This even applied to some "pro-de Gaulle" Socialist leaders. Thus at Sète, Jules Moch's constituency, the voting went as follows:

1st round:			2nd round:		
Moch (Socialist)	.	12,284	UNR	.	16,905
Communist .	.	12,239	Moch (Socialist)	.	15,244
UNR	.	7,643	Communist	.	13,676
MRP	.	6,325			
Right	.	2,744			

Or else Defferre's Marseille constituency:

1st round:			2nd round:		
Defferre (Socialist)	.	18,306	UNR	.	18,739
Communist .	.	11,235	Defferre	.	18,535
UNR	.	8,953	Communist	.	10,825
MRP	.	2,383			
Right	.	1,696			
Poujadist	.	499			

In both cases the hesitant MRP voters in particular supported the UNR, and not the Socialist in the second round.

a *Compagnon de la Libération*, who had been a paratrooper in the Free French Forces; the notorious M. Biaggi, of Algiers fame; M. de la Malène, a Councillor of the French Union, and secretary of the RPF group, first at the National Assembly, then at the Senate, and an economist of distinction; Dr. Karcher, also a *Compagnon de la Libération*; M. Vaschetti, a young member of Chaban-Delmas' secretariat; M. Habib Deloncle, lawyer, Councillor of the French Union and ex-secretary-general of the RPF parliamentary group; M. Misoffe, an industrialist and son of an Admiral; M. Le Tac, a member of the Resistance, who had been deported to Germany, and had, more recently, fought in Korea; M. Bernasconi, a "militant syndicalist" at the Simca works, a leader of the anti-Communist *Action Ouvrière* of the RPF; M. Ruais, who had been a member of de Gaulle's private secretariat back in 1942.

In the *banlieue*, the UNR deputies included a "Gaullist militant since 1947"; a surgeon; M. Peretti, Mayor of Neuilly, who was a former police inspector, and had been head of the Sûreté at Algiers in 1944; Mme Devaud, an RPF senator; M. Nungesser, nephew of the famous air ace who had disappeared over the Atlantic in 1927; M. Peyrefitte, an official of the Ministry of Foreign Affairs, besides a number of soldiers, lawyers, mayors and other important local personages, nearly all associated with the RPF.

The member for Fontainebleau was Colonel Battisti, "National President of the French of Algeria"; in the Seine-et-Oise the UNR men included M. Leduc, an active Gaullist since the Liberation; M. Jean Palewski, a former RPF deputy; M. Picard, one of the founders of the UNR; M. Ribière, a member of the Home Resistance, who was now a member of de Gaulle's secretariat (his father had been *chef de cabinet* to Raymond Poincaré). Another was M. Boscher, of M. Debré's secretariat.

In provincial France there was a higher proportion of plain "mayors", "lawyers", "doctors", "industrialists" and even a few *commerçants* or *négociants*; but, in the main, the UNR deputies still represented a certain upper-bourgeois layer, and at least partly a certain political caste with ramifications in the Army, industry, the administration, the Police and the various Government secretariats. Also, several Algiers "heroes" were returned—Thomazo, Neuwirth, Delbecque, Arrighi, etc., as well as a few people with impressive "family connexions", such as M. Raphael Leygues, grandson of a famous Minister of the Marine under the Third Republic. A small proportion among these people were local notabilities —mayors, presidents of Chambers of Commerce, etc., among these no doubt a few opportunists who jumped on the UNR bandwagon as easily as, in other conditions, they would have been Radicals.

These people represented a fairly distinct social phenomenon. There were, perhaps, a few pious old-time Christian-liberal Gaullists among them, but if so, they were in a small minority. A much greater proportion clearly belonged to the "networks"; some were plain "Algiers" Fascists; the great majority belonged to the higher income groups; many (especially the younger ones, the "third generation Gaullists") represented

a new kind of "technical *élite*". Most of the UNR had been associated
with the (largely totalitarian and anti-trade union) RPF; many of the
older ones had been members of the Free French Forces or the wartime
"networks", and only a few had belonged to the Home Resistance; the
UNR, as already said, had numerous ramifications spreading to the Army
in France and in Algeria, to the Police, to de Gaulle's inner circle and even
to his family; to Big Business and the technocracy; to the various secretariats of the Government (Chaban-Delmas's, Soustelle's, Debré's,
Michelet's, etc.). The UNR seemed to try to derive a certain prestige
value from some of its members' family association with the more
"respectable" leaders of the Third Republic (Poincaré, Leygues) or with
national heroes like Nungesser. Unlike the "Left-wing Gaullists", it
included few intellectuals in the older sense, but a great many members of
the "technological *élite*". Among them there were no "proletarians"; if
the working class was even remotely represented, it was only by leaders of
strike-breaking commandos from places like the Simca motor works.

Even without leaders like Soustelle pulling the strings, this whole group
of "new men" could not but look extremely suspect from any traditional
democratic or republican point of view.

Even apart from the numerous toughs amongst them (Thomazo,
Biaggi, etc.), most of these people of the *bonne bourgeoisie*, whether
Army men, "technicians" or provincial worthies, tended to be nationalist
in the usual hard and narrow way. In particular, they seemed united in a
stubborn, shortsighted attitude to Algeria, despite the efforts made by
M. Frey, a few days before the second round, to present the UNR as a
"centre" party—almost a "Left" party.

In 1952 the RPF had split into a "Gaullist" majority and a "conservative" minority, which went over to the "classical" Right of M.
Pinay. Only time would show whether there would not also be a split in
the UNR—not so much between "Gaullists" and "conservatives" as
between Fascists and non-Fascists, or between Algerian *ultras* and supporters of a peace policy in Algeria—provided de Gaulle genuinely intended to enforce such a policy. This, in November 1958, was still far
from certain, despite the gestures that he had made, and which the Left
had found so reassuring at the time. And, as the *Monde* had ominously
hinted, the "apparatus" of the UNR was in the hands of the extremists.
But big salaries and the fear of dissolution also counted.

Radio and TV had both enormously helped the UNR.

The role played by the French press in the success of the UNR was
rather smaller. Before the first ballot it had shown remarkably little
interest in the election, as compared with the election of 1956, and it was
not till after the first round on November 23 that the papers livened up.
Banner headlines announced in most papers on November 24 the great

success of the UNR. Even then, after the Tuesday, many papers preferred, somehow, to dwell on subjects other than the election, notably on Khrushchev's Berlin "ultimatum" which occurred between the two rounds of the French election.

The Left reacted only feebly to the UNR victory; although the *Dépêche* of Toulouse recalled that *"before the war the second round was always marked by a union of all the republican forces"* it doubted whether anything like that would happen this time, the Socialists and Radicals being often divided, and both being more or less committed to having nothing to do with the Communists. It was curious that the Radical press, aware of all the propaganda against the Fourth Republic, did not say a word this time about the "great ancestors", and the name of Herriot —whose seat at the *mairie* of Lyon Soustelle was shortly hoping to fill— was never mentioned. The traditional French republicans seemed to be suffering from an inferiority complex, and, on the face of it, not much "republican *mystique*" was left in the country—actually a somewhat erroneous impression, at least if one looked a few months ahead.

But at the time the inferiority complex of the traditional republican parties was undeniable, and the UNR's success in the first round was treated with the same kind of bewilderment as was the Poujadist success on January 2, 1956. The Right-wing press made, of course, the most of the débâcle of men like Mendès-France and Daladier.

This and three other factors were played up by practically all papers:

(1) Roger Frey's statement on November 26: "The UNR will tend to be a Left party; and I hope the Left is strong, powerful and well-organized"; or his other version that it would be "a Centre party". Several Right-wing papers tried to put across the reassuring idea that the UNR would be a reasonable party, holding the balance between Left and Right.

(2) The very large number of seats the UNR would have in the new Assembly. In flat contradiction with the prefects' forecasts before the first round, a paper like *La Liberté de l'Est* was now prophesying 140 UNR seats on the Tuesday; by Saturday it was already talking of 200 seats. A similar phenomenon could be observed in countless other papers.

(3) Most important of all, the three letters UNR, which were printed in enormous type in the headlines. This had a kind of hypnotic effect on those who were going to vote in the 2nd round: UNR came to mean victory. Almost everywhere the UNR victory came to be identified with the YES vote in the Referendum; as said before, a large part of the press started referring to the UNR as "Gaullists". There was a tendency to back the winner, especially as the winner was now being identified with de Gaulle.[1]

A good businessman like M. Pierre Lazareff, editor of *France-Soir*, and his "Socialist" minions could in their banner headlines have warned the

[1] Most of these facts on the provincial press during the election were kindly supplied to the author by M. Jacques Kayser from a study he and his students were preparing for publication by the *Fondation nationale des Sciences Politiques*.

paper's millions of readers of the UNR menace; instead, they lent the new régime a hand by speaking of the UNR as "Gaullists".

Altogether, the bulk of the Paris press did not behave very differently from the provincial press. The Big Three of the morning press—*Le Figaro*, *Parisien Libéré* and *L'Aurore*—were Right-wing, if not specifically Gaullist (*Le Figaro* was much more reserved than the other two about the UNR); *Paris-Presse* was definitely Gaullist, and *France-Soir* insidiously so; almost alone the *Monde* (and a number of weeklies) were highly dubious, while the Communist papers—*L'Humanité* and *Libération*—were, of course, openly hostile and dwelt on the Fascist danger.

Significantly, the swindle of the election in Algeria was played down nearly everywhere, even in the Socialist press.

It almost looked as though the question were irrelevant; in reality what was happening about the election in Algeria showed that de Gaulle's instructions had been ignored and disobeyed from the start, and that the Algerian elections would do nothing to bring a peace settlement nearer.

The comments on the outcome of the election were what was to be expected. The Communists, naturally, dwelt on the fact that with nearly 4 million votes they would have only ten deputies; the whole election was a swindle; they were, nevertheless, disturbed by the large number of habitual Communist voters who, as in the Referendum, had now voted for "de Gaulle", i.e. usually for the UNR. This seemed particularly true in the case of "a-political" young workers, and a good number of women.

Soustelle said it was essentially a vote for "French Algeria":

Broadly speaking, the electorate voted for those candidates who vowed that Algeria would remain French. They voted against those whose presence in Parliament might signify a slackening of the bonds between France and Algeria.

Mitterrand, one of the victims of the election, said:

We are witnessing the establishment of a new régime and of a powerful group— the UNR—which will tend to become the Single Party. People did not vote for the UNR—a meaningless label—but for men who claimed to represent de Gaulle, but whose Gaullism represents in reality a policy of the extreme Right. Two reasons for this: the errors of the Fourth Republic but, above all, the totalitarian propaganda to which France has latterly been subjected.

He thought conditions might arise when a dictatorship in France would become possible.

Claude Bourdet blamed de Gaulle himself:

De Gaulle is directly responsible for this avalanche from the Right. He broke the last used-up, feeble, but still live reflexes of parliamentary democracy by humiliating, breaking and ridiculing the last Assembly. Instead, he created in our country "plebiscite" reflexes, with their lack of character and civic intelligence. The French were people who liked to argue, albeit irresponsibly; but they were free people; now, by juggling with promises and dark, panic-producing hints, he has turned the French into respectful, credulous and fetishist people; he thus widely opened the flood-gates to all those willing to exploit his name unscrupulously.

7. DE GAULLE DEFIED IN ALGERIA

THE lopsidedness and unrepresentative nature of the new French Parliament was made even worse by what happened in Algeria. As we have seen, de Gaulle, dissatisfied with the manner in which the Referendum had been conducted there, had sent strict instructions to General Salan on October 9 demanding that genuinely free elections be held in Algeria on November 28–30. At his press conference a fortnight later he had reiterated his determination not to tolerate a "cooked" election there:

"With the approach of political and electoral contests in Algeria," he said, "the Army has had to adopt a distant, lofty, detached attitude. That is precisely what the Army has done—on orders from me."

It soon became apparent that the Army had done nothing of the sort.

It should be explained that the electoral system to be used in Algeria was different from the French *scrutin d'arrondissement*. Algeria was divided into eighteen large constituencies, in each of which electoral "lists" were to be formed, and the list heading the poll was to get all the seats of the constituency.

An elaborate and highly respectable "control commission" for supervising the elections was set up under the chairmanship of M. Hoppenot, a top-ranking diplomat. But this proved of little avail.

As November 9, the closing date for the registration of candidatures, approached, it was clear that there were plenty of *colon* and Committees of Public Safety candidates for the twenty-one "European" seats of Algeria, but no European liberals, and, worse still, no Moslem candidates for the forty-six Moslem seats—not even Moslems sitting on these Committees of Public Safety.

But—at almost the last moment, the Army produced its Moslem candidates, ranging from heavily decorated Moslem officials and gendarmes to ignorant and almost illiterate fellows who were added to the already existing, all more or less openly "integrationist", lists.

There was something of an uproar, not only among liberals in Paris, but even inside the de Gaulle Government, and around M. Hoppenot, who was very reluctant at first to accept these prefabricated "candidates". The whole thing was an act of open defiance of de Gaulle's instructions. It was asked that the Algerian elections be postponed. But at this point the lying in the press began again: it was argued that there was a sufficient "diversity" among these Moslem candidates to make the future Algerian deputies as "representative" as possible of Algerian opinion in the given circumstances. De Gaulle, though apparently nettled by what had happened, and feeling that he was being no more obeyed than a Mollet, Bourgès-Maunoury or Pflimlin, nevertheless acquiesced in what was happening; and it was not till after the election that, by way of a sort of delayed-action protest, he recalled Salan from Algeria.

There were two particularly interesting aspects to the elections in Algeria, with their sabotage of de Gaulle's instructions. One was the technique whereby certain Army leaders went about it; the other was the reasons why every one of the French liberals, who had thought of running in the Algerian elections, gave up before long.

As we have seen, de Gaulle's peremptory orders to Salan on October 9 were, on the face of it, obeyed at first. The officers and generals on the Committees of Public Safety, with General Massu at their head, *did* make a spectacular exit. But this was no more than a tactical retreat. Among the Army hierarchy the opposition to any negotiations with the FLN continued to be absolute. The fatal phrase about the "white flag" in de Gaulle's press conference had been inserted at the demand of the Army. Its real views were voiced by none other than Marshal Juin who, while the election "campaign" in Algeria had already begun, simply declared that the war in Algeria wasn't an issue at all, since it was "virtually finished".

He wrote in *L'Aurore* of November 17:

The Moslem population made a free choice both on May 13 and September 28. This means that the war is virtually over. No doubt there will still be some terrorist acts, and a few rebel hideouts to mop up, but the French Army has done all that is necessary to deal with this task.

The FLN and our enemies abroad are fully aware of this, and are trying to spread the myth of an Algeria with an "evolutionary" statute, thus hoping to undermine the choice the Moslems have already made, and to revive a war which is already finished.

The situation can no longer be reversed, and the FLN are kidding themselves. Why have they not accepted the Brave Men's Peace? Surely they know what that means in North Africa, ever since the French set foot there. Although both Abd-El-Kader and, later, Abd-El-Krim caused us great damage, they lived to appreciate the great advantages of such a peace. Brave Men's Peace means "*aman*", i.e. a pardon granted in a spirit of charity and loyalty.

Needless to say, these extravagant utterances were taken up with great gusto by the official candidates in Algeria though, privately, a few may have had some doubts whether the situation was quite as simple as that, and whether "*aman*" was really what de Gaulle had meant.

The military members of the Committees of Public Safety, after their initial exit, soon resumed contact with these organizations. Though wearing mufti, they continued to attend their meetings, and to discuss the election tactics to be adopted. In the three days before the closing of the electoral lists, many officers, no longer making any bones about it (for hadn't de Gaulle's peace offer failed?) appeared in uniform at the CPS meetings. Thus, General Massu, in full uniform, went to a meeting of the CPS at Blida and announced : "Gentlemen, here at Blida I want a single list." And when somebody proposed a rival list, Massu said: "My friend, you haven't a chance in hell."[1]

All this was, of course, in flat contradiction with de Gaulle's instructions to Salan: "The worst thing would be the establishment of single lists supported by the official authorities."

Although, in other constituencies, there were, in fact, two or more lists, the European candidates on these were, almost without exception, old-time colonialists or extremist, if not lunatic-fringe characters from the Committees of Public Safety, while the Moslems had simply been "appointed" by the Army.

A number of French and European-Algerian liberals had thought of standing for election in Algeria; but they soon gave up. M. Chevallier, the liberal ex-Mayor of Algiers, whom de Gaulle had personally tried to persuade to stand, found that it was hopeless.

The real attitude of the Army was well summarized in the note addressed by Colonel Marzloff to his subordinates in the Medea sector. This note, entitled "Elementary instructions for preparing and conducting parliamentary elections in Algeria" was (apparently through somebody's indiscretion) published in the *Monde* of November 12:

> Although the Army must remain impartial in the struggle between parties and persons . . . it must, nevertheless, promote the fusion of the two communities and act as a guide particularly to the Moslem population. . . . It must influence them to vote for candidates best qualified to defend the cause of French Algeria and to reject separatist and morally-disqualified candidates. The Army must remain in the closest contact with the Moslem masses . . . and, while keeping to an a-political line, it must maintain its closest contacts with the Committees of Public Safety.
>
> Candidates may freely express their opinions, provided . . . they respect legality and say nothing that would encourage the rebellion; otherwise they shall be liable to criminal prosecution.

[1] *L'Express*, November 13.

It is not the Army's business to choose candidates and establish lists . . . nevertheless, since the rebels may attempt to include their own camouflaged people among the candidates, you shall vigilantly watch all candidates, and inform me immediately of any suspects . . .

So, in the end, only "completely reliable" Moslem candidates were put up for election, none other having even ventured to come forward.

As for French liberals, they gave up almost immediately. M. Alain Savary, now a member of the anti-Mollet Autonomous Socialist Party and a former member of the Mollet Government, from which he had resigned to protest against the Mollet-Lacoste policy in Algeria, said why he had decided against standing as a candidate in Alger-Banlieue: "The conditions for free democratic elections just aren't there," he said.

"A psychosis of fear is dominating life in Algeria, particularly the life of the Moslems. Arrests continue to be numerous and everybody feels himself threatened. No doubt the Referendum was a great success for the Army; but the way in which people were 'conditioned' into voting YES did not strengthen people's respect for election procedures—which had never been taken seriously in Algeria, anyway. . . .

"Although no attempt was made to influence or threaten me, I must say that the military authorities are actively intervening in the election. SAS officers who were thought too liberal, were sent on leave of absence for the whole duration of the election campaign. Some people, whom the Government had released from camps and prisons, have been sent back there again."

He concluded by quoting a Moslem who told him that de Gaulle was right to have asked for fair elections; but these would not be held. On the other hand, since these elections would mean nothing anyway, people would vote any way they were told; they were not going to risk their lives by boycotting the election; it wasn't worth it."[1]

Similarly, M. Fonlupt-Esperaber, a Left-wing member of the MRP, who had thought of standing as a candidate in Algeria, gave up.

Taking a line rather different from M. Savary, he said that the Moslems did vote for de Gaulle in the Referendum; but, in doing so, they certainly did not vote for "integration".

"In the coming election, on the other hand, the situation is different. Those 'organizing' the election don't want to produce bona fide candidates with whom de Gaulle can 'do the rest'—i.e. agree on a reasonable new arrangement about Algeria. By picking their own candidates, they are trying to put across the fantastic idea that the Moslems want 'integration'.

"Although the cruder methods of the past will be avoided . . . the results of the election will be a fake, all the same. The list of candidates was drawn up with the assistance of the Army and, more frequently still, on the Army's

[1] Le Monde, November 12, 1958.

initiative, the military authorities having substituted themselves for the civilian authorities. No doubt, in the large cities, a few lists may have been formed spontaneously. But in the other places we find either a single list or two 'rival' lists denoting merely the rivalry of people representing, politically, more or less the same things. Often two lists are drawn up, simply to give the illusion that voters have a 'choice'. . . . This 'cooking' of the lists is not the only way in which the military authorities are intervening in the election. The local military authorities will rule supreme over the voting. *Colonel Marzloff's 'instructions' are not an isolated case, but the common rule.* And how can one imagine that the Moslem voters, who have been horribly ill-treated in the last four years—and I can prove that this ill-treatment is continuing—and living in deadly fear day after day, are going in any way to disobey the Army?

"The present Algerian election is going to be just as much a snare and a delusion as Algerian elections in the past."

M. Fonlupt-Esperaber went on to say that FLN rule (i.e. independence) would not solve anything in Algeria, least of all economically; but that it was absurd to refuse the Algerians the kind of generous autonomy or home rule that France had given several countries in Black Africa. He recalled that he himself had, in 1955, proposed that Algeria be given a status similar to that given by Italy to Sicily.

"But nothing," he concluded, "will be possible if a bunch of ambitious people send sixty or seventy so-called Algerian deputies to the National Assembly who will then be used as a means of inflicting on France a policy which is completely at variance, it seems, with General de Gaulle's real wishes and wholly contrary to the interests of both France and Algeria . . ."[1]

As regards his own plans for forming a liberal list at M'Zab, Fonlupt-Esperaber declared that he had met with opposition and obstruction from the military.

These took the line that the ex-MRP deputy was merely making excuses; he realized that he wouldn't get any more support from the Europeans in Algeria than from "nationalist" Algerians, since the FLN was against the Moslems taking part in the election anyway.

It would be pointless to describe in detail how this extremely phoney election was conducted; but here is an example. At Ben Chicao, in the Medéa region, a locality comprising 1,100 Moslem and 150 European voters, the choice lay between an "Integrationist" list and a "Gaullist" list, the latter stressing the importance of the Constantine Plan. Both the ballot papers and posters of the former had a broad blue stripe printed across them, and outside the local polling station only this one poster with the blue stripe was displayed, but not the other one—with the clear suggestion that the "blue stripe" was the correct ballot paper to use.

[1] Fonlupt-Esperaber in an article in *Le Monde*, November 16-17, 1958.

In the morning, practically all the Europeans hastened to vote; the Moslems did not vote until Army lorries had gone to fetch them. Inside the polling station, too, only the poster with the blue stripe was displayed; to a nosy journalist it was explained that "there hadn't been time" to print the rival poster.[1]

In the larger cities, it is true, there were some quite sharp rivalries—not between ideas, it is true, but between persons. At Oran one list was headed by a civilian, M. Fouques-Duparc, the Mayor, the other list by a soldier, the notorious General Miquel (of Toulouse fame). In the course of the campaign the former complained about the latter being "favoured" by the Army. When, in the end, Miquel's list lost by a few hundred votes, its members protested against "irregularities" which, they alleged, the "civilian" list had committed.

In one or two places, there was also a list sponsored by the Socialists and bearing the SFIO label; its representatives were typical Algerian *petits-blancs*; they received some limited support from Europeans, not much from Moslems.

In the end, Algiers-City returned two extremists, Lagaillarde and Vinciguerra, and their two Moslem stooges; Algiers-banlieue, Prof. Marcais and Prof. Lauriol, both standing for "French Algeria", and two equally tame Algerians, Mlle Sid Cara and M. Abdessalem; the rival list "Intégration et Renouveau" was beaten by a short head; at Batna, the UNR, headed by a Moslem, M. Mallem, a member of its Central Committee, won. At Medéa, a *gros colon* headed the winning list; at Constantine, the CPS list defeated the "Gaullist" list; at Oran-ville Fouques-Duparc defeated Miquel; in Oran-campagne, "Algérie Française", headed by M. Sid Cara, won; at Orléansville, there was an unopposed CSP list; at Tizi-Ouzou, there was a similar unopposed list; at Bougie, the CPS list defeated an SFIO-sponsored list; and so on.

Nearly everywhere in Algeria the "spirit of May 13" triumphed, and the election of M. Lagaillarde at *tête de liste* in Algiers was symbolic. He was given a big eve-of-the-poll boost by M. de Sérigny in the *Echo d'Alger*. Nearly everywhere CPS candidates and "Integration" candidates were helped to defeat anyone who dared speak of "Algerian personality", or even referred to the Constantine Programme.

Only in three constituencies—Philippeville, Sétif and Tlemcen—were "slightly dissident" lists elected, i.e. not lists directly blessed by the Committees of Public Safety.

The abstentions were more numerous than during the Referendum; in Algiers they amounted to some 40 per cent—which shows that the greater part of the Moslems abstained—at least until troops were sent to the Casbah to bring as many as possible to the polling stations. The confusion was great in these, especially when it came to explaining to

[1] Eugène Mannoni in *Le Monde*, November 29, 1958.

Moslem women what they were to do; sometimes officials would vote in their place—just to be helpful![1] Altogether, the Army trucks played a decisive role, as during the Referendum, in getting the Moslems to vote; even so, at Sétif, for instance, the abstentions were around 50 per cent. All the same, for the whole of Algeria, the Army managed to get a 66 per cent poll. That, at any rate, was the figure shown in the official returns.

The Algerian election had settled absolutely nothing for de Gaulle. All it had done was to strengthen by 65 or 70 seats the already inflated UNR group at the new National Assembly; between them, the two came very close to commanding an absolute majority of the Chamber.

L'Express said that, among the European deputies from Algeria, at least three were "notorious killers".

[1] Mannoni in Le Monde, December 2.

1960 EPILOGUE

HERE we may end the story of the de Gaulle "revolution" proper—that "revolution" in which "Algiers" overthrew the Fourth Republic and imposed on France the leadership of General de Gaulle. France accepted this leadership either willingly, or as a "lesser evil"—the greater evil being that authoritarian or plainly Fascist régime which the Algiers *ultras* would have preferred.

The apotheosis of this "revolution", the election of de Gaulle to the Presidency of the Republic, on December 21, 1958, by an overwhelming majority, was, of course, a foregone conclusion.

The "revolution" period of June–December 1958 was marked, as we have seen, by only some tentative beginnings of what soon came to be regarded as a new foreign policy. This came popularly to be known as the "policy of greatness", a phrase used in all seriousness by men like M. Malraux, but with an invariable touch of irony by all foreigners. Why "French greatness" in the days of H-bombs, ICBM's, Sputniks, moon rockets and the Two Giants, the USA and the USSR? Why not "British greatness" or "Italian greatness"? De Gaulle himself said the phrase was a misnomer; by "French greatness" he merely meant greater French independence.

It was already in September 1958 that de Gaulle made his first attempts to achieve "parity" with Britain and the USA; in a memorandum in September 1958 he asked London and Washington that the strategic and economic co-operation between the Big Western Powers—which must include France—be organized on a world scale; there must be no repetition of the Lebanon incident. The response to this request was half-hearted, to say the least: hence de Gaulle's subsequent refusal to act as a fully-integrated member of NATO; hence partly also the decision to back "Little Europe", despite de Gaulle's earlier prejudices against it, and the attempts to create a "Paris–Bonn Axis", the foundations of which were laid during the de Gaulle-Adenauer meeting at Bad Kreuznach in November 1958. Hence also de Gaulle's determination to act independently of anyone in exploding the first French A-bomb.

And yet nothing that was done in the foreign field since 1958 could in any way be considered as final. The "crisis" in Anglo-French relations over the Common Market could not be regarded as a final breach, any more than could be the Franco-American "crisis" over NATO. Nor could the *rapprochement* with Adenauer be treated as a final consecration of a Paris–Bonn Axis, if only because de Gaulle and Adenauer continued to hold diametrically-opposite views on the Oder–Neisse frontier.

With regard to the Soviet Union, de Gaulle also blew hot and cold, speaking almost in the same breath of the world menace of Communism and of the Russians as part of the White Race which must, some day, together with the rest of Europe, stand up to the "yellow multitudes of China". The Kremlin found him puzzling; on the one hand, he was the weakest link in NATO; on the other, he *seemed*, since Dulles's death, to have become Adenauer's last and only wholehearted supporter.

Despite the removal of Salan from Algiers at the end of 1958, and his replacement by a civilian chief, M. Delouvrier, and a major purge in the Army, the Algerian problem was no more settled by de Gaulle in 1958 and 1959 than it had been by the governments of the Fourth Republic. His "peace offer" of October 23, 1958, was to be followed by several others, including the famous (if ambiguous) "self-determination" offer of September 16, 1959. But still the war went on, and so did torture and *ratissages*; Alleg was still in prison; over a million Algerians (including children) were in horrible *camps d'hébergement* and by the beginning of 1960 France was still losing an average of fifty men a week.

The Constitution, which was completed by an avalanche of "organic laws" and ordinances taken in virtue of Article 92 during the last weeks of 1958, soon showed, in the course of 1959, that parliamentary control had become even more ineffectual than the supporters of the NO vote had prophesied; also, as Maurice Duverger pointed out (*Le Monde*, January 2, 1960), the Constitution was being repeatedly violated by both the Government and the President—for example the famous Article 2 proclaiming France to be a *laïque* Republic. The Constitutional Council was not even consulted on this issue. But although, for a time, there was a good deal of feeling over the school problem (religious schools could now make "contracts" with the State, but without being subject to any State control), the decay of Parliament—at least at first—left people singularly indifferent and there seems little doubt that *if at any time in 1959 another plebiscite for or against de Gaulle had been held, he would again have received his 80 per cent.*

Despite the Algerian war, and a shortage of funds for schools and housing, France seemed in a sound economic condition, and, rightly or wrongly, a spectacular future was being prophesied for the Sahara.

That was in Metropolitan France.

But, although very little was said about it, Algeria, and particularly Algiers, were again in a state of ferment, especially since de Gaulle's self-determination offer of September 16. This was full of mental reservations, provided for long delays in any kind of final settlement, but implicitly provided the possibility of a *partition* of Algeria, if all else failed. It was, in any case, wholly contrary to the *ultras'* conception of either "integration" or "*Algérie française*".

And it was in the first days of January 1960, when all seemed peaceful and normal in France, that things began to happen.

Although, on the face of it, there seemed no connection between the "Pinay affair" and Algeria, the savage attack launched on de Gaulle during the first week of January by the official organ of the Conservative Right—the "Independents"—which called him "Louis XIV", "Napoleon", a "monarchist", etc., and likened him to Napoleon III, showed that Duchet and his friends felt that, at last, de Gaulle had become weakened and vulnerable. Soon after this attack de Gaulle dismissed M. Pinay, his Minister of Finance, replacing him by a "technician", M. Baumgartner, the Governor of the Bank of France. Ostensibly, the change was made for purely financial reasons; in reality, Pinay, who had already disrupted de Gaulle's RPF in 1952, declared himself out of sympathy with all that de Gaulle stood for; the old Vichyite proceeded to pose as a better "republican" than de Gaulle, and is said even to have been encouraged in his rebellion against de Gaulle by Mr. Dillon of the State Department and by General Noris Norstad, head of NATO, who resented de Gaulle's over-independent attitude to the Atlantic Pact.

But was there something else behind Pinay's revolt? Did not the "Independents", with their close contacts with Algiers and M. de Sérigny, know that something very serious was brewing there again? For weeks—ever since de Gaulle's "self-determination" offer of September 16—he had been publicly denounced in thousands of leaflets printed in Algiers as "a traitor"; it was said that the biggest mistake the "Algiers patriots" had made in May 1958 was to have chosen de Gaulle as their leader.

Only a few days after Pinay's dismissal—and his humorously arrogant words of farewell: "I'm not saying good-bye, I am just saying *au revoir*"—the Massu incident broke. The wheel seemed to have turned full circle: Massu, who had been the first to acclaim de Gaulle on May 13, 1958, now declared himself wholly opposed to de Gaulle's Algerian policy in an interview given to the Munich paper, the *Süddeutsche Zeitung*. He was summoned to Paris, and, despite a (highly tortuous and ambiguous) denial of the interview, de Gaulle understandably sacked him. Did the Massu interview point to a revolt of the Army against de Gaulle, or merely to a revolt of the Algiers *ultras*?

In any case, two days later, on January 24, 1960, the *ultras* of Algiers rebelled once more. They were, as was to be expected, led by M. Orthiz, one of the "heroes" of the Bazooka Affair and of the "Declaration of the 14", who had, in October 1959, formed a new Fascist organization called the FNF (*Front National Français*), and by the even more notorious M. Lagaillarde, who had started the trouble on May 13, 1958. On January 24, the first shots were fired from the headquarters of M. Orthiz at the *gendarmes*, trying to canalize the anti-de Gaulle demonstrators. In the shooting some 25 persons were killed and 150 wounded.

In the hours that followed these anti-de Gaulle riots, a part of central Algiers, including the University, was occupied by the rioters. This area was "surrounded" by troops; but the "blockade" was a peculiar one; during the following day, January 25, trucks carrying arms and supplies of various kinds were able to enter the "rebel fortress" without difficulty. What was the Army going to do?

Like Coty and Pflimlin before him, de Gaulle was issuing orders and proclamations. But what was going to happen *this* time?

For a few days, it was touch-and-go. A part of the Army, and, above all, the paratroopers, seemed to side with the Algiers insurgents. The high command assumed, for a few days, an ominously "neutral" attitude. It was not until they had received certain assurances from de Gaulle (*via* General Ely), and had also been impressed by the fact that the overwhelming bulk of French metropolitan opinion was "for" de Gaulle and "against" the Algiers insurgents, that the Army "supported" de Gaulle. Finding themselves isolated, the insurgents surrendered. Orthiz managed to escape (who had helped him?) while Lagaillarde was sent to the Santé Prison, to be followed there by Biaggi and a number of other leading Fascists. M. Soustelle, who had openly sympathized with the *ultras*, was evicted from the Government. For a short time de Gaulle was immensely popular in France, above all with the Left. The arrest of a spluttering M. de Sérigny seemed to symbolize de Gaulle's declaration of an all-out war on the Algiers *ultras*, even though de Sérigny argued that, at the height of the January insurrection, he had done not much more in his *Echo d'Alger* than—quote earlier pronouncements by M. Debré, de Gaulle's Prime Minister!

In his famous broadcast of January 29, de Gaulle reaffirmed the principle of "self-determination"; and yet—his real intentions on Algeria remained highly ambiguous, and the zig-zag policy continued. Soon afterwards, he went to Algeria; from what he said to the Army, it became clear that he had (at least for the time being) given in to them all along the line: he spoke in terms of fighting the war to a victorious finish, if the Rebels did not lay down their arms.

Algiers was now reassured; Metropolitan France was bitterly disappointed. Here there were also other causes of discontent. To deal with the growing economic grievances among the peasantry, the majority of the deputies asked in March, under Article 29 of the Constitution, that a special session of Parliament be called. Contrary to all that had been said during the discussion of the Draft Constitution, de Gaulle rejected this "request". This seemed thoroughly unconstitutional; there was an outcry about the "presidential republic" having become a dictatorship overnight; even Guy Mollet, who now used some strong words, suddenly seemed to regret that he had placed so much confidence in de Gaulle. Even so, the general protest was disconcertingly mild.

It was not until several months later—in July—that ex-President Vincent Auriol resigned from the Constitutional Council in protest against the complete ineffectualness of this institution set up by de Gaulle, and against the *violations of the Constitution* of which he considered de Gaulle guilty, notably on the question of Article 29, and on the school issue; on several occasions, he said, the Constitutional Council had been simply by-passed by the President.

De Gaulle's popularity, which was high in France in January, as a result of the crushing of the *ultras'* plot, slumped heavily after his *tournée des popotes* in Algeria. He had not lived up to the promises made in September 1959 and again in January 1960. Was the Algerian war to go on indefinitely, "for another six, or another sixty years?" as *The Observer* put it.

And yet, in June 1960, after the breakdown of the Paris Summit meeting, de Gaulle strongly reiterated his "self-determination" offer, and his invitation to "the external organization of the Algerian Rebellion" (his description of the Algerian Government) to send representatives to Paris. This time two men—M. Boumendjel, whose brother had committed suicide in a French gaol in Algiers, and another emissary, M. Yahia, came to Paris to establish contact.

What had persuaded de Gaulle to adopt a seemingly more vigorous "new" line? Had the Summit failure persuaded him that there might be, before long, a major international crisis, in which France could not afford to have her hands tied by the Algerian war? Did he seriously believe that China first and, later perhaps, the Soviet Union, would start giving more and more direct or at least indirect help to the FLN? Did he feel that he was building on sand in Black Africa so long as the Algerian war continued? Also, did he think that, in the long run, the build-up of a major French atomic "striking force" was more important than the maintenance of an enormously costly, conventional army in Algeria—no matter how "revolutionary" it fancied itself? Here, clearly, was a possible conflict in the offing between the Army and the "technocrats".

The immediate reaction to the arrival in France of the FLN representatives (no matter how disdainful their treatment) was, of course, an explosion of fury from Soustelle, Bidault and the various political and administrative profiteers of the May '58 "revolution". Persons in Debré's entourage, if not Debré himself, were doing their utmost to persuade de Gaulle to be "intransigent". The Army remained silent—for the time being.

Despite all these pressures, was de Gaulle going to see it through this time? Popular sentiment in France, though not very articulate, except possibly in Paris (though here, too, the holiday season was having a paralysing effect), was, nevertheless, strongly "for" de Gaulle—if he truly meant Peace.

If, in spite of everything, de Gaulle at last succeeded in making peace in Algeria, would the French democratic tradition become revitalized—especially after a new Election? Or would the civic inertia, the political conformism, the "daddy-knows-best" moods engendered by the first two years of the de Gaulle régime, continue as before? And what if de Gaulle were suddenly to disappear? *Après moi le déluge* was the title of a seemingly funny, but desperately serious article in the *Canard Enchaîné* early in 1960.

A possible reply to this is, of course, that France has, in the course of her long history, already survived many a "deluge".

All the same, it is not a good school for citizenship in which a thing like this is possible: during de Gaulle's visit to the United States in April 1960, the French radio seemed to think it quite natural to start one of its news bulletins with the words: "In the absence of General de Gaulle, there is no political news in France today."

INDEX

Morice, A., 14, 25, 42, 54, 60, 66, 78, 106, 294, 364, 366, 376
Morin, E., 214
Murphy, R., 22–24, 28–32, 35, 42–44, 49–50, 53–54, 81, 108, 128, 229
Mussolini, B., 1
Mutter, A., 65, 74, 76, 97

NAEGELEN, E., 96–97, 172
Napoleon I, 342, 393
Napoleon III, ix, xi, 1, 2, 244, 327, 393
Nasser, Col. G., 12, 30, 308, 325
Naudet, 20
Neuwirth, L., 50, 85, 120, 190, 238, 258, 338, 380
New York Herald-Tribune, 19, 53
New York Times, 24, 221
Norstad, Gen. N., 393
Noury Said, 220
Nungesser, 380–1

Observer, The, 21
Olmi, M., 223, 344
Ortiz (or Orthiz), J., 46, 80, 120, 222, 352, 393–4
Ouali, Azem, 219
Ouraghi, M., 305

PAJAUD, H., 82
Palewski, J. P., 368, 380
Parachini, 120
Paris, Count of, 233
Paris-Journal, 86
Paris-Presse, 60, 92, 118, 141–2, 240, 300, 322, 383
Paris de La Bollardière, Gen., 79, 226, 271
Parisien Libéré, Le, 86, 92, 155–6, 294, 300, 330, 383
Payron, 68
Péguy, C., 359
Pelat, 137
Pelletier, 168, 330
Peretti, 380
Périllier, L., 218
Perspectives, 198
Pétain, P., ix, 41, 48, 95, 97, 110, 165, 168, 222, 233, 295, 311, 316, 318, 369
Petit, Gen., 79

Peyrefitte, 380
Pflimlin, P., 11, 25, 30, 35, 48, 54, 61–68, 71–78, 80, 84, 86–89, 92–97, 103, 106, 110, 112–18, 121, 124–8, 130–8, 140–54, 158–9, 164, 169–70, 175–6, 180–1, 191, 200, 215, 241–2, 245, 273, 290, 296, 316, 365–6, 385, 394
Philip, A., 151, 289
Philipe, G., 151
Picard, P., 357–8, 380
Pickles, D., 259
Pierrard, 148
Pinay, A., 4, 11, 28, 35, 37, 39, 49, 52, 91, 113, 117–18, 121, 129, 155, 168–9, 175, 195, 213, 241, 304, 364–6, 381, 393
Pineau, C., 11, 15, 17, 19, 32–3, 43, 54, 59, 62, 151, 172, 229, 234, 287, 289, 307, 347, 376
Pius XII, 367
Pleven, R., 11, 36, 55–60, 74, 122, 245
Poincaré, R., x, 318, 380–1
Pompidou, O., 80, 169, 195
Populaire, Le, 25, 124, 145, 150, 216
Poudonson, R., 375
Poujade, P., xii, 6, 10–11, 27, 33, 39, 42, 66, 71, 79, 123, 171–2, 218, 222, 278, 294–6, 310, 320, 368, 372–3
Primo de Rivera, J. A., 259
Profichet, 377
Proust, M., 173

QUEUILLE, H., 23

RABAH, BITAT, 308
Rabemananjera, 252
Radio-Algiers, 84, 124, 127, 132, 175, 184, 191, 240, 291, 358
Ramadier, P., 91, 142, 146–7, 164, 166, 168, 172, 283, 376
Ramdane, Abade, 247
Ramette, J., 148
Ranavulo, Queen (Madagascar), 253
Raseta, 253–4
Renault, Col., 120
Reuilly, Gen. de, 205
Reynaud, P., 21, 96, 244–5, 296, 360, 368
Ribeyre, 87

PER 840
French Studies

ernet Services:
OM HOME

01902-822303

a PC with a non-University Internet
in your workplace, you will need a
me computer to BIDS/OVID as a valid

e web page at:

s/bidsintro.htm#accesshome

v to proceed.